NEW TESTAMENT
HISTORY

Jameson Stockhaus

NEW TESTAMENT HISTORY

F. F. Bruce

*Rylands Professor of Biblical Criticism
and Exegesis,
University of Manchester*

A GALILEE BOOK
DOUBLEDAY
NEW YORK LONDON TORONTO SYDNEY AUCKLAND

A GALILEE BOOK
PUBLISHED BY DOUBLEDAY
a division of Bantam Doubleday Dell Publishing Group, Inc.
1540 Broadway, New York, New York 10036

GALILEE, DOUBLEDAY, and the portrayal of a boat
are trademarks of Doubleday, a division of
Bantam Doubleday Dell Publishing Group, Inc.

New Testament History was originally published in
England by Thomas Nelson and Sons Ltd. in 1969
and in the United States by Doubleday in 1971.
This edition is published by arrangement with
Marshall Morgan & Scott Ltd.

TO MY COLLEAGUES
IN THE FACULTY OF THEOLOGY,
UNIVERSITY OF MANCHESTER

Contents

Preface

In dedicating this book to my colleagues in the Manchester Faculty of Theology, I include past members of the Faculty as well as present ones, and think with particular gratitude of three.

First, Professor H. H. Rowley, Editor of Nelson's Library of Theology, who honoured me with the invitation to make this contribution to the series and has waited patiently for its too tardy delivery.

Second, my predecessor, the late Professor T. W. Manson. My indebtedness to him will be clear enough in the chapters on Jesus and Paul. The temptation to quote him at length is always strong, for he had the gift of putting into telling and memorable language views to which I wholeheartedly subscribe but could never express so happily as he did. I have in mind, for example, his insistence that Jesus was conceivably at least as interesting, for his own sake, to people in the first century as to historians in the twentieth, and that the Gospels are more satisfactorily studied as historical documents concerning him than as psychological case-material concerning the early Christians.

Third, my present colleague, Professor S. G. F. Brandon. I cannot think that everything in this book will command his agreement, but it owes more to him than he could realize. To be so closely associated as I have been for nine years with the author of *Jesus and the Zealots* and *The Fall of Jerusalem and the Christian Church* is a privilege of immense value to a student and teacher of New Testament literature and Christian origins.

Although this volume is written for a Library of Theology it is not a theological work. New Testament history is indeed charged with theological implications, which call for serious treatment in the proper place, but they are not dealt with here. I have written as a historian, not as a theologian; but I am persuaded that the theological implications can be the better appreciated when the historical basis is duly laid.

A special word of thanks is due to Miss Margaret Hogg, who has typed the whole work from a very rough manuscript and given great help with the indexing.

1969   F.F.B.

Principal Abbreviations

Ad Magn.	*To the Magnesians* (Ignatius)
Ad Philad.	*To the Philadelphians* (Ignatius)
Ad Rom.	*To the Romans* (Ignatius)
Ad Smyrn.	*To the Smyrnaeans* (Ignatius)
Adu. Pelag.	*Against the Pelagians* (Jerome)
AJT	*American Journal of Theology*
Ann.	*Annals* (Tacitus)
Ant.	*Antiquities* (Josephus)
Apol.	*Apology* (Justin, Tertullian)
Att.	*To Atticus* (Cicero)
BASOR	*Bulletin of the American Schools of Oriental Research*
BGU	*Berliner Griechische Urkunden*
BJ	*Jewish War* (Josephus)
BJRL	*Bulletin of the John Rylands Library*
BM	British Museum
BZNTW	*Beiheft zur Zeitschrift für die Neutestamentliche Wissenschaft*
CAH	*Cambridge Ancient History*
CBQ	*Catholic Biblical Quarterly*
C. Cels.	*Against Celsus* (Origen)
CD	*Covenant of Damascus* (Zadokite Work)
CIG	*Corpus Inscriptionum Graecarum*
CIL	*Corpus Inscriptionum Latinarum*
Clem. Hom.	*(Pseudo-)Clementine Homilies*
Clem. Recogn.	*(Pseudo-)Clementine Recognitions*
Cl. Phil.	*Classical Philology*
Conf. Ling.	*Confusion of Tongues* (Philo)
CPI	*Corpus Papyrorum Iudaicarum* (ed. V. A. Tcherikover and A. Fuks)
CSEL	*Corpus Scriptorum Ecclesiasticorum Latinorum*

DACL	*Dictionnaire d'Archéologie Chrétienne et de Liturgie*
DJD	*Discoveries in the Judaean Desert* (Clarendon Press)
Ep(p)	*Epistle(s)*
E.T.	English Translation
ExT	*Expository Times*
Flacc.	*On Flaccus* (Philo)
Fug.	*On Flight and Finding* (Philo)
Geog.	*Geography* (Strabo)
Haer.	*Against Heresies* (Irenaeus)
HE	*Ecclesiastical History* (Eusebius)
Hist.	*History, Histories* (Sallust, Tacitus, Dio Cassius)
HJP	*History of the Jewish People in the Time of Jesus Christ,* by E. Schürer (E.T.)
HNT	*Handbuch zum Neuen Testament* (ed. H. Lietzmann)
HTR	*Harvard Theological Review*
HUCA	*Hebrew Union College Annual*
IEJ	*Israel Exploration Journal*
JBL	*Journal of Biblical Literature*
JEH	*Journal of Ecclesiastical History*
JJS	*Journal of Jewish Studies*
JQR	*Jewish Quarterly Review*
JRS	*Journal of Roman Studies*
JTS	*Journal of Theological Studies*
Leg. Agr.	*On the Agrarian Law* (Cicero)
Leg. Alleg.	*Allegorical Interpretation of the Laws* (Philo)
Leg(atio)	*Embassy to Gaius* (Philo)
Migr.	*Migration of Abraham* (Philo)
Mut. Nom.	*Change of Names* (Philo)
Nat. Hist.	*Natural History* (Pliny)
NovT	*Novum Testamentum* (Leiden)
NTS	*New Testament Studies*
OGIS	*Orientis Graeci Inscriptiones Selectae* (ed. W. Dittenberger)
Pan.	*Panarion* (Epiphanius)
Pap. Herc.	Papyri published in *Volumina Herculanensia*
PEQ	*Palestine Exploration Quarterly*

Praep. Euang.	*Praeparatio Euangelica* (Eusebius)
Prouid.	*On Providence* (Philo)
Ps. Sol.	*Psalms of Solomon*
Q	Qumran (1 Q = Qumran Cave 1; 1 QH = *Hymns of Thanksgiving* from Cave 1; 1 QM = *War Scroll* from Cave 1; 1 QS = *Rule of the Community* from Cave 1; 1 QSa = *Rule of the Congregation* from Cave 1; 1 QSb = *Blessings* from Cave 1; 4 QpNah. = the *pesher* [commentary] on Nahum from Qumran Cave 4)
Quaest. Exod.	*Questions on Exodus* (Philo)
Quaest. Gen.	*Questions on Genesis* (Philo)
RB	*Revue Biblique*
Ref.	*Refutation of all Heresies*, otherwise called *Philosophumena* (Hippolytus)
RGG[3]	*Religion in Geschichte und Gegenwart*, 3rd edn (Tübingen, 1957ff)
RHPR	*Revue d'Histoire et de Philosophie Religieuses*
RThR	*Reformed Theological Review* (Australia)
Sat.	*Satires* (Juvenal)
SEG	*Supplementum Epigraphicum Graecum*
Sib.Or.	Sibylline Oracles
SNTS	Studiorum Novi Testamenti Societas
Somn.	*On Dreams* (Philo)
Strack-Billerbeck	*Kommentar zum Neuen Testament aus Talmud und Midrasch*, H. L. Strack & P. Billerbeck (München, 1922ff)
Strom.	*Stromata* (*Miscellanies*) (Clement of Alexandria)
TB	Babylonian Talmud
TJ	Jerusalem Talmud
TU	*Texte und Untersuchungen*
TWNT	*Theologisches Wörterbuch zum Neuen Testament*, ed. G. Kittel & G. Friedrich (Stuttgart, 1933ff)
Vit. Contempl.	*The Contemplative Life* (Philo)
Vit. Mos.	*Life of Moses* (Philo)
VT	*Vetus Testamentum* (Leiden)

NEW TESTAMENT
HISTORY

1 From Cyrus to Augustus

1

The latest narrative books of the Hebrew Bible deal with the period when Judaea, with the rest of Western Asia, formed part of the Persian Empire. The last monarch whom they mention by name is 'Darius the Persian' (Neh. 12:22)—either Darius II (423–405 B.C.) or, more probably, Darius III (336–331 B.C.), the last king of Persia.

When we open the New Testament, we find another world power dominating the Near East and indeed the whole Mediterranean area. The New Testament writings, from first to last, are set in the context of the Roman Empire. The story which they tell, from the closing years of the pre-Christian era to the end of the first century A.D., presupposes throughout the dominating presence of Roman power. The Third Evangelist connects the birth of Jesus with a decree issued by the first Roman Emperor Augustus, 'that all the world should be enrolled' (Luke 2:1). Jesus grew to manhood in a land where the propriety of paying to Rome the tribute which it imposed was a live political and theological issue; it was a Roman magistrate who sentenced him to death and it was by a Roman form of execution that the sentence was carried out. The most prominent character in New Testament history after Jesus himself is Paul, a Roman citizen by birth, who carried the Christian message from its Palestinian homeland through the eastern provinces of the Roman Empire until he reached Rome itself; our last certain view of Paul sees him living there in house-arrest for two years, at liberty to urge the Christian way of salvation on all who came to visit him.[1] Nor does the New Testament stop there; it carries the story forward to the following decades in which Roman law set its face against Christianity, so that a man was liable to suffer 'as a Christian',[2] without its being necessary to produce evidence of positive criminal action on his part. The Roman Empire is presented, in the powerful imagery of John's Apocalypse, as a seven-headed mon-

[1] Acts 28:30f; see pp. 361ff.   [2] I Peter 4:16; see p. 425.

ster, waging war against the people of God and all who refuse to
pay it divine honours, but doomed to go down in defeat before
'the patience and faith of the saints' as they win through to final
victory 'by the blood of the Lamb and by the word of their testimony' (Rev. 13:10; 12:11).

2

Between the last king of Persia and the extension of Roman rule
over the Near East, that part of the world had been dominated by
the Graeco-Macedonian Empire of Alexander the Great and his
successors. Alexander the Great, king of Macedonia, whose father
Philip had unified the Greek world under him by diplomatic and
military action, led an invading army of Macedonians and Greeks
into Asia in 334 B.C. In three years he had conquered the whole
Persian Empire (including Egypt); in the following years he advanced farther east and added to his empire the territories which
we now know as Afghanistan and Western Pakistan. His empire,
as a political unity, did not survive his death in 323 B.C.; but the
cultural empire which he founded lasted for nearly a thousand
years, until the rise of Islam and the Arab conquests of the seventh
century A.D.

Some of Alexander's leading generals divided his empire among
themselves soon after his death and founded dynasties, some of
which endured well into the first century B.C. Of these dynasties
the most important for our purpose were the Ptolemaic dynasty in
Egypt, founded by Ptolemy I in 323 B.C., with its capital in Alexandria, and the Seleucid dynasty in Syria, founded by Seleucus I
in 312 B.C., with its capital in Antioch. Judaea was part of the dominions of the Ptolemies until 198 B.C. In that year it changed hands, in
consequence of a Seleucid victory won at Paneion, near the sources
of the Jordan (the Caesarea Philippi of the gospel narrative),[3] and
for the next fifty years and more it belonged to the Seleucid Empire.

Under these Hellenistic dynasties, as under the Persians before

[3] Mark 8:27; see pp. 186f. Paneion, and the district of Paneas to which it
belonged (cf. mod. Banyas), were so called by the Greeks after the god Pan,
to whom (together with the Nymphs) they dedicated the grotto there in which
Nahr Banyas, one of the principal sources of Jordan, springs up. Probably the
place had always been regarded by the local inhabitants as a sacred shrine; it
may be the Baal-gad of Joshua 11:17. See p. 26.

them, Judaea enjoyed a considerable measure of internal autonomy. The country was controlled by an imperial governor, and the people had to pay taxes to the imperial exchequer; but Judaea itself—which consisted of a restricted area radiating but a few miles from Jerusalem—was organized as a temple-state, whose constitution was laid down in the priestly law of the Pentateuch.[4] The high priest, as head of the Temple administration, was head of the internal administration of the tiny Jewish state. There were many Jews outside Judaea—in Babylonia and in Asia Minor, in Alexandria and in Antioch—and their gifts helped to maintain the Jerusalem Temple and its administration; but only the Jews who lived in Judaea came directly under the jurisdiction of the high priest. The high priest was always drawn from the ancient family of Zadok—the Zadok who had been chief priest in the earlier Temple built by King Solomon about 960 B.C.

Shortly after Judaea fell under the control of the Seleucid Empire, that empire clashed in the Aegean world with the expanding power of Rome and was completely defeated at the battle of Magnesia in 190 B.C. The ensuing Peace of Apamea (188 B.C.) not only deprived the Seleucids of their wealthy provinces in Western Asia Minor, but imposed a crushing indemnity on them, which was to be paid in twelve annual instalments. As it was, the period of payment had to be extended, and many of the events of the following years can be traced to the necessity of raising the money for the indemnity. When Jason, brother of the Zadokite high priest Onias III, offered the Seleucid king Antiochus IV (175–163 B.C.) a sum of money if he would make him high priest in his brother's place, Antiochus could not afford to ignore the proffered bribe, especially as Jason undertook to speed the process of Hellenization in Judaea. When, a few years later (171 B.C.), a still more ardent Hellenizer named Menelaus, who did not belong to the Zadokite line, offered the king a larger sum if he would make *him* high priest in Jason's place, once more the bribe was accepted, and for the future no Zadokite high priest ministered in Jerusalem.

Antiochus IV, who assumed the epithet Epiphanes (which im-

---

[4] Cf. Ezra 7:14, where 'Ezra the priest, the scribe of the law of the God of heaven' (meaning perhaps secretary of state for Jewish affairs in the Persian imperial chancery) is commissioned by Artaxerxes 'to make inquiries about Judah and Jerusalem according to the law of your God, which is in your hand'.

plied that he was the manifestation on earth of Olympian Zeus),
tried to make up for his father's losses in the Aegean area by an-
nexing Egypt to the Seleucid dominions, but when he was on the
brink of success he was decisively checked by Roman intervention
(168 B.C.). News of this check prompted an attempt in Judaea to
oust the king's high-priestly nominee Menelaus in favour of the deposed Jason. Antiochus looked on this as an act of rebellion; on his
way back from Egypt he treated Jerusalem as a rebellious city,
demolishing the walls and looting the Temple treasury. More than
that, since it was important to ensure the loyalty of Judaea, which
lay on the exposed south-western frontier of his empire, he was advised to abolish the Temple constitution, ban the distinctive practices of the Jewish religion, and give Jerusalem a new constitution
as a Hellenistic city in which the thorough-going assimilationists in
the population were enrolled as citizens. The Temple, still under
the control of Menelaus, was turned over to the cult of Olympian
Zeus, identified with the Syrian deity Ba'al Shamem, 'the lord of
heaven'. For three years—from December, 167 B.C., to December,
164 B.C.—this 'appalling sacrilege' or 'abomination of desolation'[5]
(Heb. *šiqqūṣ mĕšōmēm*, a mocking pun on the name Ba'al Shamem)
dominated the holy house.

Those Jews who valued loyalty to their ancestral religion above
everything else refused to submit to the royal decrees and many of
them suffered martyrdom. Others took up arms against the king
and found leaders in Mattathias, an aged priest of the Hasmonaean
family, and his five sons—Judas Maccabaeus and his brothers.
Thanks to the genius of Judas as a guerrilla leader, which resulted
in the defeat of a succession of royal armies far larger and better
armed than his own following, Antiochus, who had plans for recov-
ering lost provinces beyond the Euphrates and had no wish to tie
down large forces on the Judaean front, saw the wisdom of coming
to terms with the Jewish insurgents. The ban on the practice of the
Jewish religion was rescinded, and the worship of the God of Israel
was resumed in the purified Temple according to the ancient ritual
(164 B.C.).[6]

[5] Gk. βδέλυγμα ἐρημώσεως (I Macc. 1:54; cf. Dan. 11:31 [8:13; 9:27;
12:11]; Mark 13:14). See p. 257.
[6] The reconstruction of the Temple has ever since been celebrated annually
by Jews on Kislew 25 as the feast of Ḥanukkah ('dedication')—an ancient
winter solstice ritual thus received a new historical significance, following a

But the Hasmonaeans, having recovered religious liberty for their people by military means, had no thought of resting content with this achievement. They continued the struggle for twenty years and more, and were greatly aided by dynastic rivalry and civil strife within the Seleucid camp, until at last national autonomy was won under Simon, the last survivor of the sons of Mattathias (142 B.C.).

The conditions of this long struggle, with the opportunities it offered to the Jewish leaders to play off one Seleucid ruler against another, tended to compromise the idealism which had marked its inception. This was particularly manifest in 152 B.C., when Jonathan, who had succeeded his brother Judas Maccabaeus eight years previously as leader of the insurgent Jews, accepted the high-priesthood as a gift from Alexander Balas, pretender to the Seleucid throne. His action must have caused grave misgivings among those pious Jews for whom the constitutional succession to the high-priesthood was part of the law of God. Yet, when national independence was secured under Simon, who succeeded to the leadership when Jonathan was taken prisoner and put to death in 143 B.C., a grateful popular assembly decreed that Simon should not only be their civil governor and military leader, but also 'high priest for ever, until a trustworthy prophet should arise' (I Macc. 14:41). That is to say, in default of a suitable candidate of Zadokite stock (since the heir to the Zadokite high-priesthood had betaken himself some twenty years previously to Egypt, there to preside over a new Jewish temple at Leontopolis),[7] Simon was recognized as founder of a heredi-

---

pattern established much earlier for Israel's sacred year (cf. I Macc. 4:42–59; II Macc. 1:18; 10:1–8; John 10:22).

[7] The temple at Leontopolis was founded by Onias IV, son of Onias III whom Antiochus IV deposed from the high-priesthood in 174 B.C. He migrated to Egypt about 161 B.C., when Alcimus was appointed high priest in Jerusalem (cf. I Macc. 7:5ff), and was welcomed by Ptolemy VI, who authorized the building of the Leontopolis temple. Here, under the ministrations of a Zadokite high priest, a sacrificial ritual modelled on that of Jerusalem persisted for 230 years, until it was suppressed by Vespasian on the morrow of the destruction of the Jerusalem Temple (Josephus, *BJ* vii, 423–32; *Ant.* xiii, 62–73). Despite its Zadokite high-priesthood, the Leontopolis temple was generally regarded as schismatic even by Egyptian Jews, many of whom would regularly go on pilgrimage, like Philo, to Jerusalem 'to our ancestral temple' (*Prouid.*, 64). In the Mishnah the Leontopolis temple is called 'the house of Onias'; priests who ministered there were debarred from ministering at Jerusalem (*Menaḥot* 13:10).

tary high-priesthood. There was no means of ascertaining the will of God in the matter, nor would there be, until the expected prophet of the end-time[8] arose to declare it; until he did, Simon and his descendants were to occupy the high-priestly office.

This they did, for over a hundred years, and for three quarters of that period they governed an independent Judaea. The earlier days of the Hasmonaean dynasty were marked by prosperity and national rejoicing. After a brief attempt by the Seleucids to reimpose their authority on Judaea, their strength rapidly diminished, partly in inconclusive campaigns against the Parthians and partly because of further armed rivalry for the throne. The Hasmonaeans, who had so recently been hard put to it to secure bare survival for their nation, now saw undreamed-of opportunities of expansion opening out before them. Simon's son, John Hyrcanus (134–104 B.C.), overran Idumaea, Samaria and part of Galilee and added them to his realm; his sons Aristobulus I (104–103 B.C.) and Alexander Jannaeus (103–76 B.C.), who took the title 'king', continued their father's conquering enterprise until the kingdom of Judaea, extending from the Mediterranean seaboard on the west into Transjordan on the east, was nearly as large as the united monarchy of David and Solomon.

These kings, however, were unprincipled characters, aping the ways of minor Hellenistic rulers, but lacking any redeeming pretensions to Hellenistic culture. Jannaeus in particular, as he besieged and destroyed one Hellenistic city after another on the perimeter of his kingdom, showed himself a complete vandal. Nor had his vandalism the excuse that it was the product of zeal for the God of Israel against the idolatries of the heathen; of all the high priests of Israel, some of whom did little to adorn their sacred office, none was unworthier than he. He showed no concern for anything but personal power and military conquest; in his unquenchable thirst for this way of life he hazarded his nation's independence more than once, exhausted the national wealth, and forfeited the respect and goodwill of the best elements in the nation.[9]

At his death in 76 B.C. he was succeeded as civil ruler by his wife Salome Alexandra (her Jewish name Salome is an abbreviation of Šělōm-Ṣiyyōn, 'peace of Zion').[10] Her elder son, Hyrcanus II, a

[8] See pp. 38, 212.
[9] See pp. 56f, 75.　　[10] See p. 76.

man singularly lacking in the characteristic family ambition, became high priest; her younger son, Aristobulus II, whose excess of ambition amply compensated for his brother's deficiency, was given a military command. Her reign of nine years was remembered as a brief golden age; her death in 67 B.C. was followed by civil war between the partisans of her two sons. While Hyrcanus was completely unambitious, he was used as a façade by the gifted Idumaean politician Antipater, who saw how useful Hyrcanus could be for the promotion of his own ambitions. Antipater saw clearly that the path of wisdom for a man with his ambitions was to co-operate with the Roman power, which at this juncture was establishing itself firmly in Western Asia. His opportunity came with the Roman occupation of Judaea in 63 B.C. The pretext for this occupation was the civil war between the two Hasmonaean brothers. Each of them invoked the support of the Roman general Pompey, who, in the course of reorganizing Western Asia, was at that time reducing Syria to the status of a Roman province. He intervened very readily, but Aristobulus and his followers soon found themselves opposing him, and their opposition led to his occupation of Jerusalem in the spring of 63 B.C., followed by the three months' siege and storming of the well-fortified Temple area. Judaea lost her independence, and became subject to Rome.

3

Pompey's presence in Syria followed his successful prosecution of a long-drawn-out war between Rome and Mithridates VI, king of Pontus.

In 120 B.C. Mithridates, then a boy twelve years old, fell heir to a kingdom which had at one time been a satrapy of the Persian Empire. It stretched along the southern shore of the Black Sea (from which it derived its name) from the lower Halys eastwards to Colchis. Alexander the Great incorporated it in his empire, but in the wars between his successors it regained its independence. When in 133 B.C. Attalus III, the last king of Pergamum, bequeathed his kingdom to the Senate and people of Rome, Mithridates V of Pontus became an ally of the Romans. He aided them in their war against Aristonicus, half-brother of Attalus, who tried to claim the kingdom of Pergamum for himself, and the Romans rewarded him with part of the territory of Phrygia.

When Mithridates V was assassinated in 120 B.C., and was succeeded by his young son, the Romans took advantage of the latter's youth to reclaim the Phrygian province which they had bestowed on his father. But Mithridates was able to compensate himself by extending his power to the east. His neighbours to the west and south—Bithynia, Galatia and Cappadocia—lay within Rome's sphere of influence and could not be interfered with, but he expanded his power eastward into Armenia and along the east and north coast of the Black Sea until the Crimea was included within his empire. He allied himself with Tigranes, king of Armenia, to whom he gave his daughter in marriage, and with the Parthian and Iberian kingdoms too. With such statesmanship and energy did he expand his power that he became the most powerful ruler in Asia—far more powerful than the warring claimants to the disintegrating Seleucid Empire, and powerful enough to challenge the might of Rome.

He came to blows with Rome when Rome prevented him from placing puppets of his own on the thrones of Cappadocia and Bithynia. The new Roman-sponsored ruler of Bithynia, with Rome's connivance, invaded the territory of Mithridates; when Mithridates's protest to Rome proved fruitless, he overran Cappadocia and Bithynia in 88 B.C., defeating a Roman army in the latter province, and then made himself master of the province of Asia. Such was the hatred of the provincials for their Roman overlords, under whose oppressive domination they had lived for forty years, that when Mithridates ordered the cities of Asia to put to death all Roman and Italian citizens resident there, they co-operated with him readily, and 80,000 persons are said to have been massacred in one day.

Athens and other city-states of Greece, thinking that this was their opportunity too to throw off the Roman yoke, welcomed Mithridates as a new liberator.

Henceforth, inevitably, it was war *à l'outrance* between Rome and Mithridates, but the war dragged on for a quarter of a century. First Sulla was sent out in 87 B.C. He defeated the Pontic armies in Greece and brought back the Greek cities to their Roman allegiance; then, carrying the war into Asia, he compelled Mithridates to give up all his conquests in the Roman province and imposed an indemnity on him (84 B.C.).

There was some further fighting between Mithridates and Roman forces in Asia Minor in the following years, but the next major phase in the struggle was precipitated by the incorporation of Bithynia, which adjoined Pontus on the west, into the Roman Empire in 75 B.C. Mithridates invaded Bithynia as champion of a prince of the former royal house who claimed the throne. Lucius Lucullus, who was sent against him this time, succeeded in driving Mithridates out of Asia Minor altogether, and pursued him into Armenia, where he had taken refuge. But Lucullus's troops mutinied, and by the end of 67 B.C. Mithridates was in possession of his home territory of Pontus once more.

Next year the Roman Senate decided to make an end of the Mithridatic war once and for all, and entrusted the conduct of operations to Gnaeus Pompeius (Pompey), who was given an unlimited command over all the Roman forces in the east in order to press the war to a successful conclusion. Pompey was marked out as the man to achieve this by the success which he had shown the previous year in clearing the eastern Mediterranean from the pirates who had infested it for long, and whose interference with the grain supply was threatening Rome itself with famine. Thanks to the extraordinary powers bestowed on him, and his own extraordinary skill as a strategist, Pompey completed his operation against the pirates in three months. His extraordinary powers were confirmed and expanded by the Manilian Law of 66 B.C. Arriving in Asia Minor, Pompey took over from Lucullus command of the Roman armies there. Mithridates was driven from Pontus, and as his son-in-law refused him entrance into Armenia, he withdrew to his Crimean dominions (65 B.C.), and there, two years later, he committed suicide.

The whole of Western Asia now lay at Pompey's mercy. Tigranes acknowledged Pompey as his conqueror, and was confirmed as king of Armenia, but had to surrender to Rome the territories which he had annexed in Cappadocia, Cilicia and Syria. Pontus was made a Roman province. In 64 B.C. Syria also was made a province, the last remnant of Seleucid power having collapsed, and the neighbouring principalities, including Judaea, had to acknowledge Roman overlordship.

4

The reputation of the Romans for rapacity had preceded them in the new areas which they now occupied. Mithridates had done his best, during his twenty-five years of intermittent war with the Romans, to prejudice his allies and neighbours against them. One sample of his anti-Roman propaganda is preserved in his letter to Arsaces XII, king of Parthia (*c.* 69 B.C.):

> The Romans have from of old known but one ground for waging war with all nations, peoples and kings—inveterate lust of empire and wealth. . . . Do you not realize that they leave nothing that they do not lay their hands on—homes, wives, land, power? that they are a gang of men with no fatherland or ancestry of their own, swept together of old to be a plague to the whole world? No law, human or divine, can stand in their way; they uproot and drag off their 'friends' and 'allies', whether they live near at hand or far away, whether they are weak or strong; they treat as their enemies all men, and especially all kingdoms, that refuse to serve them as slaves.[11]

That this was not pure invention is clear from the testimony of public-spirited Romans. For example, in his speech advocating the bestowal of extraordinary powers on Pompey for the final prosecution of the war against Mithridates, Cicero said:

> It is difficult to convey to you, gentlemen, the bitter hatred felt for us among foreign nations because of the unbridled and outrageous behaviour of the men whom we have sent to govern them during these past years. What temple in those lands do you think has had its sanctity respected by our magistrates? What state has been free from their aggression? What home has been adequately closed and protected against them? They actually look around for wealthy and flourishing cities in order to find an occasion of waging war against them and thus gratify their lust for plunder. . . . Do you suppose that when you send an army you are defending your allies against their enemies? No, you are using these enemies as a pretext for attacking your friends and allies. What state in Asia is sufficient to contain the arrogance and insolence of one ordinary military tribune—not to speak of a general or his second-in-command?[12]

[11] Sallust, *Hist.*, frag. iv. 69, 1–23 (ed. A. Kurfess, *C. Sallustius Crispus*, Bibliotheca Teubneriana [Leipzig, 1954], pp. 162–4).
[12] Cicero, *Pro Lege Manilia*, 65f (66 B.C.).

Plainly, some superior power to check the rapacity of provincial
governors was called for, if the Roman dominion was to be tolerable
at all to subject-nations.

The effectiveness of Mithridates's propaganda in Western Asia
may be judged from its echo in the Qumran commentary on Habakkuk, composed shortly before the Roman occupation of Judaea in 63
B.C., where Habakkuk's Chaldaean invaders are reinterpreted as
the 'Kitti'im' or 'Kittim', in whom it is not difficult (as in Dan. 11:30)
to recognize the Romans:

> Their fear and terror are on all the nations, and in the council all
> their device is to do evil, and with trickery and deceit they proceed
> with all peoples. . . . They trample the earth with their horses and
> their beasts: from afar they come, from the coastlands of the sea, to
> devour all peoples like an eagle, and there is no sating them. With
> wrath and anger and fury of face and impetuousness of countenance
> they speak with all peoples. . . . They scorn great ones, they despise
> mighty men, of kings and princes they make sport, and they mock at
> a great people. . . . They sacrifice to their ensigns, and their weapons
> of war are their objects of worship. . . . They apportion their yoke
> as their tribute, the source of their sustenance, on all peoples, to lay
> waste many lands year by year. . . . They destroy many with the
> sword—youths, men in their prime, and old men; women and little
> children, and on the fruit of the womb they have no compassion.[18]

Yet in the eyes of the Qumran commentator the Kittim were to
be the executors of divine judgement against the Hasmonaeans, who
usurped the high-priesthood that belonged properly to the sons of
Zadok—although he was tempted to think that the cure might
prove worse than the disease.

In the *Psalms of Solomon* (c. 50 B.C.) the Romans are also seen as
the agents of divine judgement against the Hasmonaeans, although
here the offence of the latter is not that they usurped the Zadokite
high-priesthood but that they 'laid waste the throne of David' (*Ps.
Sol.* 17:8).

> But thou, O God, wilt cast them down, and remove their seed from the
> earth,

[18] 1QpHab. iii, 4–vi, 12 (on Hab. 1:7–17). The Qumran 'Kittim' have also
been interpreted as the Seleucid forces under Antiochus IV; cf., e.g. H. H.
Rowley, 'The Kittim and the Dead Sea Scrolls', *PEQ* 88 (1956), pp. 92ff.
See p. 113.

For there has risen up against them a man alien to our race.
According to their sins wilt thou recompense them, O God;
So that it befalls them according to their deeds.
God will show them no pity;
He has sought out their seed and let none of them go free.
Faithful is the Lord in all his judgements
Which he accomplishes on earth.[14]

The man 'alien to our race' is Pompey, in whose triumphal procession Aristobulus II and his sons, with many other Jews of noble birth, were led as captives in 61 B.C. But, like the Qumran commentator, the psalmist deplores the savagery of the Romans:

The lawless one laid waste our land so that none inhabited it,
They destroyed young and old and their children together.
In the heat of his anger he sent them away to the west,
And exposed the rulers of the land unsparingly to derision.
Being an alien, the enemy behaved arrogantly
And his heart was alien from our God.[15]

One of Pompey's acts was felt to be specially shocking. When he captured the Temple area in Jerusalem, he insisted on entering the holy house, and penetrating into the holy of holies itself, the throne-room of Israel's God, which was barred to all access except once in the year, on the Day of Atonement, when the high priest entered to present a sin-offering on behalf of the nation before the invisible presence of Yahweh. That a pagan soldier should force his way in, despite the protests of the priests, was an unspeakable sacrilege. When, fifteen years later, Pompey fled to Egypt from Pharsalus in Thessaly, the field of his defeat by Julius Caesar, and was assassinated as he set foot on the Egyptian shore, there were some in Judaea who remembered his sacrilegious act and recognized that divine nemesis had caught up with him at last. Among these was one of the circle that produced the *Psalms of Solomon:*

I had not long to wait before God showed me the insolent one
Slain on the mountains of Egypt,
Esteemed less than the least, on land or sea,

[14] *Ps. Sol.* 17:8–12.
[15] *Ps. Sol.* 17:13–5. The Romans at close quarters presented a different picture from the idealized description of them given a few decades earlier in I Macc. 8:1–16.

His body tossed this way and that on the billows with much insolence,
With none to bury him, since he had rejected God with dishonour.[16]

5

After Pompey's conquest of Judaea, Hyrcanus II was confirmed
in the high-priesthood and in the titular leadership of the nation,
but the nation was now tributary to Rome, and lost its control over
the neighbouring Greek and Samaritan territories which the Hasmonaean rulers had conquered and added to their kingdom.

During the next thirty years, Judaea and the province of Syria to
which it was attached, lying as they did on the eastern frontier of
the Roman sphere of influence, were involved in imperial politics,
and in Rome's relations with the neighbouring empires of Egypt
and Parthia. Antipater, remaining the power behind Hyrcanus's
throne, played his cards astutely and made himself increasingly
useful to the Romans, pre-eminently so to Julius Caesar when the
latter was besieged in the palace quarter of Alexandria during the
winter of 48–47 B.C.

In appreciation of Antipater's services, Caesar made him a tax-
free Roman citizen with the title of procurator of Judaea. He was
allowed to rebuild the walls of Jerusalem, which Pompey had dis-
mantled; Judaea's tribute was reduced, and a number of other concessions were made to the Jews.

The assassination of Caesar in 44 B.C. was a blow to the Jews, but
Antipater continued to support the representatives of Roman power
in the East, whoever they might be at one time or another. He was
assassinated himself in 43 B.C., but his sons Phasael and Herod continued their father's policy, and when the partisans of Caesar, led by
Octavian (Caesar's adopted son) and Mark Antony, defeated the
anti-Caesarian army at Philippi in 42 B.C., and the eastern part of
the empire came under Antony's control, Phasael and Herod were
appointed joint-tetrarchs of Judaea.

In 40 B.C. the provinces of Syria and Judaea were overrun by the
Parthians, who placed the Hasmonaean Antigonus (son of Aris-
tobulus II) on the throne in Jerusalem as priest-king of the Jews.
Phasael was captured and killed; Herod escaped to Rome, where

[16] *Ps. Sol.* 2:30–2.

the Senate, on the motion of Antony and Octavian, declared him king of the Jews.

The reconquest of Judaea was no easy matter, but by October, 37 B.C., it was completed by Herod's capture of Jerusalem, with the aid of Roman troops, after a siege of three months. Antigonus was sent in chains to Antony at Antioch, and there executed at Herod's request.

Herod's reign of thirty-three years was thus inaugurated in circumstances ill-calculated to win him the goodwill of his subjects. Although he chose as his queen the Hasmonaean princess Mariamme (granddaughter of both the rival brothers, Hyrcanus II and Aristobulus II), putting away his first wife Doris in order to marry her, the Jews continued to look on him as an Idumaean upstart who had usurped the royal estate over the dead body of the rightful king, Antigonus.

Herod nevertheless showed himself an able, if ruthless, administrator, and throughout his reign the Romans had no reason to rue the day when they appointed him king of the Jews. He consistently upheld the interests of Rome at home and abroad, and indeed he found no contradiction between Rome's interests and those of his kingdom and subjects. Their interests, including the preservation of their religious freedom, would be best served, he believed, by integration into the Roman sphere of influence.

For the first few years of his reign he was subjected to considerable anxiety because of the covetous glances which Cleopatra VII of Egypt threw at his kingdom. Antony was his friend, but at the same time Antony was so much under Cleopatra's influence that there was some danger that she might at last get her way and add Judaea to her empire as her ancestors, the earliest Ptolemies, had done. She did indeed secure the revenues of some of the richest parts of Judaea, especially Jericho and the surrounding territory. She also tried to stir up strife, to her own advantage, between Herod and his eastern neighbour, the king of the Nabataean Arabs.

Herod's position was the more insecure during these years because of the friendship between Cleopatra and his mother-in-law Alexandra, daughter of Hyrcanus II. When Antigonus was deposed and put to death, Hyrcanus II could not resume the high-priesthood because his ears had been cropped by Antigonus so that he might be disqualified from ever again holding the sacred office.

The next in succession among the Hasmonaeans was Mariamme's brother, the seventeen-year-old Aristobulus III. At Alexandra's insistence, Herod in 30 B.C. appointed the boy high priest. A few months later, however, Aristobulus was drowned in a bathing accident, and Herod was widely suspected of having arranged the 'accident'. The boy's mother had no doubt at all of Herod's guilt, and made such indignant representations to Cleopatra that the latter persuaded Antony to investigate the alleged crime. Antony summoned Herod to appear before him at Laodicea in North Syria, but acquitted him of the charge of murder, remarking to Cleopatra that 'one must not inquire too closely into the actions of a king, lest he ceases to be a king'.[17] Cleopatra no doubt found this point well taken.

The growing tension in the Roman Empire between Antony and Cleopatra on the one hand and Octavian on the other came to a head in 31 B.C. at the Battle of Actium, in western Greece, where Antony and Cleopatra were completely defeated. They fled back to Egypt, where both committed suicide next year. Octavian was now undisputed master of the Roman world, and he was the representative of Roman power with whom Herod had to deal for the remainder of his life. Soon after his victory at Actium, Octavian summoned Herod to meet him at Rhodes. Herod went with some trepidation, for it was well known that he had been Antony's friend. He did not attempt to disguise from Octavian his friendship with Antony, but assured him that he would find him as good a friend and ally as Antony had done. Octavian, for his part, recognized how well the interests of Rome would continue to be served in the East if Herod remained as king of the Jews, so Herod was confirmed in his kingdom. He was given back the region round Jericho, which Cleopatra had detached from his kingdom, and he received in addition a number of Greek cities on the Mediterranean coast and on both sides of the Jordan.

6

In January, 27 B.C., Octavian, having established peace throughout the Roman world, 'handed the republic back to the Senate and

[17] Josephus, *Ant.* xv, 76.

people of Rome'.[18] He himself was acclaimed as *princeps*, chief citizen of the republic, and among other honours was given the name Augustus, by which he was thenceforth known. In fact he retained all the reins of power in his own hands, but he knew the psychological and diplomatic value of restoring the forms and no-menclature of the old republican régime.

When he handed the republic back to the Senate and people of Rome, he handed back the provinces, many of which were at the time administered by officers of his own. He was immediately asked, and consented, to undertake direct responsibility for the adminis-tration of some of the most important of these provinces. It is often said that he administered directly those provinces which required the presence of a standing army, while the more peaceful provinces came under the jurisdiction of the Senate. This is roughly true, though not completely so. Augustus was commander-in-chief of the Roman army, so provinces which required Roman arms either for external defence (as along the Rhine, Danube and Euphrates fron-tiers) or for internal security were more conveniently administered by him through one of his officers. But even those provinces (like Asia and Achaia) which were nominally under the control of the Senate and were governed by proconsuls appointed by that body were none the less really under the control of Augustus and his successors. Neither the Senate in appointing a proconsul, nor the proconsul in administering his province, could afford to ignore the will of the *princeps*.

Those provinces which required legionary troops to be posted in them (like Galatia and Syria) were administered by an imperial legate, the *legatus pro praetore*. For the sixty years following A.D. 6, when Judaea became a Roman province, it was garrisoned not by legionary but by auxiliary troops, and was governed by an officer of lower rank than an imperial legate—by a member of the eques-trian order, the *praefectus* or *procurator*.[19]

---

[18] His own account is in the *Res Gestae Diui Augusti*, completed shortly be-fore his death (A.D. 14) and preserved in the bilingual *Monumentum Ancyra-num*: 'in consulatu sexto et septimo, po[stquam b]ella [ciuil]ia exstinxeram, per consensum uniuersorum [potitus reru]m om[n]ium, rem publicam ex mea potestate in senat[us populique Rom]ani [a]rbitrium transtuli' (§ 34).

[19] *Praefectus Iudaeae* is the title given to Pontius Pilate in the inscription bearing his name which was discovered in the theatre excavations at Caesarea in 1961; the title *procurator* was probably not borne by governors of Judaea

The proconsuls of Asia and Africa were normally ex-consuls, the proconsuls of the other senatorial provinces were ex-praetors. In either case the proconsuls were members of the senatorial order. So were the imperial legates, who might be either ex-consuls or ex-praetors.

Egypt was administered by a prefect appointed directly by the *princeps*; he had a legionary garrison under his command, but was drawn from the equestrian order.

A number of territories, in the East particularly, were governed in the interests of Rome by native dynasties of 'client kings'. Judaea under the Herods, from 40 B.C. to A.D. 6 and again from A.D. 41 to 44, provides one example; another is provided by Cappadocia, which was governed by a native dynasty until Tiberius annexed most of it as a province on the death of its aged king, Archelaus, in A.D. 17. South-east of Cappadocia and north of Syria lay Commagene, whose king, Antiochus III, died about the same time as Archelaus; his kingdom was added to the province of Syria. But twenty years later the Emperor Gaius restored it to his son Antiochus IV, and added to it a westward extension of territory reaching the eastern frontier of Galatia, with a coastal strip between Pamphylia and Cilicia. Three years later, however, he was deprived of his new kingship, but Claudius restored it to him when he became emperor in A.D. 41, and he reigned for long as the friend and ally of Rome.

Some of the cities in the eastern provinces had a special status, more or less independent of the provincial administration. There were, for example, the Roman colonies—settlements of Roman citizens which received a municipal constitution modelled on that of the city of Rome itself, with two principal collegiate magistrates, the *duouiri* or, as they often preferred to be called, praetors. These colonies were sometimes established at strategic positions along the great roads to safeguard imperial interests; sometimes they provided a convenient means of disposing of veteran soldiers on their retirement. Thus, after Antony and Octavian defeated the army of Caesar's assassins (led by Brutus and Cassius) at Philippi in 42 B.C., they gave that long-standing Macedonian city a new constitution as a Roman colony (calling it *Colonia Iulia*) and settled their veterans there. Eleven years later, when Octavian defeated Antony

---

before the time of Claudius. See A. N. Sherwin-White, *Roman Society and Roman Law in the First Century* (Oxford, 1963), pp. 6ff.

at Actium, he settled in the new colony a group of Italian settlers who had supported Antony and who were now obliged to cede their lands to Octavian's veterans; the official name of the colony was amplified to *Colonia Augusta Iulia Philippensis*. Although several Roman colonies figure in the narrative of Acts, Philippi is the only one which is expressly referred to as such by Luke. Its citizens are very conscious of their superior dignity as Romans, and their two collegiate magistrates, who are referred to by the more grandiloquent title praetors, are attended, as such senior Roman magistrates were, by their lictors; it is with the lictors' rods, normally carried in bundles (*fasces*), that Paul and Silas receive a summary beating.[20]

Corinth was another Roman colony, founded as such by Julius Caesar in 46 B.C. after it had lain derelict for a century, and given the official designation *Laus Iulia Corinthus*; it was one of the colonies where Caesar settled some of the overflowing proletariat of Rome.

At various times before the Roman provincial system extended over so much of the East, a number of Greek city-states had entered into alliance with Rome, and continued to enjoy a special status as free or federate cities. Athens, for example, largely in view of her glorious past, had the status of a *ciuitas foederata* with municipal autonomy, paying no tribute to Rome and remaining independent of the provincial government of Achaia, within which it lay. Ephesus, in the province of Asia, was a free city (*ciuitas libera*) with its own senate and assembly, rejoicing in its religious prestige as 'Temple Warden (*neōkoros*) of Artemis'.[21] But these privileges were completely dependent on Roman goodwill, as appears from the narrative of the riotous assembly in the Ephesian theatre towards the end of Acts 19. The secretary of the *dēmos* shows by the terms of his conciliatory speech how anxious he is lest the Roman authorities deprive the city of her privileges as a punishment for the citizens' irregular behaviour: 'we are in danger of being charged with rioting today, there being no cause that we can give to justify this commotion' (Acts 19:40).

The history and very existence of some eastern cities was so closely

[20] Acts 16:22; the lictors are called ῥαβδοῦχοι, 'rod-bearers' (Acts 16:35, 38). See p. 307.
[21] Cf. Acts 19:35; see p. 329.

bound up with their sacred associations—as when the city had
grown up around a temple—that they had special constitutions as
temple-cities. Such a city was Hierapolis in Syria, seat of the worship of Atargatis (the 'Syrian goddess' of Lucian's treatise). Jerusalem was another. With the surrounding territory of Judaea it had
been recognized as a temple-state by the Persian Empire, as by the
Ptolemaic and Seleucid dynasties which succeeded in turn to Alexander's empire, until its special constitution was abolished by
Antiochus Epiphanes. Under this constitution the high priest was
head of the internal administration of the state, while the interests
of the imperial power were looked after by a Persian and thereafter
a Greek governor. A similar state of affairs was restored after A.D. 6,
when the high priest, presiding over the Sanhedrin, administered
the internal interests of Judaea, while the interests of Rome, which
always included the maintenance of public order, were safeguarded
by the procurator. The sacred status of Jerusalem was respected by
the Romans; for example, Roman military standards, bearing the
imperial image, were not carried into the city out of deference to
the Jewish objection, based on the Second Commandment of the
Decalogue, to 'graven images' of any kind. As it happened Hierosolyma, common Greek form of the name Jerusalem (which actually
means 'foundation of Shalem' or 'foundation of peace'), seemed to
emphasize the sacred character of the city, for it is modelled on the
analogy of compound words whose first element is *hieros*, 'sacred'.[22]

[22] The Alexandrian writer Lysimachus voices the fanciful idea that the city
was originally called Hierosyla (from Gk. ἱερόσυλος, 'temple-plunderer' or
'sacrilegious', as in Acts 19:37), 'because of the Jews' sacrilegious propensities. At a later date, when they had risen to power, they changed the name to
avoid the disgraceful imputation, and called the city Hierosolyma and themselves Hierosolymites' (quoted by Josephus, *Apion* i, 311). Tacitus mentions a
theory which derives the Jews from Crete; the Solymi, a Cretan people referred to by Homer (*Iliad* vi, 184; *Odyssey* v, 282), 'are supposed to have
founded Hierosolyma and named it after themselves' (*Hist.* v, 2).

2 The Herodian Succession

1

With Cleopatra and her malicious covetousness at last removed, with his kingdom confirmed to him by the undisputed master of the Mediterranean world, Herod might have been expected to breathe more freely. But fresh anxieties crowded in upon him to take the place of those which the victory at Actium had dispelled.

He did indeed enjoy for many years the goodwill not only of the emperor but also of the emperor's close friend and son-in-law Marcus Agrippa. He administered his kingdom capably in the interests of Rome and proved that his title of 'allied king'[1] was much more than nominal. When Augustus sent Aelius Gallus on his abortive expedition against the Sabaeans of S.W. Arabia in 25 B.C., Herod supplied a contingent of 500 auxiliaries.[2] Such, indeed, was the confidence which Augustus felt in him that, when he had crushed rebellion in the Transjordanian territories north of the Yarmuk,[3] he found no better way of ensuring their good behaviour for the future than by adding them to Herod's kingdom (23–20 B.C.), which thus approached the limits to which the united monarchy of Israel had extended a thousand years earlier under David and Solomon.

Had Herod done nothing else, he would have made a secure niche in history for himself as a great builder. Some of his buildings were designed for defence. In the early part of his reign he rebuilt the Hasmonaean fortress of Baris north-west of the Temple area in Jerusalem, and renamed it Antonia after his friend and patron Antony. Further defences were provided for Jerusalem and also for Jericho; fortresses were established at Masada (south-west of the

---

[1] *Rex socius.* In Josephus, *Ant.* xvii, 246, Herod is called Augustus's 'friend and ally', but it is not certain if he enjoyed the official designation of *socius et amicus populi Romani.*

[2] Josephus, *Ant.* xv, 317; Strabo, *Geog.* xvi, 4, 23.

[3] The districts called Trachonitis, Batanaea, Auranitis and Ituraea.

Dead Sea), Machaerus (east of the Dead Sea), Herodeion (near
Jerusalem), another Herodeion (on the Nabataean border), and
Alexandreion (near Jericho). He built several new cities: Antipatris
and Phasaelis were named after members of his own family, Agrip-
peion or Agrippias (the rebuilt Anthedon) was named after the
emperor's friend Agrippa, while Sebaste (the restored Samaria)
and Caesarea on the Mediterranean coast (formerly called Strato's
Tower) were named after the emperor himself. Caesarea, which
was provided with a great artificial harbour, took twelve years to
build (22–10 B.C.), and became the principal port of the country.

His fame as a builder extended far beyond Judaea. He erected
temples or other public buildings in Athens, Sparta, Rhodes and
other great cities of the Greek world; he repaved the main street
of Syrian Antioch and equipped it with a colonnade. While the
stricter Jews among his subjects viewed with misgivings his erecting
temples to pagan deities both overseas and in the Hellenistic cities
of Judaea, they could not complain that he expended more on them
than he did on the Temple of Israel's God in Jerusalem. The reconstruction of the national shrine was his greatest building enterprise.
The project was begun early in 19 B.C. A thousand Levites were
trained as builders, and they did their work so efficiently that the
sacred services of the Temple were carried on without interruption
all the time. The outer court was extended and enclosed by colonnades; the whole area was adorned with splendid gateways and
other structures until the whole architectural complex became
famed throughout the world for its magnificence. The first stage of
its reconstruction took ten years to complete; it was then officially
consecrated. But much more remained to be done before the work
was finished; the finishing touches, indeed, were not put to it until
A.D. 63, only seven years before its destruction.

The cost of this great building programme, as of the maintenance
of his court and the general lavishness of Herod's character and
style, must have been enormous. He had ample private means, including (from 12 B.C. onward) half the revenue from the copper-
mines in Cyprus, for which he gave Augustus 300 talents.[4] But much
of the expenditure must have been met by taxation of one kind or
another. He probably knew how oppressive a burden this was for

[4] Josephus, *Ant.* xvi, 128.

his subjects to bear, and occasionally did something to relieve it. In
20 B.C. he remitted a third of their taxes; six years later he remitted
a quarter. When the land was hard hit by famine in 25 B.C. he took
energetic measures for famine relief, even converting the palace
plate into coinage for this purpose.[5] But none of these concessions
endeared him to his Jewish subjects. The more he insisted to them
that he was a true Jew, the less pardonable in their eyes were his
acts of courtesy towards pagan religion. If he reconstructed Yahweh's Temple in Jerusalem, it was the more intolerable that he
should build idolatrous temples elsewhere. What credit was there
in his insistence that Syllaeus, the Nabataean vizier, could not marry
his sister Salome unless he consented to be circumcised, when he
allowed his own statue to be set up in a pagan temple in Batanaea?[6]

He paid respectful attention to Pharisaic scruples and held such
leading Pharisees as Pollio and Samaias[7] in high regard, refusing
even to punish them when they refused to take the oath of allegiance
to himself which he exacted of all his subjects in 17 B.C.[8] But as
he grew older he became more impatient of Pharisaic recalcitrance.
He penalized those Pharisees—practically the whole order—who
some ten years later refused to take a new oath of allegiance to
the emperor as well as to Herod.[9] When, towards the end of his
reign, a number of Pharisaic students, instigated by their teachers,
pulled down the great golden eagle which Herod had erected over
the gate of the Jerusalem Temple—a flagrant breach of the Second
Commandment in their eyes—he punished them ferociously.[10]

Herod was tragically unfortunate in his family life. His marriage
with the Hasmonaean princess Mariamme did nothing to improve
his own public image in Judaea, but it did have the result that his
children by Mariamme, having Hasmonaean blood in their veins,
enjoyed the goodwill of the Jews as their father did not. Two of
these children, who bore the good Hasmonaean names Aristobulus

---

[5] Josephus, *Ant.* xv, 299–316.

[6] *OGIS* 415: the inscription (from Si'a) reads: [βα]σιλεῖ Ἡρώδει κυρίῳ
Ὀβαίσατος Σαόδου ἔθηκα τὸν ἀνδριάντα ταῖς ἐμαῖς δαπάνα[ις]. The
donor appears to have been one of the 3,000 Idumaean colonists settled by
Herod in that region (Josephus, *Ant.* xvi, 285).

[7] These have been tentatively identified with Abtalion and Shemayah, mentioned in *Pirqē Abot* 1:10f as the pair of tradents in the generation before
Hillel and Shammai. See p. 73.

[8] Josephus, *Ant.* xv, 370.   [9] Josephus, *Ant.* xvii, 42.

[10] Josephus, *Ant.* xvii, 151–67.

and Alexander, were at an early age nominated by Herod as his heirs. Their mother was executed by her insanely jealous husband when they were young boys (29 B.C.), but they themselves were educated at Rome in a manner befitting their royal expectations. In due course, however, having been suspected of plotting against their father, they too were executed at his instance in 7 B.C.

Herod's suspicions against the sons of Mariamme were not unnaturally fomented by their elder half-brother Antipater, Herod's son by his first wife Doris, whom he had put away thirty years previously in order to marry Mariamme. Now that Mariamme's sons were out of the way, Antipater realized his ambitions and stepped into their place as heir to the throne; indeed, he was practically co-opted by his father as joint king along with him.[11]

But Herod's jealousy was soon directed in turn against Antipater, whom he suspected of plotting against his life. Antipater was therefore deprived of his status as crown prince in favour of one of his half-brothers—Herod, son of a second Mariamme (daughter of the high priest Simon Boëthus, whom Herod married in 23 B.C. in place of the Hasmonaean Mariamme). But in 5 B.C. this son too fell from grace, his mother was divorced and his grandfather deposed from the high-priesthood.[12] Herod's youngest son, Antipas, was now named heir to the throne.[13] Antipas was Herod's son by a secondary wife, a Samaritan woman named Malthake. Herod had an elder son by Malthake, Archelaus by name, but he passed him over at this stage because his mind had been poisoned against him by Antipater.

By this time Herod was in the grip of his last illness, which ended with his death in March, 4 B.C. Four or five days before his death he ordered the execution of Antipater, and changed his mind once more about the succession, for in his last will and testament his kingdom was divided between three of his sons. Antipas was to rule Galilee and Peraea as tetrarch, his full brother Archelaus was to receive Judaea (including Samaria and Idumaea) with the royal title, while Philip, Herod's son by yet another wife (Cleopatra of Jerusalem), was nominated tetrarch of the territory which Herod

[11] Josephus, *Ant.* xvii, 3.
[12] Josephus, *Ant.* xvii, 53, 78. See p. 61.
[13] Josephus, *BJ* i, 646, ii, 20; *Ant.* xvii, 146, 224.

had received from Augustus east and north-east of the Lake of Galilee.[14]

2

Herod's will could not take effect until its provisions were ratified by Augustus. Archelaus and Antipas, and later Philip, made their way to Rome to make sure that their claims were properly represented before the emperor. Antipas, indeed, angled for the kingship in rivalry to Archelaus, and was supported by several members of the royal family and others—not so much, says Josephus, because they loved Antipas as because they hated Archelaus.[15]

While the brothers were pressing their claims in Rome, there were many attempts at revolt in Palestine. The most serious was in Galilee, where an insurgent named Judas, whose father Hezekiah had been captured and put to death by Herod forty years before, raided the palace at Sepphoris and seized the armoury.[16] This rising was not put down until Varus, imperial legate of Syria, marched south with two legions to crush it and to pacify the troubled land.

Augustus, after listening to representations from various quarters, including a deputation of aristocrats from Judaea which asked for the abolition of Herodian rule in favour of a Roman governor, ratified the general terms of Herod's will, except that he bade Archelaus content himself with the title of ethnarch instead of king. Antipas and Philip governed their tetrarchies ably in the interests of Rome for forty-two and thirty-seven years respectively, but Archelaus's nine years' ethnarchate of Judaea proved so oppressive that in A.D. 6, Augustus deposed him and sent him into exile, for fear that if he were left much longer in command of Judaea there would be a large-scale revolt in the land. Archelaus had all his father's defects of character with but little of his administrative and diplomatic ability. He was, like his father, an energetic builder. He repaired the damage recently done to the Temple in Jerusalem. He restored the palace at Jericho, which had been damaged during a rising in 4 B.C.; he built an aqueduct to water the palm-groves north of the city, and in the same region he founded a settlement which he called Archelaïs, after his own name.

[14] Josephus, *Ant.* xvii, 188f.
[15] Josephus, *Ant.* xvii, 227.   [16] See p. 98.

He gave great offence to the Jews by marrying Glaphyra, a Cappadocian princess, who had previously been the wife of his half-brother Alexander, one of the sons of Mariamne. (After Alexander's death in 7 B.C. Glaphyra married Juba, king of Mauretania, but this marriage had been dissolved.) Marriage with a deceased brother's widow was not allowed in Jewish law, except when the former marriage was childless; in that case the ancient law of the 'levirate' marriage provided that a surviving brother or next-of-kin should marry the widow in order to produce a child who would be the dead man's legal heir.[17] But, since Alexander and Glaphyra's marriage had not been childless, this provision could not be invoked.

Archelaus's deposition followed the arrival of two embassies at Rome, one from Judaea and one from Samaria, both showing unwonted unanimity in their protest against Archelaus's tyrannical rule and in their plea that he be removed. Removed he was—to Vienne in the Rhone valley—and Judaea was reorganized as a Roman province under the control of a prefect or procurator appointed by the emperor, exercising capital jurisdiction[18] and commanding a body of auxiliary troops (A.D. 6).

3

Philip's tetrarchy is described in Luke 3:1 as 'the region of Ituraea and Trachonitis'. Josephus fills in the details by telling us that it included Auranitis, Gaulanitis, Batanaea and the district around Paneas;[19] in other words, his tetrarchy comprised a small area west of the upper Jordan, to the north of Lake Ḥuleh, and a much larger area east of the Jordan, between Lysanias's tetrarchy of Abilene to the north and the Decapolis federation to the south.

As his capital Philip chose the city of Paneion on the easterly

---

[17] Cf. Deut. 25:5ff; Ruth 3:9ff; Mark 12:19ff.

[18] Coponius received authority from the emperor μέχρι τοῦ κτείνειν (Josephus, *BJ* ii, 117; cf. *Ant.* xviii, 2). That the Roman prefect of Judaea reserved to himself capital jurisdiction to the exclusion of the Sanhedrin has been questioned (cf. P. Winter, *On the Trial of Jesus* [Berlin, 1961], pp. 75ff); but such an exception to imperial practice and policy as would be involved in the conceding of some measure of capital jurisdiction to the Sanhedrin could be admitted only on the ground of strong positive evidence (cf. A. N. Sherwin-White, *Roman Society and Roman Law in the New Testament* [Oxford, 1963], p. 37). See pp. 199f.

[19] *BJ* ii, 95; *Ant.* xvii, 189.

headstream of the Jordan now called Nahr Banyas.[20] Philip is said to have established that the stream flows underground from the pool of Phiale by throwing chaff into the pool which reappeared at Paneion.[21] Phiale is commonly identified with the pool now called Birket Ram, about four miles east of Banyas; but we are assured that there is no connexion between Birket Ram and the grotto at Paneion.[22] Philip refounded and enlarged Paneion and called it Caesarea in honour of the emperor; to distinguish it from the better-known Caesarea on the Mediterranean seaboard of Judaea it came to be known as 'Philip's Caesarea'—Caesarea Philippi in Latin.

Another new foundation was the city of Bethsaida ('Fishertown'), east of the point where the Jordan enters the Lake of Galilee; this city Philip rebuilt as a winter residence and renamed it Julias, after Augustus's daughter Julia.

Philip's territory was populated for the most part by Gentiles. This relieved him of the many difficulties with which his brothers Archelaus and Antipas had to cope in avoiding giving offence to the religious susceptibilities of their Jewish subjects. Philip could, for example, issue coinage bearing the heads of the emperors Augustus and Tiberius without fear of incurring his subjects' resentment.[23]

Philip was a moderate and tolerant ruler, says Josephus, the mildest of the sons of Herod. He spent most of his time in his own tetrarchy. He went on circuit periodically with a few chosen friends, taking a portable judgement-seat with him, and such cases as were submitted to him he judged on the spot, pronouncing sentence on convicted criminals and discharging those who were unjustly accused, so that no one could complain that justice was delayed.

He married his niece Salome, daughter of his brother Herod Philip[24] (son of the second Mariamme, the high priest's daughter) by Herodias (daughter of Aristobulus, one of the ill-fated sons of the first Mariamme). The number of marriages between uncle and niece in the Herod family led to a complicated series of interrelationships. Philip's marriage with Salome was childless.

---

20 See p. 2.   21 Josephus, *BJ* iii, 509–13.
22 Cf. E. Schürer, *HJP* I. ii, p. 14, n. 7.
23 F. W. Madden, *History of Jewish Coinage* (London, 1864), pp. 100–2.
24 See p. 23. Josephus calls him Herod (*BJ* i, 557, 562, etc.; *Ant.* xvii, 14, 19, etc.); Mark (6:17), followed by Matthew (14:3), calls him Philip, but does not confuse him with Philip the tetrarch, as the Slavonic addition to Josephus does (between *BJ* ii, 168 and 169).

In A.D. 34 he died in his winter palace at Bethsaida Julias; his tetrarchy was placed under the jurisdiction of the legate of Syria. His young widow married her first cousin Aristobulus, son of Herod of Chalcis, to whom she bore three sons.[25]

4

How well Antipas served Rome's interests may be gauged in part from the absence of revolt or open unrest on any serious scale in the two regions of his tetrarchy for over forty years. The troubles which beset Judaea when it became a Roman province in A.D. 6 do not appear to have affected Galilee or Peraea, even though Judas, who led the revolt in Judaea at this time, was in some sense a Galilaean, according to both Luke and Josephus.[26]

Although Antipas throughout the whole of his public career had no higher title than tetrarch, his subjects informally called him 'king', especially (no doubt) when they spoke Aramaic, in which *malkā* is a term with a wider range of meaning than Latin *rex* or even Greek *basileus*. This looser usage is reflected in the Gospel of Mark, who (followed to some extent by Matthew) calls him 'King Herod';[27] Luke, Josephus, speaks of him as 'Herod the tetrarch'.[28]

Antipas was the ablest of Herod's sons. Like his father, he was a patron of Hellenistic culture and a great builder. His chief building enterprise was the city of Tiberias, on the west shore of the Lake of Galilee, which he named in honour of the Emperor Tiberius (*c.* A.D. 22). It was a predominantly Gentile city; since it was built on the site of a cemetery, Antipas's Jewish subjects regarded it as unclean. But Jewish scruples were overcome later, and Tiberias became a famous seat of rabbinical learning. Before the end of the first century, the lake on which it stood came to be called after it— the Lake of Tiberias.[29]

Antipas also rebuilt Sepphoris, which had been destroyed in the

[25] Josephus, *Ant.* xviii, 137 (see also p. 338). This Salome is commonly, but improbably, identified with the little girl (κοράσιον) whose dancing gave such pleasure to Antipas (Mark 6:22–8).

[26] Acts 5:37; Josephus, *BJ* ii, 118; *Ant.* xx, 102. See p. 96.

[27] Mark 6:14, 22, 25, 26, 27; Matt. 14:9. But in Matt. 14:1 he is called 'Herod the tetrarch'.

[28] Luke 3:19; 9:7; Acts 13:1; cf. Josephus, *Ant.* xviii, 102, 109, 122, etc.

[29] Cf. Josephus, *BJ* iii, 57, iv, 456; John 6:1; 21:1.

fighting that followed the revolt of 4 B.C., and renamed it in honour
of Augustus. In his Peraean territory he rebuilt Beth-ramphtha (the
Old Testament Beth-haram), which had been burned by insurgents
in 4 B.C., and fortified it as an outpost against the Nabataean kingdom, calling it Julias or Livias (after the Empress Livia).[30] There
was some debatable land between Peraea and the Nabataean kingdom, and a time came when Antipas needed all the fortification he
could have against the Nabataeans.

Early in his reign he married a daughter of the Nabataean king
Aretas IV (9 B.C.–A.D. 40), but after living with her for twenty years
or more he transferred his affection to his niece and sister-in-law
Herodias. Herodias, daughter of his half-brother Aristobulus, had
married her uncle Herod Philip, who was now a private citizen, although his father had once designated him heir to the throne. On a
journey to Rome Antipas lodged with Herod Philip and, falling in
love with Herodias, proposed marriage to her. She consented, on
condition that he dismiss his Nabataean queen. But the queen forestalled them; getting wind of what was afoot she arranged to move
her residence to the Peraean palace-fortress of Machaerus[31] near
the Nabataean frontier, and from there she seized an opportunity of
crossing into her father's kingdom.

With the Nabataean lady out of the way, Herodias came to live
with Antipas as his wife. This marriage of Antipas to his brother's
wife must have been offensive to all pious Jews among his subjects.
It incurred the denunciation of John the Baptist (who lost his head
in consequence)[32] and the disapproval of Jesus. When Jesus, according to Mark 10:11f, declared that 'whoever divorces his wife
and marries another, commits adultery against her; and if she divorces her husband and marries another, she commits adultery', he
may well have had Antipas and Herodias in mind. A woman could
not divorce her husband by Jewish law, but she could do so by
Roman law; and Herodias, like all the Herods, was a Roman citizen.
In any case, the ladies of the Herod family were a law to themselves; over fifty years before, Herod the Great's sister Salome di-

[30] Josephus, *Ant.* xviii, 27.
[31] Josephus, *Ant.* xviii, 112. The manuscript reading (εἰς τὸν Μαχαιροῦντα
τῷ τε πατρὶ αὐτῆς ὑποτελεῖ) is emended in the printed editions of
Josephus to indicate that Machaerus at that time belonged to Aretas, but that
this was so is unsupported by any independent evidence.
[32] See p. 161.

vorced her Idumaean husband Costobar, 'not following her country's law', says Josephus, 'but acting on her own authority'.[33]

But Antipas's divorce and remarriage gave greatest offence of all to King Aretas, who was naturally incensed at the insult thus offered to his daughter, and he waited for a favourable opportunity to have his revenge on Antipas. The opportunity came after several years.

In the meantime Antipas made another enemy. Herodias had a brother named Agrippa, who was sent to Rome shortly after their father's death in 7 B.C. to be educated there. Their mother Berenice was a bosom friend of Antonia, widow of the elder Drusus (brother of Tiberius); Agrippa himself became very friendly with her son Claudius, the future emperor, whose exact contemporary he was, and also with the younger Drusus (son of Tiberius) and other members of the imperial family. He became so heavily involved in debt, however, that he incurred the disapproval of Tiberius, and when his protector Drusus died in A.D. 23 he had to retire to Idumaea. When Herodias came to live with their uncle Antipas as his second wife, she used her influence on Agrippa's behalf and procured for him a home, a pension, and an official status (as *agoranomos*) at Tiberias. But before long he quarrelled with Antipas and betook himself to Flaccus, legate of Syria, at Antioch. Soon, however, he quarrelled with Flaccus, and went back to Rome, having contrived to pay off his old debts by incurring new ones. He now tried to sow suspicion in Tiberius's mind against Antipas, but the old *princeps* knew his faithful servant too well to listen to such calumnies.[34] Agrippa was appointed guardian of Tiberius's grandson, Tiberius Gemellus (son of the younger Drusus), and formed a close friendship with Tiberius's grand-nephew Gaius, who was later to succeed him as emperor. An imprudent remark which he made about the succession reached Tiberius's ears, and he spent the last six months of Tiberius's reign in prison.

A good example of the way in which Antipas could be useful to his imperial overlord is provided by the course of Rome's relations with Parthia towards the end of Tiberius's reign.

In A.D. 35, at the instigation of Lucius Vitellius, legate of Syria, the subjects of Artabanus III, king of Parthia, rebelled against him, and transferred their allegiance to Tiridates III. Artabanus was

[33] *Ant.* xv, 259f.   [34] Josephus, *BJ* ii, 178.

forced to take refuge in the Scythian border-lands. But some months later he staged a comeback, with the aid of Scythian allies, and Tiridates and his supporters were forced to flee in their turn.[35]

When Tiberius heard of the restoration of Artabanus, he decided to make a treaty of friendship with him, and instructed Vitellius to enter into negotiations to this end. These overtures were warmly welcomed by Artabanus. He and Vitellius met half-way along a bridge which had been thrown across the Euphrates, the frontier between the two empires. When they had reached agreement on the terms of the treaty, Antipas entertained them at a banquet in a luxurious marquee which he had erected in the middle of the bridge.[36]

Vitellius then returned to Antioch and Artabanus to Babylon. Antipas made up his mind to be the first to send Tiberius news of the treaty, and he wrote such a detailed letter that there was nothing for Vitellius to add. When Tiberius received Vitellius's official report, he let him understand that, thanks to Antipas's exemplary promptness, he knew the whole story already. Vitellius was annoyed, and not long afterwards he found occasion to satisfy his grudge against Antipas.[37]

Later in A.D. 36 the Nabataean king seized a long-awaited opportunity to invade Peraea, where he inflicted a crushing defeat on an army of Antipas. It may well be, as Josephus says, that some of Antipas's subjects saw in this defeat the divine nemesis for Antipas's execution of John the Baptist;[38] but it is unimaginative to conclude that John's execution must therefore have been much more recent than the Evangelists indicate. The Pharisees and many other Jews believed that the mills of God ground slowly; if divine nemesis could wait fifteen years before punishing Pompey for violating the

[35] Tacitus, *Annals* vi, 31ff.

[36] Josephus, *Ant.* xviii, 96–104. According to Suetonius (*Gaius*, 14) and Dio Cassius (*Hist.* lix, 27), Tiberius had already been succeeded by Gaius when this treaty was concluded (cf. J. P. V. D. Balsdon, *The Emperor Gaius* [Oxford, 1934], p. 198, n. 2). But see E. M. Smallwood, 'The Date of the Dismissal of Pontius Pilate from Judaea', *JJS* 5 (1954), pp. 12ff, for cogent arguments in support of the view that this whole section of Josephus on Parthia (*Ant.* xviii, 96ff), including the Euphrates conference, belongs chronologically before his account of Vitellius's earlier visit to Jerusalem (*Ant.* xviii, 90ff), which she shows to have taken place towards the end of A.D. 36 rather than, as Josephus says, during Passover of that year.

[37] Josephus, *Ant.* xviii, 104f.   [38] *Ant.* xviii, 116 (see p. 152).

sanctity of the holy of holies in Jerusalem,[39] it was not extraordinary that it should have waited a mere seven years before taking vengeance for the death of John.

When news of Aretas's invasion of Peraea came to Rome, Tiberius ordered Vitellius to mount a punitive attack on Aretas for this act of aggression against one of Rome's allies. Vitellius made preparations accordingly, and set out from Ptolemais early in A.D. 37 with two legions and a number of auxiliary forces, intending to march on Petra, Aretas's capital. To avoid offending the Jews with the spectacle of the legionary standards, he sent his troops south along the maritime road, through mainly Gentile territory, while he himself went up to Jerusalem with Antipas to celebrate the Passover of April 17–18. But on the fourth day after they arrived in Jerusalem, news came of the death of Tiberius on March 16.[40] Vitellius accordingly called off his expedition against Aretas. He had cherished his own personal grievance against Antipas for forestalling him in sending news of the Parthian treaty to Rome, and had no great urge to pull the tetrarch's chestnuts out of the fire for him. Besides, although the dead emperor had been solicitous for the welfare of Antipas, Vitellius may already have had reason to know that the new emperor did not share this solicitude.

[39] Cf. *Ps. Sol.* 2:30ff (quoted on p. 12).

[40] Josephus, *Ant.* xviii, 122–4. For the date of Tiberius's death see Tacitus, *Annals* vi, 50. The news of his death, carried by the fastest means available, would take about five weeks to reach Judaea; the Passover of A.D. 37 was later than usual because of the intercalation of a second Adar in that year.

3 Judaea Under Roman Governors

1

When Archelaus was deposed and banished by Augustus in A.D. 6, Judaea was reduced to the status of a Roman province, governed by a prefect appointed directly by the emperor and responsible to him. The governor of a minor province like Judaea was regularly drawn from the equestrian order (the second order in Roman society) and not, like governors of larger and more important provinces, from the senatorial order. The troops whom he had under his command were auxiliary cohorts, not legionary troops. In an emergency beyond the capacity of the prefect's auxiliary forces to handle, legionary troops could be provided by the legate of Syria, who appears to have exercised some general supervision over the prefect of Judaea. This supervision was called for only when the prefect of Judaea was involved in serious trouble with the provincials, as happened with Pilate (A.D. 36), Cumanus (A.D. 52) and, above all, with Florus, under whom the Jews revolted against Rome (A.D. 66).

The legate of Syria at the time of Archelaus's deposition was P. Sulpicius Quirinius; he had the task of liquidating Archelaus's estate and holding a census to determine the amount of tribute which the new province might be expected to pay into the imperial exchequer.[1] It was this census that provoked the rising under Judas the Galilaean and gave birth to the Zealot movement.[2] When the rising had been suppressed and the census completed, Coponius was installed in office as first prefect of Judaea.

In addition to other prerogatives held by Archelaus, and by

---

[1] Josephus, *BJ* ii, 118, 433; *Ant.* xvii, 355; xviii, 1f, 26; xx, 102. Luke 2:2, which mentions Quirinius in connexion with an earlier census, is best translated 'This enrolment was before that made when Quirinius was governor of Syria' (cf. N. Turner, *Grammatical Insights into the Greek New Testament* [Edinburgh, 1966], pp. 23f).
[2] See p. 97.

Herod before him, Coponius took over the custody of the high priest's vestments, which were kept under seal in the Antonia fortress, the headquarters of the Roman garrison in Jerusalem. A cohort under the command of a military tribune was a sufficient garrison normally; at the great festivals, when Jerusalem was filled with crowds of pilgrims and rioting was apt to break out, this force had to be augmented, and sometimes the governor himself left his headquarters at Caesarea and took up residence in Jerusalem on these occasions, as Pilate did at the Passover season which witnessed the trial and execution of Jesus.

During one of the Passovers which fell in the governorship of Coponius, a group of Samaritans made their way into the Jerusalem Temple when the gates were thrown open after midnight. They then polluted the sacred precincts by scattering human bones about: conceivably they wished to parody Ezekiel's vision of the valley of dry bones, the account of which was prescribed for reading as a prophetic lesson among the Jews at Passovertide. The arrangements for Temple security were accordingly tightened up.[3]

Coponius was replaced about A.D. 9 by Marcus Ambivius,[4] and he made way about three years later for Annius Rufus, who was in office when Augustus died (19 August, A.D. 14). Augustus changed his provincial governors rather frequently, whereas his successor Tiberius believed in letting them continue in office for longer periods. When asked why he followed this policy, he is said to have justified it by the fable of the wounded man who lay by the roadside covered with blood-sucking insects. A compassionate passer-by who began to brush them off was begged to desist: 'These flies', said the wounded man, 'are already sated with blood, and are causing me no trouble now; but if they are driven off, a fresh swarm of hungry ones will take their place and I shall not survive *their* attentions'.[5] The rapacity of many provincial governors is only too well attested in Roman records.

About A.D. 15 Tiberius sent Valerius Gratus to govern Judaea, and

[3] Josephus, *Ant.* xviii, 29f. Temple security was in the hands of the Temple police, a picked band of Levites, assigned to twenty-one separate posts (three others were manned by priests) and commanded by the *sāgān*, or 'captain of the Temple' (see p. 67). Cf. Mishnah, *Tamid* 1:1; *Middot* 1:1.

[4] His name is uncertain, as the MS. tradition of Josephus, *Ant.* xviii, 31 is corrupt; Niese conjectured Amphiboulos.

[5] Josephus, *Ant.* xviii, 174ff.

he remained in the province for eleven years. During that period he deposed four high priests and appointed another four. It may well be that this was Gratus's method of enriching himself. The last high priest appointed by Gratus was Joseph Caiaphas (A.D. 18–36), son-in-law of Annas, whom Gratus found in possession of the sacred office when he arrived in Judaea as prefect.[6]

2

Gratus was succeeded as prefect of Judaea in A.D. 26 by Pontius Pilate, the only one of the earlier prefects of whom we have some detailed information. This is due not only to the part he plays in the New Testament narrative as the judge who tried Jesus and condemned him to death, but also to the account of his governorship given by Josephus. In addition, there is a description of his character and conduct in a letter written, according to Philo, by Herod Agrippa the elder to the Emperor Gaius in A.D. 40. There he is described as 'naturally inflexible, a blend of self-will and relentlessness'.[7]

This description occurs in Agrippa's account of Pilate's attempt to dedicate some gilded shields in Herod's palace in Jerusalem. This attempt was regarded by the Jews as a violation of the sanctity of Jerusalem. The citizens therefore, led by four sons of Herod the Great, protested to Pilate; when he refused to remove the shields, they appealed to Tiberius, who sent instructions to Pilate that the shields should be transferred to the temple of Augustus in Caesarea.[8]

But why were the shields so offensive? They had no image engraved on them—nothing but inscriptions stating by whom and to whom they were dedicated. We may suspect that they had some religious significance which was inconsistent with the status of Jerusalem as a city consecrated to the exclusive worship of the God of Israel; but the real trouble probably was that the incident was one of a series in which Pilate, either deliberately or through utter tactlessness, outraged the religious sentiments of his Jewish subjects. Ostensibly the votive shields were set up in honour of Tiberius; actually, the Jews believed, Pilate's main purpose was to cause them annoyance.

[6] See pp. 64f.   [7] Philo, *Legatio* 301.   [8] Philo, *Legatio* 299–305.

Early in his governorship, according to Josephus,[9] he introduced into Jerusalem under cover of night military standards bearing the imperial image. None of his predecessors had done such a thing because imperial policy respected the sanctity of the city and the Jewish objection to the exhibition of images, which infringed the Second Commandment. When day broke, the indignation of the people knew no bounds; they beset Pilate's residence and followed him back to Caesarea, clamouring for the removal of the images from Jerusalem. Finding that even the threat of slaughter did not dissuade them, and that he was faced with a province-wide rising if he did not remove the images, Pilate, with no very good grace, gave in to their insistence.

It has been held that this is Josephus's version of the same incident as that of the votive shields recorded in Philo's *Embassy to Gaius*;[10] but the details differ so much that it is best to regard them as two separate incidents. If the incident of the votive shields was later than that of the standards, we can understand better why such an apparently innocent action as setting up the shields in Herod's palace met with instant opposition. The people of Jerusalem had already had experience of Pilate's disregard of their city's sacred status, and suspected a fresh attempt to violate it.

Pilate's brutal overriding of well-established Jewish prerogatives has been thought to be part of the policy of Sejanus, prefect of the praetorian guard and, in the years immediately preceding his downfall in A.D. 31, the most powerful man in Rome. His ascendancy over the emperor was at its height in the earlier years of Pilate's governorship, and Pilate may well have been his nominee. Our evidence for Sejanus's anti-Jewish policy is confined to two passages in Philo's writings.[11] At the outset of his treatise on Flaccus, the prefect of Egypt under whom the anti-Jewish excesses at Alexandria took place in A.D. 38,[12] he says that Flaccus took over Sejanus's policy of

[9] Josephus, *BJ* ii, 169–74; *Ant.* xviii, 55–9.

[10] Cf. Loeb edition of Philo, x (London, 1962), p. 151, n. *c*.

[11] Philo, *Flacc.* 1; *Legatio* 159f; cf. Eusebius, *HE* ii, 5, where Philo's authority is invoked for the statement that Sejanus took steps to destroy the whole Jewish race, and Pilate's attempt on the Temple is mentioned in the same context. A judicious assessment of the question is provided by E. M. Smallwood, 'Some Notes on the Jews under Tiberius', *Latomus* 15 (1956), pp. 314–29; *Philonis Alexandrini Legatio ad Gaium* (Leiden, 1961), pp. 243f.

[12] See p. 250.

attacking the Jews. In his *Embassy to Gaius* (159f) he speaks again
of Sejanus's attack on the Jews, but adds that after Sejanus's death
the charges which he had brought against the Jews of Rome were
immediately recognized by Tiberius as slanderous lies, 'invented by
Sejanus in his desire to do away with our nation, because he knew
that it would play the sole or at least the leading part in opposing
his impious plots and actions and would defend the emperor if he
was like to be endangered by treachery'. We must make allowance
for Philo's apologetic motives in so writing; he wished to make the
point that the emperors before Gaius had always shown favour to
the Jews of Rome, and that any incidents in the reign of Tiberius
which seemed to indicate the contrary (such as, perhaps, the expulsion of Jews from the capital in A.D. 19)[13] were due, not to the
emperor's personal initiative, but to his evil genius Sejanus.

Even so, Philo has probably some factual basis for attributing an
anti-Jewish policy to Sejanus, and if he was indeed Pilate's patron,
Pilate would certainly have felt defenceless after Sejanus's fall in
A.D. 31. This situation would have made him peculiarly sensitive to
the chief priests' scarcely veiled menace at the trial of Jesus: 'If you
release this man, you are not Caesar's friend; every one who makes
himself a king sets himself against Caesar' (John 19:12). For this
reason it has been argued that, of the two most probable years for
the death of Jesus, A.D. 30 and 33,[14] the latter is to be preferred;[15] but
the situation is not so clear as to set aside *a priori* the arguments
for the earlier date.

Another clash between Pilate and the Jerusalem authorities arose
out of his construction of an aqueduct to augment the city's water-
supply.[16] The construction of this aqueduct, carrying water from
the southern highlands to Jerusalem, was the one positive boon that
his governorship brought to Jerusalem. The Temple in particular
benefited from it, because it continually required an exceptionally
large water supply—not only for the ritual ablutions prescribed for
the priests but also for keeping the area clean and fresh after the
incessant slaughtering and sacrifice of animals which went on there.

[13] See p. 137.
[14] Cf. G. Ogg, *Chronology of the Public Ministry of Jesus* (Cambridge,
1940), pp. 243ff.
[15] Cf. B. Reicke, *The New Testament Era* (Philadelphia, 1968), pp. 183f.
[16] Josephus, *BJ* ii, 175–7; *Ant.* xviii, 62.

Pilate therefore—very naturally, from his point of view—demanded that payment for the cost of the aqueduct be made from the Temple treasury. The Temple authorities protested that it was an act of sacrilege to appropriate for such a secular purpose money which had been dedicated to God; but Pilate insisted that they should pay what he demanded, and raided the fund into which each adult Jewish male throughout the world contributed half a shekel annually for the maintenance of the sacrificial services. Crowds of indignant Jews gathered in protest against the sacrilege, but their demonstration was forcibly broken up by the procurator's troops.

It is uncertain whether this is the setting of the incident mentioned in Luke 13:1, when Pilate's troops attacked a number of Galilaean pilgrims in the Temple courts, so that their blood was mixed with the blood of their sacrifices. In any case, the incident illustrates the unrest of the period, and the insensitive violence with which Pilate reacted to it. The Galilaeans were not Pilate's subjects, although they were temporarily under his jurisdiction when they visited Jerusalem, and this attack on them by Pilate probably contributed to the personal hostility between Pilate and the tetrarch of Galilee, to which Luke makes reference in his narrative of the trial of Jesus (Luke 23:12). (Another contribution to this personal hostility was no doubt supplied by Antipas's intervention, along with three of his brothers, in the matter of the votive shields.)

Immediately after referring to the incident of the Galilaean pilgrims Luke mentions the death of eighteen men when a tower in Siloam (in the south-east corner of Jerusalem) fell and crushed them. This may have been nothing more than a tragic accident, but the context in which it appears suggests that it relates to an attempt at insurrection around this time by a group of militant Jerusalemites, which was speedily and violently put down.[17]

Pilate crowned his oppressive acts by an attack on a crowd of Samaritan pilgrims on the holy hill of Gerizim.[18] They gathered there in response to the announcement of a *soi-disant* prophet that he would bring to light the sacred vessels of the Mosaic tabernacle, which the Samaritans believed had been buried on Mount Gerizim after Israel's settlement in Canaan. According to Samaritan belief, the gift of prophecy had been withdrawn on the death of Moses,

[17] See p. 188. [18] Josephus, *Ant.* xviii, 87.

and would not be manifested again until the appearance of the *Taheb* or 'Restorer', the great prophet of the end-time, to whom Moses had pointed forward when he said, 'Yahweh your God will raise up for you a prophet like me from among you, from your brethren—him you shall heed' (Deuteronomy 18:15). This man's announcement therefore probably involved the claim to be this *Taheb*; for the Samaritans it was a claim parallel to a claim to be the Messiah of David's line among the Jews,[19] and in the eyes of the provincial government it was fraught with equal dangers. So Pilate sent a detachment of infantry, supported by cavalry, against these Samaritans, who were dispersed with considerable bloodshed. The leaders of the Samaritan community sent a delegation to Lucius Vitellius, legate of Syria (A.D. 35–39), to protest against Pilate's violence.

Vitellius ordered Pilate to go to Rome and give an account of his actions to the emperor; he appointed one of his lieutenants, Marcellus by name, acting procurator in Pilate's absence.[20] It was now the end of A.D. 36.[21] Pilate set out for Rome without delay—he must have gone by the land route, since the Mediterranean was closed to navigation for the winter—but by the time he reached the capital, Tiberius was dead (March 16, A.D. 37). Pilate was not continued in office by the new emperor, Gaius; a new prefect, Marullus, was appointed,[22] and he retained the post throughout Gaius's reign. He was followed in Judaea, not by another Roman governor, but by a Jewish king.[23]

3

To estimate the size of populations in antiquity is a hazardous exercise; contemporary writers, even when they appear to give precise figures, are not always reliable, because often they had no means of making an accurate assessment. Josephus's population estimates for Palestine and Jerusalem, for example, are impossibly

[19] Cf. John 4:25.   [20] Josephus, *Ant.* xviii, 89.
[21] See E. M. Smallwood, 'The Date of the Dismissal of Pontius Pilate from Judaea', *JJS* 5 (1954), pp. 12ff (cf. p. 30 *supra*, n. 36).
[22] What Josephus says is that Gaius sent Marullus to be ἱππάρχης over Judaea; the word strictly means 'cavalry commander' but may be used more generally here of the prefect as commander of the military forces in Judaea.
[23] Herod Agrippa I. See p. 258.

inflated, as when he implies a population of three million for Galilee,[24] or estimates that at Passovertide Jerusalem (less than one square mile in area) accommodated more than two and a half million persons.[25] Joachim Jeremias, on such evidence as is available, reckons the normal population of the city in New Testament times to have been between 25,000 and 30,000,[26] a number which may have been more than trebled at the great festivals.[27] The population of all Palestine at this period, he estimates, was between 500,000 and 600,000;[28] F. C. Grant's estimate is about three times as large.[29]

When Judaea became a Roman province and its inhabitants became liable to pay tribute to the emperor, they were not relieved of their existing obligations for the maintenance of the Temple state. They had to pay two sets of dues, each of which was calculated with complete disregard of the other; the Jewish authorities were as little disposed to relax the Temple dues in the light of the imperial tribute as the Roman government was to relax the tribute in the light of the Temple dues. Herod and Archelaus, of course, had drawn their income from the territory which they governed, but it was largely derived from customs duties and sales taxes. In so far as Herod had levied taxes on individuals, the taxation was not exacted unconscionably; in a famine year Herod remitted it[30]—but this kind of precedent was not likely to be followed by the Romans.

The religious dues were heavy enough; they included obligations (like the 'first' and 'second' tithes) which were originally alternatives, or one of which was intended to replace another, but which were now combined.[31] Yet they were paid willingly enough by many pious Jews as a service to God; they might suspect that the

[24] Compare *Life*, 235, where he says there are 204 cities and villages in Galilee, with *BJ* iii, 43, where he says that the smallest of the Galilaean villages contains over 15,000 inhabitants.

[25] *BJ* vi, 422–5.

[26] 'Die Einwohnerzahl Jerusalems zur Zeit Jesu', *ZDPV* 66 (1943), pp. 24–31.

[27] *Jerusalem in the Time of Jesus* (London, 1969), p. 83, where, however, he had calculated the normal population to be about 55,000.

[28] *Jerusalem in the Time of Jesus*, p. 205.

[29] *The Economic Background of the Gospels* (Oxford, 1926), p. 83.

[30] See p. 22.

[31] The 'first tithe' is that prescribed by the priestly legislation of Lev. 27:30ff; Num. 18:24ff; the 'second tithe' is that prescribed in Deut. 14:22ff; 26:12ff; cf. the Mishnah tractate *Ma'aser Sheni*.

wealthy chief-priestly families secured more than their fair share of
the wealth so contributed, but the contributions themselves were
part of their religious duty.

The tribute to the emperor, on the other hand, was an unwelcome
impost, and the harsh and rapacious methods by which it was often
exacted made it all the less tolerable. When it was added to the
theocratic taxation it discouraged economic initiative and so
produced a situation in which it became ever more burdensome. In
the absence of data only an approximate estimate of the burden
can be attempted, but F. C. Grant is not far wide of the mark when
he calculates that *'the total taxation of the Jewish people in the time
of Jesus, civil and religious combined, must have approached the
intolerable proportion of between 30 and 40 per cent.; it may have
been higher still'.*[32]

There were thus special reasons why the Roman peace was less
attractive to the people of Judaea than to many other provincials; it
is doubtful if there were any other subjects of Rome on whom the
burden of tribute to Caesar bore so heavily as it did on them. The
weight of their double tribute, 'to Caesar and to God', as it might
have been put, combined with other forms of taxation administered
by extortionate *publicani* to bring the province to the brink of economic collapse. Popular resentment was felt not only against the
Romans but against the wealthy landed proprietors who prospered
at the expense of their poorer fellow-countrymen; this is perhaps
the situation which called forth the outburst against the rich in
James 5:1–6. The successive Zealot revolts, culminating in the war
of A.D. 66, were directed almost as much against the Jewish 'establishment' as against the occupying power.

[32] *Economic Background*, p. 105 (his italics).

4 The Philosophical Schools

Aristotle died in 322 B.C., a year later than his most famous pupil, Alexander the Great. Aristotle was to remain 'the master of them that know' for many centuries to come, but in some respects his outlook reflected a way of life and thought that had become obsolete during his lifetime. He believed, for example, that barbarians were inherently inferior to Greeks, and he looked on the Greek city-state as the perfect and final social organism. Both these convictions were undermined by the conquering careers of Philip and Alexander.

The breaking down of the old pattern of autonomous city-states in the Greek world which resulted from their conquests, and the rise of a wider sense of citizenship throughout the great empire of Alexander and his successors, led to a new sense of cosmopolitanism among thinking Greeks. This cosmopolitan outlook marks the two great schools of philosophical thought which arose in the Hellenistic age—the Epicureans and the Stoics.

1

The Epicureans acquired their name from Epicurus (341–270 B.C.), who belonged to a family of Athenian settlers on the island of Samos. His family were compelled to leave their island home when he was nineteen years old, and it has been thought that Epicureanism bears marks of a 'refugee philosophy'. During his years of wandering from one place to another he built up his system of physics and ethics, and when he settled in Athens in 306 B.C. he opened a school in the garden of his house—the 'Garden of Epicurus'. To this school slaves and women were admitted as well as freemen.

In physics Epicurus adopted the atomic theory of Democritus (c. 460–370 B.C.)—the theory that the ultimate 'principles' (*archai*) of the universe are atoms (indivisible particles of solid matter beyond all numbering and varying greatly in size and shape) moving at the dictate of necessity in the infinite void. To this theory Epicurus added the doctrine of the 'swerve'[1] to explain how the atoms, falling through the void, deviated from their straight path so as to collide and thus bring all things into existence. Epicurus's doctrine was completely materialist; living beings and lifeless things alike were produced by the fortuitous concourse of atoms. When men and other living beings died, the atoms of which their souls consisted immediately dispersed and all sensation ceased; by this denial of the immortality of souls Epicurus hoped to liberate men from the fear of death. He did not deny the existence of gods; they too were composed of fine atoms and lived in the spaces between the worlds, enjoying perfect blessedness, undisturbed by concern for mankind or worldly affairs.

The atomic theory commended itself to Epicurus as one on which peace of mind could be securely based. The highest good, according to him, was pleasure—but pleasure in the sense of peace of mind, freedom from disturbing cares, *ataraxia*. The more exciting pleasures of the flesh, with which Epicureanism came to be unjustly associated in much popular thought, were to be avoided, as they tended to bring corresponding pains in their train and were in any case incompatible with true peace of mind. 'Live unobtrusively'[2] was Epicurus's advice to his followers; in a dangerous world there was nothing to be gained by 'sticking their necks out'. For the rest, they might live free from worry, assured (in the words of the *tetrapharmakos* of Philodemus, excavated at Herculaneum a century and a half ago) that:

> There is nothing to fear in God,
> There is nothing to be alarmed at in death;
> Good is easily obtained,
> Evil is easily endured.[3]

Epicurus and his philosophy have suffered in reputation because of a debased way of life which, generations after his time, laid claim to the designation 'Epicureanism'. His name appears as a loanword

---

[1] Gk. κίνησις κατὰ παρέγκλισιν (Epicurus, frag. 280).

[2] Gk. λάθε βιώσας (Epicurus, frag. 551).

[3] ἄφοβον ὁ θεός, ἀνύποπτον ὁ θάνατος, καὶ τἀγαθὸν μὲν εὔκτητον, τὸ δὲ δεινὸν εὐεκκαρτέρητον (*Pap. Herc.* 1005, iv, 19).

in rabbinic Hebrew and Aramaic in the form *'appiqōrōs*, meaning an irreverent heretic, a libertine. But Epicurus himself was 'something of a saint, and far from carnal'.[4] Seneca, for all his Stoicism, spoke well of Epicureanism: 'I venture to say, in face of some men's opinions, that the ethics of Epicurus are sane, upright, even austere, for the man who penetrates their depths'.[5] And Lucian, the satirist of Samosata (second century A.D.), couples Epicureans and Christians as people who were unlikely to be taken in by charlatanry; when Alexander the oracle-monger institutes his fraudulent mysteries, a preliminary proclamation is made: 'If there be any atheist or Christian or Epicurean here spying on our rites, let him speedily begone'.[6] Alexander then leads the litany with the versicle, 'Christians, begone!'—to which the congregation makes the response, 'Epicureans, begone!' Lucian describes further[7] how Alexander publicly burned a copy of Epicurus's *Sovereign Principles*[8] because of its appeal to right reason against superstition, and he gives his personal testimony to Epicurus as 'that great man, a genuine saint and inspired prophet, who alone possessed and imparted true insight into the Good, and has proved a deliverer to all who consorted with him'.[9]

His last words, we are told, were 'Remember the dogmas'.[10] His disciples took him at his word; for generations they maintained his teaching without modification. Of his followers the most illustrious was the Latin poet Lucretius (c. 97–53 B.C.), whose six books *On the Nature of Things* give classical expression to his master's philosophy.

The weakest feature of his philosophy is the Epicurean theory of knowledge. Knowledge, for Epicureanism, is a matter of sensation, of feeling. But since our senses sometimes mislead us, they do not provide an infallible criterion. How then could Epicurus and his followers be so sure that their dogmas were true? There was no satisfactory answer to this question; for practical purposes, it was maintained, the senses were reliable enough. The one thing worth pursuing is pleasure; the one thing to be shunned is pain; and our senses tell us plainly enough what is pleasant and what is painful.

[4] E. M. Blaiklock, 'The Areopagus Address', *Faith and Thought* 93 (1963–4), p. 182.
[5] Seneca, *De vita beata*, 14.   [6] Lucian, *Alexander* 38.   [7] *ibid.* 47.
[8] Κυρίαι Δόξαι.   [9] *ibid.* 61.
[10] χαίρετε καὶ μέμνησθε τὰ δόγματα (*Vita Epicuri* 16).

2

Unlike the Epicureans, who refused to deviate from their master's teaching, the Stoics developed and modified their founder's philosophy throughout successive generations.

The Stoics acquired their name from the *Stoa Poikilē* (the 'Painted Portico') in the Athenian marketplace, where their founder Zeno gathered his first disciples around him. Zeno (335–263 B.C.) was a native of Citium in Cyprus; he may have been partly Phoenician by descent. In 313 B.C. he came to Athens and attended lectures in the Academy and other philosophical schools, but soon attached himself to the Cynics. A study of the works of Antisthenes, the founder of the Cynic school, moved him to pay attention to the philosophy of Socrates.

He identified the *logos* of Socrates and his followers—the rational principle in human life—with the *logos* of Heracleitus (*c.* 500 B.C.), the world-order which consists ultimately of 'ever-living fire, kindled and quenched in due measure'.[11] The course of time is recurrently punctuated at lengthy intervals by a universal conflagration (*ekpyrōsis*) followed by a regeneration (*palingenesia*) or restoration (*apokatastasis*) of all things. Man is a microcosm corresponding to the universal macrocosm; as in the macrocosm creative Reason (*logos*) exerts its force on matter and imposes form on it, so in the microcosm it is Reason that governs—or ought to govern—the life of man. Man is thus completely integrated with the world of nature; the universal law is also the law for individual life, and so the Stoic way of life could be summed up in the phrase *homologoumenōs zēn*, 'to live in harmony (with nature)'.

The true Stoic looked on himself as belonging to a community which was coextensive with the world. His *polis* was the *cosmos*— the 'world-city' or *cosmopolis*, Marcus Aurelius's 'dear city of God'.[12] What the soul was to man's body, that God was to the universe. In Alexander Pope's words:

> All are but parts of one stupendous whole,
> Whose body Nature is, and God the soul.[13]

[11] Heracleitus, frag. 20.
[12] Marcus Aurelius, *Meditations* iv, 23 (ὦ πόλι φίλη Διός).
[13] *Essay on Man*, 267f.

This Stoic conception of God as the world-soul is essentially pan- *yes*
theistic, and this should be borne in mind when Stoic language
about God or Zeus presents remarkable resemblances to the theistic
language of the Bible. Paul at Athens may quote a Stoic poet's
words about Zeus, 'for we are also his offspring' (Acts 17:28), and
apply them to the God of creation, but Aratus's God is quite differently conceived from Paul's.

The Stoic conception of God finds its most memorable and noble
expression in the great *Hymn of Cleanthes*, preserved for us in one
manuscript of Stobaeus's *Eclogues*:[14]

Most glorious of the immortals, thou of many names, almighty for
ever, O Zeus, author of nature, directing all things with law, all hail!
It is right for all mortals to address thee. For we are thy offspring,
having been allotted the likeness of thy divinity—we alone, of all mortal things that live and move on earth. Therefore I will hymn thee
and always sing of thy might.

To thee this whole world, circling round the earth, renders obedience wherever thou dost lead, and is willingly ruled by thee; such a
servant dost thou hold in thine invincible hands, the two-edged, fiery,
ever-living thunderbolt. Under its strokes all the works of nature are
brought to fulfilment. With it thou directest universal Reason, which
moves through all things, mingling with the great and the lesser lights.
. . . So great a king art thou, supreme throughout all.

Nor does any deed take place apart from thee, O Lord, on earth or
throughout the divine vault of the sky or in the sea, save what wicked
men do by their own folly. Nay, thou knowest also how to make the
odd even, and the things that lack order orderly; and things that
are unlovely are loved by thee. So hast thou fitted all things together
into one, the good with the bad, so that they become one universal
Reason, existing for ever.

As many of mortals as are wicked flee this Reason and bid it begone
—ill-fated wretches, who always yearn for the possession of good
things, but neither see nor hear the common law of God, through
obedience to which they might have a good life in company with reason. But they for their part rush on unreasoning now to this end, now
to that; some cherishing contentious zeal for glory, some turning in-
ordinately towards gain, and others towards indulgence and the pleas-
urable deeds of the body . . . and they are borne on now here, now

[14] *Ecl.* i, 25. With the opening words of the third sentence in the hymn
(ἐκ σοῦ γὰρ γένος ἐσμέν) compare the words quoted from Aratus (*Phainomena*, 5) in Acts 17:28b (τοῦ γὰρ καὶ γένος ἐσμέν).

there, eagerly striving for the exact opposite of these things which they attain.

But, O Zeus, giver of all, shrouded in dark clouds, lord of the thunderbolt, rescue men from baneful ignorance. Scatter it, O Father, from their souls, and grant that they may attain sound judgement, trusting in which thou dost direct all things with justice; so that honoured by thee we may requite thee with honour, hymning thy works continually, as is fitting for one who is mortal. For neither for mortals nor for gods is there any greater privilege than justly to hymn universal law forevermore.

There is another, much shorter, poem by Cleanthes which has been preserved to us because it was a favourite of the later Stoic writer Epictetus (c. A.D. 55-135):[15]

> Lead me, O Zeus, and thou, my destiny,
> Whate'er the path that ye ordain for me;
> Fearless I'll follow, but if I refuse,
> Still must I follow, howsoe'er I choose.

Here Zeus is little more than a personification of fate. A man's fate cannot be avoided, but it will be easier for himself if he co-operates with it and accepts it gladly instead of struggling vainly against it. At least this fate was not capricious; it was part of the universal *logos* or design. When men were convinced that they were caught up into this grand design, the conviction gave rise to great moral strength and purpose of mind, stimulating them to noble endurance and action.[16]

But if the Stoic is conscious of his duty to co-operate with destiny, he is proudly conscious of his independence of the will of other men. Self-sufficiency—*autarkeia*—was a Stoic ideal.[17] For all their

---

[15] Epictetus, *Enchiridion* 2.23.42; 3.22.95; 4.1.131, etc.

[16] With this concept of the divine essence is closely bound up the Stoic belief in 'providence' (πρόνοια). This personified providence finds its way into Hellenistic Jewish literature of the closing generations B.C. and first century A.D (Wisdom; III and IV Maccabees; Philo, Josephus) and, although it is absent from the New Testament (where the only occurrence of πρόνοια, Acts 24:2, bears a different sense), appears in the early Christian apologists and survives in the use of 'Providence' as a surrogate for the divine name. See A. Ehrhardt, *The Beginning* (Manchester, 1968), p. 169.

[17] The αὐτάρκεια which Paul claims in Phil. 4:11 (cf. II Cor. 9:8; I Tim. 6:6) is different from the Stoic ideal in that it denotes the contentment which comes from an assurance of divine guidance and provision—a 'God-sufficiency' rather than 'self-sufficiency'. R. Bultmann has pointed out that while the mat-

cosmopolitanism the Stoics were at heart sturdy individualists; they tended to put up with their brother-men rather than to love them. When conditions of life became too intolerable for a self-respecting Stoic to endure with human dignity, suicide was regarded as a proper way of release. Stoicism proper had no doctrine of immortality; the soul survived the death of the body, but was bound to disappear when the next world conflagration took place, if not earlier. Seneca and others indeed tried to find comfort in the hope of immortality, but it was not from Stoicism that they derived this hope.

In the realm of moral values they distinguished good things, which were to be pursued, bad things, which were to be shunned, and indifferent things, to be pursued or shunned as might be most expedient. Alongside these moral values they distinguished practical values—things in accordance with nature, which were to be preferred, things contrary to nature, which were to be rejected,[18] and (again) indifferent things, to be preferred or rejected as might be most expedient. Conduct which was in accordance with nature was 'fitting' (*kathekon*); conduct which was contrary to nature was 'unfitting' (*apokathēkon*). Terms akin to these appear in the codes of conduct in the New Testament epistles. For example, in Eph. 5:3f immorality, impurity and covetousness are not as much as to be named in the Christian community, 'as is fitting (*prepei*) among saints'; filthiness, silly talk and levity are deprecated as 'not fitting' (*ouk anēken*). But the Stoic terminology is apt to be given a Christian edge by the addition of a Christian phrase; thus, in Col. 3:18 wives are exhorted to be subject to their husbands because this is 'fitting (*anēken*) in the Lord'.

As for the Stoics' theory of knowledge, they began with a view of

---

ter and vocabulary common to Stoicism and primitive Christianity afforded an evangelistic bridgehead for the Christians, Christianity (unlike Stoicism) had the dynamism and enthusiasm which sprang from living faith in a personal God and enabled the individual soul, conscious of its immeasurable value in God's sight, to rise to its true life ('Das religiöse Moment in der ethischen Unterweisung des Epiktet und das Neue Testament', *ZNTW* 13 [1912], p. 191). Cf. E. Bevan, *Stoics and Sceptics* (Oxford, 1913), p. 49.

[18] Nature (φύσις) came indeed to be the most widely used term of popular Stoicism: it persists to our own day in the personification of 'Nature' with a capital 'N'. The argument of I Cor. 11:14f, based on nature's bestowal of short hair on men and long hair 'for a covering' on women, has affinities with this diffused Stoic terminology.

the human mind as being originally a *tabula rasa*, a completely blank writing-tablet ready to receive the recordings made by experience. They were quite close to the Epicureans in thinking of knowledge as based on a succession of sensations originating outside oneself, but they emphasized that the individual was responsible to adopt the proper attitude to these sensations, to decide which to accept as valid and which to reject. It is not clear what criteria were laid down for making a right decision in this regard. No doubt one who already accepted the Stoic outlook would judge sensations and all the impressions made on his mind in the course of experience in the light of that outlook. Some impressions were irresistible; they carried their own conviction with them (*phantasiai kataleptikai*).

The moral earnestness of the Stoics was congenial to the traditional Roman ideal of 'seriousness' (*grauitas*), and the political unity of the Roman Empire approximated in a considerable degree to the Stoic ideal of the *cosmopolis*. The conditions of Roman imperialism thus favoured the development of a suitably adapted Stoicism. Seneca, the tutor of Nero, the slave Epictetus, and the Emperor Marcus Aurelius were the most outstanding Stoic thinkers and writers under the Empire. Later students might trace affinities between Seneca and Paul, Epictetus's expositions of Stoic ethics may have been influenced indirectly by Christianity, but the essential incompatibility of Christianity and Stoicism was appreciated by that austere moralist Marcus Aurelius, who figures in early church history as one of the 'persecuting' emperors. Partly through the early influence of his tutor Fronto, Marcus Aurelius despised what he regarded as the crass superstition of the Christians' belief; this disqualified them in his eyes from the respect due to others who maintained their principles at the cost of their lives. Their resoluteness in face of torture and death was for him, not the fortitude of soul which would have commanded the respect of a Stoic, but perverse obstinacy which called for exemplary punishment.[19] Moreover, Marcus Aurelius's Stoicism was combined with an old-world Roman piety which looked on the Christians as dangerous revolutionaries and as a disintegrating ferment in the body politic. During the centuries, however, Marcus's *Meditations* have almost acquired in some quarters the status of a manual of Christian devotion; it is

[19] Marcus Aurelius, *Meditations* xi, 3; for Fronto's attitude see Minucius Felix, *Octavius* 9, 31.

interesting to speculate what further 'meditation' Marcus would have bequeathed to posterity could he have foreseen this development!

3

The Peripatetic school, founded by Aristotle, continued for several generations to prosecute the studies which he had inaugurated in the Lyceum at Athens. Several Peripatetic leaders, following their master, specialized in the study and classification of various departments of knowledge. Theophrastus, who succeeded Aristotle as leader of the school (322–288 B.C.), wrote treatises on botany and other sciences in addition to his famous *Characters*; and other members of the school wrote on medicine, mathematics, astronomy, geography, art and music. But while for a time they 'produced scientific results which put all their rivals in the shade',[20] their influence did not survive into the New Testament period in anything like the same degree as the influence of those rivals. The Aristotelianism of the early Middle Ages was a new revival.

4

The philosophical tradition of Plato's Academy was radically modified by Arcesilaus, head of the school for a number of years until his death in 241 B.C. Controversy with the Stoics about the nature of knowledge led him to propound a thorough-going scepticism in which all possibility of knowledge was denied. He refused the Stoic appeal to 'irresistible conviction' as a criterion of truth. Even Socrates's residual knowledge—knowing that he did not know—was held by Arcesilaus to be no true knowledge. Carneades, an Academic leader of a later generation, maintained this position, but conceded that one could reach conclusions of varying degrees of probability, which provided a guide to right conduct. In 155 B.C. Carneades visited Rome along with the heads of the Peripatetic and Stoic schools, and they introduced there the main lines of Greek philosophy.

The 'New Academy', as this sceptical phase of the Academy's life

[20] G. Murray, *Five Stages of Greek Religion* (Oxford, 1925), p. 145.

was called, came to an end in the first century B.C., when Antiochus of Ascalon (d. 69 B.C.) became head of the school and claimed to restore the 'Old Academy'. He brought to an end the main dispute with the Stoics.

A distinguished Academic of the first century B.C. was the Roman statesman Cicero. He adhered in general to the 'New Academy', but was quite eclectic in his thinking and showed some Stoic leanings.

While it was Stoicism more than any other of the Greek philosophical schools that influenced early Christian thought, affinities with the later and sceptical Academics can also be traced. The Stoic allegorization of Greek mythology was followed by the Alexandrian school in its allegorization of the Old Testament narratives, but where Greek mythology itself was concerned, the Christian apologists attacked it for its irrational and immoral tendencies as vigorously as the Academy. Cicero's treatise *On the Nature of the Gods* exhibits the characteristic Academic criticism of the Greek poets' stories about the gods (because of which Plato himself felt bound to exclude the poets from his ideal Republic), and the same essential criticism appears in one Christian apologist after another.[21]

5

Several of the leading Greek philosophers show the influence of Orphism, a body of belief traditionally traced back to Orpheus, whose visit to Hades made him a suitable hero for a cult which held out to its initiates the hope of immortality and release from punishment in the underworld or from continued imprisonment in a succession of bodies. Orphic mythology included an account of the formation of the world and of men, the latter springing from the ashes of the Titans who were destroyed by a thunderbolt from Zeus in retaliation for their killing and eating his son or grandson Dionysos Zagreus.[22]

---

[21] Cf. H. Chadwick (ed.), *Origen: Contra Celsum* (Cambridge, 1953), p. x.
[22] The character of this story indicates that Orphism had its origin in a mystery religion. The mysteries were cultic ceremonies in which the passion and triumph of a divinity were dramatically enacted before devotees in a manner which enabled them in some sense to participate in his fortunes. They were called 'mysteries' because only those who were initiated (μυέομαι) were admitted to the rites; they were promised salvation and immortality. Our information on the details of the mysteries (the most renowned of which were

The conception of the body (*sōma*) as a prison-house or tomb (*sēma*) for the soul and the belief in transmigration of souls (*metempsychōsis*) played a prominent part in the thinking of the Pythagoreans, a religious order which revered as its founder Pythagoras, who about 531 B.C. migrated from the Aegean island of Samos to Croton in South Italy. How much of Pythagorean teaching goes back to Pythagoras himself is uncertain, but we may be sure that he taught (*a*) that the soul might be delivered from the weary cycle of transmigration through the practice of purity and (*b*) that numbers were the basic principles (*archai*) of the real world.

The Pythagorean régime of purity involved the study of nature and the avoidance of certain kinds of food and other tabus, which— later, at least, if not originally—were explained in terms of the doctrine of transmigration of souls. A moral self-examination was imposed on members of the society: 'Wherein have I transgressed?' each one was exhorted to ask himself. 'What have I done? What duty have I left unfulfilled?'[23]

The influence of Orphism and Pythagoreanism can be recognized in Plato's works. At a later date Pythagorean tradition, combined with elements from the Platonic, Peripatetic and Stoic systems, enjoyed a new heyday in the form of Neopythagoreanism, which appears in Rome and Alexandria in the first century B.C. Among those thinkers who show themselves influenced by Neopythagoreanism is the Jewish philosopher Philo of Alexandria (*c.* 20 B.C.–A.D. 50).

6

Philo was in mind and practice a passionately loyal and patriotic Jew. He belonged to the leading Jewish family in Alexandria; his brother Alexander was 'foremost among his contemporaries in Alexandria for his family and his wealth'[24] and was recognized by

---

those celebrated at Eleusis, near Athens, in honour of Demeter the earth-mother and her daughter Kore) is scanty and late.

[23] πῆ παρέβην; τί δ' ἔρεξα; τί μοι δέον οὐκ ἐτελέσθη; (Diogenes Laertius, *Lives of Philosophers*, 8:22).

[24] Josephus, *Ant.* xx, 100. His reputation for wealth may be gauged from his providing the silver and gold plating for the nine gates of Herod's Temple (*BJ* v, 205) and from his ability to lend Agrippa I and his wife Cypros 200,-

the Romans as 'arabarch'[25] or chief tax-collector of Alexandria; Alexander's son Tiberius was to become in turn procurator of Judaea and prefect of Egypt.[26] Philo too played his part in public life;[27] but it is to his philosophical activity that he owes his secure place in history. His mind responded eagerly to the picture of reality presented by Greek philosophy—especially Platonism, Stoicism and Neopythagoreanism. But it was a matter of hereditary faith with him that the highest truth available to mortals was contained in the sacred writings of the Jewish people, especially in the five books of Moses. It was inevitable, therefore, that he should interpret the Torah in terms of the philosophy which by the light of native reason he recognized as the truth. The ethical injunctions of the law of Moses laid down a way of life for Israel, but in Philo's eyes the law imposed that virtue which (as he learned from the Neopythagoreans and others) consisted in the control of the lower members by the mind and the bringing of the mind into harmony with the Right Reason (*orthos logos*) which ruled in the world of nature. Not only did the laws of the Pentateuch impose this path of virtue; the narratives of the Pentateuch, allegorically interpreted, exemplified it. The story of Abraham, for instance, tells of his migration from bondage to matter, his visions of God which gave him an increasing appreciation of ultimate reality, the changing of his name to indicate that at last he had become a true sage, and his marriage to Wisdom or Virtue in the person of Sarah.[28] The fruit of this marriage, Isaac, was the son of God who required no such development as his father underwent, since he was perfect from the first.[29]

---

ooo drachmae, with no great assurance of its ever being repaid (*Ant.* xviii, 159f).

[25] In Josephus (*Ant.* xviii, 159; xx, 100, 147) ἀραβάρχης with its derivatives appears by dissimilation as ἀλαβάρχης. In the Ptolemaic Empire, as inscriptional evidence confirms, the title was given to the head of the inland revenue department (cf. also Juvenal, *Sat.* 1. 130). In form, though not in meaning, it is identical with ἀραβάρχης, 'ruler of Arabs' (used of Pompey by Cicero, *Att.* ii, 17. 2; cf. Josephus, *Ant.* xv, 167).

[26] See pp. 268, 338. Another of Alexander's sons, Marcus, was the first husband of Berenice, daughter of Agrippa I (Josephus, *Ant.* xix, 277).

[27] He led the delegation of Alexandrian Jews to the Emperor Gaius (see p. 253).

[28] See Philo's treatises *De migratione Abrahami, Quis rerum diuinarum heres, De congressu quaerendae eruditionis gratia, De fuga et inuentione, De mutatione nominum, De somniis* and *De Abrahamo.*

[29] Cf., e.g., *Migr.* 140; *Fug.* 166–8; *Mut. Nom.* 130f; *Quaestiones in Gen.* on Gen. 24. No separate treatise on Isaac survives.

The story of Jacob, on the other hand, is more like that of Abraham; it relates his progressive renunciation of the flesh and training in divine truth until at last he wins his decisive victory and in experiencing the vision of God attains union with God.[30]

Moses typifies the Logos which as a saviour liberates man from material bondage and as a hierophant leads them along the path of initiation into the knowledge of God; at the end Moses himself sheds the last vestige of materiality and becomes a complete partaker of the divine nature.[31] His laws set forth the way of virtue,[32] his sacrificial ritual and the sanctuary in which it was enacted are visible object-lessons of cosmic reality.[33]

Philo found in Plato's doctrine of the ideas, eternally subsisting in the supercelestial realm,[34] a key to the understanding of many parts of scripture. In the first chapter of Genesis (as we call it) he read of the creation by God of the ideal world, including the ideal Man, as an architect forms a plan in his mind; in the second chapter he read of the reproduction of this plan or archetype in material form.[35] The ideal Man was, in the language of Gen. 1:27, 'male and female'; the man of earth, into whom God infused the Logos, was distinctively male, divinely endowed with sovereignty over his

[30] Cf., e.g., *Migr.* 153, 208ff; *Fug.* 4ff, 39ff; *Somn.* i, 2ff, 45ff, 68ff, 115ff. Jacob's new name Israel (meaning 'God strives'), given him at Penuel (Gen. 32:28), is interpreted to mean 'the man who sees God', as though incorporating Heb. *rā'āh*, 'see' (*Migr.* 200f; *Mut. Nom.* 81f; *Somn.* i, 129). No separate treatise on Jacob survives. In *De Abrahamo* 52 Abraham, Isaac and Jacob symbolize virtue acquired respectively by teaching (διδασκαλία), nature (φύσις) and practice (ἄσκησις).

[31] See especially the treatise *De uita Mosis*. His death is described as his 'transformation' (*Vit. Mos.* ii, 288) or 'translation' (*De sacr.* 8), his shedding of the body and 'transition from mortal existence to life immortal' (*De uirtutibus* 76). In *Quaestiones in Exod.* on Ex. 24:2 Philo speaks of Moses as 'changed into the divine'. Josephus similarly says that Moses 'withdrew to the divine' (*Ant.* iv, 326)—an expression which he also uses of Enoch's translation (*Ant.* i, 85).

[32] See especially his treatises *De decalogo* and *De specialibus legibus*.

[33] Cf. *Vit. Mos.* ii, 71–108.

[34] The ὑπερουράνιος τόπος (Plato, *Phaedrus* 247c).

[35] *Leg. Alleg.* i, 31ff; ii, 4ff. But the man whom God places in the Garden (Gen. 2:8) is, surprisingly, not the man 'moulded out of earth' (Gen. 2:7) but the heavenly Man, made in the divine image (Gen. 1:26f), because, in Philo's allegorical interpretation of the narrative, only the heavenly Man can cultivate the virtues (*Leg. Alleg.* i, 88f). Paul formally contradicts Philo in I Cor. 15:45ff, where he affirms that the man of earth precedes and does not follow the heavenly Man (the man of the new creation, invested with a spiritual body, whose prototype is the risen Christ).

fellow-creatures, but disaster befell him by the forming of woman from his body, for her affinities were with earth and the material order, and through her the serpent, the symbol of sensual pleasure, brought him into the bondage from which he can be set free only by long discipline in the pursuit of truth and virtue.[36]

Philonism cannot be accounted for in terms of the various sources, Jewish and Greek, on which it drew. Philo's indebtedness to his sources is plain, but Philonism is the creative achievement of his own mind, the fusion of distinct elements producing something new. It was destined to be much more influential on Christian than on Jewish thinking; it is no accident that the writings of Philo (like those of Josephus) were preserved by Christians and not by Jews. Although Philo does not appear to have exercised direct influence on New Testament thought, his writings present a number of striking points of contact with the Pauline Epistles,[37] and some knowledge of his thought and method provides positive help for the understanding of the Fourth Gospel (although the Johannine Logos doctrine is essentially different from the Philonic)[38] and of the Epistle to the Hebrews—the work of another Alexandrian who, however, prefers the typology of salvation-history to Philonic allegory as the key to unlock the meaning of the Old Testament.[39]

7

Not only the dispersion but Judaea itself was permeated by Hellenistic culture and thought in the last three centuries B.C. Abundant evidence of the Hellenization of Palestine in the first half of the third century B.C. is provided by those Zenon Papyri which deal with the affairs of the province under Ptolemy Philadelphus

[36] *Leg. Alleg.* ii, 13ff, 71ff.

[37] See H. Chadwick, 'St. Paul and Philo of Alexandria', *BJRL* 48 (1965–6), pp. 286ff.

[38] The background of the Johannine λόγος is to be found mainly in the OT concepts of 'word' and 'wisdom' of God rather than in the λόγος of Heracleitus and the Stoics; although Philo can describe the λόγος metaphorically as 'first-born son of God' (*Conf. Ling.* 146) and even as a 'second god' (*Quaest. in Gen.* on Gen. ix. 6), he has nothing approaching the Johannine doctrine of the personal and incarnate λόγος.

[39] Cf. C. Spicq, *L'Épitre aux Hébreux* (Paris, 1952), 1, pp. 39ff (where, however, the evidence for Philo's influence on Hebrews is overstated).

(285–246 B.C.).[40] The later Palestinian Wisdom literature (not to mention that of Alexandrian Jewry) presents clear evidence of Greek influence. Although Josephus's tracing of an affinity between the Pythagoreans and the Essenes is bound up with his portrayal of Jewish religious sects in terms of Greek philosophical schools,[41] some Pythagorean influence on the Essenes need not be ruled out in the world situation of that day. Too facile a distinction between Palestinian and Hellenistic phases in primitive Christianity is unwarranted; to judge by such names as Andrew and Philip, Jesus may have had Hellenists in his immediate entourage. The Hellenistic elements in the New Testament should not be written down as accretions or intrusions; they are of the essence of Christian life from the beginning.

[40] *CPI*, 1, pp. 115ff.   [41] See p. 85 with n. 10.

5 The High Priests

1

In the post-exilic age the high priest was the most important personage in the Jewish community, and was recognized as head of the Temple-state. His position was acknowledged by the Persian Empire, and then by the Hellenistic monarchs who replaced the Persians as overlords of Coelesyria. The provincial governors appointed over Judaea by the Persian and Hellenistic kings looked after the financial and strategic interests of the imperial power, but took little to do with the administration of the internal affairs of the province.[1] Until the crisis precipitated under Antiochus IV, the high-priesthood was restricted to the dynasty of Zadok, which had provided the chief priests in Solomon's Temple from its foundation until its destruction by the Babylonians in 587 B.C. and in the post-exilic Temple from its foundation onwards. When the Sanhedrin first appears in historical records, it appears as an aristocratic senate over which the Zadokite high priest presides.[2]

The high priest's primary duties, of course, were not administrative but sacral. He was, in the words of Lev. 21:10, 'the priest that is great among his brethren'—in other words, *primus inter pares*. Most of the priestly functions—the regular sacrificial ministry, the burning of incense, and so forth—could be performed by any priest, and were in fact performed by members of the twenty-four priestly orders in rotation.[3] It was natural that the high priest should officiate on the more important occasions, such as the three great pilgrimage-

---

[1] Except in a breakdown of public order, as when the Persian governor Bagoas intervened *c.* 410 B.C. when the high priest John killed his brother Jeshua in the temple in a quarrel over the succession to the high-priesthood (Josephus, *Ant.* xi, 297ff).

[2] Josephus, *Ant.* xii, 138, 142, in a letter purporting to have been sent by Antiochus III to Ptolemy, his governor in Coelesyria and Phoenicia (198 B.C.); see p. 77.

[3] Cf. I Chron. 24:4–19; Josephus, *Ant.* vii, 366.

festivals of the Jewish year—Passover (Unleavened Bread), Pentecost and Tabernacles, especially the last-named. (It was while
Alexander Jannaeus was performing the ceremony of water-pouring
at the Feast of Tabernacles once that the people pelted him with the
citrons which they carried according to the custom of the festival,
because he poured the water on the ground beside the altar, after
the Sadducean manner, and not on the altar itself, according to the
Pharisaic rule, which was popularly approved.)[4]

But even at the great pilgrimage-festivals the high priest's presence, though desirable and normal, was not essential. The one occasion above all others when his presence *was* essential was the
annual Day of Atonement, on the 10th of Tishri, around the time of
the autumnal equinox. On this day the high priest, and none but
he, must enter into the inner compartment of the sanctuary, the
holy of holies (which was normally curtained off from the outer
compartment), and there present the blood of the sin-offering as an
atonement for himself and his people. To perform this solemn
ceremony he had to be in a state of complete ritual purity, and in
later times he was isolated for the seven days preceding the Day
of Atonement to guard against accidental contamination, and perhaps even sprinkled twice with purifying water during that period.[5]
If nevertheless he did incur defilement too late to be purified before the Day of Atonement, another priest had to deputize for him,
and for the time being that other priest was high priest *quoad sacra*,
since none but the high priest might enter the holy of holies.[6]

The solemn splendour of the high priest's appearance and ministry on the Day of Atonement under the old Zadokite régime is
illustrated by Ben Sira's panegyric on the high priest Simon II (*c.*
200 B.C.)—especially the description of Simon's glory 'when the people gathered round him as he came out of the inner sanctuary' (Sir.
50:5ff). Seldom in post-Zadokite times did the character of the high
priest match the sacredness of his intercessory ministry. Jonathan,

[4] This account is based on a combination of Josephus, *Ant.* xiii, 372f, and
TB *Sukkah* 48b.
[5] The ritual for this fast-day goes back to the apotropaic prescriptions of
Leviticus 16. The isolation of the high priest for the preceding week is laid down
in Mishnah, *Yoma* 1:1; our authority for the tradition of his being sprinkled
with *mē niddāh* on the third and seventh days of his isolation is Maimonides,
Yad ha-ḥazaqah 1, *Halakah* 4.
[6] See p. 62 (Matthias).

one of the sons of Annas, appears to have had some sense of the holiness of the office and his personal unworthiness, for when the elder Agrippa offered him a second period of office as high priest he declined, saying that it was sufficient for him to have worn the sacred vestments once.[7]

Another, but more infrequent, ceremony which called for the presence and action of the high priest in person was the slaying of the red heifer, in accordance with the ritual prescribed in Num. 19. When the red heifer was slaughtered, her body was completely incinerated; the ashes were stored in a suitable place and used from time to time for the preparation of purifying water (Heb. *mē niddāh*, literally, 'water for impurity'), the sprinkling of which was necessary for the removal of ceremonial defilement, such as might be contracted through contact with a corpse. The ashes of one heifer would suffice for the preparation of purifying water for several years. (Among the Samaritans, who continued the practice for centuries after the Jews, the ashes of the last red heifer to be killed were preserved for 250 years, until the end of the sixteenth century.)[8] According to the Mishnah, the last Jewish high priest to slay the red heifer was Ishmael ben Phiabi (*c.* A.D. 58–60).[9]

2

The last legitimate high priest of the house of Zadok to hold the office was Onias III, who was deposed by Antiochus IV about 174 B.C. and assassinated three years later.[10] He was replaced by his brother Jason, who promised to promote the king's Hellenizing policy more wholeheartedly than Onias; but Jason himself was deposed in 171 B.C. and replaced by Menelaus, who was not of Zadokite stock, and perhaps not even of priestly stock.[11] When

[7] Josephus, *Ant.* xix, 313–15.
[8] Cf. M. Gaster, *Samaritan Traditions and Oral Law* (London, 1932), pp. 195f; J. Bowman, 'Did the Qumran Sect Burn the Red Heifer?' *Revue de Qumran* 1 (1958–9), pp. 73ff.
[9] Mishnah, *Parah* 3:5. This tractate is devoted to the ritual of the red heifer.
[10] Cf. II Macc. 4:1–10, 33–8; Dan. 9:26a.
[11] According to II Macc. 4:23, Menelaus was brother to Simon, captain (προστάτης) of the Temple, who in II Macc. 3:4 is said to have been of the tribe of Benjamin. Josephus makes him a younger brother of Onias III and Jason (*Ant.* xii, 238f), but he is certainly confused in his account here. The Old Latin text of II Macc. 3:4 assigns Simon (and accordingly Menelaus) to

Menelaus at last fell from favour, Alcimus was appointed high priest in his place (161 B.C.). Alcimus, though not a Zadokite, was at least recognized by the pious in Israel as a priest of Aaron's line.[12] About the time of his appointment, Onias IV, son of Onias III, seeing that there was no hope of a restoration of the legitimate dynasty of Zadok in the Jerusalem Temple, betook himself to Egypt, where Ptolemy VI allowed him to found a temple at Leontopolis, on the model of the Jerusalem Temple. There he and his descendants maintained a priestly succession and sacrificial ritual for 230 years, until their temple was closed by the Emperor Vespasian soon after the fall of the Jerusalem Temple in A.D. 70.[13]

Alcimus died after two years in office, and the high-priesthood in Jerusalem remained unfilled for seven years. In 152 B.C. it was bestowed by Alexander Balas, pretended—or possibly genuine—younger son of Antiochus IV, on Jonathan, brother and successor of Judas Maccabaeus, whose support Balas was anxious to secure in his bid for the Seleucid throne.[14] (The Hasmonaean family, to which Judas and his brothers belonged, was a priestly family, of the order of Jehoiarib.)[15] When Jonathan's brother Simon succeeded him as leader of the Jews in 143 B.C., he succeeded him as high priest also. But when Simon secured complete independence for his nation, it was no longer seemly that he should hold office by gift of a foreign king, and a popular assembly of the Jews in September, 140 B.C., decreed that Simon should be appointed ethnarch, commander-in-chief, and hereditary high priest —'high priest for ever', as the decree phrased it, perhaps in imitation of the oracle of Psalm 110:4.[16] From Simon until the downfall of the Hasmonaeans, then, the high-priesthood remained in that family, and was usually conjoined with the chief civil power.

'the tribe of Bilgah' (known from Neh. 12:5, 18, as the name of a priestly family); this reading is preferred, e.g., by F.-M. Abel, *Les Livres des Maccabées* (Paris, 1949), pp. 316f. Cf. H. H. Rowley, 'Menelaus and the Abomination of Desolation', in *Studia Orientalia Ioanni Pedersen septuagenario . . . dicata* (Copenhagen, 1953), pp. 303ff.

[12] I Macc. 7:5, 9ff.
[13] Josephus, *BJ* i, 33, vii, 421–36; *Ant.* xii, 62–73; xx, 236. See p. 5 with n. 7.
[14] I Macc. 10:18ff.
[15] Cf. I Chron. 24:7, where the course of Jehoiarib is named as first of the twenty-four. Josephus claimed to belong to this course (*Life*, 2). See p. 139, n. 21.
[16] I Macc. 14:41.

(When Salome Alexandra ruled as queen regnant from 76 to 67 B.C., she, being a woman, was ineligible for the high-priesthood—priestesses, though not uncommon in the Near East in those days, were unknown to the Jews—and gave that office to her elder son Hyrcanus.) The *ḥasiḍim* were not greatly enamoured of the Hasmonaeans' assumption of the high-priesthood for themselves. The Pharisees tolerated the situation under protest; the community of Qumran found it so intolerable that they withdrew from association with a temple and administration defiled by a 'wicked' (i.e. illegitimate) priesthood, and maintained at least a theoretical loyalty to the Zadokite dynasty in their wilderness retreat north-west of the Dead Sea.[17]

In the strife that broke out between Hyrcanus II and his younger brother Aristobulus II after the death of their mother Alexandra in 67 B.C. the high-priesthood went to the one or the other along with the kingship. After the Roman occupation in 63 B.C., Pompey deprived Aristobulus of both offices and restored the high-priesthood to Hyrcanus. Hyrcanus was later confirmed in the high-priesthood by Julius Caesar (47 B.C.) and officially recognized as ethnarch of the Jews, but the royal title was withheld from him.

When Antigonus, son of Aristobulus II, was placed on the throne of Judaea by the Parthian invaders in 40 B.C., he became high priest also instead of his uncle Hyrcanus, whose ears were cropped to make sure that he would never be high priest again.[18] (Bodily mutilation was an absolute bar to the exercise of the priestly office.)[19] Antigonus, then, like his ancestors, reigned in Judaea as priest-king; but when Jerusalem was taken by Herod, with Roman aid, in 37 B.C., he was captured and put to death.[20]

3

Herod now entered upon the kingdom to which he had been nominated by the Roman Senate three years before. Manifestly he could not assume the high-priesthood himself, since (Idumaean as he was) he had no priestly blood in his veins. Hyrcanus, his wife's grandfather, could not be made high priest again, because he was now physically disqualified, and in any case Herod would have been

[17] See pp. 102ff.   [18] Josephus, *BJ* i, 270; *Ant.* xiv, 366.
[19] Lev. 21:16ff.   [20] See p. 14.

reluctant to bestow such an authoritative office on a potential rival to himself. He bestowed it, in fact, on an obscure priest of the Jewish diaspora in Babylonia, Hananel by name.[21]

This appointment was not to the liking of Herod's mother-in-law Alexandra, who maintained that, since her father Hyrcanus was no longer eligible, the high-priesthood belonged by right to her young son Aristobulus. At her insistence Herod took the high-priesthood away from Hananel and gave it to his own seventeen-year-old brother-in-law. The sacred office brought the boy no good fortune; in less than a year he was drowned. Whether his drowning was accidental or not we cannot be sure; his mother believed that Herod arranged it, and never forgave him.[22] But her hostility to Herod brought further disasters on herself and her family.[23]

When young Aristobulus was drowned, Hananel was restored to the high-priesthood.[24] He was succeeded a few years later by Jeshua ben Phiabi, but about 23 B.C. Jeshua was deposed because reasons of state required that the high-priesthood be conferred on Simon, son of Boëthus, member of a well-to-do family of Alexandria. Simon, who functioned from time to time as a priest in Jerusalem, had a daughter of exceptional beauty, Mariamme by name. Herod fell in love with her, and wished to marry her, making her queen instead of her hapless namesake, the Hasmonaean Mariamme. But he could not give the queenly dignity to the daughter of a commoner; accordingly he ennobled her father by making him high priest. Jeshua ben Phiabi had to step down to make room for Simon son of Boëthus.[25] Simon retained the high-priesthood until 5 B.C. By that time Herod's last illness was wellnigh upon him, and his morbid suspicion tormented him more than ever. Not long before he had nominated Herod, his son by the second Mariamme, heir to the throne in place of his eldest son Antipater, whom he believed to be plotting to poison him. But in the course of further inquiries into the matter, Mariamme was accused of having concealed some knowledge of the plot which had come her way. Herod therefore divorced her, blotted her son's name out of his will, and deposed her father from the high-priesthood, which was given to Matthias

---

[21] Josephus, *Ant.* xv, 22.   [22] Josephus, *Ant.* xv, 34–9, 50–61; see p. 15.
[23] See p. 22.   [24] Josephus, *Ant.* xv, 56.   [25] Josephus, *Ant.* xv, 322.

the son of Theophilus, a native of Jerusalem.[26] But though Simon was deprived of the high-priesthood, his family ('the house of Boëthus'), which was one of the most wealthy and powerful of the priestly families, was to provide several high priests during the following decades.

Matthias, Simon's successor, was unable to discharge his high-priestly functions on the Day of Atonement following his appointment, because he accidentally incurred a ceremonial pollution on the night preceding the fast. A relative took his place. Before another Day of Atonement came round, Matthias was deposed (12 March, 4 B.C.) because of suspected complicity in the removal and destruction of the great golden eagle which Herod had placed over one of the Temple gates. His wife's brother, Joazar, whom Herod appointed in his place, belonged to the family of Boëthus.[27] A few weeks later, Herod was dead.

During the nine years that Archelaus ruled Judaea as ethnarch, after the death of his father Herod, he changed high priests three times. First, he accused Joazar the son of Boëthus of participating in the agitation against him while he was absent in Rome, and replaced him by his brother Eleazar. But Eleazar had soon to give way to Jeshua, son of Seë. By the time of Archelaus's deposition, however, we find Joazar back in office, persuading the people to submit to the census held by Quirinius, legate of Syria, as part of the business of reorganizing Judaea as a Roman province.[28]

4

Now that Judaea was a Roman province, governed by a representative of Augustus, the high-priesthood regained much of the authority which it had enjoyed under the Persian and Hellenistic monarchs. Once again the high priest, presiding over the Sanhedrin of seventy elders, himself bringing the total to seventy-one, administered the internal affairs of the Jewish nation. The office was not so powerful, of course, as it had been in the heyday of the Hasmonaean dynasty; on the other hand, it was no longer subject to the humiliating impotence that had been its lot under Herod and

[26] Josephus, *Ant.* xvii, 78.
[27] Josephus, *Ant.* xvii, 164–6.
[28] Josephus, *Ant.* xvii, 339, 341; xviii, 3.

Archelaus. The high priest was the unquestioned representative
and spokesman of the nation not only to the provincial governor,
whether of Judaea or of Syria, but to the emperor in Rome.

But there was one limitation to his authority that his predecessors
had not known during the three centuries and a half that separated
Cyrus the Great from Antiochus IV. For the first thirty-five years of
the provincial administration of Judaea the high priests were appointed and deposed by Roman governors, who in this as in other
respects took over the prerogatives of Herod and Archelaus. In
spite of official statutes against bribery and extortion, Roman provincial governors found it difficult to resist the temptation to engage in
such practices when so many opportunities presented themselves;
and such an opportunity was provided by this arrangement for making and unmaking high priests. It is not surprising that from A.D. 6
onwards the high-priesthood came to be practically the preserve
of a small number of wealthy priestly families, adherents of the
party of the Sadducees, anxious not to do or allow anything which
might compromise them in the eyes of Rome or endanger the existing settlement.

During Herod's reign the high priest's vestments were kept in the
Antonia fortress, secured by the seals of the high priest and Temple
treasurer. The high priest was allowed to take them out seven days
before the Day of Atonement and the great pilgrimage-festivals, so
that they might be ceremonially purified before being worn for
these sacred occasions. Their retention under royal custody was a
further means of ensuring the docility of the high priest.

When Judaea became a Roman province, this practice continued;
now, however, it was not a Jewish king but a Roman governor who
exercised this additional control over the high priest. In A.D. 36
Lucius Vitellius, legate of Syria, as a conciliatory gesture to the
Jews, obtained permission from Tiberius to restore the custody of
the vestments to the Temple authorities.[29] This privilege was confirmed to the Jews by Claudius after the death of Herod Agrippa I
in A.D. 44, when the procurator Cuspius Fadus tried to have the
vestments deposited as before in the Antonia fortress under his
control.[30]

In spite of Joazar's services in persuading the people of Judaea

[29] Josephus, *Ant.* xviii, 90ff.   [30] Josephus, *Ant.* xx, 6ff.

to accept Quirinius's census, Quirinius removed him from office. Josephus says that the populace rebelled against him; perhaps the contrast between his part in the census and that played by Judas the Galilaean was so marked that they could no longer tolerate so blatant a collaborator as high priest, even though they had let him talk them into submitting to the census instead of following Judas in resisting it.[81]

In Joazar's place Quirinius appointed Annas the son of Seth.[82] Annas became the head of one of the most influential high-priestly families in the closing decades of the Second Temple. Five of his sons,[83] one son-in-law[34] and one grandson[35] became high priests at various times after him. He himself retained the high-priesthood from A.D. 6 to 15, when he was deposed by the procurator Valerius Gratus in favour of Ishmael ben Phiabi;[36] but he remained the power behind the throne for many years after. The Fourth Evangelist suggests that while Caiaphas (Annas's son-in-law) was the officiating high priest in the year of Jesus' death, Annas played a leading part in the preparations for arraigning Jesus before Pilate; and Luke ascribes to him a leading part in the earliest attempt by the Sanhedrin to repress the apostles' preaching in Jerusalem.[37]

Between Annas and Caiaphas three high priests held office in as many years, one of them being Eleazar, a son of Annas. But after conferring the office on Caiaphas in A.D. 18, Valerius Gratus left him unmolested for the remaining eight years of his procuratorship, and when he himself was replaced as procurator by Pontius Pilate in A.D. 26, Caiaphas was not removed by the new procurator; in fact Caiaphas and Pilate held their respective offices concurrently for ten years, and were deposed within a few months of each other.[88] Caiaphas's tenure of the high-priesthood for the remarkably long

[81] Josephus, *Ant.* xviii, 26.
[82] Josephus, *BJ* ii, 240; *Ant.* xvii, 26 (he is called Ananus by Josephus).
[83] Eleazar (A.D. 16–17), Jonathan (A.D. 36–7), Theophilus (A.D. 37–41), Matthias (A.D. 42–3) and Annas II (A.D. 61–2).
[84] Joseph Caiaphas (John 18:13).
[85] Matthias son of Theophilus (c. A.D. 65–8).
[86] Josephus, *Ant.* xviii, 34.
[87] John 18:13–24; Acts 4:6. In Jewish religious law the sacral character of the high priest's office and person (including the purificatory and matrimonial regulations governing him and the atoning virtue of his death) adhered to him after his deposition (cf. J. Jeremias, *Jerusalem in the Time of Jesus* [London, 1969], pp. 159f).
[88] Josephus, *Ant.* xviii, 35, 95 (where he is called 'Joseph surnamed Caiaphas'). See p. 38 with n. 21.

period of eighteen years (paralleled between 40 B.C. and A.D. 70 only by the tenure of Simon, Herod's father-in-law) may have been due in part to his personal diplomacy, in part to his influential and wealthy connexions. Presumably no rival was able to outbid him so long as Gratus and Pilate governed Judaea. He was deposed at last in A.D. 36 by Vitellius, legate of Syria. Vitellius replaced Caiaphas by Jonathan, a son of Annas, but immediately after the Passover of A.D. 37 he removed Jonathan in turn and appointed his brother Theophilus high priest in his place.[39]

During Herod Agrippa's three years as king of Judaea, he appointed three high priests—first Simon Kantheras, a third son of the former high priest Simon Boëthus, then Matthias, a fourth son of Annas, and then Elioenai, son of Simon Kantheras.[40]

5

When Judaea reverted to procuratorial rule after Agrippa's death in A.D. 44, the right to appoint the high priest was not handed back to the procurator; the Emperor Claudius conferred this authority on Agrippa's brother Herod, king of Chalcis, and when Herod died in A.D. 48 it passed to his nephew, the younger Agrippa, who exercised it until the outbreak of war in A.D. 66.

Herod of Chalcis appointed two high priests—Joseph son of Kami (c. A.D. 44–47) and Ananias son of Nedebaeus (c. A.D. 47–58).[41] The latter figures in the New Testament narrative as 'the high priest Ananias' before whom Paul appeared in A.D. 57 and who was rebuked by the apostle as a 'white-washed wall' for ordering him to be struck across the mouth (Acts 23:1ff). The rabbinical traditions tell of his rapacity in seizing for himself the sacrificial perquisites which ought to have gone to the other priests; this behaviour was lampooned in a parody of Psalm 24 which was supposed to have been heard from the Temple court:

> Lift up your heads, ye gates,
> That Yoḥanan ben Narbai, Panqai's disciple, may enter
> And fill his belly with heaven's holy things![42]

[39] Josephus, *Ant.* xviii, 95, 123. [40] Josephus, *Ant.* xix, 297f, 313ff, 342.
[41] Josephus, *Ant.* xx, 15f, 103.
[42] TB *Pesaḥim* 57a. Panqai is evidently a corruption of Phinehas, but the Phinehas envisaged is more probably the reprobate son of Eli (I Sam. 2:12ff) than the grandson of Aaron, so outstandingly zealous for the divine law (see p. 93).

Ananias lived for eight years after his deposition from the high-priesthood; he was killed by Zealots at the beginning of the war in September, A.D. 66. His son Eleazar, who was captain of the Temple at the time, avenged his death.[43]

Six men in all were appointed to the high-priesthood by Agrippa II. The first of these, Ishmael ben Phiabi II, was not only (as has been mentioned) the last high priest to kill the red heifer, but was evidently thought to be a most extraordinary person to function as high priest at all.[44] He is probably to be identified with the high priest Ishmael who, according to Josephus, was later beheaded in Cyrene—under what circumstances we do not know.[45]

The most notable of Agrippa's high priests was a son of Annas who bore his father's name. This younger Annas (Ananus) was the high priest who exceeded his authority by procuring the execution of James the Just and certain other people during the interregnum in the procuratorship which followed the death of Festus in A.D. 62. Agrippa quickly dissociated himself in the eyes of Rome from this illegal action by deposing the high priest who committed it.[46] During the war the younger Annas played a prominent part as a leader of the more moderate party among the citizens of Jerusalem and an opponent of the Zealots;[47] Josephus's account of his death early in A.D. 68 at the hands of the Zealots' Idumaean allies is accompanied by an encomium on his patriotism. In Josephus's eyes the public exposure in the streets of Jerusalem of the corpse of Annas, along with that of another ex-high priest, Jesus son of Gamaliel, was an abomination sufficient in itself to ensure the city's ruin.[48]

---

[43] See pp. 116, 379.

[44] Josephus, *Ant.* xx, 179ff. During Ishmael's high-priesthood, says Josephus, the chief priests reached such a point of shameless audacity that they sent their servants to the threshing-floors to seize the tithes due to the ordinary priests, with the result that some of the latter starved to death (*Ant.* xx, 181). This resembles the account given in the Talmud of Ananias (see above). Other passages in the Talmud speak of the priests in general as wresting the tithes from the Levites about this time (TB *Yebamot* 86a, b; *Ketubot* 26a, TJ *Ma'aser Sheni* 5:15).   [45] *BJ* vi, 114.

[46] Josephus, *Ant.* xx, 197–203. See pp. 344, 374.

[47] *BJ* ii, 563, 647ff. See p. 95. The different portrayals of the younger Annas's character in *Ant.* (unfavourable) and *BJ* (highly favourable) may have been politically motivated; see on this and on several other questions raised by the subject-matter of this chapter E. M. Smallwood, 'High Priests and Politics in Roman Palestine', *JTS*, n.s. 13 (1962), pp. 14ff.

[48] *BJ* iv, 162ff, 314ff. Josephus's account of the treatment of these two former high priests suggests that he may have seen here the fulfilment of an apocalyptic fragment which underlies Rev. 11:1–13 (the apocalypse of the two witnesses).

Jesus son of Gamaliel had been high priest from A.D. 63 to 65. A tradition preserved in the Talmud tells how his wife Martha bought the high-priesthood for him from the king for a large sum of money.[49]

The last high priest to officiate before the destruction of the Temple was a priest of peasant stock, Phanni (Phinehas) son of Samuel, who was appointed by lot.[50] Josephus regards his appointment as a wanton sacrilege, but the truth is, Josephus's aristocratic sensibilities were outraged by the elevation to the supreme office of a priest who could claim no advantage of rank or wealth. Phanni's priestly pedigree was impeccable, and his appointment to the high-priesthood cannot dispassionately be regarded as more unworthy than many of the appointments made in the preceding ninety years.

6

The wealthy families which provided most of the high priests from the accession of Simon son of Boëthus to the Jewish War also provided the captains of the Temple[51] and the Temple treasurers. This meant an unhealthy concentration of power in the hands of a few rich and influential families. When the New Testament writers speak of 'chief priests' (Gk. *archiereis*) in the plural, at any one time, they refer to the members of those families, and in particular to those who at the time held the high-priesthood and the principal Temple offices. Both within the Sanhedrin and in public life in general these 'chief priests' exercised power out of all proportion to their numbers. The common people's attitude towards them and the families to which they belonged finds expression in a satirical chant preserved in the Talmud:

> Woe is me for the house of Boëthus!
> Woe is me for their club!
> Woe is me for the house of Ḥanin [Annas]!
> Woe is me for their whisperings!
> Woe is me for the house of Kantheras!
> Woe is me for their pen!

[49] TB *Yebamot* 61a.
[50] Josephus, *BJ* iv, 153ff. In *Ant.* xx, 227 he is called Phanasos (a Hellenization of Phinehas).
[51] The captain of the Temple is probably the *sāgān* of rabbinical tradition; if so, he ranked next to the high priest. He was in charge of the Temple guard (see p. 33, n. 3).

> Woe is me for the house of Ishmael [ben Phiabi]!
>   Woe is me for their fist!
> For they are the high priests;
>   Their sons are the treasurers;
> Their sons-in-law are temple-officers;
>   And their servants beat the people with cudgels![52]

[52] TB *Pesaḥim* 57a.

6 Ḥasīdīm, Pharisees and Sadducees

1

At a time when the devotion of the post-exilic community in Judaea under the Persian Empire was but lukewarm at best, groups of pious Jews began to meet for mutual encouragement. This development is referred to in the book of Malachi (*c.* 450 B.C.) in these words: 'Then those who feared Yahweh spoke to one another; Yahweh heeded and heard them, and a book of remembrance was written before him of those who feared Yahweh and thought on his name. "They shall be mine," says Yahweh of hosts, "my special possession on the day when I act, and I will spare them as a man spares his son who serves him"' (Mal. 3:16f). The book of remembrance kept in Yahweh's presence is analogous to the official chronicle kept at the Persian court, in which services such as that which Mordecai performed for Xerxes were recorded 'in the presence of the king' (Esth. 2:23).[1] And those whose names were entered in Yahweh's book of remembrance would have cause to be grateful when the day of judgement dawned: 'for you who fear my name the sun of righteousness shall rise, with healing in its wings. . . . And you shall tread down the wicked, for they will be ashes under the soles of your feet, on the day when I act, says Yahweh of hosts' (Mal. 4:3).

In this development we may with some confidence trace the origins of the *ḥasīdīm*, the 'godly people', who were to play such an important part in the religious crisis in Israel in the second century B.C. Their passionate devotion to the Torah is well illustrated in Psalm 119, the composition of an anonymous *ḥasīd*[2] who has en-

[1] Cf. Esth. 6:1–3; Herodotus, *Hist.*, viii, 85; Thucydides, *Hist.*, i, 129.
[2] The *ḥasīd* is one who maintains loyally the covenant-bond of *ḥesed* (traditionally rendered 'loving-kindness') with Yahweh, as Yahweh does for his part (cf. Ps. 18:25 // II Sam. 22:26, 'with the loyal [*ḥasīd*] thou wilt show thyself loyal').

dured hardship and persecution for his loyalty to the divine 'testimonies', but finds those testimonies a light to his path and sweeter than honey to his taste.

The *ḥăsidīm* deplored the inroads of the Hellenistic way of life into Judaism under the Ptolemies and Seleucids, but their disapproval had but little effect. The younger men, even in the priestly families, who vied with one another in following the new fashion, looked on the *ḥăsidīm* as out-of-date spoil-sports. But when Hellenism showed another side of its nature, in the attempt of Antiochus Epiphanes and his advisers to stamp out the distinctiveness of Jewish religion and nationhood, the *ḥăsidīm* stood firm and refused to compromise. Nor was their resistance merely passive; many of them made common cause with the Hasmonaean insurgents. 'There united with them a company of Hasidaeans, mighty warriors of Israel, every one who offered himself willingly for the law' (I Macc. 2:42). This alliance endured throughout the years of guerrilla warfare, until religious liberty was regained and the Temple restored to the pure worship of Israel's God.

With this happy issue of the struggle the *ḥăsidīm* were disposed to be content. While no overt breach of their alliance with the Hasmonaeans took place for a number of years, they did not cooperate so enthusiastically with the Hasmonaeans' continued fight for political autonomy and the advancement of their own family. An instance of this weakening enthusiasm appears in the story of the appointment of Alcimus as high priest, in place of the discredited apostate Menelaus (161 B.C.). 'Then a group of scribes[8] appeared in a body before Alcimus and Bacchides [governor of Syria under Demetrius I] to ask for just terms. The Hasidaeans were the first among the sons of Israel to seek peace from them, for they said, "A priest of the line of Aaron has come with the army, and he will not harm us"' (I Macc. 7:14). The narrative goes on to relate how, in spite of Alcimus's oath that these men's lives would be safe, sixty of them were seized and put to death in one day. The extremely pro-Hasmonaean author of I Maccabees suggests that Alcimus was responsible for this treacherous act, but in all probabil-

---

[8] The 'scribes' (Heb. *sōpĕrîm*, Gk. γραμματεῖς) were the accepted teachers and interpreters of the Torah, from the time of Ezra onwards. The ideal scribe is portrayed in Sir. 39:1–11. They were represented in the Sanhedrin. See pp. 77f.

ity it was the work of Bacchides, in whose eyes the *ḥāsiḏim* were rebels against the Seleucid authority like their allies the Hasmonaeans. In any case there was no further attempt at a *rapprochement* between the *ḥāsiḏim* and Alcimus.[4]

When, after an interregnum of seven years following the death of Alcimus, Jonathan, brother and successor of Judas Maccabaeus, accepted the high-priesthood as a gift from Alexander Balas (152 B.C.), the *ḥāsiḏim*, with their reverence for religious tradition, could not look with approval on this assumption of the sacred office by one who, while belonging to a priestly family, had no legal claim to the high-priesthood—especially as he received it from a pagan ruler whose questionable authority to bestow it rested on his claim to be the son of the persecutor Antiochus Epiphanes. When, however, in 141 B.C. 'the yoke of the Gentiles was removed from Israel' and in the following year a national assembly confirmed the high-priesthood to Simon and his family 'until a trustworthy prophet should arise',[5] most of them appear to have acquiesced in this settlement. For one thing, the main line of the former high-priestly family of Zadok had gone to Egypt and installed themselves as high priests in a new Jewish temple at Leontopolis, which must have ranked as schismatic in the eyes of the *ḥāsiḏim*.[6]

Under Simon's son John Hyrcanus the alliance between the *ḥāsiḏim* and the Hasmonaeans was completely disrupted. It is at this time that the Pharisees begin to play a distinctive part in the historical record;[7] according to the usual reconstruction of events, they are the *ḥāsiḏim* who broke with John Hyrcanus, and one explanation of the name Pharisees (Heb. *pĕrūšim*, Aram. *pĕrišayyā*, 'separatists') derives it from this separation or withdrawal from the Hasmonaean alliance.[8] This, however, is quite uncertain. Other sug-

[4] In II Macc. 14:6 Alcimus complains to the king that 'those of the Jews who are called Hasidaeans, whose leader is Judas Maccabaeus, are keeping up war and stirring up sedition, and will not let the kingdom attain tranquillity'; but this may refer to those who shared the Hasmonaean policy of fighting on until political independence was gained.
[5] I Macc. 13:14; 14:41. See p. 5. [6] See p. 5 with n. 7.
[7] They first appear, along with the Sadducees and Essenes, in Josephus, *Ant.* xiii, 171f (*c.* 145 B.C.).
[8] Cf. E. Meyer, *Ursprung und Anfänge des Christentums* II (Stuttgart, 1921), pp. 283f.

gested meanings of the name are 'expounders'[9] (of the divine law)
and 'Persianizers'.[10] In the latter case the designation would have
been a taunt flung at them by their theological opponents for their
holding such doctrines as the resurrection of the body and judgement to come, and believing in hierarchies of good and evil spirits,
angels and demons, organized in two opposed 'kingdoms'.

It is possible that their opponents did deliberately misconstrue
the name 'Pharisees' as though it meant 'Persianizers'; but that this
was the origin of the name is unlikely. It is much more likely that
they were called 'Pharisees' is the sense of 'separatists' because of
their strict avoidance of everything which might convey ceremonial
impurity to them.[11] For they certainly exercised great care in matters of ritual purity, in food laws, the sabbath law and the like. In
this regard Daniel, who refused to defile himself with Nebuchadnez-
zar's food or drink, is the prototype of the ḥăsîḏîm; and the martyrologies of II and IV Maccabees centre around this very point.[12]

The Pharisees were also most scrupulous about maintaining the
ancient regulations on tithing the produce of the soil. Their scrupulousness in this regard is reflected repeatedly in the Gospel tradition, as when the Pharisee praying in the Temple says, 'I give
tithes of all that I get' (Luke 18:12), and when Jesus describes
them as tithing 'mint and dill and cummin' (Matt. 23:23).[13] They

9 Cf. W. O. E. Oesterley, *The Jews and Judaism during the Greek Period*
(London, 1941), p. 246. This view can appeal for support to the statement
of Josephus (*BJ* ii, 162) that the Pharisees 'are reputed to be the most accurate exegetes of the laws'.

10 Cf. T. W. Manson, 'Sadducee and Pharisee', *BJRL* 22 (1938), pp. 153ff;
The Servant-Messiah (Cambridge, 1953), pp. 19f.

11 In this sense the word approaches closely the root-meaning of Heb. qāḏōš,
'holy'. Thus the midrash *Sifra* on Leviticus amplifies 'you shall therefore be
holy, for I am holy' (Lev. 11:44f) to: 'as I am holy, so shall you also be holy;
as I am separate (pārûš), so shall you also be separate (pĕrûšîm).'

12 Cf. Dan. 1:8; II Macc. 6:18–7:42; IV Macc. 4:26ff.

13 Cf. Luke 11:42, 'you tithe mint and rue and every herb'. The implication
is that they tithed these garden plants in addition to the principal produce of
the earth—grain, wine and olive—specified in Deut. 14:22f. A literal application of Lev. 27:30 led to the formulating of a more comprehensive rule: 'whatever is used for food and is kept watch over and grows from the soil is liable
to tithes' (Mishnah, *Ma'aserot* 1:1). There was some difference of opinion
among the rabbis about the tithing of minor herbs (cf. Mishnah, *Ma'aserot* 4:5).
According to Mishnah *Shebi'it* 9:1 rue was exempt from the tithe; E. Nestle
('Anise and Rue', *ExT* 15 [1903–4], p. 528) suggested that the Semitic šab-
bārā behind Luke's πήγανον might be a misreading for šēḇēṭā ('dill' or 'anise',
Gk. ἄνηθον).

avoided eating food that was subject to the tithe unless the tithe
had in fact been paid on it.

They took seriously the biblical doctrine of God's government
of the universe and overruling of the actions of men for the further-
ance of his own purpose. Men might disobey his laws and oppose
his will, but his will would triumph no matter what they did.[14]

In the course of their study of the law they built up a body of
traditional interpretation and application of the law which in due
course tended to assume a validity as sacrosanct as that of the
written law itself. Later generations of rabbis, indeed, represented
this oral law as coming down from Moses, who received it on Sinai
equally with the written law; while the written law was transmitted
by copyists, the oral law was transmitted by word of mouth from
one generation to the next—from Moses to Joshua, then in turn to
the elders, to the prophets, to the men of the Great Synagogue, and
from Simon the Just, one of the last survivors of the Great Synagogue, to Antigonus of Soco, who delivered it in turn to successive
pairs of scholars, generation by generation—Jose ben Joezer and
Jose ben Johanan; Joshua ben Perachyah and Nittai the Arbelite;
Judah ben Tabbai and Simeon ben Shetach (*c.* 70 B.C.); Shemayah
and Abtalion (*c.* 40 B.C.); Hillel and Shammai (*c.* 10 B.C.).[15] The
impression given by the Mishnaic tractate *Pirqē Abot*, which opens
with this account of the tradition, is that these pairs were pairs of
collegiate teachers. In fact Hillel and Shammai, for example, were
founders of rival rabbinical schools, which differed widely from each
other in the interpretation of certain parts of the law, and in the
form in which they communicated the tradition of the elders.

Yet in their attitude to tradition and in their general way of life
and thought all the Pharisaic schools displayed a family likeness
which distinguished them from other parties among the Jews, and
especially from their principal opponents, the Sadducees.

[14] Cf. Josephus *BJ* ii, 162f; *Ant.* xiii, 172; xviii, 13. Gamaliel's advice in Acts
5:38f is characteristically Pharisaic; cf. the dictum of Rabbi Yoḥanan the Sandal-
maker in *Pirqē Abot* 4:14 ('any assembling together that is for the sake of
heaven will in the end be established, but any that is not for the sake of heaven
will not in the end be established').

[15] *Pirqē Abot* 1:1–12. Shemayah and Abtalion are perhaps to be identified
with the Samaias and Pollion of Josephus's narrative (*Ant.* xiv, 172ff; xv, 3f,
370) who flourished in the earlier part of Herod's reign (see p. 22).

2

The origin of the Sadducees is even more obscure than that of the Pharisees. Theologically they differed from the Pharisees in their rejection of tradition and exclusive acceptance of the written law. Although in the event it was the Pharisaic line which was destined to rank as normative Judaism, the Sadducees regarded themselves as 'Old Believers', and refused the doctrines of bodily resurrection and the allocation of rewards and punishments in a judgement after death as innovations imported from Zoroastrianism, together with the belief in angelic and demonic hierarchies. As against the predestinarianism of the Pharisees they insisted on man's freedom of choice to determine the course of affairs.[16]

Their theological outlook, however, which is defined in our sources only in contradiction to Pharisaic doctrine, is not so important as their political rôle. They first appear as the party supporting and advising the Hasmonaean rulers, from the time of John Hyrcanus onwards. It has frequently been held that their name betokens special attachment to the high-priestly family of Zadok, but since they make their début in history as supporters of the Hasmonaean high priests, this etymology is improbable. A more probable view is that 'Sadducees' (Heb. *ṣaddūqīm*) is a Hebraization of the Greek word *syndikoi* ('syndics', 'members of the council') and that it marks them out as the councillors of the Hasmonaeans; although they themselves came to associate the word with Heb. *ṣaddīq*, 'righteous'.[17]

According to Josephus,[18] John Hyrcanus was at first a disciple of the Pharisees, until once, while he was entertaining them at a banquet, he invited them to correct him quite frankly if they ever saw him departing from the way of righteousness. One of his guests, Eleazar, responded to this invitation on the spot and told him that, if he would maintain perfect righteousness, he ought to give up the high-priesthood and content himself with the civil power. This was because his priestly pedigree was not above suspicion, since his

---

[16] Cf. Josephus, *BJ* ii, 163f; *Ant.* xiii, 173; xviii, 16f; Mark 12:18; Acts 23:8.
[17] T. W. Manson, 'Sadducee and Pharisee', *BJRL* 22 (1938), pp. 144ff; *The Servant-Messiah* (Cambridge, 1953), p. 16.
[18] *Ant.* xiii, 288ff.

mother was alleged to have been held as a prisoner by the Seleucid officials shortly before his birth. Hyrcanus naturally took offence at this reflection on his mother's chastity and his own legitimacy. One of his friends, a Sadducee named Jonathan, assured him that Eleazar had voiced outspokenly the sentiments which the whole Pharisaic party cherished at heart, whereupon Hyrcanus broke with the Pharisees and henceforth attached himself to the Sadducees.

This story (which closely resembles one related in the Talmud about Alexander Jannaeus)[19] over-simplifies the situation, but it is certain that from this time until the death of Jannaeus in 76 B.C. the Sadducees were the party in power and the Pharisees were in opposition.

Powerful as they were, the Sadducees appear to have been confined to a few wealthy families, especially the leading priestly families, while the Pharisees enjoyed the esteem of the people at large. The distinction between the two parties has indeed been envisaged as originally social, the Sadducees being the descendants of the patrician landowners and the Pharisees being drawn from the tradesmen of the towns;[20] but whatever truth may be in this reconstruction, the differences between the two in the period when they figure in history under their proper designations is not primarily social.

The opposition of the Pharisees to the régime came to a head in the reign of Alexander Jannaeus, and they appear to have been implicated in the revolt of 94–88 B.C. during which the insurgents enlisted the aid of the Seleucid King Demetrius III against him.[21] Pharisaic participation in this revolt is indicated by a reference in the fragmentary commentary on Nahum 2:11, found in Cave 4 at Qumran, to '[Deme]-trius king of Javan, who sought to enter Jerusalem by the counsel of the Seekers after Smooth Things'. The phrase 'Seekers after Smooth Things', or 'Givers of Smooth Interpretations' (Heb. *dōrĕšē ḥalāqōṯ*), is used several times in Qumran literature of a party of which the Qumran community disapproved, most probably the Pharisees. The ferocious vengeance which Jannaeus took on the insurgents when he had crushed the revolt,

[19] TB *Qiddušîn* 66a.
[20] This thesis is defended especially by L. Finkelstein, *The Pharisees* (Philadelphia, 1946).
[21] Josephus, *BJ* i, 83ff; *Ant.* xiii, 372ff.

crucifying eight hundred of them, may be referred to later in the same Qumran fragment, where the commentary on Nahum 2:12 speaks of 'the raging lion who smote with his mighty ones and the men of his counsel', and 'took vengeance on the Seekers after Smooth Things, in that he proceeded to hang them up alive, which was never done in Israel before'.[22] It is plain from the Talmud that the occasion 'when King Jannaeus put the rabbis to death' lingered long in the national memory. 'All the wise men of Israel were massacred, and the world was desolate until Simeon ben Shetach came and restored the law to its former glory.'[23]

According to Josephus, after Jannaeus's crucifixion of the leading insurgents, the remainder fled the country, to the number of eight thousand, and did not return until after the king's death. But his death marked a reversal of the Pharisees' fortunes, for Jannaeus's widow, Salome Alexandra, who succeeded him as queen regnant, favoured the Pharisees and raised them to a position of great influence in the realm. Her reign of nine years is remembered in rabbinical tradition as a miniature golden age, and it is not surprising that she herself (*more rabbinico*) is represented as being the sister of Simeon ben Shetach.[24]

The queen's advisers, not unnaturally, used their influence to avenge themselves on their persecutors; those in particular who had abetted Jannaeus in the crucifixion of his eight hundred opponents were now put to death in their turn. (A possible reference to this has been tentatively identified in a fragmentary sectarian calendar from Qumran Cave 4, not yet published.)[25] The Sadducees in terror enlisted the aid of the queen's younger son Aristobulus, who persuaded his mother not to allow her late husband's loyal supporters to be wiped out; otherwise they might in despair go over to the Nabataean king and other neighbouring rulers who would be only too glad to strengthen themselves thus at Judaea's expense.[26]

[22] 4 QpNah., ed. J. M. Allegro, DJD, v (Oxford, 1968), pp. 37–42. Cf. below, pp. 110, 240.
[23] TB *Soṭah 47a*; *Qiddušin 66a*.
[24] TB *Berakot 48a*.
[25] Cf. J. T. Milik, *Ten Years of Discovery in the Wilderness of Judaea* (London, 1959), p. 73.
[26] Josephus, *BJ* i, 110ff; *Ant.* xiii, 401ff.

3

From the time of Salome Alexandra onwards the Pharisees had a secure position within the national council. This council, usually known by the Hebrew and Aramaic form Sanhedrin (a loanword from Gk. *synedrion*, 'council'), had been in existence since before the establishment of independence under the Hasmonaeans. When Judaea was a temple-state under the Hellenistic empires, and probably earlier under the Persians, the high priest, as head of the internal administration, had a council to advise him. Rabbinical exegesis traced this council back to the seventy elders chosen to share Moses' administrative and judicial burden during the wilderness wanderings (Num. 11:16ff); but its first appearance in history is in a letter written by Antiochus III to the governor of Coelesyria, after the battle of Paneion brought Judaea within the Seleucid dominions.[27] This letter, as reproduced by Josephus, makes repeated reference to the Jewish 'senate' (Gk. *gerousia*): 'Let all the members of the nation have a constitution in accordance with their ancestral laws, and let the senate, the priests, the Temple scribes and the Temple musicians be relieved of the poll-tax, the crown-tax and the salt-tax'. In the books of Maccabees the members of this council are probably intended in the references to 'the elders of the people'.[28] Under the Hasmonaean princes the council consisted of Sadducees, but Alexandra evidently packed it with Pharisees. For 'the elders of the Jews' who came to her on her deathbed, along with her elder son Hyrcanus the high priest, to ask what action should be taken to prevent her younger son Aristobulus from carrying out his plan to seize the kingdom,[29] were certainly not Sadducees; Aristobulus was the friend and champion of the Sadducees, who would have desired nothing more than to see him firmly established as priest-king.

After the Roman conquest, the high priest Hyrcanus retained the leadership of the nation (*prostasia tou ethnous*)[30] and presided over the Sanhedrin. When Gabinius was governor of Syria (57–55 B.C.) he greatly reduced the authority of the Sanhedrin in his reorganization of Judaea,[31] but by 47 B.C. we find it in full possession

[27] Josephus, *Ant.* xii, 138ff.
[28] I Macc. 7:23, etc.   [29] Josephus, *Ant.* xii, 428.
[30] Josephus, *Ant.* xx, 244.   [31] Josephus, *BJ* i, 170; *Ant.* xiv, 90f.

of its power as supreme court, under the presidency of Hyrcanus. For in that year Herod was summoned to appear before it on a charge of exceeding his authority as military governor of Galilee by executing the bandit chief Hezekiah without a trial, and the Sanhedrin would have condemned him had not Hyrcanus, for fear of the consequences, adjourned the court before it took this drastic action.[32]

When Herod became king of the Jews, high priest and Sanhedrin alike lost most of their authority, but the popular prestige of the Pharisees increased—partly because, when the occasion seemed to demand it, they did not shrink from opposing Herod publicly. When Judaea became a Roman province in A.D. 6, the high priest and Sanhedrin resumed their control of internal Jewish affairs, although they were ultimately responsible to the procurator. During the next sixty years the high priests were regularly selected from the wealthy Sadducean families, and these families dominated the Sanhedrin. But although the Pharisees were in the minority, their popular support was such that in the Sanhedrin as well as out of it they enjoyed an influence out of proportion to their numbers. According to Josephus, who himself adhered to the Pharisaic party from his nineteenth year onwards, Sadducean magistrates acquiesced in Pharisaic principles because they saw that this was the only way in which they could persuade the people to tolerate them.[33]

In the New Testament the Sanhedrin is variously called the 'council' (*synedrion* or *boulē*), the 'body of elders' (*presbyterion*) and the 'senate' (*gerousia*); at other times it is denoted in terms of its component elements—e.g. 'the chief priests and Pharisees' (Matt. 21:45; John 7:32), 'the chief priests and elders and scribes' (Mark 14:53), 'the chief priests and scribes' (Luke 22:2), 'the chief priests and elders' (Acts 4:23), 'the chief priests and all the council' (Acts 22:30), 'the rulers and elders and scribes' (Acts 4:5).

4

The Pharisees banded themselves together in local fellowships or brotherhoods (*ḥăḇūrōṯ*; members of a *ḥăḇūrāh* were *ḥăḇērim*).[34]

---

[32] Josephus, *BJ* i, 208ff; *Ant.* xiv, 163ff.
[33] *Ant.* xviii, 17.
[34] The *ḥāsīḏ* who composed Psalm 119 says 'I am a companion (*ḥāḇēr*) of all who fear thee, of all who keep thy precepts' (*v.* 63).

Josephus estimates their numbers at about 6,000.[85] Many no doubt followed their direction who did not belong to any Pharisaic fellowship. Moreover, many, if not most, of the scribes, the professional students and teachers of the scriptures, belonged to one or another of the Pharisaic schools and popularized their interpretations. But not all the scribes were 'scribes of the Pharisees' (Mark 2:16; cf. Acts 23:9); there were others who expounded the law in accordance with Sadducean tenets, ignoring the 'tradition of the elders' (Mark 7:3, 5).

The 'tradition of the elders' was largely designed to mitigate the rigours which a literal application of the written law would impose on people living under conditions widely different from those which obtained when the law was first promulgated. For example, the law of Ex. 16:29, 'let no man go out of his place on the seventh day', would, if literally interpreted, have prevented almost any movement outside one's home on the sabbath, had 'his place' not been interpreted in the light of Num. 35:5 to include a distance of 2,000 cubits from one's home, or whatever place a man might decide to nominate as his home for this purpose—the 'limit of the sabbath' (*tēḥūm haššabbāṯ*) or a 'sabbath day's journey' (cf. Acts 1:12).[86]

Sometimes, indeed, the interpretation was stretched so far as in practice to nullify the original wording of the commandment, or neutralize the force of a more fundamental commandment. This criticism was levelled by Jesus against a scribal interpretation which in effect enabled a man to evade giving material help to his parents by representing that the money which he might have used for that purpose was already devoted to God (*qorbān*). Such an interpretation, said Jesus, overrode the spirit of the Fifth Commandment, which enjoined reverence to parents (Mark 7:9–13). This interpretation of the law concerning vows (Deut. 23:21) was a specific application of the general principle that money vowed to sacral purposes must not be diverted to other uses. However, before the end of the first century A.D. Rabbi Eliezer ben Hyrcanus expressed the judgement that when a vow adversely affected relations between parents and children the door was open for its annulment, and he secured the assent of his colleagues.[87]

[85] Josephus, *Ant.* xvii, 42 (towards the end of Herod's life).
[86] Mishnah, *'Erubin* 4:3, etc.
[87] Mishnah, *Nedarim* 9:1.

To Hillel is assigned a legal innovation which went far to modify, if not to nullify, the ancient law that debts owed by a fellow-Israelite were to be remitted every seventh year (Deut. 15:1–6). In the changed situation of the Second Commonwealth this law bore hardly on a man who might be badly in need of a loan to tide him over a difficult period; if the sabbatical year was approaching, he would have difficulty in finding a willing lender, despite the exhortation in Deut. 15:7–11 to a wealthy Israelite not to refuse a loan in such circumstances. Hillel accordingly instituted the provision that if, *before* the execution of a loan, a declaration was made before the court (Gk. *pros boulē*, whence the provision was known by the Hebrew and Aramaic loanword *prozbul*) that the law of release of debts should not apply to it, then the debt was not liable to cancellation when the sabbatical year came round.[38]

Of the two dominant schools in New Testament times, the school of Shammai was credited with a stricter interpretation of the law and the school of Hillel with a milder. It is probable that the lawyers in the Gospel record, who 'load men with burdens hard to bear' but do not themselves lift a finger to ease their weight (Luke 11:46), are Shammaites. But in the reconstruction of national life that followed the war of A.D. 66–73 it was the school of Hillel, under Yoḥanan ben Zakkai and his associates, that became dominant. The extreme Shammaite position which insisted on the fulfilment of every jot and tittle and is reflected in James 2:10 ('whoever keeps the whole law but fails in one point has become guilty of all of it') is a far cry from the teaching of Rabbi Aqiba (c. A.D. 100), that 'the world is judged in mercy, and all is according to the amount of the work' (*Pirqē Abot* 3:19)—that is, according to the preponderance of good or bad in human acts.[39] This must be borne in mind when the contrast is marked between the picture of the Pharisees given in the Gospels and that found in the later rabbinical records. But even in the rabbinical records it is freely recognized that not all

---

[38] Mishnah, *Shebi'it* 10:3ff. (An alternative etymology, but less probable than πρὸς βουλῇ, is Gk. προσβολή, 'delivery' of goods.) Hillel's illustrious disciple and successor, Gamaliel I, modified the law restricting the movements of witnesses of the new moon on the sabbath day (Mishnah, *Rosh ha-Shanah* 4:5) and forbade the annulment of divorce proceedings without the wife's knowledge (Mishnah, *Giṭṭin* 4:2).

[39] Cf. H. Danby, *Studies in Judaism* (Jerusalem, 1922), p. 19; B. S. Easton, *Christ in the Gospels* (New York, 1930), pp. 88ff; C. G. Montefiore and H. Loewe, *A Rabbinic Anthropology* (London, 1938), pp. 595ff.

Pharisees are worthy of the name; of seven categories of Pharisee distinguished in the Talmud only one, he who is a Pharisee from love of God, receives unqualified commendation.[40]

The Pharisaic concern for ceremonial purity involved not only strict separation from Gentiles, who were beyond the pale of the law altogether, and from Samaritans, whose interpretation of the laws of purity differed from that current among the Jews, but even a considerable degree of aloofness from those of their fellow-Jews who were not so particular about the laws of purity and tithing as the Pharisees themselves were. Chief among these latter were the ordinary artisans and peasants, who could not devote much time to the study and practice of these laws, and perhaps could not bring themselves to be greatly interested in them. These people, who formed the great majority of the Jewish population of Palestine, were called 'the people of the land'—only, the old collective phrase *'am hā'āreṣ* was now used in an individual sense, of one of these people, and came to have the specialized sense of a religious ignoramus, one unversed in the law. The phrase occurs in this sense in a dictum ascribed to Hillel, 'No *'am hā'āreṣ* is pious'[41]—a dictum which is echoed in the remark of a group of ruling Pharisees in the New Testament: 'this crowd, who do not know the law, are accursed' (John 7:49).

One fact above all others stands to the credit of the Pharisees: when the Second Temple fell and the Second Commonwealth came to an end in A.D. 70, they were the only party in Jewry equal to the task of reconstituting the national life, and they accomplished it.

[40] TJ *Berakot* 9:7.   [41] *Pirqē Abot* 2:6.

7   The Essenes

Alongside the Pharisees and Sadducees there was a third party in Judaea in New Testament times which, while it played no such part in public life as they did, nevertheless presents features of great interest and importance for Jewish religion and Christian origins. This is the party of the Essenes.

The derivation of their name (Gk. *Essēnoi, Essaioi*) has long been, and still is, a matter of debate. The view that is still perhaps most widely held derives it from Aramaic *ḥasyā*, 'pious' or 'holy'—a derivation consistent with the high probability that the Essenes represent another development of the *ḥāsiḍim* of the second century B.C., but difficult to accept with confidence because *ḥasyā* is attested for Syriac (Eastern Aramaic) rather than for Western Aramaic.[1] A strong case has been made out for the alternative derivation from Aramaic *'āsyā*, 'healer'[2]—a derivation the more interesting because of its resemblance in sense to the *Therapeutai*, a pious community of Jews in Egypt to whom Philo points, as he points to the Essenes of Judaea, for confirmation of his thesis that 'every good man is free'.[3] The designation *therapeutai* could mean 'healers', as Philo points out, although he also interprets it as 'servants' or 'worshippers' of God.

Philo of Alexandria (c. 20 B.C.–A.D. 50) is our earliest informant about the Essenes; other first-century informants are Josephus and the elder Pliny, while the Christian writer Hippolytus of Rome, at the beginning of the third century, makes some contributions to our knowledge of them not paralleled in his predecessors.

[1] This derivation is preferred, e.g., by J. T. Milik, *Ten Years of Discovery in the Wilderness of Judaea* (London, 1959), p. 80, and M. Black, *The Scrolls and Christian Origins* (London, 1961), pp. 13ff; they mention an inscriptional occurrence of *ḥsy* in a verbal form in Palmyrene (a dialect of Western Aramaic).
[2] Cf. G. Vermes, 'The Etymology of "Essenes"', *Revue de Qumran* 2 (1959–60), pp. 427ff.   [3] Philo, *De uita contemplatiua*, 2ff.

1

Pliny's account comes in his *Natural History* (v. 73); it was evidently written between A.D. 73 (the year of the reduction of Masada) and 79 (the year of Pliny's death in the eruption of Vesuvius). He has just been describing the Dead Sea and its marvels, and he continues thus:

> On its west side, just far enough from its shore to avoid its baneful influences, live the Essenes. They form a solitary community, and they inspire our admiration more than any other community in the whole world. They live without women (for they have renounced all sexual life), they live without money, and without any company save that of the palm trees. From day to day their numbers are maintained by the stream of people who seek them out and join them from far and wide. These people are driven to adopt the Essenes' way of life through weariness of ordinary life and by reason of the changes of fortune. Thus, through thousands of generations—incredible to relate—this community in which no one is ever born continues without dying; other people's weariness of life is the secret of their abiding fertility! Below them was the town of Engedi, whose fertility and palm-groves formerly made it second only to Jerusalem [probably a scribal error for 'Jericho']; but now it too lies a heap of ashes. Next comes Masada, a fortress on a rock, itself also not far from the Dead Sea. And there is the frontier of Judaea.

Whoever the people may be whom Pliny is describing, his description, which is probably based on earlier sources, contains a large element of rhetorical exaggeration. For example, the Essenes had certainly not lived in that area for 'thousands of generations'; ten generations would probably be a considerable exaggeration, even if we reckoned four generations to a century.

The identification of their headquarters must depend in part on the meaning of the preposition 'below' in the statement, 'Below them was the town of Engedi' (Lat. *infra hos Engada oppidum fuit*). Since Pliny in this context is describing the Jordan valley from its source to the Dead Sea, it is reasonable to suppose that he locates Engedi south of the Essene headquarters, just as 'next' (Lat. *inde*) at the beginning of the following sentence marks Masada as lying south of Engedi. This raises the question whether these Essene headquarters may not be identified with Khirbet Qumran—the more so since Père de Vaux and other archaeologists assure us that there is no other installation west of the Dead Sea which could satisfy Pliny's description.[4] This suggested identification has important implications which must be considered later.

2

Philo of Alexandria has left us two accounts of the Essenes. One is a fairly long account, in his treatise *Every Good Man is Free* (which is commonly regarded as one of his more youthful productions); the other is shorter, and formed part of his *Hypothetica* (an apology for the Jews).

In his longer account Philo estimates the numbers of the Essenes at about four thousand, and describes them as living in villages, working hard at agriculture and similar occupations, devoting much time (especially on the sabbath, when they congregated in their synagogues) to the communal study of moral and religious questions, including the interpretation of the sacred scriptures. They paid scrupulous attention to ceremonial purity, he tells us, and held all their property—money, food and clothes—in common. They abstained from animal sacrifice, from the swearing of oaths, from military service and commercial activity. They kept no slaves, made provision for those of their number who were unable to work through sickness and old age, and in general cultivated all the virtues. They were, indeed, illustrious examples of his thesis that the truly good are the truly free.[5]

In his shorter account Philo again makes mention of several of these features, and adds that they admit none but adults to membership of their community, and that they practise celibacy, on the ground that wives and families distract men's attention from the pursuit of goodness and truth.[6]

[4] R. de Vaux, *L'Archéologie et les Manuscrits de la Mer Morte* (London, 1961), pp. 100ff. See p. 104 below.   [5] Philo, *Quod omnis probus liber sit,* 75ff.
[6] *Hypothetica (Apologia pro Iudaeis), apud* Euseb., *Praep. Euang.* viii, 11. 1ff.

3

Josephus has given us three accounts of the Essenes. His longest account comes in the second book of his *History of the Jewish War*, which was written only a few years after A.D. 70.[7] A shorter account appears in the eighteenth book of his *Jewish Antiquities*, written some twenty years later,[8] and a shorter one still in the thirteenth book of the same work, where the Essenes appear in history for the first time.[9]

Josephus gives us more detailed information than Philo does, and his information is based—in part, at least—on first-hand evidence. He claims, indeed, to have made trial of the Essenes in his youth, as of the other Jewish sects, in order that, when he had made some acquaintance with them all, he might choose the best.[10] Unfortunately, we can never read anything that Josephus tells us about himself without a certain measure of reserve; and as his 'close familiarity' with the Essenes was wedged in along with other experiences between his sixteenth and nineteenth years (c. A.D. 53–56) it does not appear to have been very extended.

Besides, while Philo for his part admittedly uses the Essenes to point a moral, Josephus in turn emphasizes those features in this as in other Jewish sects which he judged would make the greatest impression on his Gentile readers; for one thing, he persists in describing the Jewish religious sects as schools of philosophy after the Greek fashion.

For the most part, however, Josephus's description of the Essenes strikes us as being factual and reliable.

[7] *BJ* ii, 119ff, preceding descriptions of the Pharisees (162f) and Sadducees (164ff). Josephus calls the Essenes the third philosophical school among the Jews.

[8] *Ant.* xviii, 18ff, following descriptions of the Pharisees (12ff) and Sadducees (16f) and preceding an account of the 'fourth philosophy' (23ff), i.e. the Zealot movement (see pp. 93ff below).

[9] *Ant.* xiii, 171f (see p. 91).

[10] *Life* 10ff. He chose the Pharisees, 'a party resembling what the Greeks call the Stoic school'. He probably regards the Sadducees as the Jewish counterpart to the Epicureans, while he says elsewhere that the Essenes 'follow the way of life taught among the Greeks by Pythagoras' (*Ant.* xv, 371). This attempt to conform the main Jewish parties to various Greek philosophical schools probably results in some distortion in his descriptions of the former; see, however, remarks on Greek influence on p. 55.

According to him the Essenes were scattered through all the cities of Palestine. Some of them lived in Jerusalem. They practised common hospitality; an Essene from a distance would be treated as a brother by any other Essene to whose house he came. But much of Josephus's description implies a community life such as could not be followed by permanent city-dwellers, and a reasonable inference is that the fully initiated Essenes were organized in separate communities while they had attached to them associate members who lived in cities.

The Essenes, says Josephus, were even more predestinarian in their outlook than the Pharisees. Translating their belief into the Greek idiom, he says that 'the race of Essenes declares Fate to be the mistress of all things, holding that nothing befalls men except by her decree'.[11]

In the eighteenth book of the *Antiquities* he has this to say:

> The doctrine of the Essenes is that all things are left in the hand of God. They teach the immortality of the soul, and think it their duty to strive for the fruits of righteousness. When they send their votive offerings to the Temple, they present their offerings[12] in accordance with exceptionally strict purificatory rules of their own; for this reason they are excluded from the common precinct of the Temple and offer their sacrifices by themselves.[13] They excel all other men in their manner of life, and they devote themselves wholly to agriculture. A special need of admiration should be accorded to their life, without precedent among either Greeks or barbarians. Nor is this a temporary devotion; it has persisted among them for long as a settled policy. They have all things in common, so that a rich man enjoys no more of his wealth than a man who is penniless. There are more than four thousand men who follow this way of life, and they neither marry

[11] *Ant.* xiii, 172.

[12] The sixth-century Latin version and the tenth- or eleventh-century epitome add a negative: 'they do not present offerings'. But the Latin version does not contradict the sense of the Greek text; it says 'they do not celebrate sacrifices or offerings with the people'. However, all the extant manuscripts of the full Greek text omit the negative. Philo's statement that the Essenes have proved to be outstandingly servants or worshippers (θεραπευταί) of God 'not by sacrificing animals but by determining to make their minds becomingly sacred' (*Quod omnis*, 75) does not deny outright that they offered sacrifice, but is parallel to similar statements about the comparative merit of sacrifice and righteousness in the OT (cf. I Sam. 15:22; Hosea 6:6, etc.).

[13] We may connect this statement with the existence of the (unidentified) 'Gate of the Essenes' in the neighbourhood of the Temple (Josephus, *BJ* v, 145).

wives nor keep slaves, for they think that the possession of slaves tends to injustice, while marriage is an occasion of strife. But they live by themselves and serve one another. They appoint fit men to receive their revenues and the produce of the earth, and priests to supervise the preparation of their bread and other food.[14]

While Josephus confirms, in general, the statements of Philo and Pliny that the Essenes were celibates,[15] he mentions one order of Essenes, 'which, while at one with the rest in its mode of life, customs and regulations, differs from them in its views on marriage'.[16] Members of this particular order marry wives and bring up families, he says, because they reckon that otherwise the race would die out (a naïve explanation, since, on his showing, the major Essene groups appear to have propagated their species quite successfully by adopting and bringing up other people's children). These wives evidently shared the community life and ritual washings.

Anyone who sought admission to the Essene brotherhood, Josephus tell us, had to undergo three years' probation. During the first year he wore the white linen habit and loin cloth which were characteristic of the sect, and carried the small trowel which every Essene used to dig a latrine-pit, in accordance with the instruction of Deut. 23:12–14. At the end of the first year the novice was admitted to the ritual purification in water, but two more years had to elapse before he was considered ready for admission to the communal meal. And when this final stage of full initiation was reached, says Josephus,

> before he is allowed to touch the communal food, he is made to swear tremendous oaths: first, that he will practise piety towards God; then, that he will observe justice towards men; that he will do wrong to none whether on his own initiative or by another's orders; that he will always hate evildoers and help the just; that he will keep faith with all men and especially with those in authority (since no man achieves dominion save by the will of God); that, if he himself should be a

[14] *Ant.* xviii, 18–22. The last sentence in this account is textually corrupt and has been omitted.
[15] Celibacy was not traditionally regarded as a superior state of life to matrimony by religious Jews: its maintenance among the Essenes may have been due to the carrying over of regulations for the holy war in Israel into the order's spiritual militancy (cf. M. Black, *The Scrolls and Christian Origins*, pp. 17, 29f).   [16] *BJ* ii, 160f.

ruler, he will not abuse his authority or outshine his subjects in dress or by any superior decoration; that he will always love truth and expose liars; that he will keep his hands free from theft and his soul pure from impious gain; that he will conceal nothing from his fellow-Essenes and reveal none of their secrets to others, even though he be tortured to death. He swears, moreover, to transmit their rules exactly as he received them, to abstain from banditry, and likewise to preserve the books of the sect and the names of the angels. By such oaths they bind securely those who join them.[17]

As might be expected in a fellowship guarded by such oaths, the discipline was strict; yet it was notoriously and inflexibly just. The effect of the initiatory oaths on the conscience of those who were bound by them was such that an excommunicated Essene inevitably starved to death (unless his excommunication was rescinded in time), because all food prepared otherwise than according to their rule was ceremonially unclean and he could not bring himself to eat it.[18] Josephus tells how many members of the sect endured all kinds of tortures at the hand of the Romans, who tried by such means to force them to eat forbidden food or otherwise break their oath, but all to no effect.[19]

An Essene's day began before sunrise, when he rose to recite morning prayers along with his fellows, 'as though they were entreating the sun to rise'.[20] This probably means no more than that they said their prayers facing east, which was not the general Jewish practice. (Josephus's language here is reminiscent of a baptist sect elsewhere called the Sampsaeans, which probably had some affinities with the Essenes, and acquired its name, cognate with Heb. *šemeš*, 'sun', from acts of homage paid to the sun as a manifestation of divinity.[21]) Before these prayers were offered no word

---

[17] *BJ* ii, 139–42.   [18] *BJ* ii, 143f.   [19] *BJ* ii, 152.

[20] *BJ* ii, 128. Eastward prayer was not a Jewish practice, but it is attested as early as the sixth century B.C. for some 'nonconformists' in the Jerusalem Temple (Ezek. 8:16).

[21] Epiphanius, *Panarion* 19:2; 53:1. The Sampsaeans of subsequent centuries are probably to be identified with those Ebionites who accepted the angelic revelations in the Book of Elkasai, through which at the beginning of the second century A.D. certain 'Essene' doctrines were spread among Jewish Christian groups in Transjordan (cf. Hippolytus, *Ref.* ix, 12; x, 25; Origen *apud* Euseb. *HE* vi, 38; Epiphanius, *Panarion* 19:1ff; 30:17). Philo similarly says that the Therapeutai in Egypt stand at dawn facing the east 'and when they see the sun rising they raise their hands heavenwards and pray for a good day and truth and clear-sighted power of reasoning' (*Vit. Contempl.* 89).

was spoken. Then (except on the sabbath, which was very strictly observed) the brethren betook themselves to the various tasks which were assigned to them by the overseers, and worked at them until noon was approaching. Then they assembled in the community centre, bathed, and entered the refectory in their linen habits. This midday meal was a solemn occasion at which none but full members were present. It was introduced and concluded by grace, said by a priest, and the company praised God together before and after the meal, which consisted of simple fare. They ate in moderation, and their behaviour during the meal, as at all other times, was marked by quietness and sobriety. They did not all speak at once, but spoke in turn, observing the rules of seniority. For there were four grades of members, arranged in order of seniority.[22]

After the meal they laid aside their linen habits, resumed their working clothes, and continued their prescribed tasks until evening. Then they assembled for another meal, but at this meal strangers and visitors might be present.

One curious feature which Josephus relates is that the Essenes regarded oil as defiling and would not anoint themselves, even after bathing, for they believed a rough skin to be more pleasing to heaven[23] (probably they looked on the application of oil to the skin as a mark of luxurious living). They avoided oaths, apart from those which they swore at their initiation. They were great students of the sacred books and writing of the ancients, and had a reputation both for interpreting the prophets and for making predictions themselves, which were regularly verified by the event. They also paid much attention to the medicinal properties of various roots, plants and 'stones' (probably bituminous products of the Dead Sea).[24]

[22] Josephus, *BJ* ii, 10. The four grades, divided 'according to the duration of their discipline', probably denote successive stages of initiation, the fourth and highest grade comprising those who had passed through all the stages and were fully established members.

[23] *BJ* ii, 123. The avoidance of oil as defiling is perhaps attested for the Qumran community, according to one reading of *CD* xii, 16; cf. A. Dupont-Sommer, *The Essene Writings from Qumran* (Oxford, 1961), p. 155 with n. 4. Some ceremonial reason may be envisaged, if we compare the avoidance of oil by the priests mentioned by Porphyry, *De abstinentia* iv, 6, 7.

[24] *BJ* ii, 136.

4

Hippolytus's account comes in the ninth book of his treatise on *The Refutation of All Heresies*,[25] dating from the early years of the third century. Hippolytus follows Josephus for the most part, but he appears to have had access also to a reliable and independent source of information, which enabled him to correct Josephus's account in certain points, and to supplement it in others.[26] Hippolytus omits the suggestions of sun worship in their morning prayers; according to him, 'they continue in prayer from early dawn, and do not speak a word until they have sung a hymn of praise to God'.[27]

Hippolytus tells us that the Essenes in the course of their history had split up into four parties, although from his account of the four it is not easy to draw a clear distinction between them, since all appear to be equally rigorist. One of these parties, he says, manifested such a degree of intolerance of Gentiles (especially Gentiles who took the name of God upon their lips but refused to be circumcised) that its members were known as Zealots or *sicarii*.[28] If this does not indicate an actual overlapping of the Essenes and Zealots, it does at least suggest that some Essenes adopted an attitude towards Gentiles which led people to confuse them with Zealots. That the Essenes were not pacifists in principle seems to be further indicated by the appearance of an Essene named John as an energetic commander of the insurgent Jewish forces in the war against Rome.[29]

Hippolytus gives us a number of instances which illustrate the strictness with which the Essenes observed the sabbath and other laws. Some, he says, would not handle a coin which bore the likeness of the emperor or any other man, for the very act of looking at such a thing was regarded by them as one of the forms of idolatry forbidden in the Second Commandment.[30]

But his most important deviation from Josephus's account is his

[25] *Ref.* ix, 14–23.
[26] Cf. M. Black's appendix on 'The Essenes in Hippolytus and Josephus' in *The Scrolls and Christian Origins*, pp. 187ff.   [27] *Ref.* ix, 16.
[28] *Ref.* ix, 21. See p. 98.   [29] Josephus, *BJ* ii, 567; iii, 11, 19.
[30] *Ref.* ix, 21. This scrupulousness was paralleled in the main stream of rabbinic Judaism: Nahum of Tiberias, for example, was so holy that never in his life did he look at the image on a coin (TJ *'Abodah Zarah*, 3:1).

statement that the Essenes believed in the resurrection of the body, as well as in the immortality of the soul. The soul, he says, is in their view imperishable, and rests after death in an airy and well-lighted place, until the day of judgement arrives and it is rejoined by the resurrected body.[31] But Josephus tells us that the Essenes regarded the body as the temporary and perishable prison-house of the immortal soul, from which at death the latter breaks free and soars on high, rejoicing at its liberation from a long bondage. Both bear witness to the Essene belief in the natural immortality of the soul, which was not a characteristic doctrine of Judaism, but Josephus, not content with recording this Greek element in Essene belief, appears to have made a further concession to Greek thought by implying that the Essenes did not expect a bodily resurrection.[32]

5

According to Philo, the Essenes were founded by Moses.[33] No doubt, like the men who transmitted the main body of Jewish religious tradition, they represented their regulations and interpretations of the law as going back to Moses and bearing his authority. And when Josephus tells us that they honoured the name of their law-giver next after the name of God, and punished any blasphemous or unseemly use of his name with death,[34] he is probably referring to Moses. Again, the Essenes have been thought of as in the spiritual succession to people like the Rechabites, who in the days of the Hebrew monarchy abjured the settled way of life in Canaan, with the cultivation of corn and wine, and set themselves to maintain the wilderness tradition of their ancestors.[35] But the Essenes' existence as a community cannot be traced back earlier than the middle of the second century B.C. Josephus first mentions them, along with the Pharisees and Sadducees, in his account of the governorship of Jonathan (160–143 B.C.);[36] the first individual Essene known to history is a man called Judah, who lived in the

[31] *Ref.* ix, 22.
[32] *BJ* ii, 154f. Since, however, Josephus was acquainted with the Essenes at first hand, the possibility cannot be excluded that it was they themselves who made this concession to Greek thought.
[33] *Hypothetica* 11:1 ('our lawgiver').
[34] *BJ* ii, 145.   [35] M. Black, *The Scrolls and Christian Origins*, p. 15.
[36] *Ant.* xiii, 171f.

reign of Aristobulus I (104–103 B.C.) and was renowned for his ability to predict the future. Among other predictions he is said to have foretold the day and place of the death of Antigonus, one of the king's brothers.[87]

Another Essene prophet was Menahem, who, one day when Herod as a boy was on his way to school, greeted him as the future king of the Jews. Many years after, when Herod was now king, he sent for Menahem, who told him that he had twenty or thirty years of kingship before him. Herod accordingly held the Essenes in high honour, says Josephus.[88]

There may be a sequel to this incident in the New Testament. Luke tells us that among the leaders in the church at Syrian Antioch around A.D. 47 was one Manaen (a Greek spelling of Menahem), who had been *syntrophos* (foster-brother, class-mate or courtier) of Herod the tetrarch (Acts 13:1). It has been suggested that one of the ways in which the elder Herod honoured the prophet Menahem was by selecting a grandson and namesake of his to be brought up at court as companion to his own son Antipas, the future tetrarch of Galilee and Peraea.

Yet another Essene prophet was one Simon, who, shortly before the deposition of Archelaus in A.D. 6, was summoned before him with others to interpret a dream, and interpreted it correctly of Archelaus's impending downfall. Five days later Archelaus was summoned to appear before Augustus in Rome, whence he was banished to Gaul.[89]

Whereas until recently we have been almost entirely dependent for our information about the Essenes on writers who were not themselves members of the order, we have now to reckon with the possibility that a large body of Essene literature has come to light, which enables us to see them from within.[40]

[87] Josephus, *BJ* i, 78ff; *Ant.* xiii, 311ff.
[88] *Ant.* xv, 373–8.   [89] Josephus, *BJ* ii, 113; *Ant.* xvii, 346f.
[40] See pp. 101ff.

8 The Zealots

The Zealots (Gk. *zēlōtai*) called themselves by the Hebrew term
qannā'im or the Aramaic *qan'anayyā*. The apostle whom Luke calls
'Simon the Zealot' (Luke 6:15; Acts 1:13) is referred to by the other
Synoptic Evangelists as 'Simon the Cananaean' (Mark 3:19; Matt.
10:4)—'Cananaean' being the Aramaic form supplied with a Greek
ending. The Semitic and Greek words alike may denote not only
zeal in the common sense but a religious jealousy for the exclusive
honour of Israel's God against anyone or anything that threatened
to diminish his honour.

The Zealots of the first century A.D. had an ancient and noble
spiritual heritage. Their prototype was Phinehas, grandson of
Aaron, who in the apostasy of Baal-peor was animated by zeal for
Yahweh—a zeal like Yahweh's own—and took drastic action to stop
the rot (Num. 25:7–13; cf. Ps. 106:28–31). Phinehas's 'zeal' is expressed by the Hebrew verb *qinnē'* and its cognate noun *qin'āh*,
which are represented in the Septuagint by the Greek words *zēloō*
and *zēlos*.

It is no doubt the example of Phinehas's violent termination of a
mixed marriage that underlies the provision in the Mishnaic tractate
Sanhedrin (9:6) that those Jews who marry heathen women[1] may
be attacked by zealots (*qannā'in*)—presumably without formal
process of law.

In a similar context of apostasy the prophet Elijah manifested
comparable zeal for God.[2] 'I have been very zealous for Yahweh,

---

[1] Literally 'an Aramaic woman' (Heb. *'arāmiṯ*).

[2] In later Jewish tradition Elijah is compared to Phinehas or even equated
with him (cf. Targ. Jer. I Ex. 4:13; 6:18; Num. 25:12; *Pirqē de-R. Eliezer* 29;
Origen, Comm. on Jn. 1:21, listed by J. Jeremias in *TWNT* ii, *s.v.* Ἠλ(ε)ίας
p. 935 (E.T., p. 933) with n. 38; v, *s.v.* παῖς θεοῦ, p. 684 (E.T., p. 686),
n. 234). In addition to their common zeal for God, Phinehas and Elijah were
associated through a 'covenant of peace' (Num. 25:12f; Mal. 2:5) and Phinehas's thoroughness of execution is paralleled in Elijah's command to wipe out
the prophets of Baal: 'let not one of them escape' (I Kings 18:40).

the God of hosts,' he said; 'for the people of Israel have forsaken thy covenant' (I Kings 19:10); the Hebrew phrase he used was *qannō* *qinnē'tī* (LXX *zēlōn ezēlōsa*). Elijah's zeal was remembered in later ages; of his ministry to Israel Ben Sira said (Sir. 48:2):

> He brought a famine upon them,
> and by his zeal he made them few in number.

So too Mattathias, father of Judas Maccabaeus and his brothers, reminded his sons on his deathbed how 'Elijah because of great zeal for the law was taken up into heaven' (I Macc. 2:58).

Mattathias himself a year or two earlier proved his own zeal for the law when he took vigorous action against apostasy in his home town of Modin. After refusing with disdain the invitation extended to him by an officer of Antiochus IV to lead his fellow-townsmen in offering sacrifice on a pagan altar, 'he burned with zeal' and killed another Jew who was about to offer the idolatrous sacrifice, together with the king's officer, and demolished the altar. 'Thus he burned with zeal for the law, as Phinehas did against Zimri the son of Salu. Then Mattathias cried out in the city with a loud voice, saying: "Let every one who is zealous for the law and supports the covenant come out with me!"' (I Macc. 2:24-7). In this passage the Greek verb *zēloō* appears three times, and no doubt in the lost Hebrew original of I Maccabees the verb was *qinnē'*.

There was thus a well-established tradition of religious 'zeal' in Israel, and zealots for God could point to worthy precedents. We must beware of thinking that every time the word 'zealot' appears in a Jewish context in the New Testament membership of the Zealot party in the stricter sense is meant. Thus, when Paul says that in his earlier days he outstripped his contemporaries as 'a zealot for the ancestral traditions' (Gal. 1:14),[3] or when James the Just describes the thousands of believers at Jerusalem as 'all zealots for the law' (Acts 21:20), the word is used in its ordinary, non-technical sense, albeit with an unmistakably religious connotation.

The first explicit references to Zealots in the party sense relate

---

[3] With Gal. 1:14 compare Josephus's description of himself as a 'devotee' (ζηλωτής) of Bannus (*Life*, 11), and Paul's further description of his pre-Christian career, 'as to zeal a persecutor of the church' (Phil. 3:6). The question in I Peter 3:13, 'who is there to harm you if you are zealous for what is right?' may convey a warning not to be zealous in the wrong way—e.g., against the authorities.

(possibly) to the followers of Menahem who tried to take command
of the revolt against Rome in September, A.D. 66,[4] (certainly) to
the extremists among the insurgents at Jerusalem in the winter of
A.D. 66–67,[5] and (more especially) to those 'bandits' (Gk. *lēstai*),
as Josephus calls them, who gained control of the Temple towards
the end of A.D. 67 and found a leader in John of Gischala, who had
lately made his escape to the capital when Galilee was subdued by
Vespasian's forces. After describing how these 'bandits' elevated by
lot to the high-priesthood one of the common priests, Phanni ben
Samuel, Josephus records the attempts of two ex-high priests, Annas
II and Jesus son of Gamaliel, 'to incite the people against the
Zealots, for so these men called themselves, as though they were
zealous for good causes and not—as in fact they were—for evil practices to an extravagant degree'.[6] Our rabbinical sources also relate
the activities of the *qannā'im* to the period of the Jewish War; thus
the post-Talmudic *Abot de-Rabbi Nathan* (an expansion of the
Mishnaic tractate *Pirqē Abot*) says that they tried to burn the
sacred vessels when Vespasian marched against Jerusalem to fight
against it[7]—perhaps a reference to his intended investment of the
city in June, A.D. 68, which he suspended on receiving news of Nero's
death.

From his first mention of the Zealots onwards Josephus makes
frequent reference to their activities; to them he ascribes the worst
atrocities committed during the war, and on them he places the
chief responsibility for the disasters which the war brought upon
the Jewish people.[8] Yet he knows that the term 'Zealot' is primarily
an honourable one; these men, he says, took this name because they
professed to be zealous for virtue, whereas in truth 'there was no
wickedness recorded in earlier history which they did not zealously
emulate'.[9] His account of the Zealots is manifestly prejudiced. The
blame for the havoc of A.D. 70 could not be laid at the door of the
Romans, his patrons (apart from an occasional individual like the
procurator Florus), nor at the door of his own people as a whole;
but the Zealots, who persisted to the bitter end and endured the
worst reprisals, might conveniently be held responsible for the sufferings that befell the Jewish nation.

[4] Josephus, *BJ* ii, 441. See pp. 97f, 379f.   [5] *BJ* ii, 651.   [6] *BJ* iv, 160f.
[7] *Abot de-Rabbi Nathan* 6:8 (see p. 99, n. 21).   [8] *BJ* vii, 268f.
[9] *BJ* vii, 269.

While the Zealots are not mentioned by name before A.D. 66, the rise of their party is commonly traced in the events of A.D. 6. After the deposition of Archelaus, when Judaea received the status of a Roman province, a census was held in the province by P. Sulpicius Quirinius, legate of Syria, in order to determine the amount of tribute which it should contribute to the imperial exchequer. This was the occasion when, in the words of Gamaliel the elder as reported by Luke, 'Judas the Galilaean arose in the days of the census and drew away some of the people after him; he . . . perished and all who followed him were scattered' (Acts 5:37). A fuller account is given by Josephus; according to him Judas (variously described as of Galilee and of Gamala in Gaulanitis),[10] together with a Pharisee named Sadduk, raised the standard of revolt because they held it to be intolerable that tribute should be paid by the people of God to a Gentile monarch; indeed, to acquiesce in such a state of affairs would be high treason to God, who alone was Israel's king.

Josephus speaks of Judas as a 'sophist' who founded a new party, the fourth 'philosophic school' among the Jews[11]—the other three being the parties of the Pharisees, the Sadducees and the Essenes. Josephus, as we have seen, calls these parties philosophic schools after the analogy of the Greek philosophic schools.[12] The distinctive feature of this new party was its carrying the theocratic principle to a point where it was held unlawful to acknowledge the sovereignty of a Gentile ruler. It is this point of view that lies behind the question put to Jesus while he was teaching in the Temple in April, A.D. 30: 'Is it lawful to pay taxes to Caesar, or not? Should we pay them, or should we not?' (Mark 12:14f). In general the party founded by Judas shared the theological beliefs of the Pharisees, but whereas the Pharisees (wisely, as the event proved) were for the most part content to await God's good time and bear the foreign yoke as best they might until that time came, the adherents of the 'fourth philosophy' held that it was their duty to co-operate actively with what must be God's purpose—the liberation of Israel

---

[10] He is called a Galilaean in *BJ* ii, 118, 433; *Ant.* xviii, 23; xx, 102; he is called 'a Gaulanite from a city named Gamala' in *Ant.* xviii, 4.

[11] *BJ* ii, 118; *Ant.* xviii, 9, 23.   [12] See p. 85.

from the foreign yoke—and seize the initiative, like Mattathias and
his sons in the days of the Seleucid dominance, in breaking that
yoke.

To the revolt of Judas and Sadduk Josephus traces all the ills
which befell the Jews of Palestine in the following decades, culminating in the devastation of the land and the burning of the
Temple.[13] While he does not say so in so many words, it is difficult
to avoid the conclusion that the 'fourth philosophy' is identical
with the party of the Zealots, whose emergence is thus dated to
A.D. 6.

But if the Zealots emerged as a distinct party in A.D. 6, the Zealot
spirit was not born anew in that year. For Josephus, after he has
begun to speak of the Zealots in his account of the Menahem incident, 'Zealots' and 'bandits' (*lēstai*) are practically interchange-
able terms. And he has a good deal to say about the activity of such
'bandits' long before Quirinius's census. In 47 B.C. we read in his
pages of the bandit-chief (*archilēstēs*) Hezekiah, whose activities
in Galilee came to an abrupt end when the young Herod, lately appointed military prefect of that region, caught him and had him
summarily executed.[14] That Hezekiah was no ordinary bandit-chief,
but a patriotic resistance-leader, is suggested by the anger with
which the news of his execution was greeted by the Sanhedrin in
Jerusalem, although it enhanced Herod's prestige in the eyes of the
Romans.[15] Forty-three years later, on Herod's death, a son of this
Hezekiah, Judas by name, raised a band of followers and raided
the royal arsenal at Sepphoris in Galilee so as to equip them for
war. The scale of this and other simultaneous risings was such that
Quintilius Varus, legate of Syria, had to intervene; Sepphoris was
taken and burnt and its inhabitants enslaved, and the insurrection
was put down with fire and sword.[16]

Whether all the risings that were precipitated by Herod's death
can accurately be described as Zealot risings is uncertain; that some
of them were led by surviving scions of the Hasmonaean family is
conceivable, but the evidence for this view is insufficient. That

[13] *Ant.* xviii, 8.
[14] *BJ* i, 204; *Ant.* xiv, 159. The word ἀρχιληστής (for the majority reading
ληστής) is applied to Barabbas in some texts of John 19:40. See p. 203, n. 28.
[15] *BJ* i, 205ff; *Ant.* 160ff.   [16] *BJ* ii, 56; *Ant.* xvii, 271f.

the Galilaean rising in 4 B.C. under Judas son of Hezekiah was a Zealot rising in the stricter sense is, however, quite probable.[17]

It cannot be asserted as beyond all doubt that this Judas is identical with the Judas who led the revolt in Judaea in A.D. 6. (That the latter revolt took place in Judaea follows from the fact that Galilee, being part of the tetrarchy of Antipas, formed no part of the newly constituted Roman province and was not involved in the tribute dispute.) But the identification is not at all improbable. If it can be accepted, it is the more interesting to see how the hereditary principle was perpetuated in the insurgent leadership: two sons of Judas of Galilee, Jacob and Simon, were captured and crucified by the procurator Tiberius Julius Alexander about A.D. 46;[18] twenty years later another son (or grandson?), Menahem by name, played a brief but energetic part in the revolt of A.D. 66, and it was a kinsman of his, Eleazar ben Jair, who held out with his followers to the bitter end at Masada in A.D. 73.[19]

While Josephus speaks of many of the insurgents against Rome as bandits, it may well be that this latter designation acquired an honourable connotation among the people so described and those who sympathized with them—like the designation *klephtai* (literally 'robbers') given to resisting Greeks during the centuries of Turkish rule. When Barabbas, and the two men crucified along with Jesus, are called *lēstai* in the Gospels (John 18:40; Mark 15:27), we understand by the term not ordinary robbers but insurgents against the occupying power; this, indeed, is expressly indicated in the case of Barabbas when Mark tells us that he was 'among the rebels in prison, who had committed murder in the insurrection' (Mark 15:7), and it explains his popularity with the Jerusalem crowd, who clamoured for his release. Twenty years later an outbreak of insurgency under the procurator Cumanus is similarly ascribed to *lēstai*.[20]

Another term used by Josephus of such people is *sikarioi*, a Greek form of Latin *sicarii*, men armed with a *sica*, or 'dagger'. (The same

---

[17] Cf. W. R. Farmer, 'Judas, Simon and Athronges', *NTS* 4 (1957–8), pp. 147ff.   [18] *Ant.* xx, 102.

[19] *BJ* ii, 447; vii, 253, 275, 297, 320ff. See pp. 379f.

[20] *BJ* ii, 228ff; *Ant.* xx, 113, 121. Gk. λῃστής appears as a loanword in Hebrew and Aramaic (*listā*), sometimes in the sense of 'Zealot'; cf. TB *Sanhedrin* 106b where, in reference to his killing the false prophet Balaam, Phinehas the grandson of Aaron is called *listā*.

word appears also as a loanword in Hebrew and Aramaic in the plural form *siqārin*.)[21] This term is used in a stricter and in a more general sense. In the stricter sense it refers to the protagonists in a new wave of terrorism which followed energetic and temporarily effective action taken by the procurator Felix against a 'bandit' rising under one Eleazar early in Nero's reign (*c.* A.D. 54). Eleazar and his principal lieutenants were sent to Rome for punishment; many of the rank and file of his followers were captured and crucified. As open insurrection against the provincial authority was out of the question for the time being, extremists in the resistance party began to mingle with crowds in Jerusalem during festivals and similar occasions and stab the objects of their displeasure unawares with daggers (*sicae*) which they carried concealed about their clothes; they would then melt immediately into the surrounding crowds. Jewish leaders who were suspected of being hand-in-glove with the Romans, or at least insufficiently sympathetic to the patriotic cause, were the principal targets for such attacks; one of the earliest victims of the *sicarii* was an ex-high priest, Jonathan son of Annas.[22]

In the more general sense *sicarii* is used of insurgents in general. It is probably in this sense that it appears in Acts 21:38, where the military tribune in charge of the Antonia fortress in Jerusalem mistakes Paul for 'the Egyptian . . . who recently stirred up a revolt and led the four thousand men of the Assassins (*sicarii*) out into the wilderness'. In an even wider sense Josephus uses it of the whole Zealot movement, from those who revolted in the days of Quirinius[23] to the desperate defenders of Masada and the survivors of the fighting in Judaea who fled to Egypt after A.D. 70 and made a last stand there.[24] Perhaps Josephus preferred to call the Zealots *sicarii* because that term did not have the honourable associations that 'Zealot'—and probably even *lēstēs*—had; yet at the end he himself can hardly have withheld a meed of admiration from them when he describes how, under every form of torture, none of the

---

[21] In the second edition of *Abot de-Rabbi Nathan* the *qannā'in* referred to on p. 95 above are called *sīqārīn*; in TB *Giṭṭin* 56a their leader on this occasion is called *'Abbā Sīqĕrā*, 'chief of the *biryōnīm* of Jerusalem' (see p. 183 with n. 21).

[22] BJ ii, 256; *Ant.* xx, 164 (see p. 345 for the rumour that his assassination was instigated by Felix).   [23] BJ vii, 253f.

[24] BJ vii, 409ff.

sicarii who were taken captive, whether young or old, could be compelled to acknowledge Caesar as lord.[25] Those of us who are prone to admire the early Christians for persisting in just such a refusal must readily concede the constancy of those patriotic Jews, who refused to utter a confession which, in their eyes, would have been disloyalty to the God of their fathers.

The excavations carried out from 1963 to 1965 at Masada, where the Zealots held out against the Romans to the end in A.D. 73, have given us a silent but impressive picture of their courage and devotion. Far from being the godless miscreants of Josephus's account, the defenders of Masada were scrupulously observant Jews. Amid the splendours of Herod's palace they installed the apparatus of worship. Two rooms of Zealot construction have been identified with some probability as a synagogue and school respectively, while there is no room for doubt about two baths for their ritual ablutions which have also been uncovered, and which have been certified as kosher by rabbinical experts of the present day.[26]

We shall not properly understand Josephus's bitterness against them unless we recognize that their movement cannot be explained in terms of Jewish nationalism alone. Fiercely anti-Roman as they were, they were almost as hostile to the Jewish establishment—the hierarchy and the wealthy aristocrats—as to the Romans. They commanded the admiration of the common people because they were known to be champions of the common people. The war of A.D. 66–73, as Josephus describes it, was not only a war of independence against Rome but also a class war within Israel. His animus against the Zealots was the sharper because he saw in their policy and activity a mortal threat to all the privileges that he and his fellow-aristocrats prized.

[25] *BJ* vii, 418f.
[26] Cf. Y. Yadin, *Masada: Herod's Fortress and the Zealots' Last Stand* (London, 1966), pp. 164ff.

0 The Qumran Community

1

To the *ḥăsiḍim* of the second century B.C. must also be traced the ancestry of the Qumran community, a community of pious Jews of whose existence the world became suddenly aware in 1947 and the following years, as a result of manuscript discoveries and archaeological excavations in the Wadi Qumran and its vicinity, north-west of the Dead Sea.

The particular *ḥăsiḍim* among whom we should seek the ancestors of the Qumran community are probably the people referred to in the book of Daniel as the *maśkilim*, which may mean either 'the wise' or (more probably) 'those who impart wisdom'. They were people whose ambition was to understand and co-operate with the divine purpose, as they read it in the prophetic writings,[1] and to impart to others the insight which they themselves acquired. On them the persecution under Antiochus Epiphanes bore with exceptional severity. The part they played in that critical time is thus described in Dan. 11:33ff: 'the *maśkilim* among the people shall make many understand, though they shall fall by sword and flame, by captivity and plunder, for some days. When they fall, they shall receive a little help. And many shall join themselves to them with flattery, to refine and to cleanse them and to make them white, until the time of the end'. The 'little help' which they received is probably to be interpreted of the activity of Judas Maccabaeus and his brothers: the words quoted are written from the perspective of an early stage in the Hasmonaean rising, long before there was any likelihood that Judas and his followers could regain religious liberty for the nation or restore the Temple to its rightful worship. Those who joined the ranks of the *maśkilim* 'with flattery' are evi-

[1] Like Daniel studying Jeremiah (Dan. 9:2). The word *maśkil* in the sense of 'instructor' appears repeatedly in the Qumran texts. See also p. 129.

dently those who weakened under the persecution, or were persuaded to compromise in one way or another. The secession of
these unworthy members of the order made those who remained
feel the purer and the stronger for their departure.[2]

The *maśkīlīm* expected an intensification of the persecution to a
point where their survival seemed impossible: then the archangel
Michael would intervene as the champion of the people of God.
The persecutor would be brought down at the height of his power.
The resurrection age would follow, in which the *maśkīlīm* would
'shine like the brightness of the firmament; and those who turn
many to righteousness, like the stars for ever and ever' (Dan. 12:3).
The description of the *maśkīlīm* as 'those who turn many to righteousness' echoes language used of the Servant of Yahweh in Isa.
53:11 (where he will 'make many to be accounted righteous'); it
may be, indeed, that their insight into the divine purpose taught
them that they were called upon to fulfil corporately the programme
mapped out for the Suffering Servant.[3]

At any rate, the consummation for which the *maśkīlīm* looked
did not come so soon as they expected. Instead, the Hasmonaeans
were victorious. The *maśkīlīm* could not reasonably complain of
the Hasmonaean success, for they shared in the benefits it brought;
they were free once more to keep the law of God and follow their
traditional way of life without constant peril of discovery, torture
and death. But the Hasmonaean ambitions manifested themselves
in ways which gave the *maśkīlīm* cause for serious complaint, and
reached an intolerable pitch when Jonathan, brother and successor
to Judas Maccabaeus, assumed the high-priesthood in 152 B.C. by the
gift of Alexander Balas.

Offensive as this assumption of the high-priesthood was in the
eyes of the Pharisees, it was even more so in the eyes of these
maśkīlīm. For to them the high-priesthood belonged exclusively to
the family of Zadok. Zadok had been the chief priest in Solomon's
day, when the first Temple was dedicated (*c.* 960 B.C.); and the
sacred office descended from father to son in Zadok's family, apart

---

[2] Compare the thousand 'seeking righteousness and justice' who were
slaughtered to a man in the wilderness sooner than offer resistance on the
sabbath (I Macc. 2:29–38).

[3] The martyrs of II and IV Maccabees yield up their lives as a propitiation
for their fellow-countrymen (II Macc. 7:37f; IV Macc. 6:27ff; 17:22; 18:4).
See pp. 113, 130.

from the seventy years' interregnum between the fall of the first Temple and the dedication of the second (516 B.C.), until Antiochus IV deposed Onias III, the last legitimate Zadokite high priest, in 174 B.C., and his brother and supplanter Jason some three years later. They found it ironical, indeed, that a Hasmonaean should accept the sacred office at the hand of the pretended son of that king who had brought the true Zadokite régime to a violent end!

This new order was nothing like the bringing in of everlasting righteousness which the *maśkilim* had ardently expected. In the dénouement which they envisaged they had a clear idea of the part which they would play, but in this new and unexpected situation what were they to do? Acquiesce they could not; protest they must—but how?

This is perhaps the moment indicated in the Zadokite *Admonition*, part of a Qumran work which came to light in two fragmentary early mediaeval manuscripts half-a-century before the discovery of the manuscripts at Qumran.[4] In a time of apostasy, says the *Admonition*:

> God remembered the covenant made with the forefathers and caused a remnant to remain for Israel and did not give them up to be consumed. And in the epoch of wrath, 390 years[5] after he had given them into the hand of Nebuchadnezzar king of Babylon, he visited them; and he caused to sprout from Israel and from Aaron a root of his planting to possess his land and to grow fat in the goodness of his soil. They considered their iniquity and knew that they were guilty men; but they were like blind men, and like men that grope for a way for twenty years. God took note of their deeds, for they sought him with a perfect heart; and he raised up for them a teacher of righteousness to lead them in the way of his heart, that he might make known to the last generations what he was about to do to the last generation—the congregation of deceivers.[6]

This Teacher of Righteousness,[7] this rightful and reliable guide, was evidently a man of remarkable personal qualities, an organizer

[4] In the genizah of the ancient synagogue in Old Cairo. Much earlier fragments of the same work have been identified among the Qumran manuscripts.
[5] A figure probably drawn from Ezek. 4:5, but here given a new interpretation.   [6] *CD* i, 4–12.
[7] Heb. *mōrēh ṣeḍeq*, an expression perhaps derived from Hosea 10:12 (cf. RV mg., 'till he come and teach you righteousness'), or Joel 2:23 (cf. AV mg., 'he hath given you a teacher of righteousness').

and leader of men as well as an original thinker and interpreter of the prophetical writings. Under his direction many of the *maśkilim* went out to the wilderness of Judaea, to live there as a closely-knit society of 'volunteers for holiness', bound together in a 'new covenant', dedicated to the study and practice of the divine law. In this way, they believed, they would be a people prepared for the Lord, ready to be his chosen and fitted instrument when the time came for him to act decisively in the world. Biblical authority for their withdrawal to the wilderness was found in the familiar words of Isaiah 40:3:

> In the wilderness prepare the way of Yahweh;
> Make straight in the desert a highway for our God.[8]

They had sympathizers in the towns and villages of Judaea, who did not feel called upon to embrace the full rigour of community life in the wilderness. Many of these would have had family ties which kept them back. While the Qumran settlement cannot have numbered more than a few hundred at any one time, their associates and sympathizers in other parts of the country may have been ten times as numerous. But those who went out to the wilderness underwent a searching probationary period, after which they submitted to a strenuous and lifelong discipline, the details of which are preserved in the *Rule of the Community*.

The community centre survives to this day in the ruined building complex called Khirbet Qumran; the intensive archaeological research conducted on this site[9] has led to the conclusion that it served as the headquarters of the community for over two centuries. The community's first settlement there (probably during Jonathan's governorship) was on a modest scale; twenty to thirty years later, presumably as their numbers increased and their rule of life and plans for the future became more clearly defined, a more elaborate structure was built. This first phase of occupation lasted until about the beginning of Herod's reign (37 B.C.); then the site seems to have been abandoned for over thirty years, and during this interval the building was severely damaged by an earthquake—almost certainly that of 31 B.C. When the site was reoccupied about

[8] Quoted in 1 QS viii, 14.
[9] For the most authoritative account of this research see R. de Vaux, *L'Archéologie et les Manuscrits de la Mer Morte* (London, 1961), pp. 1ff.

4 B.C., considerable reconstruction was therefore necessary. This second phase of occupation lasted until the war of A.D. 66–73.

2

The *Rule of the Community* refers to a group of fifteen men—three priests and twelve laymen—who were to be established 'in the council of the community';[10] with their establishment the council of the community would be well and truly founded and would be in a position to fulfil the divine purpose. This group may have constituted a supreme inner council to direct the life and work of the community,[11] but primarily these fifteen men were probably the nucleus with which the Teacher of Righteousness made a beginning when he set about organizing the community.[12]

The organization of the community was hierarchical: there were priests (called variously 'sons of Aaron' or 'sons of Zadok'), Levites, elders, and the rank and file. Certain important matters were to be decided by lot, which was cast under the direction of the sons of Aaron. This preserved the tradition of earlier days in Israel when the will of God was ascertained by the priests by means of the sacred lot, the Urim and Thummim.

From time to time a general assembly of the community was held, the session of 'the many' (*hā-rabbim*). Rules of precedence were laid down with regard to the taking of their seats—first the priests, then the elders, then the rest of the people, each in his position—and standing orders for the conduct of the meeting were strictly enforced. Anyone who wished to speak had to stand up and say: 'I have a word to speak to the many'. If he received permission from the leaders, he might speak. And while he was speaking no other member might interrupt him.[13] Such unseemly behaviour as speaking foolishly, laughing out loud, sleeping while the session was in progress, or leaving the room too often without due cause,

[10] 1 QS viii, 1.
[11] Cf., e.g., M. Burrows, *The Dead Sea Scrolls* (New York, 1955), p. 232; P. Wernberg-Møller, *The Manual of Discipline* (Leiden, 1957), pp. 122f; K. Schubert, *The Dead Sea Community* (London, 1959), p. 47; A. Dupont-Sommer, *The Essene Writings from Qumran* (Oxford, 1961), p. 90.
[12] Cf. E. F. Sutcliffe, *The Monks of Qumran* (London, 1960), pp. xi, 152f; A. R. C. Leaney, *The Rule of Qumran and its Meaning* (London, 1966), pp. 210ff. [13] 1 QS vi, 8–13.

received appropriate punishment. Punishment commonly took the form of expulsion for a set period from the 'purity of the many', i.e. from the purificatory rites and the communal meal, or the reduction of a man's rations for a specified time.[14]

Over each of the camps into which the community was divided there was an inspector (*mĕḇaqqēr*),[15] and over them all a chief inspector (*pāqīḏ*) to see that discipline was maintained.[16]

One of the duties of this chief inspector was to examine candidates for admission to the community, to see if their motives and their lives were pure and if they understood what they were doing. Those who passed this first examination had then to appear before the general assembly of 'the many' and be accepted or refused by them. If they were accepted, they had to pass through two stages of initiation, each of them lasting one year, before they were enrolled as full members. During the first year they retained their private property; during the second year it was deposited with the community treasurer, but not until the candidate became a full member at the beginning of the third year was it merged with the common fund.[17] A stern penalty was imposed on a member who 'knowingly deceived in regard to property'[18]—but not so stern as the judgement which overtook Ananias and Sapphira when they committed this offence in the early days of the Jerusalem church.[19] The penalty at Qumran was one year's exclusion from 'the purity of the many' (perhaps from participation in their solemn acts of fellowship), together with the reduction of his rations by one quarter. For more heinous offences complete excommunication was prescribed. Even after complete excommunication, the way was open for a penitent to return on condition that he submitted to two years' severe discipline before his readmission to membership was considered. But for one who suffered excommunication after ten years' membership of the council of the community no such restoration was allowed.[20]

When a man was admitted to the covenant-community, he swore a solemn vow to return to the law of Moses with all his heart and avoid all fellowship with ungodly men. While he was thus engaged,

[14] 1 QS vi, 24–vii, 15.
[15] 1 QS vi, 12; *CD* ix, 18, etc.   [16] 1 QS vi, 14.
[17] 1 QS vi, 13–23.   [18] 1 QS vi, 24f.   [19] Acts 5:1–11.
[20] 1 QS vi, 27–vii, 2; vii, 19–25; viii, 20–ix, 2.

the priests recited an amplified form of the Deuteronomic blessings
on those who set their hearts to walk in God's ways, and the Levites
recited the corresponding curses on those who were guilty of rebellion against him.[21]

The joint property of the community was administered by the
treasurer in accordance with the direction of the council.[22] This
common stock appears to have been augmented by wages or other
income earned by members of the community after their admission.
For it is plain that they did not shirk manual labour, and were
willing to do menial service for the ungodly, showing them humble
deference outwardly, while cherishing very different sentiments towards them at heart. For all their self-denial, the men of Qumran
must have had some means of livelihood. Various kinds of work
were available around Qumran itself—work connected with the
products of the Dead Sea, work connected with the neighbouring
oasis of *'Ain Feshkha,* and work which might have been carried on
within the community headquarters. They could have worked as
agriculturalists, herdsmen, bee-keepers, potters and so forth, and
could have sold various kinds of produce and manufactured articles.
Nor need we suppose that all the members spent all the time at
Qumran. By working in more populated parts of Judaea, and hand-
ing over to the community all their earnings apart from their bare
subsistence requirements, many of them could have contributed to
the maintenance of community life. They may also have received
support from 'associate members' or sympathizers who were engaged in secular life.

The part which marriage and family life played in the community
cannot be determined with certainty. On the one hand, the *Zadokite
Work* contains its own strict interpretation of the Jewish marriage
law, and makes provision for adherents of the new covenant who
live 'in camps according to the order of the land', taking wives and
begetting children;[23] while the *Rule of the Congregation* looks forward to a time when the life of the whole congregation of Israel will
be properly regulated and women and children as well as men will
come together to listen to the exposition of the covenant law.[24]
There is also the fact that some burials of women and children have

[21] 1 QS i, 16–ii, 18; v, 7–11. [22] 1 QS vi, 19–23.
[23] *CD* vii, 6ff; see p. 120. [24] 1 QSa i, 4ff.

been identified in the borders of the Qumran cemeteries.[25] On the
other hand, it is difficult to see how those who devoted themselves
to the full rigours of community life at Qumran can have been able
to discharge the normal obligations of marriage and fatherhood.
There is no express statement in our documents that full initiation
involved celibacy, and we must beware of importing into the life
of the Qumran community features which we associate with Christian conventual and monastic life. But, while the evidence is inconclusive, it is conceivable that those adherents of the community who
lived in the towns and villages of Judaea 'according to the order of
the land' married and brought up families in the usual way (following the strict Qumran interpretation of the marriage law), whereas
those who lived in the wilderness as full members of the community
denied themselves these comforts and responsibilities, looking on
them as encumbrances for men enrolled in the *militia dei*. In that
case, they might be included among those referred to by Jesus as
having abstained from marriage and family life—as having 'made
themselves eunuchs for the sake of the kingdom of heaven' (Matt.
19:12).[26]

3

The Qumran community attached much importance to ritual
cleansing in water; in fact, the special ablutions which the levitical
law prescribes for the priests appear to have been prescribed at
Qumran for all the members of the community. This is made clear
by the *Rule of the Community*, although we cannot assume that this
was the purpose of the plentiful water supply and elaborate system
of cisterns at Khirbet Qumran. We gather that this cleansing was
not merely an initiatory rite, but one performed frequently. But it
is made abundantly plain that ritual washing alone had no efficacy
if a man's heart was not right with God. The washing of the body
was religiously acceptable only if it was the outward sign of a
purified and humble soul within.[27]

Communal meals, communal worship and communal consultation

[25] R. de Vaux, *L'Archéologie et les Manuscrits de la Mer Morte*, p. 38.
[26] See p. 87, n. 15. On the other hand, it may be of some relevance that the
communities of Therapeutai included women as well as men (Philo, *De uita
contempl.*, 68f).   [27] 1 QS iii, 1–12.

were regular features of the community. These communal activities, however, did not always involve the coming together of the whole community; they could be carried out wherever ten members were gathered together, provided that one of the ten was a priest. It was necessary, for example, that when they met for a communal meal, whether as a group of ten or as a larger number, the priest should say grace before they partook of bread or wine. And where there was such a group of ten, it had to be arranged that one of them was always engaged in the study and exposition of the holy law. This seems to have been arranged by relays, so that the study and exposition were carried on continuously. The night was divided into three watches and during each watch one-third of the membership kept awake to listen to the reading and exposition, and to voice the appointed blessings.[28]

In addition to the ordinary communal meals, there were probably special meals of a more sacred character, restricted to full members of the community. Since the *Rule of the Congregation* describes a meal in the coming age at which the priestly head of the theocracy and the Messiah of Israel would be present,[29] the special meals at Qumran may have been in some sort regarded as anticipations of this future meal. But, since the Qumran community laid such stress on the priesthood and its privileges, it is even more likely that the special meals were a continuation of the weekly eating of the shewbread. The shewbread, consisting of twelve loaves which were replaced every sabbath day on the table before the invisible Presence of Yahweh, was reserved 'for Aaron and his sons, and they shall eat it in a holy place' (Lev. 24:5–9).[30]

Again, the priests of Israel had as their perquisites not only the food from the table of shewbread, but also the flesh of various animal sacrifices. This last point may be relevant for the interpretation of collections of animal bones at Qumran, which were either placed in earthen vessels or buried under potsherds (the pottery in question is so broken that either account is feasible, though the former is more probable). The bones come from cattle, sheep and goats

[28] 1 QS vi, 1–8. The quorum or *minyān* of ten is common to Judaism; the stipulation that one of the ten must be a priest reflects the priestly origin and ideal of the Qumran community.

[29] 1 QSa ii, 17ff.

[30] Cf. M. Black, *The Scrolls and Christian Origins* (London, 1961), pp. 108ff.

(specially goats) which had been roasted; they are evidently the relics of meals.[31] The fact that it was considered worth while to collect these relics and dispose of them so carefully suggests that the meals of which they formed part were not ordinary meals but special ones. Were they sacrificial meals? This raises the difficult problem of the practice of sacrifice at Qumran. Jerusalem was the one place where sacrifice might be offered, according to the Deuteronomic law (Deut. 12:5-14). But if the temporary control of the Jerusalem Temple by an illegitimate high-priesthood made it impossible for the men of Qumran to take part in its services, did they have an altar in the wilderness (like their ancestors in the days of Moses) on which acceptable sacrifices could be offered by their own priests? Certainly no object that could be identified as an altar has been found at Qumran.[32] Perhaps their special meals could be described as 'quasi-sacrificial' (whatever meaning may be put upon that term).

The Pharisees, for all their antagonism to the chief-priesthood of the Hasmonaean, Herodian and Roman régimes, did not abstain from the regular sacrificial worship in the Temple. But the men of Qumran criticized the Pharisees not only for this compromising attitude (as they thought it to be) but also for their general laxity in legal interpretation and for choosing an easy way of righteousness.[33] So far as we can compare the Qumran interpretation of the law with that of the Pharisees, it appears that even the strictest Pharisaic school (that of Shammai) taught a milder *halakah* than that followed at Qumran. The Qumran marriage law forbade polygamy on the basis of Gen. 1:27 (taken to mean 'a male and a female he created them')—a scripture which provided Jesus with one of his arguments against divorce.[34] At Qumran marriage between uncle and niece was frowned upon,[35] although it is not explicitly forbidden in the Torah. Because it is not explicitly forbidden in the Torah, other schools of interpretation in Judaism allowed it. Marriage between uncle and niece was particularly common in the

---

[31] Cf. F. E. Zeuner, 'Notes on Qumran', *PEQ* 92 (1960), pp. 28ff.

[32] R. de Vaux, *L'Archéologie et les Manuscrits de la Mer Morte*, pp. 10f. But see F. M. Cross, *The Ancient Library of Qumran* (New York, 1958), pp. 74ff.

[33] See p. 76 for the designation *dōrĕšē ha-ḥălāqōt*; the last word could have been a derogatory pun on the Pharisaic *hălākōt*, 'rules' (in the light of Isa. 30: 10, 'speak to us smooth things').

[34] *CD* iv, 20ff; cf. Mark 10:2-9.   [35] *CD* v, 7ff.

family of the Herods,[36] and does not appear to have aroused disapproval among the religious leaders, although they were very ready to criticize many other features of the Herodian way of life. But the Qumran interpreters argued that, since the Torah does explicitly forbid marriage between aunt and nephew,[37] marriage between uncle and niece must be considered as banned by analogy.

The sabbath law of the Qumran community, too, was stricter than that of the strictest Pharisees. When the Pharisees criticized Jesus for his practice of healing people on the sabbath, he replied: 'Which of you, having an ass or an ox that has fallen into a well, will not immediately pull him out on a sabbath day?' (Luke 14:5).[38] It is a matter of common ground between his theological opponents and himself that none of them would be prevented by any interpretation of the sabbath law from performing this humane action. But just such a humane action as this, in exceptionally critical circumstances, is forbidden by the Qumran *halakah*: 'Let no one assist an animal in birth on the sabbath day. Even if she drops her new-born young into a well or a pit, let no one lift it out on the sabbath day.'[39]

While the men of Qumran would take no part in the sacrificial services so long as the Jerusalem Temple was controlled by an illegitimate high-priesthood, believing that for the time being God would accept the praises of their lips as a sufficient sacrifice, they looked forward to a day when a worthy priesthood of the house of Zadok would once again offer up acceptable sacrifices to God in a purified Temple;[40] and in their community they kept the orders of priests and Levites intact so that there would be no delay in resuming the Temple worship when the appointed time came.

They had to endure some measure of persecution at the hands of the Hasmonaean dynasty. One member of the dynasty receives special mention in the Qumran texts as the 'Wicked Priest'.[41]

[36] An earlier notorious instance was the marriage between Joseph the Tobiad and his brother's daughter (Josephus, *Ant.* xii, 186ff).

[37] Lev. 18:13, quoted *CD* v, 9.

[38] The parallel in Matt. 12:11 specifies 'one sheep'. (Cf. also Luke 13:15.) On the rabbinical attitude see I. Abrahams, *Studies in Pharisaism and the Gospels*, Series I (Cambridge, 1917), pp. 129ff; also Strack-Billerbeck 1, p. 629.

[39] *CD* xi, 13f; in 16f a concession is made where a human being is involved.

[40] This is implied in 1 QM ii, 1–6, and in fragments from various caves of the 'Apocalypse of the New Jerusalem'.

[41] This is not universally agreed; other identifications range from Menelaus in the time of Antiochus IV (cf. H. H. Rowley, *The Zadokite Fragments and*

(While every Hasmonaean high priest, and indeed every high priest after the fall of the house of Zadok, was a 'wicked priest' in the eyes of the community in the sense of being an illegitimate holder of the sacred office, one Hasmonaean is singled out as the 'Wicked Priest' *par excellence*.) It is not agreed which of the Hasmonaeans should be identified with the Wicked Priest; but the weight of the evidence seems to favour Jonathan, brother and successor of Judas Maccabaeus.[42] The Wicked Priest is said to have launched an attack on the Teacher of Righteousness on one occasion when the Teacher and his followers were observing the day of Atonement.[43] The fact that the Wicked Priest was free to behave in this way on that sacred day (when one might have expected him to be officiating in the Temple) is probably to be explained by the different calendars by the Temple authorities and by the Qumran community.

The calendar used by the Qumran community appears to have been substantially identical with that known to us from the book of *Jubilees*.[44] In this calendar the sun alone was regulative; the year was (in intention, at least) a solar year (of 364 days), but the months were conventional calendar months of thirty or thirty-one days, and were no more regulated by the phases of the moon than are the months of our Julio-Gregorian calendar. The months of the official Jewish calendar, on the other hand, were lunar; the first day of the month coincided as far as was practicable with the new moon, and the festivals were regulated by the phases of the moon. (This disparity of calendrical usage provides a further reason why the Qumran community could not take part in the regular Temple worship.)

The task to which the men of Qumran dedicated themselves was no light or ignoble one. During the present dominion of wickedness they could expect nothing but suffering as the reward for their devotion to the will of God, but they accepted this suffering as some-

---

the *Dead Sea Scrolls* [Oxford, 1952], pp. 67ff) to Eleazar, captain of the Temple in A.D. 66 (cf. G. R. Driver, *The Judaean Scrolls* [Oxford, 1965], pp. 267ff).

[42] Cf., e.g., G. Vermes, *Les Manuscrits du Désert de Juda* (Tournai-Paris, 1953), p. 94; J. T. Milik, *Ten Years of Discovery in the Wilderness of Judaea* (London, 1959), pp. 65ff; E. F. Sutcliffe, *The Monks of Qumran* (London, 1960), pp. ixff, 42ff. [43] 1 Qp Hab. xi, 4–8 (on Hab. 2:15).

[44] Cf. A. R. C. Leaney, *The Rule of Qumran and its Meaning* (London, 1966), pp. 23ff.

thing which would not only secure their own justification in God's sight but also effect propitiation for the land of Israel as a whole.[45]

They believed that the iniquities of the Wicked Priest and his associates would bring the judgement of God upon them. As time went on, they came to see clearly who would be the instruments of God's judgement. God was raising up the 'Kittim' for this purpose, and by the 'Kittim', as has been said above, they probably meant the Romans.[46] It was indeed the Romans who, by their occupation of Judaea in 63 B.C., put an end to Hasmonaean domination; but the Qumran community could see the shape of things to come before that date. They also saw that the Romans would exceed the terms of their commission and incur the divine judgement themselves because of their impiety and rapacity. And the agents of the divine judgement against the Kittim would be the elect of God, among whom the Qumran community occupied the front rank.[47] Just how the elect of God would execute his judgement against the Kittim and other 'sons of darkness' is forecast in detail in the Qumran *Rule of War*, which is in part an extended *midrash* on Dan. 11:40-12:3. In this regard it might be said that the community looked forward to fulfilling the rôle of 'the people of the saints of the Most High', to whom final judgement and eternal dominion are committed in Dan. 7:22, 27.

The various designations by which the men of Qumran are named in their literature combine to make it plain that they regarded themselves as the righteous remnant and the true Israel of God. They appear, for example, as the saints of the covenant, the poor of the flock, the sons of light, the men of truth, the community of Israel and Aaron (in this last title 'Israel' stands for the laity and 'Aaron' for the priests among them).

Thanks to the instruction which they received from the Teacher of Righteousness, they could read their God-given duty clearly in the prophetic scriptures. The biblical commentaries found at Qumran are of extraordinary interest for this purpose. They throw no light on the original meaning of the books expounded, but they throw much light on the beliefs of the commentators and their companions. They believed themselves to have entered the last days, the days to which all the prophets pointed forward; and they eagerly

---

[45] Cf. 1 QS v, 6f; ix, 3-5.   [46] See p. 11.
[47] Cf. 1 Qp Hab. ii, 12-vi, 12.

awaited the signal which would herald the dawn of the new age, the signal which would at the same time summon them to arms against the enemies of God. Even after the death of the Teacher of Righteousness (c. 100 B.C.?) they continued to look forward with undiminished faith to this dénouement.[48]

But the dénouement for which they looked did not take the form which they had come to expect. The last days of their community life can be reconstructed only with difficulty. The one certain fact is that their headquarters at Qumran were attacked and destroyed by sword and fire during the war of A.D. 66–73.[49] Whether the community remained in occupation to the end we cannot say; it is perfectly conceivable that when the revolt against Rome broke out they concluded that now was the time to come to the help of the Lord against the mighty. Another possibility is that Khirbet Qumran was commandeered by the Zealots to serve as a strong-point in the war. The evidence of the 'copper scroll' from Qumran Cave 3 may be relevant here, if (in accordance with a very reasonable interpretation of its text) it contains an inventory of temple treasure and the like stored by the insurgent leaders in various hiding places to serve as sinews of war.[50] As for the other scrolls, belonging presumably to the community's library, it is uncertain whether it was members of the community themselves or other Jews who stored them in the adjoining caves—in some instances, especially in Cave 4, 'dumped' them would be the better expression. Probably the members of the community hoped that one day it would be possible to return and regain possession of them. What happened to the community, or to such of its members as survived the war, can only be conjectured. Some survivors may have made common cause with those members of the church of Jerusalem who about the same time left the doomed city and found refuge east of the Jordan; certain beliefs and practices of the Ebionites could be explained by an infusion of the Qumran ethos into the lifestream of early Jewish Christianity.[51]

[48] Cf. the references to his death in *CD* xix, 35f; xx, 14.
[49] Cf. R. de Vaux, *L'Archéologie et les Manuscrits de la Mer Morte*, pp. 28ff; H. H. Rowley, 'The History of the Qumran Sect', *BJRL* 49 (1966–7), pp. 202ff.
[50] Cf. J. M. Allegro, *The Treasure of the Copper Scroll* (New York, 1960), pp. 120ff.
[51] Cf. O. Cullmann, 'Die neuentdeckten Qumran-Texte und das Judenchristentum der Pseudoklementinen', *Neutestamentliche Studien für R. Bultmann* = *BZNTW* 21, ed. W. Eltester (Berlin, 1954), pp. 35ff; 'The Significance

4

The Qumran community has been identified in turn with every religious party in Judaism in the later period of the Second Commonwealth—with the Sadducees,[52] Pharisees,[53] Zealots[54] and Essenes.[55]

With the Sadducees of history, however, they have nothing in common apart from the resemblance between the designation 'Sadducee' (whencesoever derived) and the name Zadok which the community held in high honour. Even if the Sadducees claimed to be 'sons of Zadok' (which is unlikely), the expression meant something very different among them from what it meant at Qumran. All the relevant evidence indicates that the community's bitterest enemies were associates of the Sadducees.

With the Pharisees they had in common their concern for the law of God. But their interpretation of the law was stricter than that of any Pharisaic school known to us. In their biblical exegesis, too, they gave the prophetic writings a permanent and independent place which links them with Jesus and his first followers rather than with the Pharisees. Their criticism of the contemporary Temple order was more radical than that of the Pharisees, from whom their calendrical practice also sets them apart. If, moreover, the Pharisees are the people whom the men of Qumran described as 'seekers after smooth things' or 'givers of smooth interpretations' (and it is difficult to see who else could be intended), their identification with the Pharisees, or even with a particularly strict school of Pharisees, is excluded.

It has, however, been confidently maintained by some scholars of

---

of the Qumran Texts for Research into the Beginnings of Christianity', *The Scrolls and the New Testament*, ed. K. Stendahl (London, 1958), pp. 18ff. See p. 391.

[52] Cf. R. North, 'The Qumrân "Sadducees"', *CBQ* 17 (1955), pp. 164ff; A. M. Habermann, *Megillot Midbar Yehuda* (Jerusalem, 1959), pp. xv, 25ff.

[53] Cf. C. Rabin, *Qumran Studies* (Oxford, 1957), pp. 53ff.

[54] Cf. C. Roth, *The Historical Background of the Dead Sea Scrolls* (Oxford, 1958), pp. 22ff; G. R. Driver, *The Judaean Scrolls* (Oxford, 1965), pp. 237ff.

[55] This is the majority view; among the first to propound or suggest it were E. L. Sukenik, *Megillot Genuzot* i (Jerusalem, 1948), p. 16, and A. Dupont-Sommer, *Observations sur le Commentaire d'Habacuc découvert près de la Mer Morte* (Paris, 1950), pp. 26ff.

high repute that the men of Qumran are to be identified with the Zealots. The best-known presentation of this thesis identifies the Teacher of Righteousness with the Zealot leader Menahem, son of Judas the Galilaean, who was done to death in September, A.D. 66, by the followers of the rival insurgent leader Eleazar, captain of the Temple; or with Menahem's kinsman Eleazar ben Jair, who escaped when Menahem was caught and killed, and held out at Masada until it was stormed by the Romans in May, A.D. 73. The Wicked Priest is identified with Eleazar, captain of the Temple. This Eleazar's attack on Menahem and his followers is seen as the occasion when the Wicked Priest attacked the Teacher when the latter, with his disciples, was celebrating the day of Atonement. The time of year is near enough, but Eleazar's hostility to Menahem was intensified by the fact that Menahem or his followers had, a few days previously, attacked and killed Eleazar's father Ananias, a former high priest.[56]

Apart from this discrepancy between the two incidents, the character and career of the Teacher of Righteousness, in so far as they can be reconstructed from the Qumran literature, do not correspond to those of Menahem or Eleazar ben Jair. The Teacher appears to have been a priest; it is nowhere hinted that Menahem or his kinsmen came of priestly stock. Menahem's claims were regal rather than priestly; perhaps he hoped to be accepted as the warrior-Messiah of Israel. Josephus calls him a 'sophist' (a designation which he gives also to his father Judas),[57] but since Josephus presents the various Jewish sects as philosophical schools, their leaders had correspondingly to be presented as philosophers.

The Qumran Teacher of Righteousness was the effective founder of his community.[58] If, then, the Qumran community is to be identified with the party of the Zealots, the Teacher of Righteousness

[56] For the persons and events concerned see Josephus, *BJ* ii, 433ff (pp. 379f below). Cf. H. E. Del Medico, *The Riddle of the Scrolls* (London, 1958), pp. 140ff; C. Roth, *The Historical Background of the Dead Sea Scrolls* (Oxford, 1958), pp. 6ff, 66ff, 74f; G. R. Driver, *The Judaean Scrolls* (Oxford, 1965), pp. 241ff.

[57] *BJ* ii, 118; the text of ii, 433, where σοφιστής is used of Menahem, is debatable and according to some MSS. it is used here too of Judas.

[58] The 'effective founder' because, while the faithful groped blindly for twenty years before he arose (*CD* i, 9f), they do not appear to have had a leader at that time; it was the Teacher who organized them as a coherent community.

should more properly be identified with Judas, or even with Judas's father Hezekiah,[59] than with Menahem or Eleazar ben Jair.

Again, some of the Qumran literature—notably the Zadokite work—was composed some time after the Teacher's 'gathering in' (an expression which suggests a natural death rather than a violent one).[60] But between Menahem's death and the final collapse of the Zealot resistance at Masada less than seven years elapsed—too short a time for the composition of the literature in question. And the destruction of Khirbet Qumran was not later than the fall of Masada; it was most probably four or five years earlier.

Another obstacle in the way of the Zealot hypothesis is the palaeographical evidence. The palaeographers differ somewhat in their dating of the Qumran manuscripts, but they do not differ by more than a generation. If the Zealot hypothesis in its current form be sustained, the palaeographers are a hundred and fifty years out. The wealth of Qumran manuscripts, however, has made it possible to establish a *relative* palaeographical chronology, while the manuscripts from other areas west of the Dead Sea, which are expressly dated in terms of the second Jewish revolt (A.D. 132–135),[61] have helped greatly to establish an *absolute* chronology for the Qumran documents. The clash between the Teacher of Righteousness and the Wicked Priest was a thing of the past when the manuscript of the Qumran commentary on Habakkuk was copied out—and this manuscript should almost certainly be dated before 50 B.C.[62] The Teacher of Righteousness was dead when the Zadokite work was written, and the earliest manuscript of this work is dated early in the first century B.C.—too early, in fact, to admit of the Teacher's identification even with Hezekiah (d. 47 B.C.), not to speak of any of Hezekiah's descendants.

The Zealot hypothesis is far from satisfying all the evidence. Any acceptable hypothesis must satisfy not only the internal evidence of the documents as interpreted by philologists and historians, but also the palaeographical evidence as interpreted by palaeographers, and the archaeological evidence as interpreted by

[59] See p. 97.   [60] *CD* xix, 35f; xx, 14.
[61] Especially from Murabba'at and En-gedi.
[62] The commentary itself is earlier still, probably before 63 B.C., since the Roman occupation of that year seems to be expected rather than recorded as something which has taken place.

archaeologists. The identification of the men of Qumran with Essenes—not with the whole Essene order, but with one group of Essenes—satisfies more of the evidence than does any rival identification.

Almost from the early days of the discoveries in Cave 1 at Qumran, an identification of the community with the Essenes has been suggested. Père de Vaux and others have identified Khirbet Qumran with the Essene headquarters mentioned by Pliny. In addition to the argument that no other identification of Pliny's Essene headquarters is archaeologically feasible, there are others, some of them weightier than this.

There is a rather precarious chronological argument: the Essenes are known to have flourished during the time when the Qumran community was in being—to make their appearance in history about the same time as the beginning of the Qumran movement, in the second half of the second century B.C., and were still flourishing in the second half of the first century A.D.

More important is the argument based on the similarity between the beliefs and practices of the Essenes, as contemporary writers describe them and those of the Qumran community, as attested in their own literature.

There are striking similarities (which do not, however, amount to complete identity) between the two in respect of the long period of probation, the solemn oaths sworn on initiation, the strict discipline, the ceremonial ablutions, the common meal, the hierarchical organization with exact observance of the rules of precedence, the place of honour and responsibility given to priests, the community of goods, the rigorous interpretation of the sabbath law, and the pursuit of an unusually high and exacting standard of righteousness. Since the *Rule of the Community* makes it clear that a common penalty at Qumran was the reduction of rations, we can easily understand how a member whose offence was so serious as to warrant complete withdrawal of rations for a sufficiently long time could be in danger of death by starvation, as Josephus tells us. Sometimes the similarity between the two disciplinary codes extends to matters which we should regard as trivial; thus Josephus's statement that the Essenes avoided spitting 'into the midst' or to the right[63] is paralleled by the regulation in the *Rule of*

[63] *BJ* ii, 147.

the Community that a man who 'spits into the midst of the session of the many' shall be punished—presumably by suspension from a share in the communal meal—for thirty days.[64]

From Josephus's statement that 'if ten are in session together, no one of them will speak if the other nine are against it'[65] we might reasonably infer that ten was a normal grouping of the Essenes' membership, and recall that at Qumran ten might engage in the regular communal activities provided that the ten included a priest; but since ten was a recognized number for communal activity among the Jews in general (to this day it is the quorum necessary for a synagogue congregation among orthodox Jews), no weight can be put on this coincidence.

Josephus's testimony to the Essenes' intensive study of the ancient scriptures,[66] particularly the prophetic writings, may find ample illustration in the Qumran texts. On the other hand, the instances he gives of the Essenes' gift of prophecy appear trivial in comparison with the forecasts of coming events, based on the interpretation of Old Testament prophecy, which we find in the Qumran texts. His reference to the Essene interest in angels[67] is in keeping with the attention which was paid at Qumran to late Jewish works in which angels figure prominently.[68] The Essenes' interest in healing also appears to have analogies at Qumran.[69]

Hippolytus tells us that the Essenes expected a universal conflagration at the time of the last judgement;[70] this belief finds occasional expression in the Qumran *Hymns of Thanksgiving*, in terms which suggest Zoroastrian influence.[71]

But all the similarities and parallels that can be adduced do not amount to an outright identification of the Qumran community with the Essenes. Where prominent features of the one body are not related at all in the sources of our information about the other, we cannot reach indisputable conclusions. Again, both bodies

[64] 1 QS vii, 13.　[65] *BJ* ii, 146.
[66] *BJ* ii, 136.　[67] *BJ* ii, 142.
[68] For the place given to angels in the Qumran liturgy cf. J. Strugnell, 'The Angelic Liturgy at Qumran, 4 Q Serek Šîrôt 'Olat Haššabbāt', *VT Supplement* 7 (1960), pp. 318ff; another fragment of this document was found at Masada in 1963.
[69] *BJ* ii, 136; cf. 4 Q *Therapeia* (also 4 Q *Or. Nab.*; 1 Q *Gen. Apoc.* xx, 28f).
[70] *Ref.* ix, 22.
[71] Cf. 1 QH iii, 29ff (where, however, the conflagration may not be eschatological).

no doubt modified their beliefs and practices to some extent in the course of the years, so that we should not lay too much emphasis, perhaps, on divergencies between the Essenes and Qumran with regard to the frequency and significance of ceremonial lustration, the years during which a man's probation lasted, sacrificial doctrine and procedure, the attitude towards the government (Jewish or Gentile) and the use of force. Yet there are so many hints in ancient writings of a rich variety of messianic and 'baptist' communities with their headquarters in the Jordan valley and Dead Sea region that we should be cautious before we make a complete identification of two of these communities concerning which we are now better informed than we are about the others.

It has been suggested that the Qumran community should be identified with the marrying Essenes of whom Josephus speaks. Those marrying Essenes were plainly very exceptional Essenes, for not only Pliny and Philo but Josephus himself record celibacy as one of the characteristic features of Essenes in general. There is no evidence that the men of Qumran were celibate on principle, although, as we have seen, there are practical considerations which make it not unlikely that those of them who were fully initiated did abstain from marriage and family life. Another possibility is that Josephus's marrying Essenes were those associate members of the brotherhood who did not withdraw from the ordinary ways of life in the world.

The Essenes are mentioned only in Greek and Latin documents. It may be asked whether the Qumran community can be identified with any group mentioned in Jewish rabbinical literature, which is written in Hebrew and Aramaic. Here too we are unable thus far to say anything certain. We may think of those people known to rabbinical tradition as the 'morning bathers' (*ṭōḇĕlē šaḥărīn*) because they indulged in a ritual washing at dawn before they took the name of God upon their lips—thus exceeding the righteousness of the Pharisees, with whom they entered into controversy.[72] But in view of the variety of such sects in the Judaism of those days, a verdict of 'Not Proven' is all that our present knowledge warrants.

[72] Tosefta, *Yadaim* 2:20; possibly to be associated with the ἡμεροβαπτισταί ('daily bathers') of Epiphanius *Anacephalaeoses*, 17 (cf. *Clem. Hom.* ii, 23, where John the Baptist is called a ἡμεροβαπτιστής).

The term 'Essenes' was plainly a comprehensive one. Hippolytus, as we have seen, distinguishes four divisions of Essenes, and there may have been other groups which were loosely designated by the same name. When the known resemblances and apparent differences between the Qumran community and the Essenes are considered and assessed, a reasonable conclusion is that the Qumran community was one Essene group, and an important one at that, though it may have diverged in a number of features from other Essene groups.[73]

If the men of Qumran were not Zealots in the party sense, they were certainly in the non-party sense zealots for God, for his law and for his cause. As for their readiness to take the leading part in the eschatological struggle against the sons of darkness, this does not rule out their identity with Essenes. According to Hippolytus, some Essenes received the name and acted the part of zealots and *sicarii*;[74] and we may be sure that John the Essene was not the only member of his order to take arms against Rome in A.D. 66.

[73] I agree with A. R. C. Leaney that the Qumran community was 'a special form of a movement which originally existed in different branches in various towns and villages of Palestine. This movement may well have been identical with or part of that which Josephus calls the Essenes' (*The Rule of Qumran and its Meaning*, p. 33). Branches may have existed also outside Palestine—in Egypt, perhaps, and most probably at Damascus, if the Damascus migration of some followers of the Teacher of Righteousness (*CD* vi, 5, 19; vii, 19; xix, 34; xx, 12) is to be understood literally. [74] *Ref.* ix, 21. See p. 90.

10 The Messianic Hope

1

The designation 'Messiah' represents a Hebrew (or Aramaic) verbal adjective meaning 'anointed'.[1] When applied to persons, it denotes their sacral function: it indicates that the office which they hold is held, as we should say, 'by the grace of God'. In the Old Testament it is applied exceptionally to prophets,[2] occasionally to the chief priest[3] and most commonly to the king of Israel, 'the Messiah of Yahweh'.[4]

It is with the kingship in Israel, and especially with the royal dynasty founded by David, that the historic 'messianic hope' is most closely related. The hope is bound up with the promise of perpetual sovereignty made to David's house in Nathan's oracle preserved in prose in II Samuel 7:8–16 and quoted in (presumably earlier) poetical form in Psalms 89:19–37; 132:11ff. When, from the days of the Assyrian menace onward, the fortunes of David's house began to wane, the contrast between the high hopes of the dynastic oracle and the existing state of affairs became more and more painfully obvious. But it was in these depressing circumstances that prophets began to speak most confidently of a coming day in which David's fallen house would be rebuilt and its vanished glories restored and surpassed in a second and greater David.[5]

Another contrast was felt between the ideal kingship of Yahweh in his people Israel and over the world, which was celebrated in the national worship, and the imperfect manner in which his kingship was represented, and sometimes even caricatured, by his hu-

---

[1] Heb. *māšiaḥ* from the verb *māšaḥ*; Aram. *měšiḥā*.
[2] E.g. Ps. 105:15 for the parallelism 'anointed ones' // 'prophets'. Cf. I Kings 19:26 for an (exceptional) instance of anointing to the prophetic succession.
[3] Lev. 4:3, 5, 16; 6:22.   [4] E.g. I Sam. 16:6; 24:10; Lam. 4:20, etc.
[5] Cf. Amos 9:11f (quoted in Acts 15:16f as fulfilled in the apostles' Gentile mission); Hosea 3:5.

man vicegerents. This contrast too stimulated the expectation of a day—the day of Yahweh—when the ideal would be realized, and the vindication of Yahweh's cause in the world would bring his people security. As Amos pointed out, Yahweh's people were inclined to make too facile an identification of his victory with their well-being.[6]

These two forms of hope—the hope of the day of Yahweh and the hope of the revival of David's sovereignty—tended to merge. They do so in some of Isaiah's oracles. The 'prince of the four names' is to establish David's throne for ever, thanks to the zeal of Yahweh of hosts, his concern to fulfil his pledged word (Isaiah 9:6f); the 'shoot from the stump of Jesse', on whom the Spirit of Yahweh will rest in rich fulness, will inaugurate a golden age in which not Israel only but all the earth will rejoice in the knowledge of Yahweh (Isaiah 11:1–10).

Isaiah's portrayal of the righteous king of the future is closely related to his teaching about the righteous remnant of Israel. In the disastrous flood about to break upon the disobedient nation, only a remnant will survive, but at least a remnant will survive, and carry in its midst the hope of Israel into the new age. It will be not only a surviving remnant, but a believing remnant, the foundation stone of the restored Zion. Thus, when the son of David appears, he will have a holy city as his capital and a righteous nation as his subjects.[7] This close association between king and people has its counterpart in other pre-Christian expressions of the hope of Israel, as well as in the New Testament portrayal of the Servant-Messiah and his servant-people.

Even though the days that followed Isaiah's ministry grew darker, not brighter, the hope to which he gave voice did not die. Jeremiah hails the advent of a prince of the house of David who will bear worthily the name *Yahweh-ṣidqēnū* ('Yahweh is our righteousness') so unworthily borne by the contemporary Zedekiah (*ṣidqī-Yāhū*), the last crowned king of the Davidic dynasty. 'In his days Judah will be saved, and Israel will dwell securely' (Jeremiah 23:5f; 33:14–16). Similarly, his younger contemporary Ezekiel, contemplating the downfall of the perjured Zedekiah, sees

[6] Amos 5:18–20.   [7] Isa. 4:3; 10:20ff; 28:16; 32:1ff.

the crown of David remaining without a wearer for long, but not for ever: 'A ruin, ruin, ruin I will make it; there shall not be even a trace of it until he comes whose right it is; and to him I will give it' (Ezekiel 21:27). The words 'until he comes whose right it is' are probably Ezekiel's interpretation of the clause 'until Shiloh comes'[8] in the blessing of Jacob, where a ruler of the tribe of Judah is in view (Genesis 49:10). Elsewhere Ezekiel gives this coming ruler the name of David and pictures him as the good shepherd of Israel, the flock of Yahweh (Ezekiel 34:23f; 37:24f).

When Cyrus authorized the return of the Judaean exiles and the rebuilding of the Temple in Jerusalem, it was natural that a restoration of David's dynasty should be looked for at the same time. Indeed, Zerubbabel, grandson of the former king Jehoiachin, and governor of Judaea at the beginning of the reign of Darius I (521 B.C.), is hailed in Zechariah 6:12 as 'The Branch'—the title already given by Jeremiah to the coming prince *Yahweh-ṣidqēnū*.[9] Whereas his grandfather Jehoiachin had been rejected, signet-ring on Yahweh's right hand though he might be (Jeremiah 22:24ff), Zerubbabel receives the promise through the prophet Haggai that Yahweh has chosen him as his signet-ring (Haggai 2:23). Zerubbabel never wore the crown of his royal ancestors, but to the returned exiles the sight of a scion of David's house acting as governor in Judaea was a token that the promises made to that house had not been forgotten.

After Zerubbabel, however, the house of David passes into obscurity. The later oracle of Zechariah 9:9 probably refers to a Davidic prince:

> Rejoice greatly, O daughter of Zion!
> Shout aloud, O daughter of Jerusalem!
> Lo, your king comes to you;
> triumphant and victorious is he—

but centuries were to pass before this call found an echo. With the rise to power of the Hasmonaeans, the hopes attached to the house of David bade fair to be eclipsed by the present glories of a family

---

[8] Meaning perhaps 'until the prince comes' or, with RSV, 'until he comes to whom it belongs'.
[9] Jer. 23:5; 33:15 (Heb. *ṣemaḥ*).

of the tribe of Levi, in which the kingship was combined with the high-priesthood.

This combination of the kingship with the high-priesthood in the tribe of Levi is probably alluded to in a passage in the *Testament of Reuben* (6:7–12), where Reuben addresses his sons thus:

> To Levi God gave the sovereignty. . . . Therefore I command you to listen to Levi, because he will know the law of the Lord and give ordinances for judgement and offer sacrifice for all Israel until the consummation of the times, as the anointed high priest, of whom the Lord spoke. . . . Draw near to Levi in humbleness of heart, that you may receive a blessing from his mouth. For he will bless Israel and Judah, because it is he whom the Lord has chosen to be king over all the nation. And bow down before his seed, for on your behalf it will die in wars visible and invisible, and will be among you as an eternal king.[10]

But not all Judaeans were content with the Hasmonaean priest-kingship. The Qumran community, for example, cherished the expectation of a priestly and a royal Messiah, two distinct personages who would arise in the end-time and, under God, inaugurate the new age, but the Hasmonaean family was the last family in the world with which they associated the priestly Messiah. He would be, in their expectation, a priest of the house of Zadok, and would be head of state in the age to come, superior even to the Davidic Messiah.[11] Another pious community, from which comes the collection of hymns called the *Psalms of Solomon*, excoriated the Hasmonaeans for arrogantly 'laying waste the throne of David', and saw in the Roman occupation of 63 B.C. a divine judgement on them. The Romans themselves acted no less arrogantly, but their days were numbered; they would be overthrown and expelled

[10] The *Testaments of the Twelve Patriarchs* are extant in their entirety only in a Christian Greek recension. Fragments of earlier, pre-Christian, recensions of some of the *Testaments* have survived, including fragments of the *Testament of Levi* in Aramaic from the Cairo genizah and from Qumran and of the *Testament of Naphtali* in Hebrew from Qumran.

[11] Thus, in 1 QSa ii, 11ff, 17ff, 'the priest' takes precedence over 'the Messiah of Israel' at meetings of the council and at community banquets; and in 1 QSb ii, 24ff, v, 20ff, the blessing invoked on the high priest and 'the sons of Zadok the priests' precedes that invoked on 'the prince of the congregation'. Where 'the Messiah' is mentioned absolutely in the Qumran texts, the Davidic Messiah is intended.

from the land of Israel by the Davidic Messiah. So the psalmist prays (17:23f, 32–6):[12]

See, Lord, raise up for them their king, the son of David,
  In the time which thou knowest, O God,
  To reign over Israel thy servant;
and gird him with strength to shatter the unjust rulers . . .

He will possess the nations, to serve beneath his yoke;
  He will glorify the Lord with the praise of all the earth.
He will cleanse Jerusalem in holiness, as it was of old,
  That the nations may come from the ends of the earth to see his glory,

Bearing as gifts her sons who had fainted,
  And to see the glory of the Lord with which God has glorified her.
A righteous king, taught by God, is their ruler,
  And there will be no unrighteousness among them all his days,
  For all will be holy, and their king the Anointed Lord.

These last words, 'the Anointed Lord' (Gk. *christos kyrios*) are identical with those used in the angelic annunciation to the shepherds of Bethlehem in Luke 2:11, 'to you is born this day in the city of David a Saviour, who is Christ the Lord'.[13] And this may be more than a coincidence, for the atmosphere of Luke's nativity narrative is quite close to that of the *Psalms of Solomon*; the pious Israelites depicted in this narrative—Zechariah and Elizabeth, Joseph and Mary, Simeon and Anna—who look for 'the consolation of Israel' and 'the redemption of Jerusalem', apparently belonged to a pious group of 'the quiet in the land' not unlike the group which produced the *Psalms of Solomon*. The aspirations of the *Psalms of Solomon* are voiced afresh in the canticles of Luke's nativity narrative, but now they are on the verge of fulfilment. Gabriel, announcing the birth of Mary's son (Luke 1:32f), says:

He will be great, and will be called the Son of the Most High;
  and the Lord God will give to him the throne of his father David,
and he will reign over the house of Jacob for ever;
  and of his kingdom there will be no end.

[12] The Psalms of Solomon have commonly been regarded as Pharisaic compositions, but they may more generally express the sentiments of any pious community cherishing the hope of Israel.

[13] In both places χριστὸς κύριος has been frequently emended to χριστὸς κυρίου ('the Lord's anointed'); cf. Luke 2:26.

In these words we catch an echo of Isaiah's oracle of the 'prince of the four names', whose righteous government 'upon the throne of David, and over his kingdom' is to endure 'from this time forth and for evermore' (Isaiah 9:7). And the same note is struck in Zechariah's hymn of praise (Luke 1:68–71):

> Blessed be the Lord God of Israel,
>   for he has visited and redeemed his people,
> and has raised up a horn of salvation for us
>   in the house of his servant David,
> as he spoke by the mouth of his holy prophets from of old,
>   that we should be saved from our enemies,
> and from the hand of all who hate us . . .

Such were the noblest expressions of the messianic hope on the eve of the birth of Jesus. His interpretation and fulfilment of them cannot be properly appreciated, however, without reference to another form which the hope of Israel takes in the Old Testament and intertestamental writings.

2

One of the prophets of Israel describes the messianic hope as 'the sure mercies of David' (Isa. 55:3)—the sum-total of the promises made by Yahweh to David and secured to him by a dynastic covenant. These words occur towards the end of the corpus of prophetic oracles which opens with the message of consolation to Jerusalem, assuring her of the imminent end of her desolations and the return of her deported citizens from their exile in Babylonia: 'Comfort, comfort my people, says your God' (Isa. 40:1). This restoration is to be the redemptive act of Israel's God; to accomplish it he has raised up Cyrus, founder of the Persian Empire. As Cyrus marches from victory to victory, he does not realize that his triumphant progress is directed by a God whom he does not know, the only true God, by contrast with whom all the gods of the nations are nonentities. Nevertheless, it is Yahweh who has anointed Cyrus and held his right hand, in order to bring him to a position of world dominion from which he may give effect to Yahweh's purpose and restore the Jewish exiles to their homeland. The effect of this restoration will be that all nations will know that Yahweh alone is God.

The joyful news thus proclaimed to Zion will find an echo throughout the world; it is, indeed, joyful news not for Zion only but ultimately for all mankind.[14]

But how can the rise of a Gentile conqueror or the return of a few thousand displaced Jews have such universal implications? Because by these movements, whatever their intrinsic importance may be, the stage is set for something more important—for the introduction of a figure who puts Cyrus in the shade, the Servant of Yahweh whose mission it is to spread the knowledge of the true God to the ends of the earth. Cyrus has served Yahweh unconsciously; here is one who will serve him willingly and intelligently. Cyrus has promoted the divine purpose by the temporary and limited methods of military conquest and imperial power; here is one who will promote it in a far different way—not by making a noise in the world but in obscurity and patient obedience; not by imposing his will on others but by uncomplaining endurance of contempt, injustice, suffering and death. Such is the fate meted out to him by others for his obedience to God; but more than that: submission to this treatment is his crowning obedience; for this he has been chosen by Yahweh and endowed with his Spirit (Isaiah 42:1). His suffering is the very means by which he fulfils the purpose of God in a more abiding fashion than Cyrus could ever achieve, and so brings blessing and liberation to multitudes.[15]

Who is this Servant? Occasionally he is addressed as 'Israel', as in Isaiah 49:3, where Yahweh says to him:

> You are my servant,
> Israel, in whom I will be glorified.

But he is not the personified nation of Israel *simpliciter*: Israel as a whole has been a disobedient servant, and the task of carrying the knowledge of God to the world is entrusted to one who in his own person realizes the ideal Israel and conveys the saving grace of God to the nation of Israel and the other nations alike (Isaiah 49:6):

> It is too light a thing that you should be my servant
> to raise up the tribes of Jacob
> and to restore the preserved of Israel;

[14] Isa. 45:1ff.
[15] Isa. 42:1–4; 49:1–6; 50:4–9; 52:13–53:12.

I will give you as a light to the nations,
that my salvation may reach to the end of the earth.

This Servant of Yahweh, then, is closely associated with the nation of Israel and yet distinguished from the nation; indeed, it is in part for the sin of the nation that he suffers—'stricken to death', says the prophet, 'for the transgression of my people' (Isaiah 53:8).[16] He is, in fact, Israel's king, portrayed in sacral terms, who can both represent his people and suffer vicariously for them;[17] he is the one whose ministry ensures the fulfilment of 'the sure mercies of David'. If, in the first of the four 'Servant Songs', it is he who 'will bring forth justice to the nations' (Isaiah 42:1), so, in an adjacent oracle not included within these Songs, Yahweh says of him (Isaiah 55:4):

> Behold, I made him a witness to the peoples,
> a leader and commander for the peoples.

In whatever sense these words were true of the original David, they are much more applicable to the Servant who, triumphant through suffering, establishes truth and righteousness on earth.

Two statements made about the Isaianic Servant are echoed in the book of Daniel. 'My Servant', says Yahweh at the beginning of the fourth Servant Song (Isaiah 52:13), 'will act wisely (*yaśkīl*)'.[18] The plural particle of this Hebrew conjugation, *maśkīlīm*, is used in Daniel 11:33; 12:3 of those who bear the brunt of the attack when Antiochus Epiphanes attempts to abolish the Jews' religion, and by precept and example encourage others to stand firm and refuse to violate the law of their God.[19] Although these *maśkīlīm* suffer severely, their reward is sure: when the resurrection age dawns, they will 'shine like the brightness of the firmament; and those who turn many to righteousness, like the stars for ever and ever' (Daniel 12:3). The words 'those who turn many to righteousness', which stand in synonymous parallelism with 'those who are wise' (the *maśkīlīm*), are reminiscent of Yahweh's words in

[16] Reading, with LXX, *lammāwet* ('to death') for MT *lāmō* ('to him').
[17] Cf. C. R. North, *The Suffering Servant in Deutero-Isaiah* (Oxford, 1948), pp. 207ff; A. Bentzen, *King and Messiah* (London, 1955), pp. 48ff; H. H. Rowley, *The Servant of the Lord and Other Essays on the Old Testament* (Oxford, 1965²), pp. 1–94 and especially pp. 61ff.
[18] The same form *yaśkīl* is used of the messianic 'Branch' in Jer. 23:5 ('he shall . . . deal wisely'). [19] See p. 101.

Isaiah 53:11, 'the righteous one, my servant, will make many to be accounted righteous'. The persecuted *maśkīlīm* may well have thought of themselves as corporately filling, in some degree, the rôle of the Servant of Yahweh.

These *maśkīlīm* may be identified with the people referred to in an earlier vision of Daniel as 'the saints of the Most High' who receive judgement and everlasting dominion after the downfall of the last pagan world-empire (Daniel 7:22, 27). But the phrase 'the saints of the Most High' appears in the interpreting angel's explanation of Daniel's dream in which, after the rise and fall of four wild beasts depicting the pagan world-empires, eternal and universal dominion is given to 'one like a son of man' (Aram. *kĕ-ḇar 'ĕnāš*, i.e. a man-like figure), who comes with the clouds of heaven and is presented before the 'Ancient of Days' (Daniel 7:13f).

It is not necessary to look outside Israel—to Iranian conceptions of a Primal or Heavenly Man, for example—for the sources of this figure 'like a son of man'.[20] So far as the wording is concerned, we may think of such a passage as Psalm 80:17, where in prayer to Yahweh, the 'Shepherd of Israel', the psalmist speaks of Israel as 'the man of thy right hand, the son of man whom thou hast made strong for thyself' ('son of man', Heb. *ben 'āḏām*, stands here in synonymous parallelism with 'man', Heb. *'īš*), or Psalm 8:4, where the 'son of man' (Heb. *ben 'āḏām*), in parallelism with *'man'* (Heb. *'ĕnōš*), made but 'little less than God', exercises dominion over the lower creation, realizing the ideal of man as God intended him to be. But a more direct antecedent, though designated in different terms, may be recognized in the Servant of Yahweh, especially if we bear in mind the tendency of Hebrew thought to oscillate between corporate and individual personality—in this case, between the nation and its representative.

Daniel's 'one like a son of man' is not expressly viewed as a suffering figure, but 'the saints of the Most High', his counterpart in the angelic interpretation of Daniel's vision, are attacked and overpowered in the dream by the 'little horn' on the head of the fourth imperial beast—the persecutor Antiochus. Only by divine intervention is the situation reversed, so that the persecutor is de-

[20] Cf. R. Otto, *The Kingdom of God and the Son of Man* (London, 1943[2]), pp. 185ff; also S. Mowinckel, *He that Cometh* (Oxford, 1956), pp. 335ff, 346ff.

stroyed and the persecuted saints vindicated and exalted. In any case, if we look not so much at the words or symbols as at the reality which they convey, it is not going too far to find in this 'one like a son of man' yet another embodiment of Israel's messianic hope.

3

The vision of Daniel 7 probably lies behind a number of passages in the *Similitudes of Enoch*. This is the title commonly given to I Enoch 37–71, a section in many respects distinct from other parts of the composite corpus of Enoch literature which we call I Enoch. It may or may not be significant that, while fragments of all the other main sections of I Enoch have been identified among the Qumran manuscripts, no fragment of the *Similitudes* has been found. Although this section may be of different authorship and date than the rest of I Enoch, it is probably pre-Christian.[21]

In the *Similitudes* the fallen angels who figure so prominently elsewhere in I Enoch do not appear. God, the 'Lord of spirits', is described in the *Similitudes* as 'One who had a head of days' (or, more briefly, as 'the Head of days') whose head is 'white like wool' (46:1). This designation is apparently based on Daniel 7:9, where Daniel sees God as 'one that was ancient of days' with 'the hair of his head like pure wool'. With him Enoch sees 'another being whose countenance had the appearance of a man' (46:2). This being is referred to as 'that son of man', an expression no doubt echoing Daniel 7:13, but 'that son of man' is not a title in the *Similitudes*; it means 'that particular son of man (human being) who appears in the company of the Head of days', 'the son of man who has righteousness', as he is called in 46:3, evidently identical with the being who is otherwise called 'the Righteous One . . . whose elect works hang upon the Lord of spirits' (38:2), the 'Elect One of righteousness and faith' who has 'his dwelling-place under the wings of the Lord of Spirits' (39:6f), and the 'Anointed One' (Messiah) of the Lord of Spirits (48:10; 52:4).[22] This son of man is to be a support

[21] See E. Sjöberg, *Der Menschensohn im äthiopischen Henochbuch* (Lund, 1946), pp. 35ff.
[22] See M. D. Hooker, *The Son of Man in Mark* (London, 1967), pp. 33ff, for a lucid account of the Son of Man in I Enoch.

to the righteous and a light to the nations (48:4)—here we catch an echo of the second Isaianic Servant Song (Isa. 49:6)—but the executor of divine judgement on the ungodly (I Enoch 48:8–10).

> From the beginning the son of man was hidden,
> And the Most High preserved him in the presence of his might,
> And revealed him to the elect (62:7).

But on the day of visitation this son of man is manifested as vindicator of the righteous and judge of the wicked:

> And one portion of them shall look on the other,
> And they shall be terrified,
> And they shall be downcast of countenance,
> And pain shall seize them,
> When they see that son of man
> Sitting on the throne of his glory (62:5).

Language like this is remarkably similar to the language in which Jesus speaks of the time when the Son of Man will sit on 'the throne of his glory' to execute judgement along with twelve assessors (Matt. 19:28), while all nations are gathered before him to be divided into two groups 'as a shepherd separates the sheep from the goats' (Matt. 25:31ff).

The son of man in the *Similitudes* 'was named before the Lord of Spirits, and his name before the Head of days . . . before the sun and the signs were created, before the stars of heaven were made' (I Enoch 48:2f). But his name is kept secret until near the end of the *Similitudes*; in chapter 71 Enoch is translated to heaven and greeted by God with the words: '*Thou* art the son of man who art born for righteousness; righteousness abides over thee, and the righteousness of the Head of days forsakes thee not' (71:14). This identification of the son of man with Enoch[23] is sufficient proof that we are not dealing with the work of a Christian author in the *Similitudes*.

Like the 'one like a son of man' in Daniel, the 'son of man' in the *Similitudes* is to be understood in terms of corporate personality, as the community of the righteous and elect ones, named and 'hidden'

[23] We may compare the portrayal of Enoch as servant of the Lord in Wisdom 4:10–15 (cf. 2:13).

in God's presence from all eternity,[24] which can be individualized from time to time in someone who is outstandingly righteous, like Enoch, who in another section of I Enoch is commissioned because of his righteousness to pronounce judgement on the fallen angels,[25] and who in the *Similitudes* has been chosen to pronounce judgement on all the ungodly at the end-time. In the *Similitudes* the son of man is closely associated with the faithful community: if he is righteous, so are they (38:1ff, etc.); if he is elect, so are they (38:3, etc.).

In one of the visions of the Ezra Apocalypse (II Esdras 13:1–53), a later development of the 'son of man' of Daniel and Enoch is seen in a 'man' who comes up from the sea and flies with the clouds of heaven to judge the ungodly and deliver creation. He is acknowledged by God as 'my Son' and described as 'he whom the Most High has been keeping for many ages'—language which in other parts of the same apocalypse is used of the Messiah (II Esdras 7:28f; 12:32f).

The Ezra Apocalypse, however, was composed in the period following A.D. 70 and is too late to have influenced the gospel tradition. The title 'Son of Man' in the gospel tradition, where it is found only on the lips of Jesus, marks a creative advance in its use and significance.[26]

4

No single form of messianic expectation was cherished by Jesus' contemporaries, but the hope of a military Messiah predominated. The promises of a prince of the house of David who would break the oppressor's yoke from his people's neck seemed to many to be designed for such a time as theirs, whether the yoke was imposed by a Herodian ruler or by a Roman governor. But among a minority of 'the quiet in the land' expectations of a more spiritual order were voiced from time to time. Luke's nativity canticles have room not only for the Davidic theme sounded by Gabriel and Zechariah, but

[24] Cf. Eph. 1:4 where the people of God are chosen in Christ before the world's foundation.
[25] Cf. I Peter 3:18f, where this function is performed by Christ, 'made alive in the spirit' after being 'put to death in the flesh'.
[26] See pp. 173ff.

also for Simeon's *Nunc dimittis* with its echo of the Servant Songs (Luke 2:30–2):

> Mine eyes have seen thy salvation
>   which thou hast prepared in the presence of all peoples,
> a light for revelation to the Gentiles,
>   and for glory to thy people Israel.[27]

It was in the spirit of these words, which Luke must have found specially congenial, that the messianic hope was to be realized in the first Christian century.

[27] See pp. 276f for a further application of Isa. 49:6.

11 Judaism at the Beginning of the Christian Era

1

At the beginning of the Christian era all Jews throughout the world looked on Palestine and Jerusalem as their home, but the majority of them lived farther afield.[1] The list of nations in Acts 2:9–11 from which worshippers came to Jerusalem for the feast of Pentecost seven weeks after the death of Jesus has interesting literary affinities,[2] but it does indicate clearly the wide area of Jewish dispersion (Gk. *diaspora*), from the territories of the 'Parthians and Medes and Elamites' in the east to Rome in the west, with Mesopotamia, Asia Minor, Crete, Arabia, Egypt and Cyrene receiving special mention between these limits.

Jews had lived continuously in Mesopotamia and the adjoining lands since the days of the Assyrian and Babylonian deportations from the eighth to the sixth century B.C. Many descendants of those deported did not avail themselves of the opportunity to return from exile under the Persian Empire. Artaxerxes III of Persia settled a number of Jewish captives in Hyrcania, on the Caspian Sea (*c.* 350 B.C.).[3] It was for the benefit of these Jews, living among 'the up-country barbarians', that Josephus composed the first (Aramaic) edition of his *Jewish War*.[4]

---

[1] Passages from contemporary authors attesting the extent and size of the Jewish *diaspora* are collected in Schürer, *HJP* II. ii, pp. 220ff.

[2] S. Weinstock ('The Geographical Catalogue in Acts 2:9–11', *JRS* 38 [1948], pp. 43ff) mentions a marginal note in F. C. Burkitt's hand in an offprint of F. Cumont, 'La plus ancienne géographie astrologique', *Klio* 9 (1909), pp. 263ff—an article dealing with the division of the nations among the signs of the zodiac. Burkitt's note tabulates the catalogue of Acts 2:9–11 alongside the list of nations, arranged according to the signs of the zodiac, given in Paul of Alexandria's *Apotelesmatica* (4th cent. A.D.). The implication of the note seems to be that Luke 'meant in fact to say "the whole world" . . . all nations who live under the twelve signs of the zodiac'.

[3] Jerome, *Chronicle* (Olympiad 105).   [4] Josephus, *BJ* i, 3.

The Jewish settlements in Egypt date from the beginning of the sixth century B.C. The 'Elephantine papyri' reveal the fortunes of one such settlement—a body of Jewish mercenaries and their families enlisted by Psamtek II of Egypt (594–588 B.C.) to help him in a war against the Ethiopians and then to guard his southern frontier. These Jews, on whom Josiah's religious reformation of 621 B.C. appears to have made remarkably little impact, built a temple and altar to Yahweh on the Nile-island of Elephantine and continued to live there and at Syene (Aswan) until about 400 B.C.[5] They may be included among the addressees of the message delivered (c. 586 B.C.) by Jeremiah to the Jews living in both Lower and Upper Egypt when he was compelled to accompany the Judaean leaders and their followers who went down to Egypt to escape the Babylonian vengeance after the assassination of Gedaliah, appointed governor of Judaea by Nebuchadrezzar (Jer. 44).

With the conquering campaigns of Alexander the Great and the incorporation of Egypt and Cyrenaica in his empire, many more Jews settled in these lands, especially in Alexandria (founded by Alexander in 331 B.C.) and Cyrene. Philo of Alexandria estimated about A.D. 38 that there were at least a million Jews in Egypt and the neighbouring territories.[6] We may subject this figure to a substantial discount, but the Jewish population of Egypt was certainly very great. In Alexandria itself at that time one out of the five wards of the city was entirely Jewish and a second was very largely so.[7] The Ptolemies encouraged Jewish settlement in Alexandria, especially during the period when Judaea formed part of their empire; Ptolemy I (323–285 B.C.) settled a number of Jews in Cyrenaica to ensure its loyalty.[8] In the early decades of the second century B.C., when the Seleucid king Antiochus III had wrested Judaea and Coelesyria from the Ptolemies, he similarly encouraged Jewish settlement in Antioch and other cities of his empire. Even before his conquest of Coelesyria he moved many Jews from the eastern area of his empire into Phrygia and Lydia in Asia Minor to secure the loyalty of these provinces.[9] The Jews of Phrygia were reputed to be exceptionally lax in their devotion to the law and prone to assimilation with their neighbours; the barriers between Judaism

---

[5] See A. E. Cowley, *Aramaic Papyri of the Fifth Century B.C.* (Oxford, 1923); E. G. Kraeling, *The Brooklyn Museum Aramaic Papyri* (Oxford, 1953).
[6] Philo, *Flaccus*, 43.   [7] Philo, *Flaccus*, 55; cf. Josephus, *BJ* ii, 495.
[8] Josephus, *Apion* ii, 44.   [9] Josephus, *Ant.* xii, 149ff.

and paganism there were not impenetrable, although we cannot be sure that the *Prugita* whose wines and baths, according to the Talmud, had separated the ten tribes from their fellow-Israelites[10] is to be identified with Phrygia.[11]

As for Rome, with which the Jews had established diplomatic relations in the days of Judas Maccabaeus, the Jewish colony there was greatly augmented after Pompey's conquest of Judaea in 63 B.C., and by 59 B.C., according to Cicero, it formed an influential element in Roman society.[12] It is estimated that by the beginning of the Christian era the Jews of Rome numbered between 40,000 and 60,000.[13] In addition to literary evidence, the study of six Jewish catacombs in Rome has made a substantial contribution to our knowledge of the Roman Jews.[14] Three of these catacombs in particular have yielded valuable information—the Monteverde catacomb on the Via Portuensis, first discovered in 1602 and rediscovered in 1904, the catacomb on the Via Appia, discovered in 1859, and that on the Via Nomentana, discovered in 1919. The Roman Jews generally were Greek-speaking and bore Greek names, but (to judge by inscriptions in the catacombs) they tended to give their children Latin names. A public scandal in A.D. 19, when four Roman Jews persuaded a wealthy proselyte named Fulvia to make a generous donation to the Jerusalem Temple but appropriated it themselves, moved the Emperor Tiberius to expel the whole Jewish community from Rome; four thousand of them were drafted into military service in Sardinia, to take part in suppressing the brigandage in that island.[15] In a few years, however, the Jewish community was back in Rome, as numerous as ever.[16]

---

[10] TB *Shabbat,* 147*b.*

[11] Cf. A. Neubauer, *Géographie du Talmud* (Paris, 1868), p. 315. M. Jastrow (*A Dictionary of the Targumim,* etc. [New York, 1926], p. 1217) locates Prugita in northern Palestine. For the assimilationist tendencies of Phrygian Jews see also W. M. Ramsay, *Cities and Bishoprics of Phrygia* ii (Oxford, 1897), pp. 637ff, 649ff, 673ff; in view of the epigraphic data he presents he says (p. 674): 'We may then take the marriage of the Jewess Eunice at Lystra to a Greek, and the exemption of her son Timotheus from the Mosaic law as typical of a relaxation of the exclusive Jewish standard in Lycaonia and Phrygia and an approximation to the pagan population around them' (cf. Acts 16:1–3; II Tim. 1:5; see p. 305).   [12] Cicero, *Pro Flacco,* 66.

[13] H. J. Leon, *The Jews of Ancient Rome* (Philadelphia, 1960), pp. 135f.

[14] H. J. Leon, *op. cit.,* pp. 46ff.

[15] Josephus, *Ant.* xviii, 81–4; cf. Tacitus, *Ann.* ii, 85. 5; Suetonius, *Tiberius* 36.   [16] See p. 295.

2

At the heart of Jewish national life stood the Temple in Jerusalem, on the site where King Solomon had built his house 'exceeding magnifical' for Yahweh nearly a thousand years before. That house, burned down by the Chaldaean armies in 587 B.C., had been replaced some seventy years later by the more modest sanctuary of Zerubbabel. This second Temple remained in being, profaned though it was for three years by Antiochus Epiphanes (167–164 B.C.) and embellished from time to time by benefactors—preeminently by Herod, who rebuilt and greatly extended the sacred precincts—until its destruction by Roman soldiers in A.D. 70. As restored by Herod, it outdid in magnificence even the earlier house that Solomon had built—

> far off appearing like a Mount
> Of Alabaster, top't with golden Spires.

Here day by day, in the Court of the Priests, the *tāmîḏ*, the continual burnt-offering, was presented to Israel's God—a lamb every morning at daybreak and another lamb every afternoon 'at the hour of prayer, the ninth hour' (Acts 3:1).[17] The details of these two daily sacrifices are given in the Mishnah tractate *Tamid*; although the contents of this tractate, like the rest of the Mishnah, were not set down in writing until the end of the second century A.D., the tractate preserves in substantially reliable form an oral tradition going back to the days when the Temple still stood. The *tāmîḏ* was accompanied each morning by choral singing and congregational prayers; it was preceded by an offering of incense and followed by a *minḥāh* or cereal offering (a cake of wheaten flour and oil), paid for by the high priest and presented to God on his behalf, and a libation of wine; then came a prayer-service in the 'hall of hewn stone' (*liškaṯ hag-gāzîṯ*) which included the *Shemaʿ* ('Hear, O Israel . . .') and the blessing of the people, and a service of praise with musical accompaniment, concluding with the appointed psalm for the day. The afternoon service was similar, except that the incense-offering followed the sacrifice of the lamb instead of preceding it.

[17] The biblical prescription for the *tāmîḏ* is given in Num. 28:3–8.

On the sabbath[18] two lambs were offered in the morning and two again in the afternoon; on new moons[19] and festival days[20] the sacrifices were greatly multiplied.

The priests were divided into twenty-four divisions or 'courses'; each course served a week at a time.[21] Most of the priests thus ministered for two weeks in the year, except that at the great festivals all the courses were on duty because of the increased sacrificial activity at these times.

In addition to the stated sacrifices, there were many others offered at the instance of private individuals, especially by way of thanksgiving for deliverance from danger or for other benefits and in fulfilment of vows,[22] like the Nazirite vow of the four men of Acts 21:23ff whose expenses Paul undertook to pay. Outstanding among all these individual offerings was the daily sacrifice on behalf of the Roman Emperor from Augustus to Nero;[23] its termination in the summer of A.D. 66 was tantamount to official renunciation of his authority.[24]

The three great pilgrimage-festivals were (i) the seven-days Feast of Unleavened Bread, inaugurated by the Passover Feast, about the time of the spring equinox, (ii) the Feast of Pentecost seven weeks later, and (iii) the Feast of Tabernacles, or Booths, about the time of the autumnal equinox. Originally these three festivals were agricultural; they marked respectively (i) the beginning and (ii) the end of the barley and wheat harvest, and (iii) the end of the vintage and olive harvest, with which the whole annual

---

[18] Cf. Num. 28:9f.   [19] Cf. Num. 28:11–15.   [20] Cf. Num. 28:16–29:38.
[21] Cf. I Chron. 24:7–19; Mishnah, *Ta'anit* 4:2. To the first of the divisions, that of Jehoiarib, the Hasmonaean family belonged (I Macc. 2:1), as also did Josephus (*Life,* 2). The divisions did not always total twenty-four; twenty-two are indicated in the lists of Neh. 12:1–7 (in Zerubbabel's time), 12:12–21 (early 5th century B.C.), and 10:3–9 (c. 430 B.C.). The Qumran community made provision for twenty-six divisions (1 QM ii, 2)—an adaptation to the 'Jubilees' calendar with its 52 weeks in the year (see p. 112). The official Jewish calendar had a 354-day year of 12 lunar months, with a thirteenth month intercalated at appropriate intervals. See also E. J. Vardaman, 'Introduction to the Caesarea Inscription of the Twenty-Four Priestly Courses', and M. Avi-Yonah, 'The Caesarea Inscription of the Twenty-Four Priestly Courses', in *The Teacher's Yoke,* ed. E. J. Vardaman and J. L. Garrett (Waco, 1964), pp. 42ff, 46ff.
[22] Several of the canonical psalms appear to have been composed for such occasions (e.g. Ps. 66, especially verses 13–20); cf. also Jonah 2:2–9, especially verse 9.   [23] See p. 253.   [24] See p. 378.

'ingathering' was completed. But by New Testament times—and as regards the first and third of these festivals much earlier—their agricultural significance had been overlaid by historical commemoration: the Feast of Unleavened Bread commemorated the unleavened cakes which the Israelites baked in their hasty departure from Egypt (Exodus 12:39), the Feast of Pentecost commemorated the giving of the law at Sinai (Exodus 19:1ff)[25] and the Feast of Tabernacles commemorated the booths in which the Israelites lived during their wilderness wanderings (Lev. 23:42f).

Yet the agricultural significance was not wholly forgotten. For example, the ceremony of water-pouring, which was performed on seven mornings during the Feast of Tabernacles,[26] was an acknowledgement that no amount of work on the land would produce a harvest unless rain fell in the proper season. That the due observance of the Feast of Tabernacles (including presumably the water-pouring ceremony) guaranteed rain for the ensuing year is implied in Zech. 14:17: 'if any of the families of the earth do not go up to Jerusalem to worship the King, Yahweh of hosts, there will be no rain upon them'.[27] This water-pouring forms the background to Jesus' proclamation on the eighth and last day of the Feast of Tabernacles in A.D. 30 (the day, it appears, on which the ceremony was not carried out):

> He who is athirst, let him come to me,
> And let him drink who believes in me (John 7:37f).

In the earliest days of Israel's national history every male was directed to be present at the sanctuary on these three occasions,[28] and even in the vastly altered conditions of the first century A.D. great numbers of Jews from all parts of the Diaspora made the effort to come to Jerusalem for one or another of these festivals. With them would come some proselytes and even God-fearing Gentiles: 'visitors from Rome, both Jews and proselytes' (Acts 2:10),

[25] The recognition of Pentecost as the anniversary of the law-giving appears first in Jubilees 1:1 with 6:17; cf. also TB *Pesaḥim* 68*b*; Midrash *Tanḥuma* 26*c*; it is probably implied in the narrative of Acts 2:1–11. For the Jewish sacred calendar see Appendix to this chapter, p. 151.

[26] Cf. Mishnah, *Sukkah* 4:9.

[27] Since the Egyptians depended for their harvest on the annual overflowing of the Nile, and not on rainfall (on the land of Egypt, at least), their penalty for non-attendance was to be plague, not drought (Zech. 14:18f).

[28] Exodus 23:17; 34:23; Deut. 16:16.

were in Jerusalem at Pentecost in A.D. 30, and seven weeks earlier mention is made of some Greeks 'among those who went up to worship at the feast' of Passover and asked to see Jesus (John 12:20f). More than once Paul made a point of returning from his Gentile mission-field to be in Jerusalem for one of the festivals.[29]

In addition to the pilgrimage-festivals there was New Year's Day at the beginning of the autumnal month Tishri (perhaps the un-named 'feast of the Jews' in John 5:1), the Feast of Ḥanukkah ('Dedication') about the time of the winter solstice, commemorating the re-dedication of the Temple under Judas Maccabaeus in 164 B.C. after its profanation by Antiochus IV[30] (cf. John 10:22) and the Feast of Purim in early spring, commemorating the deliverance of the Jews from the malice of Haman, according to the story told in the book of Esther.[31] No occasion in the whole year was so solemn as the Day of Atonement, on the tenth day of Tishri (five days before the beginning of the Feast of Tabernacles), when the high priest entered the holy of holies, the inner compartment of the sanctuary, to make atonement for the sins of the whole people.[32]

The incident with which the Third Gospel opens, the offering of incense in the holy place by Zechariah, father of John the Baptist, is better understood when it is realized that this was the red-letter day of his whole priestly career. There were so many priests in each 'course' that none of them could hope to exercise the privilege of ministering at the golden incense-altar more than once. The angelic annunciation was made to Zechariah when his division—'the division of Abijah' (cf. I Chron. 24:10)—was on duty, and 'it fell to him by lot to enter the temple of the Lord and burn incense' (Luke 1:9).

The Temple services were maintained chiefly by the capitation tax of one half-shekel payable annually on the first day of Adar (February–March) by each male Jew of twenty years old and up-ward.[33] Jews from all parts of the world paid this tax, and its collection and conveyance to Jerusalem were facilitated by the Roman

[29] Acts 18:21, Western text ('I must by all means keep this coming feast [Passover or Pentecost] in Jerusalem'); 20:16 ('he was hastening to be at Jerusalem, if possible, on the day of Pentecost').
[30] Cf. I Macc. 4:36–59; II Macc. 1:18; 2:16–18; 10:1–8.
[31] Esther 9:17–32.   [32] Cf. Leviticus 16; Mishnah, *Yoma.*
[33] Cf. Exodus 30:11–16; II Chron. 24:6; Josephus, *Ant.* xiv, 110; Mishnah, *Sheqalim.* At one time, c. 430 B.C. (cf. Neh. 10:32f), the annual tax was one-third of a shekel.

142   *New Testament History*

authorities. The coinage most acceptable for this purpose was the silver tetradrachm of Tyre, equivalent in value to a shekel; two Jews normally combined to pay their contributions with this coin. This was the coin which, in the incident of Matt. 17:24–7, Peter was instructed by Jesus to give to the collectors 'for me and for yourself'.

The wood-offering for the sacrifices was also a public donation, contributed annually on the fifteenth day of Ab (July–August).[34]

A further source of support was the freewill offerings, which were given in various ways. There were large, widely publicized donations;[35] in addition, there were thirteen trumpet-shaped containers in the Temple treasury, situated in the Court of the Women, into which coins might be placed,[36] as by the widow of Mark 12:41–4, who by putting in two tiny copper coins contributed 'everything she had, her whole living'.

The priests derived their emoluments from a number of sources: sin-offerings and reparation-offerings were normally their perquisites; so were a considerable part of the cereal offerings, the shewbread, the breast and right shoulder of thank-offerings, the skins of the animals sacrificed as burnt-offerings, the first-fruits of grain and other produce of the earth (*tĕrūmāh*) and of dough (*ḥallāh*), the firstborn of cattle (or the money equivalent), the five shekels ransom money for human firstborn, part of the proceeds of sheep-shearing and a large number of occasional dues.[37] The tithe (a ten per cent. income tax) was allotted mainly to the Levites, the non-priestly Temple servants; they paid one tenth of it to the priests.[38] The tithe of Deuteronomy (14:22ff; 26:12ff) was at this time interpreted as a second tithe (which it was not originally), to be expended on animals slaughtered for ordinary use (as distinct from those slaughtered for sacrifice), of which the priests received certain portions (Deut. 18:3).[39]

The chief priests increasingly appropriated the lion's share of these perquisites and emoluments for themselves; this tendency

[34] Neh. 10:34; Josephus, *BJ* ii, 425; *Megillat Ta'anit* 11; Mishnah, *Ta'anit* 4:5, 8.
[35] Like the gold and silver donated by Alexander of Alexandria (Philo's brother) to adorn the Temple gates (Josephus, *BJ* v, 205). See p. 51, n. 24.
[36] Of these thirteen containers seven were for various legal dues and six for voluntary gifts (Mishnah, *Sheqalim* 6:1, 5).
[37] Most of these provisions are laid down in the priestly legislation of the Pentateuch.   [38] See p. 348.   [39] See Mishnah, *Ma'aśer Shenī.*

reached its peak, as we have seen, in the high-priesthood of Ananias son of Nedebaeus, when many of the ordinary priests were reduced to desperate straits.[40]

3

The Temple represented the heart of Jewish religious life while it remained standing, but it could not play the part in the regular religious life of most Jews that it had done in King Josiah's day, when Jerusalem, where he centralized the national worship, was within manageable distance for everyone in the kingdom of Judah. The Jews of the dispersion in particular could pay only occasional visits to the Temple. The centre of their ordinary religious and community life was the synagogue.

The origins of the synagogue are obscure,[41] but it is reasonable to look for them in the circumstances of the exile and its aftermath. How did the exiled Jews preserve their religious loyalty, to a point where those who ultimately returned from exile considered 'the people of the land' too lax or syncretistic in their practice to merit participation in the rebuilding of the Temple? If in their exile they met together for mutual encouragement, to recite appointed prayers and sing the songs of Zion even in a foreign land, this would constitute a synagogue in embryo at least. The synagogue developed throughout the post-exilic centuries and became an invariable feature of Jewish life not only in the Diaspora but in Palestine and even in Jerusalem itself. There on sabbaths and festivals services of worship were held in which the prayers and praises of the Temple services were repeated; but whereas in the Temple these prayers and praises were adjuncts to the sacrifices, in the non-sacrificial liturgy of the synagogue they constituted the indispensable elements. In addition, place was provided in the synagogue service for the reading and exposition of the Law. The Law was read through consecutively—according to a yearly cycle in the synagogues east of Palestine, according to a triennial cycle in the lands farther west.[42]

[40] See pp. 65, 348.

[41] The earliest literary reference to synagogues may be Psalm 74:8 (frequently held to be of Maccabaean date): 'they have burned all the meeting places of God (*mōʿăḏē ʾĒl*) in the land'.

[42] Cf. A. Büchler, 'The Reading of the Law and Prophets in a Triennial Cycle', *JQR* 5 (1892-3), pp. 420-68; 6 (1893-4), pp. 1-73; J. Mann, *The*

In Palestine and the east the reading of the Hebrew text was accompanied by an oral rendering (a *targum*) in Aramaic; in the Greek-speaking provinces of the west the Greek version popularly called the Septuagint was used.[43] The lesson from the Pentateuch was followed each sabbath by a lesson from the Prophets (a *haphṭarah*); the prophetic lessons, however, were not read in consecutive order, but each of them was chosen because of some link with the appointed Pentateuchal lesson. Some details of two synagogue services are given in the Lukan writings of the New Testament—one in Luke 4:16ff, where on a sabbath day in Nazareth Jesus stands to read the second lesson (the opening clauses of Isaiah 61) and sits down to expound it, the other in Acts 13:14ff, where in the synagogue of Pisidian Antioch Paul and Barnabas are invited by the 'rulers of the synagogue' to give a word of exhortation' after the reading of the two lessons and Paul stands up to address the congregation.[44]

A synagogue service at this time began with the call to worship and the recitation of the *Shema'* and associated benedictions, together with the Decalogue;[45] it continued with the appointed prayers and benedictions, the reading of the law and the prophets, a 'word of exhortation' or exposition, and concluded with a blessing.[46] Though a general pattern could no doubt be discerned in synagogue services throughout the Jewish world, there was considerable variation; Israel Abrahams could speak of 'the freedom of the synagogue'.[47] But the general sequence of the synagogue service had an importance beyond the confines of Jewish history; it in-

---

Bible as Read and Preached in the Old Synagogue (Cincinnati, 1940); A. Guilding, *The Fourth Gospel and Jewish Worship* (Oxford, 1960).

[43] Greek would be used also in the Hellenistic synagogues of Palestine, such as the Jerusalem synagogue of the Freedmen from Cyrene, Alexandria, Cilicia and Asia where Stephen debated with his opponents (Acts 6:9); indeed, the fact that Greek was the language of these synagogues may have been a principal reason for their members being designated Hellenists (see pp. 217f).

[44] See p. 273.

[45] The recitation of the decalogue was later discontinued. Cf. TB *Berakah* 3c; C. W. Dugmore, *The Influence of the Synagogue upon the Divine Office* (Oxford, 1944), pp. 21f; M. Simon, 'The Ancient Church and Rabbinical Tradition' in *Holy Book and Holy Tradition*, ed. F. F. Bruce and E. G. Rupp (Manchester, 1968), p. 110. See p. 388.   [46] Cf. Mishnah, *Megillah* 4:3.

[47] *Studies in Pharisaism and the Gospels* 1 (Cambridge, 1917), pp. 1ff.

fluenced to some extent the order of early Christian worship.[48] Invocation, prayer, thanksgiving, scripture reading, exhortation, blessing have from the beginning been integral to the Christian liturgy, although the central place is given to the distinctively Christian ordinance of the Eucharist.

The synagogues throughout the world brought the knowledge of Israel's God and Israel's religion to all the Gentile cities in which there were Jewish communities. 'From early generations Moses has had in every city those who preach him, for he is read every sabbath in the synagogues' (Acts 15:21). The picture given in the Acts of the Apostles, of Paul and his colleagues making for the synagogue in each new city they came to, and using it as their base of operations as long as they were permitted, harmonizes perfectly with the picture given by archaeology and literary and epigraphic evidence. Even Athens, which Jewish residents would probably have found less congenial than many Greek cities, had its synagogue, according to Acts 17:17, and evidently some Athenians were sufficiently attracted by Jewish worship to attend it regularly as 'God-fearers'. Philippi appears to have been an exception: according to the most probable reading of Acts 16:13[49] Paul and three companions, finding no regular synagogue there, went outside the city on the sabbath to 'a place where prayer was habitually offered' on the riverside according to the Jewish custom and 'sat down and spoke to the women who had come together'. This seems to mean that, in the absence of a sufficient number of Jewish men (ten of whom must be present before a synagogue congregation can be properly constituted), some women—Jewesses and God-fearers—came together and said the appointed prayers for the sabbath. Although they could not form a synagogue, they did form the nucleus of the Christian church in Philippi. The quorum for a church was 'two or three' (Matt. 18:20), much smaller than a Jewish *minyān*,[50] and so far as the privileges of church membership were concerned, Paul himself laid it down that in Christ there was 'neither male nor female', just

[48] Cf. C. W. Dugmore, *op. cit.*

[49] The evidence of Codd. אAB suggests that the Alexandrian reading ἐνομίζομεν προσευχὴν εἶναι ('we thought there was a prayer-house') is a revision of an earlier text which is probably preserved in the Byzantine reading ἐνομίζετο προσευχὴ εἶναι ('prayer was wont to be made', AV).

[50] See p. 119.

as there was 'neither Jew nor Greek, . . . neither slave nor free' (Gal. 3:28).[51]

The narrative of Acts speaks of synagogues also in Damascus, Cyprus, Iconium, Thessalonica, Beroea, Corinth and Ephesus.[52] In Rome we have inscriptional evidence for eleven synagogues,[53] most of which appear to have been on the right bank of the Tiber, where Philo informs us the Jewish quarter was.[54] As at Corinth,[55] there was a 'synagogue of the Hebrews', perhaps the earliest of the synagogues of Rome. Some were named after patrons, like the synagogues of the Augustenses (who claimed the emperor as their patron) and of the Agrippenses (after the emperor's friend and adviser Agrippa). Others bear the names of the areas from which their congregations came—the synagogues of the Suburenses (called after the Subura, a slum on the slope of the Esquiline hill) and of the Campenses (who presumably lived around the Campus Martius). No remains of any of the Roman synagogues have been identified, although in 1963 there was excavated at Ostia (the seaport of Rome at the mouth of the Tiber) a synagogue of the fourth century A.D., erected on an earlier foundation of the late first century A.D. which also proved to be a synagogue.[56]

4

When Paul rose to speak in the synagogue at Pisidian Antioch, he addressed the congregation as 'Men of Israel and you that fear God' (Acts 13:16). In many synagogues the congregation would include not only Jews and proselytes (converts from paganism to Judaism) but God-fearers—Gentiles who were loosely attached to the Jewish worship and way of life without going so far as to 'take upon themselves the yoke of the kingdom of heaven' by being in-

---

[51] It is tempting to suppose that Paul is here denying the threefold privilege possessed by the pious Jew who in the course of his morning prayers thanks God for not making him a Gentile, a slave or a woman (cf. S. Singer, ed., *Authorised Daily Prayer Book* [London, 1939], pp. 5f)—if this thanksgiving can be dated so early as A.D. 50.

[52] Acts 9:2, 20; 13:5; 14:1; 17:1, 10; 18:4ff, 26; 19:8.

[53] Cf. Schürer, *HJP* II. ii, pp. 247ff; H. J. Leon, *The Jews of Ancient Rome*, pp. 135ff.   [54] Philo, *Legatio* 155.   [55] See p. 314.

[56] Cf. M. F. Squarciapino, 'The Synagogue at Ostia', *Archaeology* 16 (1963), pp. 194ff.

corporated as proselytes in the Jewish community. Since for men circumcision was normally involved in becoming a proselyte,[57] it is natural that more women than men should take the final step. Those who were content to remain God-fearers, no matter how great their devotion to Jewish ethical and religious practices or their generosity in giving to Jewish good causes, were nevertheless outsiders. Cornelius, the centurion of Caesarea, was 'a devout man who feared God with all his household, gave alms liberally to the [Jewish] people, and prayed to God constantly' (Acts 10:2), but he was still technically a pagan.

To such people in synagogue after synagogue the gospel made an instant appeal. Without requiring them to be circumcised or to submit to the distinctively Jewish features of the Mosaic law, it offered them salvation and membership in the people of God on the ground of faith, making no difference between them and believing Jews. Their adherence to Paul and other missionaries was frequently resented by the synagogue authorities, who naturally hoped that they, or at any rate their children, might be won to full membership in the commonwealth of Israel. As late as the beginning of the second century the Roman satirist Juvenal describes the process:[58] a father keeps the sabbath and refuses pork but remains a God-fearer; his son goes all the way, accepts circumcision and becomes a complete proselyte. But if such a father believed the gospel and so became a member of the Christian community, his family was lost to the synagogue.

The synagogue, then, provided the apostle of the Gentiles with a base of operations as he prosecuted his mission, and in one city after another it was in the God-fearing fringe of the synagogue congregation that he found the nucleus of the church.

One thing more must be said about the synagogue: when in A.D. 70 the Temple and its ritual came to an end, Judaism survived, because the institution on which its survival, and Jewish community life in general, depended was already well established. The Temple had outlived its usefulness; it was the synagogue that continued to

---

[57] In addition to a purifying bath and the offering of a sacrifice in the Temple at Jerusalem, both of which ceremonies were required of female proselytes. For the bath ('proselyte baptism'), see pp. 156, 266.

[58] *Satire* xiv, 96ff.

serve the most abiding interests of Judaism as it had already been
doing for generations.

5

In view of the important part played in the synagogue by the
reading and exposition of the sacred scriptures, it was necessary to
know which writings were included among these and which were
not. The final delimitation of the canon of Hebrew scripture, like
the standardization of its text, belongs to the period after A.D. 70 and
is traditionally associated with the establishment of the new rabbinical Sanhedrin at Jamnia under the leadership of Yoḥanan ben
Zakkai and his followers. Yet the main outlines of the canon appear
to have been widely accepted at the beginning of the Christian
era. The threefold division of the Hebrew Bible into the Law, the
Prophets and the Writings is attested as early as the time of the
grandson of Jesus ben Sira who, after migrating to Alexandria in
132 B.C., translated his grandfather's 'Wisdom' book (Ecclesiasticus)
from Hebrew into Greek and composed a preface for this Greek
version in which he describes his grandfather as a devoted student
of 'the law, the prophets and the other books of our fathers'. Indeed,
by the time when he wrote, it appears that the contents of 'the law
itself, the prophecies and the rest of the books' had already been
translated into Greek.

In the Gospels there is no hint of any difference between Jesus
and his theological opponents with regard to the limits of holy writ;
it was on its interpretation that they disagreed. Even if the reference in Luke 24:44 to 'the law of Moses and the prophets and the
psalms' is the Evangelist's formulation, it corresponds to the facts
of Jesus' ministry. Jesus' words about all the martyr blood shed since
the beginning of time, 'from the blood of Abel to the blood of
Zechariah, who perished between the altar and the sanctuary'
(Luke 11:51; cf. Matt. 23:35), are best understood if his Bible, like
the traditional Hebrew Bible, began with Genesis and ended with
Chronicles;[59] for as Abel is the first martyr to appear in this se-

[59] In the traditional order of the Hebrew Bible, the Law comprises the
Pentateuch, the Prophets comprise the four 'Former Prophets' (Joshua, Judges,

quence of books (Gen. 4:8), so Zechariah the priest (the son of Jehoiada) is the last (II Chron. 24:20–4).[60] It is difficult on any other basis to see why Zechariah should mark the end of the 'noble army of martyrs' as Abel marks the beginning. Chronologically there are later martyrs named in canonical scripture,[61] not to mention the martyrs under Antiochus IV[62] and others still more recent.[63]

What uncertainty there is attaches to a few documents in the third division, such as Ecclesiastes and Esther. It is possible that the Qumran community did not recognize Esther as a canonical book,[64] and there is no reference to it in the New Testament. Yet the rabbis of Jamnia were no innovators when their synod confirmed the inclusion of these books in the Bible. 'Its discussions have not so much dealt with acceptance of certain writings into the Canon, but rather with their right to remain there.'[65] When Josephus in his treatise *Against Apion* enumerates the sacred books of his people as twenty-two,[66] he probably is not dependent on the debates of Jamnia which were going on at the time of his writing, nor does the fact that his enumeration falls short of the traditional Jewish total of twenty-four mean that he excluded two books which Jamnia in-

---

Samuel, Kings), and the four 'Latter Prophets' (Isaiah, Jeremiah, Ezekiel, the Twelve), while the Writings begin with Psalms, Proverbs and Job, continue with the five *Megillot* ('rolls'), namely Song of Songs, Ruth, Lamentations, Ecclesiastes, Esther, and end with Daniel, Ezra-Nehemiah, Chronicles.
[60] Cf. TB *Sanhedrin* 96b. It is quite improbable that any other Zechariah is intended. 'Zechariah the son of Barachiah' (Matt. 23:35) is due to a confusion of the martyr son of Jehoiada with the later prophet Zechariah (Zech. 1:1); there is no reference here to Zechariah son of Baris, put to death by Zealots in A.D. 67–8 (Josephus, *BJ* iv, 335ff). A reference to Zechariah the father of John the Baptist is even more excluded; the legend of his assassination (Protevangel of James 23:1ff) is probably based on a misinterpretation of Luke 11:51.
[61] E.g. Uriah the prophet (Jer. 26:20ff).
[62] II Macc. 6:18–7:42; cf. Heb. 11:36ff.
[63] E.g. Onias the rain-bringer c. 66 B.C. (Josephus, *Ant.* xiv, 22ff).
[64] Esther is the only book of the Hebrew Bible not identified among the Qumran manuscripts; any inference drawn from its absence must suffer from the limitations of any argument from silence.
[65] A. Bentzen, *Introduction to the Old Testament*, i (Copenhagen, 1948), p. 31. For a fuller discussion see G. F. Moore, *Judaism in the First Centuries of the Christian Era*, i (Cambridge, Mass., 1927), pp. 238ff. The debate among the rabbis on the retention of Ezekiel probably had to do with its being read in synagogue; the canonicity of the Prophets, to which Ezekiel belongs, was by now too securely established to be reopened. [66] *Apion* i, 37–41.

cluded;[67] he simply adopts a different method of counting, following in large measure the arrangement of the Greek version which
he used.[68] In his earlier days in Palestine Josephus counted himself an adherent of the party of the Pharisees, and he probably held
the view current among them about the limits of the canon.

How far the Sadducees agreed with the Pharisees in this regard is
not certain. Hippolytus, Origen, Jerome and other early Christian
writers say that they acknowledged the Pentateuch only,[69] but
this is probably due to a misunderstanding of Josephus. When Josephus says that the Sadducees hold that only the written law is to be
observed, the Pentateuch (the written law) is not set over against
the prophetical books but against the oral regulations which the
Pharisees accepted as 'handed down by former generations and not
recorded in the laws of Moses'.[70]

It is sometimes suggested that when Jesus countered the Sadducean objection to the doctrine of resurrection by an appeal to the
Pentateuch (Exodus 3:6) rather than to such more 'obvious' passages as Isa. 26:19 ('Thy dead shall live, their bodies shall rise') or
Daniel 12:2 ('many of those who sleep in the dust of the earth shall
awake'), it was because the Sadducees did not accept the Prophets
or the Writings. We may indeed doubt whether they accepted the
book of Daniel, but Jesus, instead of quoting one or two of the
more conventional proof-texts, placed the whole matter on a firmer
basis by grounding the doctrine in the being and nature of God:
'He is not God of the dead, but of the living' (Mark 12:26f).

[67] To judge from his detailed reproduction of the story of Esther (*Ant.* xi,
184–296), he does not seem to have excluded this book. He probably treated
Ruth as an appendix to Judges and Lamentations to Jeremiah.
[68] There is no evidence of any authoritative delimitation of the Greek canon
among Alexandrian Jews. Philo's Bible, so far as the evidence indicates, had
substantially the same limits as the Hebrew Bible.
[69] Cf. Hippolytus, *Ref.* ix, 24; Origen, *c. Cels.* i, 49; Jerome, *Comm. on Matt.*
22:31f.   [70] *Ant.* xiii, 297.

THE SACRED YEAR IN ISRAEL

Hebrew name of month in post-exilic age	Gregorian equivalent	Day of Feast or Fast	Name of Feast or Fast
I Nisan	March–April	14	Passover
		15–21	Unleavened Bread
		17 (approx.)	Firstfruits
II Iyyar	April–May		
III Siwan	May–June	7 (approx.)	Feast of Weeks (Pentecost)
IV Tammuz	June–July		
V 'Ab	July–August	9	Fast for Destruction of Temple
VI 'Elul	Aug.–Sept.		
VII Tišri	Sept.–Oct.	1	New Year (Feast of Trumpets)
		10	Day of Atonement
		15–22	Sukkot (Tabernacles, Booths)
VIII Marḥešwan	Oct.–Nov.		
IX Kislew	Nov.–Dec.	25	Ḥanukkah (Dedication)
X Ṭebet	Dec.–Jan.		
XI Šebaṭ	Jan.–Feb.		
XII 'Adar	Feb.–March	14–15	Purim

12 John the Baptist

Of all the religious movements in Palestine on the eve of the coming of Christianity none is more directly relevant to Christianity itself than the ministry of John the Baptist. All four Gospels preface their narrative of the ministry of Jesus with a brief summary of the ministry of John,[1] and the evidence of Acts suggests that this reflects primitive Christian preaching. In Acts both Peter and Paul are represented as introducing their accounts of Jesus' activity with a reference to the baptism of John;[2] and when the question arises of filling the vacancy in the apostolic college created by the defection of Judas Iscariot, it is laid down that the man to be chosen must be one of those 'who have accompanied us during all the time that the Lord Jesus went in and out among us, beginning from the baptism of John' (Acts 1:21f).

John's place in the Gospels and Acts is due to the part that he played as Jesus' 'forerunner'; but his ministry made a deep, if short-lived, impression in its own right on many of the Palestinian Jews.

Outside the New Testament, our only reliable source of information about John is a passage in the *Antiquities* of Josephus, where the defeat of Herod Antipas by his outraged father-in-law Aretas IV is narrated.[3] Josephus goes on:

> Now some of the Jews thought that it was God who had destroyed Herod's army, and that it was a very just punishment to avenge John, surnamed the Baptist. John had been put to death by Herod, although he was a good man, who exhorted the Jews to practise virtue, to be just one to another and pious towards God, and to come together by baptism. Baptism, he taught, was acceptable to God provided that they underwent it not to procure remission of certain sins but for the purification of the body, if the soul had already been purified by righteousness. When the others gathered round John, greatly stirred as they

[1] Matt. 3:1–12; Mark 1:2–8; Luke 3:1–20; John 1:6–8, 19–36; 3:23–30.
[2] Acts 10:37; 13:24f.   [3] See p. 30.

listened to his words, Herod was afraid that his great persuasive power over men might lead to a rising, for they seemed ready to follow his counsel in everything. Accordingly he thought the best course was to arrest him and put him to death before he caused a riot, rather than wait until a revolt broke out and then have to repent of permitting such trouble to arise. Because of this suspicion on Herod's part, John was sent in chains to the fortress of Machaerus . . . and there put to death. The Jews therefore thought that the destruction of Herod's army was the punishment deliberately sent upon him by God to avenge John.[4]

According to Luke, John was a 'wonder-child', born to a priestly couple in their old age, who spent the years before he began his public ministry 'in the wilderness' (Luke 1:80)—presumably the wilderness of Judaea, since his parents' home was in the Judaean hill-country. Whether his wilderness life was solitary or spent in community with others we are not told. More especially since the discovery of the Qumran texts it has been frequently suggested that he was brought up in the Qumran community or in some similar Essene group.[5] This can be neither proved nor disproved. John's wilderness retreat would not have been far from Qumran, and a young man of priestly birth might have found something specially congenial in a movement which attached such importance to the maintenance of a pure priesthood.

But, whatever substance there may be in these speculations, the ministry by which John made his mark cannot be brought within an Essene framework. His ministry was distinctively a prophetic ministry. When 'the word of God came to John the son of Zechariah in the wilderness' (Luke 3:2), as it had come to many a prophet in earlier days, that word proclaimed the necessity for something different from the teaching or practice of Qumran.

[4] *Ant.* xviii, 116–19. The additional passage about John in the Slavonic (Old Russian) version of Josephus (11th–12th cent.), following *BJ* ii, 168, is too full of historical errors (e.g. Herodias's first husband is said to have been Philip the tetrarch) to receive serious consideration. Another addition in the Slavonic version, following *BJ* ii, 110, describes a wild man of the woods who flourished during the ethnarchate of Archelaus (4 B.C.–A.D. 6); R. Eisler identified him with John the Baptist (*The Messiah Jesus and John the Baptist* [London, 1931], pp. 223ff); he also identified John with the Teacher of Righteousness of the Zadokite document (*op. cit.*, pp. 254f, 575).

[5] Cf. W. H. Brownlee, 'John the Baptist in the New Light of Ancient Scrolls', *Interpretation* 9 (1955), pp. 71ff, reprinted in *The Scrolls and the New Testament*, ed. K. Stendahl (London, 1958), pp. 33ff; A. S. Geyser, 'The Youth of John the Baptist', *NovT* 1 (1956), pp. 70ff.

To John, as to the men of Qumran and other Essenes and related groups, the wilderness was the expected place of the divine epiphany.[6] But John chose for the inauguration of his ministry the most public part of the wilderness of Judaea, the crossing of the Jordan north of the Dead Sea, where traffic between Judaea and Peraea passed this way and that; and he addressed his message to all who would hear, including the 'men of the pit' from whom the pious sectaries of Qumran swore to keep aloof.[7] If John had previously been associated with a community like that of Qumran, now was the time to break with his former associates and follow a new path. The multitudes which flocked to the Jordan valley to hear him from all parts of Palestine did so because men recognized in his preaching a note of authority the like of which had not been heard in Israel for centuries: 'all held that John was a real prophet' (Mark 11:32). It is not as a disciple of any other Teacher of Righteousness, but as a new teacher of righteousness with his own following of disciples, that we know the historical John the Baptist.

John's preaching was eschatologically based. The day of judgement, he proclaimed, was about to dawn. The judgement would be executed by the 'Coming One', for whom John was preparing the way. The Coming One fulfils the function assigned to Daniel's 'one like a son of man' (Dan. 7:13ff), although John is not recorded as using the designation Son of Man. Yet, when the Fourth Evangelist records John as speaking of the pre-existence of the Coming One— 'He who comes after me ranks before me, for he was before me' (John 1:15, 30)—there may be some contact with the Son of Man of the *Similitudes of Enoch*, whose name was named in the presence of the Lord of Spirits before the sun and the stars were made (I Enoch 48:3).[8]

The Coming One would hew down all the fruitless trees—all those whose lives did not produce the fruits of righteousness. Or, to change the figure, he would treat the world as his threshing-floor, winnowing the wheat from the chaff. The wheat—the righteous— would be gathered into his granary, but the chaff, blown away by

[6] Cf. J. Steinmann, *St. John the Baptist and the Desert Tradition* (London, 1958); W. H. Brownlee, *The Meaning of the Qumran Scrolls for the Bible* (New York, 1964), pp. 112ff. For the Qumran use of Isa. 40:3 (applied to John the Baptist in Mark 1:3; John 1:23) see p. 104 above.

[7] *CD* vi, 14f.   [8] See p. 131.

the wind, would be swept up and burned. Therefore, let Israel repent. Before this coming judge the merits of the fathers would not avail: descent from Abraham was irrelevant. Nothing would meet the challenge of the hour, nothing would avert the wrath to come, but sincere repentance. And this repentance, to be effective, must be expressed by baptism.[9]

John's picture of the Coming One has also been compared with the Qumran expectation that at the end-time a man would appear in whom some of the community's most characteristic functions would be embodied—a man who in several respects resembles the Isaianic Servant of Yahweh:

> At that time God will purify by his truth all the deeds of a man, and will refine him for himself more than the sons of men, in order to destroy every evil spirit from the midst of his flesh and to cleanse him through the Spirit of holiness from all evil practices. He will sprinkle upon him the Spirit of truth as purifying water, so as to cleanse him from every false abomination and from being contaminated with the spirit of impurity, so that he may give to the upright insight into the knowledge of the Most High and into the wisdom of the sons of heaven, in order to make wise the perfect of way.[10]

This passage does not teach that the man who receives this special endowment of the Holy Spirit will himself baptize others with the Spirit, as John says the Coming One will do; but this is not the only respect in which John's prophetic insight goes beyond anything that was envisaged at Qumran.

The baptism of John was a new thing in Israel, although it had antecedents in some degree. Cleansing lustrations, by means of the water of purification[11] and otherwise, were prescribed in the Law,

---

[9] Cf. Matt. 3:7-12 // Luke 3:7-9, 16f.

[10] 1 QS iv, 20-2; W. H. Brownlee, 'The Servant of the Lord in the Qumran Scrolls', *BASOR* 135 (Oct. 1954), pp. 33ff (especially pp. 36f); J. P. Audet, 'Affinités littéraires et doctrinales du Manuel de Discipline', *RB* 60 (1953), pp. 41ff (especially p. 74); cf. J. A. T. Robinson, 'The Baptism of John and the Qumran Community', *HTR* 50 (1957), pp. 175ff (especially pp. 188f), reprinted in *Twelve New Testament Studies* (London, 1962), pp. 11ff (especially pp. 23f). But instead of 'a man' in the first clause of the quotation we should perhaps render the generic 'man', paralleled by 'some of the sons of men' in the next clause instead of 'more than the sons of men' (i.e. treating the preposition *min* as partitive, not comparative); in that case the passage may point to the fulfilment of the promise of the outpouring of the Spirit in Joel 2:28.   [11] See p. 58.

and in some pious communities the observance of such rites was intensified. The Pharisees attached great importance to frequent ablutions,[12] and some smaller and even more radical groups insisted on them to a point where they were characterized as 'daily bathers', 'morning bathers' and the like.[13]

A further analogy to John's baptism may be sought in the practice of Jewish proselyte baptism. A Gentile who was converted to Judaism had to be circumcised (if he was a male) and to offer a special sacrifice in the Temple (while it stood), and also to undergo a ceremonial bath. The date when this bath or self-baptism was instituted is disputed, but as it was a matter of debate between the school of Shammai and the school of Hillel it must have antedated the fall of Jerusalem and goes back at least to the beginning of the Christian era.[14] Some members of the school of Hillel went so far as to maintain—for the sake of the argument, but hardly in practice—that it was by this baptism rather than by circumcision that a Gentile became a Jew.[15]

In so far as proselyte baptism provides an analogy to John's baptism John was saying in effect to true-born Jews, proudly conscious of their descent from Abraham: 'Your impeccable pedigree is irrelevant in God's sight; if you wish to be enrolled in the new Israel of the age that is about to dawn, you must take the outside place, acknowledging that you are not better in his eyes than Gentiles, and you must enter the end-time community of his people by baptism, as they have to do.'

But John's baptism was distinctive in that he administered it to others, and in its eschatological significance. Ezekiel promised that, at the dawn of the new age, the God of Israel would purify his people from their defilement with clean water and give them a new heart and a new spirit—his own spirit.[16] It is probably this promise that underlies the words in John 3:5 about the new birth

---

[12] Cf. Mark 7:3f; C. G. Montefiore, *The Synoptic Gospels* (London, 1927[2]), i, pp. 133–44.   [13] See p. 120.

[14] See H. H. Rowley, 'Jewish Proselyte Baptism and the Baptism of John', *HUCA* 15 (1940), pp. 313ff, reprinted in *From Moses to Qumran* (London, 1963), pp. 211ff.

[15] Cf. the *baraita* (extra-Mishnaic tradition from the generation after A.D. 70) in TB *Yebamot* 46a (see Rowley, *From Moses to Qumran*, p. 216).

[16] Ezek. 36:25ff.

'of water and spirit'—words which in their original context may have
borne some relation to John's baptism. Those who heeded John's call
to repentance and accepted baptism at his hands would form the
righteous remnant of the end-time, the 'people prepared' whom
John was charged 'to make ready for the Lord' (Luke 1:17). This
is probably the point of Josephus's statement that John called upon
his hearers 'to come together by baptism'.[17] When, however, Josephus says that John's baptism procured bodily cleansing for those
whose souls had already been purified by righteousness, he may be
influenced by what he knew of the significance of the Essene washings: at Qumran it was emphasized that all the washings in the
world would never convey cleansing to a man whose heart remained stubborn against God.[18] John indeed would have cordially
agreed that the baptism which he administered availed nothing for
any who accepted it without heart repentance, but Mark's description of his baptism as 'a baptism of repentance for the forgiveness of
sins' (Mark 1:4) is consistent with all the evidence we have for
John's ministry.

Those who confessed their sins and received John's baptism in
token of their repentance were required to 'bear fruits that befit
repentance' (Luke 3:8), to live lives which accorded with the 'way
of righteousness' inculcated by John (Matt. 21:32).

This way of righteousness did not differ essentially from that on
which the earlier prophets insisted—to do justice, to love kindness,
and to walk humbly with God.[19] John taught his hearers to share
their food and clothes with those in greater need than themselves;
he did not command tax-collectors to abandon their calling but forbade them to exact a little extra for themselves over and above the
appointed taxes; he did not command soldiers to give up their military career but told them to be content with their rations and pay
and not to extort money from civilians by violence or by threats of
denunciation.[20] (These soldiers were probably auxiliary forces
under the command of the procurator of Judaea; the suggestion
that they were members of Jewish Zealot bands, to whom John
acted as field-chaplain, involves a wholesale reading into our basic

[17] Josephus, *Ant.* xviii, 117; in the phrase βαπτισμῷ συνιέναι the dative
probably denotes means rather than purpose.
[18] 1 QS iii, 4–6.   [19] Micah 6:8.   [20] Luke 3:12–14.

texts of something that is not there;[21] Josephus, moreover, would not have described an insurgent field-chaplain as 'a good man'!)

While the common people, and even some who were classed as social outcasts, were greatly moved by his preaching, and sought baptism at his hands in great numbers, the religious leaders of the nation, the teachers of the law and especially the Pharisees, remained unimpressed.[22] They had their own ideas of what constituted the way of righteousness, and would not recognize in John's baptism any improvement on their own ritual washings.

Most of John's hearers went home after listening to him, to await the advent of the Coming One. But some stayed with him and became his disciples.[23] How numerous John's disciples were we cannot be sure, but they formed a recognizable community, comparable in this respect to the disciples of the great Pharisaic teachers and, later, to the disciples of Jesus. John taught them a form of prayer[24] in which, we may be sure, the eschatological note of his preaching was struck, and evidently imposed a régime of fasting on them as a periodic duty.[25] But it is unlikely that he required them to share the full vigour of his own asceticism, for he wore a coat of camel's hair, and, eschewing bread and wine, ate such food as the wilderness provided—locusts and the honey of wild bees.[26] The fact that he had no objection to eating locusts shows that his asceticism did not involve vegetarianism as a principle of life, although the Encratites in the second century made him a near-vegetarian like themselves by emending the locusts and honey to 'milk and honey', the reading of Tatian's *Diatessaron*.[27]

From the New Testament writers' point of view, the climax of John's ministry was his baptism of Jesus, who came from his Galilaean home at Nazareth to the Jordan valley and asked John to baptize him. This event marks also the beginning of Jesus' public ministry. Why Jesus should have sought baptism at John's hands was a problem which some early Christian writers found difficulty

---

[21] Cf. R. Eisler, *The Messiah Jesus and John the Baptist* (London, 1931), pp. 245ff.   [22] Cf. Luke 7:29f.
[23] Cf. Mark 6:29; John 1:35; 3:25f.   [24] Luke 11:1.
[25] Mark 2:18.   [26] Mark 1:6; Matt. 11:18 // Luke 7:33.
[27] In the *Gospel of the Ebionites* (*ap.* Epiphan. *Pan.* 30. 13. 4f) the 'locusts' (ἀκρίδες) are transformed into 'pancakes' (ἐγκρίδες).

in explaining.[28] It is most probable that Jesus recognized John as a prophet and acknowledged his baptismal ministry as a work of God. We may go further and say that he knew that with John's preaching the hour had struck for his own mission; hence he associated himself in the most public and unmistakable way with John's ministry by accepting baptism at his hands: 'we do well to conform in this way with all that God requires' (Matt. 3:15, NEB).

If such was Jesus' conviction, it was more than confirmed by what he experienced as he came up out of the river.[29] Nor is there any good reason to doubt that John for his part thenceforth recognized in Jesus the Coming One of whom he had spoken. The message which he later sent to Jesus from prison, 'Are you the Coming One, or must we look for someone else?' (Matt. 11:3 // Luke 7:20), does not suggest that he had not previously looked on Jesus as the Coming One. It suggests rather that, having once acknowledged him as such, he was now beginning to entertain doubts, because the reports brought to him about Jesus' Galilaean activity bore but little resemblance to his own description of the ministry of judgement which the Coming One would discharge.

John continued his ministry after the baptism of Jesus not only in the Jordan valley but in other parts of the country. The Fourth Evangelist preserves a brief but valuable record of a phase of John's baptismal ministry 'at Aenon near Salim', which is most probably to be identified with the Wadi Far'ah, east of Shechem, for, in the Evangelist's words, there is 'much water there' (John 3:23).[30] This means that he preached and baptized in the region of Samaria. Even if the Samaritans were ceremonially unclean from the viewpoint of 'normative Judaism', it would not follow that Jewish nonconformists took the same line; and in fact recent discovery and research have pointed to a considerable degree of affinity between

[28] Cf. Matt. 3:14f. In the *Gospel of the Nazarenes* (*ap.* Jerome, *adu. Pelag.* iii, 2), 'the mother of the Lord and his brothers said to him, "John the Baptist is baptizing for the remission of sins; let us go and be baptized by him". But he said to them, "Wherein have I sinned that I should go and be baptized by him?—unless what I have said is (a sin of) ignorance".'

[29] See p. 167.

[30] Cf. W. F. Albright, 'Recent Discoveries in Palestine and the Gospel of St. John', in *The Background of the New Testament and its Eschatology*, ed. W. D. Davies and D. Daube (Cambridge, 1954), pp. 153ff; *The Archaeology of Palestine* (Harmondsworth, 1960), pp. 247f.

certain aspects of Samaritan teaching and of Jewish noncon-
formity.[31]

While John was active there, Jesus remained in Judaea and carried on a brief baptismal ministry of his own. Some young men who
had formerly been John's disciples had by now attached themselves
to Jesus, and a not unnatural tension developed between them and
their former associates who still regarded themselves as disciples of
John. Learning that this tension was being exploited by some Pharisees to drive a wedge between himself and John, Jesus withdrew to
the north.[32]

John's Samaritan ministry probably did not last long, but it laid
the foundation for further important developments in that area in
the next few decades, of which we are given hints in the brief accounts of the ministries there of Jesus (John 4:30ff) and Philip (Acts
8:5ff).[33]

One part of Palestine which John does not appear to have visited
was Galilee. Yet it was at the hands of Herod Antipas, tetrarch of
Galilee, that he met his death. Antipas's tetrarchy included not only
Galilee but Peraea, and John's ministry in the Jordan valley was
carried on on the Peraean bank of the river as well as on the west
bank (John 1:28). John, if we may so reconstruct the course of
events, returned from Aenon to Peraea, and there he was arrested
by the tetrarch's orders. Antipas might well be afraid, as Josephus
says, that John's ability to gather multitudes around him would
lead to a revolt; the Synoptic Evangelists add more precisely that
John denounced Antipas's marriage to his sister-in-law Herodias.[34]
The law of Lev. 18:16 and 20:21 forbade a man to marry his
brother's wife. The law applied even when the brother had died;
there was deep disapproval several years earlier when Antipas's
elder brother Archelaus had married Glaphyra, widow of the ill-
starred Alexander, son of Herod the Great and Mariamme. (The
levirate law of Deut. 25:5–10 was an exception, which covered only
the case where the deceased brother had left no children.) It was

[31] Cf. M. Black, *The Scrolls and Christian Origins* (London, 1961), pp. 54ff.
[32] John 1:35ff; 3:25f; 4:1ff.
[33] Cf. J. A. T. Robinson, 'The "Others" of John 4:38', in *Twelve New Testament Studies*, pp. 61ff; a different point of view is expressed in O. Cullmann,
'Samaria and the Origins of the Christian Mission', in *The Early Church* (London, 1956), pp. 185ff.
[34] Mark 6:18; Luke 3:19.

an even more blatant breach of the law when the brother whose wife the woman had formerly been was still alive.[35]

John's denunciation of the marriage did not simply affect the private life of Antipas and Herodias; it had political implications, as we have seen already.[36] The allegiance of Antipas's subjects could well be alienated from a ruler who was denounced by a prophet for a flagrant breach of the holy law. It was unsafe to leave John at large, so he was seized and imprisoned at the Peraean fortress of Machaerus. Antipas was unwilling to proceed to more extreme measures, and for a time John was able to communicate with the outside world through his disciples, as when he sent two of them to interview Jesus and report on his activity in Galilee. According to Mark, it was Herodias who ultimately encompassed John's death, against the better judgement of her husband, who 'went in awe of John' and 'liked to listen to him, although the listening left him greatly perplexed' (Mark 6:20, NEB).

The memory of John remained for many years with those who had heard him; a quarter of a century after his death we learn of a group of people as far away as Ephesus who claimed to have been baptized with John's baptism.[37] Later still in the same area it has been inferred that there was a 'Johannite' group against whom the Fourth Evangelist polemicized, but there is no independent evidence for its existence. John's disciples probably survived as a self-conscious community for a generation or two, apart from those who, recognizing in Jesus the Coming One of whom John spoke, became disciples of Jesus. The connexion between John's disciples and various schismatic Jewish groups of which some information is preserved by Christian writers such as Justin, Hegesippus, Hippolytus and Epiphanius, is difficult to establish. Still more problematical is the historic connexion between John's followers and the Gnostic sect of Mandaeans, surviving to this day in Iraq. The Mandaeans hold John in high veneration, but all the information about him contained in their literature seems to be derived from the Gos-

[35] As Herodias's first husband was (Josephus, *Ant.* xviii, 136).
[36] See p. 28.
[37] Acts 19:1–7; but they are not called disciples of John. When Luke introduces them as 'some disciples', he intends us, in accordance with his regular use of 'disciple(s)' in the absolute, to understand that they were disciples of Jesus (cf. A. Ehrhardt, *The Framework of the New Testament Stories* [Manchester, 1964], p. 159).

pels, more particularly from Luke, mediated through some form of Syriac-speaking Christianity which had been influenced by Marcionism and Manichaeism.[38]

In the eyes of Jesus, John's ministry marked the end of the era of the law and the prophets; there followed the new era of the kingdom of God on the threshold of which John stood as the last and greatest in the long succession of those who foresaw and foretold its advent (Luke 16:16). And it is with Jesus that the last word about John may safely be left: 'What did you go out into the wilderness to behold? A reed shaken by the wind? What then did you go out to see? A man clothed in soft raiment? . . . What then did you go out to see? A prophet? Yes, I tell you, and more than a prophet. . . . I tell you, among those born of women none is greater than John; yet he who is least in the kingdom of God is greater than he' (Luke 7:24–8).[39]

[38] Cf. F. C. Burkitt, 'The Mandaeans', *JTS* 29 (1928), pp. 228ff; *Church and Gnosis* (Cambridge, 1932), pp. 100ff; C. Colpe, 'Mandäer', *RGG*[3] iv (Tübingen, 1961), cols. 709–12.

[39] See the excellent summing up of John's significance by T. W. Manson in *The Servant-Messiah* (Cambridge, 1953), p. 47; also his essay, 'John the Baptist', *BJRL* 36 (1953–4), pp. 395ff.

13 Jesus and the Kingdom of God

1

Apart from the New Testament writings and later writings dependent on these, our sources of information about the life and teaching
of Jesus are scanty and problematic. So far as the wider Roman
world is concerned, this is not surprising. Perhaps the situation can
be illustrated by an episode of more recent times.

In the closing years of British rule in India some trouble was being caused in the Waziristan section of the North-West Frontier
by a self-styled 'Champion of Islam' named Haji Mirza Ali Khan,
Fakir of Ipi. He figured from time to time in the British and Indian
press when he was engaged in upsetting the *pax Britannica* in those
parts. Then for years he faded into oblivion, until his death was
briefly announced in April, 1960.[1] It is unlikely that he will play a
prominent part in histories of the twentieth century.

The Fakir of Ipi was a holy man, and his devotees no doubt
thought him a very important person indeed. If they had begun to
propagate a cult in which he played a central part; if their mission
had proved unexpectedly successful; if it had led to riots in Karachi
and Delhi; if it had been carried to London and begun to cause
trouble in the Indian and Pakistani communities of Britain—then
the name of the Fakir of Ipi would have become familiar and ultimately found its way into historical writings. But such a process
would require a little time.

Similarly in A.D. 30 the name and activity of Jesus of Nazareth
would have meant no more to people living at the heart of the
Roman world than the Fakir of Ipi meant to people in England. A
religious leader who won a following by his claim to be a king, and
who was conveniently executed, was no exceptional phenomenon
in the Palestine of those days. But when his followers, claiming that

[1] See *Illustrated London News*, April 30, 1960.

he had risen from the dead, began to proclaim him as the Deliverer
for whom the world was waiting, when their mission met with as-
tonishing success, when it was carried not only to Antioch and
Alexandria, but to Rome itself, and led to riots there, then the name
of Christ (as the Gentiles called him)[2] and of his followers the
Christians became familiar at the heart of the Roman Empire. But
this process required a little time. And, while Christ and the Christians did ultimately come to be mentioned in Roman historical writing, the first Roman 'literature' in which we might expect to find
any reference to them would be what we should call the police
news. This is what in fact we find.

The introduction of Christianity into the Jewish community at
Rome appears to have led to rioting in that community about A.D.
49—rioting which Suetonius, writing about A.D. 120, ascribes to the
instigation of 'Chrestus'.[3] The significance of this reference will be
discussed more fully in a later chapter; it was probably to 'police
records' that Suetonius owed it.[4]

Suetonius's contemporary, Tacitus, writing his *Roman Annals* between A.D. 115 and 117, mentions the Great Fire of Rome in A.D. 64
and Nero's attempt to fasten the blame for it on the Christians.
Then, to explain the origin of this name, he says that they got it
'from Christus, who was executed by sentence of the procurator
Pontius Pilate when Tiberius was emperor. That checked the pernicious superstition for a short time [he goes on], but it broke out
afresh—not only in Judaea, where the plague first arose, but in
Rome itself, where all the horrible and shameful things in the world
collect and find a home.'[5]

When police news becomes sufficiently significant it provides
material for history, and this is illustrated by these words of Tacitus. Not only was the action of Nero's police against the Christians
of Rome worth recording (the more so in view of the dimensions
to which Christianity had grown by the time of Trajan,[6] under
whom Tacitus wrote), but the police action which had been carried out over thirty years previously, when Pilate governed Judaea,
now acquired a significance which no Roman could have foreseen

---

[2] Gk. χριστός, the equivalent of Heb. *māšiaḥ*, was originally applied to Jesus
as a title ('the Anointed One'), but soon came to be used as his name.
[3] Suetonius, *Claudius* 25.   [4] See p. 297.
[5] Tac. *Ann.* xv, 44.   [6] Emperor, A.D. 98–117.

in A.D. 30. It is unlikely that Tacitus acquired his accurate information about the execution of Christ from Christians (in view of the contemptuous and hostile tone which he adopts in speaking of them); if some account of the matter survived to his day in official archives, a man of his standing could have had access to it.

Another contemporary of Suetonius and Tacitus, the younger Pliny, supplies a sort of 'police record' of his own in the report which, as proconsul of Bithynia about A.D. 112, he sent to the Emperor Trajan about the advance of Christianity in his province.[7] In the course of his report he tells how some Christians, who had turned 'emperor's evidence', revealed what went on at Sunday meetings of Christians—things harmless enough in themselves, though perversely superstitious in Pliny's eyes, including the reciting of an antiphonal hymn 'to Christ as God' (or 'to Christ as to a god'). These are the earliest references to Christ in pagan literature.[8]

The references to him in Jewish traditions of the Tannaitic period (c. A.D. 70–200) amount to this: Jesus of Nazareth was a transgressor in Israel, who practised magic, scorned the words of the wise, led the people astray, and said he had come neither to take away from the law of Moses nor to add to it (or, according to another reading, not to take away from the law of Moses but to add to it). He was hanged on Passover Eve for heresy and for misleading the people. His disciples (of whom five are named—Mattai, Naqai, Neṣer, Buni and Todah) are said to have healed the sick in his name. This account is much what one might expect from the heirs of Jesus' theological opponents as they are portrayed in the Gospels.[9]

Two earlier Jewish references to him appear in the manuscript

[7] Plin. *Ep.* x, 96. See pp. 423ff.

[8] More problematical are the references to Jesus in the lost history of Thallus (c. A.D. 52), quoted by Julius Africanus (F. Jacoby, *Die Fragmente der griechischen Historiker* II B [Berlin, 1929], §256), and in the letter of Mara bar Serapion to his son some time after A.D. 73 (preserved in a seventh-century British Museum Syriac MS., Additional 14, 658).

[9] The rabbinical references are conveniently summarized in J. Klausner, *Jesus of Nazareth* (London, 1929), pp. 18–47; cf. T. W. Manson, *Studies in the Gospels and Epistles* (Manchester, 1962), pp. 16ff. The most important single passage relating to Jesus in rabbinical literature is TB *Sanhedrin* 43a, where a *baraita* tells how 'they hanged Yeshu on Passover Eve' after a herald for forty days had vainly called on anyone who would speak in his defence to come forward and do so.

tradition of the *Antiquities* of Josephus (composed *c.* A.D. 93). In
one of these James of Jerusalem ('James the Just' of later Christian
writers) is described as 'the brother of Jesus the so-called Christ';[10]
the other, a paragraph about Jesus himself, was evidently modified
and interpolated at an early stage in the course of transmission to
suit Christian tastes.[11] It cannot therefore be adduced with confidence as evidence, but in the light of its context, where various
Jewish troubles in the principate of Tiberius are described, it may
originally have been worded something like this:

> About this time there arose a source of further troubles[12] in one
> Jesus, a wise man[13] and a wonder-worker, a teacher of those who gladly
> welcome strange things.[14] He led away many Jews, and also many of
> the Gentiles. This man was the so-called Christ.[15] When Pilate, acting
> on information supplied by the chief men among us, condemned him
> to the cross, those who had attached themselves to him at the first did
> not abandon their allegiance,[16] and the tribe of Christians, which has
> taken this name from him, is not extinct even today.[17]

[10] *Ant.* xx, 200.

[11] *Ant.* xviii, 63f. See J. Klausner, *Jesus of Nazareth*, pp. 55ff.

[12] 'A source of fresh troubles', which fits Josephus's context, is a conjectural
supplementation of R. Eisler, *The Messiah Jesus and John the Baptist* (London,
1931), pp. 50f.

[13] The extant text adds 'if indeed we should call him a man'.

[14] The extant text reads 'welcome the truth' (ΤΑΛΗΘΗ, here emended to
ΤΑΑΗΘΗ).

[15] The extant text reads 'This man was the Christ'. The phrase 'the so-called
Christ' appears in the reference to James in *Ant.* xx, 200 and is supported here
by Jerome's reading *'credebatur esse Christus'* (*De uiris illustribus*, 13). According to Origen (*contra Cels.*, i, 47), Josephus did not believe in Jesus as
the Christ—not that Origen's testimony on this point is necessary.

[16] The extant text adds 'for he appeared to them on the third day alive again,
the divinely-inspired prophets having spoken these and thousands of other
wonderful things about him'.

[17] The additional references to Jesus in the Slavonic version of Josephus's
Jewish War (see p. 153, n. 4) represent interesting Christian traditions but
have no substantial claim to authenticity. Of these additions two may be mentioned. One, appearing after *BJ* ii, 174, is an amplification of the passage in
Ant. xviii, 63f. It includes a summary of the trial and execution of Jesus according to which Pilate (grateful to Jesus because he had healed his wife)
refuses to convict him, but allows 'the teachers of the law' to work their will
on him; they accordingly crucify him. This exoneration of Pilate at the expense
of the Jewish leaders is a familiar Christian tendency. In the course of Josephus's
description of the Temple another reference to Jesus is inserted in *BJ* v, 195;
after his account of the notices warning Gentiles not to trespass in the inner
precincts we are told that 'above these inscriptions a fourth inscription was
hung in the same letters [Greek, Latin and Hebrew], which said: "Jesus, a

Of independent Christian information about Jesus, beyond what the New Testament writers supply, there is nothing apart from a number of sayings attributed to him. The best-known collection of these belongs to the second century, and is extant in a fourth-century Coptic translation from the Greek, the *Gospel of Thomas* discovered about 1945 along with many other documents, mostly Gnostic in character, near the site of the ancient Chenoboskion, in Upper Egypt. Some of these, unparalleled in the New Testament texts, may well be genuine, but to decide on the authenticity of any given one is a precarious critical undertaking, since for the most part they appear with no life-context.[18]

2

We are thus thrown back on the New Testament writings as our primary documents, and we may congratulate ourselves on having such a well-tested and thoroughly analysed body of source-material at our disposal.[19]

Jesus' first public appearance was at his baptism by John in the river Jordan, an event which is commonly, and rightly, regarded as marking the beginning of his ministry. According to Mark's account, when he came up from the water, 'immediately he saw the heavens opened and the Spirit descending upon him like a dove;

king who did not reign, was crucified by the Jews because he foretold the destruction of the city and desolation of the Temple".' Here too the statement that Jesus 'was crucified by the Jews' cannot be ascribed to Josephus. The wording of the inscription in its Greek form, ΙΗΣΟΥΣ ΒΑΣΙΛΕΥΣ ΟΥ ΒΑΣΙΛΕΥΣΑΣ ('Jesus a king who did not reign') supplied the title of R. Eisler's great German work (Heidelberg, 1928-9) which used these Slavonic additions, appropriately emended, as source-material for his reconstruction of Christian origins; cf. the abridged English edition, *The Messiah Jesus and John the Baptist* (London, 1931), and the critique by J. W. Jack, *The Historic Christ* (London, 1933).

[18] See A. Guillaumont *et alii* (edd.), *The Gospel according to Thomas* (Leiden, 1959); R. McL. Wilson (ed.), *New Testament Apocrypha* i (London, 1963), pp. 511ff.

[19] The NT writings were not, of course, designed as historians' source-material, and apart from Luke-Acts are not written in historiographical style; but historians will not be deterred on that account from using them as source-material; nor will they be intimidated by theologians who assure them that their task is impossible and illegitimate. See F. F. Bruce, 'History and the Gospel' in C. F. H. Henry (ed.), *Jesus of Nazareth: Saviour and Lord* (London, 1966), pp. 87ff.

and a voice came from heaven, "Thou art my beloved Son; with thee I am well pleased"' (Mark 1:10f). The rent heavens denote a divine manifestation, as in Isa. 64:1, 'O that thou wouldst rend the heavens and come down. . . !' The descent of the dove suggests a special endowment of the Spirit of God for a distinctive ministry, like that of the 'shoot from the stump of Jesse' in Isa. 11:1ff ('and the Spirit of Yahweh shall rest upon him') or of the Servant introduced in Isa. 42:1ff, of whom Yahweh says: 'I have put my Spirit upon him'. Yahweh's introduction of his Servant in the latter passage seems to lie behind the language of the heavenly voice at Jesus' baptism, which is probably to be understood as a *baṭ qōl*, an 'echo' of the divine utterance from heaven.[20] If the acclamation 'Thou art my Son,' addressed to Yahweh's Anointed in Psalm 2:7, marks Jesus out as the Davidic Messiah, the following words are reminiscent of Isa. 42:1, 'my chosen, in whom my soul delights', and give notice that Jesus is to discharge his messianic function in terms of the Servant's career.[21]

That the implication of the heavenly voice is not merely part of Mark's representation of Jesus' ministry, but deeply influenced that ministry as a historic fact, accounts best for the following course of events. Jesus recognized in the vision and the voice his call to a unique ministry—the divine response, it may be, to his expressed readiness to conform 'with all that God requires'.

Jesus' baptism was followed by a forty days' solitary withdrawal to the wilderness of Judaea, where he underwent the experiences so vividly depicted in the temptation narrative.[22] From his wilderness retreat he emerged with his baptismal resolution confirmed. The ministry to which he knew himself called must be discharged in a spirit of complete trust in God. He would not exploit it as an instrument for his own advantage; he would not demand its validation by any spectacular sign; he would not fulfil it by the methods

[20] The *baṭ qōl*, 'daughter of the voice', is the designation given by rabbis to an utterance from heaven by which God made his will known after prophecy had ceased.

[21] We need not be guilty of the anachronism of attributing to men of the first century the recognition of the four 'Servant Songs' delimited by B. Duhm if we assume that they saw a connexion between the two passages beginning 'Behold my servant' (Isa. 42:1; 52:13).

[22] The detailed temptation narratives of Matt. 4:1–11 and Luke 4:1–13 are commonly recognized to be derived from the 'Q' source.

of military conquest or political power, which the Messiah of popular expectation was expected to employ.

There followed a period of activity in association with John, and when John moved from the Jordan valley to the neighbourhood of Shechem, Jesus and his disciples remained for a time in the Jordan valley, as we have seen. But when the ensuing tension between his disciples and John's was likely to be exploited by the Pharisees to the disadvantage of both John and Jesus, Jesus withdrew from Judaea.[23] John's ministry in the neighbourhood of Shechem was followed by a short but fruitful visit by Jesus himself to the same district. His words to his disciples during this visit, 'others have laboured, and you have entered into their labour' (John 4:38), have commonly been assigned an original life-setting in the early apostolic age, in Philip's evangelization of Samaria (Acts 8:5ff); but the setting which the Fourth Evangelist gives them can be confidently defended.[24] With John's ministry at Aenon, Jesus' visit to those parts has its place at the beginning of the insufficiently documented history of Christian and para-Christian movements in Samaria.

3

The main phase of Jesus' ministry, however, began in Galilee after the arrest and imprisonment of John the Baptist.[25] It is striking that the news about John should have sent him at once into Galilee, for if John had incurred the hostility of Antipas by his activity in Peraea, then Jesus chose the other, and more important, part of Antipas's tetrarchy to take up where John left off. Why he chose Galilee rather than Judaea must be a matter of speculation. Galilee was the region where he had lived from his childhood, and he may well have judged that a firmer foundation could be laid for his work in Galilee than in Judaea; the mention in Isa. 9:1 of 'Galilee of the nations' as the recipient of divine light may also have been in his mind, as it certainly came to the mind of the First Evangelist (Matt. 4:12–16).

The burden of Jesus' preaching during the earlier months of his Galilaean ministry was the kingdom of God. 'The appointed time

23 John 3:22–4:3 (see p. 160).
24 See p. 160 with n. 33.   25 Cf. Mark 1:14f.

has fully come', he said, 'and the kingdom of God has drawn near;[26] repent, and believe in the good news' (Mark 1:15). To hearers who had some knowledge of the Old Testament writings, these words could have meant one thing only: the time had come, as the book of Daniel foretold, for the God of heaven to set up on the ruins of the successive Gentile world-empires a kingdom which would never be destroyed or superseded by another, a kingdom which would endure for ever (cf. Dan. 2:44; 7:14, 18, 27). In Daniel's own words, of which Jesus' proclamation may be an intentional echo, 'The appointed time came for the saints to receive the kingdom' (Dan. 7:22).

What was the nature of the kingdom which Jesus proclaimed? In all his recorded teaching there is not one reference to the restoration of David's kingdom, although this idea was vividly present to the minds of many of his contemporaries, including his own disciples. The nature of the kingdom of God, as he conceived and preached it, can best be inferred from the character of his ministry, and the main emphasis of his teaching.

Nothing in Jesus' teaching about the kingdom of God is more determinant than his teaching about the God to whom the kingdom belongs. So far as we can gather from the evidence, Jesus was unique in applying to God the designation *'abbā*—not the liturgical form *'aḫīnū* ('our Father') by which God was addressed in certain synagogue prayers, nor even the more personal *'āḫī* ('my Father'), but the domestic word by which a father was called within the affectionate intimacy of the family circle. He addressed God as *'abbā*[27] and apparently referred to him in the third person as *'abbā*, thus expressing his own sense of loving nearness to God and his implicit trust in him; but more than that, he taught his disciples similarly to call God *'abbā* and to look to him with the same trustful expectation as children show when they look to their fathers to provide

---

[26] Gk. ἤγγικεν, which, in the light of ἔφθασεν in Matt. 12:28 // Luke 11:20 (cf. also Mark 9:1, ἐληλυθυῖαν), C. H. Dodd takes to mean that the kingdom of God 'has come' (*Parables of the Kingdom* [London, 1935], pp. 44ff; 'The kingdom of God has come', *ExT* 48 [1936–7], pp. 138ff). But the issue of 'realized eschatology' depends not merely on the translation of individual words but on the overall interpretation of the gospel record. The general viewpoint of Mark and the other evangelists seems to be that the kingdom of God during the ministry of Jesus was in the process of inauguration, but was fully inaugurated only with his death and resurrection.

[27] Cf. Mark 14:36.

them with food and clothes. This attitude is specially inculcated in the Lord's Prayer (itself a brief compendium of the teaching of Jesus),[28] where his disciples are taught almost in the same breath to pray for the consummation of God's eternal purpose in the world (the coming of his kingdom) and to ask him for their daily bread, the forgiveness of their sins and deliverance in temptation's hour. *'Abbā*—originally an Aramaic form but used freely also in post-biblical Hebrew as a hypocoristic for 'father'—was so distinctively a locution of Jesus and his disciples when applied to God that it passed unchanged into the vocabulary of Gentile Christianity; Paul, for example, says that when Christians (in the context, Gentile Christians) call God *'abbā*, that is a token that they have received the Spirit of Jesus, the Spirit that makes them in their turn sons of God (Gal. 4:6; Rom. 8:15f). 'Here we see who the historical Jesus was: the man who had the power to address God as *abba* and who included the sinners and the publicans in the kingdom by authorizing them to repeat this one word, "Abba, dear Father".'[29]

As for the character of his ministry, especially during the first months in Galilee, it is summed up in his message to John the Baptist. John, hearing reports of the ministry of Jesus in his prison at Machaerus, and recognizing that it did not tally completely with the ministry of judgement which he himself had forecast for the Coming One, sent two of his disciples to ask him, 'Are you the Coming One, or must we look for someone else?' Before the eyes of John's messengers Jesus 'cured many of diseases and plagues and evil spirits, and on many that were blind he bestowed sight. And he answered them, "Go and tell John what you have seen and heard: the blind receive their sight, the lame walk, lepers are cleansed, and the deaf hear, the dead are raised up, the poor have good news preached to them. And blessed is he who takes no offence at me"' (Luke 7:19–23; cf. Matt. 11:2–6). When they brought back their report to John, he would surely recognize that these were the things

---

[28] Cf. J. Jeremias, 'The Lord's Prayer in Modern Research', *ExT* 71 (1959–60), pp. 141ff.

[29] J. Jeremias, *The Central Message of the New Testament* (London, 1965), p. 30; for a more detailed study see the same author's *Abba: Studien zur neutestamentlichen Theologie und Geschichte* (Göttingen, 1966), pp. 15–67; cf. also C. F. D. Moule, *The Phenomenon of the New Testament* (London, 1967), pp. 47ff.

which the Hebrew prophets had associated with the New Age; in particular, the emphasis on the preaching of good news to the poor marked Jesus out as the Spirit-anointed speaker of Isa. 61:1f, who is commissioned to discharge a ministry of precisely this kind—'to proclaim liberty to the captives, and the opening of the prison to those who are bound; to proclaim the year of Yahweh's favour'.[30] There is a hint here at a messianic ministry, for the speaker is the Lord's anointed; but it is a messianic ministry widely different from that to which so many in Israel were looking forward at the time. The language of Isa. 61:1f might indeed have been used of one who undertook to liberate the oppressed subjects of Rome and Antipas from their yoke, but of this kind of liberation there is not a whisper.

The same emphasis on the presence of the kingdom of God in the actual circumstances of the ministry appears in a controversy between Jesus and some of the scribes about his power to relieve people who were demon-possessed. 'If it is by the finger of God that I cast out demons', said he, 'then the kingdom of God has come[31] upon you' (Luke 11:20).

Such words as these can only mean that in the ministry of Jesus the kingdom of God was already present; in his curing the sick and the possessed and preaching to the poor the 'powers' of the kingdom were at work, engaged in a holy war, invading the realm of evil and releasing its prisoners. The same point is reiterated in many of his parables of the kingdom.[32] In keeping with this is his declaration to a group of Pharisees, who asked him when the kingdom of God was coming, that it would not come 'with signs to be observed; nor will they say "Lo, here it is!" or "There!" for behold, the kingdom of God is in the midst of you'[33] (Luke 17:20f).

Yet this did not mean that in his current ministry the hope of the ages was fully realized. Although the kingdom of God was pres-

[30] This is the text of Jesus' programmatic sermon in the Nazareth synagogue in Luke 4:16ff; he began his exposition of it with the words: 'Today this scripture has been fulfilled in your hearing'.

[31] Gk. ἔφθασεν (cf. p. 170, n. 26).

[32] Cf. J. Jeremias, *The Parables of Jesus* (London, 1963²).

[33] This is the most probable meaning in the context of ἐντὸς ὑμῶν. While ἐντός means 'within', the fact that the pronoun is plural suggests the meaning 'in the midst of you' rather than 'within each of you (individually)'. Another possible rendering is 'within your grasp'.

ent and active, it was only in process of inauguration. One day, as
he told his disciples, it would come 'with power', and some of them
at least would live to see that day (Mark 9:1). So, too, he taught
his disciples to pray to God, 'Thy kingdom come' (Luke 11:2), and
assured them that, 'little flock' though they were by comparison
with the big battalions of political power and religious establishment, it was for them that the kingdom was designed by their heavenly Father's decree (Luke 12:32). Yet they must not think that
promotion in the kingdom of God would mean privilege and status
and the right to command the service of others; in his kingdom the
way to honour was the way of humble and self-giving service; in
fact, the service *was* the honour. In this he set them a worthy example, coming as he did not to receive service but to give it, and
to give the highest service of all by surrendering his life as 'a ransom for many' (Mark 10:45). In Origen's great word, Jesus was
the *autobasileia*,[84] the kingdom in person; for the principles of the
kingdom of God could not have been more completely embodied
than in him who said to his Father, 'Not my will, but thine, be
done',[85] and accepted the cross in that spirit.

At present the kingdom of God, and Jesus himself, were beset by
limitations. One day these limitations would be removed. 'I have a
baptism to be baptized with,' said Jesus, 'and how I am constrained
until it is accomplished!' (Luke 12:50). That this baptism was his
death is clear enough from the terms in which he once asked his disciples James and John if they were able to drink his cup or be baptized with his baptism (Mark 10:38f). His death would be the
means of unleashing the powers of the kingdom of God and of
bringing liberation and blessing to many more than could be
touched by his current ministry in Galilee or Judaea.

4

These two phases of the kingdom of God in the teaching of Jesus
are closely related to what he has to say about the Son of Man. The
figure of the Son of Man in his teaching, like his proclamation of
the kingdom of God, goes back to the book of Daniel. The Son
of Man, as we have seen, is portrayed further in the *Similitudes of*

[84] Origen, *Comm. in Matt.* xiv, 7 (on Matt. 18:23).   [85] Mark 14:36.

Enoch;[36] it is unlikely, however, that Jesus' thinking was influenced by the latter work, although its language may be echoed in the Matthaean phraseology about the Son of Man sitting 'on the throne of his glory' (Matt. 19:28; 25:31). But the Son of Man in the teaching of Jesus probably owes something of his distinctive character to his identification with the Isaianic Servant of Yahweh, who (unlike the Son of Man in the *Similitudes*) gives his life as a reparation offering (*'āšām*) on behalf of others, and thus crowns his ministry (Isa. 53:10).[37]

As we trace the development of the Gospel tradition, we mark an increasing tendency to make the designation 'the Son of Man' on the lips of Jesus a surrogate for the pronoun 'I'.[38] Thus, whereas in Mark 8:27 Jesus asks his disciples, 'Who do men say that I am?' (similarly in Luke 9:18), in Matt. 16:13 his question appears as 'Who do men say that the Son of Man is?' This tendency may have set in even before the earliest Gospel strata took written shape; at any rate we find a 'Q' passage (Matt. 11:18f // Luke 7:34f) where Jesus contrasts the ascetic John the Baptist with 'the Son of Man' (that is, himself), who 'has come eating and drinking'. Here 'the Son of Man' simply means 'I'. Since the ordinary Aramaic word for 'a man' (*bar 'ĕnāš*) means literally 'son of man', it is conceivable that on an occasion like this Jesus used some such periphrasis as 'this man' for the first personal pronoun singular; but this has little to do with his eschatological use of the designation 'the Son of Man'.

It has, indeed, been argued that Jesus' eschatological use of the designation is entirely questionable, since nowhere in the Gospel record does he mention the kingdom of God and the Son of Man in the same context. Since it cannot be seriously doubted that he spoke about the kingdom of God, it must accordingly be seriously doubted whether he ever spoke of the Son of Man.[39] This argument

[36] See pp. 131ff.

[37] For this identification see T. W. Manson, *The Teaching of Jesus* (Cambridge, 1935), pp. 229ff; J. Jeremias in W. Zimmerli and J. Jeremias, *The Servant of God* (London, 1957), pp. 88ff; for a critique of the identification and other views generally associated with it see M. D. Hooker, *Jesus and the Servant* (London, 1959).

[38] Occasionally 'I' in one of the later Synoptic Gospels may replace 'the Son of man'; compare Matt. 10:32f. ('I also will acknowledge . . . I also will deny . . .') with Mark 8:38; Luke 12:8f.

[39] Cf. H. B. Sharman, *Son of Man and Kingdom of God* (New York, 1943); P. Vielhauer, 'Gottesreich und Menschensohn in der Verkündigung Jesu',

carries little conviction. If there is any significance in the fact that
the kingdom of God and the Son of Man are not mentioned together, it may simply be that either implies the other, so that it was
unnecessary to mention both at once.[40]

According to Jesus, those who acknowledge him in the presence
of men will be acknowledged by the Son of Man in the presence of
God (Luke 12:8). This rôle is discharged by the Son of Man in the
one New Testament passage where he appears outside the Gospels;
in Acts 7:55f Stephen, maintaining the claims of Jesus before the
Sanhedrin, sees 'the heavens opened, and the Son of Man standing
at the right hand of God'—standing, that is to say, as Stephen's advocate in the heavenly court.[41]

But if the Son of Man is the advocate of the faithful and righteous, he is the judge of the faithless and unrighteous: 'whoever is
ashamed of me and of my words in this adulterous and sinful generation, of him will the Son of man also be ashamed, when he comes
in the glory of his Father with the holy angels' (Mark 8:38). The
Son of Man would be a 'sign' to that generation—the only sign that
would be granted to it (Luke 11:30)—but his coming would take
them all by surprise (Luke 12:40; 17:24–30).

So far, Jesus' references to the Son of Man, though cryptic, did
not depart noticeably from what had been written concerning the
Son of Man. But the Son of Man's coming in glory and judgement
was not all that had been written concerning him: it was also 'written of the Son of man, that he should suffer many things and be
treated with contempt' (Mark 9:12).[42] With increasing emphasis in
the later phase of his ministry Jesus told his disciples that 'the Son
of man must suffer' (Mark 8:31; cf. 9:31; 10:33),[43] and announced
at the Last Supper that 'the Son of man goes as it is written of him'
(Mark 14:21). This insistence that the suffering of the Son of Man

---

Festschrift für Günther Dehn (Neukirchen, 1957), pp. 51–79. This implies
that the juxtaposition of Mark 8:38 and 9:1 is the evangelist's work.
[40] Cf. C. K. Barrett, *Jesus and the Gospel Tradition* (London, 1967), p. 31.
[41] See C. F. D. Moule, 'From Defendant to Judge—and Deliverer', *SNTS
Bulletin* 3 (1952), pp. 40ff, especially pp. 46f.
[42] Cf. Luke 17:25; before the 'day' of the Son of Man 'first he must suffer
many things and be rejected by this generation'.
[43] On the pre-Hellenistic and pre-Easter stratum of tradition discernible in
these passion-announcements see J. Jeremias in Zimmerli and Jeremias, *The
Servant of God*, pp. 100ff; *The Central Message of the New Testament*, pp. 42f.

is something that is 'written' concerning him implies a reference to Hebrew scripture, and if in fact the reference is to the suffering Servant of Isa. 52:13–53:12 the situation is clear. 'How is it written of the Son of man, that he should suffer many things, and be treated with contempt?' is a question easily answered, if the Son of Man is the Servant of Yahweh. Jesus was not the only teacher in Israel in those days to posit a unitive exegesis of the Son of Man and the Servant; the Qumran community appears to have identified the two figures in substance, though without explicit use of the two titles.[44]

As the end of Jesus' ministry approached, he made it increasingly clear that the rôle of the suffering Son of Man was one which he himself would fulfil. Yet, even in the last week, according to the Fourth Evangelist, his language on this subject—at least to the general public—was sufficiently enigmatic for them to ask him, 'Who is this Son of man?' (John 12:34).

When, however, at the court of inquiry after his arrest the high priest asked him whether or not he was the Messiah, he replied, 'I am, and you will see the Son of man sitting at the right hand of Power, and coming with the clouds of heaven'.[45] This is the Markan version of his answer (Mark 14:62); according to Luke, he said: 'But *from now on* the Son of man shall be seated at the right hand of the power of God' (Luke 22:69).[46] The impending suffering of the Son of Man would inaugurate the new order in which he would be vindicated by God and visit his people as Saviour and Judge. In the language of the Fourth Gospel, the hour had come for the Son of Man to be glorified: 'when you have lifted up the Son of man, then you will know that I am he' (John 12:23; 8:28).

By the same token, it was with the suffering of the Son of Man that the kingdom of God, hitherto subject to limitations in spite of all Jesus' mighty works, would come 'with power'. Moreover, it was

[44] See p. 113.
[45] When we compare Mark's 'I am' with Matthew's 'You have said so' (Matt. 26:64) and Luke's 'You say that I am' (Luke 22:70), the question of the original wording behind these three formulations is raised. It may be that Jesus indicated that 'Messiah' was the term of their choice; as for himself, he preferred to speak of the vindication of the Son of Man. See p. 198.
[46] Cf. Matt. 26:64, 'hereafter (ἀπ' ἄρτι, corresponding to Luke's ἀπὸ τοῦ νῦν) you will see the Son of Man seated at the right hand of Power . . .'.

in the suffering of the Son of Man that the mystery of the kingdom
of God was unveiled.[47]

Those who had continued with Jesus in his trials, even if at the
end their nerve failed and they could not then drink his cup or
share his baptism, were nevertheless the heirs of the kingdom which
he bequeathed to them (Luke 22:28–30); it was for them henceforth to share his ministry and propagate the message of the kingdom of God not only (as in the earlier phase of limitation) to the
people of Israel but to all the nations.

For Jesus evidently envisaged an interval between the inauguration of the kingdom of God by the passion and vindication of the
Son of Man and the consummation of the kingdom at the last
judgement, when the Son of Man would be finally revealed.[48] This
raises the further question whether he intended to found a 'church',
a community of his disciples or a 'new Israel'. If the Baptist endeavoured to form a baptismal community, it is not antecedently improbable that Jesus cherished a similar purpose. That he did so is
indicated very clearly by the fact that from the general body of
his disciples he chose twelve men, not only to be trained by him
and to share his ministry of preaching and healing, but also to be
the leaders of the new Israel. This is the plain implication of the
well-authenticated *logion* in which he tells them that when the new
order dawns, they will 'sit on thrones judging the twelve tribes of
Israel' (Luke 22:30; cf. Matt. 19:28). That such honour depended
on their being servants of all—indeed, consisted in their being servants of all—was something of which Jesus left them in no doubt.[49]
But the designed coincidence of their number, twelve, with the
totality of the tribes of Israel, implied that there would be an 'Israel' for them to lead. That they themselves appreciated this is suggested by the care which they took, after the defection of Judas
Iscariot, to fill the vacancy and keep the number up to twelve.[50]

[47] Cf. T. W. Manson, 'Realized Eschatology and the Messianic Secret', in
Studies in the Gospels: Essays in Memory of R. H. Lightfoot, ed. D. E. Nineham (Oxford, 1955), pp. 209ff.
[48] Cf. W. G. Kümmel, *Promise and Fulfilment* (London, 1957), pp. 64ff; his
argument is criticized in C. K. Barrett, *Jesus and the Gospel Tradition*, pp. 74ff.
[49] Cf. Mark 10:42–5; Luke 22:24–7.   [50] Acts 1:15–26.

14 Jesus and the Kingdoms of the World

1

Jesus' proclamation of the kingdom of God did not take place in a historical vacuum. Even if he did not envisage the 'fifth monarchy' in a way that the Zealots would have appreciated, any proclamation of a new kingdom was bound to arouse expectant, if unintelligent, enthusiasm in some quarters, suspicion and hostility in others. The life and ministry of Jesus cannot be adequately interpreted without reference to the critical situation in which he lived and ministered.

'The apocalyptic movement in the time of Jesus', wrote Albert Schweitzer in the first decade of this century, 'is not connected with any historical event. . . . The period offers no events calculated to give an impulse to eschatological enthusiasm.'[1] This was an extraordinary statement to make, for the historical event calculated to give just such an impulse stares one in the face: it is, in general, the Roman occupation of Palestine from 63 B.C. onwards and, more particularly, the replacement of Herodian rule in Judaea by direct Roman administration in A.D. 6.[2]

This at least should have been as clear in the first decade of our century as it is today; but today we have evidence which was not available then of a 'general eschatological movement' of which Dr. Schweitzer could find no trace. In the Qumran community the events of 63 B.C. and the years immediately following brought the conviction that the unprecedented 'time of trouble' foretold in Daniel 12:1 had now set in, and the *Rule of War* shows how some of

[1] *The Quest of the Historical Jesus* (London, 1910), p. 368.
[2] Cf. H. G. Wood, *Jesus in the Twentieth Century* (London, 1960), p. 123, where the point is made, in the course of an appreciation of T. R. Glover's *The Jesus of History* (London, 1917), that it 'does not sufficiently relate the mission of Jesus to the crisis in Israel's history which incorporation in the Roman Empire involved' and is 'not sufficiently permeated with the sense of crisis'.

them took steps to prepare for the eschatological dénouement which must swiftly follow.[3]

That there was any direct contact between Jesus and the men of Qumran or other Essene communities is uncertain, either during his forty days of testing in the wilderness of Judaea or at any other time. Probably he was born and brought up in the general milieu of 'nonconformist' Judaism to which these communities also belonged. But we have only to compare Jesus' attitude to the law with the strict interpretation of Qumran—stricter than that of the Pharisees[4]—to realize how far removed his thinking was from the ideals of Qumran. It has, indeed, been suggested that some of his polemic against an oppressive application of the Torah was originally directed against the Qumran community, and redirected against the Pharisees by the early Palestinian church.[5]

This may have happened in some instances, but the Gospel representation of the Pharisees as his principal *theological* opponents may confidently be regarded as historical.[6] If he charged the Pharisees with imposing on men's shoulders 'burdens hard to bear' (Matt. 23:4; Luke 11:46) and invited his hearers rather to take up his own 'easy' yoke (Matt. 11:30), we can imagine what he would have said of the Qumran *halakah*, in comparison with which the Pharisees were indeed 'givers of smooth interpretations'.[7]

Of all the parties in Israel at this time, none was more self-sacrificingly devoted to the ideal of the coming kingdom of God than that of the Zealots. In their eyes, talk about waiting God's good time was not what the present crisis demanded. The Sadducean chief-priesthood might collaborate with the occupying power; the Pharisees might submit under protest; the Essenes in their desert retreat might remain aloof from public affairs. But what the situation called for, the Zealots maintained, was violent action against the enemy; God would not fail to aid those who undertook his cause and devoted themselves to the establishment of his kingdom, as he had not failed to aid Judas Maccabaeus and his brothers in an earlier crisis.

[3] See p. 113.   [4] See p. 111.
[5] W. D. Davies, *The Setting of the Sermon on the Mount* (Cambridge, 1964), pp. 208ff.
[6] The Sadducees, indeed, were further from him theologically as well as politically. But theological opposition tends to be sharper between parties who share a considerable area of common belief and practice.   [7] See p. 75.

In Jesus' eyes, this was not the way of the kingdom. When he
himself, on more than one occasion, had the opportunity of leading
a militant force he refused to do so, and lost many followers by his
refusal. The question of paying tribute to Caesar was of minor importance to him: since the tribute money bore Caesar's name, it
manifestly belonged to him; let him have it back.[8] The things
that are God's', the interests of his kingdom, were paramount; let
a man put these first, and the necessities of life would not be lacking. Not that the interests of the kingdom of God were other-
worldly; they had to do with earth as well as with heaven, and
were to be promoted in this life by the doing of his will. But these
interests would not be at all diminished by returning to a pagan
monarch coinage which in any case bore his image. Perhaps the
question about the image on the denarius which was handed to
Jesus when he asked to see a sample of the tribute-money had an
implication beyond the immediate topic. There were some Jews
whose conscience was so scrupulous that they would neither touch
nor look at a coin bearing a human image, because it infringed the
Second Commandment.[9] Did Jesus suggest that such coinage was fit
only for Gentiles to handle, so that the best thing a law-abiding Jew
could do with it was to turn it over to them at once? Everyone knew
that it was unfit for sacred purposes; no Jew, for example, could
pay his temple dues with Caesar's money. Caesar's money seemed
best designed for paying Caesar's tribute.

We may go further and say that Jesus recognized that Caesar exercised his current overlordship over the Jewish people, and would
continue to exercise it, so long as divine providence permitted it.
The misplaced but genuine incident of Jesus' confrontation with
the adulterous woman is perhaps relevant here.[10] Of her guilt there
was apparently no question; of the law of Israel in such a case there
was no question. The law required that she be put to death by
stoning.[11] Her accusers sought Jesus' ruling in the matter, we are

[8] This may be the force of 'render' (ἀπόδοτε) in Mark 12:17.
[9] See p. 90.
[10] Its position after Luke 21:38 in family 13 may reflect its historical life-
setting fairly accurately.
[11] Stoning is explicitly prescribed for the betrothed maiden convicted of
adultery (Deut. 22:21, 24); by analogy the same mode of execution was meted
out for adultery in a married woman, which was similarly a capital offence
(Deut. 22:22; Lev. 20:10).

told, 'that they might have some charge to bring against him' (John 8:6). Either he must clash with the law of Moses, or he must clash with the law of Rome, which as a matter of course withdrew the right to inflict capital punishment from the Jewish authorities when Judaea became a province.[12] Jesus refused to be impaled on either horn of the dilemma. By all means let the sentence of Moses' law be executed, he said—executed, however, only by those whose own hands are clean in this regard.

The Jesus of the Gospels taught his followers to take a contrary line to the Zealots, not to resist violence or retaliate against it, but to turn the other cheek and volunteer to go a second mile when their services were conscripted by the military for one mile. If this way of peace were disregarded, if the way of revolt against Rome were preferred, then, he warned his hearers, destruction would fall upon the land of Israel as surely as it fell on the rioting Galilaeans who were cut down by Pilate's troops in the Temple court.[13] That this picture should, within a couple of generations at the most, have successfully replaced an earlier and more historically accurate picture of a Zealot sympathizer is as probable as that, fifty years after the Dublin rising of Easter week, 1916, an attempt should be made, with any hope of success, to portray Michael Collins and other leaders of the Irish independence struggle as pacifists who inculcated in their followers an attitude of sweetness and light towards the 'Saxon foe'.

2

Jesus' Galilaean ministry had not long begun before he found the synagogue authorities of the region increasingly disinclined to let him use the synagogues as a platform for his proclamation of the kingdom. He had recourse, therefore, to the hillside or the shores of the Lake of Galilee in order to address the multitudes. He challenged the accepted standards of Pharisaic orthodoxy at too many points, especially by the sovereign liberality with which he inter-

---

[12] See J. Jeremias, 'Zur Geschichtlichkeit des Verhörs Jesu vor dem Hohen Rat', *ZNTW* 43 (1950–1), pp. 145ff, especially pp. 148ff; cf. also T. W. Manson, 'The Pericope de Adultera (Joh. 7, 53–8, 11)', *ZNTW* 44 (1952–3), pp. 255f.
[13] Luke 13:1–3. See pp. 37f.

preted the sabbath law and by his seeking out and consorting with disreputable characters from whom most religious people preferred to keep their distance.

Instead of following the sabbath law as expounded in the schools of Hillel or Shammai, Jesus insisted that, since the sabbath was given to men for their relief and well-being, any action which promoted that end was specially appropriate to the sabbath day. The rabbis would have agreed that, in an urgent case of life or death, medical attention might be given on the sabbath day, but if the patient could without danger wait until the next day, then the healing action should be postponed.[14] Jesus argued on the contrary that the sabbath was a pre-eminently suitable day for the performance of such works of mercy, whether the case was urgent or not, since such works were so completely in keeping with God's purpose in giving the day.[15] On the other hand, anything that tended to make the sabbath law burdensome conflicted with that purpose. 'The sabbath was made for man, and not man for the sabbath' (Mark 2:27).

As for his consorting with disreputable persons, among whom tax-collectors were commonly reckoned, he must have given considerable offence when he actually called a tax-collector to be one of the twelve.[16] Even if Levi abandoned his career as a tax-collector in order to be a companion of Jesus, the fact that he had once been a tax-collector would be, in the eyes of many pious people, an indelible black mark against him. Tax-collectors in Galilee, while Herod Antipas was tetrarch, could not be charged with collaboration with the Romans; but the conditions of tax-collecting meant that extortion was practically inseparable from a tax-collector's way of life. Tax-collectors might not hold any office of communal responsibility, nor was their testimony admissible in a Jewish law-court.[17] The question whether it was possible for such depraved characters to experience true repentance was seriously debated in the rabbinical schools, and even those who allowed that it was possible agreed that it was very difficult, since it would not normally be practicable for a penitent tax-collector to restore all the money

---

[14] Cf. Mishnah, *Yōmā* 8:6, 'whenever there is doubt whether life is in danger, this overrides the sabbath'.   [15] Cf. Luke 6:9; 13:10–16; 14:1–6.
[16] Mark 2:13ff.   [17] Cf. Mishnah, *Nedarim* 3:4.

which he had unjustly extorted.[18] Jesus' consorting and eating with such people, and with other 'Jews who had made themselves Gentiles', was a cause of great scandal to his most religious contemporaries.

What the fishermen whom Jesus called from their calling on the lake of Galilee thought of this new companion, to whom they had so often been compelled to pay taxes on their catches of fish on the quayside of Capernaum, may with some effort be imagined. It must have been even more difficult for Simon the Zealot,[19] another member of the inner circle, to tolerate his company. That a Zealot should have been one of the twelve illustrates the catholicity of Jesus' choice, and Simon the Zealot must have found some of the teaching of his new master strangely different from much of what he had previously learned. Theologically the Zealots differed but little from the Pharisees, and neither a Pharisee, a Zealot nor an Essene need violate his basic theological tenets in order to recognize in Jesus a teacher sent by God. A Sadducee, on the other hand, could not have accepted Jesus' teaching while remaining theologically a Sadducee, for the hope of a life to come, which was common to the creed of Jesus and that of the other three parties, was repudiated by the Sadducees.

In so far as we know anything of the twelve personally, they appear to have been a company of rugged individualists, far removed from the plaster saints in whose guise they have conventionally been cast. James and John, the 'sons of thunder' or 'sons of tumult'[20] were an impetuous pair, and the first of the apostles himself bore a patronymic, Barjona, which is strikingly similar to a term used in rabbinical literature to denote a class of rebel.[21] 'Iscariot', Judas's sobriquet, has sometimes been derived from *sicarius*, but if Josephus is right in dating the rise of the *sicarii* in the procuratorship of Felix (A.D. 52–59), this derivation is anachronistic.[22] It is in any

[18] Zacchaeus was an exception (Luke 19:8).
[19] Called 'Simon the Cananaean' in Mark 3:18 // Matt. 10:4 (see p. 93).
[20] Gk. βοανηργές probably represents a Galilaean pronunciation of Aram. *bĕnē regeš* (see G. H. Dalman, *Jesus-Jeshua* [London, 1929], p. 12).
[21] See p. 99, n. 21, for the activity of *biryōnim* during the siege of Jerusalem. But the *biryōnim* appear only in later Babylonian tradition, and *Barjona* (Matt. 16:17) is best treated as an ordinary patronymic, 'son of John' (so John 1:42; 21:15–17).
[22] Moreover, the initial vowel of 'Ἰσκαριώτης would in this situation be prothetic, but a prothetic vowel develops when the word in question begins with

case better to accept the ancient etymology attested in *Codex Bezae*[23] and interpret 'Iscariot' as *'ĭš Qĕriyyōṯ*, 'the man of Kerioth'. If this is the Kerioth of Josh. 15:25, Judas may have been the one Judaean among the twelve; and, if we may judge from his betrayal of Jesus to the Temple authorities, he is as likely to have been 'a zealot of the right' as a zealot of the 'left' (to use modern political jargon).[24]

The twelve received the designation 'apostles' (probably the equivalent of Heb. *šĕlīḥîm*)[25] when Jesus sent them out two by two through the towns and villages of Galilee to proclaim the kingdom of God and heal the sick in his name. It is evident that he expected them to find sympathizers in many of the places which they were to visit, so that they would not need to carry with them provisions for the road: 'whatever town or village you enter, find out who is worthy in it, and stay with him until you depart' (Matt. 10:11). The precise force of the adjective 'worthy' in this saying calls for consideration. We are reminded of Josephus's statement that, when Essenes went on a journey, they had no need to take supplies with them, since in every city there was one of their order appointed to entertain travelling members of the brotherhood.[26]

But who would perform for the twelve apostles the service that these 'associate members' of the Essene orders discharged for their

---

two adjacent consonants (cf. the form Σκαριώθ in the 'western' text), not when there is a full vowel between the first two consonants, as there is in *sicarius*/σικάριος/*sīqār*/*sīqĕrā*. Some Coptic versions curiously call 'Judas *not* Iscariot' in John 14:22 'Judas the Cananaean'.

[23] For 'Ισκαριώτης Cod. D. reads ἀπὸ Καρύωτου in John 12:2; 13:2, 26; 14:22. The same reading is found in ℵ*, family 13, and the Harclean margin of John 6:71, where D has Σκαριώθ (as repeatedly in the Synoptic Gospels). The reading 'Ισκαριώθ in Mark 3:19; 14:10; Luke 6:16 further supports the etymology *'ĭš Qĕriyyōṯ*. According to John 6:71; 13:26 Judas's father Simon was also surnamed Iscariot.

[24] These expressions are borrowed from an article by J. A. Findlay, 'Why did Jesus tell His Disciples to buy Swords?' in *The British Weekly*, March 16, 1950. By 'a zealot of the right' he meant 'a fanatical supporter of the Temple', who 'betrayed Jesus to the Government because he honestly believed that Jesus intended to destroy the Temple'.

[25] Cf. K. H. Rengstorf in *TWNT* I (Stuttgart, 1933), *s.v.* ἀπόστολος, pp. 413ff. Although one cannot argue from the institution of the *šāliaḥ* in rabbinical Judaism to that of the apostle of Jesus, they share the common principle that their authority is derived entirely from the one who sends them and can be exercised only within the terms of their commission.

[26] *BJ* ii, 124f.

brethren? We may most naturally think of men who had been impressed by the preaching of John the Baptist, and returned home to wait for the manifestation of the Coming One announced by John. Galilee is not specifically mentioned among the regions from which people came in large numbers to listen to John, but one man at least came from Galilee to be baptized by him—Jesus himself—and if one came, there may have been more. More generally we may expect that in Galilee there were those who, like Simeon and Anna and Joseph of Arimathaea farther south,[27] were 'waiting for the kingdom of God' and would welcome those who announced its arrival. Nor would it be at all surprising if some of those 'worthy' people were connected with the Essenes.

Confining their activity, in accordance with their commission, to their fellow-Israelites, and avoiding the Gentile communities in Galilee and the Samaritan areas on its southern border, the apostles had a reception which filled them with enthusiasm and enabled them to bring a glowing report to Jesus when their mission was fulfilled. But in their zeal they probably said and did things which disturbed the tetrarch of Galilee when he heard of them, and made him suspect that he had a new John the Baptist on his hands, in place of the original one whom he had recently executed.[28] An unnatural alliance was formed against Jesus by the Herodian party, who promoted Antipas's interests in Palestine, and the Pharisees. Jesus therefore took the twelve across the Lake into Philip's territory, where the political atmosphere was quieter.

But such excitement had been aroused by the mission of the twelve that a large body of Galilaeans followed them across the Lake. Plainly these were leaderless men who were desperately anxious for someone to put himself at their head and inaugurate the promised kingdom without delay; Jesus' compassionate recognition of them as 'sheep without a shepherd' (Mark 6:34)[29] implies, as T. W. Manson used to insist, not a congregation without a pastor but an army without a captain.[30] He knew that if they found the wrong kind of captain they could be led to disaster; and the kind of captain

[27] Luke 2:25, 38; 23:51.   [28] Mark 6:14–16.

[29] Cf. the same phrase in I Kings 22:17, where it denotes Ahab's army after he is killed.

[30] T. W. Manson, *The Servant-Messiah* (Cambridge, 1953), p. 70: 'What Jesus saw on the shore of the lake was a maccabean host with no Judas Maccabaeus, a leaderless mob, a danger to themselves and everyone else.'

they would have liked to find is shown by the Fourth Evangelist's account of how, after Jesus had fed them there in the wilderness, they tried to compel him to be their king (John 6:15).[31] But he would not be the kind of king they wanted, and they had no use for the only kind of king he was prepared to be; therefore, as John says, many of his Galilaean followers left him from that time forth.[32]

This crisis appears to have marked the end of Jesus' public ministry in Galilee; Jesus took the twelve farther into Philip's tetrarchy, to the vicinity of his capital, Caesarea Philippi. They might well have wondered whether they had not been totally misled by their master; why had he refused such a golden opportunity of putting himself at the head of an army of eager patriots and leading them against the Romans? Some of their fellow-disciples, completely disillusioned, had given up following Jesus after that incident; why should they continue in his company? Jesus tested their loyalty, and Peter, acting as their spokesman, affirmed that, in spite of so much that went contrary to their presuppositions, they believed him to be the Messiah.[33] But plainly the meaning of the term had begun to change in Peter's mind, if the title could be according to one who had declined to fill the rôle which was popularly associated with the Messiah. In Peter's confession, in fact, we can trace the beginning of the process by which, among the followers of Jesus, the meaning of 'Messiah' has been changed to conform with his character and achievement. At the time, however, when to most people 'Messiah' was the Davidic warrior who would lead his people to victory over their Gentile overlords, it was natural that Jesus should warn Peter and the other apostles not to repeat in public what they had said about his being the Messiah. But he said more than that: according to Mark, it was from now on that he began to tell his disciples that, far from attacking and overthrowing the power of Rome, he himself would be repudiated and put

[31] Cf. H. W. Montefiore, 'Revolt in the Desert?', *New Testament Studies* 8 (1961–2), pp. 135ff.   [32] John 6:66.

[33] E. Haenchen, 'Die Komposition von Mk viii 27–ix 1 und Par', *NovT* 6 (1963), pp. 81ff, conducts a form-critical analysis of this section which leads him to the conclusion that it is 'a composition of the evangelist' (who admittedly used available traditions in constructing it), designed to convey a theological message. The coincidence of the Markan and Johannine traditions at this point, which both present as a crisis in the ministry, is an important piece of evidence that the core of the narrative antedates its evangelic presentation.

to death. When Peter told him to stop talking like that, he insisted
that this was the path of God's will for him, and added that those
who were still determined to follow him must realize clearly what
lay ahead for their leader, so that they might count the cost for
themselves and be prepared one day to carry a cross to the place of
execution as he was prepared to carry his.

3

Not long afterwards, Jesus and the twelve left Galilee for Judaea,
and arrived in Jerusalem during the feast of Tabernacles in the autumn of (probably) A.D. 29.[34] For the next six months they remained in Judaea or Peraea, visiting the capital for the feasts—for
example, the Feast of Dedication, in December of the same year
—and spending the intervening weeks in the Jordan valley or near
the Judaean wilderness.[35] On his visits to Jerusalem Jesus enjoyed
the hospitality of the famous family of Bethany, on the eastern
slopes of the Mount of Olives (about two miles from Jerusalem);
the days were spent in the Temple precincts, where like many
other rabbis he taught those who gathered round him. Jesus was
not a complete stranger in Jerusalem, and as a result of his earlier
visits to the city there were a number of people in it who counted
themselves his disciples. But during these last months he concen-
trated his teaching activity in Jerusalem—at least at those times
when the crowds of pilgrims made it safe for him to do so without
the risk of surreptitious arrest by the Temple police. His teaching
was not at all congenial to the Temple authorities and leaders of
the Sanhedrin, who feared that any talk of a new kingdom would
excite revolutionary sentiments among the people and bring down
reprisals from the Romans. But his popularity with the crowds was
such that they dared not take overt action against him.

As Galilee had heard the good news of the kingdom, so Jerusalem
must now hear the things that concerned its peace. There were too
many popular and influential enthusiasts going about whose teaching, for all their confident optimism, meant anything but peace for

[34] Cf. Mark 10:1; John 7:2ff.
[35] Cf. M. Goguel, *Life of Jesus* (London, 1953), p. 400. T. W. Manson, 'The
Cleansing of the Temple', *BJRL* 33 (1950–1), pp. 271ff, argues that it was
about the time of the Feast of Tabernacles, and not during Holy Week six
months later, that the cleansing of the Temple took place.

the city. It may be that the collapse of the tower of Siloam, briefly
mentioned in Luke 13:4 as having taken place shortly before Jesus'
arrival in Judaea, was connected with an attempt at revolt against
the Romans; some of the insurgents who had occupied the tower
were crushed in its fall when the Romans undermined it. This, it
must be conceded, is a speculative amplification of Jesus' reference
to 'those eighteen upon whom the tower in Siloam fell and killed
them'; but it is supported by his warning that the same kind of
disaster awaited his hearers unless they changed the direction of
their minds. If their minds remained bent upon resistance to Rome,
then ruin would befall their city and themselves. Why not rather
follow the way of the Son of Man, the way of submission and service, and thus establish the new kingdom—not as a *result* of obedience to God's will but *in* obedience to his will?

The last feast which brought Jesus to Jerusalem was the Passover
of early April in A.D. 30. With his disciples he joined the pilgrim
crowds who were going up for the feast, and as they approached
Bethany tremendous excitement was unleashed, for the people
there were talking freely of a miracle which he had lately performed
in their town, by calling his friend Lazarus back to life from the
tomb where he had been laid three days before. As Jesus rode into
Jerusalem on an ass[36] which had been provided for him at Bethany, the pilgrims recognized his enactment of a late Old Testament
oracle, in which Jerusalem is called upon to greet with joy her king
who comes to her 'humble and riding on an ass' (Zech. 9:9). Whatever the original life-setting of that oracle may have been, Jesus
by his action was presenting himself to the people of Jerusalem as
their Messiah, if only they would choose the way of peace in preference to the way of war, which would have been indicated had his
mount been a war-horse rather than a peaceful ass. But neither the
pilgrims nor the people of Jerusalem were in a mood to appreciate
such a fine distinction. If at last the prophet of Nazareth was offering himself as their leader, then their leader let him be; and the

---

[36] W. Bauer's argument that πῶλος ('colt'), used without qualification as in
Mark 11:2ff, means 'horse' ('The Colt of Palm Sunday', *JBL* 72 [1953], pp.
220ff) is rebutted by O. Michael, 'Eine philologische Frage zur Einzugsgeschichte', *NTS* 6 (1959–60), pp. 81f; cf. H. W. Kuhn, 'Das Reittier Jesu in
der Einzugsgeschichte des Markusevangeliums', *ZNTW* 50 (1959), pp. 82ff,
for evidence that the Markan account draws on Gen. 49:11 as well as on
Zech. 9:9.

ancient festal cry *Hosanna* ('give victory, O Lord!')[37] took on a new significance. Surely now Jerusalem's redemption was at hand—and they could envisage only one way in which that redemption could be attained.

The hopes of the enthusiastic pilgrims were matched by the apprehensions of the chief priests and rulers of the people. Whatever Jesus' intention might be, it seemed to them that now he was being pushed by his followers into the kind of action which would attract swift and sharp reprisal from the Romans. He must be arrested and put out of harm's way as soon as possible, although his arrest would have to be carried out in such a way as to avoid a popular rising, and this (they thought) would be impossible until the feast was over.

Jesus was not unaware of their deliberations, but took care that his programme of action in the few days remaining before the celebration of the Passover should not be interrupted. His 'cleansing of the Temple', which figured prominently on this programme, was bound to bring him into collision with the Sanhedrin, and indeed it confirmed them in their conviction that he was too dangerous to be left at large.

This action was far from being an attack on the sanctity of the Temple; it was rather a protest against its desecration. It can best be understood as a 'prophetic action' of a type familiar enough in the Old Testament records.[38] The part of the sacred precincts affected by it was the outer court, sometimes called the Court of the Gentiles, because Gentiles were permitted to enter it, as they were not permitted (on pain of death) to enter the inner courts. Jesus' ban on the use of the outer court as a market or bazaar, or as a short-cut for porters and messengers, was calculated to restore this court to its proper function as the area where Gentiles could

---

[37] Cf. Ps. 118:25, *hôšī'āh-nnā*.

[38] While a symbolic action of this kind could easily have been interpreted as a political action, and was so represented to the Sanhedrin (and perhaps to Pilate), the rulers appear to have had some inkling of its character and purpose when, instead of calling in the Temple police (cf. John 7:32, 45), they challenged his authority to act thus (Mark 11:27ff). A prophet could conceivably have performed such an action with divine authority. Jesus countered their challenge with a question about the authority of John the Baptist, who was popularly regarded as a prophet. There is no hint that the temple-cleansing was a riotous proceeding such as would inevitably have attracted the intervention of members of the Roman garrison in the adjoining Antonia fortress.

approach the living God.[39] That this was his purpose is confirmed
by the fact that, as he taught the crowds the meaning of his action,
he quoted the prophetic words of Isa. 56:7, 'My house shall be
called a house of prayer for all the nations'. If he added, 'But you
have made it a den of robbers', he was but repeating Jeremiah's
severe words in the oracle which gave warning of the imminent
destruction of Solomon's Temple (Jer. 7:11).[40] It is not implied
that the commercial activity in the court was a racket designed to
line the pockets of the Temple authorities; much of the activity,
such as the selling of sacrificial animals and the changing of money,
was no doubt a considerable convenience to the worshippers.[41]
But the diversion of the sacred precincts to such business was an act
of robbery in that the Gentiles' opportunity of approaching God
was restricted and God was deprived of the worship which he
might have received from them. And perhaps some of the God-
fearing Gentiles who were in Jerusalem at this time appreciated the
significance of Jesus' action. For although the Fourth Evangelist,
probably for programmatic reasons, places the cleansing of the Temple two years earlier than this Passover, he tells how during Jesus'
last week in Jerusalem some Greeks who had come up 'to worship
at the feast' approached Philip, one of Jesus' disciples, requesting
an interview with Jesus.[42] The Evangelist records this incident for
a purpose of his own, but the approach of these Greeks may well
have been prompted by Jesus' gesture on behalf of Gentile worshippers like themselves.

Even if the chief priests were not personally affected by the
'cleansing of the Temple', Jesus' act compelled them to review the

[39] Mark 11:39 (cf. Mishnah, *Berakot* 9:5). Cf. E. Lohmeyer, *Lord of the
Temple* (Edinburgh, 1961), pp. 36ff, for the suggestion that Jesus wished to
prepare for the eschatological influx of 'all nations' to the mountain of the
house of Yahweh (Isa. 2:2; Micah 4:1).

[40] This is not the only point of resemblance between Jesus and Jeremiah:
compare Jesus' policy of non-resistance to Rome with Jeremiah's advice to his
king and people to submit to Nebuchadrezzar. No wonder that in Matthew
16:14 the disciples say to Jesus, 'Some say that you are . . . Jeremiah'.

[41] There is no ground for connecting the market-stalls in the outer court
with the 'booths of the sons of Annas' mentioned repeatedly in rabbinical
literature; these were set up on the Mount of Olives and were destroyed (by
Zealots) in A.D. 67 (TJ *Peah* 1:6; *Sifre* on Deut. 14:22). But cf. V. Eppstein,
'The historicity of the Gospel account of the cleansing of the Temple', *ZNTW*
55 (1964), pp. 42ff.

[42] John 12:20ff.

situation urgently. The danger of a popular rising and Roman reprisal, which they had feared when Jesus entered the city a day
or two before amid the clamorous enthusiasm of the pilgrims, was
now much greater. A recent small-scale revolt,[43] in the course of
which some people were assassinated, had been put down by the
Romans with little trouble, and the leaders were now in prison
awaiting execution; if Jesus were allowed to go on unhindered,
something much worse might break out. We may indeed wonder
how many willing helpers Jesus had as he drove the merchants and
money-changers out of the Temple court, and whether they all
appreciated his intention. The leaders of the Sanhedrin still saw
no way of getting Jesus into their power until after the feast, although they may well have wondered if by then events would not
have passed out of their control.

It was now that Judas Iscariot, perhaps for his part too thinking
that Jesus had allowed himself to be pushed by popular enthusiasm
into a course of action which might be fatal for his associates as well
as for himself, played for safety and offered to facilitate Jesus' arrest *before* the feast in circumstances which would involve no danger of a public tumult. The authorities eagerly accepted his offer.

Jesus knew very well that he had a traitor in the camp, and he
took special precautions as he made his remaining arrangements.
He was resolved to celebrate the Passover meal with his disciples in
Jerusalem—the last Passover before the kingdom of God was inaugurated—and nothing must prevent the carrying out of this plan.
A secret rendezvous had been arranged in a house belonging to a
well-disposed citizen; shortly before the appointed time for meeting there he sent two trusted disciples to prepare the meal. They
were not even told the street where the house stood, but were instructed to follow a certain man who would come to meet them,
carrying a water-jar. When they had completed their task, they
were joined by Jesus and the rest of the twelve.[44]

If, as seems clear, this Passover celebration took place at least
twenty-four hours before the official celebration, the meal would
have to be taken without the Passover lamb—since the lambs had to
be sacrificed in the Temple precincts at the time prescribed by

---

[43] The 'insurrection' in which Barabbas 'had committed murder' (Mark 15:7);
the two ληστσί crucified with Jesus may also have been involved in it.
[44] Mark 14:12ff.

the official calendar, according to which in that particular year the Passover was to be eaten after sunset on the Friday evening. The eating of the Passover without the lamb was not unprecedented; it was indeed the rule rather than the exception, for the lamb was perforce missing from every Passover table in the world outside Jerusalem.[45]

It may be that Jesus and his disciples celebrated the Passover according to another calendar than the official one; it may be that Jesus, knowing that he would be no longer alive on Friday evening, the official time for celebrating it, deliberately arranged to eat it with his disciples earlier in the week.[46] During and after the meal he gave them some of the bread and wine on the table around which they reclined, representing it to them as a token of his life which he was about to sacrifice for the establishment of the new covenant between God and man. His enemies were bent on taking his life, but he would not permit them to take the initiative and gain their end as they planned; instead, he would offer his life to God as an atonement for his people, as 'a ransom for many' (Mark 10:45). To meet death in this spirit would not bring his ministry to an abrupt termination; it would crown his ministry and bring the mission of the Son of Man to a triumphant conclusion.

During the meal Judas slipped away from the house; only Jesus knew the errand on which he was bent. He stayed for some time with the others and warned them of the crisis that lay immediately ahead. He had previously described them as the 'little flock' on whom the Father had chosen to bestow the kingdom; now he spoke of the imminent scattering of this flock in terms of Zech. 13:7, where Yahweh says, 'I will strike the shepherd, and the sheep will be scattered' (Mark 14:27). To this Markan saying Luke's counterpart is the conversation between Jesus and his disciples about the two

[45] That the Last Supper had the character of a Passover meal (cf. J. Jeremias, *The Eucharistic Words of Jesus* [London, 1966²]) is clearly indicated, although the lamb is not expressly mentioned. Cf. E. Stauffer, *Jesus and His Story* (London, 1960), p. 94, for the suggestion that Jesus, being a heretic in the eyes of the Temple authorities, was denied the privilege of a paschal lamb.

[46] Cf. A. Jaubert, *La Date de la Cène* (Paris, 1957), for the thesis that Jesus and his disciples, following the calendar of the book of Jubilees and the Qumran community (cf. pp. 112ff), celebrated Passover on the *Tuesday* evening of Holy Week. See also A. Jaubert, 'Jésus et le calendrier de Qumrân', *NTS* 7 (1960–1), pp. 1ff; E. Ruckstuhl, *Die Chronologie des Letzten Mahles und des Leidens Jesu* (Zürich, 1963).

swords (Luke 22:35-8). On an earlier occasion, he reminded them, he had sent them out to proclaim the kingdom of God without any supplies in hand—with neither purse, bag, nor sandals—and yet they had lacked nothing. But now they would need more substantial equipment, for he himself was about to be condemned as a law-breaker, and his followers would find themselves outlaws; they could no longer depend on the charity of sympathetic fellow-Israelites. Purse and bag would now be necessary—and if any of them had no sword, he would do well to sell his cloak and buy one. According to Josephus, although Essenes on a journey had no need to take provisions with them, they did carry arms on account of robbers. But Jesus now does not envisage robbers as the kind of people against whom his followers would have to defend themselves; they themselves would be lumped together with bandits by the authorities and they might as well act the part properly.[47] Taking him over-literally, they revealed that they already had two swords—which, by the way, suggests how far they were from resembling a Zealot band, which would have been much more adequately equipped. Seeing that they had failed to catch the purport of his words, Jesus said 'Enough of this!'[48] and dropped the subject. In contrast to the days when they had shared their Master's popularity, 'they are now surrounded by enemies so ruthless that the possession of two swords will not help the situation'.[49]

But the shepherd would return and gather his scattered flock together again: 'after I am raised up', he said, 'I will lead you forth to Galilee' (Mark 14:28). The verb 'lead forth' (Gk. *proagō*) is one naturally used of a shepherd going before his sheep, or of a captain going before his men. The promise that the little flock would inherit the kingdom was not to be frustrated. In the angelic interpretation of Daniel's vision it was through suffering and persecution that the 'people of the saints of the Most High' were to receive the kingdom; in the New Testament fulfilment the Son of Man absorbs the greater

[47] Cf. the saying of Yoḥanan ben Zakkai in TJ *Sanhedrin* 1:4, *šuttap listis kēlistis*, 'the associate of a bandit is (reckoned) as a bandit'. Cf. S. G. F. Brandon, *Jesus and the Zealots* (Manchester, 1966), pp. 340ff, for another interpretation.
[48] Ck. ἱκανόν ἐστιν. T. W. Manson translates it 'Well, well' (*Ethics and the Gospel* [London, 1960], p. 90). Cf. Deut. 3:26, 'Let it suffice you (ἱκανούσθω σοι); speak no more to me of this matter.'
[49] T. W. Manson, *Ethics and the Gospel*, p. 90.

part of this suffering in his own person, and thus wins the glory of the kingdom for his followers as well as for himself—although for them too it remains true that 'through many tribulations we must enter the kingdom of God' (Acts 14:22).

15 Trial and Execution of Jesus

After the Last Supper Jesus and his disciples left the house where they had eaten it together and made for a spot on the slopes of the Mount of Olives, where they had spent the night on similar occasions before. The authorities, meanwhile, had not been idle. When Judas, fresh from the upper room, told them that now was their opportunity to arrest Jesus without a public commotion, they sent a posse of Temple police, armed with swords and clubs, to go with him and carry out the arrest. The Johannine account, according to which the officers of the Sanhedrin were accompanied by a *speira* (John 18:3, 12), has been taken to mean that Roman soldiers were also present, members of the cohort on duty in the Antonia fortress, for the Greek *speira* is the proper equivalent of Latin *cohors*, which in Judaea (where legionary troops were not stationed under the procurators) would be an auxiliary cohort with a paper strength of 760 infantry and 240 cavalry. Some translations seem reluctant to give *speira* its proper force, or at least to express its proper force unambiguously; thus RSV translates it, as do the earlier English versions, by 'band', and in representing Judas as 'procuring a band of soldiers and some officers from the chief priests and the Pharisees' (verse 3), suggests to the ordinary reader that the Sanhedrin provided this 'band'. The situation becomes a little clearer in verse 12, where RSV probably intends a distinction to be made between 'the band of soldiers and their captain' on the one hand and 'the officers of the Jews' on the other; in fact, 'the band of soldiers and their captain' were the cohort and its 'chiliarch' or (to use the Roman term) its military tribune.[1] We need not take John to mean that the

---

[1] Cf. Acts 21:31ff, where Claudius Lysias, military tribune in command of the Antonia garrison in A.D. 57, is called the χιλίαρχος. In John 18:3 NEB translates σπεῖρα by 'detachment of soldiers' but rightly punctuates so as to distinguish it from the 'police provided by the chief priests and the Pharisees', who are mentioned next; similarly in v. 12 the punctuation distinguishes between 'the troops with their commander' and 'the Jewish police'.

whole cohort turned out to arrest one man with a handful of followers, even if they expected them all to be armed to the teeth, but he implies a detachment of soldiers of the cohort sizeable enough to warrant the presence of their commanding officer. This account runs so much counter to the later tendency to reduce Roman responsibility for Jesus' arrest and execution to a minimum that the strongest arguments would be necessary to cast doubt on its historicity.[2] But if it is historical, it follows that the chief priests had already been in consultation with the Roman authorities about Jesus and the most effective way of dealing with him.

The arrest was effected with surprising ease. The presence of Roman soldiers may have been due to the expectation of armed resistance, but in the event, after a mere scuffle which Jesus himself sharply checked, his disciples took to their heels and escaped, leaving their Master to his enemies. He expressed surprise at the arms they carried—'Did you think you were coming to overpower a bandit?' he asked[3]—and submitted to them. Determined to take no chances, they handcuffed him and took him to the house of Annas the former high priest, still the most influential leader of the chief-priestly group in the Sanhedrin.[4] There an unofficial inquiry was held before Jesus was sent on to Caiaphas, president of the Sanhedrin. If a case against him was to be presented to Pilate, it would carry official weight if the high priest in office presented it on behalf of the supreme court.[5]

But the case proved unexpectedly difficult to prepare. Haste was imperative, because Passover was due to be celebrated the following evening, and it was desirable to have the whole affair concluded before that. Moreover, people in Pilate's position transacted business early in the day and concluded it by noon. A night session of the court—or at least of a quorum—was therefore held.[6]

In the house of Annas, Jesus had been questioned about his teaching, in hope that he might admit some element which could be construed as seditious. But he appealed to the fact that for the past week (as also on earlier visits to the capital) he had taught

[2] Cf. P. Winter, *On the Trial of Jesus* (Berlin, 1961), p. 45.
[3] Mark 14:48.   [4] John 18:13.   [5] John 18:24.
[6] Cf. A. H. Sherwin-White, *Roman Society and Roman Law in the New Testament* (Oxford, 1963), p. 45; he regards the incidental reference to the fire at which Peter warmed himself (Mark 15:54, 67; Luke 22:55) as an undesigned coincidence supporting the evidence for a night inquiry.

publicly in the Temple court and had nothing to hide.[7] At the inquiry before Caiaphas an attempt was made to convict him of a threat to the safety or sanctity of the Temple, on the ground that he had undertaken to destroy it and replace it in three days with 'a house not made with hands'.[8] But it proved impossible to get witnesses to agree on what he had actually said. He had certainly foretold the destruction of the Temple, and that in itself was as dangerous an utterance for the speaker as Jeremiah's similar language about Solomon's Temple had been over six hundred years before.[9] He had also spoken, according to John the Evangelist, of building a new Temple in three days.[10] But a charge of speaking 'against' the Temple could not be fastened on him; had such a charge been proved it would have been constructive blasphemy in Jewish law and would also have been an offence in Roman law, which protected the safety and sanctity of the Temple.[11]

There was another possible way of procuring a conviction against him. He himself had always been reticent about the Messiahship, whatever claims his enthusiastic followers might make on his behalf. If only a straightforward claim to be the Messiah were forthcoming from him, this could readily be represented to Pilate as a claim to be king of the Jews, and Pilate could be relied upon to take appropriate action. Caiaphas accordingly asked Jesus directly if he was the Messiah. Jesus' affirmative reply may have been couched in terms which threw the responsibility for choosing that word on the high priest—but it was sufficiently affirmative to give the high priest and his colleagues the pretext they sought for bringing a watertight case against him before Pilate. Jesus, however, said more, and gave his judges material for convicting him also of blasphemy, a capital crime in Jewish law (as the claim to be Messiah was not). 'From now on', said Jesus, 'you will see the Son of Man sitting at the right hand of Power, and coming with the clouds of heaven'.[12]

The claim to be Messiah carried with it the claim to be the one addressed by God in the oracle of Psalm 110:1, 'Sit at my right

[7] John 18:19.
[8] Mark 14:58.　[9] See p. 190 with n. 39.　[10] John 2:19.
[11] Cf. Acts 6:11ff, where Stephen's 'blasphemous words against . . . God' consist in his speaking 'against this holy place' and in particular predicting its destruction. See p. 221.
[12] Mark 14:62 // Matt. 26:64 // Luke 22:69. See p. 176.

hand, till I make your enemies your footstool'. That the person so addressed was the Messiah appears to have been generally agreed upon by Jewish interpreters at this time. One who claimed to be the Messiah might therefore, as a corollary, speak of sitting at God's right hand; but to speak thus explicitly would be regarded as going to the very limit of daring, and the same attitude would be taken to one who, claiming to be the Messiah, accepted the corollary that because the Messiah is addressed by God as his Son in Psalm 2:7, he himself therefore was the Son of God. But Jesus evidently drew both these corollaries.[13] Not only so; in speaking of the Son of Man as coming with the clouds of heaven he applied to himself the language of Daniel 7:13f. There is evidence for certain strands of Jewish interpretation of Daniel's reference to 'one like a son of man' which viewed this figure as almost the peer of God. This interpretation appears, for example, in the older Greek version of Daniel, where the 'one like a son of man' comes on to the scene 'as an ancient of days'.[14] We may have an echo of it in Revelation 1:12ff, where John has a vision of 'one like a son of man' (identified by him with the risen Christ) who is described in terms partly borrowed from Daniel's description of the Ancient of Days; we may have a further echo of it in the shocked reaction of Rabbi Aqiba's colleagues when he suggested that the 'thrones' which were placed in Daniel 7:9, immediately before the judgement scene, might be intended respectively for the Ancient of Days (as the context shows) and for 'David', that is the Davidic Messiah. 'Aqiba', they protested, 'how long will you profane the divine glory?'—for the interpretation which identified the 'one like a son of man' with the Messiah was felt to border on blasphemy, the more so in view of the Christian acceptance of it.[15]

Jesus, then, was pronounced guilty of blasphemy, and might have been executed by stoning (although the Roman governor's sanction would technically have been necessary before the execution could

[13] In the high priest's question, 'Are you the Messiah, the Son of the Blessed?' (Mark 14:61), the designation 'the Son of the Blessed' is an official synonym of 'Messiah'. To Jesus himself the consciousness of being in a special sense the Father's Son was no merely official relationship but something intensely personal, the basic assurance of his inner life (see the discussion of *Abba* on p. 170).

[14] Gk. ὡς παλαιὸς ἡμερῶν, where the Theodotionic version has the literal ἕως τοῦ παλαιοῦ τῶν ἡμερῶν.

[15] TB *Ḥagigah* 14a; *Sanhedrin* 38b.

be carried out). But his acceptance (whether expressed or implied) of the messianic title suggested a way in which the odium
of putting him to death could be transferred to the Romans. While
the Messiah in Jewish eyes was mainly a religious figure (albeit
with political implications), in Roman eyes he would be a political
figure, for the Messiah was by definition the rightful king of Israel,
and not merely a political figure but a political rebel, since sovereignty over the Jewish people was at present exercised by the Emperor Tiberius. The point of the high priest's insistence that the
terms of Jesus' reply to his question constituted blasphemy was
probably to satisfy members of the Sanhedrin who would not have
approved of the delating of Jesus to Pilate simply because he
claimed to be Messiah.

As soon as daylight dawned on Passover Eve, Jesus was brought
before Pilate, and the chief priests appeared to make formal accusation against him. Invited by Pilate to state their charge, they replied
that he had endeavoured to sow disaffection throughout the province, forbidding the Judaeans to pay tribute to the emperor and
claiming to be himself the anointed king of the Jews.[16]

Since these were offences against Roman law, the much-debated
question whether the Sanhedrin had or had not the right to carry
out the death-sentence without the procurator's ratification is not of
the first importance. The chief priests did not come to Pilate asking
him to ratify a sentence of the Sanhedrin. It was a little later that
this question arose, when it looked as if Pilate did not find much
serious substance in the original charge, and spoke of inflicting a
lighter penalty on Jesus, which would teach him to speak and act
more cautiously in future. The title 'king of the Jews' implied that
the accused man was leader of a resistance movement, but a few
minutes' questioning convinced Pilate that it was no resistance
leader who stood before him. 'I will teach him a lesson', he said,
'and let him go' (Luke 23:16). Jesus' accusers then protested that
he had in any case been convicted of a crime against Jewish law,
and when Pilate replied, 'Then take him and punish him yourselves', they protested that he had incurred the death penalty,

---

[16] The fullest statement of the charge before Pilate is given in Luke 23:2.
The charge would normally have been stated in response to such a question as
that asked by Pilate in John 18:29, 'What accusation do you bring against this
man?'

which they had no authority to carry out. 'It is not lawful for us to put any man to death' (John 18:31).[17]

This account of the situation, given by the Fourth Evangelist, has been vigorously contested. But the question is not to be dealt with by adducing detailed references from various quarters bearing on the execution of offenders in Judaea between A.D. 6 and 66, and weighing one set against another, without considering the context within which the whole matter is to be considered. That context is Roman provincial procedure. The right of jurisdiction in capital cases was most jealously reserved by provincial governors; permission to provincials to exercise it was a very rare concession, conceded only to such privileged communities as free cities within the empire. Jerusalem was no free city, and a turbulent province like Judaea was most unlikely to be granted such a concession. Most of the incidents appealed to as evidence for the Sanhedrin's retention of capital jurisdiction have features which stamp them as exceptions.[18] Even in Judaea it is probable that a concession was

17 John 18:31 is corroborated by a *baraita* preserved in TJ *Sanhedrin* 1:1; 7:2, to the effect that 'forty years before the destruction of the Temple the right to inflict the death penalty was taken away from Israel'. As a *baraita* (earlier than A.D. 200), this tradition is too early to be regarded as a corollary from the comment of R. Isaac ben Evdemi (c. A.D. 250) on the tradition that 'forty years before the destruction of the Temple the Sanhedrin abandoned the hall of hewn stones and established itself in a bazaar'. This, said R. Isaac, 'teaches that it no longer adjudicated in laws relating to fines. Laws relating to fines, do you say? Say rather, it no longer adjudicated in capital cases!' (TB *Sanhedrin* 12a, 41a). See J. Jeremias, 'Zur Geschichtlichkeit des Verhörs Jesu vor dem Hohen Rat', *ZNTW* 43 (1950–1), pp. 145ff.

18 Among these incidents are the stoning of Stephen (Acts 7:54ff) and that of James the Just (Josephus, *Ant.* xx, 200). The stoning of James took place in the interval between two procuratorships, and even so was an excess of jurisdiction which would have incurred penal action by the Roman authorities had not Agrippa II averted it promptly by deposing the high priest responsible (see pp. 66, 346). The view that the stoning of Stephen took place in the interval between Pilate's being sent to Rome and the appointment of his successor (cf. B. Reicke, *The New Testament Era* [Philadelphia, 1968], pp. 191f) is not altogether cogent (see p. 225). The execution of a priest's daughter for unchastity (cf. Lev. 21:9), witnessed as a boy by Rabbi Eliezer ben Zadok who was lifted on his father's shoulder to see it (Mishnah, *Sanhedrin* 7:2; Tosefta *Sanhedrin* 9:11a), may well belong to the reign of Herod Agrippa I (A.D. 37–44). As for executions carried out within the Essene order (cf. Josephus, *BJ* ii, 145), they had no more status in the law of the land than had assassinations carried out by the *sicarii*, or than private executions within a secret society would have in a modern civilized state. In any case, the province was not so thoroughly policed that an occasional excess of jurisdiction in Jewish circles was out of the question;

made in regard to violations of the sanctity of the Temple, for which even Roman citizens were liable to execution under Jewish law;[19] but there is no suggestion that at any point this kind of sacrilege figured in Jesus' trial before Pilate.

If Pilate was not disposed to treat the charge of sedition as seriously as the chief priests expected, he was even less disposed to ratify the death sentence for a theological offence against Jewish law. But in the end it was on the charge of sedition that Jesus was condemned. The chief priests' hint that the emperor would not regard as his friend a judge who had discharged a claimant to kingship over the Jews was sufficient to make Pilate's mind up. 'If you release this man, you are not Caesar's friend; every one who makes himself a king sets himself against Caesar' (John 19:12).[20] So he took his seat on the tribunal or platform from which formal sentence had to be pronounced, and sentenced Jesus to death—by crucifixion, as was customary for seditious provincials, especially in that part of the world. The precise charge on which sentence was pronounced is indicated by the wording of the *titulus* placed above Jesus' head on the cross: 'The King of the Jews'.

Two incidents in the course of the trial call for special mention— the sending of Jesus to Antipas (recorded by Luke alone) and the Barabbas episode (recorded by all the Evangelists, and therefore a feature common to the Markan and Johannine traditions).

When Jesus' accusers told Pilate that he had stirred up disaffection all the way from Galilee to Jerusalem, Pilate asked if he was a

cf. Origen's evidence (*Letter to Africanus*, 14) of capital trials carried out secretly (λεληθότως) before the president of the (later) Sanhedrin, 'neither entirely openly, nor yet without the emperor's knowledge'.

[19] Cf. Josephus, *BJ* vi, 124–6, and the Greek inscription (*OGIS* 598, *SEG* vιιι, n. 169) warning Gentiles that any of them caught trespassing in the inner courts would have himself to blame for his ensuing death. Jewish trespassers in the holy of holies, where only the high priest had the right of entry, were similarly liable to the death penalty (Philo, *Legatio ad Gaium*, 307).

[20] If by this time Sejanus had fallen from power (which he did in October, A.D. 31), Pilate's position was perhaps the more delicate, as he may have owed his appointment to Sejanus's influence (see p. 36). (Cf. B. Reicke, *New Testament Era*, pp. 175f, 183f; P. L. Maier, 'Sejanus, Pilate and the date of the Crucifixion', *Church History* 37 [1968], pp. 3ff.) But it is not necessary to link Pilate's fear of Tiberius's suspicion with Sejanus's fall; a date of A.D. 30 for the crucifixion of Jesus is more likely than any later one. On the significance of the 'notable political term' *Caesaris amicus* cf. A. N. Sherwin-White, *Roman Society and Roman Law in the New Testament*, p. 47.

Galilaean, and on learning that he was, he sent him to Antipas, who also was resident in Jerusalem at that Passover season. Pilate was probably under no obligation to refer the case to Antipas, but did so as a courteous gesture when he learned that some of the offences alleged against Jesus had been committed in his home territory of Galilee, part of Antipas's tetrarchy.[21] Antipas may have inherited, so far as his tetrarchy was concerned, some of the extraordinary rights of extradition conferred on his father by Augustus, but such rights would have to be invoked before being granted. As it was, Pilate's gesture was complimentary. Antipas appreciated the compliment, but was too wise to presume upon it. He recognized the superior authority of the emperor's representative, and sent Jesus back to Pilate, after trying in vain to make him do or say something worthy of the rumours of his wonder-working activity which had come to his ears.

Antipas evidently allowed Pilate's courtesy to wipe out the sense of grievance which he had cherished against the procurator for some time, probably ever since Pilate's troops had used unnecessary violence against some of his Galilaean subjects six months or a year earlier, during a pilgrimage festival when their 'blood was mixed with their sacrifices' in the outer court of the Temple.[22] Pilate, for his part, may have borne a grudge of longer standing against Antipas, ever since the latter, with three of his brothers, had persuaded the emperor to bid Pilate remove the votive shields which he had displayed publicly in Jerusalem, thus offending the religious susceptibilities of its inhabitants.[23] The standing feud between the two men was removed by the present exchange of courtesies.

Luke, who records this incident in his Gospel and refers to it in Acts,[24] knows more about the Herod family than any other New Testament writer does. He was acquainted with one or two people who had fairly close contact with the family, such as Joanna, whose husband Chuza was steward (*epitropos*) in Antipas's ménage in Galilee,[25] and pre-eminently the tetrarch's foster-brother or boyhood friend Menahem who in later years became a Christian and occupied a position of leadership in Luke's home church of Syrian

---

[21] Cf. A. N. Sherwin-White, *op. cit.*, pp. 28ff.
[22] Luke 13:1.   [23] Philo, *Legatio ad Gaium*, 300.
[24] Luke 23:6–12, 15a; Acts 4:27.   [25] Luke 8:3.

Antioch.[26] The incident of Pilate's referring the case of Jesus to
Antipas can therefore by no means be dismissed as a piece of
fiction.

The Barabbas incident constitutes a problem which still awaits
its solution. We have no certain reference outside the Gospels to
the release of a prisoner to the people each Passovertide. The existence of such a custom is attested independently in the Markan and
Johannine passion narratives: 'at the feast', says Mark, 'he [Pilate]
used to release for them any one prisoner whom they asked' (Mark
15:6). Whereas in Mark the people take the initiative in asking
that the custom be observed, it is Pilate who mentions it first in
John (John 18:39). The origin and purpose of this *privilegium
paschale* elude us; that it was nothing more than an apologetic invention in the gospel tradition is most unlikely.[27] Mark and John
agree that the man whose release was demanded by the people was
Barabbas. 'Barabbas', says John, 'was a robber' (John 18:40)—that
is, a bandit (Gk. *lēstēs*) in the sense in which Josephus so often
uses the term, meaning a Zealot insurgent.[28] This is in keeping with
Mark's fuller statement that Barabbas was one of 'the rebels in
prison, who had committed murder in the insurrection' (Mark
15:7). This 'insurrection' is not documented elsewhere, but it must
have been quite recent, since the leaders had not yet been executed. The two bandits—*lēstai*, as Mark calls them (Mark 15:27)—

---

[26] Acts 13:1 (cf. p. 92).

[27] Barabbas is a patronymic; it is a material factor in the situation that, according to several textual witnesses for Matt. 27:16f, his personal name was
Jesus. An attempt has been made to relate the Barabbas episode to the provision
in Mishnah, *Pesaḥim* 8:6, that the paschal lamb may be slaughtered 'for one
whose release from prison has been promised' as well as for others potentially
hindered from eating it, but not specifically by name, lest he be unable to eat
and so the sacrifice be invalidated. Cf. J. Blinzler, *The Trial of Jesus* (Cork,
1959), pp. 218ff, and, for a critique of this thesis, P. Winter, *On the Trial of
Jesus*, p. 91. See further J. Merkel, 'Die Begnadigung am Passahfeste', *ZNTW*
6 (1905), pp. 293ff. The Barabbas episode is the only serious problem left un-
touched by A. N. Sherwin-White in his otherwise very illuminating chapter 'The
Trial of Christ in the Synoptic Gospels', *Roman Society and Roman Law in the
New Testament*, pp. 24–47.

[28] A reading in the margin of the Syriac Peshitta and in the text of Barṣalibi
presupposes a variant ἀρχιλῃστής—the same term as Josephus uses of Hezekiah
the father of Judas (*BJ* i, 204; *Ant.* xiv, 159). In Matt. 27:16 Barabbas is given
the epithet ἐπίσημος ('notorious'), used by Josephus (e.g.) of John of Gischala
and others like him (*BJ* ii, 585).

who were crucified with Jesus were probably involved in the same incident.

But, for all the obscurities of the Barabbas episode, there is dramatic fitness in the opposition Barabbas *versus* Jesus, as the evangelists present it. They represented two irreconcilable reactions to the Roman occupation—the way of attack and the way of non-resistance. It is not surprising that the people, faced with such a choice, preferred Barabbas; what is surprising is that Pilate should have found himself in a position where he had to release a declared enemy of Rome. It was Jesus who was crucified; and a significance beyond anything that Pilate could have envisaged was to be attached to the wording of the indictment fixed to his cross: 'The King of the Jews'.[29]

[29] On the subject of this chapter, see now S. G. F. Brandon, *The Trial of Jesus of Nazareth* (London, 1968).

16   The Primitive Jerusalem Church

1

If Caiaphas and his colleagues thought that with the death of Jesus the whole movement which he had led was suppressed for good, they were wrong, but they had sound reasons for thinking so. After a hot-headed but abortive attempt at armed defence by one of Jesus' followers, their nerve failed and they took to their heels. We have a glimpse of some of them a day or two later, secreted behind barred doors somewhere in Jerusalem, for fear of the Jewish authorities. No more effective way could have been devised for discrediting Jesus and all that he stood for than his followers' demoralized flight when he was seized and crucified. 'The pernicious superstition', says Tacitus, 'was checked for a short time' by the execution of Jesus, but perhaps his sources did not tell him how very short the time was before it 'broke out afresh'.[1]

None of the authorities, whether Roman or Jewish, could have reckoned with the event that confounded all their calculations: Jesus' rising from the dead and appearing to his disciples 'alive again after his passion'.[2] Not even the disciples themselves had reckoned with it; it took them quite by surprise. But it transformed them almost on the spot from a crowd of demoralized and frightened people into a band of men with a mission and purpose in life which, without delay, they proceeded to translate into action. This

[1] Tac. *Ann.* xv, 44.
[2] Acts 1:3. These appearances were granted now to individuals (like Peter, James the Just and, belatedly, Paul), now to groups of people ('the twelve' or 'all the apostles'), once to a large number, 'more than five hundred brethren at one time', of whom the majority were alive twenty-five years later, when the list of resurrection appearances 'received' by Paul was recorded by him in I Cor. 15:5ff. Some were located in or near Jerusalem, others in Galilee; they did not always have the same form (for example, at times Jesus was recognized immediately, at others not until he made himself known). But they all conveyed the unshakeable assurance that Jesus, crucified and buried, had burst the bonds of death.

'resurrection faith' of the disciples is a historical fact of prime importance, but to identify it with the resurrection event is to confuse cause with effect.[3] Were it not for the resurrection event there would have been no resurrection faith. But the resurrection faith brought the scattered followers of Jesus together again, and within a few weeks after his death they appear as a coherent, vigorous and self-propagating community in Jerusalem.

At quite an early stage, it appears, this community was designated by one of the terms which in the Old Testament are applied to the whole 'assembly' (*qāhāl*) or 'congregation' (*'ēḏāh*) of Israel. The Greek word *ekklēsia*, traditionally rendered 'church' in English, reflects one of these Hebrew words, or the Aramaic equivalent *kĕništā*, and expresses the community's conviction that it was the true remnant of the people of God, the Israel of the new age.[4]

2

One determinant fact which pervades all our evidence about this primitive church of Jerusalem is the disciples' consciousness that with the completion of the Messiah's work on earth the age of the Spirit had come. The dawn of this age had been foretold in Old Testament prophecy, notably in Joel 2:28f, where Yahweh promises that in days to come, when he visits his people to bless them,

> I will pour out my spirit on all flesh;
> your sons and your daughters shall prophesy,
>   your old men shall dream dreams,
>   and your young men shall see visions.
> Even upon the menservants and maidservants
>   in those days, I will pour out my spirit.

That this Spirit of Yahweh was the Spirit by whose power the earlier prophets had spoken is implied in the promise that those on whom the Spirit comes will prophesy. Behind Joel's oracle, indeed,

[3] Paul makes the distinction between the resurrection fact and the resurrection faith in I Cor. 15:17, where he emphasizes that without the former the latter is illusory: 'if Christ has not been raised, your faith is futile'.
[4] Occasionally συναγωγή was used in the same sense (cf. Jas. 2:2; perhaps also ἐπισυναγωγή in Heb. 10:25); but it was specialized in Greek as a designation for a Jewish meeting-place in the 'synagogue' in distinction from the 'church'. See p. 394 with nn. 3, 4.

there may be the memory of Moses' words in Numbers 11:29, 'Would that all Yahweh's people were prophets, that Yahweh would put his spirit upon them!'

The expectation of the age of the Spirit, stimulated by such words as Joel's, was cherished in a number of Jewish communities on the eve of the coming of Christianity. The Qumran documents in particular provide ample evidence of this. The members of the community, or at least some of them, believed that God had already poured out his holy Spirit upon them; repeatedly in the *Hymns of Thanksgiving* the singer praises God because the Spirit he has received enables him to know the divine mysteries and to stand fast when he might otherwise stagger and fall. The Spirit is variously called the Spirit of holiness, of truth, of counsel, of knowledge, of mercy, of uprightness.[5] It is through the Spirit that the sins of man are cleansed; in those who have received this gift sin is doubly offensive, for it is a pollution of the Spirit of holiness.[6] But this outpouring of the Spirit within the frontiers of the community is preliminary to a fuller outpouring when the new age dawns;[7] how extensive this outpouring will be is not made clear, but if all the wicked are to be exterminated before the dawn of the new age, then the Spirit may well be envisaged as poured out on 'all (surviving) flesh'.

The outpouring of the Spirit is announced in the preaching of John the Baptist. He baptizes with water, he says, but the Coming One will baptize with the Holy Spirit.[8] The Gospels present Jesus as the Coming One who himself is 'anointed' with the Spirit in order to fulfil his appointed ministry.[9] And when Jesus sends John's messengers back to their imprisoned teacher to report all that they have seen and heard while in Jesus' company, he intends John to understand by what they tell him that he is indeed the one on whom, in the words of Isaiah 61:1, the Spirit of God has come to enable him to accomplish the work which John had predicted for the Coming One.[10] It is by the Spirit of God that Jesus, in particular, expels the demons; that is why those who attribute his power in this respect to the aid of Beelzebub are guilty of blasphemy

[5] Cf. 1 QH vii, 6f; ix, 32; xii, 11f.   [6] CD v, 11; vii, 3f.
[7] 1 QS iv, 20–3; see p. 155.   [8] Mark 1:7f.
[9] Luke 4:18; cf. Acts 10:38.   [10] Luke 7:22; see p. 171.

against the Holy Spirit.[11] The outpouring of the Spirit and the coming of the kingdom of God are two different ways of viewing the ministry of Jesus;[12] both are manifested in partial measure before his death, but only after his death—his being 'glorified', in Johannine terminology—will the kingdom come with power, will the Spirit be poured out in fulness.[13] In the fourth Gospel Jesus, in his farewell discourse to the disciples, promises to send the Spirit as their advocate or friend at court (Gk. *paraklētos*) on whose help they can always rely (John 14:16, 26; 15:26; 16:7); in the Synoptic record this function of the Spirit is implied in the promise that when, in days to come, they are brought to trial and required to make their defence, they need not anxiously think out in advance what they are to say—'for it is not you who speak, but the Holy Spirit' (Mark 13:11; cf. Matt. 10:20).[14]

In the Acts of the Apostles, the fulness of Jesus' impartation of the Spirit takes place after he has passed through suffering and death to exaltation at the right hand of God, in response to the invitation of Psalm 110:1.[15] The impartation takes place at the festival of Pentecost, seven weeks after the Passover which witnessed his death. In post-exilic Judaism Pentecost came to be celebrated as the anniversary of the giving of the law and confirmation of the covenant at Sinai. It has been suggested that the annual ceremony of covenant renewal at Qumran took place at Pentecost,[16] which is the more likely since one of our earliest authorities for identifying Pentecost with the anniversary of the law-giving is the book of *Jubilees,* according to which the same day is the anniversary of the covenant with Noah: 'for this reason it is ordained and written on the heavenly tablets that the feast of weeks should be celebrated in this month [the third month, Siwan] once a year, to renew the covenant every year' (Jubilees 6:17).[17] In the events of the first Christian Pentecost, according to Acts 2, God, who once spoke at Sinai, now spoke again to the nations and confirmed his covenant to pour out his Spirit on all flesh. The putting of God's Spirit within

[11] Mark 3:22ff; Matt. 12:31f.

[12] Cf. J. E. Yates, *The Spirit and the Kingdom* (London, 1963).

[13] Mark 9:1; John 7:39.

[14] In the parallel passage in Luke 21:15 Jesus says, 'I will give you a mouth and wisdom' (cf. Acts 6:10).   [15] See pp. 176, 198.

[16] Cf. A. R. C. Leaney, *The Rule of Qumran and its Meaning* (London, 1966), pp. 95ff.   [17] Cf. TB *Pesaḥim* 68b.

men was a sign of the new covenant, as a comparison of Jeremiah
31:31ff with Ezekiel 11:19f and 36:25ff makes plain; in view of
Jesus' promise it was also a token that he had now been enthroned
by God as Lord and Messiah, the effective Baptizer with the Spirit.
The call therefore came to the whole house of Israel to repent, to
accept baptism in the name of Jesus, and thus receive not only
the forgiveness of their sins but also the gift of the Spirit.

The contrast in the words of John the Baptist between his own
baptism in water and the Coming One's baptism with the Holy
Spirit might have prepared us for the discontinuance of baptism in
water when once the gift of the Spirit was bestowed. In fact, baptism in water was not discontinued; it was carried over into the
new age but received a further significance. Now it was not only
associated with the forgiveness of sins, as it had been in John's ministry; it became the sacramental sign by which believers in Jesus
were incorporated into his Spirit-baptized community.[18]

Any tendency which baptismal terminology might have encouraged to think of the Spirit as a substance, a fluid comparable to
water, was counteracted by the intense awareness of his personal
presence among them. The community's decisions are primarily the
decisions of the Spirit;[19] an offence committed within the fellowship is an offence against the Spirit;[20] later, the disciples' missionary
activity is directed by the Spirit.[21] The utterances of prophets in the
church are recognized as the voice of the Spirit; indeed the
prophet, as the channel of communication, need not be mentioned;
it suffices to say that the Holy Spirit spoke.[22]

3

Among the questions about the primitive community on which
we are almost completely uninformed is that of the part which
Jesus' followers in Galilee played. Our knowledge of the earliest
days of the community comes from Luke, whose account of its beginnings, like his account of resurrection appearances, is confined
to Jerusalem and its neighbourhood.[23] Granted that the apostles

---

[18] Cf. Acts 2:38; I Cor. 12:13.   [19] Cf. Acts 15:28.
[20] Cf. Acts 5:3.   [21] Cf. Acts 16:6f.   [22] Cf. Acts 13:2.
[23] Cf. E. Lohmeyer, *Galiläa und Jerusalem* (Göttingen, 1936); R. H. Lightfoot, *Locality and Doctrine in the Gospels* (London, 1938), pp. 78ff; H. Conzelmann, *The Theology of Saint Luke* (London, 1960), pp. 18ff.

and several of their adherents (including members of the family of Jesus), Galilaeans though they were, henceforth made their head-quarters in Jerusalem, Jesus had many more followers in Galilee than in Jerusalem, and not all his Galilaean followers migrated to Jerusalem. What did they do? Their faith, too, was restored after the resurrection, for some of Jesus' resurrection appearances took place in Galilee, but their subsequent story must be left largely to the imagination. We may envisage their faith and practice as dif-fering in a number of details from the faith and practice of their brethren in Jerusalem, and perhaps some of the forms of Christian life and teaching which appear in the apostolic history as defective by the standards of Jerusalem could be traced back to Galilee.[24]

4

The leaders of the community were the twelve apostles, desig-nated by Jesus as judges of 'the twelve tribes of Israel' in the new age.[25] That the Jewish Christians continued for decades to regard themselves as the true remnant of Israel, the 'twelve tribes', is im-plied by the superscription of the Epistle of James. The defection of Judas Iscariot made it necessary to co-opt one of their fellow-disciples to fill the vacancy; two were nominated, and the lot cast, after prayer, between the two pointed to Matthias as the new twelfth apostle. (Two stated qualifications of Matthias and of his unsuccessful co-nominee were that they should have been followers of Jesus and companions of the apostles since the time of John the Baptist's ministry, and that they should be personal witnesses to Jesus' resurrection.)[26] Some years later, when James the son of Zebedee, another member of the twelve, was executed by Herod Agrippa the elder, his death did not create a vacancy;[27] a faithful apostle carried his office over into the resurrection life. A succession in the apostleship was not envisaged.

At a very early stage in the community's life the brothers of Jesus are specially mentioned among its members.[28] This is the more striking since it is evident that they had no place among his follow-ers before his death; their attitude to him appears to have been re-

[24] Cf. Acts 18:24ff; 19:1ff (see pp. 321f, 327f).
[25] Matt. 19:28; Luke 22:30.
[26] Acts 1:21f.   [27] Acts 12:2.   [28] Acts 1:14.

served, if not hostile.[29] Paul's statement that Jesus in resurrection
'appeared to James' (I Cor. 15:7) provides an explanation of their
change of heart. James was apparently the eldest as well as the
most prominent of Jesus' four brothers, and was destined to occupy a prominent position in the Jerusalem church. He appears
in a few years' time as one of the three 'pillars' of that church, along
with the apostles Peter and John:[30] indeed, Paul designates him
an apostle as a matter of course.[31] (Paul's use of the term 'apostle'
embraces more than the twelve.) A few years later still James
emerges as the undisputed leader of the Jerusalem church, perhaps
president of the Sanhedrin of the new Israel.[32]

5

The community of goods which was practised in the earliest days
of the Jerusalem church was in part a continuation of the practice
of the twelve in the days when they had gone about with Jesus.
They shared a common purse, and Judas Iscariot was its custodian.[33]
It was also the spontaneous response of many of the new converts
to the forgiving grace which they had experienced. Many handed
their property over to the apostles, who put the proceeds into a
common pool from which a daily dole was distributed to the poorer
members of the community.[34] Unlike the highly organized and
obligatory community of goods at Qumran, this was unsystematic
and voluntary; on the other hand, the fate which befell Ananias
and Sapphira when they tried to gain public credit for greater generosity than was their due was more drastic by far than the penalty
prescribed in the Qumran *Rule* (one year's exclusion from the common meal and the docking of rations by one-fourth) for those
who 'knowingly deceived in regard to property'.[35]

6

The handicap with which the disciples embarked upon their
public witness to Jesus can scarcely be exaggerated. They were

[29] Mark 3:21; John 7:4.   [30] Gal. 2:9.   [31] Gal. 1:19.
[32] Acts 15:13ff; 21:18.
[33] John 12:6; 13:29.   [34] Acts 2:44ff; 4:32ff.
[35] Acts 5:1ff; cf. 1 QS vi, 24f (see p. 106).

bound to compromise themselves in the eyes of the Romans by proclaiming themselves the followers of a man whose execution had
followed his conviction in a Roman court on a charge of sedition.
And the idea of commending to their fellow-Jews as the long-
expected Messiah of Israel a man who had been crucified would,
on all rational grounds, have been ruled out as absurd and scan-
dalous. A crucified Messiah was a contradiction in terms.[36] Practically by definition, the Messiah of Israel was one on whom the
divine favour rested in an unparalleled degree; equally by definition, a crucified man was one on whom the divine disfavour rested,
for the sentence stood unambiguously in the Torah: 'a hanged man
is accursed by God' (Deut. 21:23). To many Jews the suggestion
that the crucified Jesus was the Messiah must have been intoler-
ably blasphemous. Yet the followers of Jesus, freely acknowledging
that their Master had been crucified, maintained that, by raising
him from the dead, God had reversed the death-sentence passed
upon him together with all that that death-sentence implied. To
Jesus' resurrection they themselves could bear first-hand witness,
and Old Testament *testimonia* were available to prove that his resurrection marked him out as the promised Messiah.[37]

Not only was he the promised Messiah; he was the prophet like
Moses of Deuteronomy 18:15-19 and the Isaianic Servant of Yahweh. The threefold identification of Jesus as Messiah, Prophet and
Servant is made in Peter's Temple-speech in Acts 3:12-26, following on the healing of a lame man in Jesus' name. The manifest
power of Jesus' name is explained as evidence that, in the language
of Isaiah 52:13, the Servant of Yahweh has been exalted and lifted
up and made very high. Through ignorance of his true character,
the leaders of the people had handed him over to Pilate and procured his execution. But the speaker and his companions could
bear witness that God had raised him from the dead, and a further
witness was provided by the healing sign which had been effected
in his name. 'What God foretold by the mouth of all the prophets,
that his Messiah should suffer, he thus fulfilled. Repent therefore,
and turn again, that your sins may be blotted out, that times of re-
freshing may come from the presence of the Lord, and that he may

[36] I Cor. 1:23.
[37] Cf. C. H. Dodd, *According to the Scriptures* (London, 1952); B. Lindars,
New Testament Apologetic (London, 1961).

send Jesus, your appointed Messiah, whom heaven must receive until the time for establishing all that God spoke by the mouth of his holy prophets of old'. Among those prophets was Moses, who spoke of the prophet to be raised up by God, to whom all must pay the utmost heed; 'and all the prophets who have spoken, from Samuel and those who came afterwards, also proclaimed these days'. Let the sons of the prophets, the heirs of God's covenant with Abraham, accept the blessing now made available through the one to whom all the prophets bore witness.

The Christology of this speech, with its emphasis on Jesus as servant and prophet, has been described as 'the most primitive Christology of all'.[38] Particularly noteworthy is the suggestion that, if Israel (or a representative number in Israel) would now repent, God would send Jesus from heaven as their Messiah to fill the rôle for which he had been designated. His coming would mark the establishment, or restoration, of all that God had promised through the prophets, and inaugurate a period of respite—presumably before the final cataclysm. The language here is similar to that used elsewhere of Elijah, who was expected to come to earth and restore all things to their proper status 'before the great and notable day of Yahweh' (Malachi 4:5; Mark 9:12).

7

If we call the early disciples 'Christians', we may use this as a term of convenience, but such use at this stage is an anachronism. The name 'Christian' did not come into use until the Gentile mission began, several years later; it was Greek-speaking inhabitants of Syrian Antioch who coined it.[39] The disciples themselves called their movement 'The Way';[40] to their fellow-Jews they were known as Nazarenes or, more precisely, Nazoraeans. The origin of this designation raises some knotty problems. Jesus was known as 'Jesus the Nazarene' or 'Jesus the Nazoraean'—both these forms appear in the Gospels, where they are synonymous with 'Jesus of Nazareth'.

[38] J. A. T. Robinson, *Twelve New Testament Studies* (London, 1962), pp. 139ff.
[39] Acts 11:26.
[40] Acts 9:2; 19:9, 23; 24:14, 22. Cf. E. Repo, *Der 'Weg' als Selbstbezeichnung des Urchristentums* (Helsinki, 1964).

The form 'Nazarene' is derived directly from the place-name
Nazareth (or Nazara); the form 'Nazoraean' may also be so derived,
by metathesis.[41] The disciples of Jesus may in their turn have been
called Nazarenes because they were followers of the Nazarene, but
the situation is complicated by evidence of a variety of groups bearing similar names. In some cases the name may mean 'observants'
(from Heb. *nāṣar*); in others it may mean 'Nazirites' (Heb. *nāzîr*,
'separated', 'consecrated'). There is no original connexion between
these two names, as they come from quite distinct roots; they may,
however, have been confused in later times especially when translated, or rather transliterated, into Greek. Even in the application
of the designation 'Nazoraean' to Jesus, one of the evangelists
presents us with a problem which has never been solved with complete satisfaction: according to Matthew, the holy family settled in
Nazareth of Galilee after returning from Egypt, 'that what was
spoken by the prophets might be fulfilled, "He shall be called a
Nazoraean"' (Matt. 2:23). No prophetic oracle with this precise
wording is known from the Old Testament or elsewhere; the favoured explanation of Matthew's reference is that it is a play on
words, relating Nazareth (*nṣrt*) and Nazoraean (*nṣwry*) to a word
with the same radical letters in Isaiah 11:1, where the promised
Davidic Messiah is described as 'a shoot from the stump of Jesse
and a branch (Heb. *nēṣer*)[42] . . . out of his roots'. In a Greek
writer like Matthew, however, we cannot rule out a word-play on
nāzîr ('Nazirite'), appearing in an Old Testament annunciation
formula in such a phrase as 'he shall be a Nazirite to God from
birth' (cf. Judges 13:7).

The problem is further complicated by evidence that there was
a Jewish sect of 'Nasaraeans' before the time of Christ.[43] Probably
we have to do with a designation given to adherents of various non-

[41] Cf. G. F. Moore, 'Nazarene and Nazareth' in *The Beginnings of Christianity*, ed. Foakes Jackson and K. Lake, 1 (London, 1920), pp. 426ff; W. O. E.
Oesterley, 'Nazarene and Nazareth', *ExT* 52 (1940–1), pp. 410ff; W. F. Albright, 'The Names "Nazareth" and "Nazoraean",' *JBL* 65 (1946), pp. 397ff;
M. Black, *An Aramaic Approach to the Gospels and Acts* (Oxford, 1967³),
pp. 197ff; H. H. Schaeder, *s.v.* Ναζαρηνός, Ναζωραῖος, *TWNT* IV, pp. 879ff
(E.T. 874ff).
[42] This word *nēṣer* appears in a special community sense in 1 QH vi, 15; vii,
19; viii, 6, 8, 10.
[43] Epiphanius, *Pan.*, 19. 3. 1f, where they are distinguished from Nazoraeans;
cf. M. Black, *The Scrolls and Christian Origins* (London, 1961), pp. 66ff.

conformist movements in Israel because of their 'observant' tendencies; a modern survival of this usage may be found among the Mandaeans, who call themselves by preference *nāṣōrāiā*. It might in any case have been applied to Jesus in this sense, but it adhered to him the more readily and distinctively because he was also a 'Nazarene' in the local sense, having been brought up in Nazareth.

If the ranks of the disciples of Jesus were augmented by a large number of nonconformist Jews, those who called them 'Nazarenes' may well have interpreted the term in the established sense of 'observants', with no special emphasis on Jesus' association with Nazareth. In the Christian tradition the designation is restricted to certain groups of Jewish Christians—more particularly to those who were regarded by their Gentile brethren as more orthodox than the Ebionites.[44] But in the Semitic-speaking world the designation has remained the general one for Christians, whether of Jewish or of Gentile stock; thus they are called *Naṣrānī* in the Qur'ān, where the word is interpreted to mean 'helpers' (*anṣar*).[45]

8

The disciples' public witness met with widespread acceptance in Jerusalem, and their following increased rapidly. Many of those who joined them may well have belonged to those pious communities which had for long waited for the kingdom of God—adherents of nonconformist movements in Israel. Some of these perhaps joined them *en masse*. But they also won over a number of Pharisees, and even a considerable body of priests.[46] Whether these priests continued to discharge their Temple duties, or would have been permitted to do so, we cannot be sure.

The one group that showed direct hostility to the new community was the Sadducean party, especially the chief priests and Temple authorities. They were the more disturbed as they witnessed the swift advance of a movement which they thought had been suppressed for good with its founder's death. They objected on religious grounds to people who made such a point of resurrection,

---

[44] Cf. Jerome, *De uiris illustribus* 3 (on the Nazarenes of Beroea = Aleppo). For the Ebionites see pp. 114, 391.
[45] Sura 3:45; cf. 11:14; also the Coptic *Gospel of Philip*, logion 47.
[46] Acts 6:7.

not content with maintaining it (like the Pharisees) as a future event, but underlining it by their assertion that in the case of one man, Jesus, resurrection had already taken place.[47] They objected to their activities on grounds of public order, since great crowds gathered to listen to them in the Temple precincts, especially in Solomon's colonnade, at the east end of the outer court.[48] And they objected to them because their preaching constituted a threat—indefinable, perhaps, but none the less radical—to the Jewish establishment of which they themselves were custodians. But the disciples enjoyed widespread goodwill; they were pious and practising Jews, attending the Temple services regularly, and could not be convicted of law-breaking. Attempts were made to repress them, to browbeat them into discontinuing their preaching, but they refused to be intimidated and persisted in proclaiming Jesus, crucified by men but raised to life by God, as Israel's true Messiah. In due course a more favourable opportunity for a campaign of repression presented itself, but this resulted from the adhesion to the community of a body of Hellenistic Jews, whose challenge to the establishment was much more explicit than was that of the apostles.

[47] Acts 4:2.   [48] Acts 3:11; 5:12.

17 Stephen, Philip and the Hellenists

1

At a very early stage in its existence the community of Jesus' disciples in Jerusalem embraced both 'Hellenists' and 'Hebrews'. These terms are introduced suddenly, without explanation, by Luke in Acts 6:1, where he mentions the complaint voiced by the Hellenists against the Hebrews in the primitive community, because in the daily distribution made from the common pool of property the widows of the Hellenistic group were being neglected.[1]

This division between Hebrews and Hellenists was primarily linguistic and cultural, but probably it had theological implications too. The Hebrews were evidently Jews who habitually spoke Aramaic, whose homeland was Palestine (or any other area where Aramaic-speaking Jews lived). The Hellenists, on the other hand, were Jews who spoke Greek and whose way of life, in the eyes of stricter Palestinians, smacked too much of Greek customs. Many of them would belong to the Greek-speaking Diaspora, even if they resided in Palestine for longer or shorter periods; but Palestine had

[1] Cf. W. Bauer, W. F. Arndt, F. W. Gingrich, *Greek-English Lexicon of the New Testament* (Chicago, 1957), s.v. Ἑλληνιστής': 'a Greek-speaking Jew in contrast to one speaking a Semitic language' (p. 251). See also G. P. Wetter, 'Das älteste hellenische Christentum nach der Apostelgeschichte', *Archiv für Religionswissenschaft* 21 (1922), pp. 410ff; H. J. Cadbury, 'The Hellenists', in *The Beginnings of Christianity*, ed. Foakes Jackson and K. Lake, v (London, 1933), pp. 59ff; H. Windisch, s.v. Ἑλληνιστής', *TWNT* II (Stuttgart, 1935), pp. 508f (Eng. tr. [Grand Rapids, 1964], pp. 511f); E. C. Blackman, 'The Hellenists of Acts vi, 1', *ExT* 48 (1936–7), pp. 524f; M. Simon, *St. Stephen and the Hellenists in the Primitive Church* (London, 1958), pp. 1ff; C. F. D. Moule, 'Once More, Who Were the Hellenists?' *ExT* 70 (1958–9), pp. 100ff; C. S. Mann, ' "Hellenists" and "Hebrews" in Acts vi, 1' = Appendix VI in J. Munck, *The Acts of the Apostles* (New York, 1967), pp. 301ff (where there is too ready an acceptance of A. Spiro's identification of 'Hebrews' and 'Samaritans' in Appendix V to the same commentary, pp. 285ff—for all the striking affinities between Stephen's exposition and Samaritan tradition to which Spiro draws attention).

its native Greek-speaking Jews.[2] If we ask when and how so many of these Hellenists were enrolled as disciples of Jesus, we may find the answer in Luke's narrative of the day of Pentecost, according to which Jews of the Diaspora formed a large, if not the main, part of Peter's audience.

There was no hard-and-fast linguistic barrier dividing Palestinian Jewry—as late as the Second Jewish Revolt of A.D. 132–135 Hebrew, Aramaic and Greek appear to have been used with equal facility in the insurgent ranks[3]—but there was a feeling that to use Hebrew or Aramaic was more 'patriotic'. An interesting sidelight is thrown by Luke on the situation in Jerusalem when he describes how Paul in A.D. 57, rescued by the Roman soldiery from the crowd that threatened to lynch him in the court of the Gentiles, was permitted by the military tribune to address the crowd from the top of the steps leading up from that court to the Antonia fortress. 'Paul, standing on the steps, motioned with his hand to the people; and when there was a great hush, he spoke to them in the Hebrew language, saying: "Brethren and fathers hear the defence which I now make before you". And when they heard that he addressed them in the Hebrew language, they were the more quiet' (Acts 21: 40–22:2). They had expected him to speak Greek, and presumably they would have understood him well enough had he done so, but his using the 'Hebrew language'—which in this context probably means Aramaic—was more congenial to them, whether it was more intelligible or not. Like Paul himself (despite his Tarsian origin),

[2] The presence of Hellenists in Palestine as early as the reign of Ptolemy Philadelphus (285–246 B.C.) is amply attested in the Zenon papyri (cf. V. Tcherikover, *Hellenistic Civilization and the Jews* [Philadelphia, 1959], p. 60, with n. 53 on pp. 427f for bibliography). Long before the foundation of Hellenistic empires in Egypt and Asia Minor there were Jewish settlements in those territories (cf. Jer. 44:1; Obad. 20), but they became much more numerous after the foundation of Greek cities there after Alexander's conquests. According to Josephus, Jews were settled in Cyrenaica by Ptolemy I and in Phrygia by Antiochus III to ensure the loyalty of those areas (*Ap.* ii, 44; *Ant.* xii, 147ff). There were Jews in Rome in the second century B.C.; their number increased greatly after Pompey's conquest of Judaea in 63 B.C. (cf. H. J. Leon, *The Jews of Ancient Rome* [Philadelphia, 1960]). The evidence of ossuaries in and around Jerusalem for the period preceding A.D. 70 indicates that Jews from the Diaspora liked to come home to Jerusalem if only to die and be buried there; they tended to be even more devoted to the Temple than the Pharisees and rabbinate.

[3] Cf. *Discoveries in the Judaean Desert* II: *Les Grottes de Murabba'at* (*Texte*), ed. P. Benoit, J. T. Milik, R. de Vaux (Oxford, 1961), *passim*.

they were 'Hebrews', not 'Hellenists'. The distinction is made not only in Greek documents but in Hebrew: in the Mishnah, for example, *'ēdīm 'ibrīm* are (Jewish) witnesses whose common language is Aramaic (or Hebrew), while *'ēdīm yěwānīm* are (Jewish) witnesses whose common language is Greek.[4]

The dissension over the unequal allocation of charity to the widows of the two groups introduces, in Luke's narrative, the appointment of seven men to take charge of the daily distribution. The seven may be judged by their names to have been Hellenists; one of them, indeed (Nicolaus), was a proselyte from Syrian Antioch. But they appear to have been much more than almoners (*septem uiri mensis ordinandis*); they may well have been the elected leaders of the Hellenistic group. That they maintained a more liberal outlook than the 'Hebrews', including the apostles, is evident from the sequel to the narrative of their election, which indeed is used by Luke as an introduction to the beginnings of the Gentile mission. Nicolaus, the Antiochene proselyte, figures in second-century Christian literature as the founder of the Nicolaitans,[5] who (as we learn from the Letters to the Seven Churches of Asia in the Apocalypse) endeavoured to relax the requirements of the Council of Jerusalem.[6] But the only two of the seven of whom we have detailed knowledge are Stephen and Philip. Stephen's short public career was marked by a vigorous attack on the Temple cultus in Jerusalem; Philip's career as an evangelist carried the gospel beyond the limits of Judaism.

Luke's account of Stephen's career is immediately preceded by the statement that 'a great many of the priests were obedient to the faith' (Acts 6:7). This statement belongs to one of the characteristic summaries of progress which punctuate Luke's history, but attempts have been made to relate it more closely to its context and to the Hellenistic party. The priests who adhered to the Christian faith have been associated, for example, with the recipients of the Epistle to the Hebrews, or with the Qumran community, or with

---

[4] Mishnah, *Gittin* 9:6, 8.
[5] Cf. Irenaeus, *Haer.* i, 26. 3; iii, 10. 6; Clement of Alexandria, *Strom.* iii, 4. 25f (cit. ap. Euseb., *HE* iii, 29). The derivation of the word from this particular Nicolaus may have been little more than a guess.
[6] Rev. 2:6; 3:15.

both.[7] If they were associated with the Qumran community, then their attitude to the Temple and its cultus, it is held, would have been similar to Stephen's. But the Qumran criticism of the Temple and cultus was due in the main to the contemporary dominance of an illegitimate high-priesthood; the community looked forward to a day when the true high-priestly line of Zadok would preside over an acceptable cultus in a purified Temple. Stephen's criticism was much more radical; it was directed against the Temple as such. Moreover, in spite of the prestige of Professor Cullmann's name and the weight of his arguments, it is very difficult to see any close connexion between the intensely conservative and exclusive community of Qumran and the missionary-minded liberalism of the Hellenists in the primitive church.[8] If, on the other hand, the priests of Acts 6:7 were Hellenists, they may have shared Stephen's outlook, in which case presumably they relinquished their Temple duties. But we have no evidence that they did so.

Stephen belonged to a Hellenistic synagogue in Jerusalem called the Synagogue of the Freedmen; its membership embraced Jews from Cyrene, Alexandria, Cilicia and proconsular Asia.[9] It was in this synagogue that he first publicly voiced his criticism of the Temple order and his conviction that that order had now been decisively superseded by the coming of Jesus. This led to a regular debate in the synagogue in which Stephen's arguments proved irrefutable. The next step was his formal indictment before the supreme court, which met under the presidency of the high priest (almost certainly Caiaphas). Stephen was charged with twofold blasphemy—against God, because he affirmed that Jesus had come to abolish the Temple and all that it stood for, and against Moses, because he affirmed similarly that Jesus had come to abrogate the customs laid down for Israel to keep in Moses' law.

To what extent he taught the abrogation of the Jewish Law we do not know. We know that some liberal Jews of the Diaspora taught

---

[7] Cf. K. Bornhäuser, *Empfänger und Verfasser des Briefes an die Hebräer* (Gütersloh, 1932); C. Spicq, *L'Épître aux Hébreux* I (Paris, 1952), pp. 226ff, and 'L'Épître aux Hébreux: Apollos, Jean-Baptiste, les Hellénistes et Qumrân', *Revue de Qumran* I (1958–9), pp. 365ff.

[8] Cf. O. Cullmann, 'The Significance of the Qumran Texts for Research into the Beginnings of Christianity', in *The Scrolls and the New Testament*, ed. K. Stendahl (London, 1958), pp. 18ff, especially pp. 25ff.

[9] Acts 6:9. See p. 236, n. 7.

that the external requirements of the law might be dispensed with, provided that the spiritual lessons conveyed by those requirements were observed. Philo criticizes such people: 'let us not abolish the law of circumcision', he says, 'on the ground that circumcision signifies the cutting away of pleasure and passions of every sort and the destruction of ungodly glory'.[10] Ananias, the Jewish instructor of Izates, king of Adiabene, advised him to worship God according to the Jewish law without being circumcised.[11] But more than this form of liberalism is implied in the case of Stephen. According to his accusers, the abrogation of 'the customs' which he announced was bound up with 'this Jesus of Nazareth'[12]—that is, with Jesus acknowledged as Messiah. There is evidence for one strand of thought in rabbinic Judaism according to which the age of the Messiah would supersede the age of Law.[13] If one who had been brought up to accept this doctrine came to believe in Jesus as the Messiah, then he would hold that the coming of Jesus abrogated the Law. This was probably Paul's experience, and it may have been Stephen's too. But no details are recorded of this part of the charge brought against Stephen. We can believe, however, that this point of view was represented among the Hellenists to whom he belonged, and it would inevitably cause tension between them and the more traditionalist 'Hebrews' in the church, not to speak of the bulk of Jerusalem Jewry.

The other part of the charge against Stephen bears a noteworthy resemblance to the charge which was unsuccessfully pressed against Jesus a few years before; 'we have heard him say that Jesus of Nazareth will destroy this place' (Acts 6:14) echoes the words of the witnesses at Jesus' trial: 'we heard him say, "I will destroy this temple that is made with hands, and in three days I will build another, not made with hands"' (Mark 14:58). At both trials the witnesses are called 'false witnesses'; any one who bears testimony against a witness for the truth is *ipso facto* a 'false witness'. (It is striking that in the Lukan account of the trial of Jesus no word is said about his destroying the Temple; this is one of sev-

---

[10] *De migr. Abr.*, 92.
[11] Josephus, *Ant.* xx, 41. See p. 282.   [12] Acts 6:14.
[13] TB *Sanhedrin* 97a, *Shabbat* 151b; cf. L. Baeck, 'The Faith of Paul', *JJS* 3 (1952), pp. 93ff; W. D. Davies, *The Setting of the Sermon on the Mount* (Cambridge, 1964), pp. 446ff.

eral instances of Luke's deferring for his second volume a theme
which his fellow-Synoptists treat in the context of Jesus' ministry.)

Stephen was given the opportunity of answering the witnesses'
allegations. The apologia in Acts 7, which is formally his reply to
the charges brought against him, might be regarded as a manifesto
of the Hellenistic group to which he belonged. It cannot be regarded
without qualification as a manifesto of Hellenistic Judaism in general, although no doubt there were certain elements in Hellenistic
Judaism which took the same radical attitude to the Temple as
Stephen did. Justin, in the second century, knows of Jews in the
Diaspora who interpreted Malachi 1:10f to mean that God had rejected the Temple sacrifices in favour of the prayers of his people
living among the Gentiles.[14] But what was decisive in Stephen's
attitude was his belief that Jesus by his coming and ministry had
sounded the death-knell of the Temple order.

So far as the charge of blasphemy against Moses is concerned,
Stephen's reply takes the form of a *tu quoque*; such a charge, he
suggests in irony, comes well from the offspring of those who, on
the testimony of their own sacred scriptures, so persistently opposed
Moses both in Egypt and in the wilderness, refusing to recognize
in him their divinely appointed judge and deliverer, and calling for
his supersession by a captain who would lead them back to Egypt.
Moses was but the first of many spokesmen of God who had to
endure similar opposition from Israel, and this pattern of behaviour
had now reproduced itself definitively in the national rejection of
Jesus, the final prophet to whom Moses and his successors had
pointed forward.[15]

This argument is not only a good example of early Christian apologetic and polemic against Jewish criticism; in its emphasis on Jesus
as the 'prophet like Moses' it reminds us of the Christology of the
Ebionites at a later date, and also of the Samaritan doctrine of the
Taheb.[16]

Interwoven with this theme in Stephen's apologia is his polemic
against the Temple order, more particularly against the state of mind
which the Temple order too easily fostered. The God of their fathers,
he reminded his hearers, was not confined to any single place; he
revealed himself to Abraham in Mesopotamia, he was with Joseph

[14] *Dialogue with Trypho* 41:2.   [15] Acts 7:37.   [16] See pp. 38, 213.

in Egypt, he spoke to Moses in the wilderness, where indeed the people of Israel had all that was requisite for true worship—the angel of the divine presence, the 'lively oracles', and the movable tabernacle, which was a much more fitting shrine for a pilgrim people than a permanent structure of stone, fixed to one spot. Even after the settlement in Canaan a mobile tent served them as a sanctuary until the days of David and Solomon. This is in line with the divine oracle spoken through Nathan to David: 'I have not dwelt in a house since the day I brought up the people of Israel from Egypt to this day, but I have been moving about in a tent for my dwelling' (II Sam. 7:6). Other prophets and righteous men in Israel had condemned or ridiculed the idea that the Most High could be accommodated in a material building or located at one specially hallowed spot,[17] but so long as the Jerusalem Temple continued to be in the eyes of the majority of the people the place which their God had chosen out of all others as his abode, it was difficult for them to resist the temptation of thinking that they had him at their disposal, just where they wanted him.

It is not plain from Stephen's apologia what conception of the divine dwelling-place he wished to recommend to his hearers instead of that which he deprecated. It may be that, like others in the apostolic age, he envisaged the community of the people of God as constituting the new Temple, but of this we cannot be sure, although a form of teaching which is common to the Pauline writings, the Epistle to the Hebrews, I Peter and the Apocalypse may well be regarded as primitive.[18] At any rate, Stephen's attitude to the Temple betokens a much clearer appreciation of the incompatibility of the old order with the implications of the teaching of Jesus than appears to have been common among the early disciples in Jerusalem. There is a contrast—perhaps a deliberate one—between the leading apostles who still attended the Temple services and this young Hellenist who proclaimed that with the coming of the Christ the Temple and all that it stood for had lost whatever status it might ever have possessed. There is a contrast, too, between Stephen and James the Just who, according to Hegesippus, was assiduous in his attendance at the Temple and commanded the esteem

[17] Cf. I Kings 8:27; Isa. 66:1; Jer. 7:4.
[18] Cf. A. Cole, *The New Temple* (London, 1950); B. Gärtner, *The Temple and the Community in Qumran and the New Testament* (Cambridge, 1965).

of the Jews in general for his devotion to the law and his constancy in prayer.[19]

The contrast between Stephen and James is all the more striking when we consider the affinities between Luke's account of the execution of Stephen and Hegesippus's account of the execution of James. Both bear witness before the Sanhedrin concerning the Son of Man at the right hand of God; both are executed by stoning in accordance with the traditional procedure. But the importance of these affinities should not be exaggerated; we must bear in mind the possibility that the later account of the martyrdom of James is influenced by Luke's description of the condemnation and death of Stephen.[20]

Stephen's reply concludes with the denunciation of his judges, whose recent rejection of the 'Righteous One' is completely in keeping with their fathers' rejection of the prophets who foretold his advent. Such language could not fail to provoke their anger, and Stephen, seeing their hostility and realizing the certainty of an unfavourable verdict, appealed from their judgement to that of the heavenly court, where Jesus stood as witness or counsel for the defence: 'I see the heavens opened', he said, 'and the Son of man standing at the right hand of God' (Acts 7:56). These words would inevitably remind the hearers of Jesus' words spoken in the same place a few years previously: 'From now on the Son of man shall be seated at the right hand of the power of God' (Luke 22:69). It is noteworthy that this is the only passage in the New Testament outside the Gospels where the title 'the Son of Man' occurs, and that Stephen is the only person apart from Jesus himself who is recorded as using it. It is equally noteworthy that, for Stephen, the Son of Man's rôle is an intercessory one. It cannot be reasonably doubted that the Son of Man whom he sees is the exalted Jesus; that is to say, Jesus appears to him as that Son of Man of whom Jesus himself spoke when he said: 'every one who acknowledges me before men, the Son of man also will acknowledge before the angels of God' (Luke 12:8). But the fact that the title is here used by a Hellenist throws but little light on its origin; the title is so thoroughly Ara-

---

[19] Eusebius, *HE* ii, 23. 4ff.

[20] This is more probable than H. J. Schoeps's view that Stephen in Acts is a 'substitute-figure' for James (*Theologie und Geschichte des Judenchristentums* [Tübingen, 1949], p. 441).

maic that it cannot be derived from a Hellenistic source. If a Hellenist uses it, that simply proves that it was such a characteristic locution of Jesus that it was early translated literally from Aramaic into Greek by the Hellenistic believers in Palestine. If Hegesippus's account of the martyrdom of James is to be trusted, the title continued to be used in the Palestinian church throughout the apostolic age;[21] its absence from the New Testament outside the Gospels and Acts 7:56 is probably due to the fact that such a distinctively Semitic idiom was too unintelligible for use in the Gentile mission.

As the words about the Son of Man on Jesus' lips sealed his conviction for blasphemy, so they did on Stephen's lips. But Stephen's sentence was executed by stoning, in accordance with the ancient law against the blasphemer. It was the duty of the witnesses to throw the first stones,[22] and Luke notes that as they prepared to do so, they laid their outer garments down 'at the feet of a young man named Saul' (Acts 7:58), who thus makes his début in the narrative of Acts. As a native of Cilicia, Saul may have been a member of the synagogue where Stephen held debate; in any case, he was acquainted with Stephen's views and abominated them, holding that Stephen was justly put to death.

The question naturally arises how Stephen's death sentence could have been executed without reference to the Roman governor if capital jurisdiction was withheld from the Jewish authorities.[23] There was no hiatus in Roman jurisdiction after Pilate left for Rome at the beginning of A.D. 37 of which Caiaphas or his successor could have taken advantage,[24] as a later high priest took advantage of the interregnum following the death of Festus in 62 to procure the conviction and execution of James the Just and some others.[25] In fact, during the period following Pilate's departure, Vitellius, governor of Syria, was taking an unusual personal interest in the affairs of Judaea. It is, in any case, difficult to date the death of Stephen and the conversion of Saul of Tarsus as late as 37. It has been suggested —e.g. by Joseph Klausner[26]—that Stephen's stoning was not the

---

[21] James says to his questioners: 'Why do you ask me about the Son of Man?' (Hegesippus *ap.* Euseb., *HE* ii, 23. 13).
[22] Deut. 17:7; cf. the details of later practice in Mishnah, *Sanhedrin* 6:1–4.
[23] See p. 200. [24] See pp. 38f. [25] See pp. 347, 373.
[26] *From Jesus to Paul* (London, 1944), p. 292.

execution of a regular death sentence but the action of a group of zealous hot-heads who took the law into their own hands. There are indeed some features of Luke's narrative which lend themselves to this interpretation, but it is nevertheless highly unlikely. The most probable account of the matter is that during the closing part of Pilate's administration, especially when he was resident in Caesarea, the Jewish rulers knew that they could take certain discreet liberties. After the fall of his patron Sejanus in A.D. 31, Pilate's position *vis-à-vis* Tiberius was too precarious for him to be over-scrupulous about intervention in internal matters of Jewish judicial procedure at Jerusalem. He was more than ever dependent on favourable— or, at least, not too unfavourable—reports to Rome from the high priest and Sanhedrin. Where public order was not imperilled, an incident like the stoning of Stephen would be over and done with long before it reached the procurator's ears, and on such a *fait accompli* he may well have judged it wise to turn a blind eye.

2

The death of Stephen was the signal for a campaign of repression by the authorities in Jerusalem against those who were of his way of thinking. Luke does not say explicitly that the Hellenists in the Jerusalem church were the principal targets of this campaign, but it emerges fairly clearly from his narrative that this was so. He represents Saul of Tarsus as taking the lead in the campaign, and this agrees with the account given by Saul (Paul) himself of his activities before his conversion: 'I persecuted the church of God violently and tried to destroy it' (Gal. 1:13). The Hellenistic disciples in particular were forced to leave Jerusalem. Although they were the chief victims in the persecution, their 'Hebrew' fellow-disciples did not pass through it unscathed. When Paul tells how 'the churches of Christ in Judaea' referred to him later as our former persecutor' (Gal. 1:22f), it is unlikely that he has none but Hellenistic communities in mind; the context shows that he includes the Jerusalem church, which by this time had very few Hellenists remaining in it.

One result of this short but sharp outburst of persecution was that from this time forth the Jerusalem church was predominantly

'Hebrew' in colour,[27] much more conservative than it might have been had the Hellenists been able to stay and play their full part in it. Another, and happier, result was that the evicted Hellenists carried the gospel with them to the neighbouring regions and provinces where they sought refuge, so that before long it took root in non-Jewish soil.

With Stephen's disappearance, Philip emerges as the outstanding man among the leaders of the Hellenists. He left Judaea for Samaria, and began to preach the gospel in one of the Samaritan cities. The best attested text of Acts 8:5 says that he went down to 'the city of Samaria',[28] without naming the city. It can hardly have been the ancient capital of that name, for it was now called Sebaste. Since the city in question was that in which Simon Magus had been active for a considerable time, we may think of his native town of Gitta,[29] some six miles west of Nablus; but that is no solid ground for concluding that it was here that Philip preached. In view of the evidence of the Fourth Gospel that both John the Baptist and Jesus engaged in brief ministries in Samaria,[30] it may seem more probable that Philip built on the foundation which they laid; we cannot be sure. At any rate, his preaching met with conspicuous success.

Simon Magus, according to Luke, was known by his devotees as 'that power of God which is called Great' (Acts 8:10). This is a curious form of words; Luke normally uses the expression 'which is called' to apologize for a foreign word, and it may be, as A. Klostermann suggested in 1883, that we have to do here not with the Greek adjective *megalē*, 'great', but with the Aramaic or Hebrew participle *mĕgalleh*, 'revealer'.[31] Whether this suggestion is accepted or not, Simon probably did claim to be the revealer of an esoteric form of advanced knowledge which would liberate those who acquired it from the domination of the evil world and raise

[27] But not exclusively so, as is shown by the mention of 'Mnason of Cyprus' in Acts 21:16.
[28] τὴν πόλιν τῆς Σαμαρίας (A B 69 etc.). Even so, H. von Soden and J. H. Ropes prefer the reading 'a city of Samaria' (πόλιν τῆς Σαμαρίας) of C D 81 byz. sah. boh.
[29] Justin, *Apol.* i, 26:2; Justin himself was a native of Flavia Neapolis (mod. Nablus) in Samaria (*Apol.* i, 1).
[30] See pp. 159, 169f.
[31] *Probleme im Aposteltexte* (Gotha, 1883), pp. 15ff.

them to the upper world of light. It would be anachronistic to think
of his teaching in terms of the elaborately developed Gnostic systems of the second century, but it could reasonably be described as
a species of 'incipient Gnosticism', which superficially bore a sufficiently close resemblance to the apostolic gospel to be somehow
syncretized with it. Before that gospel reached them, Simon's followers already 'believed in the coming of a Divine revelation
through a Divinely inspired human agent'.[32]

The accounts of Simon given by the apologists and church fathers
must be scrutinized with the utmost caution. Because they regarded
him as the father of Gnosticism, they tended to ascribe to him a
more fully developed system of Gnostic teaching than is probable for
the middle third of the first Christian century. But some of their
statements have historical probability in their favour. According to
the pseudo-Clementine *Recognitions*, he was a disciple of Dositheus;[33] according to the pseudo-Clementine *Homilies*, both Dositheus and he were at one time disciples of John the Baptist.[34] The
very existence of an individual named Dositheus has been doubted;
his name has been interpreted as a back-formation from the Dosithean sect.[35] At least the existence of the Dositheans is not in
serious doubt; they were a Samaritan sect characterized by features
not unlike those of the Essenes of Judaea. We have one or two
suggestive signposts here, but the lettering on them is too obscure
for us to be sure where they are directing us.

At the time of Philip's mission, Simon was probably the acknowledged leader of a Dosithean group, to which he imparted distinctive
teaching over and above their inherited beliefs—teaching of a rec-
ognizably 'Gnostic' hue. The Christian fathers regard him as the
father of Gnosticism; the description which they give of his system
of teaching suggests that it was 'nothing more or less than an assimilation of imperfectly understood Christian doctrines, to a funda-
mentally pagan scheme'.[36] It is perhaps going beyond the evidence

[32] A. Ehrhardt, *The Framework of the New Testament Stories* (Manchester,
1964), p. 163. G. Delling, *s.v.* μαγεία, *TWNT* iv (Stuttgart, 1942), p. 363
(Eng. tr. [Grand Rapids, 1967], p. 359), suggests that Simon regarded himself
as the *Taheb* (cf. p. 38).   [33] *Clem. Recogn.* ii, 8, 11f.
[34] *Clem. Hom.* ii, 23f.
[35] Cf. M. Black, *The Scrolls and Christian Origins* (London, 1961), p. 57.
[36] R. McL. Wilson, *The Gnostic Problem* (London, 1958), p. 100; cf. his article, 'Simon, Dositheus and the Dead Sea Sect', *ZRG* 9 (1957), pp. 21ff.

to say, as A. Ehrhardt does, that Philip 'admitted a pre-Christian
Gnostic sect into the communion of his Gospel'; but we may agree
with him that the record of Philip's mission, together with other
allusions in the New Testament writings to an early association of
Samaritans with the gospel, raises 'the question of the existence and
extent of Samaritan influences upon Primitive Christianity in general, and upon the Fourth Gospel in particular'.[87]

Whether any sort of contact was maintained between Philip and
Simon in later years is unknown; it was made clear, however, that
there was no room for Simon in the apostolic fellowship. The apostles remained in Jerusalem when the Hellenists and their leaders
were dispersed, but they maintained an active interest in the forward movement carried on by the Hellenists outside Judaea and
felt their responsibility to direct it. When news of Philip's Samaritan
mission reached them, Peter and John, two of the leading apostles,
visited Samaria and manifested their approval of Philip's work and
their welcome of his converts into their fellowship by laying their
hands on those who had received baptism 'into the name of the
Lord Jesus'.[99] The imposition of apostolic hands on these Samaritans
was immediately followed by visible or audible signs such as had
marked the descent of the Spirit on the apostles and their companions in Jerusalem on the day of Pentecost. Some special evidence
of this kind was probably necessary to convince the Samaritans, so
long accustomed to being despised as outsiders by Jerusalem, that
they were fully incorporated into the new community of the people
of God.[39] Luke may intend by this narrative to show that a new
nucleus of the expanding Church was established in Samaria, from
which the gospel proceeded to radiate in various directions.

But the visit of the apostles was the occasion for a breach between
them and Simon Magus, who showed by his reaction to the spiritual
manifestations which accompanied the imposition of their hands
that he had no comprehension of the inwardness of the Christian
faith. To him the gift of the Spirit was a superior kind of magic
which he hoped they would sell to him so that he could operate it
too. He appears in Christian tradition as the inveterate opponent
of the apostles, especially Peter, throughout their missionary travels.

[87] *The Framework of the New Testament Stories*, pp. 163f.
[88] Acts 8:16.
[89] Cf. G. W. H. Lampe, *The Seal of the Spirit* (London, 1951), p. 72.

That he himself travelled as far as Rome and taught his rival gospel
there is suggested by the presence in Rome over a century later
of a sect called the Simonians, who perpetuated his doctrines—
though whether the Simon whose followers they were was the Simon
who figures in Luke's narrative has been questioned, so problematical is our evidence.[40] But probably he was, and the brief appearance of Luke's Simon in the account of the evangelization of
Samaria may suggest how, at a very early date, a form of incipient
Gnosticism could strike roots in Hellenistic Christianity.

3

His Samaritan mission over, Philip is next found near Gaza, baptizing a God-fearer from the kingdom of Meroë on the Upper Nile,
who was on his way home from a pilgrimage to Jerusalem when
Philip met him and 'told him the good news of Jesus' on the basis
of the Isaianic Song of the Suffering Servant, which he was reading
at the moment when Philip encountered him.[41]

From Gaza Philip then made his way north along the Palestinian
seaboard, evangelizing the cities on the way until he reached Caesarea. There he appears to have settled down, no doubt making
Caesarea his base for further evangelistic activity; at any rate, it is
there that we meet him twenty years later, known to his fellow-
Christians as 'Philip the Evangelist'; known also as the father of four
daughters with the gift of prophecy.[42]

The population of the Palestinian seaboard, and especially of
Caesarea, was largely Gentile. The evangelization of this territory,
therefore, involved a greater extension of the scope of the gospel
than Philip's Samaritan mission. But the initiative in evangelizing
Gentiles is ascribed by Luke not to Philip but to the apostle Peter,
who, when the persecution in Judaea had died down, visited the
dispersed communities of disciples in Lydda, Joppa and other areas
in the Plain of Sharon, and while thus engaged was called to Caesarea to visit a God-fearing Roman centurion, Cornelius by name.
When Peter preached the gospel to Cornelius and his household,
they believed the message, and their belief was attended by such

[40] Cf. Justin, *Apol.* i. 26:2ff; Iren. *Haer.* i, 23. 1ff; Origen, *c. Cels.*, i, 57; see
H. Waitz, 'Simon Magus in der altchristlichen Literatur', *ZNTW* 5 (1904),
pp. 121ff.   [41] Acts 8:26ff.   [42] Acts 21:8f.

audible tokens of the power and approval of the Holy Spirit that
Peter had no option but to have them baptized, without raising
the question of circumcision.[43] The date of this incident is uncertain, but even if Cornelius was not the first Gentile convert to
Christianity, for Luke he was the first such convert of sufficient
note to be appealed to as a precedent, and the events in his home
constituted 'the Pentecost of the Gentile world'.[44] Philip's convert
from Meroë may have been baptized earlier than Cornelius, but his
baptism was a private action on Philip's part and thereafter he continued his journey home, whereas Peter's baptism of Cornelius took
place at the seat of the provincial government of Judaea, and was
held by many to represent an act of policy on the part of the whole
Jerusalem apostolate.

But the first large-scale evangelization of Gentiles took place not
in Caesarea but in Syrian Antioch, and the evangelists were neither
Peter nor Philip, but unnamed 'men of Cyprus and Cyrene' (Acts
11:20), members of the Hellenistic community that had fled from
Jerusalem and Judaea after Stephen's death. When these men, who
had made their way north through Syria and Phoenicia evangelizing
the Jewish communities on their way, reached Antioch, they began
to tell the story of Jesus to Gentiles as well as Jews, and large numbers of Gentiles welcomed the good news and hailed Jesus as the
Saviour who could meet their spiritual need.[45] In a great Greek
metropolis like Antioch—the third largest city in the world—there
were many competing cults and mystery religions which held out
the promise of salvation. The message which the men of Cyprus
and Cyrene brought was thus cast in terms which were not entirely
unfamiliar, but there was something about the Christ of whom the
visitors spoke which was peculiarly attractive and not paralleled in
any of the Lords and Saviours named in those other cults. To the
Gentiles of Antioch 'Christ' sounded like a personal name, not an
official designation as it properly was; naturally, therefore, in Anti-

[43] Acts 9:32–10:48.
[44] F. H. Chase, *The Credibility of the Acts of the Apostles* (London, 1902),
p. 79.
[45] If a distinctively Antiochene Christology can be detected in the New Testament, it may be regarded as a development of the doctrine of Stephen, Philip
and their associates; cf. D. Georgi, 'Der vorpaulinische Hymnus Phil. 2, 6–11',
in *Zeit und Geschichte: Dankesgabe an R. Bultmann*, ed. E. Dinkler (Tübingen
1964), pp. 263ff, especially p. 292.

och those people who had so much to say about *Christos* were
called *Christianoi*, 'Christ's people', and the name stuck. It is a
characteristically Gentile appellation, and would never have been
devised by Jews—even Greek-speaking Jews—since for Jews to call
Jesus' followers Christians would have seemed like an acknowledgement that Jesus, whom they followed, was indeed the *christos*, the
'Anointed One'.[46]

The men of Cyprus and Cyrene had started something the end
of which could not be foreseen. The Jerusalem apostles, who reserved supervisory rights over all the extensions of Christianity from
its mother-city, realized that this new extension in Antioch must be
controlled and directed if it was not to get out of hand and develop
into some wild syncretism. But instead of sending one or two of
their own number, as they had done when Philip's preaching in
Samaria proved so successful, they sent Barnabas, a foundation-
member of the church at Jerusalem. Barnabas was himself a Cypriot
by birth, and therefore probably a Hellenist, although he is also
said to have been a Levite, and bore the uncompromisingly Jewish
name Joseph. Barnabas, says Luke, was the sobriquet given him by
the apostles because of his 'encouraging' character. How precisely
Barnabas means 'son of encouragement', as Luke says it does (Acts
4:36), is a nice philological problem;[47] but all that is recorded of him
confirms the accuracy of this summing up of his character. No happier choice could have been made of a delegate to go to Antioch
to take charge of the Christian advance there. True to his name, he
was delighted at what he found there and encouraged the missionaries and the converts to go on as they had begun. Under his
guidance a vigorous church began to develop in Antioch—a church
in which from the outset a large proportion, if not the majority, of
the membership was Gentile by birth. The atmosphere of such a
cosmopolitan city as Antioch was vastly different from that of Jerusalem and the atmosphere of the new church of Antioch must have
been almost equally different from that of the mother-church of

[46] See pp. 126, 164.
[47] Gk. υἱὸς παρακλήσεως. The nearest affinity to Barnabas is the Palmyrene
Bar-Nebo, suggesting the sense 'son of (the) prophet'; perhaps 'exhortation',
one of the meanings of παράκλησις, is near enough to 'prophecy'. Alternatively,
one may think of a form of the Semitic root *nwḥ*, like Syriac *nawḥā*, which
might be rendered 'consolation' (another meaning of παράκλησις), but this is
less probable.

Jerusalem. This state of affairs was bound, sooner or later, to lead to tensions between the two churches.

At the moment these tensions lay in the future. Barnabas pressed ahead with the work of building up the church in Antioch, but he soon found the task more than he could perform single-handed. He knew a man who would make an admirable colleague. This man lived in Tarsus, so Barnabas went there to find him and bring him to Antioch. His name was Saul—that Saul of Tarsus who first makes his appearance in our records as an approving spectator at the execution of Stephen but who, under his Roman name Paul, was to make an indelible mark in world-history as the great apostle of the Gentiles.

18 Paul: The Early Years

1

'Saul, who is also called Paul',[1] was born in Tarsus, the principal city of Cilicia, probably in one of the first few years of the Christian era. His native city boasted a high antiquity; it had been subject at various times to the Assyrians and Persians, to Alexander the Great and the Seleucids. About 170 B.C. Antiochus Epiphanes gave it a new constitution as a free city, and it retained this status after it became part of the Roman Empire in 64 B.C. About the time of Paul's birth it enjoyed considerable fame as a centre of learning; its schools were devoted to philosophy, rhetoric and (in Strabo's words) 'the whole round of education in general'[2]—it was more or less what we should call a university city. It did not attract students from other parts of the Graeco-Roman world, as Athens and Alexandria did; on the other hand, some of its philosophers had a widespread reputation. Such were Athenodorus the Stoic and, after him, Nestor the Academic. Athenodorus, who could number the Emperor Augustus among his pupils, returned to his native Tarsus in 15 B.C. and reformed the civic administration. Among other things, a property qualification was now required for the exercise of full citizen rights.

As in other eastern cities, those citizens of Tarsus who also possessed the privilege of Roman citizenship would naturally form an aristocratic élite. Paul, as a Tarsian, was in his own words 'a citizen of no mean city' (Acts 21:39); but he was also a Roman citizen by birth (Acts 22:28).

How the Roman citizenship came into Paul's family we have no means of knowing. Cilicia fell within the *prouincia* of more than one Roman general in the first century B.C.—Pompey and Antony, for example—and the bestowal of Roman citizenship on approved individuals was included in the supreme authority (*imperium*) legally

[1] Acts 13:9.   [2] *Geog.* xiv, 5. 13.

exercised by these generals. But whether it was one of these, or someone else, who granted the citizenship to Paul's father or grandfather, we cannot tell; neither can we tell why it was so granted. As reasonable a suggestion as any was made by Sir William Calder: 'Had not his father (or possibly grandfather) been made a citizen by Antony or Pompey? Were they not a firm of *skēnopoioi* [tentmakers], able to be very useful to a fighting proconsul?'[3] But it is no more than a reasonable suggestion.

As a Roman citizen, Paul had three names—*praenomen* (first name), *nomen* or *nomen gentile* (family name) and *cognomen* (additional name or surname). Familiar examples of such threefold Roman names are Gaius Julius Caesar and Marcus Tullius Cicero. But of Paul's three names we know only his *cognomen*, *Paullus* in Latin. If we knew his *nomen gentile*, we should have some idea of the circumstances in which his family obtained the citizenship, for newly made citizens usually adopted the family name of their patron —and quite often his *praenomen* too. Thus if, for the sake of illustration, Paul's father had had the citizenship conferred on him by Antony, Paul's threefold name might have been Marcus Antonius Paullus.

Each legitimately born child of a Roman citizen had to be registered within thirty days (apparently) of birth. If he lived in the provinces, his father or some duly appointed agent made a declaration (*professio*) in the appropriate record office (*tabularium publicum*) to the effect that the child was a Roman citizen. This declaration was recorded in the official register (*album professionum*) and the father or his agent received a certified copy in the form of a diptych (folding tablets).[4] This certificate was legal evidence that a man was a Roman citizen. It is conceivable that, on the occasions when Paul appealed to his Roman citizenship, he was able to produce this certificate in confirmation of his claim.[5]

[3] In a personal letter dated February 18, 1953. He added, with reference to a publication of the addressee, 'You don't bring out enough that Paul was a great *swell*—compare recently, *mutatis mutandis*, a Hindu K.B.E.'

[4] F. Schulz, 'Roman Registers of Births and Birth-Certificates', *JRS* 32 (1942), pp. 78ff; 33 (1943), pp. 55ff.

[5] So F. Schulz, *JRS* 33 (1943), pp. 46f (cf. Acts 16:37; 22:25ff); A. N. Sherwin-White thinks it more probable that such certificates were normally kept in the family archives (*Roman Society and Roman Law in the New Testament* [Oxford, 1963], p. 149). A further uncertainty lies in the apparent fact that this registration of Roman citizens at birth was enacted by the *Lex Aelia Sentia*

In addition to his Roman names, Paul had a Jewish name, by which he was known in his family circle and in Aramaic-speaking circles such as the Christian communities of Damascus and Jerusalem. His Jewish name was Saul; it may be that his parents, who belonged to the tribe of Benjamin (Rom. 11:1; Phil. 3:5), gave their son this name because it was the name of the most illustrious member of that tribe in their nation's history, Israel's first king.

Paul describes himself as a 'Hebrew' (II Cor. 11:22), 'a Hebrew born of Hebrews' (Phil. 3:5). According to Jerome,[6] Paul's family belonged to Gischala in Galilee and emigrated to Tarsus at the time of the Roman conquest of Palestine; it is not known whether he derived this interesting piece of information from a reliable source or not. But Paul's statement that his parents were 'Hebrews' implies that they were Aramaic-speaking—not exclusively Aramaic-speaking, for no one could live for long in Tarsus without speaking Greek, but certainly, and perhaps by preference, Aramaic-speaking.[7] By all accounts they were as far as possible from imitating the assimilationist tendencies exhibited by many Jewish residents in Asia Minor. According to Luke's report of Paul's appearance before the Sanhedrin in Acts 23:6 they were associated with the Pharisaic party,[8] and this is corroborated by the fact that it was not to one of the schools of philosophy or rhetoric in Tarsus that they sent their promising son, but to the school of Gamaliel in Jerusalem. Gamaliel was the most distinguished disciple of Hillel, and succeeded him as head of the school which bore his name.

How early in Paul's life he was sent, or brought, to Jerusalem is a debatable point. Attempts to find in his later language and outlook traces of the influence which his native city exerted on him in his

---

of A.D. 4 and the *Lex Papia Poppaea* of A.D. 9. If Paul was born a year or two before the earlier of these laws, would he have been registered in this way? On the whole question see A. N. Sherwin-White, *The Roman Citizenship* (Oxford, 1939).

[6] *De uiris illustribus*, 5.

[7] C. F. D. Moule ('Once More, Who Were the Hellenists?' *ExT* 70 (1958–9), p. 100) suggests (what seems eminently reasonable) 'that the Ἑλληνισταί of the Acts were Jews living in Jerusalem who were chiefly distinguished by reading the Scriptures and worshipping in synagogue only in Greek, whereas the Ἑβραῖοι could use and understand Aramaic and perhaps Hebrew, even if they easily used Greek Scriptures also (as Paul evidently did).'

[8] He there calls himself 'a Pharisee, a son of Pharisees' (cf. Phil. 3:5, 'as to the law a Pharisee').

boyhood are not too cogent. It may be that Tarsus influenced him more in his thirties than it did in his earliest years, when his strict Jewish upbringing must have insulated him against much that another boy of the same age would have seen and heard there. Besides, the opening words of his address to the hostile crowd in the Temple court at Jerusalem, reported by Luke in Acts 22:3, suggest that he came to Jerusalem at an early age: 'I am a Jew, born at Tarsus in Cilicia, but brought up in this city at the feet of Gamaliel, educated according to the strict manner of the law of our fathers' —especially if they are punctuated, as perhaps they should be, 'I am a Jew, (*a*) born at Tarsus in Cilicia, but (*b*) brought up in this city, (*c*) educated at the feet of Gamaliel according to the strict manner of the law of our fathers'.[9] According to this punctuation he was brought up in Jerusalem—presumably for some years—before he entered Gamaliel's academy.[10]

How apt a pupil Paul was may be learned from his own account: 'I advanced in Judaism beyond many of my own age among my people, so extremely zealous was I for the traditions of my fathers' (Gal. 1:14). To master the corpus of law, both written and oral, was difficult; to observe it in detail was more difficult still; but twenty years and more after he became a Christian Paul could look back on his earlier days and sum up his conduct in the words: 'as to righteousness under the law blameless' (Phil. 3:6).

It is just possible that Paul's education under Gamaliel is recalled in a Talmudic reference to an unnamed pupil of that rabbi who exhibited 'impudence in matters of learning'.[11] If so, this passage reflects rabbinical disapproval of Paul's defection from his original course; his wrong attitude to the law (as it appeared) during his apostolic career was projected back to his student days.

At the feet of Gamaliel, in addition to rabbinical learning he and his fellow-students could well have been given prophylactic courses in Greek culture. We learn from the Talmud that his son Simeon had pupils who learned 'the wisdom of the Greeks';[12] and it is most

[9] This is the punctuation of the Nestle Greek text and of the 1958 edition of the Greek New Testament published by the British and Foreign Bible Society.
[10] Cf. W. C. van Unnik, *Tarsus or Jerusalem: The City of Paul's Youth* (London, 1962).
[11] TB *Shabbat*, 30*b*; cf. J. Klausner, *From Jesus to Paul* (London, 1944), p. 310.
[12] TB *Soṭah*, 49*b*.

probable that Simeon's father had such pupils too. Paul may well have acquired the rudiments of Greek learning in his school. There is no evidence that Paul ever received anything in the way of formal education from Greek teachers; the knowledge of Greek literature and culture that his letters reflect was part of the common stock of educated people in the Hellenistic world at that time, whether they were Jews or Gentiles.

In due course Paul appears to have been ordained to the rabbinate.[13] That he occupied some such position is suggested by the authority given him by the high priest to go to Damascus as his commissioner, in order to procure the extradition by the leaders of the Jewish community there of refugees from the persecution in Jerusalem which was precipitated by Stephen's condemnation and death. It has even been inferred from some passages in Acts— especially from Acts 26:10, where Paul says of the Jerusalem believers who were victims of that persecution, 'when they were put to death I cast my vote against them'—that he was a member of the supreme Sanhedrin; but this is not at all probable.[14]

In the narrative of Acts there is a sharp contrast between Gamaliel's moderate and temporizing policy towards the disciples of Jesus (Acts 5:34ff) and his pupil's intolerant attitude. Gamaliel's policy was more in consonance with the general Pharisaic point of view; but Paul's different attitude may have been due not only to a difference in temperament on his part but also to his keener appreciation of the threat implicit in the new movement to those features of his ancestral religion that he held most dear—above all, the supremacy of the Torah. To him the incompatibility of the old order and the new was as patent as it was to Stephen, to whose arguments he may have listened in the Synagogue of the Freedmen. But the two young men drew directly opposite practical conclusions from the conviction which they held in common. If Stephen argued, 'The new has

[13] According to tradition, the rabbinate could be entered only on condition that the candidate had a comprehensive knowledge of the written and oral law, was conversant with the *talmîḏê ḥăḵāmîm* ('disciples of the wise'), and was forty years old. Paul had not fulfilled the third qualification, but it is questionable whether the tradition goes back beyond A.D. 70. Cf. E. Lohse, *Die Ordination im Spätjudentum und im Neuen Testament* (Berlin, 1951), and critique by A. Ehrhardt, *The Framework of the New Testament Stories* (Manchester, 1964), pp. 132ff.

[14] A 'young man' (νεανίας, Acts 7:58) would scarcely belong to the council of elders (γερουσία).

come; therefore the old must go', Paul argued, 'The old must stay; therefore the new must go'.

After the death of Stephen, Paul figures as the leader in the persecution of the disciples of Jesus in Judaea. His activity at that time was something he never forgot; not only does he revert to it in public preaching and private prayer in the narrative of Acts, but in his epistles he repeatedly refers to it: 'I am the least of the apostles', he says, 'unfit to be called an apostle, because I persecuted the church of God' (I Cor. 15:9). His persecuting career, however, was brought to a sudden stop and he was turned round in his tracks when, outside the city of Damascus, he was, as he put it himself, 'apprehended by Christ Jesus' (Phil. 3:12). Three times over the story of his conversion is told in Acts—once in the third person and twice on his own lips—so great, we may judge, was the importance attached to this event by Luke. Briefly, Luke's account tells how, as he approached Damascus with the high priest's commission to arrest 'any belonging to the Way' there and bring them in chains to Jerusalem, a blinding light flashed around him. He fell to the ground, and heard the risen Lord take him to task for persecuting him, using the Aramaic vernacular to do so: 'Šā'ūl, Šā'ūl, mā'att rāḍĕpinnî?' In that moment Paul became the lifelong bondslave of a new master, whose commands brooked no questioning: he was told to continue his journey into Damascus and await further orders there. 'Blasted with excess of light' he was led by his companions to his lodging in the 'street called Straight',[15] and remained sightless and fasting for three days. He was then visited by a disciple in Damascus named Ananias, 'a devout man according to the law' (Acts 22:12), who greeted Paul as a brother and laid his hands on him. Paul immediately recovered his sight and was able to take food and drink. Ananias also acted as the mouthpiece of Christ, giving Paul the further orders which he had been told to expect, bidding him be baptized and conveying to him Christ's commission to be his witness to the world.[16]

[15] The name persists today in the Darb al-Mustaqim.

[16] Since Damascus was the place where Paul was first welcomed into Christian fellowship, one may speculate whether this was a factor in the Qumranic affinities which have been discerned in his writings. Such speculation would depend on the assumption (not unreasonable in itself) that the Damascus to which, according to the *Zadokite Work*, some at least of the followers of the Teacher of Righteousness migrated (*CD* vi, 5, 19; vii, 19; viii, 21; xx, 12), was

A number of attempts have been made to explain this experience in medical and psychological terms. Of greater practical moment is the meaning which it had for Paul. To him it was the occasion when Christ, who had earlier appeared in resurrection to his original apostles and other followers, appeared 'last of all' to Paul himself (I Cor. 15:8), the occasion when he 'saw the Lord' (I Cor. 9:1), when God, who had set him apart for his special ministry before he was born, 'was pleased to reveal his Son' in him so that he might be his herald among the Gentiles (Gal. 1:15f). To Paul his conversion from Judaism and his call to be an apostle of Christ were part of a single revolutionary experience.

Revolutionary indeed, for it meant not only a sudden and total change of attitude towards Jesus and his followers, but the occupation by Jesus of the central place which hitherto the Law had held in Paul's life and thought. It was the Law that had dictated his previous attitude to Jesus: according to the Law 'a hanged man is accursed by God' (Deut. 21:23), and these words were clearly applicable to Jesus.[17] Whether Jesus was put to death justly or unjustly was, in comparison with this, an academic question; what was important was that since he was put to death by crucifixion, he had died under the curse of God, and therefore could not conceivably be the Messiah, upon whom, almost by definition, the blessing of God rested in unique measure. To claim that Jesus was the Messiah was therefore blasphemous; those who made such a preposterous claim deserved to suffer as blasphemers. For they were not simply deluded fools; they were deceivers and impostors. They bolstered up their claim that Jesus was the Messiah by asserting that he had risen from the dead—that, in fact, they themselves had seen him in resurrection. But such an assertion could not be listened to for a moment; the Law nowhere hinted that the divine curse pronounced upon 'a hanged man' could ever be reversed, as his being raised from death would imply. Paul had no doubt at all of the rightness of his course while he was engaged in stamping out this blasphemy, as he saw it; his conscience was clear as he thus manifested his

the literal Damascus. Were Ananias and his associates, it might be asked, followers of the Teacher of Righteousness before becoming disciples of Jesus? See E. Repo, *Der 'Weg' als Selbstbezeichnung des Urchristentums* (Helsinki, 1964), pp. 84ff.

[17] These words are interpreted as covering crucifixion ('hanging men alive') in 4 Qp Nahum. See p. 76 with n. 22.

zeal in the service of God and the Law. The 'introspective conscience of the West'[18] may imagine that Paul had subconscious
misgivings about his conduct while he was active as arch-persecutor,
but nothing that Paul himself says in later life about this conduct
supports any such idea.

And then, without warning, the Crucified One appeared to him
in a form too compelling to admit of any doubt, and identified
himself to Paul as 'Jesus of Nazareth, whom you are persecuting'
(Acts 22:8; cf. 26:15). The disciples had been right after all: the
hanged man' had indeed risen from the dead, and must consequently be acknowledged as Lord and Messiah. The pronouncement
of the divine curse on the hanged man still stood in the Law; it must
therefore be accepted that the Messiah had incurred this curse, but
now this paradox had to be considered and explained. Sooner rather
than later, Paul saw the solution of the problem in the argument
which he expounds in Gal. 3:10–14, where he says that Christ, in
accepting death by crucifixion, voluntarily submitted to the divine
curse and thus released his people from the curse which the Law
pronounces on all who break it (Deut. 27:26) by 'becoming a curse'
on their behalf.

Not only so, but for Paul the belief that the Messiah had come
carried with it the corollary that the era of the Law had come to
an end. There is some evidence that some rabbinic schools of
thought maintained this point of view—that the validity of the Law
would cease when the days of the Messiah dawned—and it may be
that Paul had learned this doctrine.[19] But whether he had learned
it previously or not, he maintained it vigorously in his Christian
life and teaching. 'Christ is the end of the law, that everyone who
has faith may be justified' (Rom. 10:4). Therefore, any attempt to
impose the Law on believers in Christ, as a means of acceptance
in God's sight, was in effect, even if not in intention, a denial that
the Messiah had come—a denial that Jesus was the Messiah.

That Jesus was the Messiah, and that accordingly he had superseded the Law as the way of life, was cardinal to Paul's thinking
from his conversion onward. Hitherto all his thinking had been

[18] Cf. K. Stendahl, 'The Apostle Paul and the Introspective Conscience of
the West', *HTR* 56 (1963), pp. 199ff.

[19] Cf. L. Baeck, 'The Faith of Paul', *JJS* 3 (1952), pp. 93ff; see p. 221 with
n. 12.

organized around the Law as its central and directive principle. When that principle was displaced, the component parts of his thinking fell apart, only to begin immediately to be reorganized in a new pattern around the risen Christ, the new central and directive principle. Henceforth, for Paul, life was—Christ (Phil. 1:21).

2

According to Paul's own account, his conversion was followed by his departure for Arabia (Gal. 1:17). It has commonly been supposed that he went to the desert, so that in the light of his conversion he might commune with God and re-think his whole attitude to life in the solitudes where Moses and Elijah had communed with God in the earlier days of his nation's history. This may be so, but there is some evidence that it was not only for solitary meditation that he left Damascus for Arabia. For when he returned from Arabia to Damascus (Gal. 1:17), he had an adventure which suggests that he had done something to attract the unfriendly attention of the Arabian king: 'the ethnarch of King Aretas',[20] he tells us elsewhere, 'guarded the city of the Damascenes in order to seize me, but I was let down in a basket through a window in the wall, and escaped his hands' (II Cor. 11:32f).

The reference to King Aretas suggests that the 'Arabia' to which Paul went was the Nabataean kingdom, which came up to the walls of Damascus and may even at this time have included the city itself. This last inference has been drawn from the absence of Damascene coins bearing the image of the Roman emperor between A.D. 34 and 62, and it would explain why an 'ethnarch' of Aretas had such authority in Damascus as Paul implies.[21] (Another suggestion is that the ethnarch was waiting to arrest Paul the moment he stepped out of Damascus into Nabataean territory, but this is not the natural implication of Paul's language.)[22] If, then, Paul so quickly became *persona non grata* in the eyes of the Nabataean authorities, may he not have begun to fulfil his commission to

[20] Nabataean king 9 B.C.–A.D. 40 (see p. 28).
[21] Cf. E. Schürer, *HJP* II. i. p. 98.
[22] According to Acts 9:23 the Damascene Jews were watching the city gates to assassinate Paul.

---

preach to the Gentiles during this visit to 'Arabia', and in so doing incurred their hostility?

From Damascus, in the third year after his conversion, he made his way to Jerusalem. His reception there was bound to be difficult. His old friends would now look on him as a renegade, but where was he to find new friends? Among those whom he had so recently persecuted? But would they be so ready to let bygones be bygones, even if they believed in the genuineness of his conversion? At this juncture it was Barnabas, the Levite from Cyprus, who proved himself a friend in need to Paul, and assured the Christian leaders in Jerusalem that he was no *agent provocateur*. Barnabas had presumably known Paul before his conversion—perhaps he too was a member of the synagogue which Stephen and Paul attended. Thanks to Barnabas's good offices, Peter was now sufficiently persuaded of Paul's *bona fides* to entertain him as his guest for a fortnight. It was indeed principally to meet Peter that Paul visited Jerusalem at this time.[23] The only other apostle whom he met during his visit was James the Just,[24] who, although he had not been one of the twelve appointed by Jesus, nevertheless rapidly attained such eminence in the Jerusalem church and beyond it that he ranked as an apostle alongside them.

Paul's desire was not only to make Peter's acquaintance, but to acquire information which Peter was specially competent to impart. For all Paul's insistence on his independence of the Jerusalem apostles, he knew the importance of being well-informed on the facts of Jesus' ministry, passion, and resurrection appearances—and who was better able to give him this information than Peter? Even James, brother of Jesus though he was, was not so useful in this respect as Peter, since James had not been a companion of Jesus during his ministry. But one thing neither Peter nor James could impart to him, and that was apostolic authority, for this, Paul insists, he had already received direct from the risen Lord.

Paul must have distinguished in his mind between the sense in which he did not receive the gospel from man, since it came to him

[23] Gal. 1:18, where he says he went up to Jerusalem ἱστορῆσαι Κηφᾶν, 'to interview Cephas', 'to make inquiry of Cephas'. Cf. G. D. Kilpatrick, 'Galatians 1:18 ΙΣΤΟΡΗΣΑΙ ΚΗΦΑΝ' in *New Testament Essays in Memory of T. W. Manson*, ed. A. J. B. Higgins (Manchester, 1959), pp. 144ff; W. D. Davies, *The Setting of the Sermon on the Mount* (Cambridge, 1964), pp. 453ff (Appendix IX, 'The Use of the Term ἱστορῆσαι in Gal. 1. 18'). [24] Gal. 1:19.

without mediation, 'through a revelation of Jesus Christ' (Gal. 1:12), and the sense in which he did receive it as something to be transmitted to others as it had been transmitted to him (I Cor. 15:3).[25] If he had been asked to elucidate this distinction between the gospel as 'revealed' and the gospel as 'received', he would probably have said that the essence of the gospel, 'Jesus Christ the risen Lord', was revealed to him in his conversion experience, while the factual details were related to him by first-hand witnesses who were 'in Christ' before he was. In this latter sense he reminds his Corinthian converts how he had 'delivered' to them 'as of first importance what I also received,[26] that Christ died for our sins in accordance with the scriptures, that he was buried, that he was raised on the third day in accordance with the scriptures, and that he appeared to Cephas [Peter], then to the twelve; then he appeared to more than five hundred brethren at one time . . . Then he appeared to James, then to all the apostles' (I Cor. 15:3-7).

This summary of resurrection appearances falls into two series, headed respectively by the individual appearances to Peter and to James. Since this is something which Paul says he 'received', nothing is more likely than that he was told it by Peter and James during that fortnight in Jerusalem. Hence he goes on to emphasize that, whatever differences might exist in other respects between himself on the one hand and Peter, James and their colleagues on the other hand, they were all agreed unanimously in the proclamation of these basic facts: 'whether then it was I or they, so we preach and so you believed' (I Cor. 15:11).

If, however, Paul had begun to preach before he met Peter and James, what did he preach? On the basis of his knowledge of the Old Testament prophets, interpreted in the light of his Damascus revelation, he was able to proclaim 'Jesus Christ the risen Lord' without any delay. This agrees with the account given by Luke,

---

[25] Cf. H. Lietzmann, *HNT: An die Korinther I–II*[2] (Tübingen, 1923), p. 58; P. H. Menoud, 'Revelation and Tradition: The Influence of Paul's Conversion on his Theology', *Interpretation* 7 (1953), pp. 131ff; B. Gerhardsson, *Memory and Manuscript* (Lund, 1961), pp. 272ff. O. Cullmann argues that the tradition stemming from the historical Jesus was at the same time validated by the exalted Lord (*The Early Church* [London, 1956], pp. 66ff).

[26] The verbs rendered 'deliver' (παραδίδωμι) and 'receive' (παραλαμβάνω) are the Greek equivalents of Heb. *māsar* and *qibbēl*, the technical terms for the process of transmitting rabbinical tradition.

that 'for several days' after his conversion and baptism 'he was with
the disciples at Damascus; and in the synagogues immediately he
proclaimed Jesus, saying, "He is the Son of God"' (Acts 9:19f).
After meeting Peter and James, however, he was able to fill in further details, delivering to others what he himself had received.

After this brief visit to Jerusalem, Paul returned to his native
Tarsus. According to Luke, his departure from Jerusalem was ex-
pedited by his new friends, who got wind of a plot against his life
made by a group of Hellenists—perhaps members of that synagogue
in which he and they had once opposed Stephen.[27]

For a number of years—eight or ten—Paul now disappears almost
entirely from view. That they were not inactive years is plain from
his statement that news kept on coming to the churches of Judaea
that their former persecutor was now 'preaching the faith he once
tried to destroy' and gave them cause to praise God (Gal. 1:22–4).
These years were spent in the north-western part of the province
Syria-Cilicia (Eastern Cilicia formed a single administrative unit
with Syria from 38 B.C. to A.D. 72). To this period belongs the ecstatic experience described by Paul in II Cor. 12:2ff, when he received an unutterable revelation which evidently he prized highly,
but which left its mark on him for the rest of his life in an embarrassing physical disability.[28] In this period too we should probably date
some of the sufferings which he enumerates in II Cor. 11:23–7, including beatings at the hands of both Jewish and Gentile authorities.
And it is very probable that in these years, while he was engaged in
his mission to the Gentiles in and around Tarsus, Paul came into
closer contact with Hellenistic culture than he had been permitted
to do in his earliest years in Tarsus. But the main direction of his
faith and life was already too firmly fixed—first by his training in
rabbinical Judaism and then by his confrontation with the risen
Christ—to be radically influenced by Hellenism. We recognize in
his writing concepts and phrases, especially from a Stoic background, which were in the air at the time and which he was quite
ready to use in a Christian context; but Paul's gospel, while it was
pre-eminently the gospel for the Hellenists, was no Hellenized gos-

[27] Acts 9:29f.
[28] His 'thorn in the flesh'; if it had been possible to identify this satisfactorily,
the right identification would have imposed itself long ago.

pel. It was this very fact that gave it the quality of 'folly' in the eyes of those hearers of his who set some store by worldly wisdom.

From the obscurity of these years he emerges about A.D. 45, when Barnabas came to Tarsus to look for him, and brought him back to Syrian Antioch to be his colleague in the pastoral ministry with which he had been entrusted among the Gentile Christians of that city.

10 Crisis Under Gaius

1

The Emperor Tiberius left a will in which his eighteen-year-old grandson Gemellus and his twenty-five-year-old grand-nephew Gaius were named as his joint heirs.[1] But after his death the Senate was persuaded, principally by Sertorius Macro, Sejanus's successor as prefect of the Praetorian Guard, to set aside the will on the pretext of Tiberius's alleged insanity and to bestow the principate on Gaius. Gemellus was the son of Tiberius's late son Drusus, but Gaius was the son of Tiberius's nephew Germanicus, popular commander-in-chief of the Army of the Rhine, and his late father's popularity now stood him in good stead. He succeeded to the supreme power amid widespread rejoicing, and high hopes were entertained of a welcome change from the oppressive rule of the morose and suspicious Tiberius.

As a little boy, Gaius, with his mother Agrippina the elder and his brothers and sisters, lived at his father's headquarters on the Rhine, and was dressed in diminutive military uniform, boots and all. Hence the soldiers called him Caligula ('Little Boots'),[2] and the nickname has stuck to him ever since, although naturally he disowned it when he grew up, and especially after he became emperor.

For the first six months of his reign the high hopes which had attended its inception bade fair to be realized. In October of A.D. 37, however, he became seriously ill, and when he recovered there was a change in his character. Josephus, after describing the magnanimity and moderation which he showed and the popularity which he enjoyed at the beginning of his reign, goes on to say that 'with the passage of time he no longer thought of himself as an ordinary man, but was driven by the greatness of his power to

[1] Suetonius, *Tiberius*, 76.   [2] Suetonius, *Gaius*, 9.

deify himself'.[3] There is no doubt that he became progressively unbalanced, and when his madness reached a point at which he could no longer be tolerated, since there was no constitutional way of removing a living emperor, he was assassinated.

At the beginning of his principate Gaius released Herod Agrippa from the prison into which he had been thrown for offending Tiberius,[4] and heaped great honours on him in token of his undying friendship. Not only did he present him with a chain of gold equal in weight to the iron chain with which he had recently been bound; he appointed him ruler of the territory which his uncle Philip had governed as tetrarch until his death three years previously, together with the more northerly territory of Abilene which had formerly been the tetrarchy of Lysanias. With these territories, Gaius gave Agrippa the title 'king'.[5]

Agrippa's sister Herodias now urged her husband Antipas to petition the emperor to raise *his* title from tetrarch to king. For more than forty years Antipas had ruled Galilee and Peraea in Rome's interests, incurring the ill-will of his neighbours by acting as the emperor's faithful agent and informer in that part of his dominions. It would be but a small requital for such long and thankless service rendered to Rome if Antipas were now, at the end of his days, to receive the royal style. If the emperor had so readily bestowed this style on his spendthrift boon-companion Agrippa, surely he would recognize Antipas's more solid claim to equal honour.

So Herodias argued; but Antipas, who was not called 'that fox' by Jesus for nothing,[6] told her that it was wisest to leave well alone. She persisted, however, and at last he was persuaded against his better judgement to set out for Rome to present his request. As he had feared, it was his undoing. Instead of receiving what he sought, he lost what he already had. For Agrippa now gratified his long-standing animosity by sending a letter to poison the emperor's mind against Antipas. Antipas, said this letter, had been confederate with Sejanus before Sejanus fell from power in A.D. 31, and he was now conspiring to Rome's disadvantage with Artabanus III of Parthia. Moreover, in his arsenal at Tiberias, Antipas had armour sufficient for 70,000 men.

When Antipas appeared before Gaius at the emperor's country

[3] *Ant.* xviii, 256. [4] See p. 29.
[5] Josephus, *BJ* ii, 181; *Ant.* xviii, 236ff. [6] Luke 13:32.

house at Baiae, Gaius was reading Agrippa's letter. He looked up and asked Antipas if this report about the armour in the arsenal was true. Antipas could not deny it, and was sentenced on the spot to exile at Lyons. As for Herodias, the emperor told her that he proposed to treat her as the sister of his friend Agrippa and not as the wife of his enemy Antipas; she might retain her property and continue to live in the style to which she was accustomed. Herodias, like other ladies of her family, had the qualities of her defects; she assured the emperor disdainfully that she preferred to accompany her husband into exile. This she did, and in exile Antipas and Herodias disappear from history. Antipas's tetrarchy of Galilee and Peraea, with the rest of his property, was added to Agrippa's kingdom (A.D. 39).[7]

Agrippa's character thus far appears unattractive; nevertheless, his friendship with Gaius was to turn out greatly to the Jews' advantage in a crisis which came to a head not long after Antipas's banishment.

2

The large Jewish community of Alexandria in Egypt had lived there for generations as a distinct civic corporation (*politeuma*) administered by its own senate (*gerousia*) under an ethnarch, within the larger civic corporation of Alexandria.[8] The situation is obscured somewhat by the language of Jewish apologists like Philo and Josephus, who are inclined to exaggerate the privileges traditionally enjoyed by the Alexandrian Jews, but it seems clear that membership of the Jewish community did not necessarily carry with it fellow-citizenship with the Greeks of Alexandria. Indeed, the majority of Alexandrian Jews were probably well content with their own civic status and did not covet a share in that of their Greek neighbours, which would have involved more association with pagan practices than an orthodox Jew could countenance. Some distinguished Jews of Alexandria did indeed enjoy membership of both *politeumata*, like Philo's brother Alexander, who was chief

---

[7] Josephus, *BJ* ii, 182f; *Ant.* xviii, 240ff.

[8] Ps.-Aristeas, *Ad Philocratem* 310 (cf. Josephus, *Ant.* xii, 108); Philo, *Flaccus* 74. Cf. E. M. Smallwood, *Philonis Alexandrini Legatio ad Gaium* (Leiden, 1961), pp. 5ff.

customs officer (*arabarchēs* or *alabarchēs*) of Alexandria. But other ambitious members of the Jewish community, especially (we may infer) of an assimilationist tendency, maintained that the privileges of full Alexandrian citizenship should be granted them by right, even if they were not prepared to accept all the social responsibilities which that citizenship normally implied.

Under the Ptolemies, the Jews and Greeks of Alexandria lived together peaceably enough. But the circumstances in which Egypt fell under Roman control inevitably poisoned relations between the two communities; for the Jews consistently took the Roman side, and profited by the incorporation of Egypt within the Roman Empire after the Battle of Actium in 31 B.C. and the suicide of Cleopatra, the last monarch of the Ptolemaic dynasty, in the following year. While the Romans confirmed the privileges of the Alexandrian Jews, they tended to despise the Alexandrian Greeks.[9] Those Alexandrians who most resented Roman rule tended also to be anti-Jewish. One of these was a schoolmaster named Apion, whose literary attacks on the Jewish nation were answered several decades later by Josephus in his treatise *Against Apion*. In this situation any move to increase Jewish privileges in Alexandria was bound to be met with hostile opposition.

In A.D. 32 or 33 Aulus Avillius Flaccus was sent to Alexandria by Tiberius as prefect of Egypt.[10] The earlier years of his governorship were relatively uneventful, apart from some brushes with Alexandrian 'nationalists', among whose leaders Isidore and Lampo are well known by name. But with the accession of Gaius, his position became precarious, for he had some years before taken part in the prosecution of Gaius's mother which resulted in her banishment to Pandateria in A.D. 29 and her death by starvation there three years later. So long as his friend Macro remained in office as prefect of the Praetorian Guard, Flaccus felt reasonably safe; but when Macro fell a sudden victim to Gaius's caprice early in A.D. 38, Flaccus was panic-stricken. One wonders if he knew that, shortly before Macro's execution, Gaius tried to put him off his guard by appointing him prefect of Egypt in Flaccus's place.

The terror under which Flaccus now lived was detrimental to the efficiency of his administration. One symptom of this may be seen

9 Cf. Cicero, *Pro Rabirio Postumo*, 35.
10 For the following narrative cf. Philo, *Flaccus*, *passim*.

in his omission to transmit to Rome the resolution which the Jews of Alexandria passed in honour of Gaius at his accession. Flaccus promised to forward the resolution, together with a covering letter containing his personal testimony to the Jews' loyalty. His failure to keep his promise is attributed by Philo to anti-Jewish malignity; more probably it was due to sheer forgetfulness arising from pre-occupation with his own precarious position, for there is no reason to credit him with anything in the nature of anti-Jewish sentiment or activity until after Macro's death.

It was then that the leaders of the anti-Jewish movement among the Alexandrian Greeks approached him and undertook to repre-sent him in the most favourable light to Gaius if he would adopt an anti-Jewish policy. The wretched Flaccus agreed. To begin with, his policy consisted in little more than 'working to rule' where Jews were concerned. By use and wont they had acquired privileges in Alexandria beyond what was expressly specified in the various laws and edicts which regulated their status; Flaccus now insisted on dealing with them according to the strict letter of the law.

At this juncture (August, A.D. 38) the emperor's friend Agrippa paid a visit to Alexandria on his way to Palestine to take possession of the kingdom which Gaius had bestowed on him the previous year. The Alexandrian Jews treated his visit as a golden opportunity to lodge a complaint against Flaccus's vexatious treatment of them —a complaint which they were sure would be conveyed to the emperor. Flaccus, for his part, had no option but to greet the Jewish king publicly in a manner befitting the latter's rank and his friend-ship with Gaius. This was balm to the souls of the Alexandrian Jews, but gall and wormwood to their enemies, who staged a public dem-onstration in parody of Agrippa's royal estate. They seized a local idiot named Carabas, dressed him up with mock robe, diadem and sceptre, and paid homage to him in the gymnasium with loud cries of *mari* or *maran* ('my lord' or 'our lord' in Aramaic).[11]

It was clear to all thinking men in Alexandria that this public in-sult to Agrippa would give him deep offence, and that Gaius would not treat lightly this mockery of the royal dignity which he had conferred on his friend. But in the present mood of the city mob, the leaders, and Flaccus himself, felt themselves obliged to go along

[11] *Marin*, says Philo (*Flaccus*, 39); this looks like a cross between *mari* and *maran*.

with their followers. Flaccus made a proclamation defining the
status of Jews in Alexandria as that of aliens, with no rights except
those which had at one time or another been specifically granted
to them. They were herded into the one ward of the city in which
they had originally received permission to reside, and their property in other wards was looted. Synagogues were destroyed, while
those in the Jewish ward were invaded and desecrated. A favourite
method of desecration was to set up portraits or images of Gaius in
the synagogues; if the Jews removed them, their action could be
represented as disloyalty towards an emperor who was known to
take his divinity very seriously. There were numerous acts of violence and outrage against individual Jews, culminating in the public scourging of thirty-eight Jewish elders on August 31, during the
emperor's birthday celebrations.[12]

The riots began to die down after this, and a decisive change in
the situation followed the arrival in mid-October of a company of
Roman soldiers led by a centurion, with orders to arrest Flaccus and
take him to Rome. There he was tried and sentenced to banishment
on the Aegean island of Andros, where he was later put to death.
The fact that his arrest coincided with the Feast of Tabernacles in
A.D. 38 was found highly significant by the Jews of Alexandria.[13]
After his departure they were probably able, gradually and dis-
creetly, to return to their former abodes throughout the city. The
new prefect of Egypt, C. Vitrasius Pollio, held a detailed inquiry
into the origin and course of the riots, after which he permitted
two embassies—one of five Alexandrian Greeks (including Isidore
and Apion) and the other of five Alexandrian Jews (headed by
Philo)—to go to Italy to state their respective cases before the emperor. Each embassy was given two hearings, separated perhaps
by Gaius's expedition to the German frontier and the English Channel, on which he set out in September, A.D. 39. The second hearing
is precisely datable in September of A.D. 40, but by this time an
event had taken place which meant that Gaius was in no mood to
listen to Jewish protestations of loyalty.

[12] Philo, *Flaccus*, 74.   [13] Philo, *Flaccus*, 116.

3

The city of Jamnia, in western Palestine, had a mixed Gentile and Jewish population. The Gentiles, to celebrate Gaius's German campaign, set up an altar in his honour; some Jews of the city, indignant at this flaunting of idolatry, pulled it down. In due course news of their action reached Gaius, whose northern expedition had made him surer than ever of his divinity. He retaliated by sending instructions to Publius Petronius, Vitellius's successor as legate of Syria (A.D. 39–42), to march with an adequate legionary force into Judaea and set up a gigantic statue of Gaius in the Jerusalem Temple.[14]

Philo has given an account of the two Alexandrian delegations in his treatise commonly called *The Embassy to Gaius*. Gaius gave the two delegations a second hearing simultaneously in the gardens of Maecenas and Lamia on the Esquiline hill in Rome, where he was supervising extensive alterations to one of his residences. The Gentile delegation accused the Alexandrian Jews of disloyalty on the ground that they had omitted to hold sacrifices of thanksgiving for the emperor's recovery from illness at the beginning of his reign; the Jews retorted that this was a lie: they had sacrificed whole burnt-offerings on his behalf not only then but also earlier on his accession and later in anticipation of his victories in Germany—not to mention the sacrifices which the Jewish nation had offered twice daily for the emperor since the time of Augustus. 'What is the use of that?' asked Gaius. 'You offered sacrifices *for* me, it is true, but you offered none *to* me.'[15] The hearing was inconclusive, but the Jewish delegates were dismissed in less unfavourable terms than they had feared: 'These fellows are not criminals', said the emperor; 'they are pitiable fools, or else they would have recognized my divine nature'.[16]

Both delegations were left to cool their heels until it pleased the emperor to call them for a further hearing. Meanwhile, matters in Judaea mounted to a crisis the like of which had not been known since Antiochus Epiphanes set up the altar of Olympian Zeus on top of the great altar of burnt-offering in Jerusalem over two cen-

[14] Philo, *Leg. ad Gaium*, 200–3.
[15] Philo, *Leg. ad Gaium*, 357.   [16] Philo, *Leg. ad Gaium*, 367.

turies before. Petronius, in obedience to the imperial orders, marched south with two legions, but at Ptolemais he was met by deputations of Jews, including members of the Herod family and other influential men, who assured him that the whole Jewish nation would rise as one man and die as one man sooner than allow the Temple to be desecrated by the imperial statue. The demonstrations at Ptolemais were followed by similar ones at Tiberias. Petronius, although obedience to superior orders was second nature to him, was so impressed by these protests that he temporized; he sent a letter to the emperor suggesting that it would be well to wait until the cereal and fruit harvests (of A.D. 40) were reaped; otherwise the year's agricultural activities would be neglected or the crops might even be destroyed throughout the land. Gaius was annoyed, and sent Petronius a letter insisting that the erection and dedication of the statue should take precedence over everything else.[17]

It was now that Herod Agrippa proved that he had come to the kingdom for such a time as this. He was the only man who had any hope of dissuading Gaius from his foolish policy, and he took his life in both hands to do so.

According to Philo, Agrippa knew nothing about Gaius's plan until after the despatch of Gaius's second letter to Petronius; he was then told of it by Gaius himself on an occasion when he waited on the emperor to pay him the routine courtesies. When he heard of it, he fainted on the spot (perhaps suffering a cerebral haemorrhage) and did not recover for several days. Then he wrote a letter to the emperor in such discreet but persuasive terms that the emperor agreed to call off his plan for setting up his statue in Jerusalem. He sent a third letter to Petronius to this effect, adding, however, that if any of his loyal subjects in Judaea outside Jerusalem wished to set up statues or portraits of himself, or sacrificial altars in his honour, they might do so freely, and any attempt to remove them should not only be visited with capital punishment for the perpetrator but he followed by the irrevocable erection of his image in Jerusalem.[18]

Josephus, on the other hand, adopts a familiar narrative motif by telling how Agrippa gained his end by entertaining Gaius at a

[17] The story is told by Josephus, *BJ* ii, 184ff, *Ant.* xviii, 261ff, as well as by Philo.
[18] *Leg.*, 261ff.

magnificent banquet which so delighted his distinguished guest that he bade Agrippa ask what boon he pleased, and it should be granted him.[19] Agrippa thereupon asked him to desist from his plan to set up his statue in Jerusalem. Gaius was taken aback, but could not well refuse the boon Agrippa sought; accordingly he sent a letter to Petronius countermanding his order.

While Philo and Josephus differ on the details of Agrippa's interposition—probably they knew only the general outline and reconstructed the details variously—they agree that it was his interposition that decided Gaius not to proceed with his scheme.

Gaius's letter to Petronius cancelling his order crossed one from Petronius to Gaius. Further urgent representations made to Petronius by leading men in Judaea made it clear that the carrying out of the emperor's order would precipitate a war in which the whole land would be devastated. Petronius accordingly sent a further letter to Gaius pointing this out and adding that the revenue which was derived from the province would be lost in consequence. Gaius was enraged by the receipt of this letter, and sent a reply in which he threatened Petronius with death for his insubordination, unless he took the only honourable course now open to him by committing suicide.[20]

Fortunately for Petronius, this last letter from Gaius was held up by stormy weather, and took three months to reach him. Twenty-seven days before it arrived, news was received in Syria of Gaius's assassination, which took place on January 24, A.D. 41.[21] If this news took about the same time to reach Syria as the news of Tiberius's death four years previously,[22] it will have been received about the end of February; it was nearly the end of March when Petronius received the advice to commit suicide, and by this time he could safely ignore it.

Gaius's assassination was the fruit of a conspiracy hatched by a number of his influential enemies at Rome during the winter of A.D. 40–41. One of them was one of the prefects of the Praetorian Guard, and it was military tribunes of the guard who executed the

---

[19] *Ant.* xviii, 289ff. For the motif we may compare the account of Herod Antipas's birthday party in Mark 6:21ff.

[20] Josephus, *Ant.* xviii, 302ff.

[21] Josephus, *BJ* ii, 203; Suetonius, *Gaius*, 58.   [22] See p. 31.

plot. Some of the conspirators had the vague idea, shared with the assassins of Julius Caesar eighty-four years earlier, that the removal of a 'tyrant' would automatically ensure the restoration of liberty. The Senate, it was imagined, would once more become the effective government of Rome. But all that the Senate succeeded in doing was to have Gaius's wife and young daughter put to death. The praetorian soldiers showed where the seat of power was by seizing Gaius's uncle Claudius, a member of the imperial family whom no one took seriously because of his pedantic interests and ungainly movements (the result, it may be, of infantile paralysis), and hailed him as their new *princeps*. Next day the Senate found itself compelled to recognize the praetorians' choice, and one of Claudius's first actions was to call some of its members to his new residence on the Palatine hill to join him in passing the death-sentence on Cassius Chaerea, the tribune who had struck the first blow against Gaius.[23]

Herod Agrippa, who was in Rome at the time, did not forget what Gaius had done for him, and paid his dead body the last respects which friendship and courtesy dictated, at a time when others felt it unsafe to do anything of the kind.[24] But the Jews in general—in Alexandria and Judaea especially—were relieved to learn of Gaius's death. The terror of those weeks when it seemed that nothing could prevent him from carrying out his threat to set up his statue in the Temple at Jerusalem was not quickly forgotten, and in the minds of some apocalyptists Gaius's attempt, together with the outrage perpetrated by Antiochus Epiphanes in the second century B.C., provided a pattern of what might be expected in the great distress of the end-time. Philo probably has Antiochus's action in mind when he says that Gaius was prepared to convert the Jerusalem Temple into a sanctuary bearing his own name, under the designation of *Zeus Epiphanes Neos*, 'the young Zeus made manifest'.[25] (Antiochus IV claimed to be the manifestation of Olympian Zeus, whose features he bears on some of his coins.)

It was very probably during these anxious days of A.D. 40 that some Judaean Christians first circulated in written form certain collected words of Jesus which they thought had a direct bearing on

---

[23] The story of Gaius's death and Claudius's accession is told in great detail by Josephus, *Ant.* xix, 15–273.   [24] Josephus, *Ant.* xix, 237.
[25] *Leg.*, 346; cf. 197, 281.

the present crisis. 'When you see the appalling sacrilege[26] set up where he ought not to be', Jesus had said, 'then let those who are in Judaea flee to the mountains; let him who is on the housetop not go down, nor enter his house, to take anything away; and let him who is in the field not turn back to take his mantle. . . . For in those days there will be such tribulation as has not been from the beginning of the creation which God created until now, and never will be' (Mark 13:14–19).[27] To the mention of the 'appalling sacrilege' (the phrase used in Daniel's visions and in I Maccabees 1:54 of Antiochus's idolatrous installation) the compiler added the parenthesis, 'let the reader understand'—let him understand, that is to say, that Jesus' prophecy is now on the eve of fulfilment. And to make the point even more unmistakable, he violated Greek grammar so as to make the desolating sacrilege personal: it was not so much the statue that was to be worshipped as the emperor whom it portrayed.[28] In the event, the prophecy of Jesus was not fulfilled in A.D. 40, but his words were remembered afresh a generation later and given a new interpretation when idolatrous objects actually were set up in the sacred precincts.[29]

[26] Gk. τὸ βδέλυγμα τῆς ἐρημώσεως, literally 'the abomination of desolation'. See p. 4 with n. 5.

[27] See G. R. Beasley-Murray, *Jesus and the Future* (London, 1954), pp. 172ff; *A Commentary on Mark Thirteen* (London, 1957), pp. 54ff, 59ff.

[28] In Mark 13:14 the participle ἑστηκότα is masculine although it refers to the neuter substantive βδέλυγμα (the parallel in Matt. 24:15 makes the participle neuter). See p. 309.   [29] See p. 383, n. 56.

20   Herod Agrippa, King of the Jews

The Emperor Claudius and Herod Agrippa were born in the same year (11–10 B.C.) and had known each other from boyhood. When Agrippa's father Aristobulus was executed in 7 B.C., he was sent to Rome with his mother Berenice (daughter of Herod's sister Salome and her Idumaean husband Costobar). Berenice became a bosom friend of Claudius's mother Antonia (daughter of Mark Antony and Octavia, sister to Augustus), and Agrippa grew up in close and friendly association with the imperial family, not least with his contemporary Claudius.

One of the first actions of Claudius on achieving supreme power was to add Judaea to Agrippa's kingdom, with the result that Agrippa now governed a realm practically coextensive with his grandfather's.[1] At the same time he raised Agrippa to consular rank (he had received praetorian rank from the Roman Senate four years earlier), and bestowed the kingdom of Chalcis, in the Lebanon valley, on Agrippa's brother Herod.[2] Claudius was moved to transfer Judaea from Roman provincial administration to rule by a Jewish king partly, no doubt, from motives of friendship and gratitude towards Agrippa, who had been helpful to him in the difficult situation which followed the killing of Gaius, but mainly because recent troubles in Judaea had made it plain to him that the Jews were best governed in Rome's interest by one of themselves who understood their religious scruples. It was an act of great political wisdom on Claudius's part—more so even than the appointment of Herod the Great as king of the Jews in 40 B.C. For, unlike his grandfather, Agrippa was *persona grata* with his subjects. He was a Herod, indeed, but more important in their eyes was the fact that he was a Hasmonaean, through his unhappy grandmother, Princess Mariamme.

A story told in the Mishnah illustrates the popular attitude towards

[1] *BJ* ii, 214; *Ant.* xix, 274.   [2] *BJ* ii, 217; *Ant.* xix, 277.

him. It is prescribed in Deuteronomy 31:10f that at the autumnal
Feast of Booths or Tabernacles following the end of a sabbatical
year the Deuteronomic law must be read aloud to the people assembled at the central sanctuary. Accordingly, at the Feast of
Booths in October, A.D. 41 (fifteen days after the end of the sabbatical year A.D. 40–41), Agrippa, as king of the Jews, undertook this
duty. A wooden platform was set up in the Temple court, and on it
a throne was placed. He stood up to receive the scroll of Deuteronomy from the high priest; but instead of sitting down to read the
appointed selections from it, as a king was permitted to do, he remained standing while he read them. When he came to Deuteronomy 17:14–20 ('the law of kingship') he burst into tears as he read
verse 15–'One from among your brethren you shall set as king over
you; you may not put a foreigner over you, who is not your brother'
–for he remembered his Idumaean ancestry. But the people cried
out, 'Fear not; you are our brother, you are our brother!'–for they
thought of his Hasmonaean ancestry through Mariamme.[8]

Agrippa's decision to remain standing while he read the law illustrates his respectful deference to Jewish religious sentiment, and
it received due commendation from the sages in Israel. But a note
is attached to this incident in the Tosefta and the Babylonian Talmud, according to which one rabbi taught that Israel incurred the
penalty of destruction for thus flattering Agrippa.[4]

Agrippa's token of respect for the Torah was but one of many
acts of piety which were counted to him for righteousness by the
religious leaders in Israel. Earlier he had dedicated in the Temple
the gold chain, equal in weight to the iron chain with which he had
been fettered by Tiberius's order, with which Gaius presented him
on his accession to the principate.[5] Later, on entering Jerusalem as
king of Judaea, he offered sacrifices of thanksgiving in the Temple
and paid the expenses of several Nazirites whose vows were on the

[8] Mishnah, *Soṭah* 7:8. Even as a descendant of Idumaeans he had by now
qualified for recognition as their 'brother', in terms of the law of Deut. 23:7f
('the children of the third generation'). In Mishnah, *Bikkurim* 3:4 we are told
how at the festival of firstfruits he carried his basket on his shoulder into the
Temple court like any ordinary Jew.

[4] Tosefta, *Soṭah* 7:16; TB *Soṭa* 41b. It is unlikely that this complaint should
be connected with that of Simon the Pharisee recorded by Josephus, *Ant.* xix,
332ff; Simon maintained that Agrippa should have been excluded from the
Temple because he had contracted ritual impurity.

[5] Josephus, *Ant.* xix, 294f.

point of expiry and whose consequent hair-cutting had to be accompanied by appropriate thankofferings.[6]

Yet, outside the purely Jewish areas of his kingdom and in the territories adjoining it, Agrippa was no more restrained by Jewish religious scruples than his grandfather had been. While the coins of his reign minted in Jerusalem bore no image, those minted at Caesarea and elsewhere bear either his image or the emperor's.[7] Statues of members of his family were set up at Caesarea.[8] He was especially munificent in his gifts to the citizens of Berytus (Beirut); he built them a theatre, an amphitheatre, public baths and colonnades, and at the dedication of these buildings he exhibited shows of various kinds which were far removed from the standards of Jewish piety.[9]

All this, however, does not appear to have jeopardized his popularity with his Jewish subjects. To have a Jewish king after thirty-five years of government by Roman officials was too wonderful a blessing for objection to be taken (except possibly by purists among the orthodox) to his accommodation to Gentile ways in Gentile cities. He showed himself generally amiable in disposition, and remitted part of the taxes habitually levied on the householders of Jerusalem.[10] It was his Gentile subjects who most disliked him, despite his lavish donations to their cities; his death in A.D. 44 was followed by unseemly demonstrations of scornful delight in Caesarea and Sebaste.[11]

Among his prerogatives as king of the Jews was the gift of the high-priesthood; during the three years of his reign in Judaea he deposed three high priests and appointed three.[12]

He married his first cousin Cypros, daughter of his father's full sister Salampsio (whose husband was her first cousin Phasael); by her he had one son, the younger Agrippa, and three daughters— Berenice, who married her uncle Herod of Chalcis; Mariamme, who

[6] Josephus, *Ant.* xix, 294. A similar act of piety was recommended to Paul when he visited Jerusalem in A.D. 57, so that it might be seen that (contrary to report) he was an observant Jew (Acts 21:23ff); see p. 354.

[7] Cf. J. Meyshan, 'The Coinage of Agrippa the First', *IEJ* 4 (1954), pp. 186ff. His imageless coins mostly bear the inscription Βασιλέως Ἀγρίππα ('King Agrippa's'); some of his Caesarean coins bearing his image describe him as Βασιλεὺς μέγας Ἀγρίππας Φιλοκαῖσαρ ('Great King Agrippa, friend of Caesar').

[8] Josephus, *Ant.* xix, 357.   [9] Josephus, *Ant.* xix, 335ff.
[10] Josephus, *Ant.* xix, 299.   [11] Josephus, *Ant.* xix, 356ff.
[12] See p. 64.

married one Julius Archelaus, son of Hilkiah; and Drusilla, who appears later in our story as the wife of the procurator Felix.[13]

The one reference to Agrippa in the New Testament has to do with his hostile policy towards the Jerusalem church. He appears in Acts 12:1ff as 'Herod the king' who executed one of the twelve apostles, James the son of Zebedee, and imprisoned another, Peter. The evidence adduced in support of the view that James's brother John shared his fate at this time is too slender to bear the weight that some have placed on it.[14] Peter owed his life to Agrippa's decision to postpone his public execution until the festal week of Unleavened Bread had run its course. Before the week was out, Peter escaped from prison in circumstances which, in Agrippa's eyes, pointed to inside sympathizers.

According to Luke, Agrippa took this action because 'he saw that it pleased the Jews'[15] (Acts 12:3). Whereas, a few years previously, the apostles were unmolested in the campaign of suppression that followed Stephen's death, now they were evidently the principal targets of attack. Luke's account of how, shortly before this, Peter had fraternized with Gentiles in Caesarea and his fellow-apostles had acquiesced in his action, provides a sufficient explanation of their sudden unpopularity with many Jews who had formerly respected them. From this time forth James the brother of Jesus, widely esteemed in Jerusalem as a strictly observant Jew, appears as principal leader of the church of Jerusalem.[16]

In the Phoenician seaport of Dora, not far from Agrippa's northern frontier, an incident took place about A.D. 42 of a kind which had precipitated the serious crisis of Gaius's principate. Some youths

[13] Acts 24:24. See pp. 344f.
[14] Apart from the view that this is implied by Mark 10:39, cf. E. Schwartz, 'Über den Tod der Söhne Zebedaei', *Abh. d. kgl. Gesellschaft d. Wissenschaften zu Göttingen*, phil.-hist. Kl., N.F., Bd. 7, No. 5 (1904); 'Noch Einmal der Tod der Söhne Zebedaei', *ZNTW* 11 (1910), pp. 89ff; the evidence is derived from the De Boor fragment of the Epitome of the History of Philip of Side (c. A.D. 450), according to which 'Papias in his second book says that John the divine and James his brother were killed by the Jews' (cf. the statement of the ninth-century Georgios Hamartolos, according to the *Codex Coislinianus* 305, that John was 'deemed worthy of martyrdom, for Papias, in the second book of his *Dominical Oracles*, says that he was killed by the Jews'). Certainty as to what Papias really said must await the rediscovery of his long-lost *Exegesis of the Dominical Oracles*.
[15] Perhaps more particularly the chief-priestly families.
[16] Cf. Acts 12:17; Gal. 2:2.

set up an image of Claudius in the synagogue of that city. Agrippa protested to Petronius, in whose province Dora was situated, and Petronius dealt sharply with the offenders, in accordance with the edict in which Claudius on his accession safeguarded the rights of the Jews of Alexandria.[17]

Soon afterwards, Petronius was succeeded as legate of Syria by C. Vibius Marsus (A.D. 42–44). Agrippa's relations with him were not so happy; on two occasions Marsus intervened to prevent Agrippa from acting in a manner which seemed prejudicial to the interests of Rome.

One of these occasions concerned the 'third wall' which Agrippa began to build to the north of Jerusalem (more or less following the line of the present north wall of the Old City) so as to enclose the suburb of Bezetha, north of the Temple area. Marsus suspected that the strength and height of this wall were such as to encourage excessive feelings of independence among the people of Jerusalem, and he sent instructions to Agrippa to carry it no farther.[18]

The other occasion was a conference of client kings which Agrippa convened at Tiberias, no doubt to discuss matters of common interest. It was attended by the kings of Commagene, Emesa, Lesser Armenia, Pontus, together with Agrippa's brother Herod of Chalcis and Agrippa himself. The conference had scarcely begun when Marsus arrived at Tiberias and ordered the visiting kings to return home.[19]

Agrippa's death took place in dramatic circumstances which are related by both Luke and Josephus; each historian supplies details omitted by the other, but they agree on the main facts.[20] It may be that Agrippa's intervention in the affair at Dora had annoyed the Phoenicians, but since they were dependent for food supplies on the fertile districts of Galilee, as their ancestors had been a millennium before in the days of Hiram and Solomon,[21] they could not afford to quarrel with Agrippa for long. Accordingly they availed themselves of the good offices of Agrippa's chief chamberlain, and came to give public testimony of their reconciliation with the king at a festival of games held in Caesarea in honour of the emperor—

[17] Josephus, *Ant.* xix, 300ff.
[18] Josephus, *Ant.* xix, 326f.   [19] Josephus, *Ant.* xix, 338ff.
[20] Acts 12:20ff; Josephus, *Ant.* xix, 343ff.   [21] I Kings 5:9ff.

probably Claudius's birthday celebrations on August 1.[22] (An alternative account is that these were the quinquennial games in the emperor's honour instituted by Herod the Great at Caesarea on the occasion of the city's foundation on March 5, 9 B.C.[23]—but A.D. 44 would not have been a quinquennial year in the era of Caesarea.) Josephus describes how the king took his seat in the theatre at daybreak on the second day of the games, wearing a robe woven of silver thread, which reflected the rays of the rising sun so that the people (Gentiles, of course) invoked him as a god.[24] Luke says that he made a speech from his throne to the Phoenician delegates, which was greeted with the shout: 'The voice of a god, and not a man!' (Acts 12:23). Both writers agree that it was at that moment that he was seized by mortal pain, and indicate that this was because he did not repudiate the divine honours accorded him by the crowd.[25] He was carried home at once, and died five days later. The cause of death has commonly been diagnosed as peritonitis resulting from a perforated appendix,[26] although various other suggestions have also been made. Agrippa's death at the age of fifty-four was a tragedy for Judaea; had he lived as long as his grandfather, the disasters of the following decades might well have been averted. Claudius was dissuaded by his advisers from bestowing Agrippa's kingdom on his seventeen-year-old son, on the ground that he was too young to be entrusted with the responsibility of managing so difficult a realm as Judaea. He could hardly have man-

[22] Suetonius, *Claudius* 2:1.

[23] Cf. E. Meyer, *Ursprung und Anfänge des Christentums* III (Stuttgart, 1923), p. 167. For the era of Caesarea see Josephus, *Ant.* xvi, 136.

[24] Cf. for a fascinating but unconvincing interpretation of the narrative J. Morgenstern, 'The Chanukkah Festival and the Calendar of Ancient Israel', *HUCA* 20 (1947), pp. 1ff, especially pp. 89f, n. 167; 'The King-God among the Western Semites and the Meaning of Epiphanes', *VT* 10 (1960), pp. 138ff, especially pp. 156ff.

[25] Josephus tells how an owl, which had once appeared to him as a messenger of good fortune when he was thrown into chains by Tiberius (*Ant.* xviii, 195), now reappeared as a messenger of disaster (*Ant.* xix, 346).

[26] So E. M. Merrins, 'The Deaths of Antiochus IV, Herod the Great, and Herod Agrippa I', *Bibliotheca Sacra* 61 (1904), pp. 561f. Arsenical poison (on orders from Rome) is suggested by J. Meyshan, 'The Coinage of Agrippa the First', *IEJ* 4 (1954), p. 187, n. 2 (cf. *PEQ* 92 [1960], pp. 86f); acute intestinal obstruction by A. R. Short, *The Bible and Modern Medicine* (London, 1953), pp. 66ff; a hydatid cyst, by a medical colleague at Sheffield University in a private communication.

aged it less acceptably than the procurators who were appointed in succession to his father. As a consolation prize, the younger Agrippa received the kingdom of Chalcis when his uncle Herod died in A.D. 48.[27]

27 Josephus, *BJ* ii, 223; *Ant.* xx, 104.

21 Early Gentile Christianity

1

The north Syrian city of Antioch, at the head of navigation on the river Orontes, was founded in 300 B.C. by Seleucus Nicator, first ruler of the Seleucid dynasty. From its earliest days its population included Greeks and Macedonians on the one hand and Syrians on the other, together with veteran Jewish soldiers in Seleucus's army, who received land in the neighbourhood of the city and settled there. Antioch was thus a centre of the Jewish dispersion from its inception, and the Jewish population increased greatly over the years, especially after 200 B.C., when Judaea was incorporated in the Seleucid Empire, which had its seat of government at Antioch.[1] Seleucia Pieria, at the mouth of the Orontes, was its seaport.

By virtue of its land and sea communications it became an important commercial centre. Its importance in this respect was not reduced under the Roman government, for when Syria became a Roman province in 64 B.C., Antioch became the capital of the province, the residence of the imperial legate. Its cosmopolitan population and material wealth provided an apt setting for cultural exchange and religious syncretism. One pointer to the activity of the Jews of Antioch in this respect is implied by the presence of the Antiochene proselyte Nicolaus among the seven Hellenistic leaders in the primitive Jerusalem church.[2]

Paul was a powerful adjutant to Barnabas, when he joined him at Antioch, and the number of converts continued to increase. They were organized as a church—probably the second church to be statedly organized in Christian history, and one which from the outset included a large proportion of Gentiles. If the pattern which recurs repeatedly in the Pauline mission-field in later years was

[1] Cf. Josephus, *BJ* vii, 43–5.
[2] Acts 6:5. He is the only one of the seven whose place of origin is specified—perhaps because the author of Acts was himself an Antiochene (see p. 267).

manifested at Antioch, many of those Gentile converts would
have been drawn from the ranks of the 'God-fearers'[3]—Gentiles
who, in Antioch as in other places where there were Jewish communities, were attracted by the Jewish monotheistic worship and
way of life and attached themselves loosely to the synagogue without actually becoming proselytes.

Proselytes undertook to observe the Jewish law in its entirety
and were accepted as full members of the religious community of
Israel. Their initiation involved circumcision (in the case of men),
a special sacrifice at the Jerusalem Temple, and (probably by the
beginning of the Christian era) a purificatory bath or baptism.[4] The
crucial feature of the initiation was circumcision, which partly explains why full proselytization was more common among women
than among men.[5]

To those Gentiles who were satisfied with a looser attachment
to Judaism as 'God-fearers' Christianity made an inevitable appeal,
for it held out to them the privilege of incorporation among the
people of God on the same terms as Jews, without their being required to accept circumcision. Naturally, this privilege was vigorously contested by many Jewish believers, especially in the church
of Jerusalem, but it is clear that, from the earliest days of Gentile
evangelization in Antioch, no attempt was made to impose circumcision as a requirement for admission to the church. When it is considered that the evangelists were all circumcised Jews, this is the
more remarkable; but an important precedent, of which Barnabas
at least was aware, had been established a year or two earlier at
Palestinian Caesarea, where Peter and some companions brought
the gospel to the 'God-fearing' centurion Cornelius and his family,
and baptized them as fellow-believers without requiring them to be
circumcised.[6] Peter was sharply criticized for his behaviour by his
colleagues in Jerusalem, but defended himself by telling how he
had virtually been faced with a divine *fait accompli*; he had not
finished telling the household of Cornelius the story of Jesus when

[3] Called in Acts εὐσεβεῖς, φοβούμενοι τὸν θεόν, σεβόμενοι τὸν θεόν or, more
briefly, σεβόμενοι.
[4] Cf. H. H. Rowley, 'Jewish Proselyte Baptism and the Baptism of John', in
From Moses to Qumran (London, 1963), pp. 211ff (reprinted from *HUCA* 15
[1940], pp. 313ff); T. F. Torrance, 'Proselyte Baptism', *NTS* 1 (1954–5),
pp. 150ff.   [5] See pp. 147, 156.   [6] Acts 10:1–48.

the Spirit of God manifestly took possession of his Gentile audience, producing the same kind of glossolalia as had been heard on the day of Pentecost in A.D. 30; then 'who was I', asked Peter, 'that I could withstand God?'[7]

To one Gentile convert of Antioch, who may have been a 'God-fearer' before he became a Christian, we may well owe much of our limited knowledge of the beginnings of Gentile Christianity. Not only have we the statement of the anti-Marcionite prologue to the Third Gospel that Luke the physician was a native of Antioch;[8] immediately after the account of Paul's coming from Tarsus to join Barnabas at Antioch the Western text of Acts introduces an earlier 'we' section than those which appear in the other text-types: 'in these days prophets came down from Jerusalem to Antioch. There was great exultation, and when we were gathered together one of them, named Agabus, prophesied through the Spirit' (Acts 11:27f).[9] This is not the original reading, but it does indicate the acceptance, quite early in the second century, of the tradition associating Luke with Antioch.

According to Luke, it was in Antioch that 'the disciples'—i.e. the followers of Jesus—first received the designation 'Christians'. This is what we should expect; the designation was one which could originate only in a Gentile environment. It is formed from the title *Christos* by the addition of the colloquial suffix *-ianos* (the naturalized Greek form of the Latin suffix *-ianus*). The suffix was used among other things to denote a man's slaves and other members of his household; *Caesariani*, for example, is the Latin equivalent of the Greek phrase in Phil. 4:22, translated 'those of Caesar's household'.[10] *Christos*, the Greek verbal adjective corresponding to the Hebrew *māšîaḥ*, was constantly on the Hellenistic disciples' lips when they spoke of Jesus as the Anointed One or the Messiah; since they also spoke of him as their *Kyrios* or 'Lord',[11] they were evidently his servants—servants of *Christos* and so *Christianoi*.

But they would not have been given this name in a Jewish setting,

[7] Acts 11:1–18.

[8] Ἔστιν ὁ Λουκᾶς Ἀντιοχεὺς Σύρος, ἰατρὸς τῇ τέχνῃ . . . ; cf. Eusebius, *HE* iii, 4; Jerome, *De uiris illustribus* 7.

[9] The chief witnesses for this Western reading are D p Aug.

[10] οἱ ἐκ τῆς Καίσαρος οἰκίας.

[11] Cf. F. F. Bruce, 'Jesus is Lord' in *Soli Deo Gloria*, ed. J. McD. Richards (Richmond, Va., 1968), pp. 23ff. See p. 280 with n. 3.

not even among Greek-speaking Jews, for that would have implied
on the part of Jews an admission of the disciples' claim that Jesus
was the Messiah. To Jews they remained 'the party of the Nazarenes'. In Gentile ears, however, *Christos* was not so much a religious title as a rather odd second personal name borne by Jesus—
so odd, indeed, that it was naturally confused with its homophone
Chrestos, which meant 'useful' and was in wide currency as a slave-
name.[12]

Not until the second century do we find Christians using this designation themselves.[13] In the New Testament it occurs only three
times, and each time it is either expressly or by implication used
by non-Christians. In addition to Acts 11:26, where it is said to have
been coined in Antioch, it is used in Acts 26:28, where the younger
Agrippa says jestingly that Paul is trying to make him 'play the
Christian',[14] and in I Peter 4:16, where a situation is envisaged as
imminent in which a man may have to suffer not for any known
crime but simply 'as a Christian'.[15]

2

The reign of Claudius, says Suetonius, was marked by successive
droughts and bad harvests.[16] One of the resultant famines hit Palestine and the neighbouring territories with special severity during
the procuratorship of Tiberius Julius Alexander (46–48), probably
not long after he arrived in the province. Josephus makes special
mention of it because Helena, the queen-mother of Adiabene beyond the Tigris, a proselyte to Judaism, showed her devotion to her
fellow-religionists at this time by sending her servants to buy grain
in Alexandria and figs in Cyprus for distribution among the poor
of Judaea, who could not afford the high prices charged for the little
food available. At the same time her son Izates, king of Adiabene,

---

[12] Cf. *impulsore Chresto* in Suetonius, *Claudius* 25:4 (see p. 297). In Acts
11:26 χρηστιανούς appears in some manuscripts (including ℵ) as a variant of
the proper spelling χριστιανούς.

[13] First in the apologists (cf. Aristides, *Apol.* 2:1; 15:1f; Justin, *Apol.* i, 4:5,
etc.), *Epistle to Diognetus* (1:1; 2:5, etc.), *Letter of Churches of Lyons and
Vienne* (*ap.* Euseb. *HE* v, 1. 19, 20, 26). Ignatius uses χριστιανισμός (*Ad
Magn.* 10:1, 3; *Ad. Philad.* 6:1).

[14] ἐν ὀλίγῳ με πείθεις χριστιανὸν ποιῆσαι is best rendered 'In short, you are
urging me to play the Christian' (cf. the force of ποιεῖν βασιλέα in III Reg. 20:7).

[15] See p. 425.   [16] *Claudius* 18:2 (*assiduae sterilitates*).

also a proselyte, sent a large sum of money to the leading men of Jerusalem for the similar relief of the poorer citizens.[17]

Parallel action was taken about the same time, if on a more modest scale, by the church of Antioch. Hearing of the impending famine from Agabus, a prophet from Jerusalem who paid a visit to their city, the Antiochene Christians determined to send what they could to the elders of the Jerusalem church for the relief of their brethren in Judaea; Barnabas and Paul were chosen as delegates to take this gift to Jerusalem.[18]

A visit by the leaders of the Gentile mission to Jerusalem provided an opportunity for a discussion between them and the Jerusalem leaders. This particular visit may be the one described by Paul in Gal. 2:1 as taking place 'after fourteen years'—that is, probably, in the fourteenth year from his conversion, which would bring us to c. A.D. 46.[19] Paul describes the visit with an apologetic purpose, in order to show the Galatian churches that (contrary to reports which had reached them) on none of the occasions when he visited Jerusalem after his conversion did the leaders of the church there confer any authority on him. But from his account it is plain that he and Barnabas had a conference with James (the brother of Jesus), Peter and John, who were styled 'pillars' by their followers —perhaps being recognized as pillars in the new temple 'not made with hands'.[20] Paul and Barnabas told the Jerusalem leaders about the progress of the work at Antioch and of the terms in which the gospel was presented to the Gentiles there. It was imperative that full understanding and agreement should be preserved between the two parties; Christianity could not be allowed to develop into two rival movements, one based on Jerusalem and the other on Antioch. In fact Paul, for all his concern to vindicate his independence of Jerusalem, acknowledges that, when he laid before the Jerusalem leaders the gospel as he preached it among the Gentiles, he did so

[17] *Ant.* iii, 320f; xx, 51–3, 101. Helena's visit to Jerusalem at this time was presumably the occasion when, as related in Mishnah, *Nazir* 3:6, she undertook a Nazirite vow.

[18] Acts 11:27–30.

[19] Another interpretation makes it fourteen years after the visit of Gal. 1:18, which took place three years (or in the third year) after his conversion (see p. 242).

[20] Cf. C. K. Barrett, 'Paul and the "Pillar" Apostles', in *Studia Paulina in honorem J. de Zwaan*, ed. J. N. Sevenster and W. C. van Unnik (Haarlem, 1953), pp. 1ff.

'lest somehow I should be running, or should prove to have run, in vain' (Gal. 2:2). These words express his recognition that all the devotion and energy with which he had prosecuted his apostolic mission to the Gentiles, and hoped to prosecute it further, would be labour for naught if it involved a cleavage with the mother-church. For him, independence of Jerusalem must not mean dissociation from Jerusalem.

In the event, all went well. The Jerusalem leaders recognized that Barnabas and Paul had as evidently been called by God to evangelize Gentiles as they knew themselves called to evangelize their fellow-Jews. In mutual recognition of this, the two sides exchanged 'the right hand of fellowship', on the understanding, says Paul, 'that we should go to the Gentiles and they to the circumcised' (Gal. 2:9).

For us, there is an ambiguity in these words as they stand. Was this demarcation of the two spheres of activity a geographical one or a racial and religious one? Was it understood that, as Paul and Barnabas evangelized Syria and Cilicia and perhaps territory farther afield, they should carefully avoid preaching the gospel to Jews in those provinces? Probably not; at any rate, Paul and Barnabas did not understand the agreement in this sense, for their policy appears to have been to visit the synagogue first in every Gentile city to which they came and try to make it their base of operations in evangelizing that city. In their eyes, the demarcation was mainly geographical. Whether this was equally plain to the Jerusalem leaders is uncertain; perhaps there was sufficient ambiguity in the terms of their agreement to cause misunderstanding later.

Paul asserts that the Jerusalem leaders imposed no conditions on Barnabas and himself: 'only', they said, 'please go on remembering[21] the poor' (Gal. 2:10a). This request, which Paul records at the end of his account of the conference, makes the famine-relief visit the more appropriate as a setting for it, the more so as he adds immediately, 'And in fact I had made a special point of doing this very thing' (Gal. 2:10b).[22] For Paul, the bringing of the contribution from Antioch to Jerusalem was no isolated incident; it was part of a settled policy on his part, to encourage his Gentile converts to acknowledge their spiritual debt to Jerusalem, from which

[21] This is probably the sense of the present tense in ἵνα μνημονεύωμεν.
[22] This is probably the force of the aorist tense in ὃ καὶ ἐσπούδασα αὐτὸ τοῦτο ποιῆσαι.

the gospel had come to them, by making some material gift to the church there. 'The poor' on the lips of the Jerusalem leaders may have indicated the needier members of the church, or it may even have become already a designation for the Jerusalem church as a whole. In later generations one branch of Jewish Christianity was known as the 'Ebionites'[23]—a Graecized form which derives from their Hebrew self-description as *hā'ebyōnîm,* 'the poor'. This term was probably intended to denote not only their economic status (which was depressed enough) but also their ideal of humble piety. As early as some parts of the Old Testament Psalter poverty and piety are regular companions, and Matthew's Gospel conveys the true connotation of Jesus' beatitude on 'the poor' (Luke 6:20) by expanding it to 'the poor in spirit' (Matt. 5:3).

But here again an opportunity for misunderstanding may have presented itself. For Paul such contributions from Gentile Christians to Jerusalem were voluntary gifts, called forth by a sense of brotherly love and fellowship; James and his colleagues, on the other hand, may have thought of them as a tribute due, an initial instalment of the 'wealth of the nations' which, according to Isa. 60:5, 11, would make its way to Jerusalem in the new age.

What might have been an occasion of major disagreement at the conference did not, in fact, lead to any trouble. This was the presence in Jerusalem with Paul and Barnabas of a Greek Christian from Antioch, Titus by name, who was over a period of many years to prove himself one of Paul's most trusted lieutenants. How would the Jerusalem believers react to the presence of an uncircumcised Gentile? A few years later the demand that Gentile converts should be circumcised was warmly pressed by a determined minority in the Jerusalem church, but on this occasion the question of circumcising Titus seems hardly to have been raised. Paul's reference to this matter is none too clear, and his words have been interpreted in contrary senses;[24] but they may be paraphrased thus:

Titus, who was with me, was a Greek; but the idea of compelling him to be circumcised simply did not arise. When the question of circum-

[23] Cf. Irenaeus, *Haer.* i, 26. 2; iii, 11. 7; Hippolytus, *Ref.* vii, 8, 34; Origen, *De principiis* iv, 3. 8 (where he explains that the Ebionites are so called because they are 'poor in spirit'), etc.

[24] Cf. F. C. Burkitt, *Christian Beginnings* (London, 1924), p. 118: 'who can doubt that it was the knife which really did circumcise Titus that has cut the syntax of Gal. ii. 3–5 to pieces?'

cision did arise later on, that was not the act of responsible leaders, but of some counterfeit brethren who had been smuggled in. They infiltrated into our company in order to spy on the freedom which is ours in Christ and bring us into bondage if they could. But to them we never submitted for a moment; we were resolved that the truth of the gospel should remain in undiminished power.[25]

3

This later situation to which Paul refers was the sequel to a wide extension of the Gentile mission which was initiated soon after he and Barnabas returned from their famine-relief visit to Jerusalem. The Gentile evangelization which had already been undertaken was not confined to Antioch itself, but was carried on in various parts of the double province of Syria and Cilicia. But there were territories farther west to which the gospel must also be carried, and Paul and Barnabas were released by the church in Antioch to evangelize these territories. Luke ascribes this action to a prophetic utterance at a meeting of the principal teachers of that church, which directed that these two men should be set apart for the work to which the Spirit had called them.[26] This was the work of Gentile evangelization in which they were already actively engaged, but the recent conference with the Jerusalem leaders encouraged them to prosecute it even more energetically and over an even wider area than heretofore.[27]

Accordingly Paul and Barnabas set sail for Cyprus, then a senatorial province,[28] and travelled through the island from Salamis in the east to Paphos in the west. Their policy was to visit the Jewish synagogue in each place to which they came, because there they could usually be sure of finding a group of 'God-fearing' Gentiles who might become the nucleus of a Christian church. But no details are recorded of their synagogue-preaching in Cyprus or of its effect.

[25] Cf. T. W. Manson, *Studies in the Gospels and Epistles* (Manchester, 1962), pp. 175f.

[26] Acts 13:2.

[27] T. W. Manson (*op. cit.*, pp. 176f) suggests that the conference immediately preceded this missionary extension, and that Paul's statement that he went up to Jerusalem 'by revelation' (Gal. 2:2) refers to the prophetic call to release him and Barnabas for this new outreach.

[28] It had been so since 22 B.C., when Augustus transferred it (and Gallia Narbonensis) to the Senate in exchange for Dalmatia or Illyricum (see p. 335).

The one incident of their journey which Luke records in some detail concerns their interview with the proconsul of the island, Sergius Paullus—probably the Lucius Sergius Paullus who figures on a Roman inscription a few years earlier as one of the curators of the Tiber.[29] He was favourably impressed by the two preachers, despite the efforts of his court astrologer to prejudice his mind against them.

From Cyprus Paul and Barnabas took ship for Asia Minor. When they reached Perga, a city of Pamphylia, they had to dispense with the company and ministration of Barnabas's young cousin, John Mark of Jerusalem, who had served them as aide-de-camp ever since their famine-relief mission, but perhaps felt that he had now had enough experience, for the present at any rate, of sharing the hardships and uncertainties of apostolic travel, and so returned to Jerusalem. But the two older men struck up country and crossed the southern frontier of the province of Galatia.

The province of Galatia derived its name from the Celtic kingdom established in the heart of Asia Minor by invaders from Europe in 278–277 B.C. and the following years. The kingdom of Galatia expanded throughout the second and first centuries B.C., especially when its rulers became allies of Rome. It ultimately comprised a far wider territory than 'ethnic Galatia' (the area around Ancyra) —Phrygians, Lycaonians and other native Anatolians made up a large part of its population, together with Armenians to the east and Hellenized cities to the south. But the Celtic minority remained the dominant caste in the kingdom until 25 B.C., when Amyntas, the last Galatian king, fell in battle against the Homonades, an unruly tribe on his south-east frontier. The greater part of his kingdom was then taken over by Augustus and reconstituted, along with some adjacent territory, as the Roman province of Galatia.

It was to the Hellenized cities in the southern and quite non-Celtic part of the Roman province that Paul and Barnabas journeyed inland from the Pamphylian coast. Antioch-near-Pisidia, the first of these cities which they visited, lay 3,600 feet above sea-level in the Phrygian region of the province.[30] As its name implies, it was founded at the time when that region was part of the Seleucid

[29] *CIL* vi, 31545.
[30] It was not actually in Pisidia (one of the regions making up Roman Galatia), but in Phrygia Galatica.

Empire and called after one of the Antiochi of that dynasty, but no more explicit details of its foundation are available. Augustus made it a Roman colony (Colonia Caesarea Antiochia), and it was the civil and military centre of the district to which it belonged.

Iconium (modern Konya), the next city to be visited, lay at the western end of the Plain of Lycaonia, just on the Phrygian side of the frontier between Phrygia Galatica and Lycaonia Galatica. Then as now it was an important centre of communications. About this time it was granted the honorary imperial prefix and became known as Claudiconium.

Two other cities which Paul and Barnabas visited on this occasion lay in the Lycaonian region of the province—Lystra (modern Hatun Sarai), which, like Pisidian Antioch, had been created a Roman colony by Augustus, and Derbe (modern Devri Şehri), near the eastern frontier of Roman Galatia, which, like Iconium, received from Claudius the right to use his name as a prefix and so was called Claudio-Derbe.

In the cities of the Phrygian region, if not in Lystra and Derbe, there were large Jewish colonies. Shortly before 200 B.C. Antiochus III gave orders for the transfer of 2,000 Jewish families from the Mesopotamian and Babylonian regions of his empire to Phrygia and Lydia, to be a stabilizing influence in those territories when there was much disaffection there. They were to garrison the fortresses, have full liberty to pursue their ancestral way of life, and enjoy certain liberal reliefs from taxation.[81] This Diaspora in Asia Minor expanded rapidly in numbers and influence, and the impression which Luke gives of the size and importance of the Jewish communities in Pisidian Antioch and Iconium is confirmed by all the other relevant evidence.[82]

In both Pisidian Antioch and Iconium Paul and Barnabas visited the synagogues and seized the opportunity to convey their message that Israel's messianic hope had at length found its fulfilment in Jesus. The detailed account in Acts 13:14–48 of their experience in the synagogue of Antioch, while it does not belong to one of the 'we' sections of Acts, is no doubt based on Luke's knowledge of Paul's recurrent procedure when he came to a city where there was a Jewish colony and synagogue. The synagogue service which Paul

[81] Josephus, *Ant.* xii, 149ff.   [82] Cf. Cicero, *Pro Flacco* 66–8; *CIG* 9270.

and Barnabas attended the first sabbath day after their arrival in
the city ran its normal course until the two scripture lessons—the
seder (from the Law) and the *haphṭarah* (from the Prophets)—
had been read. Then the *archisynagogi*[33] sent the attendant to the
two visitors inviting them to deliver a 'word of exhortation'[34] (apparently an expression denoting a synagogue homily). Paul accepted the invitation and, perhaps taking his cue from something
in the lessons, rehearsed God's dealings with his people Israel from
the Exodus to the reign of David—a sequence of events which was
already well established in Old Testament times as a recital of the
mighty acts of God.[35] Then, mentioning God's dynastic promise to
David, he announced its fulfilment in the coming of Jesus, and to
the recital of God's mighty acts in the past he added a recital of his
more recent acts, extending from the ministry and witness of John
the Baptist to the death and resurrection of Jesus. In Jesus the
'holy and sure blessings' promised to David[36] were embodied; in
Jesus forgiveness of sins was assured to all who believed this good
news.

In addition to the Jewish members of the congregation there
were many Gentile 'God-fearers' present, and Paul's words were addressed to them as explicitly as to the Jews. These 'God-fearers'
were especially attracted by what they heard, and spread the news
around, so that next sabbath the synagogue was nearly swamped
by Gentiles. This offended the Jews and led to a breach between
them and the missionaries. But many of the Gentiles, believing the
message which they heard, adhered to Paul and Barnabas and were
formed into the Christian church of Pisidian Antioch.

The relation of this procedure to the agreement with the Jerusalem 'pillars' presents a problem with no obvious solution. The
delimitation of mission-fields was evidently geographical rather
than communal. In the event it was Gentiles more than Jews who
were converted by Paul's preaching, but at the outset probably more
Jews than Gentiles in one city after another heard the gospel. What

[33] These 'rulers of the synagogue' made arrangements for public worship.
The office, inscriptions testify, was sometimes hereditary; the title was sometimes held in an honorary sense even by women and children (cf. Schürer,
HJP II ii, pp. 63ff, 251ff).
[34] A λόγος παρακλήσεως (Acts 13:15); cf. Heb. 13:22.
[35] Cf. G. E. Wright, *God Who Acts* (London, 1952), p. 76.
[36] Isa. 55:4, quoted in Acts 13:34 (cf. p. 127).

if in certain cities the Jewish communities had accepted the gospel *en masse*? Would Jerusalem have regarded this as a breach at least of the spirit of the agreement? (In at least one city, Beroea in Macedonia, the Jewish community gave a favourable hearing to Paul's preaching, but the impression is given that this was an exceptional reaction.)[37] Paul's answer would probably have been that if the Jews accepted the gospel, then theirs would be the privilege of evangelizing their Gentile neighbours; as it was, he and his colleagues were obliged to evangelize the Gentiles directly. On the other hand, Paul's Gentile mission was no mere obligation arising from force of circumstances; it was the prime object of his apostolic vocation. Indeed, Luke represents him and Barnabas, in the context of the breach at Pisidian Antioch, as claiming the language of the second Isaianic Servant Song (Isa. 49:6) as warrant for their evangelization of Gentiles: 'I have set you to be a light for the Gentiles, that you may bring salvation to the uttermost parts of the earth' (Acts 13:47).[88]

It is over-simplifying the issue to dismiss the Lukan account of Paul's procedure as unhistorical because of the difficulty of squaring it with Paul's own account of the Jerusalem agreement. In fact, the charge against the Jews in I Thess. 2:15f, that they 'drove us out, and displease God and oppose all men by hindering us from speaking to the Gentiles that they may be saved', is in remarkably close agreement with Luke's account of what happened in Pisidian Antioch and a number of other places. Moreover, knowing himself called to evangelize Gentiles, Paul recognized in the 'God-fearers' on the fringe of synagogue congregations a providentially prepared bridgehead into the Gentile world. By attending the synagogue and listening to the reading and exposition of the sacred scriptures, these Gentiles, already worshippers of the 'living and true God', were familiar with the messianic hope in some form. They could not inherit this hope and the blessings which accompanied it until they became full converts to Judaism, and this was more than most of them were prepared for. But when they were told that the messianic hope had come alive in Jesus, that in him the old distinction between Jew and Gentile had been abolished, that the fullest bless-

---

[37] Acts 17:10ff.

[88] For Paul's conviction of his eschatological significance cf. J. Munck, *Paul and the Salvation of Mankind* (London, 1959), pp. 40ff *et passim*.

ings of God's saving grace were as readily available to Gentiles as
to Jews, such people could not but welcome this good news, just
as every ancestral instinct moved Jews to refuse it on these terms.
Only by visiting the synagogues could Paul find these Gentile 'God-
fearers'. When the almost inevitable breach with the synagogue authorities followed, he detached these believing Gentiles from the
synagogue, together with a minority of Jews who also believed, and
constituted a new congregation in which the distinction between
Jew and Gentile played no part. The Gentile believers now provided a channel of communication with other Gentiles, not 'God-
fearers' like themselves but worshippers of pagan deities, who now
'turned . . . from idols, to serve a living and true God' (I Thess.
1:9).

This, then, was the pattern of evangelization in Pisidian Antioch
and Iconium; in Lystra and probably also in Derbe there was no
such bridgehead of 'God-fearers' and the message had to be presented to pagans. The *magnalia Dei* in Israel's history and the
words of the prophets meant nothing to such people; with them,
another point of contact had to be sought. When Paul and Barnabas
found the indigenous population of Lystra enthusiastically engaged in a pagan rite,[39] they pressed upon them the

> good news, that you should turn from these vain things to a living God
> who made the heaven and the earth and the sea and all that is in them.
> In past generations he allowed all the nations to walk in their own
> ways; yet he did not leave himself without witness, for he did good
> and gave you from heaven rains and fruitful seasons, satisfying your
> hearts with food and gladness (Acts 14:15–17).

There is a difference of emphasis (considering the different groups
addressed), but not a material difference, between these words
and Paul's statement in Romans 1:19f that the knowledge of God
is accessible to men in his works of creation and providence, so
that their ignorance of him is wilful and blameworthy.

Having reached the frontier of Roman Galatia at Derbe, Paul
and Barnabas retraced their steps, revisiting the cities where they

[39] The Lystrans' identification of Barnabas and Paul with Zeus and Hermes
is illustrated by epigraphic material in that region; cf. W. M. Calder, 'A Cult
of the Homonades', *Classical Review* 24 (1910), pp. 76ff; 'Christians and Pagans in the Graeco-Roman Levant', *Classical Review* 38 (1924), p. 29, n. 1; 'A
Text: Acts 14[12]', *ExT* 37 (1925–6), p. 528.

had preached the gospel and encouraging and organizing the young
churches so recently planted there.[40] Then they made their way to
the coast, took ship for Syria, and gave their friends in Antioch a
report of their extended tour. The church of Antioch had now become a mother-church with a large number of daughter-churches,
not only in the dual province of Syria-Cilicia but possibly in Cyprus
and certainly in South Galatia.

[40] In particular, they appointed 'elders' (πρεσβύτεροι) in each of them,
probably on the pattern of Jewish synagogues (Acts 14:23).

22 The Jerusalem Decree

1

The advance of the gospel into central Asia Minor had momentous implications for Christianity. If it did not mean that there were now more Gentile Christians in the world than Jewish Christians, it suggested that the time was not far distant when this would be so. The character and ethos of the church were bound to be affected by this influx of Gentile converts, and, unless the greatest care were taken to safeguard the position, Christian doctrine and Christian practice might be radically changed.

So far as Christian doctrine was concerned, the danger was that of syncretism. In presenting the gospel to Gentiles—especially to Gentiles who had no contact with the synagogue—language which was meaningful to Jews could not be used with any assurance that its significance would be grasped. What would Gentiles understand by the proclamation that Jesus was the long-expected Messiah of Israel? 'What is that to us?' would have been their reaction—unless indeed they knew of the imperialist ideas involved in some forms of Israel's messianic hope, in which case the proclamation would have been highly uncongenial to them. 'Messiah', moreover, was a foreign term, and *Christos* its Greek equivalent, had no religious associations for Gentiles; to them it was a personal name, and rather an odd one at that, unless (as has been mentioned above) it was identified with the slave-name *Chrestos*.[1] On the other hand, the proclamation 'Jesus is Lord' (*Kyrios*), or 'Jesus is the Son of the Most High God (*Theos Hypsistos*)',[2] was immediately intelligible.

[1] See pp. 267f.
[2] The usefulness of Θεὸς ὕψιστος as a 'bridge-term' between the Judaeo-Christian and the Greek religious vocabularies is illustrated by the street-cry of the soothsaying slave-girl of Philippi: 'These men [Paul and his companions] are servants of the Most High God, who proclaim to you the way of salvation' (Acts 16:17); see p. 307. Among the Jews the phrase was the equivalent of

Again, such a phrase as 'the kingdom of God' or 'the kingdom of heaven' had none of the associations in Gentile minds that it had for Jews familiar with the visions of Daniel and later apocalyptists. But if it were replaced by 'eternal life', that would be a much more intelligible expression.

But how could one be sure that the affirmation 'Jesus is Lord' or the expression 'eternal life' would convey the same sense to Gentile minds as was intended by the speaker? Jesus was called 'Lord' by the earliest Aramaic-speaking disciples, as is shown by the importation and naturalization in the vocabulary of Greek-speaking Christianity of the invocation *marana-tha*, 'Come, our Lord'. This invocation, appearing in the New Testament in Aramaic in I Cor. 16:22 and in Greek in Rev. 22:20, is best understood as belonging to the primitive eucharistic liturgy; the *Didache*, which quotes the Aramaic phrase (10:7) in a eucharistic context, most probably reflects primitive usage in this as in some other respects. But when the words 'Jesus is *Kyrios*' was used in an environment in which there were 'many lords (*kyrioi*)', as Paul reminds his Corinthian converts (I Cor. 8:5), there was a tendency to think that Christians worshipped Jesus as Lord just as others worshipped the Lord Sarapis, the Lord Osiris, the Lady Isis or (especially in Ephesus) the Lady Artemis.[8] And when 'eternal life' was spoken of in such an environment, there was a tendency to understand it not in its original Hebraic sense of 'the life of the age to come' or the resurrection life which, thanks to the resurrection of Jesus, could be possessed and enjoyed in anticipation by his followers even now, but in the sense of that 'immortality' which the popular mystery cults of the day guaranteed to their initiates. The pressure to recast Christianity as one among many mystery religions was indeed so strong, albeit unobtrusively so, that the wonder is not that there was so much accommodation as there was but rather that the original essence of Christianity as a faith and life based not on a mystery drama but on a historical person and datable events triumphed as it did. Whatever tendencies to syncretism might appear, Christians

---

Heb. *'ēl 'elyōn*; among the Greeks it denoted the supreme deity of mythology or philosophy.

[8] Cf. W. Foerster, *s.v.* κύριος, *TWNT* III (Stuttgart, 1938), pp. 1049ff. (Eng. tr. [Grand Rapids, 1965], pp. 1050ff); also F. Hahn, *Christologische Hoheitstitel* (Göttingen, 1966), pp. 68ff. (See p. 267 above with n. 11.)

continued to confess Jesus as Lord in a unique sense, implying a lordship which could no more be shared with the lords of the mystery cults than it could with the Roman emperor. To his followers Jesus remained Lord of all, exalted by God to supremacy over the universe.[4]

If, however, Christian doctrine was liable to be compromised by the widespread Gentile mission, this was more obviously true of Christian ethics. Jewish converts to faith in Christ already inherited in their ancestral law a sound basis for decent living, to put it no higher. 'God-fearing' Gentiles who frequented the synagogue and conformed in some measure to the Jewish way of life did so largely because they appreciated its superiority to current pagan morals. The unflattering picture of current pagan morals which Paul, like many other Jewish and (later) Christian apologists, draws in Romans 1:18–32 can be paralleled in contemporary Greek and Latin writers, by whom it is equally reprobated. But it seemed obvious that the ethical standard of Christianity would decline rapidly if too many converts were admitted into church membership direct from their pagan ways, without a period of strict training and probation.

The situation was viewed with great misgivings by many members of the Jerusalem church. Some of these had been—and perhaps still were—associated with Pharisaic brotherhoods. One interesting feature of New Testament history is that, while the Pharisees figure in the Gospels as Jesus' most vehement theological opponents, in Acts they appear (with the exception of the persecuting Saul of Tarsus) much less hostile to the Christians, certainly less hostile than the Sadducean chief priests. The Christians' insistence on the doctrine of resurrection commended them to the Pharisees, even if the Pharisees did not agree that the firstfruits of the final resurrection had already been manifested by the rising of Jesus. A few of them, indeed, were persuaded that this was so, and they adhered to the apostles and their followers.[5] They were accepted as natural leaders by many other members of the Jerusalem church who set high store by the ancient law of Israel. That some parts of it—in particular the sacrificial legislation—had been abrogated by Jesus they might

---

[4] Cf. Col. 2:10, where Christ is called 'the head of all rule and authority'—i.e. of the 'archons' who dominate the life of the world.
[5] Cf. Acts 15:5.

well concede; even apart from the implication of Jesus' teaching
and death there were those in Israel whose attitude to the sacrificial
law was not unlike that of the great prophets of Israel, from Amos
to Jeremiah. But the law as a way of life was to them a sacred trust
which it was their duty to preserve and hand on unimpaired to
generations yet unborn. The influx of Gentile converts must not be
permitted to work to the detriment of the law. On the contrary, if
proselytes to Judaism had from ages past been obliged to 'take upon
themselves the yoke of the commandments', why should not Gentile
converts to Christianity accept the unspeakable boon of Israel's law?
It was no code based on mere human convention; it was imparted
by divine revelation. Gentiles should feel themselves honoured by
receiving this law to keep. Besides, if a period of training and probation was called for before Gentile converts were admitted to full
church fellowship, what more appropriate form could such training
and probation take than a course of instruction in the principles of
the law? Hence the demand began to be voiced in Jerusalem and
Judaea that it was 'necessary to circumcise them, and to charge
them to keep the law of Moses' (Acts 15:5).

Nor was this demand confined to Jerusalem and Judaea, where,
after all, there were relatively few Gentile converts. It had to be
voiced where it was most needed, so Antioch was visited by men
from Judaea whose teaching in the church of that Gentile city is
summarized by Luke: 'Unless you are circumcised according to the
custom of Moses, you cannot be saved' (Acts 15:1).

This insistence on circumcision was new; the question had not
been raised at the beginning of the Gentile mission. It may have
been partly with the idea of imposing a check on the rising number
of Gentile church members that it was raised now; Gentiles were
more reluctant to submit to circumcision than to accept other Jewish
ways. There were indeed some Jewish teachers who thought that
for proselytes the rite of circumcision might be dispensed with, provided its spiritual and moral significance were safeguarded. In debates between the school of Shammai and the school of Hillel the
latter maintained that proselyte baptism was valid without circumcision.[6] About A.D. 40 Ananias, the Jewish instructor of King Izates of
Adiabene, advised him to worship God according to the Jewish

[6] TB *Yebamot* 46a (cf. p. 156, n. 15).

religion without being circumcised, so as not to offend his subjects; but when a Galilaean visitor, Eleazar, assured him some time afterwards that God would not be content with such half measures, Izates had himself circumcised.[7] Even Philo, for all his readiness to re-state Jewish religion in terms of Greek thought, criticizes those *avant-garde* Jews who would give up the literal observance of ceremonial laws on the plea that it was enough to learn and practise their true and inward lessons.[8]

It is probably in the setting of the visit to Antioch of the Judaean Christians who urged the circumcision of Gentile converts that we should place the episode related by Paul in Gal. 2:11–14. Peter had come to Antioch some time before these other visitors from Judaea. To begin with he had been quite happy to share a common table with Gentile Christians—as might be expected in the man who, according to the narrative of Acts 10, a few years earlier learned on a house-top in Joppa not to call anything 'common or unclean' if God had purified it, and immediately afterwards put this lesson into practice by accepting the invitation to enter the house of Cornelius, the Roman centurion of Caesarea. In principle, Peter was as liberal in this respect as Paul was. But when these visitors came from Judaea, one or more of them conveyed a personal message to Peter from James and his colleagues in Jerusalem. The message was couched in some such words as these: 'News has reached us in Jerusalem that you are consorting with Gentiles in Antioch and even sharing common meals with them. This is causing grave scandal to many of our brethren here, and since it has become known also to Jews who are not believers, it is embarrassing us in our relations with them. Please have some consideration for your friends at home and desist from your present practice'.[9]

Naturally, Jews who took the law seriously, including the food-regulations, could not sit at a table where the food would not be *kosher*, and in their eyes a fellow-Jew who did such a thing could not be regarded as pious or observant. He and his associates could not be expected to command the respect or attention of Jews whom they wished to influence in favour of the Way of Jesus. Jesus him-

[7] Josephus, *Ant.* xx, 34ff.   [8] *De migr. Abr.*, 92 (see p. 220).
[9] Cf. T. W. Manson, *Studies in the Gospels and Epistles* (Manchester, 1962), pp. 178ff; he prefers the reading of Gal. 2:12 according to which James's message was conveyed to Peter by one person.

self, indeed, had made a pronouncement about food which implied the abrogation of the levitical food-laws; but it was in the light of later developments that it came to be realized that when he said that a man was defiled by what came out of his heart, not by what went into his stomach, he 'declared all foods clean' (Mark 7:19). At present, those Judaean disciples who condemned table-fellowship with Gentiles did not know that their Master had already made their position untenable.

Peter was impressed by the visitors' representations. While he himself had lost his former scruples about eating with Gentiles, he recognized that many of his friends were not so emancipated in conscience as he was; he was therefore quite ready to ease the embarrassment which his behaviour caused them by forgoing his liberty in this matter. Accordingly, he withdrew, at least for the time being, from table-fellowship with Gentile Christians.

We have not Peter's account of the incident, but if we had, this is probably the impression we should receive. As it is, we have Paul's account. If Peter was concerned about the effect his free and easy ways with Gentiles were producing in Jerusalem, Paul was concerned with the effect that Peter's sudden withdrawal from table-fellowship would have on Gentile Christians in Antioch and elsewhere. In their minds the implication of his act would be that they ranked as second-class Christians. But the effect of Peter's withdrawal on Jewish Christians at Antioch was equally disturbing: 'the rest of the Jews', says Paul (meaning Jewish Christians), 'joined in this play-acting; even Barnabas was carried away with them in their play-acting' (Gal. 2:13). He uses the word 'play-acting'[10] because, as he saw it, Peter and Barnabas and the others were acting a part which did not reflect their personal convictions. They gave up table-fellowship with Gentiles not because they believed it to be wrong but because they judged it in the circumstances to be inexpedient.

No one was readier than Paul to forgo his liberty in the interests of others; but here was a situation in which the interests not merely of Gentile believers but of the gospel itself were threatened by the action of Paul's companions. In the long run such a concession on the terms of fellowship compromised the saving message of for-

---

[10] Gk. ὑπόκρισις (RSV 'insincerity').

giveness through faith in Christ—the message which Peter accepted
and proclaimed in principle as wholeheartedly as Paul did. The
common allegiance of Jewish and Gentile Christians to Jesus as Lord
was given visible expression in their united breaking of the bread;
if this act of fellowship were no longer possible, the unity of the
believing community was in danger. Ultimately circumcision could
validly be required as a condition of social intercourse only if it
was necessary for salvation. Peter's concession, well-meant as it was,
would prove to be the thin end of the wedge; refusal to share a
common table with uncircumcised believers might be followed ere
long by refusal to acknowledge them as believers at all or to recognize them as fellow-members of the church. Hence, as Paul puts it,
he 'withstood Peter to the face, because he was self-condemned'
(Gal. 2:11). 'If you', he asked him publicly, 'Jew though you are,
follow the Gentile and not the Jewish way of life, how can you
compel Gentiles to follow the Jewish way of life?' (Gal. 2:14).

2

Since the dispute had become so serious, a 'summit meeting' was
imperative. Delegates from the Antiochene church, led by Barnabas
and Paul, went up to Jerusalem to debate the issue with the apostles
and elders there. Those who advocated the circumcision of Gentile
converts, led by 'some believers who belonged to the party of the
Pharisees' (Acts 15:5), stated their case, but the verdict went
against them. This was due partly to the argument of Peter, who
spoke from personal conviction and experience, but chiefly to the
judicious terms in which James summed up the debate. It was evident that uncircumcised Gentiles had repeatedly manifested tokens
of the entry of the Spirit into their lives; this was sufficient proof
that God had accepted them on the ground of faith in Jesus as
Lord, without imposing further conditions. Why should others insist on conditions which God had not required?

Moreover, that the Gentile mission lay within the sphere of God's
will was shown, said James, not only by contemporary experience
but also by prophetic scripture. For to James is attributed a remarkable interpretation of an oracle of blessing at the end of the book
of Amos. The Massoretic text describes how Yahweh will one day
raise up David's fallen tent—that is, restore the fortunes of David's

dynasty—and once more grant David's dynasty sovereignty over all
the neighbouring nations, Edom and others, which it ruled in its
early days. The Septuagint version, partly by following variant Hebrew readings, universalizes and spiritualizes this oracle so that it
becomes a promise of the day when all mankind will seek the true
God and be called by his name.[11] In Acts 15:16–18 the Gentile
mission is viewed as the fulfilment of this promise; the fallen fortunes of the house of David are restored by the raising up of Jesus
as the Messiah of David's line, who extends his sovereignty over the
nations through the Gentile mission, so that men everywhere are
now seeking the true God and being called by his name in virtue of
their faith in Jesus.[12]

Circumcision, then, was not to be demanded of Gentile converts.
This was the main issue, and it was decided in a manner acceptable to Paul and the other leaders of the Gentile mission.

But did this necessarily mean that henceforth table-fellowship
and other forms of social intercourse between circumcised Jewish
Christians and uncircumcised Gentile Christians could be enjoyed
without impediment? Apparently no; for this certain additional safe-
guards were required.

For many Jewish Christians, who may have felt nothing but goodwill for their Gentile fellow-believers, the problem of table-
fellowship was much more acute than it was for such emancipated
souls as Peter and Paul. Centuries of devotion to the laws governing
food and purity had bred in them an instinctive revulsion from eating with Gentiles which could not be immediately overcome. Gentiles quite happily ate certain kinds of food which Jews had been
taught to abominate, and the laxity of Gentile morals, especially
where relations between the sexes were concerned, made the idea
of reciprocal hospitality between them and Jewish Christians dis-
tasteful. An attempt was therefore made to remove some of these
obstacles to fellowship.

The precise nature of the provisions recommended by James and
his colleagues to this desirable end is somewhat ambiguous because

[11] Amos 9:11f. The LXX version universalizes the scope of the prophecy by
vocalizing 'ĕdōm ('Edom') as 'ādām ('mankind') and spiritualizes it by reading
yidrĕšû ('that the remnant of mankind may *seek* Yahweh') in place of yîrĕšû
('that they may *possess* the remnant of Edom').

[12] A good example of Christian *pesher* (the form of OT interpretation now
familiar to us from the Qumran sect's commentaries).

of textual variations in Luke's narrative at this point. According to the Western text, it was recommended that Gentile Christians should abstain from three major offences—idolatry, fornication and bloodshed. These ethical provisions are reminiscent of the 'Noachian precepts'[13]—the precepts given by God to Noah and his sons which, according to rabbinical tradition, were binding on all their descendants; in other words, on the whole human race, both Jews and Gentiles. To these three prohibitions the Western text adds a negative form of the Golden Rule: 'Do not do to others those things which you do not wish to have done to yourselves'.[14]

While the Western text here, as elsewhere in Acts, reflects familiarity with Jewish thought and practice, it is unlikely that it represents the original wording here. Such elementary ethical requirements as these must have been included in the rudiments of the instruction received by Gentile converts about the Christian way of life; any violation of them was a bar to church fellowship. It is more probable that the Western reading represents a revision of the original provisions at a time when they no longer had the relevance that they had in the early apostolic age. The original provisions, as preserved in the other types of text, enjoin abstention from the flesh of animals offered in sacrifice to pagan deities and from eating flesh from which the blood had not been completely drained (which would be inevitable when an animal had died by strangulation).[15] To these two may have been added abstention from 'fornication'—here intended not in the common sense of the word (for abstention from that was in any case stringently enjoined on all Christians), but in the sense of transgression of the degrees of consanguinity and affinity prohibited in Leviticus 18:6–18.[16]

---

[13] The prohibition of 'blood' in the sense of eating 'flesh with its life' is also included in the Noachian precepts (Gen. 9:4).

[14] The negative form of the Golden Rule appears in Tobit 4:15; Didache 1:2; TB *Shabbat* 31a; *Abot de R. Nathan* 2:26. A Jewish instance of the positive form (best known from Matt. 7:12) is provided by Maimonides, *Hilekot 'Abel* 14:1 (Mishnah Torah 2).

[15] P. H. Menoud, 'The Western Text and the Theology of Acts', *SNTS Bulletin* 2 (1951), pp. 19ff (especially pp. 22ff), argues that the decree originally covered only the two kinds of forbidden food (meat with blood and idolothyta), and that this twofold prohibition was later expanded in various ways to which our authorities for the text bear witness; cf. C. S. C. Williams, *Alterations to the Text of the Synoptic Gospels and Acts* (Oxford, 1951), pp. 72ff.

[16] Gk. πορνεία here and elsewhere in NT (e.g. Matt. 5:32; 19:9; I Cor. 5:1) probably reflects Heb. *zĕnūṭ* used to denote such transgressions, or transgres-

These marital prohibitions were basic to the Jewish marriage law and have been part of Christian canon law from the time of this Jerusalem decree.

The Jerusalem decree dealt with two questions—the major one, 'Must Gentile Christians be circumcised and undertake to keep the Mosaic law?' and the subsidiary one, 'What are the conditions with which Gentile Christians should comply if Jewish Christians are to have easy social relations with them?' The second question would not have been raised had the first question been answered in the affirmative. If Gentile Christians had been required to follow the example of Gentile proselytes to Judaism, then, when these requirements were met, table-fellowship and the like would have followed as a matter of course. But when it was decided that Gentile Christians must not be compelled to submit to circumcision and the general obligations of the Jewish law, the question of table-fellowship, which had caused the recent trouble in Antioch, had to be considered. It was decided, on James's motion, that table-fellowship might be allowed if Gentile converts abstained from certain practices which were specially offensive to Jews, and to the majority of Jewish Christians. Such practices which were particularly relevant to the matter of table-fellowship were the eating of food which had been 'contaminated' by idolatrous associations and the eating of flesh with blood still in it. In addition, since the sexual laxity of much contemporary paganism was also highly offensive to Jews, ordinary social intercourse between Jewish and Gentile Christians would be promoted if the latter conformed to the Jewish marriage code.

The decree formulated by the Jerusalem leaders embodied the answers to these two questions. On the first score, the yoke of the law was not to be imposed on Gentile believers; on the other score, said they, 'it has seemed good to the Holy Spirit and to us to lay upon you no greater burden than these necessary things'[17]—avoidance of idolatrous food and meat containing blood, and abstention from 'fornication'.

---

sions of the approved interpretation of these laws (cf. *CD* iv, 17ff for its use to cover polygamy and marriage between uncle and niece).

[17] Perhaps we should follow a slightly different text and read: '. . . to lay upon you no greater burden than these things: it is necessary (ἐπάναγκες) to abstain . . .'.

James and others like-minded may well have considered that they were making a liberal concession by limiting the obligations of Gentile Christians to 'those necessary things'. Did Paul, and those like-minded with him, consider that they on their part were making a concession in accepting them? Perhaps they did, but it was a concession well worth making. For one thing, the fundamental principle had been conceded: Gentile converts were free of any legal obligation. Their status as members of the redeemed community was assured, as was the status of their Jewish fellow-members, by their acknowledged faith in Jesus as Lord. That the Jerusalem leaders would confirm this, as they did, was by no means a foregone conclusion; the decree must therefore have been greeted by Paul and his friends as a victory for gospel freedom.

For another thing, Paul was the most conciliatory and adaptable of men where what he regarded as the essence of the gospel was not compromised. There, he was unyielding; elsewhere, his exhortation to his fellow-Christians, as it was his own consistent practice, was to consider the conscience and spiritual well-being of others and voluntarily forgo personal freedom for their sakes. If Gentile Christians found that their practices in food matters raised difficulties for the weaker consciences of Jewish Christians, then let them abstain from these practices, not indeed under compulsion but by their free choice, as a gesture of Christian charity.[18] (To be sure, the reference to 'these necessary things' in the decree suggests that the Jerusalem leaders had in mind something more than a voluntary gesture of charity on the part of Gentile Christians, and this may have been a cause of subsequent misunderstanding.) As for the prohibition of 'fornication', Paul's reaction a few years later to a particularly offensive instance of such an illicit union at Corinth makes it plain that he was in complete sympathy with this requirement.[19]

It was not contemplated that Jewish Christians should be liberated from the obligation to maintain the Jewish way of life. The decree did not take them into its purview. The majority of Jewish Christians at this time were far from sharing the emancipated attitude of Paul, who was equally happy to live as a Gentile in a Gentile environment and to follow the Jewish way of life in the company

[18] Cf. Paul's teaching on this subject in I Cor. 8:7ff and Rom. 14:13ff.
[19] I Cor. 5:1 (see p. 325).

of Jews. To him it was religiously indifferent which way of life he followed; these things, and especially food-regulations, were completely subordinate to the main purpose of his life and to the spiritual health of the people in whose society he found himself. During the years that followed, considerable hostility developed towards him at Jerusalem because news came from time to time that he urged Jews—more particularly, no doubt, Jewish Christians —in the provinces which he evangelized not to circumcise their children or go on observing the ancestral customs.[20] James and his fellow-elders assured Paul that they themselves knew that these reports were false; but the very behaviour, apart from the teaching, of a man who sat so loose to traditional Judaism as Paul did must have encouraged other Jewish Christians to follow his example.

For the present, however, Paul accepted the decree, and recommended it to the acceptance of Gentile Christians, at least within the area to which it was addressed. It was addressed 'to the brethren who are of the Gentiles in Antioch and Syria and Cilicia'.[21] This might mean in effect the church of Antioch and her daughter-churches; was it intended that the recently founded churches of South Galatia should be included? According to Acts 16:4, these churches had the terms of the decree delivered to them when Paul, accompanied by Silas, paid them a visit not long afterwards; but it has been argued that this passage is a duplicate of Acts 15:41, where, according to the fuller reading of the Western text, it is the churches of Syria and Cilicia that have the decree delivered to them.[22]

The upshot of the decree was that the circumcision issue could no longer impede the progress of the Gentile mission. It might indeed be raised from time to time, but henceforth those who pressed circumcision on Gentile Christians could not invoke the authority of the apostles and elders at Jerusalem.

[20] Cf. Acts 21:21 (see p. 354).   [21] Acts 15:23.
[22] A. S. Geyser, 'Paul, the Apostolic Decree and the Liberals in Corinth', in *Studia Paulina in honorem J. de Zwaan*, ed. J. N. Sevenster and W. C. van Unnik (Haarlem, 1953), pp. 124ff, especially pp. 136ff.

23 Claudius and Christianity

1

When Claudius succeeded his nephew Gaius as emperor, he did his best to allay the strife that had raged between the Gentile and Jewish inhabitants of Alexandria during the principate of Gaius. He issued an edict directing the two communities to desist from further conflict and reaffirming the traditional privileges of Alexandrian Jews.

This edict is reproduced by Josephus in a form which appears to be substantially, though not absolutely, accurate:[1]

Tiberius Claudius Caesar Augustus Germanicus, pontifex maximus, vested with the tribunician power, decrees as follows:

Whereas for a long time now, from the earliest times, the Jews of Alexandria, called Alexandrians, have lived together with the Alexandrians and received from the kings [the Ptolemies] equality in civil rights with them, as is evident from those kings' letters and edicts; and whereas, ever since Alexandria was subjected to our empire by Augustus, they have kept their rights under all the governors sent there from time to time, without any dispute being raised concerning these rights; and whereas, when Aquila [prefect of Egypt, 11–10 B.C.] was at Alexandria and the ethnarch of the Jews died, Augustus did not prevent the nomination of ethnarchs, because he desired that all his subjects should be able to remain faithful to their respective customs without infringing their ancestral laws; and whereas the Alexandrians rose against the Jews of their city under the principate of Gaius (who in his extreme folly and madness humiliated the Jews for refusing to transgress their ancestral religion by invoking him as a god); now therefore I decree that the Jewish people be deprived of none of their rights because of Gaius's madness but that they retain the same privileges as before, remaining faithful to their national customs, and I command the two parties to beware most carefully of provoking any trouble after the publication of my edict.

[1] *Ant.* xix, 279ff.

It is unlikely that Claudius represented the Ptolemies as having granted the Jews of Alexandria equality of civil rights with the Alexandrian Greeks, unless this simply means that the Alexandrian Jews had their own separate administration, established by the same royal authority as the constitution of the Greek city itself. It is noteworthy that the Jews who enjoyed these special privileges as a self-contained community within the wider city community are called 'Alexandrians'—by contrast, it may be supposed, with immigrants who swelled the Jewish population of Alexandria but were not entitled to the privileges confirmed by the Ptolemies on the established Jewish residents of the city.

Again, what really happened on the death of the ethnarch in 11–10 B.C., according to Philo, was that, instead of authorizing the nomination of a new ethnarch, Augustus replaced him by a senate (*gerousia*).[2]

It appears, then, that the text of the edict as Josephus gives it has undergone some editing, but apart from one or two points like those mentioned, Josephus's text is reliable enough.

But we have a copy of another document from the same period which throws further light on the situation. This is a letter sent by Claudius to the people of Alexandria, published by order of the prefect of Egypt, and copied on the verso of a papyrus roll which was acquired by the British Museum in 1921. The letter was sent to the Alexandrians in response to an embassy which they had sent to Claudius to congratulate him on his accession, to ask his permission to pay him various honours, and to state the city's case with regard to the recent outbreaks against the Jews. (They probably judged this last matter to be particularly urgent in view of the close friendship which was known to exist between Claudius and Herod Agrippa, king of the Jews.) The letter, as it stands in the papyrus, has no date, but the prefect's preamble is dated 'Year 2 of Tiberius Claudius Caesar Augustus Germanicus Imperator, 14th day of the month *Neos Sebastos*' (i.e. November 10, A.D. 41).

In the letter[3] Claudius deals one by one with the points raised by the embassy of Alexandrians. The section which concerns us con-

---

[2] Philo, *Flaccus*, 74.
[3] *Editio princeps* in H. I. Bell, *Jews and Christians in Egypt* (London, 1924), pp. 1ff; cf. *CPI* II, no. 153.

tains his reply to their representations about the anti-Jewish excesses in their city. It runs thus (lines 73–104):

> With regard to the question which of the two sides was responsible for the rioting and civil strife—or rather, if the truth must be told, the war—against the Jews, I am not disposed to conduct a strict inquiry, although your ambassadors, especially Dionysius the son of Theon, pleaded your cause zealously and at length against the other side. But I do reserve irrevocable anger against those who started it again. Now I tell you plainly that if you do not desist from this destructive and obstinate animosity against one another, I shall be compelled to show what a benevolent ruler is capable of when he is moved to righteous anger.[4] Therefore I adjure you now once more that the citizens of Alexandria for their part conduct themselves in a considerate and neighbourly manner towards the Jews who have lived in the same city for a long time, and offer them no outrage in the practice of their customary divine worship but allow them to follow their customs as they did in the time of the deified Augustus—customs which I too have confirmed after listening to both parties. The Jews, on the other hand, I bid for their part not to agitate for more than they have previously enjoyed, and never again to send two embassies, as though they lived in two separate cities—the like of which has never happened before. Moreover, they must not engage in contests presided over by gymnasiarchs or games directors, since they already receive what belongs to them by right and enjoy an abundance of all good things in a city which is not theirs. They must not bring in or invite Jews who sail in from Syria or Egypt; this is the sort of thing which will compel me to have my suspicions redoubled. Otherwise I will proceed against them with the utmost severity for fomenting a general plague which infests the whole world. If on both sides you are willing to desist from this behaviour and live in mutual consideration and neighbourliness, I for my part will show that long-standing friendly interest in your city with which my family has had close relations since my ancestors' days.

Much in this section of the letter, relating to the constitutional relations between the Jewish and Greek communities in Alexandria, is irrelevant to our present purpose. But one part of it would have a direct relevance, if a certain interpretation of it could be estab-

---

[4] Claudius's threat 'to show what a benevolent ruler is capable of when he is moved to righteous anger' is illustrated by his severe action against the Greek Alexandrians Isidore and Lampo (see p. 250) after a fresh outbreak of racial strife in the city in A.D. 53. See H. A. Musurillo, *Acts of the Pagan Martyrs* (Oxford, 1954), pp. 18ff; *CPI* II, no. 156.

lished. This is the ban which Claudius places on the introduction into Alexandria of Jews from Syria or Egypt. This has been interpreted by some scholars[5] as a reference to disturbances within the Jewish community of Alexandria caused by the introduction of Christianity to that city, and confirmatory evidence has been sought by linking the emperor's severe words about 'a general plague which infests the whole world' with the language used by Tertullus when he was conducting the Sanhedrin's prosecution of Paul before Felix: 'we have found this fellow a perfect plague' (Acts 24:5).

The origins of Alexandrian Christianity form an obscure and fascinating subject.[6] There is certainly every probability in the view that Christianity had found its way to Alexandria by A.D. 41. Hellenistic disciples who had left Jerusalem after Stephen's death (c. A.D. 33) are as likely to have gone to Alexandria as to Antioch; the appearance of the Alexandrian disciple Apollos at Ephesus and Corinth in A.D. 52 (Acts 18:24ff) is a factor of special importance in this connexion. But it is difficult to trace any allusion to Christians in the emperor's letter. The unrest to which he refers was unrest between the Greek and Jewish communities of the city, not within the Jewish community. The Jews who were sailing in from Syria are placed on the same footing as the Jews who sailed down the Nile to Alexandria from other parts of Egypt. There were many Jews in Egypt apart from those of Alexandria, but they did not en-

[5] Especially G. de Sanctis, 'Claudio e i Giudei d'Alessandria', *Rivista di filologia* 52 (1924), pp. 473ff, and S. Reinach, 'La première allusion au christianisme dans l'histoire', *Revue de l'histoire des religions* 89 (1924), pp. 108ff; *Orpheus* (London, 1931), p. 244. Cf. also S. Loesch, *Epistula Claudiana* (Rottenburg, 1930); S. G. F. Brandon, *The Fall of Jerusalem and the Christian Church* (London, 1951), pp. 222f; H. J. Cadbury, *The Book of Acts in History* (New York, 1955), pp. 116f; E. M. Blaiklock, *Out of the Earth* (London, 1957), p. 37 ('This letter . . . appears to contain the first secular reference to Christian missionaries'). Some writers who discern a reference to Jewish Christians here are prone to lay more stress on the sailing in of Jews from Syria than on the sailing of others down the Nile from other parts of Egypt.

[6] According to the Western text of Acts 18:25, Apollos, when he came to Ephesus c. A.D. 52, had been taught the Christian message 'in his home city' (ἐν τῇ πατρίδι). Cf. also W. Bauer, *Rechtgläubigkeit und Ketzerei im ältesten Christentum*[2] (Tübingen, 1964), pp. 49ff; S. G. F. Brandon, *The Fall of Jerusalem and the Christian Church* (London, 1951), pp. 217ff; H. E. W. Turner, *The Pattern of Christian Truth* (London, 1954), pp. 46ff; R. P. C. Hanson, *Tradition in the Early Church* (London, 1962), pp. 166f; A. Ehrhardt, *The Framework of the New Testament Stories* (Manchester, 1964), pp. 174ff.

joy the special privileges granted to their brethren in Alexandria. The significance of the illegal Jewish immigration into Alexandria from Syria and the rest of Egypt is probably to be found in the statement of Josephus that the Jews of Alexandria, having obtained no satisfaction from Gaius, took up arms when the news of his death arrived.[7] That is to say, they prepared to attack the Greek Alexandrians, and in these circumstances it was only natural that they should try to augment their strength by inviting their fellow Jews from other parts of Egypt and from Syria and Palestine to come to their aid. Such a situation would amply account for the severity of the emperor's admonition to stop this at once.

But why should Claudius speak of this situation in terms of 'a general plague which infests the whole world'? The language suggests that there had already been trouble with Jews in other parts of the Empire. Have we any evidence of such trouble elsewhere?

2

The late second-century historian Dio Cassius supplies us with what may be a piece of relevant information here. Dealing with the first year of Claudius, he gives some examples of the emperor's moderation, and adds:

> When the Jews (*sc.* of Rome) had again multiplied to a point where their numbers made it difficult to expel them from the city without a riot, he did not directly banish them, but forbade them to gather together in accordance with their ancestral way of life.[8]

The point of Dio's statement that the Roman Jews had *again* multiplied is, no doubt, that they had been banished from the city by Tiberius some twenty-two years previously.[9] That earlier edict of expulsion had, however, become a dead letter, especially (we may suppose) after the fall of Sejanus in A.D. 31.[10] But why should their increasing numbers move Claudius to place restrictions on them?

[7] *Ant.* xix, 278.
[8] Dio, *Hist.* lx, 6.
[9] Philo, *Legatio* 159ff; Josephus, *Ant.* xviii, 65, 81ff; Tacitus, *Ann.* ii, 85; Suetonius, *Tiberius*, 36. E. M. Smallwood, 'Some Notes on the Jews under Tiberius', *Latomus* 15 (1956), pp. 314ff, suggests that Jewish proselytizing activity was the reason for Tiberius's action. See also E. T. Merrill, 'The Expulsion of the Jews from Rome under Tiberius', *Cl. Phil.* 14 (1919), pp. 365ff.
[10] See p. 137.

Perhaps because there were already signs of that unruly and turbulent behaviour which led him, about eight years later, to decree their absolute expulsion from the capital. Christianity was not the only messianic movement abroad among the Jews in this period, although it is as probable that Christianity had reached Rome by the beginning of Claudius's reign as that it had reached Alexandria by that date. At any rate, if Claudius had already experienced some trouble with the Jews of Rome, we can understand better the sharpness with which he warned the Jews of Alexandria not to foment a similar plague there by an illegal increasing of their numbers.

But it may be asked whether it is probable that Claudius took such drastic action so early against the Roman Jews in view of his promptitude in confirming, at the beginning of his reign, the privileges granted by his predecessors to Jews throughout the Empire, and even more so in view of his friendship with Herod Agrippa. Agrippa was in Rome at the time of the assassination of Gaius and the accession of Claudius in January of A.D. 41, and not only performed for the corpse of the dead emperor such elementary decencies as others were afraid to perform, but encouraged Claudius to accept the imperial power which was being thrust upon him by the Praetorian Guards.[11] Is it likely that Claudius would so quickly place restrictions on the fellow-nationals and co-religionists of a man whom he himself delighted to honour? May it not be that Dio Cassius has antedated the action against the Jews of Rome which other writers ascribe to a later point in Claudius's reign? The answer to this latter question is that it is unlikely that Dio is referring to the same occasion as those other writers: they say that Claudius expelled the Jews from Rome; Dio says that he did not expel them, but put restrictions on their assembling together. It is a reasonable inference that, when these measures proved inadequate to deal with the trouble, he took more drastic steps later. As for the suggested inconsistency between restrictions on their liberty so early in his reign and the official and unofficial acts which reveal his goodwill at that time to the Jews in general and to Herod Agrippa in particular, it may be said that no amount of goodwill on the emperor's part or personal influence on Herod Agrippa's part could make the emperor close his eyes to anything that seemed to threaten the

[11] Josephus, *Ant.* xix, 236ff (see p. 256).

public peace of the capital. Professor Momigliano's observation is apposite: 'Judaism was at once a faith and a people. True to his policy of favouring provincials, Claudius desired to remain on good terms with the people but to suppress any proselytizing activities of the faith, now increased by the new ferment of a Christianity still indistinguishable from the synagogue'.[12] The reference to 'the new ferment of a Christianity still indistinguishable from the synagogue' is more relevant to Claudius's later action against the Jews of Rome, but that the earlier trouble was bound up with some aspect of the Jewish religion may be inferred from Dio's statement that Claudius 'forbade them to gather together in accordance with their ancestral way of life'.

When we come to Claudius's later action against the Jews of Rome, we find ourselves on firmer ground with regard to Christianity. According to Acts 18:2, it was just after Paul came to Corinth that he met Aquila and Priscilla, who had recently had to leave Rome in consequence of Claudius's edict of expulsion. Paul nowhere suggests that Aquila and Priscilla were converts of his, and the impression we gain is that they were already Christians when he made their acquaintance. That Christianity had been brought to Rome by this time—that, in fact, its propagation within the Jewish community of the capital had much to do with Claudius's edict—is the natural inference from the statement of Suetonius that 'because the Jews of Rome were indulging in constant riots at the instigation of Chrestus (*impulsore Chresto*) he expelled them from the city'.[13]

Although Christianity was indistinguishable from Judaism in the time of Claudius, it was perfectly distinguishable by the time Suetonius wrote (*c.* A.D. 120), and it was well known that it had been founded by Christ (*Christus*, not unnaturally confused with the common slave-name *Chrestus*, which was pronounced in practically the same way). It is just conceivable that the riots mentioned by Suetonius were caused by the activity of an otherwise unknown Chrestus, but in that case he would probably have said 'at the instigation of a certain Chrestus' (*impulsore Chresto quodam*). It is more natural to suppose that he intended his readers to understand that Chrestus who, as a matter of general knowledge, was the

12 A. Momigliano, *Claudius* (Cambridge, 1961²), p. 30.
13 Suetonius, *Claudius*, 25:4.

founder of Christianity. To be sure, Christ was not in Rome in the
time of Claudius;[14] but Suetonius, writing seventy years later, may
have thought that he was. If his sources indicated that the riots
which provoked Claudius's edict of expulsion were due to the introduction and propagation of Christianity in the capital, he could
well have drawn the mistaken inference that it had been introduced
there by Christ in person. Tacitus was better informed; he knew
that Christ was crucified under Tiberius;[15] but such accuracy required a degree of research for which others had neither the interest nor the inclination. At any rate, our inference from Suetonius
that the riots were due to the recent introduction of Christianity
into the Jewish colony at Rome agrees well enough with our independent inference from the New Testament that Aquila and Priscilla were Christians before they came to Corinth.[16]

When did this expulsion of Jews from Rome take place? Paul's
residence of eighteen months in Corinth can be dated within fairly
narrow limits by inscriptional evidence for the date of Gallio's proconsulship of Achaia;[17] we shall not be far out if we say that Paul
arrived in Corinth in the late summer or autumn of A.D. 50. But
when he arrived, Aquila and Priscilla were already in residence
there; the decree of expulsion therefore cannot be dated later than
A.D. 49. This, as it happens, is precisely the year to which Orosius
dates it. 'In his ninth year', says Orosius, 'Claudius is reported by
Josephus to have expelled the Jews from the capital'.[18] The reference to Josephus is strange; our extant texts of Josephus contain no
mention of Claudius's expulsion of the Jews, although Josephus
does record Tiberius's similar action thirty years before. Perhaps

---

[14] To the contrary R. Graves and J. Podro, *Jesus in Rome* (London, 1957),
pp. 38ff. H. W. Montefiore ('Josephus and the New Testament', *NovT* 4
[1960], p. 139, n. 2) says, 'Suetonius is here referring to the influence of the
risen Christ'—but that is the Christian commentator's interpretation, not the
pagan writer's intention.   [15] *Ann.* xv, 44.
[16] Cf. A. Harnack, 'Probabilia über die Adresse und den Verfasser des He-
bräerbriefs', *ZNTW* 1 (1900), pp. 16ff.
[17] In a rescript of Claudius to the Delphians dated to Claudius's 26th acclamation as *imperator* (W. Dittenberger, *Sylloge Inscriptionum Graecarum* II³,
801), Gallio is mentioned as proconsul of Achaia. The evidence of other inscriptions (*CIL* iii, 476, vi, 1256) points to the first seven months of A.D. 52 as the
period of Claudius's 26th imperatorial acclamation. As a proconsul nominally
entered on his office on July 1, it is just possible that Gallio became proconsul
of Achaia on 1 July, A.D. 52, but more probable that he did so twelve months
earlier.   [18] *Hist.* vii, 6. 15f.

Orosius's memory played him false; but his dating of Claudius's edict is probably right.

We have no certain means of dating the first introduction of Christianity to Rome. 'Ambrosiaster' was no doubt right in saying that the Roman believers 'had embraced the faith of Christ, albeit according to the Jewish rite, although they saw no sign of mighty works nor any of the apostles'.[19] But when they 'embraced the faith of Christ' we cannot tell. The fact that 'visitors from Rome, both Jews and proselytes' are listed by Luke[20] among those who were present at the first Christian Pentecost in Jerusalem in A.D. 30 may have a bearing on the question; one cannot be sure. But in its earliest stages Roman Christianity was thoroughly Jewish, and long after the apostolic age it continued to exhibit certain features of its Jewish provenance—features, moreover, which seem to be more characteristic of nonconformist Judaism than of the main stream.[21]

This first, and almost completely unchronicled, chapter in the story of Roman Christianity comes to an end with Claudius's edict in A.D. 49. Christian and non-Christian Jews alike were expelled from the city. But it is plain that, before many years had passed, both Christian and non-Christian Jews were back in Rome in full force, together with many Christians of Gentile stock. When Paul writes to the Roman Christians at the beginning of A.D. 57, he obviously writes to a flourishing community which includes many Gentiles, although it is not forgotten that its base was Jewish.[22]

We need not suppose that Claudius's edict of expulsion was formally rescinded, to permit a return of Jews to Rome. Just as the similar edict of Tiberius thirty years previously appears to have become a dead letter with the passing of time, and certainly with that emperor's death, so Claudius's edict probably lapsed for practical purposes with his death. A new chapter in the history of Roman Christianity opens in A.D. 54.[23]

[19] Preface to Commentary on Romans (ed. H. J. Vogels in *CSEL* lxxxi, 1 [Vienna, 1966], p. 6). The whole preface suggests that Ambrosiaster had access to reliable tradition on the Jewish origin of Roman Christianity. [20] Acts 2:10.
[21] Important evidence is provided by the Hippolytean *Apostolic Tradition* (especially 20:5); cf. R. J. Zwi Werblowsky, 'On the Baptismal Rite according to St. Hippolytus', *Studia Patristica* II = *TU* 54 (1957), pp. 93ff; M. Black, *The Scrolls and Christian Origins* (London, 1961), pp. 91ff.
[22] Cf. Rom. 1:8; 11:13, 18. [23] See pp. 393ff.

3

Shortly after Claudius's edict expelling the Jews from Rome, disturbances not unlike those which precipitated that edict broke out at Thessalonica. Paul and his companions, who brought the gospel to that city in the spring of A.D. 50, incurred opposition from the leaders of the local Jewish community, who brought a serious charge against them before the civic magistrates (the 'politarchs'): 'These men who have been subverting the whole world have come here also, . . . they all flout Caesar's decrees and proclaim a rival emperor, Jesus' (Acts 17:6f). The wording of the charge fits well into the picture of unruly movements within Jewish communities throughout the empire, more or less 'messianic' in character (if the adjective be used in its wider sense), which constituted a threat to public order in places where Jews were resident, and which were deplored and denounced by responsible Jewish leaders who knew the importance of maintaining acceptable relations with the Roman power. These movements were probably linked with the resurgence of Zealot activity in Palestine in the period that followed the death of Herod Agrippa I in A.D. 44, and more especially during the procuratorship of Cumanus (*c.* 48–52).[24]

4

Something should be added about a document which has been considered to be a further piece of evidence for Christian activity under Claudius; if that were so, it would be of peculiar interest and importance, because it would suggest that the emperor himself was compelled to take cognizance of Christianity and to devise means of checking it.

In the Cabinet des Médailles in Paris there has been since 1878 an inscribed marble slab, part of the Froehner collection. The only evidence of its provenance is the note referring to it in Froehner's manuscript inventory: *Dalle de marbre envoyée de Nazareth en 1878.* The first person to pay serious attention to it was evidently M. Rostovtzeff, about fifty years after it was brought to Paris. He drew F. Cumont's attention to it, and Cumont published it in the

---

[24] Cf. Josephus *BJ* ii, 223ff; *Ant.* xx, 105ff (see pp. 341ff).

Revue Historique for 1930, under the title 'Un rescrit impérial sur la violation de sépulture'.[25] The inscription, which is in Greek, but was probably composed originally in Latin, bears the heading 'Decree of Caesar'[26] and runs as follows:

> It is my pleasure that sepulchres and tombs, which have been erected as solemn memorials of ancestors or children or relatives, shall remain undisturbed in perpetuity. If it be shown that anyone has either destroyed them or otherwise thrown out the bodies which have been buried there or removed them with malicious intent to another place, thus committing a crime against those buried there, or removed the headstones or other stones, I command that against such person the same sentence be passed in respect of solemn memorials of men as is laid down in respect of the gods. Much rather must one pay respect to those who are buried. Let no one disturb them on any account. Otherwise it is my will that capital sentence be passed upon such person for the crime of tomb-spoliation.

The inscription is said to have been 'sent from Nazareth' to Paris; was it *found* in Nazareth? And if so, was it originally set up in Nazareth? If it was, then we may reach certain fairly precise conclusions about its date. The form of the letters suggests that the inscription belongs to the earlier half of the first century A.D.[27] But Nazareth is in Galilee, and we should not expect an imperial decree to be set up in Galilee before A.D. 44. Only in that year did Galilee become part of the province of Judaea, and so directly subject to imperial rule; before that it had formed part of the kingdom of Herod Agrippa (A.D. 39–44); previously it had formed part of the tetrarchy of Herod Antipas (4 B.C.–A.D. 39), and earlier still it had belonged to the kingdom of Herod the Great (37 4 B.C.). If the inscription belongs to the earlier half of the first century and yet cannot be dated before A.D. 44, the emperor whose decree it records would be Claudius.

Why, in that case, should it be necessary for a decree against tomb-spoliation to be given such publicity in Nazareth? And why should the penalty specified for the offence be so severe? Tomb-

---

[25] *Revue Historique* 163 (1930), pp. 241ff.
[26] Gk. Διάταγμα Καίσαρος (cf. the δόγματα Καίσαρος of Acts 17:7, mentioned below, p. 308).
[27] G. de Sanctis, *Rivista di filologia* 58 (1930), pp. 260f; 59 (1931), p. 134; 60 (1932), p. 129.

spoliation was no novelty; from ancient times tombstones and sar-
cophagi contained inscriptions warning offenders not to interfere
with the contents.[28] Epitaphs from Hellenistic times repeatedly
contain the warning that those caught in the act of tomb-spoliation
will be fined a specified amount. But here the emperor in person
takes tomb-spoliation in Palestine so seriously that he issues an edict
threatening the death-penalty against it. Why?

One suggested answer is that the spread of Christianity had come
to Claudius's notice, and that—antiquarian as he was—he made
some inquiry into the origins of the movement. Finding that it had
to do with one Jesus who was dead, whom his followers affirmed to
be alive,[29] he would be told, in response to further questions, that
what had actually happened was that when the body of Jesus had
been buried, his disciples came by night and stole him away while
the watchmen at the tomb were overcome by sleep.[30] Considering,
then, that an act of tomb-spoliation had fostered a plague which
was now infesting the whole world, he determined to impose specially heavy penalties on any repetition of such a crime, in Palestine
at any rate. His order to this effect may have taken the form of a
rescript to the procurator of Judaea or the legate of Syria; copies
would be set up in those places in Palestine which were closely associated with the gospel story—in Jerusalem and Bethlehem, we may
suppose, as well as in Nazareth.[31] There are too many uncertainties
about the inscription to justify more than a tentative consideration

---

[28] Cf. the sarcophagus of Ahiram, king of Byblos (10th century B.C.) and
the inscribed tablet found on the Mount of Olives in 1931 marking the reburial
of the bones of Uzziah, king of Judah. King David's tomb, while opened apparently with impunity by John Hyrcanus (Josephus, *BJ* i, 61; *Ant.* xiii, 249),
proved less tolerant of Herod's similar attempt to rob it (*Ant.* xvi, 179ff, 188;
cf. *BJ* vii, 392–4). Cf. W. M. Ramsay, *Cities and Bishropics of Phrygia* ii (Oxford, 1897), pp. 496ff.

[29] Cf. the puzzled language of Festus in Acts 25:19.

[30] For the currency of this story see Matt. 28:13.

[31] This interpretation was accepted by A. Momigliano, *Claudius* (Oxford,
1934), pp. 34ff; but in the latest edition (Cambridge, 1961) he regrets 'having
attributed the Nazareth inscription on violation of tombs to Claudius' time.
There was never any good reason to do so, and the inferences some scholars
have drawn from this attribution make me even keener to dissociate myself from
it' (p. ix). He does not say what positive considerations led to his change of
mind. Cf. also H. J. Cadbury, *The Book of Acts in History*, pp. 117f; E. M.
Blaiklock, *Out of the Earth*, pp. 32ff. Some reservations are expressed by F. de
Zulueta, 'Violation of Sepulture in Palestine at the Beginning of the Christian
Era', *JRS* 22 (1932), pp. 184ff.

of the possibility that it might have some bearing on the spread of Christianity in Claudius's reign, but this interpretation does at least fit in rather suggestively with other hints from ancient writers relating to the same period.

It may be that the Nazareth inscription (if it was originally a Nazareth inscription) was set up not earlier than A.D. 44. But perhaps it was set up not much later. For if Claudius had indeed developed an interest in the origins of Christianity, he did not have to look far for someone who could give him the sort of information he desired. His great friend Herod Agrippa certainly knew something about early Palestinian Christianity. He took Palestinian Christianity seriously enough to try to wipe out its leaders,[32] and it is quite conceivable, not to say probable, that he had some conversation with Claudius about this subversive movement, even if the decree against tomb-spoliation was not set up until after Agrippa's death. But Agrippa could distinguish Jewish Christianity from the main stream of Judaism more easily than Claudius could. When, some years after Agrippa's death (A.D. 44), the spread of Christianity within the Jewish colony in Rome led to increasingly frequent breaches of the peace, Claudius did not attempt to isolate the Christians in Rome and deal with them, but ordered the whole Jewish community to leave.

5

When Claudius became emperor in A.D. 41 Christianity was just beginning to spread into the Gentile world. It was taking root among the Gentiles of Syrian Antioch, and it may well have found its way already into the Jewish communities of Rome and Alexandria. When Claudius died, thirteen years later, the situation had changed very greatly. The southern cities of Galatia had been evangelized; so had the principal cities of Macedonia and Achaia, thanks largely to the activity of Paul. In most of these cities there were Christian churches whose membership was more Gentile than Jewish. And by the time of Claudius's death (October, A.D. 54) Paul had been hard at work for two years, with a number of colleagues, evangelizing Ephesus and the other cities of Asia to such good effect that for centuries that province was one of the strongest citadels of

[32] Acts 12:1ff.

Christianity in the world. Little more than two years after Claudius's death Paul could tell the Roman Christians that his work in the Aegean world was finished, and he proposed to set out for Spain to repeat in the western Mediterranean area the programme which he had lately brought to a conclusion in the east, 'from Jerusalem and as far round as Illyricum'.[33] For all the interest that Claudius may have taken in Christianity, he can hardly have realized how firm a hold it was taking of the Mediterranean world during his reign.

[33] Rom. 15:19, 23f.

1

Antioch on the Orontes had served as a base for the evangelization of Cyprus and South Galatia, but it was less well suited to be a
base for the evangelization of the provinces bordering the Aegean
Sea, which Paul had in view as his next sphere of apostolic activity.
He and Barnabas found it no longer possible to work together,[1]
although the breach of partnership did not imply any diminution
in personal esteem, as is plain from Paul's references to Barnabas
in I Corinthians, written four or five years after they parted company.[2] Paul found another congenial colleague in Silvanus (the
'Silas' of Acts), a member of the Jerusalem church, with whom he
journeyed westwards through South Galatia, revisiting the churches
which he and Barnabas had recently founded there. In one of these
churches (Lystra) was a young man of mixed Jewish and Gentile
parentage, Timothy by name, who had made such progress in Christian faith and life since his conversion to Christianity during Paul
and Barnabas's stay in his home-town that Paul took him along as a
further companion, discerning in him those qualities which would
make him a reliable adjutant. With a view to Timothy's greater usefulness in this capacity, Paul circumcised him—an action so surprising in the writer of the letter to the Galatians that some quite
exceptional reason for it must be sought. Luke points to Timothy's
mixed parentage as the reason: his father (by this time probably
dead) was a Greek, and his mother was a Jewess (such a mixed
marriage is a symptom of the assimilationist tendencies among the
Jews of central Asia Minor).[3] He had, moreover, been brought up
in the Jewish religion; this fact, coupled with his mother's being a

---

[1] In Acts 15:36ff their parting company is explained by their inability to agree
about taking John Mark with them again after his earlier defection (see
pp. 273f); the dissension at Antioch (Gal. 2:13) must also be borne in mind.
[2] I Cor. 9:6.   [3] Acts 16:3. See p. 137, n. 11.

Jewess, made him practically a Jew in every point but circumcision. Paul, despite his principle that in Christ there was neither Jew nor Greek, considered it expedient to regularize Timothy's position in the existing state of society by circumcising him—thereby also legitimizing him in Jewish eyes. To Paul, circumcision was in itself neither here nor there: 'in Christ Jesus', he tells the Galatians, 'neither circumcision nor uncircumcision is of any avail' (Gal. 5:6; cf. I Cor. 7:19). It was only when it was imposed on Gentile Christians as a religious obligation that he resisted it as a subversion of the gospel. In Timothy's case it was nothing more than a minor surgical operation performed for a practical purpose. Even so, we can understand how Paul's performing it perplexed people who were more concerned with the outward action than with the inward motive (as it continues to perplex some modern commentators), and gave his critics occasion to charge him with being 'all things to all men' (cf. I Cor. 9:22).

It was apparently the intention of Paul and his companions to pursue a westward course into the province of Asia along the road which led from Pisidian Antioch and Apamea to the Maeander basin, and eventually to Ephesus. The evangelization of proconsular Asia might well have seemed the logical sequel to the earlier evangelization of South Galatia. But they were prevented from following this road, so from Pisidian Antioch they turned north, crossing the Sultan Dag range to Philomelium, from which they struck north-west in the direction of Bithynia, another province which, with Jewish communities and synagogues in its great cities,[4] might have seemed ripe for receiving the gospel. But the way was barred across the Bithynian frontier, so (perhaps from the road-junction of Dorylaeum) they turned west and reached the Aegean coast at Troas. In the obstacles or inhibitions which had forbidden them to advance towards Ephesus or cross into Bithynia they recognized the negative guidance of the Spirit of Christ;[5] at Troas, however, the guidance became positive, for Paul in a night-vision received a clear indication that he and his companions were to cross

---

[4] Cf. Philo, *Leg. ad Gaium*, 281.

[5] The precise nature of the obstacles is not recorded: they were 'forbidden by the Holy Spirit to speak the word in Asia' and 'the Spirit of Jesus did not allow them' to enter Bithynia; the former prohibition may have been conveyed through prophetic utterance (cf. Acts 13:2), but the change of phraseology may suggest that the second one took a different form.

the North Aegean and preach the gospel in Macedonia. By this
time the company included Luke, the physician of Syrian Antioch
and author of Acts,[6] who records in the first person plural how they
embarked at Troas and landed in two days' time at Neapolis (Ka-
valla), the port of the Roman colony of Philippi, where Antony and
Octavian had settled their veterans after their defeat of Brutus and
Cassius in 42 B.C. The constitution of a Roman colony was modelled
on that of the city of Rome, with two collegiate magistrates at the
head; the *duo uiri* of Philippi (by courtesy called praetors)[7] and
their attendant lictors appear in the account of Paul and Silvanus's
arraignment before them on a charge of bringing unacceptable
teaching and causing trouble in the city by interference with property rights—their offence was that of exorcizing the 'pythonic spirit'
which spoke very profitably through a fortune-telling slave-girl,
with the result that her owners could derive no further income from
their exploitation of her 'gift'.[8] This earned the two missionaries a
beating with the lictors' rods and a night in the town jail—summary
treatment for which the chief magistrates had to apologize next
morning when they discovered that the men were Roman citizens
like themselves.[9]

How long Paul and his companions stayed in Philippi is uncertain, but when they moved on they had established a promising
church there. Luke appears to have remained in Philippi when the
others left.[10] The latter travelled along the Via Egnatia to Thessalonica, the principal city of Macedonia. A few weeks in Thessalonica
sufficed for disturbances to break out within the Jewish community
there, similar in character, it may be, to those at Rome which had
recently led to Claudius's edict expelling Jews from the capital.[11]

[6] The transition from third person to first follows the account of Paul's night-
vision in which 'a man of Macedonia' besought him to come over and help them:
'when he had seen the vision', says the narrator, 'immediately we sought to go
on into Macedonia' (Acts 16:10).
[7] Like those of Capua (Cicero, *De leg. agr.* ii, 93).   [8] See p. 279, n. 2.
[9] Luke's irony expresses itself in the contrast between the slave-owners' complaint, 'These men, Jews as they are . . . advocate customs which it is not lawful
for us to accept or practise, Romans as we are' (Acts 16:21), and Paul's protest,
'They have beaten us publicly, without a trial (ἀκατακρίτους), Romans as we
are' (Acts 16:37).
[10] It is noteworthy that the first 'we' section of Acts ends in Philippi (16:17)
and the second one begins there (20:5f). If the Epistle to the Philippians was
written in the interval between these two points, Luke may be the 'true yoke-
fellow' of Phil. 4:3.   [11] See p. 297.

At the instance of the Jewish authorities in Thessalonica, those citizens who had given hospitality to Paul were brought before the politarchs (as the chief magistrates in Thessalonica and other Macedonian cities were called)[12] and charged with harbouring the men who had 'turned the world upside down',[18] men who flouted Caesar's decrees and proclaimed a rival emperor, one Jesus (Acts 17:5-7). The language of the prosecutors, as Luke records it, suggests that subversive characters had been active elsewhere among the Jewish communities of the Empire, and Paul and his companions were represented as being of their number. Paul's friends got him out of Thessalonica quickly for his own safety—and theirs. The accusation was a most serious one, and the politarchs could not afford to treat it lightly. The language in which it is couched fits very well into the general picture that can be built up of movements within the Judaism of the day, more or less 'messianic' in character, which constituted a threat to public order in places where there were Jewish communities, and which were deplored and denounced by those responsible Jews who knew the importance of maintaining acceptable relations with Rome. Paul the Roman citizen was certainly as appreciative of the *pax Romana* as any of those responsible Jews; but it could not be denied that his apostolic progress from city to city was, more often than not, attended by public disturbances, and this could easily be turned to his detriment.

The two letters to the Thessalonian Church, which were written only a few weeks, or months at the most, after Paul's departure from their city, bear witness to an intense eschatological excitement among the Christians there, which may have been in evidence among the Jews also. Both letters insist on a more sober outlook on the last things, and it is pointed out (more particularly in the second epistle) that certain events must take place before the day of the Lord dawns.

That day will not come, unless the rebellion comes first, and the man

[12] The word is not found earlier in Greek literature, but is amply attested in Macedonian inscriptions from the 2nd century B.C. to the 3rd century A.D. Thessalonica was administered by five politarchs under Augustus; in the following century, under the Antonines, by six. Cf. E. D. Burton, 'The Politarchs', *AJT* 2 (1898), pp. 598ff.

[18] Gk. ἀναστατόω, used in Acts 21:38 of the Egyptian insurgent mentioned below, p. 339. On the charge that they flouted 'Caesar's decrees', cf. the 'decree of Caesar' quoted above, p. 301.

of lawlessness is revealed, the son of perdition, who opposes and exalts himself against every so-called god or object of worship, so that he takes his seat in the temple of God, proclaiming himself to be God. Do you not remember that when I was still with you I told you this? And now you know what is restraining him so that he may be revealed in his time. For the mystery of lawlessness is already at work; only he who now restrains it will do so until he is out of the way (II Thess. 2:3–7).

There are few New Testament passages which can boast such a variety of interpretations as this; but its life-setting and meaning should not be too difficult to determine. The personal 'appalling sacrilege', or 'abomination of desolation, standing where he ought not',[14] described by Jesus in Mark 13:14, must have appeared to many to be on the point of emerging when Gaius in A.D. 40 ordered the erection of his image in the Jerusalem Temple. This order was cancelled just in time, but the terror and anxiety of those days must have left an abiding impression on Jews and Christians alike, and coloured their views of what would happen when Antichrist did in fact arise. When Paul visited Thessalonica ten years after that crisis he told his converts there about the coming day when lawlessness would manifest itself in all its evil, incarnated in the 'man of lawlessness' who would go so far as to enthrone himself in the temple of God and claim divine honours beyond those paid to anyone or anything else. Now, in this letter, he repeats the same teaching and adds that the day of the Lord will not come until Antichrist has appeared to lead the great eschatological rebellion against God: the forces of lawlessness and anarchy, in fact, are already active beneath the surface, but a restraining power prevents them from breaking forth. One day, however, this restraining power will be removed, and those evil forces will riot unchecked.

Paul tells his readers that they know what this restraining power actually is; perhaps he had already told them by word of mouth. But his readers today have not had the advantage of his oral instruction, and they are left to infer from the context the identity of the restrainer. The context suggests that it is the power of imperial law and order that at present imposes a check on the turbulent forces that are always threatening to break loose. This identification

[14] See p. 256.

is further suggested by the fact that the restraining power is referred
to both in the neuter gender, 'you know *what is restraining* him'[15]
and in the masculine, '*he who* now *restrains* it'.[16] The imperial
power was embodied in the emperor, and could thus be described
in personal as well as in impersonal terms. This too could explain
the very guarded language in which the restrainer's identity is
hinted at. To speak openly in a letter about the coming removal
of the imperial power or of the emperor himself would be impolitic;
in view of the charges of seditious activity recently pressed against
Paul and his friends in Thessalonica, the consequences for the Thessalonian Christians would be serious if a letter which seemed to
lend colour to these charges fell into the wrong hands. On the
other hand, if one of the current interpretations of the restraining
power is adopted—if, for example, Paul was referring to himself
and his own apostolic ministry[17]—there would be no reason why
he should not say so outright.

But if Paul had the imperial power and the emperor in mind, he
was not thinking necessarily of Claudius himself, although some
have envisaged a play on the idea of 'restraint' and the name Claudius.[18] And he was certainly not looking forward to Nero,
Claudius's stepson and eventual successor, as the 'man of lawlessness', for Nero at this time was only thirteen years old. Paul was
thinking much more of his own experience of Roman justice, which
encouraged him to think of the empire as being—temporarily, at
any rate—a safeguard against the unruly forces which endeavoured
to frustrate the progress of the gospel. On the strength of this experience he could write of the imperial authorities several years
later—when Nero had already been emperor two years and more—
as 'ministers of God';[19] on the strength of this experience, too, he
confidently appealed towards the end of A.D. 59 to have his case
transferred from the jurisdiction of the procurator of Judaea to the
emperor's court in Rome.[20]

Paul was embarrassed by his enforced departure from Thessalonica for it might easily look as if he had taken steps for his own

---

[15] Gk. τὸ κατέχον.   [16] Gk. ὁ κατέχων.
[17] Cf. O. Cullmann, 'Le caractère eschatologique du devoir missionnaire et
de la conscience apostolique de S. Paul', *RHPR* 16 (1936), pp. 210ff; J. Munck,
Paul and the Salvation of Mankind (London, 1959), pp. 36ff.
[18] Cf. Lat. *claudere*, 'close' 'conclude', 'keep off'; *claudicare*, 'limp'.
[19] Rom. 13:4, 6.   [20] See p. 357.

safety and left his converts to face unpleasant mockery, if not positive persecution. But his hosts, without consulting him, had given security for his leaving the city forthwith, and his hands were tied. It may be this course of events that is referred to in I Thess. 2:18, where he tells his converts that he would have liked to return to them, 'but Satan hindered us'. If one asks how he distinguished between some obstacles as placed in his path by the Spirit of God and others as due to the malignity of Satan, the answer may be that the former proved in the event to promote his apostolic work while the latter frustrated it. His Thessalonian converts had not received as much instruction and confirmation as he had intended to impart to them, and he feared that their faith might fail through discouragement and disillusionment. As it was, when he sent Timothy back from Athens to Thessalonica to find out how his converts were faring, he was overjoyed by Timothy's report: not only were they standing fast, but they were energetically propagating their faith,[21] despite some doubts and questions about their relation to Christ's *parousia*, of which Paul had told them something but (because of the unwelcome cutting short of his time with them) not enough.[22]

2

From Thessalonica Paul was taken to Beroea,[23] and thence to the coast and south by sea to Athens, where he spent a few days waiting for his companions to rejoin him.

Luke's account of Paul's stay in Athens,[24] and especially of his appearance before the Court of the Areopagus, is marked throughout by touches of local colour which classical scholars have generally found so authentic that, like Eduard Meyer, they have difficulty in understanding 'how this scene could ever have been explained as an invention'.[25] Paul is described as entering into debate with Athenians whom he met in the Agora, including adherents of the Stoic and Epicurean schools, to whom he gave the impression of being a pedlar of some new-fangled cult. He was brought before the venerable Court of the Areopagus (so called because its original meeting-place was on the hill or Ares, west of the Acropolis), which retained

---

[21] I Thess. 3:1–8.   [22] I Thess. 4:13ff.
[23] See p. 276.   [24] Acts 17:15–34.
[25] *Ursprung und Anfänge des Christentums* III (Stuttgart, 1923), p. 105.

from antiquity special competence in the realm of religion and
morals. Invited to expound his teaching to members of this court,
he gave a discourse on the knowledge of God, taking his cue from
an altar-dedication 'To an Unknown God' which he had seen in
the city. 'The divinity whom you worship thus, acknowledging him
to be unknown, is the one whom I make known to you' (Acts
17:23).[26]

He went on to tell them, in language principally based on the
Old Testament but reminiscent in various ways of Greek concepts
and beliefs, of the one supreme God, creator of the universe, who
could not be accommodated in 'temples made with hands' and
stood in need of nothing that men could give him—on the contrary,
it was from him that men received everything necessary for life on
earth. He had made the human race from one common ancestor
and provided the nations with the habitable zones of the earth as
their dwelling-place. The quotation from Epimenides, 'In him we
live and move and have our being',[27] should not be construed as
teaching a 'God-mysticism' to be set in contrast with the 'Christ-
mysticism' of the Pauline epistles;[28] it simply underlines the lesson
of man's utter dependence on God, as does also the companion
quotation from Paul's fellow-Cilician Aratus, 'For we are also his
offspring' (Acts 17:28).[29]

In the light of God's kindly providence, men's acknowledged ignorance of him was not free from blame, but God had overlooked
this ignorance up to the present time. Now, however, the revelation
of himself given in Christ had inaugurated a new era; repentance

[26] The literature on Paul's Areopagus speech is immense in quantity; cf.
A. J. Mattill and M. B. Mattill, *A Classified Bibliography of Literature on the
Acts of the Apostles* (Leiden, 1966), pp. 430–9 (items 6029–6179).
[27] The quatrain which is concluded by this verse, an address to Zeus, survives in the Syriac translation of Ishodad of Merv (ed. M. D. Gibson, *Horae
Semiticae* x [Cambridge, 1913], p. 40), from which it is not too difficult to reconstruct the Greek original (with help from Callimachus, who echoes the
passage in his *Hymn to Zeus*, 7f); its purport is:

> 'They fashioned a tomb for thee, most holy and most high—
> The Cretans, always liars, evil beasts, idle gluttons!—
> But thou art not dead; for ever thou art alive and risen,
> For in thee we live and move and have our being'.

(For the second verse, cf. Titus 1:12.)
[28] As it is by A. Schweitzer, *The Mysticism of Paul the Apostle* (London,
1931), pp. 6f.
[29] Aratus, *Phainomena*, 5 (the exordium of this poem is, like the quatrain
from Epimenides quoted in n. 27, an address to Zeus).

was required of all mankind because Christ had been designated as final judge of all; the world had been given a pledge of this by his resurrection from the dead.

The mention of such an unacceptable idea as resurrection made it plain to the court that this man's views were not to be treated seriously. It was specially out of place to bring it up before the Areopagus: on the legendary occasion when that court was founded by the city's tutelary goddess Athene, Apollo (according to Aeschylus) had affirmed:

> When the dust drinks up a man's blood,
> Once he has died, there is no resurrection.[30]

In several respects Paul's *Areopagitica* anticipates the Christian apologies of the second century. Some scholars who recognize this couple with this recognition an inability to credit Paul with the authorship of the speech.[31] But there is nothing peculiar to the second century about the speech; it is well designed as an introductory lesson in Christianity for cultured pagans of the first century. As for its ascription to Paul, if the author of Romans 1:18–2:16 found himself called upon to give an account of his teaching to such an audience as the Athenian Areopagus, he would most probably have spoken along the lines of Acts 17:22–31. In writing to Christians he quotes the Old Testament; in addressing the Areopagus he quotes Greek poets, but Paul would not have been the effective missionary he was if he had not known the value of finding and exploiting a point of contact with his hearers, whether in a Jewish synagogue or in a Greek marketplace. In the Areopagitica as in Rom. 1:19–23 men are blamed for not holding fast to the knowledge of God that was available in his works of creation and providence; in the Areopagitica as in Rom. 3:25 God shows his forbearance by passing over sins committed before the coming of Christ, but has now inaugurated a new era in his dealings with mankind.[32]

[30] Aeschylus, *Eumenides*, 647f. The last word of the couplet, ἀνάστασις, is Paul's word for resurrection (Acts 17:18).

[31] Cf. M. Dibelius, *Studies in the Acts of the Apostles* (London, 1956), pp. 26ff, and, more generally, J. C. O'Neill, *The Theology of Acts in its Historical Setting* (London, 1961).

[32] Cf. B. Gärtner, *The Areopagus Speech and Natural Revelation* (Lund, 1955).

3

From Athens, which even under the Roman Empire retained
some traces of the great glory of her classical past, Paul went on to
Corinth. Corinth, a great seaport on the isthmus of Corinth with
harbours on the Saronic and Corinthian Gulfs, to east and west respectively, situated at the junction of land-routes north and south,
had been a maritime and commercial rival to Athens in earlier days
but was destroyed by the Romans under L. Mummius in 146 B.C.,
when the revolt of the Achaean League was put down. It lay
derelict for a century, until in 46 B.C. it was refounded by Julius
Caesar and given the status of a Roman colony. In 27 B.C. it became
the seat of government of the province of Achaia. After its restoration it soon regained its former economic prosperity, and regained
also its former reputation for unrestrained sexual licence, for which
it gave a verb to the Greek language.[33] The temple of Aphrodite
in Corinth, which lent religious sanction to this kind of behaviour,
was devoted to a Hellenized form of the Syrian cult of Astarte. No
greater contrast could be imagined than that between this cult and
another cult from the Levant—the reading and exposition of the
Jewish Torah which took place every sabbath day in the synagogue
of Corinth from which came the fragmentary door-inscription 'Synagogue of the Hebrews',[34] now in the Corinth Museum. The inartistic
quality of the lettering suggests that the synagogue congregation
was not wealthy enough to command the services of an expert en-
graver in stone.

To this or another Corinthian synagogue Paul found his way soon
after his arrival in the city. He was not the only Jewish newcomer;
the Pontic Jews Aquila and his wife Priscilla, recently forced to
leave Rome by Claudius's edict of A.D. 49, had also taken up residence in Corinth.[35] During Paul's first days in Corinth, he was glad
to join these fellow-craftsmen and pay his way as a 'tent-maker' or
leather-worker. After a short time, however, Silvanus and Timothy
returned from Macedonia and brought Paul gifts from his converts
there which enabled him to devote himself entirely to his ministry.

---

[33] Gk. κορινθιάζεσθαι, whence the noun κορινθιαστής.
[34] [ΣΥΝΑ]ΓΩΓΗ ΕΒ[ΡΑΙΩΝ]; cf. A. Deissmann, *Light from the Ancient
East* (London, 1927), p. 16.   [35] See pp. 297f.

This ministry was carried on for some weeks in the synagogue, until the familiar pattern of events repeated itself and Paul was compelled to leave the synagogue. One of his converts, a 'God-fearing' Gentile named Gaius Titius Justus,[36] presumably a citizen of Roman Corinth, placed at Paul's disposal his own house which stood conveniently next door to the synagogue. Gaius was one of Paul's first converts in Corinth; another was Crispus, ruler of the synagogue. Paul mentions these two men, along with 'the household of Stephanas', as the only Corinthian converts whom he himself baptized (I Cor. 1:14–16).

A longer reading in the Western text of Acts 18:4 says that in the Corinthian synagogue Paul 'inserted the name of the Lord Jesus' as the scriptures were read. This may well represent what actually happened: when a scripture was read or quoted which Christians recognized as fulfilled in Jesus, Paul indicated that this was so by an appropriate insertion. Such a practice was familiar in those synagogues where the reading of the Hebrew scriptures was accompanied by an Aramaic targum. For example, where Yahweh says 'Behold my servant' in Isaiah 42:1 and 52:13, the Targum of Jonathan adds the interpretative word 'Messiah'. In Corinth the scriptures were read in the Greek version, which required no translation, but Paul might well interpret such words as 'Behold my servant' by adding: 'That is to say, Jesus'. And when he detached his adherents from the synagogue and taught them in the house of Gaius he would have much greater freedom in expounding the law and the prophets so as to present in them the substructure of his gospel.

Thus the number of believers continually increased, not only from the ranks of Jews and 'God-fearers' but from pagans too. Corinth might have seemed, from an ethical point of view, an unpromising environment for a Christian church to take root, and no doubt many of Paul's friends contemplated with apprehension the prospects for Christian standards of morality when so many converts, newly and all too imperfectly delivered from the traditional Corinthian way of life, were added to the church.

Probably less than a year after Paul's arrival in Corinth a new proconsul of Achaia took up his official residence in the city. Lucius

[36] This threefold name is constructed on the assumed identification of Titius Justus of Acts 18:7 with Gaius of I Cor. 1:14 and Rom. 16:23. Cf. E. J. Goodspeed, 'Gaius Titius Justus', *JBL* 69 (1950), pp. 382f.

Junius Gallio was a son of the elder Seneca and brother of Seneca the philosopher and of Mela (father of the poet Lucan). He was born in Cordova, and came to Rome with his father in the reign of Tiberius. In Rome he was adopted by his father's friend, the rhetorician L. Junius Gallio, and assumed his adoptive father's name in place of that which he originally bore (Marcus Annaeus Novatus). His brother Seneca praises his virtuous and lovable character: 'no mortal is so agreeable to any one person as this man is to everybody'.[37] The date of his entry upon the proconsulship of Achaia, after his tenure of the praetorship at Rome, can be dated by the aid of the inscription at Delphi already mentioned to (most probably) July 1, A.D. 51, or (just possibly) twelve months later.[38] He did not remain in this office long, for ill-health obliged him to relinquish it.[39]

It was during Gallio's proconsulship that Paul had what was probably his most impressive experience of Roman justice. Shortly after Gallio's arrival in his province, the Jewish leaders in Corinth accused Paul before him of 'persuading men to worship God contrary to the law' (Acts 18:13). Their charge, as reported by Luke, is ambiguous; which law—Jewish or Roman—was Paul accused of breaking? On the whole, it is more likely that he was accused of breaking Roman law. Gallio, on dismissing the case, told them that he was not minded to be a judge in questions of Jewish law; but the prosecutors would have known that already. Their hope lay in convincing him that Paul's activity constituted a contravention of Roman law, which it was Gallio's business to maintain. Paul, that is to say, was charged with propagating an illegal religion—the implication was that what he was preaching was certainly not Judaism, which enjoyed the recognition and protection of imperial law except when its practice or propagation endangered public order.[40]

Gallio, however, summed the situation up quickly, as he thought. To him, Paul was a Jew like his accusers, and spoke the same sort

---

[37] Seneca, *Nat. Quaest.* 4a, praef. 11.   [38] See p. 298.

[39] Cf. Seneca, *Ep. Mor.* 104:1; he caught a fever and went on a cruise to recuperate. At a later date (after his consulship) he went on a cruise from Rome to Egypt because of threatened phthisis. On the death of Seneca in A.D. 65, Gallio's life was spared (Tacitus, *Ann.* xv, 73) but not long afterwards, with his other brother Mela, he fell victim to Nero's suspicions.

[40] Cf. S. L. Guterman, *Religious Toleration and Persecution in Ancient Rome* (London, 1951), pp. 75ff *et passim*; A. N. Sherwin-White, *Roman Society and Roman Law in the New Testament* (Oxford, 1963), pp. 78ff; J. C. O'Neill, *The Theology of Acts in its Historical Setting*, pp. 170ff, especially p. 172, n. 1.

of language as they did. If there were differences between Paul and them, these differences concerned interpretations of Jewish law and religion, and it was no part of Gallio's responsibility to pronounce judgement on questions like these. If public order had been endangered, if crime or misdemeanour had been involved, Gallio would certainly have taken the matter up.[41] But it seemed clear to him that, although Paul's accusers tried to represent the apostle as offending against Roman law, the matter at issue was one of Jewish law. Accordingly, he had them ejected from the court, and turned a blind eye[42] when the ruler of the synagogue[43] was mobbed by the bystanders.

Sir William Ramsay regarded Gallio's ruling as 'the crowning fact in determining Paul's line of conduct',[44] because it provided a precedent for other magistrates, and thus guaranteed Paul's freedom to prosecute his apostolic mission with the assurance of the benevolent neutrality of the imperial authorities for several years to come. One thing at least is certain: if Gallio had given an adverse verdict against Paul, it would have been pleaded as a precedent by Paul's opponents for the rest of his life; and a precedent established by so exalted and influential a magistrate as Gallio—a much more important personage than the politarchs of Thessalonica—would have carried great weight. The mere fact that Gallio refused to take up the case against Paul may reasonably be held to have facilitated the spread of Christianity during the last years of Claudius and the earlier years of his successor.

[41] This is the force of ἀνεσχόμην ὑμῶν (Acts 18:14); cf. W. Bauer-W. F. Arndt-F. W. Gingrich, *Greek-English Lexicon of the New Testament* (Chicago, 1957), *s.v.* ἀνέχω, *fin.*

[42] This is the force of 'Gallio paid no attention to this' (Acts 18:17), paraphrased in the Western text, 'Gallio pretended not to see'.

[43] The ruler's name was Sosthenes (Acts 18:17); if he is identical with the Sosthenes of I Cor. 1:1 (which is not certain), then he subsequently followed the example of Crispus (Acts 18:8; cf. I Cor. 1:14) and became a Christian.

[44] W. M. Ramsay, *St. Paul the Traveller and the Roman Citizen* (London, 1920[14]), p. 260; cf. A. N. Sherwin-White, *Roman Society and Roman Law in the New Testament*, pp. 99ff.

25 End of the Aegean Mission

1

Encouraged by Gallio's decision, Paul spent several more months in Corinth, establishing the Christian community which he had planted in that unpromising city.

Either when the appearance before Gallio was pending, or at some other crisis during his stay in Corinth, Paul undertook a vow which required for its fulfilment a ceremony in the Temple in Jerusalem. Accordingly, when the seas were open for navigation in the early spring of 52, he left Corinth with Aquila and Priscilla. Before embarking at Cenchreae, the eastern seaport of Corinth, he cut his hair, which he had allowed to grow long for the duration of his vow.[1] The cutting of his hair—which indicates that it was a temporary Nazirite vow that he had undertaken—was a partial discharge of his obligation, but full discharge called for a sacrifice in the Temple. (That Paul's conversion to Christianity necessitated his giving up all his ancestral customs, including such a voluntary act of private devotion as a Nazirite vow, is a curious idea which should be entertained only on the basis of strong and explicit evidence of a kind that is not forthcoming.) They sailed across the Aegean to Ephesus, where Aquila and Priscilla stopped, but Paul declined a pressing invitation to stay too. A ship was about to leave the harbour at Ephesus which might take him to Palestine in time for Passover, so he set sail, promising to come back and spend longer time in Ephesus.[2]

Having landed at Caesarea he went up to Jerusalem, greeted his friends there and discharged his private business; then he went

[1] Acts 18:18; cf. pp. 259f, 355.
[2] The Western text of Acts 18:21 makes Paul say, 'I must by all means keep the coming festival at Jerusalem'; since Passover fell at the beginning of April in A.D. 52 and navigation did not begin until about 10 March, this could explain Paul's haste.

north to Syrian Antioch, from which he travelled overland through
Asia Minor, visiting and encouraging the churches planted there on
earlier apostolic campaigns, and so in due course reached Ephesus.
There he settled down for the best part of three years, giving him-
self to the intensive evangelization of that city and the province of
Asia.[3]

Ephesus was at this time the greatest commercial city of Asia
Minor, although its harbour required constant dredging because of
the alluvium carried down by the Cayster, at the mouth of which it
stood. (How necessary this dredging was is graphically illustrated
by the fact that, in consequence of its cessation, the former harbour
of Ephesus now lies some seven miles inland.) Standing on one of
the main routes from Rome to the eastern imperial frontier, Ephesus
enjoyed political importance in addition to its economic advantages.
It was the seat of administration of the province of Asia, while it
remained a free Greek city, with its own senate and civic assembly;
it was also an assize town.[4] Its chief municipal officer was the
grammateus, the secretary of the *dēmos* or 'town clerk', who also
acted as liaison officer between the city government and the Roman
administration of the province.[5] The principal citizens of Ephesus
were included among the Asiarchs, the leading citizens of the cities
of the province, who formed the council (*koinon*) of Asia, an institution antedating the Roman administration and surviving under
it.[6]

Yet Paul could not give completely undivided attention to the
evangelization of Ephesus; the cares of his other churches kept
breaking in upon him, and especially those of the church in
Corinth.

2

Thanks to Paul's surviving correspondence with the church in
Corinth we are better informed on its early history than we are with

[3] Cf. Acts 19:8, 10; 20:31.
[4] That is, it was one of the cities in which the *conuentus* (κοινόν) of leading citizens in the province met as a judicial body under the presidency of the
proconsul. [5] Cf. Acts 19:35ff.
[6] Cf. Acts 19:31. From their ranks were drawn the high priests of the provincial cult of Rome and Augustus; cf. L. R. Taylor, 'The Asiarchs', in *The Beginnings of Christianity*, ed. Foakes Jackson and K. Lake, v (London, 1933),
pp. 256ff.

regard to most of Paul's other churches. Perhaps it can hardly be
viewed as typical of Paul's churches. For example, at the time when
I Corinthians was written, at least two years after Paul's departure
from Corinth, the church does not seem to have had recognized
leaders; towards the end of that letter Paul mentions some of its
members who are worthy to receive recognition from the others as
leaders because they had devoted themselves to serving their fellow-
Christians.[7] The natural inference is that while, on Paul's own
testimony, the Corinthian Christians were a singularly gifted community,[8] the gift of leadership was slow in manifesting itself among
them, and slower still was a readiness on the part of the rank and
file to submit to those who possessed the qualities of spiritual authority.

Among the gifts which were enjoyed in such abundance by the
Corinthian church was the gift of ecstatic utterance, particularly in
the form of glossolalia.[9] Glossolalia, resulting from some exceptional
influence on the speech centres of the brain, consists of articulate
speech not normally understood by the speaker. It may be in some
recognizable language which is a foreign tongue to him, or it may
be in no recognizable language, and the sounds when analysed
may not conform to any pattern known to the science of language.
From Paul's statement in I Cor. 13:1 that, in the absence of love,
it is useless to speak with the tongues of men or angels, it has been
inferred that some forms of glossolalia were explained in terms of
angelic language, and corroboration of this has been found in the
Testament of Job (first century B.C.), where Job's three daughters
are presented with a girdle which enabled them to speak with the
tongues respectively of angels, of principalities, and of 'those on
high' (or cherubim).[10]

In one form or another, glossolalia was apparently a familiar
phenomenon in some of the earliest Christian communities: Paul
himself was more than usually proficient in it—we should not have

---

[7] I Cor. 16:15–18.   [8] I Cor. 1:5–7.

[9] There is a large body of literature on this subject; cf. K. Lake, *The Earlier
Epistles of St. Paul* (London, 1911), pp. 241ff; M. Barnet, *The Living Flame*
(London, 1953), pp. 27ff, 98ff; T. W. Manson, *Studies in the Gospels and
Epistles* (Manchester, 1962), pp. 203ff; R. H. Gundry, ' "Ecstatic Utterance"
(N.E.B.)?' *JTS*, n.s. 17 (1966), pp. 299–307; J. P. M. Sweet, 'A Sign for Un-
believers: Paul's Attitude to Glossolalia', *NTS* 13 (1966–7), pp. 240–57.

[10] *Test. Job* 47–50, ed. M. R. James, *Apocrypha Anecdota* II (Cambridge,
1899), pp. 134–6.

known this had he not mentioned it incidentally in a passage where
he tries to teach his Corinthian converts to put the phenomenon in
its proper place, which is quite low down in the hierarchy of 'spiritual gifts'. A spiritual exercise which he regards as much more
valuable is 'prophecy', which took the form of utterances in the
habitual language of the speakers and their hearers, in which the
congregation recognized the mind of God declared in the power
of the Spirit. Prophecy was immediately intelligible and profita-
ble; as for glossolalia, Paul wished to restrict it to private devotion
unless someone were available to interpret the strange language to
the congregation, and if it was no known language this would require a separate supernatural endowment. Paul would not suppress
altogether what he believed to be a genuine gift of the Spirit, but
the depreciatory terms in which he refers to it were calculated to
dampen the Corinthians' enthusiastic assessment of it as the most
important spiritual gift, if not as an indispensable manifestation of
the Spirit's indwelling presence.[11]

Not long after Paul's departure from Corinth, the church there
was visited by a Jewish Christian of Egyptian Alexandria named
Apollos.[12] Apollos was well versed in the Old Testament writings
(presumably in their Greek form) and interpreted them in such a
way as to show that Jesus was the Messiah and deliverer to whose
advent they pointed. It is a natural supposition that Apollos's methods of biblical exegesis were those characteristic of his native city,
as supremely exemplified in Philo, but on this, as on other features
of Apollos's teaching, we are insufficiently informed. According to
the narrative of Acts, when he visited Ephesus shortly before his
arrival in Corinth, Paul's friends Priscilla and Aquila realized that,
despite his mastery of the Jewish scriptures and his familiarity with
the story of Jesus, his knowledge of 'The Way' was defective in that
the only baptism known to him was John's; so they invited him to
their home and gave him the further instruction which they
deemed necessary. According to the consentient testimony of Paul
and Acts, he made a great impression on the Corinthian Christians
and proved a tower of strength to them in their public witness, especially in his capacity for confuting their Jewish opponents with
his arguments that Jesus was the Messiah. In their enthusiasm some
Corinthian Christians thought him a greater man than Paul;

[11] I Cor. 14:1-33.   [12] Acts 18:24-8.

Apollos's line was the line for them, and they called themselves Apollos's men. This tendency to exalt one teacher at the expense of another was deplored by Paul, even when he himself was the teacher so exalted; but there is no evidence of personal rivalry or tension between him and Apollos; when he mentions Apollos in his letters to the Corinthians he does so in terms which betoken friendship and mutual confidence.[13]

We are not informed whether it was in Alexandria or elsewhere that Apollos first came to know of Christianity; since he first appears in the New Testament records about A.D. 52 it could well have been in his home town.[14] This would raise questions about the form in which Christianity first reached Alexandria. Alexandrian Christianity was for long regarded as defective, if not heterodox, by proponents of what came to be mainstream Christianity.[15] This suggests that the gospel reached Alexandria from another source than that from which the missions recorded in Acts stemmed; one possibility is that Alexandria, in common with some other places, was evangelized from Galilee, not from Jerusalem. Jesus had many disciples in Galilee who did not form part of the primitive Jerusalem church, and they are as likely to have propagated his message as the Jerusalem disciples were.

However that may be, Paul appreciated the help that Apollos gave to his Corinthian converts after his own departure: 'I planted the seed', he said, 'and Apollos watered it'—adding characteristically, 'but it was God who made it grow' (I Cor. 3:6).

But there were others who came to work in the Corinthian garden about whose activity Paul was much less complacent. Changing the metaphor, he speaks of the Corinthian church as a building whose foundation stone he himself had laid—and that foundation was Jesus Christ. In using this language he may have had in his mind the oracle of Isaiah (Isa. 28:16) in which the God of Israel undertakes to establish in Zion

a stone, a tested stone,
a precious corner stone, of a sure foundation.[16]

[13] I Cor. 3:6; 4:6; 16:12.
[14] The Western text of Acts 18:25 says explicitly that it was so (see p. 294, n. 6).
[15] Cf. A. Ehrhardt, *The Framework of the New Testament Stories* (Manchester, 1964), pp. 174ff.
[16] Cf. S. H. Hooke, 'The Corner Stone of Scripture', in *The Siege Perilous* (London, 1956), pp. 235ff.

In the oracle this secure foundation-stone is the faithful remnant, elsewhere embodied in its ruler, the coming prince of the house of David; in the New Testament it is repeatedly applied, together with other 'stone' passages from the Hebrew scriptures, to Christ.[17] No fault could be found with the foundation Paul had laid, but he had serious misgivings about the quality of the material which some of the builders who came after him were using for the superstructure. When the day of testing came, only the soundest workmanship, only the most durable materials, would survive. Paul thinks of an eastern town in which a fire might suddenly break out and sweep through the narrow street. Buildings of stone and similar material would emerge unharmed; flimsy wooden shacks would go up in smoke. The builder who looked for commendation on the day of final review would do well to see that his work was designed to stand such a fiery test.[18]

Who are the 'builders' whom Paul has in view? In addition to a party at Corinth which followed Apollos and another which claimed Paul as its leader, there was yet another whose members declared: 'I belong to Cephas'—that is, Peter.[19] Whether Peter in person visited Corinth and taught there shortly after Paul's departure cannot be decided with certainty.[20] It does appear that in the fifties of the first century Peter embarked on a more extended ministry and played little further part in the life of the Jerusalem church. His apostolate was exercised among the Jews, as Paul's was among the Gentiles, but since there were so many places where Jews and Gentiles lived side by side, the line of demarcation between his mission-field and Paul's must have been difficult to determine. If Peter himself did not visit Corinth, others certainly taught there in his name, and represented his authority as superior to Paul's. The modern reader of Paul's correspondence is in difficulties because he is inadequately informed on the details of a situation with which Paul and those to whom he wrote were perfectly familiar, and also (in the present regard) because Paul restrains

[17] Cf. Rom. 9:33; I Peter 2:6; also Eph. 2:20.
[18] I Cor. 3:10–15.   [19] I Cor. 1:12.
[20] E. Meyer found it incomprehensible that anyone could doubt that Peter himself came to Corinth (*Ursprung und Anfänge des Christentums*, iii [Stuttgart, 1923], p. 441), but Paul's language is not clear enough to us—it was unambiguous, of course, to his first readers who knew whether Peter had been in Corinth or not.

his language when he refers to the 'Peter' party, probably because of an unwillingness to say anything that might be construed as personal criticism of Peter. The 'Peter' party did not try to impose circumcision, like the trouble-makers in Antioch and the Galatian churches who claimed the authority of James; Peter's name could not be invoked for any teaching of this kind—nor indeed could James's after the issue of the Jerusalem decree. But the Jerusalem decree included provisions which Paul was suspected of relaxing outside the area explicitly named in the apostolic letter, especially where the eating of idolatrous food was concerned. In Paul's eyes such food was completely innocent in itself, and might be eaten with a good conscience; it was to be avoided only in situations where the eating of it would injure the conscience either of the eater or of someone who might be influenced by his example, or would in one way or another compromise the Christian confession.[21]

The activity of the Peter party had to be contested, since it tended not only to weaken Paul's apostolic authority among his converts but to make them think that material things, like food, could be evil in themselves. But the situation was made more difficult because of the presence in the Corinthian church of a vocal group of *illuminati*, who pressed to extremes Paul's teaching about Christian liberty without giving equal weight to his insistence on Christian charity and the good name of the Christian mission in the Gentile world. 'All things are lawful for me', was these people's slogan.[22] They prided themselves on their 'knowledge' (*gnōsis*)—which does not necessarily mean that we should recognize in them precursors of the second-century Gnostics—and Paul is at pains to remind them that *gnōsis* must be balanced by *agapē*: by 'knowledge' in itself men were merely inflated, but they were built up by love.[23] It may have been this respect for 'knowledge' that led some of them to reject with distaste the Jewish doctrine of resurrection.[24]

Among the parties formed in the church of Corinth after Paul's departure there was one whose members adopted the slogan, 'I belong to Christ'.[25] What would have been laudable as a declara-

---

21 Cf. I Cor. 8:7ff; 10:23ff; Rom. 14:2ff.   22 I Cor. 6:12; 10:23.
23 I Cor. 8:2.   24 I Cor. 15:12.
25 I Cor. 1:12. Some, like C. H. Turner (*Catholic and Apostolic* [London, 1931], p. 214, n. 1), take ἐγὼ δὲ χριστοῦ to be Paul's response to these partisan

tion by the whole community became reprehensible when it was used as a party-cry in competition with others—more reprehensible, indeed, than the slogans which made use of the names of Paul, Apollos and Peter. But what was this 'Christ-party'? In the context where it is mentioned no indication is given of its character. The first manifesto of the Tübingen school of the nineteenth century was F. C. Baur's monograph on the 'Christ-party' at Corinth, in which he argued that it was the party of the extreme Judaizers.[26] But if we try to correlate the various parties with those tendencies in the church with which Paul takes issue in his Corinthian letters, the process of elimination may lead us to the conclusion that the 'Christ-party' embraced the *illuminati* mentioned above—'a group for whom Christ meant something like "God, freedom and immortality", where "God" means a refined philosophical monotheism; "freedom" means emancipation from the puritanical rigours of Palestinian barbarian authorities into the wider air of self-realisation; and "immortality" means the sound Greek doctrine as opposed to the crude Jewish notion of the Resurrection'.[27]

Thus, while some members of the church were in danger of transforming the freedom of the Spirit into the bondage of legalism, either in a Judaizing sense or by reaction against the laxity of their former way of life—it is the latter tendency, and not Judaizing influence, that must be responsible for the attitude, 'It is well for a man not to touch a woman' (I Cor. 7:1)—others went to the extreme of permissiveness, like those who regarded it as rather a fine assertion of Christian liberty when one of their number cohabited with his father's wife (I Cor. 5:1). Paul found it necessary to deal with both tendencies simultaneously, saying 'Liberty, not bondage' to the one group and 'Liberty, not licence' to the other. During the two or three years after his departure from Corinth, news kept coming to him at Ephesus from Corinth, either through visitors, like the members of Chloe's household (I Cor. 1:11) and Stephanas, Fortunatus

---

watchwords: you may claim to belong to this or that leader, but I, Paul, belong to Christ, and recognize no other name. The words that follow ('Is Christ divided?') make this interpretation less likely.

[26] F. C. Baur, 'Die Christuspartei in der korinthischen Gemeinde', *Tübinger Zeitschrift für Theologie*, 1831, Heft, 4, pp. 61–206. His characterization of the Christ-party depends on its identification with those who, according to II Cor. 10:7, claim to be distinctively 'Christ's'.

[27] T. W. Manson, *Studies in the Gospels and Epistles*, p. 207.

and Achaicus (I Cor. 16:17), or by letter (I Cor. 7:1ff), and he had to deal with the situation as reported to him, both by a succession of letters (of which the Corinthian correspondence in the New Testament comprises all that survives)[28] and by at least one visit to Corinth, which was a painful experience for himself and for the Corinthian church.[29]

3

Paul's Ephesian ministry, extending from the late summer of 52 to the spring or early summer of 55, was in many respects an important phase of his apostolic career. The christianization of the province of Asia was carried out during those years by Paul and his colleagues so thoroughly that for centuries the churches of Asia were among the most influential in the world; they survived the Turkish conquest and did not come to an end until the exchange of populations which followed the Graeco-Turkish war in 1923. Unfortunately we have little detailed information about the course of Paul's activity in Ephesus. It is not included among the 'we' narratives of Acts, and Luke restricts himself to a few vivid incidents.

Luke has been compared to a narrator who uses lantern slides to do most of his narrating for him.[30] He throws one picture after another on the screen, and provides coherence by the few well-chosen words of summary which he inserts between each picture and its successor. This is certainly an apt description of his account of Paul's Ephesian ministry, which consists for the most part of four such pictures.

---

[28] We have evidence of at least four, and more probably five, letters written by Paul to the church at Corinth: (*a*) the previous letter referred to in I Cor. 5:9, (*b*) I Corinthians, (*c*) the sorrowful letter referred to in II Cor. 2:3f; 7:8ff, (*d*) II Cor. 1–9, (*e*) II Cor. 10–13 which, if not part of the same letter as II Cor. 1–9, may be identified with part of the sorrowful letter that preceded it or, more probably, with part of a still later letter (see p. 334 with nn. 54, 55). For a more radical analysis of his extant correspondence with Corinth cf. G. Bornkamm, 'The History of the Origin of the So-called Second Letter to the Corinthians', in *The Authorship and Integrity of the New Testament*, SPCK Theological Collections 4 (London, 1965), pp. 73ff; a more conservative account of the matter is given in the same collection by A. M. G. Stephenson, 'A Defence of the Integrity of 2 Corinthians' (pp. 82ff).

[29] II Cor. 2:1; cf. 12:14; 13:1.

[30] Cf. W. C. van Unnik, 'The "Book of Acts" the Confirmation of the Gospel', *NovT* 4 (1960–1), pp. 26ff, especially p. 35.

The first portrays Paul's encounter with twelve 'disciples' who, like Apollos, knew of no baptism but John's and had not heard of the Holy Spirit.[31] Whence these disciples—who, if Luke uses this word as he normally does, regarded themselves as disciples of Jesus rather than of John the Baptist[32]—had derived their knowledge of the Way, imperfect as it was by Jerusalem standards, is one of the things we should like to know. With the reference to Apollos, this encounter warns us that there were other versions of the gospel circulating in the Hellenistic world than that which bore the authority of Jerusalem. Although Jerusalem may not have appreciated the fact adequately, Paul was, among other things, 'one of the greatest assets'[33] for the mother-church, for under his influence, when not by his personal action, non-Jerusalem versions of the gospel were brought into conformity with that which he and the Jerusalem leaders held in common.[34] Whether there was any significance in the number of these disciples at Ephesus is uncertain; Luke, at any rate, by characteristically saying that there were '*about* twelve of them in all', discourages his readers from speculating on this point. It is evident that neither their numbers nor their activity gave Paul cause to fear that in Ephesus he might be 'building on another man's foundation' in breach of his settled principle.

The second picture is the familiar one of Paul's expulsion from the synagogue after three months' preaching and debate there.[35] On this occasion it was to no private residence that he transferred his converts and followers, but to the lecture hall of one Tyrannus. Tyrannus was evidently a public teacher to whose hall students came regularly for lectures in the cooler parts of the day—the earlier morning and the later afternoon. The Western text of Acts 19:9 says that Paul had the use of it during the hottest part of the day, from 11 a.m. to 4 p.m. Whether there was any documentary basis for this gloss or not, it states what probably took place. It says much for Paul's stamina as well as his hearers' if they frequented Tyrannus's hall day by day for two years at a time when most citizens would be taking their siesta.

[31] Acts 19:1–7.   [32] See p. 161 with n. 37.
[33] A. Ehrhardt, *The Framework of the New Testament Stories*, p. 94.
[34] Cf. I Cor. 15:11 for the essential agreement between Paul and the Jerusalem leaders on the basic facts of the gospel.
[35] Acts 19:9.

The third picture presents Paul's conflict with the magicians.[36] Ephesus had a great reputation in antiquity for magical practice; written collections of spells composed in Ephesus ('Ephesian letters') fetched high prices.[37] It is not surprising to find strolling Jews among these practitioners, including some who claimed to belong to one or another of the chief-priestly families. It was well known throughout the Near East that Jewish high priests had access to the secret name of the God of Israel and its true pronunciation, and by all magical canons the command of such a secret carried with it enormous power over the spirit-world. Paul's invocation of the name of Jesus in healing the sick seemed to some of these Jewish practitioners to fit admirably into their scheme of things, but when they tried to use it they came to grief.[38] But many of the magicians, acknowledging the superior power of the gospel, joined the disciples; they deprived their secret spells of their potency by publicly divulging them[39] and made a bonfire of their magical scrolls. The picture, drawn in a few lines, fits perfectly into its Ephesian background; it is a good illustration of Luke's skill in the matter of local colour.

The same is true of the fourth and most famous of the pictures, the riotous assembly in the great open-air theatre.[40] The theatre, capable of accommodating 25,000 people, was the regular meeting-place of the civic assembly (*ekklēsia*). A bilingual inscription of A.D. 103–104 records how a Roman official presented the city with statues, including a silver image of Artemis, the great goddess of Ephesus, 'to be set up on their pedestals in the theatre at each meeting of the *ekklesia*'.[41] Silver images and the goddess Artemis figure prominently in the incident recorded by Luke. Ephesian Artemis bore the same name as the 'queen and huntress, chaste and fair' of Greek mythology, but, far from being a virgin-goddess, she was a

---

[36] Acts 19:13ff.

[37] Cf. Shakespeare's *Comedy of Errors*, Act I, Scene 2, 97ff. For Ἐφέσια γράμματα cf. Anaxilas ap. Athen., *Deipnosophistae* xii, 548c; Plutarch, *Quaest. conviv.* 706e; Clement of Alexandria, *Strom.* v. 8. 45. 2.

[38] Acts 19:13f. Parallels to the exorcistic formula of the sons of Sceva are found in the great magical papyri; cf. the Paris papyrus 574, lines 3018ff, 'I adjure thee by Jesus the God of the Hebrews'.

[39] Acts 19:18; Gk. ἀναγγέλλοντες τὰς πράξεις αὐτῶν means probably 'divulging their spells'.

[40] Acts 19:23ff.

[41] Cf. A. Deissmann, *Light from the Ancient East* (London, 1927), pp. 112f.

local manifestation of the great mother of gods and men who had been worshipped in Asia Minor from time immemorial. Her many breasted image at Ephesus, 'the sacred stone that fell from the sky' (Acts 19:35), was housed in a shrine which ranked as one of the seven wonders of the world. An earlier shrine had been burnt down in 356 B.C.—on the very night, men said, in which Alexander the Great was born—by a young man, Herostratus, who said he did it in order that his name might go down in history; but it was replaced by a new one which outstripped it in magnificence. Not only in Ephesus and the province of Asia, but in many other parts of the ancient world, Ephesian Artemis was worshipped, and Ephesus prided itself on nothing so much as its title 'Temple Warden (*neōkoros*) of Artemis'.[42]

But the gospel made such progress in Ephesus during Paul's residence there that many former devotees of Artemis worshipped her no longer. The guild of silversmiths in the city found that the demand for silver objects which they manufactured for use in the cult of Artemis was diminishing, and, led by their president, Demetrius (who may have been a member of the temple 'vestry'),[43] they held an indignation meeting to protest against this outlandish propaganda which so threatened the majesty of the great goddess. The indignation spread to the general population, who rushed to the theatre and there demonstrated not only against Paul and his associates but against the Jews in general (who notoriously had no respect for Artemis). The Jewish community in Ephesus was large and influential, and its privileges were safeguarded by the Roman authorities,[44] but an angry mob tends to overlook questions of legality. Alexander, a leader of the Jewish community, was put up to address the mob and dissociate himself and his fellow-Jews from the objects of the popular indignation, but was howled down. When Paul tried to do the same, he was prevented from entering the theatre by some of his friends among the Asiarchs. Two of Paul's companions, Gaius and Aristarchus, were dragged into the theatre

[42] For the title νεωκόρος see *CIG* 2972; the widespread cult of the goddess, 'not only in her home city . . . but also among Greeks and barbarians', is attested by BM Insc. iii, 482b (cf. Pauly-Wissowa II, cols. 1385f, for a list of 33 places where she was worshipped).

[43] Cf. E. L. Hicks, 'Demetrius the Silversmith: An Ephesian Study', *Expositor*, Series iv, 1 (1890), pp. 401ff.

[44] Cf. Josephus, *Ant.* xiv, 224–30, 234, 237–40, 262–4, 304f.

by the demonstrators, but luckily suffered no serious harm; it may well have been from them that Luke obtained so vivid a description of what went on—the crowd keeping up the cry 'Great Artemis of Ephesus' for two hours until at last the secretary, alarmed lest the Roman authorities might take sharp reprisals for this unruly behaviour, quieted the angry citizens and sent them home.

The gaps in Luke's narrative can be made up in some degree by the evidence of Paul's own writings but the reconstruction is doubtful. The only extant letter of his certainly written from Ephesus is I Corinthians, and it contains two references only to his Ephesian ministry—one matter-of-fact and the other enigmatic. Towards the end of the letter he says, announcing his intention of visiting Corinth in the near future, 'I will stay in Ephesus until Pentecost, for a wide door for effective work has opened to me, and there are many adversaries' (I Cor. 16:9).

Both the open door and the many adversaries can be illustrated from Luke's account (including his report in Acts 20:19 of Paul's reference to 'trials which befell me through the plots of the Jews'); but no doubt there were opportunities and perils which Luke does not mention. One peril is hinted at in the enigmatic reference in I Cor. 15:32 where, in the course of his defence of the resurrection hope, Paul asks, 'What do I gain if, humanly speaking, I fought with beasts at Ephesus?' That Paul was actually exposed to wild beasts, or was in danger of being so exposed, is most improbable (although the second-century author of the fictitious *Acts of Paul* took the words literally);[45] Roman citizens like Paul had certain indefectible rights. But whatever the words mean in their figurative sense ('humanly speaking'), they do point to some great danger faced by Paul—conceivably, but not certainly, in connexion with the Demetrius riot.

Again, in II Cor. 1:8–11, written in Macedonia some time after Paul's departure from Ephesus, he refers to the affliction which, he says, 'we [probably meaning "I"] experienced in Asia; for we were so utterly, unbearably crushed that we despaired of life itself. We received indeed the sentence of death; but that was to make us rely not on ourselves but on God who raises the dead; he delivered us from so deadly a peril, and he will deliver us. . . .' This deadly

[45] R. McL. Wilson (ed.), *New Testament Apocrypha* II (London, 1965), pp. 370ff.

peril may indeed have been an illness which almost proved mortal;[46] it may equally well have been some threat to his life on the part of powerful enemies from which he could see no way of escape—so that when, beyond all expectation, deliverance came, he greeted it as a miracle of resurrection.

Certainty is unattainable because of the scarcity of explicit evidence; it may be, as some have thought, that in the interregnum which followed the poisoning of Junius Silanus, proconsul of Asia, at the instance of Nero's mother Agrippina early in her son's principate (October, A.D. 54), Paul was exposed to grave personal danger.[47] It is even more probable that, of the frequent imprisonments which he mentions in II Cor. 11:23, not long after the conclusion of his Ephesian ministry, one if not more was endured by him in Ephesus. A strong, though not conclusive, case can be made out for dating the Epistle to the Philippians during an Ephesian imprisonment. If so, it was certainly not written at a time when Paul despaired of life, for he confidently expects to be delivered and to see his friends at Philippi again (Phil. 1:19, 26).[48]

4

Whether indeed the perilous crisis at Ephesus mentioned in II Cor. 1:8–11 constituted such a psychological watershed in Paul's life as C. H. Dodd has argued[49] is debatable; the thesis depends in large measure on the relative dating of certain passages in Paul's correspondence, especially the first nine chapters of II Corinthians and the last four chapters. The relation between these two sections of II Corinthians is a complicated problem of literary criticism—a problem whose solution evades us because it depends on our reconstruction of Paul's dealings with the Corinthian church at this juncture, and II Corinthians itself presents the data for this reconstruction.

About the same time as I Corinthians reached Corinth, the church there received a visit from Timothy. Either from Timothy on his return, or from some other informant, Paul learned that the party-

[46] So C. H. Dodd, *New Testament Studies* (Manchester, 1953), p. 68.
[47] So G. S. Duncan, *St. Paul's Ephesian Ministry* (London, 1929), pp. 100ff.
[48] Cf. J. H. Michael, *The Epistle of Paul to the Philippians* (London, 1928), pp. xiiff *et passim*. [49] *New Testament Studies*, pp. 81f.

spirit in Corinth, far from being checked by his letter, had recently been intensified. This was due to the arrival in Corinth of some Jewish-Christian teachers whose conception of the Gentile mission in the purpose of God was radically different from Paul's. According to them, the resurrection of Jesus marked the restoration of the kingdom of God to Israel—not in the sense of the old Davidic or Hasmonaean imperialism, but in the sense of Israel's spiritual primacy over the Gentiles in the new order inaugurated by the resurrection. How such a conception could be justified may be understood in the light of James's application of Amos 9:11f at the Council of Jerusalem (Acts 15:16ff). There, as we have seen,[50] the re-erection of David's fallen tent and the re-extension of his sovereignty over Israel's Gentile neighbours are viewed as fulfilled in the Gentiles' acknowledgement of the lordship of Jesus as the Messiah, the Son of David. Luke's narrative goes no further than this, but it is easy to see how some Jewish Christians could go on to argue that, just as David's rule over the Gentiles involved the exaltation of his people to the status of a master-race, so the extension of the spiritual sovereignty of the Son of David through the Gentile mission involved the spiritual primacy of the nation to which he belonged—at least of those members of the nations who confessed Jesus as Lord and Christ. In this new order the Mosaic law retained its place as the supreme revelation of God's will, even if the Gentile converts were not obliged to submit to it in its fulness. The Jerusalem decree exempted them from any such thorough-going obligation, and in particular from the requirement to be circumcised; but to those who regarded the bestowal of the Torah as a signal token of God's special love for Israel[51] this exemption would in itself imply the inferiority of Gentile Christians in his sight. Certainly any relaxation of the Torah for Jewish believers, such as Paul was suspected of encouraging, and any relaxation of the terms of the Jerusalem decree for Gentile believers, such as Paul was known to encourage, could not be tolerated. These visitors had no hesitation in asserting their primacy as Israelites, and some members of the Corinthian church were disposed to submit to them. They sug-

[50] See p. 286.
[51] Cf. Aqiba's dictum: 'Beloved are Israel, for to them was given the desirable instrument [the Torah] . . . through which the world was created' (*Pirqē Abot* 3:18).

gested, moreover, that if Paul, unlike them, did not assert his rights as a Hebrew Christian, that showed that he was not himself convinced of the validity of his claim to be an apostle. Paul's description of himself as the Gentiles' 'slave' (II Cor. 4:5) was a reversal of what these 'apostles' regarded as the proper order. That Gentile converts should make donations to the mother-church in Jerusalem was certainly right, but such donations were a tribute due, and not (as Paul represented) a voluntary offering, to be requested but not exacted.[52]

The acceptance of such teaching inevitably undermined Paul's authority among his Corinthian converts. At the same time there was the constant pressure from the other side of the party of 'enlightenment', who criticized Paul's ethical insistence as a regrettable relic of his earlier education in Judaism, something really incompatible with the total freedom logically implied in the gospel of Christ. This pressure too tended to erode his authority. Nothing would serve, he decided, but a personal visit to Corinth. This visit brought the opposition to a head. Paul appears to have been grossly insulted and humiliated at a meeting of the church; it is impossible to determine from which direction this action came. Plainly nothing was to be gained by further attempts at conciliation on the spot.

Paul withdrew, and sent the church a stinging letter, written with the full weight of his apostolic authority, in which he demanded in the name of Christ that the church should put itself in the right by taking severe disciplinary action against the offenders. So sharp was the tone of the letter that, after he had sent it by the hand of Titus, he began to fear that he had gone too far in severity. By this time he had left Ephesus, and had hoped to undertake some missionary activity in Troas and the vicinity, where there were promising opportunities for evangelism, but his anxiety over Corinth prevented him from settling down to this work. His mind could not rest until Titus returned with news of the reception given to his letter. He waited at Troas until Aegean navigation ceased for the winter of A.D. 55–56; then, knowing that Titus could not come across the open sea direct from Corinth or Athens, he himself took the overland route into Europe (which involved no more travel by sea than the crossing of the Dardanelles) and met Titus in Mace-

[52] Cf. D. W. Oostendorp, *Another Jesus* (Kampen, 1967), pp. 75ff; see also pp. 350ff, below.

donia. Titus's news brought him overwhelming relief: the Corinthian church had been stung to such a sense of shame and indignation by Paul's letter that there was a complete revulsion of feeling in his favour. The required disciplinary action had been taken against the offending party, and especially against their ringleader, to the point where Paul himself cried 'Hold, enough!'[53] It may seem strange that a letter should have been so effective after the failure of his visit; perhaps there was some substance in the observation of those critics who said, 'His letters are weighty and strong, but his bodily presence is weak, and his speech of no account' (II Cor. 10:10). In his joy at Titus's news Paul wrote a letter of affection and reconciliation; in the warmth of his emotion he lays bare his heart more than anywhere else in his writings, and reveals the inner springs which nourished his faith and hope and the constraint of the love of Christ which was the motive of his apostolic ministry.

It would be pleasant indeed if we could be sure that the note of reconciliation which sounds in II Cor. 1–9 continued henceforth to mark relations between Paul and the Corinthian church. But the complete change of tone from the relaxed confidence and gladness of these chapters to the painful contents of chapters 10–13—the biting attack on his adversaries as 'sham apostles, crooked in all their practices, masquerading as apostles of Christ' (10:13, NEB), the uncongenial self-vindication, the reluctant boasting 'as a fool', and the warning of what will happen at his next visit if they do not mend their ways—this demands an explanation. That both sections can belong to the same letter is hardly credible. There is much to be said for the view that the last four chapters of II Corinthians represent part of the severe letter which preceded the letter of reconciliation.[54] The acceptance of this view permits us to envisage a happy ending for Paul's difficult passages with his Corinthian converts; but there are some references in II Cor. 10–13 which suggest that these chapters belong to a letter sent some time *after* the letter of reconciliation.[55] If that is so, the reconciliation was not so com-

[53] II Cor. 2:5ff.
[54] Cf. J. H. Kennedy, *The Second and Third Epistles to the Corinthians* (London, 1900), pp. 79ff.
[55] E.g., what Paul says in II Cor. 12:18 about his having sent Titus to Corinth seems to refer back, after some lapse of time, to the visit of Titus announced as impending in II Cor. 8:17ff. L. P. Pherigo, 'Paul and the Corinthian Church',

plete or permanent as Paul had reason to hope when he wrote II Cor. 1–9.[56] But, however we reconstruct the story of Paul's relations with Corinth, it provides an eloquent commentary on his own remark that, above the other burdens which weighed on him in the course of his apostolic service, 'there is the daily pressure upon me of my anxiety for all the churches' (II Cor. 11:28).

5

Paul did, of course, retain his loyal friends in Corinth, and with one of them, Gaius, he spent the winter months of A.D. 56–57. His movements during A.D. 56 are almost completely undocumented.[57] All that Luke says is that Paul, having come into Macedonia, 'went through these parts and gave them much encouragement' (Acts 20:2). To Paul himself we owe one piece of information about a journey which must probably be dated in the course of this year. In Rom. 15:19, written probably in the following winter, he sums up the range of his ministry to date in these words: 'from Jerusalem and as far round as Illyricum I have fully preached the gospel of Christ'. But for this remark of his, we should not have known that at this stage of his career he travelled as far west as Illyricum. Since he uses the Roman form Illyricum and not the Greek Illyria or Illyris, even though he is writing Greek, he probably means the Roman province, which lay along the eastern shore of the Adriatic, north of the westernmost region of Macedonia. In Greek nomenclature, Illyria embraced the westernmost region of Roman Macedonia (including the seaport of Dyrrhachium, one of the western termini of the Egnatian Way). Paul would in any case have had to pass through part of this region to reach the Roman province of Illyricum. If he crossed the provincial frontier, he would have found himself for the first time in his apostolic career in a province where the culture was more Latin than Greek. It is in the context of his reference to reaching Illyricum with the gospel that he tells the Roman Christians of his plan to visit Spain and repeat there the evangelistic

---

JBL 68 (1949), pp. 341ff, went so far as to find the life-setting of II Cor. 10–13 in the period following Paul's (hypothetical) release from his (first) Roman imprisonment—an unacceptably late date.

[56] Cf. C. K. Barrett, 'Christianity at Corinth', *BJRL* 46 (1963–4), pp. 269ff.

[57] See pp. 351f.

programme which he had completed in the Aegean world. Illyricum would have given him some idea of what it would be like to evangelize a province, such as Spain was, where the culture was wholly Latin and not at all Greek.

Paul's plan to evangelize Spain was bound up with his settled policy of pioneering. His ambition was always to preach Christ where his name had not previously been heard, instead of 'building on another man's foundation' (like some people whom he could mention).[58] We may reasonably infer that those parts of the Eastern Mediterranean world which Paul himself had not evangelized had by this time been evangelized by others (including Alexandria and Cyrene with their hinterlands); hence his decision to go to the west. Spain was the oldest Roman province and the main bastion of Roman civilization in the Western Mediterranean; to Paul's strategic eye it presented itself as his next mission-field. On the way there he hoped to visit Rome and make the acquaintance of the Christians there, and he sent them a letter to prepare them for his coming; but first he had to visit Judaea.

A plan to sail there from Achaia after his winter in Corinth was changed because of news of a plot against his life; instead, he went north to Macedonia and set sail from Neapolis, the seaport of Philippi, 'after the days of Unleavened Bread' (Acts 20:6)—about mid-April, A.D. 57. From Neapolis the ship took him to Troas, where, a week later, he boarded a fast ship which he reckoned would bring him to Caesarea in time for him to reach Jerusalem by Pentecost.

With him, Luke tells us, there travelled to Jerusalem a number of Gentile Christians, representing the main areas of his Aegean mission-field: representatives from Macedonia (Thessalonica and Beroea), Galatia (Derbe) and Asia are specially mentioned.[59] We could hardly gather from Luke's narrative why so many Gentile Christians accompanied Paul on this occasion; to grasp the importance of their presence we have again to consult Paul himself.[60]

[58] See pp. 322f.   [59] Acts 20:4.   [60] See pp. 353f.

26 Judaea: The Later Procurators

1

Cuspius Fadus, the first procurator to be appointed over Judaea after the death of Herod Agrippa, governed the whole territory which had formed Agrippa's kingdom. Now, for the first time since the accession of Herod the Great, Galilee became part of the province of Judaea. Fadus's first instructions were to administer a severe reprimand to the Gentile citizens of Caesarea and Sebaste (Samaria), who had not concealed their exultation at Agrippa's death: forgetting that they owed their very foundation to Herod the Great, they felt it a humiliation to be ruled by a Jewish king.[1]

But his actions in Peraea augured ill for the acceptance of the new order by the Jews. A frontier dispute between the people of Philadelphia (Amman), one of the Gentile cities of the Decapolis, and the Jewish inhabitants of Zia, a village some fifteen miles to the west of it, led to fighting and bloodshed. Fadus condemned the Jews as aggressors, although they believed themselves to be in the right, and executed one of their leaders and exiled two others.[2]

Elsewhere in the province Agrippa's death seems to have been followed by a fresh outburst of insurgent activity: Josephus sets it to Fadus's credit that he 'purged Judaea of robber-bands'.[3] One of these was led by a 'bandit-chief' (*archilēstēs*)[4] named Ptolemy, who had been a thorn in the sides of the Idumaeans and Arabs—presumably there had been no point in attacking the forces of the ruling power during the reign of a pious Jewish king. Ptolemy was taken prisoner, brought before Fadus and sentenced to death.

Fadus made some attempt to secure custody of the high-priestly vestments, following the precedent of earlier procurators, but Claudius (persuaded by the advocacy, it is said, of the younger Agrippa

[1] See p. 260. Cf. Josephus, *Ant.* xix, 364.
[2] Josephus, *Ant.* xx, 2–4. [3] *Ant.* xx, 5.
[4] Cf. Hezekiah (p. 97), Barabbas (p. 204), Eleazar (p. 345).

and his cousin Aristobulus,[5] who were in Rome at the time) gave orders that they should remain in Jewish custody.[6]

Fadus was succeeded as procurator (*c.* A.D. 46) by Tiberius Julius Alexander, member of the most illustrious Jewish family of Egyptian Alexandria, being the son of Alexander the *arabarchēs*[7] and nephew of the philosopher Philo. The appointment of this procurator of Jewish blood, however, was not at all acceptable to the Jews of Judaea, for Alexander was an apostate from Judaism and took care to let it be seen that his apostasy was genuine. At the beginning of his term of office Judaea was suffering from the famine already mentioned.[8] The only other noteworthy event recorded during his procuratorship is his crucifixion of Jacob and Simon, two sons of Judas the Galilaean—presumably because of their involvement in the same kind of Zealot activity as their father.[9]

Although we have no details of the action which brought the sons of Judas to their death, there was an increase in militant messianism in the period following A.D. 44. This is indicated especially by the number of insurgent movements based on the wilderness of Judaea. During the procuratorship of Fadus one Theudas, described by Josephus as a charlatan,[10] persuaded a large number of followers to take their movable property with them and march with him across the Jordan. He claimed to be a prophet (perhaps the eschatological prophet like Moses), and assured them that at his word of command the river would be divided and they would cross it dry-shod, as their ancestors had done in Joshua's day, and seize control of the land. Fadus, however, took the initiative and sent a squadron of cavalry who attacked and dispersed them. Theudas

[5] The son of Herod of Chalcis and second husband of Salome (daughter of Herodias); see p. 27.   [6] Josephus, *Ant.* xx, 6–14 (see p. 63).

[7] Cf. p. 52.   [8] See p. 268.

[9] Josephus, *Ant.* xx, 102 (see p. 98). In the Old Russian version of Josephus, sections 221 and 222 of *BJ* ii are replaced by a report that in the time of Fadus and Alexander 'many followers of the wonder-worker mentioned earlier [see p. 166 with n. 17] appeared and spoke to the people about their Master, claiming that he was risen although he was dead, and saying, "He will free you from your bondage". Many of the multitude listened to their preaching and paid heed to their injunctions . . . But when these noble procurators saw the falling away of the people, they determined, together with the scribes, to seize and kill them . . . they sent them away, some to Caesar, others to Antioch to be tried, and others [they banished] to distant lands'.

[10] Gk. γόης (Josephus, *Ant.* xx, 97f). The Theudas of Acts 5:36 is dated earlier, before the rising of Judas the Galilaean (therefore perhaps *c.* 4 B.C.).

was captured and killed, and his head was brought to Jerusalem.

But the example of his failure did not deter others. Under Felix in particular a succession of 'deceivers and impostors'[11] (as Josephus calls them) 'fomented revolutionary changes under the pretext of divine inspiration, and persuaded the populace to behave as though they were possessed, leading them out to the wilderness, where (they claimed) God would show them sure tokens of liberations. But Felix sent cavalry and heavy-armed infantry against them, regarding their behaviour as preliminary to rebellion, and so destroyed a great number'.[12] This kind of situation is reflected in the Matthaean version of the eschatological discourse, where Jesus says: 'Then, if any one says to you, "Lo, here is the Messiah!" or "There he is!" do not believe it. For false Messiahs and false prophets will arise and show great signs and wonders, so as to lead astray, if possible, even the elect . . . So, if they say to you, "Lo, he is in the wilderness", do not go out . . .' (Matt. 24:23-6).

One of these 'impostors' against whom Felix took action was an Egyptian 'charlatan'[13] (presumably an Egyptian Jew and messianic pretender) who, having gained a reputation as a prophet, mustered several thousand followers in the wilderness, whence he led them by a circuitous route round the Mount of Olives, promising that he would force his way into Jerusalem and overcome the Roman garrison in the Antonia fortress; then he would rule as king and his followers who helped him to gain his kingdom would be his bodyguard. But when Felix attacked them with an infantry force, they were scattered with much loss of life; their leader with a few companions escaped. Some time later, when Paul, on his last visit to Jerusalem, was set upon in the Temple court by a hostile crowd and snatched from their hands by Roman soldiers from the Antonia fortress, the commanding officer of the garrison jumped to the conclusion that the charlatan had reappeared in Jerusalem and was receiving rough justice at the hands of those whom he had duped. He was surprised when Paul addressed him in educated Greek: 'Are you not the Egyptian, then', he asked, 'who recently stirred up a

[11] Gk. πλάνοι καὶ ἀπατεῶνες (Josephus, *BJ* ii, 259; in *Ant.* xx, 160 he calls them λῃστήριοι καὶ γόητες ἄνθρωποι ['brigands and charlatans']).
[12] Josephus, *BJ* ii, 259f.
[13] Gk. γόης (used also of Theudas), Josephus, *BJ* ii, 261; cf. *Ant.* xx, 169ff.

revolt and led the four thousand men of the *sicarii*[14] out into the wilderness?' (Acts 21:38). Four thousand is a more reasonable estimate of the Egyptian's army than Josephus's thirty thousand;[15] even so, it was the most serious rising of its kind during Felix's procuratorship; in view of the threat to Jerusalem it is not surprising that on this occasion the citizens supported Felix's action.

A movement similar to those led by Theudas and the Egyptian is recorded for the procuratorship of Festus (A.D. 59–62): 'Festus sent a force of cavalry and infantry against the dupes of a certain charlatan who promised them deliverance and cessation from evils if they would consent to follow him to the wilderness'; leader and followers alike were wiped out.[16]

Perhaps something of this wilderness mystique was in the minds of those defenders of Jerusalem who, during the siege, asked Titus for permission to pass through the Roman lines with their families so that they could settle in the wilderness;[17] and when, after the fall of the city, some fugitive *sicarii* incited the Jews of Cyrene, and one of them, Jonathan the weaver, 'persuaded some of the poorer of their number to follow him into the desert, where he promised to show them "signs and apparitions",' we may recognize the same pattern of thought and action.[18]

2

About the same time as Alexander was replaced as procurator of Judaea (A.D. 48), Herod, king of Chalcis, brother of the late Agrippa, died. Since the death of Agrippa, this Herod had exercised the privilege of appointing the Jewish high priest. When Herod himself died, this privilege was transferred to the younger Agrippa, who retained it until the war of A.D. 66. Not only so, but Herod's kingdom of Chalcis, a tiny principality in the plain between the Lebanon and Antilebanon ranges, was given to Agrippa, together with the royal title. Claudius thus compensated the son of his old friend for his decision not to give him his father's kingdom of Judaea

[14] See pp. 98f, 356.
[15] If these numbers were expressed by means of letters of the Greek alphabet, 4,000 would be written ,Δ and 30,000 ,Λ.
[16] Josephus, *Ant.* xx, 188.   [17] Josephus, *BJ* vi, 351.
[18] Josephus, *BJ* vii, 438.

four years before.[19] In A.D. 53 Agrippa relinquished the kingdom
of Chalcis in exchange for a larger realm farther south, consisting
of the territory of Abilene (the tetrarchy of that Lysanias who is
mentioned in Luke 3:1) and the former tetrarchy of Philip, with
its capital at Caesarea Philippi.[20] When Nero succeeded Claudius,
he increased Agrippa's kingdom further by giving him the Peraean
city of Julias (Betharamphtha) with the surrounding countryside,
and the cities of Tarichaea and Tiberias on the west shore of the
Lake of Galilee. As a mark of gratitude for this imperial bounty
Agrippa renamed his capital Neronias.[21]

For a number of years Agrippa succeeded in combining loyalty to
Rome with patriotic services to the Jewish cause. Like his father, he
styled himself 'Great King, Pious Friend of Caesar and Friend of
Rome';[22] at the same time he earned the testimony expressed in
Paul's words 'expert in all customs and controversies of the Jews'
(Acts 26:3). Even before he was appointed king of Chalcis he used
his influence with Claudius to prevent Fadus from securing custody
of the high-priestly robes; later he intervened decisively on the
Jewish side in a dispute between the procurator Ventidius Cumanus, Alexander's successor, and his provincial subjects.

Cumanus's procuratorship was punctuated by a succession of
clashes between his soldiers and the Jews. One of these was provoked by the indecent gesture of one of the soldiers who were
guarding the outer court of the Temple during the Passover festival.
This caused a riot, in which the Roman garrison was pelted with
stones; when Cumanus called up reinforcements, the panic-stricken
crowds of worshippers fled from the Temple precincts in such disorder that many were crushed to death in the gateways.[23]

Some time later, an officer of the imperial household was way-
laid and robbed by brigands in the pass of Beth-horon, about twelve
miles north-west of Jerusalem. Cumanus sent a body of troops to
execute reprisals upon the neighbouring villages; while this was
going on, a soldier seized a scroll of the Law from a synagogue,
and publicly tore it up and burned it. Enraged by this outrage upon
their religion, which enjoyed imperial protection, the Jewish leaders

[19] Josephus, *Ant.* xx, 104.   [20] Josephus, *Ant.* xx, 138.
[21] Josephus, *BJ* ii, 252; *Ant.* xx, 159, 211; *Life*, 38.
[22] Cf. Schürer, *HJP* I. ii, p. 196.
[23] Josephus, *BJ* ii, 225ff; *Ant.* xx, 108ff.

waited on Cumanus at Caesarea and demanded satisfaction. Cumanus ordered the offending soldier to be beheaded in the presence of his accusers; this shows clearly enough that much of the trouble between the Roman authorities in the province and their Jewish subjects was due not to deliberate malice on the part of the former but to mismanagement and a general lack of tact.[24]

More serious—especially, in the event, for Cumanus himself—was the conflict which occasioned Agrippa's intervention. Jewish pilgrims from Galilee, on their way through Samaria to Jerusalem to celebrate the festivals there, were liable to be treated inhospitably by the Samaritans, as Jesus and his disciples found on one occasion.[25] Some Galilaean pilgrims going south to Jerusalem for a festival—probably the Feast of Tabernacles in the autumn of A.D. 51 —were roughly handled in a Samaritan village just south of the Plain of Esdraelon, and at least one of them was killed.[26] Cumanus was petitioned to punish the aggressors, but when he dismissed the affair as one of little importance, two Zealot leaders, Eleazar and Alexander, led their followers against the Samaritans of that district and massacred them indiscriminately.

This action was serious enough for Cumanus to intervene in person with a detachment of cavalry; many of the Zealot raiders were killed and others taken prisoner. The Samaritans, for their part, lodged their complaint with Ummidius Quadratus, legate of Syria, before whom also a party of Jewish dignitaries, led by the ex-high priest Jonathan, stated the Jewish case. Quadratus deferred judgement until he visited Caesarea and Lydda; there he executed all Cumanus's Jewish prisoners who had offered armed resistance to the Romans, and ordered the Jewish and Samaritan leaders, together with Cumanus and a military tribune named Celer, who for some unspecified reason had rendered himself specially obnoxious to the Jews, to go to Rome and submit themselves to the judgement of the emperor. Quadratus then went up to Jerusalem; finding the people there quietly celebrating the Passover of A.D. 52, he returned to Antioch.

When the case came up for hearing before Claudius, Agrippa appeared as a powerful advocate on the Jewish side, and also en-

---

[24] Josephus, *BJ* ii, 228f; *Ant.* xx, 113ff.   [25] Luke 9:52f.
[26] So Josephus, *BJ* ii, 232f (perhaps relying on Roman sources), but in *Ant.* xx, 118 he says that many were killed.

listed the support of Agrippina, Claudius's wife. Claudius gave judgement against the Samaritans as being the aggressors in the first instance, and three unfortunate leaders of the Samaritan community whom Quadratus had sent to Rome were sentenced to death. Cumanus was deposed from his procuratorship and banished; the tribune Celer had to expiate his offence by being sent to Jerusalem to suffer humiliation and execution at the hands of the Jewish authorities.[27] In Judaea, as in Alexandria, the Jews had no occasion to complain of Claudius's arbitration.

3

During these events one Roman played a part which impressed his superiors and the Jews alike. Felix, like his brother Pallas (now an extraordinarily influential member of the imperial civil service) was a freedman of Claudius's mother Antonia (from whom they took the *nomen gentile* Antonius).[28] He appears to have occupied some administrative post in Samaria under Cumanus[29] and, according to Tacitus, was one of the judges appointed by Quadratus to help Claudius in coming to a decision.[30] Jonathan the ex-high priest, who had been sent to Rome as leader of the Jewish deputation together with his colleagues Ananias son of Nedebaeus, the reigning high priest, and the latter's son Ananus, captain of the Temple, was so impressed by Felix's conduct that he requested Claudius to send him to be Cumanus's successor as procurator of Judaea.[31] It was an unheard-of thing for a freedman to occupy a governorship which was normally held by a member of the equestrian order. Nevertheless, thanks chiefly to his brother Pallas's influence at court (especially with the Empress Agrippina), Felix was appointed procurator of Judaea.

Despite his servile origin, Felix married into the highest families. Suetonius, referring to the favour with which he was regarded by

---

[27] Josephus, *BJ* ii, 234–46; *Ant.* xx, 119–36.

[28] Josephus, *BJ* ii, 247; *Ant.* xviii, 182; Tacitus, *Ann.* xii, 54; *Hist.* v, 9.

[29] Tacitus (*Ann.* xii, 54) says that Judaea was divided between Cumanus and Felix, the former governing Galilee and the latter Samaria. Josephus unambiguously makes Felix the successor of Cumanus as procurator of Judaea; Tacitus's statement may be explained if Felix first held a post under Cumanus.

[30] Tacitus, *Ann.* xii, 54.   [31] Josephus, *Ant.* xx, 162.

Claudius, adds that he was 'the husband of three queens'[32]—by which he means ladies of royal birth. Who all three were we do not know: one of them, however, was a granddaughter of Antony and Cleopatra (and therefore related to the Emperor Claudius),[33] while his third wife, Drusilla, was the youngest daughter of Herod Agrippa the elder.[84] Drusilla had been betrothed by her father at a tender age to Epiphanes, crown prince of Commagene, but only on condition that Epiphanes submitted to circumcision; when he refused, the betrothal was cancelled. She was then given in marriage by her brother, the younger Agrippa, to Azizus, king of Emesa in Syria, who did comply with the condition which Epiphanes had rejected. But not long after Felix's arrival in Judaea, he persuaded her, through the good offices of a Cypriot Jew named Atomos, a magician by profession, to leave Azizus and marry him instead, promising her, if she did so, every 'felicity' (with a play on his own name).[85] No question arose of compelling Felix to be circumcised! Drusilla, who was now sixteen years old, had led an unhappy life hitherto; we can only hope that Felix kept his promise. They had a son named Agrippa, who with his wife perished in the eruption of Vesuvius (A.D. 79).[86]

Those Jews who had welcomed the idea of Felix's appointment as procurator soon had reason to change their minds. Felix makes a more sympathetic appearance in the New Testament than he does elsewhere in ancient literature. True, Luke does not cast him in heroic mould, depicting him as prone to venality, procrastination and opportunism; yet there is something appealing about the picture of Felix and Drusilla's repeated summoning of Paul to their presence during his two years' custody in Caesarea (A.D. 57–59) and trembling as Paul 'argued about justice and self-control and future judgement' (Acts 24:25).

Luke also describes how Tertullus, the orator who presented the Sanhedrin's case against Paul before Felix, began his speech for the prosecution with a flowery exordium: 'Since through you we enjoy much peace, and since by your provision, most excellent Felix, re-

---

[82] Suetonius, *Claudius* 28, where Claudius is said to have conferred on Felix various military commands as a token of his regard for him.

[83] Also called Drusilla, according to Tacitus (*Hist.* v, 9). Claudius's mother was a daughter of Antony.   [84] See pp. 261, 357.

[85] Josephus, *Ant.* xix, 355; xx, 139–43; Acts 24:24.

[86] Josephus, *Ant.* xx, 144.

forms are introduced on behalf of this nation, in every way and everywhere we accept this with all gratitude' (Acts 24:3) This was a flattering reference to the ruthlessness with which, from the outset of his procuratorship, he put down every attempt at Zealot or other insurgent activity. The Zealot leader Eleazar,[87] who had led the reprisal raid on the Samaritans, was taken prisoner by a ruse and sent to Rome for punishment, with many of his associates. 'Of the bandits whom he crucified', says Josephus, 'and of the common people who were convicted of association with them and likewise punished, the number was incalculable'.[88] Open revolt was thus stamped out, but being driven underground the insurgent spirit was forced to express itself in the less heroic exploits of the *sicarii*, who seized the opportunity provided by the crowded pilgrimage-festivals to assassinate their opponents with their daggers (Lat. *sicae*).

One of their first victims was the ex-high priest Jonathan; the part he had played in having Felix appointed as procurator was no doubt a black mark on his record. But Josephus reports a curious and improbable piece of gossip: Jonathan's conscience was uneasy because he had requested Claudius to appoint Felix to this post, and to guard against popular resentment on this account he used to lecture Felix on the best way to administer the province, hoping thus to mitigate his harshness. At last Felix, annoyed by these incessant lectures, bribed a friend of Jonathan's to arrange his assassination.[89]

The picture of Felix's severity given by Josephus is confirmed by Tacitus, who says that he 'stimulated outbreaks by injudicious disciplinary measures' and sums up his character in the incisive epigram: 'plunging into every form of cruelty and lust, he exercised the power of a king with the spirit of a slave'.[40] His recall from office was the sequel to his violent intervention in a quarrel between the Jewish and Greek communities in Caesarea.[41] The date of his recall and replacement by Porcius Festus is disputed, but a change in the provincial coinage of Judaea attested for Nero's fifth year

---

[87] Josephus, *BJ* ii, 253 (where Eleazar is called an ἀρχιλῃστής); *Ant.* xx, 161.
[88] *BJ* ii, 253.
[89] Josephus, *Ant.* xx, 162f.   [40] Tacitus, *Ann.* xii, 54; *Hist.* v, 9.
[41] See pp. 377f.

points to A.D. 59.[42] By this time Felix's brother Pallas no longer
occupied the influential position at the imperial court which he had
enjoyed seven years before. He was involved in Agrippina's fall
from Nero's favour and deposed from his high office in the civil service (A.D. 55). His power was still so great, however, that on relin-
quishing his post he successfully stipulated that there should be no
scrutiny of his conduct in office and that his accounts with the state
should be treated as balanced.[43]

4

Festus is known to us only from Luke and Josephus.[44] He appears to have been a man of higher principle than his predecessor,
but was unable to do anything effective to allay the mounting popular resentment against Rome which Felix's repressive actions had
stimulated, or to check the increasing excesses of the *sicarii*, despite
the military action which he took against them.

A lighter note is supplied by a quarrel between Agrippa and the
Temple authorities.[45] Agrippa's town house in Jerusalem, a former
palace of the Hasmonaeans, stood on the western brow of the Tyro-
poeon valley and overlooked the Temple on the other side of the
valley. He built a sun-lounge on to the palace from which, as he
reclined at meals, he could watch the priests discharging their
sacrificial duties. The priests were annoyed at being spied on thus,
and the Temple authorities built a high wall which not only blocked
Agrippa's view, but also the view from the top of the colonnade on
the west side of the outer court, where Roman soldiers were posted
during festivals to keep public order. Festus, therefore, as well as
Agrippa, objected to the wall, and gave orders for its demolition.
But the Jewish authorities sent a delegation of ten men, headed by
Ishmael the high priest and Hilkiah the Temple treasurer, to make
representations to Nero. They procured the good offices of Poppaea
Sabina, Nero's mistress and, after A.D. 62, his wife, who was reputed to be a sympathizer with the Jewish religion; Josephus, in-

---

[42] Cf. F. W. Madden, *History of Jewish Coinage* (London, 1864), p. 153;
cf. H. J. Cadbury, *The Book of Acts in History* (New York, 1955), p. 10.

[43] Tacitus, *Ann.* xiii, 14; cf. Josephus, *Ant.* xx, 182, where Pallas's intercession is said to have saved Felix from worse punishment than deposition.

[44] Acts 25:1–26:32, Josephus, *BJ* ii, 271; *Ant.* xx, 182–97.

[45] Josephus, *Ant.* xx, 189ff.

Judaea: The Later Procurators

347

deed, calls her a 'God-fearer'.[46] She persuaded Nero to grant their request, and so the wall remained in position.

Festus died in office in ▲ ᴅ. 6₂ and three months elapsed before the arrival of Lucceius Albinus as his successor. It was during this interval that James the Just was executed in Jerusalem by sentence of the court illegally convened by the high priest Annas (Ananus) II.[47] News of this action reached the new procurator as he was on his way from Alexandria, where he had held an administrative post, and he wrote an angry letter threatening to punish Annas and his associates for thus arrogating to themselves the capital jurisdiction which was the prerogative of the governor. Agrippa hastily did what he could to conciliate Albinus by removing Annas from office.

Albinus took severe action against the *sicarii*.[48] Josephus tells how a party of these kidnapped the secretary or adjutant of Eleazar, captain of the Temple, and sent a message to Eleazar's father —Ananias, son of Nedebaeus—promising to release their captive if Albinus released ten *sicarii* whom he had taken prisoner. Ananias persuaded Albinus—certainly by means of bribery—to release his prisoners, but this piece of blackmail emboldened the *sicarii* to further ventures of the same kind, and disorder increased throughout the province.[49]

Towards the end of Albinus's procuratorship, the restoration of the Temple, begun by Herod over eighty years before, was completed. This threatened a large number of workmen with sudden unemployment—an undesirable situation in the prevailing unrest. Therefore, to provide them with further work, the authorities urged Agrippa to raise the height of the eastern colonnade—'Solomon's Portico'—which overlooked the Kidron ravine. Agrippa refused to finance this operation, but agreed to pave the city with white marble. A year or two later, however, when the Temple foundations showed signs of sinking, Agrippa at great expense imported wood

[46] *Ant.* xx, 195; the term he uses is θεοσεβής. Cf. p. 266. At her death in A.D. 65 she was not cremated in the customary manner but buried, says Tacitus, 'after the fashion of foreign royalty' (*Ann.* xvi, 6). Proper caution in evaluating this evidence is counselled by E. M. Smallwood, 'The Alleged Jewish Sympathies of Poppaea Sabina', *JTS*, n.s. 10 (1959), pp. 329ff.

[47] See pp. 66, 373. [48] Josephus, *Ant.* xx, 200–3.

[49] Josephus, *BJ* ii, 272–6; *Ant.* xx, 204–10. A. Momigliano (*CAH* x [1934], p. 855 with n. 1) interprets Josephus's evidence to mean that Albinus 'initiated in his brief term a policy of mildness which caused him to be accused of corruption'.

from Lebanon to underpin them. The work of underpinning was interrupted by the revolt against Rome in September, A.D. 66, and the remainder of the wood was used for the defence of the Temple area four years later when it was besieged by Titus.[50]

Jerusalem was not the only city to benefit by Agrippa's munificence. As a matter of course he enlarged and beautified his own capital, Neronias (Caesarea Philippi); he also presented Berytus (Beirut) in Syria, on which his father had conferred similar favours, with a theatre and many works of art.[51]

Apart from his contributions to the material structure of the city and Temple of Jerusalem, he raised the status of the Levites. He persuaded the Sanhedrin to permit the Temple-singers to wear linen vestments like the priests, and to allow some Levites who were ancestrally assigned to other Temple duties to be enrolled in the guilds of Temple-singers. Josephus, himself a priest, records these concessions to Levites with disapproval, and suggests that this breach of religious tradition was contributory to the judgement which a few years later befell the city and Temple.[52]

In addition to this dispute between the priests and Levites, disputes of a still more rancorous nature broke out between the wealthy members of the chief-priestly families and the poorer priests, as well as between rival candidates for the high-priesthood and their partisans. Whereas in accordance with ancient prescription it was the Levites that formerly received the tithes paid by the people for the maintenance of the Temple order,[53] it appears that by the first century A.D. the collection of the tithes was carried out by priests.[54] But the high priests of the fifties and sixties, led by Ananias the son of Nedebaeus, are charged by Josephus with sending their servants to the threshing-floors when the tithes of grain were being set aside in order to seize them by force, so that some of the poorer priests, deprived of their regular means of subsistence, died of starvation.[55] Rapacious conduct of this general character (though not this particular activity) is denounced in the

[50] Josephus, *Ant.* xx, 219–22.   [51] Josephus, *Ant.* xx, 211f (cf. p. 260).
[52] Josephus, *Ant.* xx, 216–18. J. Jeremias may be right in suggesting that Agrippa upgraded the Levites in order to administer a snub to the priests (*Jerusalem zur Zeit Jesu* II B [Leipzig, 1929], p. 76).
[53] Cf. Lev. 18:21; Num. 18:26ff; Neh. 10:38f.   [54] Cf. Josephus, *Life*, 80.
[55] Josephus, *Ant.* xx, 181, 205ff. Cf. E. M. Smallwood, 'High Priests and Politics', *JTS*, n.s. 13 (1962), 14–34, especially p. 27.

diatribe against the rich in James 5:1–6 and, whatever view be held of the authorship of that epistle, the social iniquity of these years provides a setting for the arrest and condemnation of James the Just by the high priest Annas II.[56]

When the successor of Annas, Jesus the son of Damnaeus, was deposed in his turn by Agrippa, contention between various rivals for the succession broke out into street-fighting, in which the partisans of Ananias the son of Nedebaeus once more distinguished themselves.[57] Other disorders accompanied this unseemly strife, and certain members of the Herod family figured as gang-leaders, perhaps presuming on their kinship with Agrippa.[58]

About this time Josephus, now twenty-six years old, visited Rome as one of a delegation charged with intervening on behalf of some Jewish priests who, for an unspecified offence, had been sent to Rome in chains. During their imprisonment there, Josephus says, they had avoided eating ceremonially unclean food by restricting their diet to figs and nuts. Through a Jewish actor named Aliturus, Josephus relates, he obtained an audience with the Empress Poppaea, and she consented to use her influence to procure the release of the priests.[59]

Albinus was succeeded as procurator about A.D. 65 by Gessius Florus, who is said to have owed his appointment to his wife's friendship with Poppaea. When Albinus knew that he was to be replaced, he amnestied all except the most criminal among his prisoners who were awaiting trial or serving jail-sentences; this act of clemency was widely represented as a further instance of bribery.[60] Josephus has nothing good to say of Albinus, but admits that when they began to experience his successor's misgovernment the Jews looked back on Albinus as a public benefactor.[61]

It was under Gessius Florus that the revolt against Rome took place, and his misrule provided the immediate occasion for it.[62]

---

[56] Cf. S. G. F. Brandon, *Jesus and the Zealots* (Manchester, 1967), pp. 115ff; 'The Death of James the Just: A New Interpretation', *Studies in Mysticism and Religion*. G. G. Scholem Festschrift (Jerusalem, 1967), pp. 57ff. See also p. 391, n. 87.   [57] Josephus, *Ant.* xx, 213.   [58] Josephus, *Ant.* xx, 214.
[59] Josephus, *Life*, 13–16.   [60] Josephus, *Ant.* xx, 215.
[61] Josephus, *BJ* ii, 277.   [62] See pp. 377f.

27 Paul: The Last Phase

1

The plea which James, Peter and John urged on Paul and Barnabas towards the end of their conference in Jerusalem about A.D. 46, 'Please go on remembering the poor' (Gal. 2:10), found an eager response. Indeed, the form in which the plea was expressed implied that Paul and Barnabas had already begun to remember 'the poor' —the rank and file of the Jerusalem church—before this conference; and the evidence of Acts is in agreement with this reading of the situation, for it records the famine-relief mission of these two leaders when the Christians of Syrian Antioch appointed them to convey their donation to Jerusalem.[1]

How seriously Paul continued to take this responsibility is plain from the importance which he attached to the 'collection for the saints'[2] which we find him organizing throughout his Gentile mission-field towards the end of his Ephesian ministry. This collection appears to have been associated in his mind with the impending completion of his work in the Aegean lands. At an undefined point in the course of his Ephesian ministry 'Paul', says Luke, 're-solved in the Spirit to pass through Macedonia and Achaia and go to Jerusalem, saying, "After I have been there, I must also see Rome"' (Acts 19:21). It is only with the help of Paul's epistles that we can interpret Luke's words as relating to (i) Paul's realization that his work in the Aegean lands was almost done, (ii) his plan to embark on the evangelization of Spain and to visit Rome *en route* (while Rome is the goal of Luke's history it was only a transit point, or perhaps an advanced base, in Paul's strategy), and (iii)

[1] See p. 270.
[2] By 'the saints' Paul means in the first instance the members of the mother-church of Jerusalem; if he calls Gentile Christians 'saints' (as he frequently does), it is because they have become 'fellow citizens with the saints' (Eph. 2:19). See further K. F. Nickle, *The Collection: A Study in Paul's Strategy* (London, 1966).

his resolve, before setting out for Rome and Spain, to go to Jerusalem with the contributions of the Gentile churches. Luke says nothing explicit about these contributions, although there are hints in his narrative which, in the light of the epistles, we can recognize as veiled allusions to them.

The first reference to the collection in the epistles is in I Cor. 16:1 where it is introduced in such a way as to suggest that the Corinthian Christians had asked about it in their letter to Paul. 'We have heard about the collection you are organizing for Jerusalem', they wrote; 'please tell us what action you wish us to take'.[3] Paul's reply was: 'I am giving you the same instructions as I have already given to the churches of Galatia'. The Galatian churches had probably received their instructions by letter—a later letter than the Epistle to the Galatians—rather than by word of mouth from Paul when he passed through their territory on his way to Ephesus in A.D. 52 (Acts 18:23). 'On the first day of each week', he went on, 'you should set aside a sum of money, in proportion to your income, and store it up so that, when I come to you, the accumulated sum will be ready and there will be no need to have a special emergency collection. Then, when I come to you, you must appoint delegates to carry your gift to Jerusalem, and I will provide them with letters of introduction—indeed, I may judge it advisable to go with them myself'. He then tells them that he will visit them after passing through Macedonia—this is in harmony with Luke's statement in Acts 19:21—but that he proposes to remain in Ephesus till Pentecost. This Pentecost is perhaps the Pentecost of A.D. 55 (about seven weeks after Paul wrote),[4] but we should probably reckon with some dislocation of his plans.[5] No more is heard of the collection until a later phase of his Corinthian correspondence. Naturally the strained relations between him and a substantial part of the church in Corinth made it impolitic to mention the collection until mutual confidence was restored; accordingly, he reverts to the subject at the end of his letter of reconciliation (II Cor. 1–9). This letter was sent to Corinth from Macedonia, and Paul introduces the subject

[3] Cf. J. C. Hurd, *The Origin of 1 Corinthians* (London, 1965), pp. 200ff.
[4] The theme of firstfruits and harvest in I Cor. 15:20ff would be specially appropriate at Passovertide (cf. also I Cor. 5:7f).
[5] He may indeed have paid the 'sorrowful visit' implied in II Cor. 2:1, etc., after Pentecost of A.D. 55, but this visit led to a change of plan, as the context from II Cor. 1:15 onwards makes plain.

by enlarging on the generosity of the Macedonian churches. Paul
may have wondered whether he ought to ask the Macedonian
churches to contribute, because of their present critical poverty,
but they took the initiative and insisted that their gifts should be
accepted towards the relief of the poverty of their fellow-Christians
in Jerusalem. They wanted to know how the other churches in
Paul's mission-field were responding to the appeal, and Paul—always ready to boast of his converts behind their backs, however
severely he might have to criticize them to their faces—told them
that the churches of Corinth and other parts of Achaia had been
ready since the previous year. In his letter he tells the Corinthians
how he has been boasting about them; he is sure they will not let
him down. He is sending Titus and two others (one of whom may
have been Luke)[6] to pay them a further visit and help them to
complete the collection, so that, when he himself arrives, accompanied probably by delegates from the Macedonian churches, neither he nor the Corinthians will be embarrassed by any discrepancy
between his boasting and the actual situation.

Paul expresses himself diplomatically, insisting that the whole
merit of any donation to 'the collection for the saints' lies in its being given 'not as an exaction but as a willing gift' (II Cor. 9:5).
Nevertheless some of the Corinthians who were not in whole-
hearted sympathy with the collection must have felt that he was
putting them on the spot. Echoes of this reaction may be detected
in the later chapters of II Corinthians. They could find no fault
with him on the score of probity. Paul plainly had a keen sense
of delicacy where money was concerned, and saw to it that the
whole procedure of gathering the collection and transmitting it to
Jerusalem should be above suspicion. And Titus was as scrupulous
in the matter as Paul himself. True enough, said some, but that was
just Paul's cunning: 'granting that I myself did not burden you, I
was crafty, you say, and got the better of you by guile' (II Cor.
12:16). So Titus evidently told Paul when he reported on this
further visit.

[6] The 'brother whose praise in the gospel is spread through all the churches'
(II Cor. 8:18) was identified with Luke by Origen (*ap.* Euseb. *HE* vi, 25. 6),
but on unconvincing grounds; a better case than Origen's could be made out
(cf. A. Souter, 'A Suggested Relationship between Titus and Luke', *ExT* 18
[1906–7], p. 285; 'The Relationship between Titus and Luke', *ibid.*, pp. 335f).

Paul assures them that he has no intention of being a burden or
an embarrassment to them when he comes; it is their love, not
their money, that he seeks. What the response was when he arrived in Corinth for his three months' winter visit at the end of
A.D. 56 we are not told definitely. But in the course of that visit
he told the Roman Christians in his letter to them that he must
go to Jerusalem 'with aid for the saints' before he can carry out
his plan of visiting the capital on his way to Spain. He explains
that 'Macedonia and Achaia[7] have been pleased to make some
contribution for the poor among the saints at Jerusalem; they were
pleased to do it, and indeed they are in debt to them, for if the
Gentiles have come to share in their spiritual blessings, they ought
also to be of service to them in material blessings' (Rom. 15:25-7).

The collection was not designed by Paul only as something
that would forge a bond of fellowship between his Gentile mission and the mother-church, greatly as he desired this. In his eyes
it was fraught with eschatological meaning. It was the tangible
'fruit' of the Aegean phase of his ministry which was now completed; his ministry thus far would be 'sealed' by the presentation
of this 'fruit' at Jerusalem. In a sense the money collected might
be called the offering of the Gentiles, but when Paul tells the Romans of his aim 'that the offering of the Gentiles may be acceptable, sanctified by the Holy Spirit', he is speaking of the Gentile
believers themselves as the offering which he himself is presenting
'in the priestly service of the gospel of God' (Rom. 15:16). The
collection for Jerusalem was but an outward and visible sign of
this more sacred offering.

In Hebrew prophecy the ingathering of the Jews from the lands
of their dispersion is occasionally described in terms of the Gentiles'
escorting them to Jerusalem as an 'offering to Yahweh' (Isa. 66:20;
cf. Zeph. 3:10).[8] But Paul's vision is more magnificent and surprising; to him Gentiles are an integral part of the people of God,
and since the ingathering of the Gentiles was his special respon-

[7] The reference to Macedonia and Achaia alone does not necessarily mean
that Asia and Galatia had dropped out of the scheme; Macedonia and Achaia
were the two provinces chiefly in Paul's thought at this time.
[8] Cf. also *Ps. Sol.* 17:34, where the Gentiles are foreseen as coming to Jerusalem to see the Messiah's glory, 'bringing as gifts her sons who had fainted'
(see p. 126).

sibility the offering which he would present to the Lord consisted
not of Jews from the Gentile lands but of Gentiles themselves.

Nor did Paul think of presenting this offering anywhere but in
Jerusalem. He could not take all his Gentile converts there with
him, but he could take representative converts from the various
provinces of his apostolic service; and his fellow-travellers who
are named in Acts 20:4 probably went to Jerusalem in this capacity as well as to carry their respective churches' contributions.
(Is there a special, or even unhappy, significance in the absence
of any Corinthian representative from Luke's list?)[9]

When Paul told the Roman Christians of his impending Jerusalem visit and its purpose, he asked for their prayers 'that I may
be delivered from the unbelievers in Judaea, and that my service
for Jerusalem may be acceptable to the saints' (Rom. 15:31).
These misgivings were not allayed as the party approached Jerusalem, for at one port after another at which they put in the
resident Christians tried to dissuade him from proceeding, and
'prophets' in the various churches warned him that 'imprisonment
and affliction' awaited him in Jerusalem (Acts 20:23; 21:4, 10–14).
But Paul would not be deterred; Luke describes Paul's last journey to Jerusalem in terms which recall his earlier description of
how Jesus 'set his face' to go there (Luke 9:51).

Impelled by a sense of spiritual constraint,[10] Paul entered Jerusalem with his friends, and there they were welcomed by James
and his fellow-elders.[11] No doubt these Jerusalem leaders were
grateful for the Gentiles' gift, but they were concerned about rumours which had come to Judaea which suggested that Paul not
only interpreted in the most liberal manner the provisions of the
earlier apostolic decree regarding Gentile Christians but encouraged Jewish Christians to give up circumcising their children and
observing the ancestral customs. James and his colleagues plainly
did not believe these rumours, but since the disciples in Jerusalem
included so many who were 'zealots for the law'—as Paul himself
had once been—they suggested that Paul should give the lie pub-

---

[9] The list comprises members of the churches of Macedonia (Beroea and
Thessalonica), Galatia (Derbe) and Asia. Perhaps Luke himself, who accompanied them, represented Philippi.

[10] Cf. Acts 20:22, 'I am going to Jerusalem, bound in the Spirit'.

[11] Acts 21:17ff.

licly to the rumours by showing himself to be an observant Jew. This he could do if he associated himself with four of the Jerusalem disciples who were about to discharge a Nazirite vow in the Temple, taking part in the appropriate sacrifice and paying their expenses. This was regarded as a pious action—we recall that it was counted to Herod Agrippa the elder for righteousness that he paid the expenses of Nazirites[12]—and Paul himself had undertaken such a vow on at least one earlier occasion.[13] He would have no conscientious difficulties about being a Jew to the Jews[14] in this particular way, whatever might be thought of the practical wisdom of the action at this juncture.

In fact, Paul may have accepted the advice of James and the other elders the more readily because it would give him an opportunity of rendering an account of his stewardship in the Temple where, over twenty years before, the Lord appeared to him in a vision and sent him 'far away to the Gentiles' (Acts 22:21). The men who had come to Jerusalem with him could not accompany him there, but there he himself by an act of devotion could consummate 'the offering of the Gentiles' who had believed through his ministry thus far, and seek grace and strength for the new ministry on which he planned to enter in the Western Mediterranean. He might even have hoped that on a later occasion, when the contemplated evangelization of Spain had been completed in its turn, he would again visit the Temple and render a further account of his stewardship, perhaps the final account. If this final account marked the coming in of 'the full number of the Gentiles' which would precipitate the return and salvation of 'all Israel', then Jerusalem would witness the climax of saving history (Rom. 11:25-7).

2

Paul could not foresee, at the moment of his entry into the Temple with the four Nazirites, that the sequel would be far from corresponding with his high hopes. While he was engaged in the ceremony, some Asian Jews, visiting Jerusalem for the Pentecost festival, raised a hue and cry against him and charged him with

[12] See p. 260.   [13] See p. 318 (Acts 18:18).   [14] I Cor. 9:20.

profaning the sacred precincts by taking Gentiles within the forbidden bounds. For Gentiles to trespass into the inner courts was a capital offence,[15] and so would be the aiding and abetting of such a trespass. Paul was set upon by an angry crowd, who dragged him into the outer court and would have made an end of him there and then had he not been rescued in the nick of time by soldiers from the Antonia garrison, who intervened when their commanding officer heard the uproar and carried Paul shoulder-high up the steps leading from the outer court to the fortress.

The military tribune in charge of the garrison, who was the chief representative of Roman power in Jerusalem in the procurator's absence, had to deal as best he could with this situation. At first he thought Paul was the Egyptian agitator who had caused considerable trouble a year or two previously,[16] but when he found him to be a Jew from Tarsus, he brought him before the Sanhedrin, hoping that so he might discover the cause of the uproar against him. The Sanhedrin could not agree about him, although the high priest Ananias made no attempt to conceal his animosity.[17] Paul's life seemed to be endangered if he remained in Jerusalem, so the military tribune, not caring to be responsible for the safety of so unpopular a Roman citizen, sent him under armed escort to Felix at Caearea.

After a few days the high priest led a deputation to Caesarea to press two charges against Paul: the particular charge of violating the sanctity of the Temple and the more general one of being a ringleader of the Nazarene sect and a subverter of public peace, a perfect pest throughout the whole Jewish dispersion. Paul returned a firm plea of Not Guilty on both counts. 'This I admit to you', he said, 'that according to the Way, which they call a sect, I worship the God of our fathers, believing everything laid down by the law or written in the prophets, having a hope in God which these themselves accept, that there will be a resurrection of both the just and the unjust.[18] So I always take pains to have a clear

[15] See p. 201 with n. 19. [16] See p. 340.
[17] See pp. 65, 348.
[18] This is the only place in the New Testament where Paul is expressly credited with a belief in the resurrection of the unjust as well as of the just; there is, of course, no improbability in his holding this belief, as did many Pharisees, on the basis of one possible interpretation of Dan. 12:2; but, as it happens, it nowhere finds expression in his extant letters.

conscience toward God and toward men. Now after some years I came to bring to my nation alms and offerings. As I was doing this, they found me purified in the temple, without any crowd or tumult . . .' (Acts 24:14–18).

A specially interesting feature of this defence is the mention of 'alms and offerings'. This is the only reference in Acts to the collection, and from it we should gather that the money was designed for the Jews of Judaea as a whole. Paul certainly regarded 'the saints' as the true Israel, comprising those who were Jews inwardly; but the vague generality of the reference suggests that apologetic interests have dictated the form in which Luke has summarized Paul's defence. If the collection was represented by Paul's accusers as a diversion into the wrong channels of money that should have gone to the Temple treasury in Jerusalem, part of the proceeds of the annual half-shekel whose collection and safe-conduct were authorized and protected by Roman law,[19] Luke would wish to be careful about the way he introduced it into his narrative.

Felix does not appear to have taken the charges against Paul too seriously, but he deferred judgement—hoping, says Luke, to receive a bribe for acquitting him. Perhaps Felix knew enough about the collection to imagine that a man who had access to financial resources in Macedonia and Achaia would find no difficulty in paying for his release. But the months slipped by, and while it was enjoyable, or at least amusing, for Felix and Drusilla to summon Paul for religious conversation it did not help Paul. Then Felix was recalled in A.D. 59, and his successor Festus found himself with a problem on his hands for which nothing in his previous experience had prepared him.

Festus reopened the case, with every intention of proceeding in accordance with the strictest standards of Roman justice. But when he spoke of holding the inquiry in Jerusalem, and implied that he might treat the Sanhedrin as his *consilium*,[20] Paul became alarmed lest the new governor's inexperience might put him into the power

[19] The seriousness with which the Romans safeguarded this fund appears clearly in Cicero's speech *Pro Flacco* (59 B.C.): Flaccus, Roman governor of Asia, confiscated some of the money collected by Asian Jews for this purpose and was prosecuted at Rome for his actions.
[20] Acts 25:9; cf. A. N. Sherwin-White, *Roman Society and Roman Law in the New Testament* (Oxford, 1963), p. 67.

of his enemies. Accordingly, availing himself of a Roman citizen's privilege, he made a momentous decision. 'Standing before Caesar's tribunal', he said, 'I stand where I ought to be tried . . . If then I am a wrongdoer, and have committed anything for which I deserve to die, I do not seek to escape death; but if there is nothing in their charges against me, no one can give me up to them. I appeal to Caesar' (Acts 25:10f).

The citizen's right of appeal (*prouocatio*) to the emperor appears to have grown out of the earlier right of appeal to the sovereign people. According to Dio Cassius, Augustus in 30 B.C. was granted the right to judge on appeal.[21] A few years later there was enacted the *lex Iulia de ui publica*,[22] which forbade any magistrate to kill, scourge, chain, torture or even sentence a Roman citizen who had announced his intention to appeal, or prevent him from going to Rome to lodge his appeal there within a fixed time.[23] It has been concluded[24] that, from the date of this enactment, a Roman citizen anywhere in the Empire was protected against a magistrate's arbitrary infliction of summary punishment (*coercitio*), although a provincial magistrate might deal with cases which involved a plain breach of established statute law. By the beginning of the second century A.D. it evidently became the regular practice for citizens in the provinces, charged with offences not covered by statute law, to be sent to Rome almost automatically, without having to take the initiative in appealing to Caesar.[25] But there was a steady erosion of citizen privileges as the number of citizens increased throughout the second century[26]—a tendency which cul-

[21] *Hist.* li, 19. The Greek phrase is ἔκκλητον δικάζειν, which may be the equivalent of *ex prouocatione cognoscere*.

[22] Its title indicates that it was introduced either by Julius Caesar or by Augustus: reasons for dating it under Augustus, and after 23 B.C., are given by A. H. M. Jones, *Studies in Roman Government and Law* (Oxford, 1960), pp. 97f.

[23] *Digest*, xlviii, 6, 7; Paulus, *Sententiae*, v, 26. 1.

[24] By A. H. M. Jones, *Studies in Roman Government and Law*, p. 59.

[25] Cf. Pliny, *Ep.* x, 96. 4 (see p. 423).

[26] In A.D. 177 the Roman citizens among the Christians rounded up in the cities of the Rhone valley were not sent to Rome for trial, as those in Bithynia had been 65 years before; they were kept in prison until the emperor's ruling could be obtained (Euseb., *HE* v, 1. 44), and even after he had ruled that they were to be beheaded, instead of being tortured to death like the others, one of them, Attalus, was exposed to the wild beasts because the mob so demanded (*HE* v, 1. 50).

minated in A.D. 212 with Caracalla's extension of the franchise to all freemen in the Empire. In this as in other respects the picture given in Acts is true to the period with which the narrative deals; Luke's account of Paul's appeal not only fits in with what is known of the situation in the mid-first century A.D. but is worthy to be accepted as a substantial contribution to the available evidence.

The provincial judge was obliged to send to Rome an explanatory statement of the case (*litterae dimissoriae*) along with the accused man, and the inexperienced Festus was glad to be helped in drafting this document by the younger Agrippa, who with his sister Berenice paid the procurator a complimentary visit soon after his arrival in the province.[27] Agrippa sought and was granted an opportunity of hearing Paul for himself, and agreed with Festus that he could not reasonably be convicted on any of the charges brought against him: indeed, he might have been discharged there and then had he not taken the matter out of Festus's hands by appealing to Caesar.[28]

3

Why did Paul appeal to Caesar? He did not appeal while Felix was in office, presumably because Felix had virtually decided on his innocence and was simply postponing his formal acquittal and release. One day, Paul might reasonably have hoped, Felix's procrastination would come to an end and Paul would be discharged and be able to carry out his compulsorily deferred plan of visiting Rome and the west. But with Felix's recall and his supersession by Festus a new and dangerous situation developed; hence Paul's appeal.

From what we know of Paul, we may be sure that his own safety was not the chief motive of his appeal to Caesar. What he had most at heart in this as in other situations was the interest of the gospel. Seven or eight years previously he had experienced the benevolent neutrality of Roman law in the decision of Gallio at Corinth.[29] Why should not the verdict of the supreme court at Rome be equally favourable? Besides, even a less intelligent man than Paul must have realized that the considerations which had weighed with Gallio would not be valid much longer. Gallio had ruled in effect that

[27] Acts 25:26f.   [28] Acts 26:32.   [29] See p. 316.

what Paul preached was a variety of Judaism, and therefore not
forbidden by Roman law. But, thanks in large measure to Paul's
own activity, it would soon be impossible to regard Christianity as
a variety of Judaism, since it was becoming manifestly more Gentile
than Jewish. A favourable hearing from the emperor in Rome might
win recognition for Christianity, if not as the true religion of Israel
(which in Paul's eyes it was), at least as a *religio licita* in its own
right.[30] Not only so: if Caesar in person heard Paul's defence, what
might the outcome not be? The younger Agrippa had politely declined to admit the logic of Paul's argument, but Gentiles had regularly shown themselves more amenable to the gospel than Jews,
and a Roman emperor might be more easily won than a Jewish
client-king. It would be precarious to set limits to Paul's high hopes,
however impracticable they may appear in retrospect to us, who
know more about Nero than Paul knew in A.D. 59.

To Rome, then, Paul was sent, under the custody of a centurion
named Julius, perhaps a member of the corps of *frumentarii* who
were charged with the organization of the Roman grain supply[31]—
if we may make such an inference from the fact that the voyage, or
the greater part of it, was made on board a grain-ship plying between Alexandria and Italy, on which Julius exercised considerable
authority.[32]

The adventures on the way to Rome—especially the disabling of
the grain-ship and its wreck at Malta—are vividly described by
Luke, whose account of the voyage remains one of our most important primary documents for the knowledge of ancient seaman-
ship.[33] The ship's company spent the three winter months in Malta,

[30] Cf. S. L. Guterman, *Religious Toleration and Persecution in Ancient Rome*
(London, 1951), pp. 121f. Cf. p. 316 with n. 40.
[31] T. Mommsen, *Gesammelte Schriften* vi = *Historische Schriften* III (Berlin,
1910), pp. 546ff, followed by W. M. Ramsay, *St. Paul the Traveller and the
Roman Citizen* (London, 1920[14]), pp. 315, 348, takes Julius to be a member
of the corps of *frumentarii* in the later sense (not attested before the 2nd century A.D.) of the corps of centurions who served as liaison officers between the
capital and the armies in the imperial provinces, thus interpreting the 'Augustan
cohort' of Acts 27:1.   [32] Acts 27:6, 38.
[33] Cf. J. Smith, *The Voyage and Shipwreck of St. Paul* (London, 1880[4]).
M. Dibelius's conclusion that 'truly literary criticism will lead us to suppose
that the nautical description is taken from the numerous accounts of sea-voyages
in literature and not from experience' is coupled with a stricture on 'the older
school of criticism, which thinks only of the event, and not of the account'
(*Studies in the Acts of the Apostles* [London, 1956], p. 107); this stricture

and early in A.D. 60 continued the journey to Italy in another ship of Alexandria, which had wintered in the harbour of Valletta They disembarked at Puteoli, from which they reached Rome by the Via Appia. There, according to the Western text, Paul was handed over by the centurion to an official called the stratopedarch, or camp-commandant. Which camp is intended is not plain—it may have been the *castra peregrinorum* on the Caelian hill,[34] or the headquarters of the Praetorian Guard. In any case, Paul was allowed a form of house-arrest, 'outside the camp', as some Western authorities add (Acts 28:16), with a soldier to guard him. He was thus free to receive visitors, although he was not at liberty to move about himself.

According to Luke, among his earliest visitors was a deputation of Roman Jews, whose debate with Paul forms the last scene in Acts—plainly with programmatic intent. The pattern of Jewish refusal of the gospel and Gentile acceptance of it, which has recurred earlier in Luke's history, unfolds itself once more, and definitively, in Rome, with Paul's last word (after quoting Isa. 6:10):[35] 'Take knowledge, then, that this salvation of God has been sent to the Gentiles; *they* will listen to it' (Acts 28:28).

Luke then concludes his history with the summary statement that Paul 'lived there two whole years at his own expense, and welcomed all who came to him, preaching the kingdom of God and teaching about the Lord Jesus Christ quite openly and unhindered' (Acts 28:30f). He has achieved the aim of his writing when he has brought Paul to Rome and left him there carrying on his apostolic task without let or hindrance under the eyes of the imperial authorities. But he has left us asking questions which he did not regard it as his business to answer, and to which no other writer provides a satisfactory answer.

4

What happened to Paul? Did his case come to trial, or was it allowed to lapse? Was he convicted or acquitted? If it did come to trial, did Nero himself conduct it?

---

might be countered with the charge that it is equally onesided to think only of the account and not of the event.

[34] The headquarters of legionary officers on furlough in Rome.

[35] Cf. the application of this passage in Mark 4:11f (and Synoptic parallels) and John 12:40.

From the fact that Paul appealed to Caesar, it would not necessarily follow that Caesar heard the appeal in person. According to Tacitus, Nero announced at the beginning of his principate that he would not judge cases *in propria persona*, as Claudius had done; and during his first eight years he generally delegated them to others.[36] It was evidently a new departure for Nero when in 62 he himself judged the case of Fabricius Veiento.[37] Thus if Paul came to trial before the early part of 62 (towards the end of his two years' detention) his case was probably heard by someone other than Nero.[38] This person might be the prefect of the Praetorian Guard, as W. M. Ramsay suggested, 'representing the Emperor in his capacity as the fountain of justice, together with the assessors and high officers of court'.[39] If it was the prefect of the Praetorian Guard, it would make a mighty difference whether it was the honest Afranius Burrus or the infamous Tigellinus, who succeeded him in 62. Chronological probability would point to Burrus rather than Tigellinus;[40] but we cannot be sure that, if indeed Paul's case was delegated at all, it was delegated to the praetorian prefect.

As for the 'two years' during which Paul remained under house-arrest in Rome, attempts have been made to relate this period to a supposed statutory time-limit of eighteen months within which the prosecutors were obliged to appear, or at least to give notice of their intention to proceed with the case. On the one hand there is the suggestion that the prosecutors did give such notice and duly arrived in Rome, that they pressed their case successfully, that Paul was condemned and executed as a disturber of the peace of the provinces.[41] On the other hand it has been argued that the case did not come to trial because the prosecutors failed to take action within the statutory period, realizing that if local pressure had been ineffective in Judaea, the chances of success would be even

[36] Tacitus, *Ann*. xiii, 4. 2.   [37] Tacitus, *Ann*. xiv, 50. 2.
[38] Cf. A. N. Sherwin-White, *Roman Society and Roman Law in the New Testament*, p. 112.
[39] W. M. Ramsay, *St. Paul the Traveller*, p. 357.
[40] Sofonius Tigellinus's succession to the office on the death of Burrus probably came after the expiry of the two years of Acts 28:30. For three years (A.D. 62–65) Faenius Rufus was joint-prefect with Tigellinus, but Tigellinus was the more powerful of the two (Tacitus, *Ann*. xiv, 51. 5f; xv, 50. 4).
[41] Cf. J. V. Bartlet, 'Two New Testament Problems: 1. St. Paul's Fate at Rome', *Expositor*, series viii, 5 (1913), pp. 464ff.

smaller in Rome, and fearing that they might incur the penalties decreed by Roman law against frivolous prosecutors.[42]

On this last point it should be said that no prosecution would be so frivolous as one in which the prosecutors failed to appear; and Roman law insisted that they should appear. Apart from that, the hypothesis of the eighteen-month statutory period lacks substance. It is based on a papyrus document which records an imperial edict fixing a time-limit of eighteen months for criminal cases from the provinces submitted to the emperor either by way of appeal or by reference as to a court of first instance.[43] As Mommsen recognized,[44] the edict belongs to the third century, and the 'appeal' which it has in view is the later process of *appellatio* against a sentence already passed, not the earlier process of *prouocatio*, which prevented the court of first instance from trying the case at all.[45] There does not appear to be first-century evidence for any procedure permitting a case to lapse automatically by default. The available evidence indicates that everything was done to compel the appearance of prosecutors and defendants and to prevent the abandonment of charges. A prosecutor who did not put in an appearance would be penalized, but this would not involve the automatic discharge of the defendant.

The prolongation of Paul's stay in Rome over two full years could have been due to congestion of court business as much as anything. At the end of the two years he was presumably either released or condemned—unless those are right who suppose that the end of the two years marked the completion of Luke's history and that Paul was still in custody when he published it (but this is not the natural inference from his language). 'Perhaps', as Mr. Sherwin-

---

[42] Cf. K. Lake, 'What was the End of St. Paul's Trial?', *Interpreter* 5 (1908–9), pp. 147ff; W. M. Ramsay, 'The Imprisonment and Supposed Trial of St. Paul in Rome', *Expositor*, series viii, 5 (1913), pp. 264ff (the article to which Bartlet's article cited in the previous note was a reply), reprinted in *The Teaching of Paul in Terms of the Present Day* (London, 1913), pp. 346ff; H. J. Cadbury, 'Roman Law and the Trial of Paul', in *The Beginnings of Christianity*, ed. Foakes Jackson and K. Lake, v (London, 1933), pp. 297ff, especially 326ff.

[43] *BGU* II, 628 *recto*; for the text cf. H. J. Cadbury in *The Beginnings of Christianity* v, pp. 333f; H. Conzelmann, *Die Apostelgeschichte* (Tübingen, 1963), pp. 157f.

[44] T. Mommsen, *Le Droit Pénal Romain* II (Paris, 1907), p. 158, n. 5.

[45] For the distinction see A. H. M. Jones, *Studies in Roman Government and Law*, p. 57.

White says, 'Paul benefited from the clemency of Nero, and secured a merely casual release. But', he adds, 'there is no necessity to construe Acts to mean that he was released at all'.[46] If he was not released, but convicted and executed, then his martyrdom was not, as has been traditionally held, an incident in the imperial assault on the Christians of Rome which followed the great fire of A.D. 64, for Paul's two years of detention in Rome cannot be dated as late as this. This is no argument against dating his execution as early as 62, if the evidence points in this direction. But the evidence is so scanty as to be quite inconclusive. If, however, his detention was followed immediately by his conviction and execution, Luke's failure to mention this is very odd; any apologetic advantage that his omission of the fact might have been thought to bring would be more than offset by the general knowledge that the case went against Paul.[47]

5

Something of our indebtedness to Luke's narrative may be assessed from the slough of uncertainty in which we are engulfed as soon as his narrative is no longer available to us. The evidence of Paul's 'captivity epistles', such as it is, is ambiguous because of lack of agreement about the time and place at which each of them was written. In Phil. 1:19–26 release from prison and a further visit to Philippi are expected and hoped for—but the Roman provenance of Philippians is particularly doubtful. If it was from Rome that Paul wrote to Philemon, then he envisages not a continuation of his westward journey to Spain but a return to the province of Asia. The Colossian Christians are urged to pray 'that God may open to us a door for the word, to declare the mystery of Christ, on account of which I am in prison, that I may make it clear, as I ought to speak'

[46] A. N. Sherwin-White, *Roman Society and Roman Law in the New Testament*, p. 119; his whole lecture on 'Paul and the Proconsul Gallio, and Paul at Rome' (pp. 99–119) is most important for the subject of his chapter.

[47] Immediate acquittal and immediate execution do not exhaust the possibilities; his *libera custodia* might have been replaced by a much stricter confinement, such as is implied in his reference to Onesiphorus, who 'was not ashamed of my chains, but when he arrived in Rome, he searched for me eagerly and found me' (II Tim. 1:16f), or he might have been exiled (in I Clem. 5:6 exile is included in a list of Paul's afflictions).

(Col. 4:3f), and a similar request for prayer is made in Eph. 6:18–20, 'that utterance may be given me in opening my mouth boldly to proclaim the mystery of the gospel, for which I am an ambassador in chains; that I may declare it boldly, as I ought to speak'. These words might refer not only to Paul's general apostolic activity but to his expected appearance before the supreme court, if not before Caesar himself. It was of the utmost importance—for the sake of the gospel rather than for his own release—that on this occasion the right words should be spoken in the right way. And an answer to these prayers could perhaps be recognized in II Tim. 4:16f: 'At my first defence no one took my part; all deserted me. May it not be charged against them! But the Lord stood by me and gave me strength to proclaim the word fully, that all the Gentiles might hear it. So I was rescued from the lion's mouth'.[48]

The bearing of the Pastoral Epistles on Paul's last movements is uncertain, not only because of doubts about their date and authorship but also because their contents may not be chronologically and geographically homogeneous.[49] It has been maintained that most of Paul's movements to which reference is made in them can be dated between the closing part of his Ephesian ministry and his last voyage to Judaea;[50] it has been maintained, on the other hand, that these movements belong to the interval between the end of Paul's two years' custody in Rome (supposing him to have been released) and his death some time after the great fire and ensuing outbreak of persecution.[51] In the latter event, one would have to suppose that he revisited the Eastern Mediterranean. A further visit to Ephesus is not necessarily implied in I Tim. 1:3 ('As I urged you when I was going to Macedonia, remain at Ephesus . . .'), for Paul's departure from Ephesus mentioned here could conceivably be the

[48] The reference to his 'first defence' implies that these words were written between the *prima* and *secunda actio*. The *prima actio* or preliminary investigation had apparently resulted in an inconclusive verdict and a deferment of the case for further inquiry, but Paul has no reason to hope that the verdict of the *secunda actio* will be other than adverse.

[49] Cf. P. N. Harrison, *The Problem of the Pastoral Epistles* (Oxford, 1921), p. 109.

[50] Cf. J. V. Bartlet, 'The Historic Setting of the Pastoral Epistles', *Expositor*, series viii, 5 (1913), pp. 28–36, 161–7, 256–63, 325–47.

[51] Cf. J. N. D. Kelly, *A Commentary on the Pastoral Epistles* (London, 1963), pp. 6ff; C. F. D. Moule, 'The Problem of the Pastoral Epistles: A Reappraisal', *BJRL* 47 (1964–5), pp. 430ff, especially pp. 434, 450.

occasion referred to in Acts 20:1. But II Tim. 4:19 ('Trophimus I left ill at Miletus') cannot refer to the Milesian visit of Acts 20:15ff, for on that occasion Trophimus continued to travel to Jerusalem with Paul. A visit by Paul to Crete is implied in Titus 1:5; this could with difficulty be accommodated within the framework of Paul's career before A.D. 62 as it can be reconstructed from other data, and was evidently more extended than anything that can be fitted into the coasting along the south shore of that island on the way to Rome, with a brief stay at Fair Havens, described in Acts 27:27ff. Titus's mission to Dalmatia (II Tim. 4:10) is probably represented as later than his activity as apostolic delegate in Crete. The combined evidence of the Pastoral Epistles implies visits by Paul to Crete, Asia Minor, Macedonia and Epirus—but at what time or in what order must be matters of precarious reconstruction.

There is no solid evidence that he was able to carry out his plan of evangelizing Spain. The Muratorian list of New Testament books, compiled at Rome towards the end of the second century, refers to his setting out from Rome for Spain as something that is not recorded in Acts—but this reference is probably based on the apocryphal *Acts of Peter*, a romance written some ten years before, and quite devoid of historical worth.[52] A century earlier Clement of Rome reminds the Corinthian church how Paul, 'having preached in the east and the west, attained the noble renown won for him by his faith, teaching righteousness to the whole world, and reaching the farthest limit of the west [or, reaching his goal in the west]'.[53] This last expression, it might be argued, coming from a man who was resident and writing in Rome, would (however translated) most naturally point to a place farther west than Rome.[54]

[52] The Muratorian fragmentist evidently tries to explain why Luke in the canonical Acts does not record two important incidents found in the *Acts of Peter*—Paul's departure from Rome for Spain and Peter's martyrdom: his explanation is that Luke recorded only those things that took place under his own observation! These two incidents are related in the seventh-century Latin portion of the *Acts of Peter* preserved at Vercelli; cf. R. McL. Wilson (ed.), *New Testament Apocrypha*, ii (London, 1965), pp. 279ff.   [53] I Clem. 5:6f.

[54] Cf. W. K. Lowther Clarke, quoted in J. Stevenson (ed.), *A New Eusebius* (London, 1957), pp. 4f. On the meaning of τὸ τέρμα τῆς δύσεως see P. N. Harrison, *The Problem of the Pastoral Epistles*, pp. 107f; he translates it 'his western goal', which certainly fits the athletic figure which Clement sustains throughout this passage, and remarks that 'the goal of this race [Paul's] was certainly not Spain, but Rome, from whatever point in the world-stadium one happened to be regarding it'. This last statement is too dogmatic, in view of

Clement, however, does not expressly mention Spain, and his rhetorical and allusive style makes it difficult to draw from his language straightforward historical inferences such as might otherwise have been made from an author writing only some thirty years after Paul's death.

'Reaching the farthest limit of the west', Clement continues, 'he bore witness before rulers, and thus passed from the world, and went to the holy place, having shown himself a wonderful pattern of patience'.[55] No city other than Rome claims to be the place of Paul's martyrdom. Gaius of Rome, writing to the Montanist Proclus late in the second century, says that he can point out Paul's 'trophy', the monument marking the scene of his death, on the road from Rome to Ostia[56]—no doubt near the spot now marked by the basilica of San Paolo fuori le Mura. Contemporary with Gaius was Dionysius, bishop of Corinth, who mentions in a letter to the Roman church that Peter and Paul, both of whom were associated (*happily* associated) with his own church,[57] thereafter taught in Rome, where they were martyred about the same time. Paul's martyrdom in Rome under Nero is said to have been expressly attested by Origen in the third volume of his commentary on Genesis.[58] Summing up these earlier writers and the consensus of tradition, Eusebius says: 'They record that under Nero, Paul was beheaded at Rome itself, and Peter likewise was crucified, and this record is accredited by the attachment, until this day, of the names of Peter and Paul to the burial-places there'.[59]

Some time in the second half of Nero's reign, we may confidently say, Paul was tried, sentenced and executed at Rome.

---

the fact that Spain, not Rome, was Paul's own goal; but Clement's language is best understood to mean that Paul, having reached the τέρμα τῆς δύσεως, suffered martyrdom there.

[55] I Clem. 5:7.

[56] *Apud* Euseb. *HE* ii, 25. 7. The *'trophy'* (Gk. τροπαῖον) is the monument commemorating the scene of his victory. See pp. 406f.

[57] Eusebius, *HE* ii, 25. 8. See p. 405.

[58] Eusebius, *HE* iii, 1. 3.   [59] *HE* ii, 25. 5.

28 End of Church and Temple in Jerusalem

1

The fortunes of Judaean Christianity during the twenty years between the promulgation of the Jerusalem decree and the destruction of the Temple and city by the Romans under Titus are for the most part unchronicled. Luke's narrative mentions Jerusalem during these years only when Paul visits it, and no account of the Jewish mission comparable to Luke's account of Paul's Gentile mission has survived, even if such a thing ever existed.

In the early fifties of the first century James the Just appears as the undisputed leader of the Jerusalem church. A few years before, he is named along with Peter and John as one of the 'pillars' of the church.[1] But one of the enigmas of apostolic history is what happened to the original apostles who survived to mid-century. Of most of them we know absolutely nothing, however willing second-century legend is to supply the gaps in our information. Concerning Peter, we have some evidence;[2] he appears to have embarked about this time on a more extended apostolic ministry—presumably among the Jewish communities of the Dispersion. Concerning John we have rather less evidence, and that of ambiguous quality.[3] Still scantier, even where some is forthcoming, is anything that can be called evidence in relation to the others; but it seems certain that they were no longer in Jerusalem.[4]

James's rôle as leader of Judaean Christianity is emphasized and amplified by later tradition in the memoirs of Hegesippus and the

[1] Gal. 2:9.   [2] Cf. Gal. 2:11ff; I Cor. 9:5; see pp. 282ff, 323, 396.
[3] The problem of the possible confusion in tradition of John the apostle with another John, such as Papias's 'John the elder' (*apud* Euseb. *HE* iii, 39. 4), remains unresolved (cf. Irenaeus, *Letter to Florinus*, [*apud* Euseb. *HE* v, 20. 4–8]; *Haer.* ii, 33. 3; iii, 1. 2; 3. 4; v, 33. 4). See also p. 376 with n. 36.
[4] The tradition of Thomas's association with eastern (Syriac) Christianity may have some factual basis, but what it is remains quite uncertain.

Pseudo-Clementine literature. The type of argument by which his primacy was supported in later generations is illustrated by one of the *logia* in the *Gospel of Thomas*, where, in reply to the disciples' question who will be chief among them after he himself has gone away, Jesus says: 'In the place to which you have gone, you will go to James the Just, for whose sake heaven and earth came into being'.[5]

James's discipleship appears to have begun when he saw Jesus risen from the dead; the evidence of the Gospel tradition is that he and his brothers were not followers of Jesus before that. But after the resurrection he and his brothers are found associated with the other disciples and indeed playing a prominent part among them.[6] The New Testament reference to Jesus's appearance in resurrection to James is Paul's brief statement in I Cor. 15:7, which probably depends on information supplied by James itself. A second-century embellishment of this bare account is provided by the *Gospel according to the Hebrews* where James swears an oath that he will eat no bread until he sees Jesus 'rising from those who sleep'. Jesus accordingly, appearing in resurrection to James, 'took bread and blessed it and broke it and gave it to James the Just and said to him, "My brother, eat your bread, for the Son of Man has arisen from those who sleep".' This account (which further represents James as having been present at the Last Supper) is designed to enhance the prestige of the Jerusalem church over against Gentile Christianity.[7]

The impact which James made on his fellow-members of the Jerusalem church and their descendants for a century after his death is reflected in the account given of him by Hegesippus.[8] According to Hegesippus, the charge of the church [of Jerusalem] passed to James 'together with the apostles'. James is described in terms which portray him as a lifelong Nazirite. James, says Hegesippus, 'was holy

[5] Logion 11 (R. M. Grant and D. N. Freedman, *The Secret Sayings of Jesus* [London, 1960], pp. 124f); this exaltation of James may be derived from the *Gospel according to the Hebrews*.
[6] John 7:5; Acts 1:14; I Cor. 9:5. Perhaps he was first accorded the leadership at the time of Peter's imprisonment by Agrippa I and subsequent departure from Jerusalem (Acts 12:17). Cf. O. Cullmann, *Peter: Disciple, Apostle, Martyr* (London, 1953), pp. 37ff.
[7] The quotation is preserved by Jerome, *De uiris illustribus*, 2. See R. M. Grant and D. N. Freedman, *The Secret Sayings of Jesus*, p. 32.
[8] *Apud* Euseb. *HE* ii, 23. 4–7.

from his birth; he drank no wine or strong drink, neither did he eat flesh. No razor came near his head; he did not anoint himself with oil or go to the baths. He alone was permitted to enter the sanctuary, for he wore garments of linen, not of wool; he would enter the Temple alone and was often found on his knees praying for forgiveness for the [Jewish] people . . . Because of his unsurpassed righteousness he was called "the Just" and . . . "Bulwark of the People".[9]

How much of this tradition is trustworthy is uncertain. In addition to his Nazirite life he apparently practised other forms of asceticism; if his avoidance of oil links him with the Essenes, his avoidance of the baths marks him off from them. Most striking of all is the statement that he had the right to enter the sanctuary.[10] This he certainly had not; in the language of the writer to the Hebrews, 'it is evident that' James like his elder brother 'was descended from Judah, and in connection with that tribe Moses said nothing about priests' (Heb. 7:14). But Hegesippus is not showing his capacity for creative fiction here; he (or the tradition on which he draws) has simply put a literal construction on figurative language. The linen clothing with which James is credited consorts strangely with the general asceticism of his life; it is much more likely to be a metaphorical expression for his piety, after the manner of Revelation 19:8 ('the fine linen is the righteous deeds of the saints'). Similarly, his access to the sanctuary may denote no more than his constant intercession for Israel in the presence of God: for him, as for the prophets and Stephen, the Most High was not confined to temples made with hands.

But Hegesippus's language, rightly understood, conveys more than this: it reflects the early tradition which envisaged the divinely

[9] 'Bulwark of the People' (περιοχὴ τοῦ λαοῦ) is Eusebius's interpretation of *Oblias*, a corrupt form of a Semitic designation given to James (as though it were in Hebrew '*ōpel 'am*). H. J. Schoeps, 'Jacobus ὁ δίκαιος καὶ 'Ωβλίας', *Biblica* 24 (1943), pp. 398ff, and K. Baltzer and H. Köster, 'Die Bezeichnung des Jakobus als 'Ωβλίας', *ZNTW* 46 (1955), pp. 141f, are among those who have in recent years propounded ingenious, but scarcely convincing, solutions of this problem.

[10] Epiphanius (*Pan.* 29:4), more precisely, makes him enter the holy of holies once a year. The attempt to establish a genealogy for Jesus (and accordingly for James) in the tribe of Levi as well as Judah is attested as early as Hippolytus (*On the Blessings of Isaac, Jacob and Moses. Patrologia Orientalis* 27 [1954], pp. 72, 144ff).

appointed high-priesthood as being transferred from Caiaphas and his colleagues to James and his successors. True, however early this view emerged in the believing community, there could be no question of James entering the earthly sanctuary to minister there: its custodians were the last people to entertain such an idea about a transference of the high-priesthood. The earliest apostolic succession-lists, in compiling which Hegesippus was a pioneer, appear to have been modelled on succession-lists of Jewish high priests in the post-exilic age, and the earliest apostolic succession-lists emphasized the primacy of James, as the fountain-head of apostolic authority.[11] When Eusebius says that James was 'the first to be allotted the bishop's throne in Jerusalem after our Saviour's assumption',[12] the language he uses is that of his own day (for it is most improbable that James was called *episkopos* during his lifetime), but the tradition expressed in that language antedates Eusebius's day by several generations. Antioch and Rome might invoke the primacy of Peter, but the Jerusalem tradition had no doubt where the primacy originally rested, and none could deny that the church of Jerusalem was the mother-church of Christendom.

In the Acts of the Apostles James is given no such exalted status; he appears as president, or *primus inter pares*, of the elders of the Jerusalem church; these constituted a kind of Nazarene sanhedrin, not necessarily so numerous as the supreme court of the nation. James and his fellow-elders had a delicate responsibility in their administration of the large community of disciples in Jerusalem. When they are described in Acts 21:20 as 'myriads' strong the figure should not be pressed too literally: if we accept the calculation that Jerusalem's normal population around this time was about 30,000,[13] 'how many myriads' literally understood would account for all its inhabitants—and indeed it has been argued, without any textual support, that the original reference of 'how many myriads' was not to the disciples but to the whole population of the city.[14] The im-

[11] Cf. A. Ehrhardt, *The Apostolic Succession* (London, 1953), pp. 28ff; *The Apostolic Ministry* (Edinburgh, 1958), p. 35. If Jesus was the prophet like Moses, was James cast in the rôle of Moses' brother Aaron?

[12] *HE* ii, 1. 2; iii, 5. 2; vii, 19. 1. Cf. *Clem. Recogn.* iv, 35, where no teacher must be credited unless he brings from Jerusalem the testimonial of James or his duly appointed successor.   [13] See p. 38.

[14] Cf. J. Munck, *Paul and the Salvation of Mankind* (London, 1959), pp. 240ff.

pression given by the narrative of Acts is that the Jerusalem church
constituted a substantial minority of the city's population, and it
embraced a wide variety of outlook and temperament, belief and
practice, within its membership. Even after the expulsion of most
of the believing Hellenists in the campaign of repression that followed Stephen's death, there were people like the Cypriot Mnason
who acted as host to Paul and his Gentile companions when they
came to Jerusalem with the 'collection for the saints' in A.D. 57 and,
at the other extreme, 'zealots for the law' who had only reluctantly
acquiesced in the terms of the apostolic decree freeing Gentile
converts from the requirement of circumcision.[15] If some of the disciples belonged to the 'quiet in the land', others no doubt sympathized with the resistance movements which were so brutally put
down by Felix. To lead such a variegated community must have
called for firmness and tact, but James seems to have succeeded,
commanding the respect not only of his fellow-believers but of the
general Jerusalem populace.

Of the Jewish mission with which James, Peter and John were
entrusted, according to Paul's account in Gal. 2:1–10, we know very
little. James does not appear to have travelled far afield, though
Peter and John probably did so; yet there may be a hint of a wider
sphere of authority for James than Jerusalem and Judaea in the
superscription of the Epistle of James: 'James . . . to the twelve
tribes in the dispersion'.[16] This wider authority may have been
exercised by duly accredited messengers, like the 'certain men' (or
'certain man') who 'came from James' to Antioch at an early stage
in the Gentile mission and persuaded Peter to withdraw from table-
fellowship with Gentile Christians (Gal. 2:12).[17] On the analogy
of authorized messengers from the Sanhedrin to Jewish communities in the dispersion, these messengers from the Jerusalem church
were probably called *šĕlūḥim* or *šĕlīḥim*,[18] and perhaps it is to some
of them, who went beyond their proper bounds into Paul's Gentile
mission-field, and tried to impose their policy on his converts, that

[15] Acts 21:16, 20.
[16] James 1:1. 'The twelve tribes in the dispersion' may here be more particularly the sum-total of Jewish believers in Jesus, considered as the new Israel.
[17] See p. 283 with n. 9.
[18] Cf. K. H. Rengstorf, *Apostleship* (London, 1952), pp. 12ff; T. W. Manson, *The Church's Ministry* (London, 1948), pp. 31ff. See p. 184.

Paul refers in his scathing denunciation of 'false apostles . . . disguising themselves as apostles of Christ' in II Cor. 11:13.

Yet when Paul and his Gentile companions came to Jerusalem in the spring of 57, they received a friendly welcome from James and the other elders; and when the latter suggested that Paul associate himself with the four Nazirites in the Temple precincts their intentions were excellent; they could have had no inkling, any more than Paul had, that this action would have such a tempestuous sequel. When, a few days later, Paul was taken from Jerusalem to Caesarea, they probably breathed a sigh of relief. Paul seemed to attract trouble wherever he went, and Jerusalem was a quieter place without him. The donation which he and his companions brought was perhaps more welcome than Paul himself was.

What Paul's fellow-visitors did when he was arrested we are left to surmise. Probably most of them left Jerusalem as quickly and unobtrusively as they could. Trophimus the Ephesian must have been specially exposed to danger in view of the charge that Paul had taken him, Gentile though he was, into the inner courts of the Temple.[19] Luke probably remained in or near Caesarea for the duration of Paul's imprisonment there, and so too perhaps did Aristarchus of Thessalonica; at any rate Aristarchus as well as Luke accompanied Paul when at last he sailed from Caesarea for Italy.[20]

But James and his associates compromised themselves in the eyes of the Sanhedrin by receiving Paul when he came to Jerusalem. Tertullus, spokesman of the Sanhedrin, charged Paul before Felix with being 'a ringleader of the sect of the Nazarenes' (Acts 24:5). The ringleader escaped their hands by his appeal to Caesar, but the central Nazarene community lay within their jurisdiction, there in Jerusalem. Yet little fault could be found with them; they were humble, pious and patriotic Jews, led by a man whose asceticism and holiness of life won him the esteem of all who knew him.

When, however, Festus died suddenly in office in A.D. 62, the high priest Annas (Ananus) the younger, as Josephus tells us, 'thought he had a favourable opportunity . . . He convened a council (*synedrion*) of judges and brought before it the brother of Jesus the so-called Christ, a man called James, together with certain others, and handed them over to be stoned on a charge of having

---

[19] Acts 21:29.   [20] Acts 27:2.

broken the law'.[21] Josephus gives no hint of the nature of their alleged crime, but makes it plain that the high priest's action offended 'those citizens who were reputed to be most fair-minded and to be strict in their observance of the law'—so it was scarcely of a flagrant breach of the religious law of Judaism that James and the others were accused. On the other hand, if they had been accused of anything in the nature of zealotry or sedition (comparable to the charge on which Jesus had been executed thirty years before), the anger of the incoming procurator Albinus would not have been so greatly feared. As it was, Agrippa took immediate steps to put himself and the Jewish commonwealth in the right with the Romans by removing Annas from office; the high priest had no right to exercise capital jurisdiction, whether a procurator was resident in Judaea or not.[22]

The sober account of Josephus may be accepted without question. It is otherwise with later embellishments of the incident. Clement of Alexandria says that 'James the Just was thrown down from the "pinnacle" of the Temple and beaten to death with a fuller's club';[23] this is a summary of the more detailed narrative of Hegesippus, who tells how the 'scribes and Pharisees' staged a public debate with James at Passovertide[24] and set him on the 'pinnacle' of the Temple so that he might be seen and heard by all who had come up for the festival. When he was asked 'What is the door of Jesus?' he replied in a loud voice: 'Why do you ask me about the Son of Man? He is sitting in heaven at the right hand of the Great Power and will come on the clouds of heaven'. At this the crowd cried out 'Hosanna to the Son of David', and James's enemies, realizing that their plan to discredit him had misfired, threw him down and began to stone him, the *coup de grâce* being given him by a fuller with his club.[25]

The narrative is plainly dependent on the New Testament ac-

---

[21] Josephus, *Ant.* xx, 200.

[22] Josephus, *Ant.* xx, 201–3 (see pp. 25, 66, 199).

[23] *Hypotyposes* vii, *apud* Euseb. *HE* ii, 1. 5.

[24] Some details of this debate are preserved in *Clem. Recogn.* i, 66–71, which H. J. Schoeps (*Theologie und Geschichte des Judenchristentums* [Tübingen, 1949], pp. 405ff) considers to be extracted from an early Ebionite 'Acts of the Apostles' known to Hegesippus.

[25] Hegesippus, *apud* Euseb. *HE* ii, 23. 8–18. The 'door of Jesus' has been variously emended to 'the door of salvation (Heb. *yešū'āh*)' or 'the law of Jesus' (Gk. θυρά emended to θωρά, i.e. Heb. *tōrāh*).

counts of the trial of Jesus and the trial and stoning of Stephen, the more so because James, while the stones were being thrown at him, knelt down and prayed: 'I beseech thee, Lord God and Father, forgive them for they know not what they do'.[26] The *motif* of the public debate figures later in the Pseudo-Clementine literature, and has an interest of its own, but is irrelevant to the history of A.D. 62.

Hegesippus implies that this violent ending of James's ministry of intercession on behalf of his people rendered the tragedy of A.D. 70 inevitable. 'At once', he says, 'Vespasian began to besiege them'.[27]

The death of James was a demoralizing blow to the Jerusalem church. Another member of the holy family (the *desposynoi*), Symeon the son of Clopas, was elected to succeed him, but probably not at once.[28] At some point between James's death and the outbreak of the revolt in A.D. 66, Eusebius says, the church received an oracle, given by revelation to those in Jerusalem who were 'approved', bidding them leave the doomed city and settle in Pella, one of the cities of the Decapolis, east of Jordan.[29] That some Christians did settle in Pella in due course is certain; from one of them, Ariston of Pella (a second-century apologist against the Jews),[30] Eusebius may have derived the information. But in view of the rioting between Jews and Gentiles which broke out in Pella, as in other Gentile cities of that region, at the beginning of the war,[31] it seems more likely that they sought refuge at first in the less-frequented parts of Transjordan; indeed, the flight of the

[26] With Eusebius, *HE* ii, 23. 16 cf. Acts 7:60 (and Luke 23:34); see p. 225 with nn. 21, 22.

[27] *Apud* Euseb. *HE* ii, 23. 18. According to Origen (*c. Cels.* i, 47) and Eusebius (*HE* ii, 23. 20), Josephus says that the disasters of A.D. 66–73 'befell the Jews to avenge James the Just, brother of Jesus the so-called Christ, for the Jews killed him in spite of his great righteousness'. No such statement exists in any manuscript of Josephus; it is quite inauthentic.

[28] Eusebius, *HE* iii, 11; his account is probably derived from Hegesippus, whom he quotes for the statement that Clopas was brother to Joseph, the husband of Mary. The designation and dignity of the δεσπόσυνοι are mentioned by Julius Africanus, *apud* Euseb. *HE* i, 7. 14.

[29] *HE* iii, 5. 3 (this oracle can scarcely be identified with the commandment to 'flee to the mountains' in Mark 13:14).

[30] Eusebius (*HE* iv, 6. 3) quotes Ariston as his authority for the events of the second Jewish revolt (A.D. 132–135).

[31] Josephus, *BJ* ii, 458; cf. S. G. F. Brandon, *The Fall of Jerusalem and the Christian Church* (London, 1951), pp. 168ff.

mother-church into the wilderness and her preservation there during the period of tribulation is reflected in the apocalyptic language of Rev. 12:14. Egypt could also have provided a haven for some refugees;[32] Egypt and Transjordan in later generations were two main centres of 'Ebionite' Christianity—a form of Jewish Christianity which combined some of the traditional theology of the Jerusalem church with elements of Samaritan or Essene character.[33] But many members of the church remained where they were—in Judaea, if not in Jerusalem itself.

Another migration of Palestinian Christians took place about the same time to the province of Asia, where a number of 'great luminaries' of the apostolic age spent their closing years and had their tombs pointed out with pride by Asian Christians of later generations.[34] Some of these migrants disapproved of the laxity of Christian practice in some churches of the province: the severe language used of the Nicolaitans and others in the Letters to the Seven Churches in the Apocalypse bespeaks the attitude of those who held fast to the conditions imposed on Gentile Christians in the Jerusalem decree and disapproved of any relaxation of them.[35] 'John the disciple of the Lord', the traditional author of the Apocalypse, was outstanding among these migrants; his tomb was later pointed out in Ephesus.[36] The majority of these migrants, however, appear to have been Hellenists who represented a much less Judaistic interpretation of Christianity than the refugees from the Jerusalem church. Among these Hellenists were Philip and his daughters, whose tombs were later pointed out at Hierapolis in Phrygia. If, as seems probable, this Philip is 'Philip the evangelist' of Acts 21:8 (rather than 'Philip, one of the twelve apostles', with whom Polycrates, bishop of Ephesus c. A.D. 190, identified him),[37]

---

[32] Cf. S. G. F. Brandon, *The Fall of Jerusalem*, pp. 217ff.

[33] See pp. 115, 271, 391f.

[34] Eusebius, *HE* iii, 31. 2ff; v, 24. 2ff.

[35] Rev. 2:6, 14f, 20ff.

[36] Eusebius, *HE* iii, 1. 1; 31. 3; v, 24. 3. In fact, two places were pointed out in Ephesus as the site of his tomb (Dionysius of Alexandria *apud* Euseb. *HE* vii, 25. 16); we may compare the situation in Rome, where for a time the *Memoria Apostolorum ad Catacumbas* rivalled in popular appeal the officially approved monuments on the Vatican hill and the Ostian Way respectively as marking the burial-places of Peter and Paul. See pp. 408ff.

[37] Polycrates *apud* Euseb. *HE* iii, 31. 3; v, 24. 2. But Eusebius understood Philip and his daughters to be those of Acts 21:8, for he quotes this passage

part of the Christian community of Caesarea joined in this migration to proconsular Asia. Caesarea certainly cannot have been a comfortable place for Christians—especially Christians of Jewish birth—in the period preceding and following the outbreak of war in A.D. 66.

2

During Paul's two years' detention in Caesarea he must have heard echoes from time to time of the trouble which developed at that time between the Jewish and Gentile inhabitants of the city. Caesarea was in the main a Gentile city, but the Jewish community held itself entitled to special privileges because Herod, the city's royal founder, was a Jew. The dispute about these privileges led to rioting, in which Felix's soldiery intervened to the disadvantage of the Jews. Such intervention naturally made the situation worse, and Felix sent the leaders of both communities to Rome to have the dispute investigated and settled by Nero. When the investigation began, Felix was recalled from Judaea and relieved of his office, probably because of the excesses which marked his intervention in the dispute. Nevertheless the emperor's judgement favoured the Gentile case; according to Josephus, the emperor's secretary was bribed by the Caesarean Greeks to procure an annulment of the grant of equal civic rights (*isopoliteia*) to the Caesarean Jews.[88] More probably the imperial rescript did not annul such a grant already made, but refused a Jewish claim to *isopoliteia* now put forward. In any case, the Caesarean Greeks could not resist the temptation to crow over their Jewish fellow-townsmen, now officially stamped as second-class citizens, and seized every opportunity of annoying and insulting them by a series of vexatious and humiliating pinpricks. When, on one occasion, they sacrificed a bird outside the synagogue door, with the implication that the Jews were lepers who required to be purified by this rite, the Jews appealed for redress to the procurator, for their religion was protected by imperial law against such outrages. The procurator at this time was Florus,

---

as the biblical reference to this family in *HE* iii, 31. 5, after quoting the statement of Proclus the Montanist that the tombs of Philip and his four daughters were at Hierapolis (*HE* iii, 31. 4).

[88] *Ant.* xx, 183f.

whose venality was so notorious that the petitioners knew that it was useless to appeal to him without bribing him. Accordingly they handed over with their appeal eight talents of silver. Florus took the money readily enough, but ignored their appeal.[39]

The Caesarean trouble is rightly reckoned by Josephus[40] among the causes of the war against Rome which broke out in September, A.D. 66. The contrast between Nero's ruling on Caesarea and Claudius's favourable decision in respect of the Jews of Judaea and Alexandria[41] suggested a change in imperial policy towards the Jews and strengthened popular support for the Zealots. But the immediate occasion of the war must be sought in Jerusalem, and the man chiefly responsible for precipitating it just then was Florus. While the roots of the trouble go back to the early days of Roman occupation, and sixty years of Zealot resistance and military repression preceded the outbreak of war, when the crisis came to a head it was not a Zealot leader but a pillar of the Temple establishment who decisively repudiated the sovereignty of Rome. This unexpected turn of events must be attributed to the blind folly of Florus.

Florus's lust for wealth was such that all the resources of bribery and extortion were exploited to gratify it. Breaking-point came when he raided the Temple treasury and seized seventeen talents, claiming that they were required for the imperial service. This may mean that the tribute due to the imperial exchequer fell short by that amount, which he insisted in making good in this way. But his action—sacrilegious in Jewish eyes—provoked a riotous demonstration which he treated as a display of rebellion; he seized a number of leading citizens indiscriminately and crucified them, and handed over part of the city to his troops to plunder. The people then destroyed the communications between the Antonia fortress and the outer court of the Temple, to prevent the soldiers from making a sudden incursion and occupying the Temple area.[42]

Urgent appeals for restraint were made to the angry citizens by Neapolitanus, a military tribune sent from Antioch by Cestius

[39] Josephus, *BJ* ii, 284–8.   [40] Josephus, *Ant.* xx, 184.
[41] Especially his severe action against Romans and Samaritans in the Judaean troubles of A.D. 52 (see p. 342) and against the leaders of the anti-Jewish faction at Alexandria in the riots of A.D. 53; cf. *CPI* II, 156 (see p. 293 with n. 4).   [42] Josephus, *BJ* ii, 293–332.

Gallus, governor of Syria, to investigate the troubles, and by the younger Agrippa. The people were disposed to listen to Agrippa's exhortation to pay their arrears of tribute and restore the broken colonnades connecting the Temple area with the Antonia fortress, but when, in answer to explicit questions, he admitted that submission to Rome meant submission to Florus until the emperor saw fit to replace him, he was shouted down and driven from the city.[43]

It was at this point that Eleazar, captain of the Temple, persuaded the priests to discontinue offering the daily sacrifice for the emperor's welfare. This was an open declaration of revolt against the Romans. Many of the most responsible citizens were appalled at its implications and took desperate measures to reverse the trend of revolt, but the insurrectionary spirit spread with rapidly increasing momentum and the point of no return was passed when, early in September, the insurgents seized the Antonia fortress and wiped out its Roman garrison.[44]

Another fortress which had been taken from the Romans a short time before was Masada, west of the Dead Sea. The Jews who took Masada were Zealots, who, learning of the revolt in Jerusalem, felt that this was the hour for which they had long been waiting. Armed with weapons from the arsenal at Masada, they marched on Jerusalem, with Menahem, a descendant of Judas the Galilaean, at their head, and occupied the western part of the city. Eleazar did not relish the presence of a rival leader of revolt, and he and Menahem came to blows. Menahem was caught and killed, with some of his chief lieutenants, after a fortnight's violent activity (during which Eleazar's father Ananias, a leader of the peace-party, was killed by a Zealot band); those Zealots who escaped made their way back to Masada, which held out against the Romans until the spring of 73.[45]

It may seem incredible that the insurgents should have hoped for any success in resisting the might of Rome. The hopelessness of their dream, as an issue of practical politics, was spelt out for them by Agrippa and others. Josephus, recently returned from a two years' visit to Rome,[46] claims to have warned the hotheads of the utter madness of exposing themselves and their families and country

[43] Josephus, *BJ* ii, 333–407.   [44] Josephus, *BJ* ii, 409–32.
[45] Josephus, *BJ* ii, 408, 433–48. For the view that this Menahem was the Teacher of Righteousness of the Qumran sect see p. 116 with n. 56.
[46] See p. 349.

to catastrophe by pursuing their reckless policies—although, when once the war had started, he accepted an insurgent command in Galilee.[47]

True, when war fever mounts men are impatient of appeals to reason. But the leaders of the Jewish revolt could muster some impressive arguments in favour of their policy. They believed that God was on their side—or rather, that they were on God's side. Josephus, Tacitus and Suetonius combine to tell how they were encouraged by an ancient oracle in their sacred writings to the effect that 'at that very time'[48] a man or men from Judaea would gain supreme world-dominion. The oracle is probably the angelic prophecy in Dan. 9:24-7 announcing that seventy heptads of years would elapse before the establishment of everlasting righteousness (i.e. under the promised kingdom of the saints which the God of heaven would set up); calculations in the sixties evidently led some to believe that this period was approaching completion. Josephus tells us how he came to the conclusion that the oracle really pointed to the Roman commander-in-chief Vespasian (sent to Judaea by Nero early in 67 to put down the revolt), who was proclaimed emperor in the summer of 69;[49] Tacitus and Suetonius put the same construction on the oracle. But the insurgents took it to mean that the hour of Israel's liberation was at hand.[50]

Again, the memory of the victories of Judas Maccabaeus and his

[47] Whereas in *BJ* ii, 568 Josephus represents himself as commander-in-chief of the insurgent forces throughout Galilee and emphasizes the vigour with which he discharged the duties of this appointment, he tries in his *Life*, 17ff, to show that whereas ostensibly he held an insurgent command, his intentions and, to a large extent, his actions were pro-Roman throughout. In the earlier work the exaggeration of his insurgent zeal enhanced the magnanimity of Vespasian and Titus; in the later work it was more important to allay Domitian's anti-Jewish suspicions.

[48] Josephus, *BJ* vi, 312 (κατὰ τὸν καιρὸν ἐκεῖνον); Tacitus, *Hist.* v, 13 (*eo ipso tempore*); Suetonius, *Vespasian* 4:5 (*eo tempore*).

[49] *BJ* ii, 351-4; cf. iv, 616-21; Tacitus, *Hist.* ii, 74ff; Suetonius, *Vespasian*, 6:3.

[50] Josephus, *BJ* vi, 313: 'They took this to portend the triumph of their own race, and many of their scholars were widely out in their interpretation; the oracle in fact pointed to the accession of Vespasian, who was in Judaea when he was acclaimed emperor'. The Slavonic version says instead: 'Some understood that this meant Herod; others, the crucified wonder-worker Jesus; others again, Vespasian'. We may compare the astrological assurances given to Nero that, if he were compelled to leave Rome, he would find another throne in the east, some even specifying Jerusalem (Suetonius, *Nero*, 40).

brothers was recalled. They too originally took the field repeatedly
against overwhelmingly larger forces than they themselves commanded; but God fought for them, and not only did they remove
the reproach that had been brought upon them by the profanation
of the Temple and the ban on the practice of their religion, but they
won independence for Israel. What had been done then could be
done again in face of another imperial oppressor. And indeed it
might well have appeared that history was about to repeat itself:
when, in November 66, Cestius Gallus marched south from Syria
with legionary forces to deal with a situation which the procurator
of Judaea could no longer control, he occupied Bezetha, the northern suburb of Jerusalem, but then suddenly withdrew (reckoning
probably that with the troops he had brought he could not reduce
the remainder of the city and the separately fortified Temple area).
As he marched north, his army was ambushed by Jewish insurgents
in the Pass of Beth-horon (leading from Jerusalem to the coast road),
where Judas Maccabaeus in his day had won more than one victory,
and suffered severe losses. This initial success for the revolt discredited the moderates and leaders of the peace-party in the public
eye, and encouraged the insurgents to organize the whole Jewish
population of Palestine for the war of liberation.[51] When Vespasian
arrived the following spring to take charge of operations, he steadily
reduced Galilee, Peraea, western Judaea and Idumaea, but when
he was ready to besiege Jerusalem itself, news came of the death
of Nero (June 9, 68) and the civil war that followed. Vespasian
suspended operations for a year to see how events would turn out,
and as the insurgents in Jerusalem received reports (garbled and
exaggerated, it may be) of the internecine strife in and around Rome
as rival claimants contended for the imperial throne, they might
have been pardoned for thinking that, as dynastic rivalry had weakened the house of Seleucus two centuries before and played into
the hands of the Hasmonaeans, a similar pattern was now about
to unfold. Even so they might have spared themselves the luxury
of indulging in civil strife themselves: during Vespasian's inactivity
three rival leaders established themselves respectively in the city
(Simon bar Giora), the outer Temple court (John of Gischala, Jo-

[51] Josephus, *BJ* ii, 499–568.

sephus's enemy) and the inner courts (the Zealot leader Eleazar son of Simon).[52]

But when Vespasian resumed his task of putting down the revolt in June, 69, he swiftly became master of all Palestine except Jerusalem itself and the three strongholds of Herodeion, Masada and Machaerus. In the summer of that year he was proclaimed emperor by the Roman commanders and armies of the eastern provinces, one after another (beginning with Tiberius Julius Alexander in Alexandria on 1 July), and, when his partisans had seized Rome on his behalf, he left Judaea to assume personal control of affairs in the capital, entrusting the final liquidation of the Jewish revolt to his elder son Titus.[53]

Titus began the siege of Jerusalem in April, 70. The defenders held out desperately for five months, but by the end of August the Temple area was occupied and the holy house burned down, and by the end of September all resistance in the city had come to an end. The reduction of the three remaining strongholds followed: the last of them to fall was the almost impregnable Masada, the defenders of which held out until April or May, 73, and, when they saw that no hope was left, committed mass suicide rather than fall into the hands of the conquerors.[54]

Josephus, who records the progress of the war in detail, is obviously moved by the heroism of his people and the magnitude of the disaster which overtook them, while at the same time he is concerned to put the best face on his own inglorious part and enhance the magnanimity of Vespasian and Titus. When he was taken prisoner by Vespasian's forces in Galilee in 67, he hailed his captor in the name of God as emperor-designate.[55] Vespasian was sufficiently impressed to spare Josephus's life, and when the prediction was fulfilled two years later he heaped honours on the prophet, who had a grandstand view of the siege and fall of Jerusalem, and spent the rest of his life in Rome as a pensioner of the imperial house.

Josephus, as prone as his predecessors were to trace the hand of

[52] The strife between these factions bears many of the features of a class-war; we may contrast the egalitarianism of the Zealots with the monopolistic enterprise credited by Josephus to John of Gischala (*BJ* ii, 585–94; *Life*, 70–6).

[53] Josephus, *BJ* iv, 658; Tacitus, *Hist.* v, 10; Suetonius, *Titus*, 5:2.

[54] Josephus, *BJ* vii, 304–406.   [55] *BJ* iii, 399–402.

God in history, must account in moral terms for the horrors of the revolt and its reduction, and endeavours to do so by painting in the blackest hues the iniquities of the Zealots. It was their misdeeds that brought this retribution not only on themselves but on their people; it was their repeated and increasing profanation of the Temple during their occupation of the inner courts that constituted the 'abomination of desolation' which could be purged only with blood and fire.[56] Nothing in Josephus's narrative is so repulsive as this heaping of obloquy on men who—however ill-advised their policy was and however unscrupulous their action in defence of the cause to which they had dedicated themselves—were braver and nobler men than himself. The uncovering of their last outpost at Masada has made it plain that, far from being the impious criminals of Josephus's portrayal, they were men of piety, scrupulously observant of the finest details of their ancestral religion.[57]

3

According to Josephus, when the Temple was set on fire by the Roman soldiery, Titus was dismayed and tried to save it.[58] This was no doubt what Titus later wished to be believed. But a historical fragment preserved by Sulpicius Severus (sometimes, but doubtfully, thought to be taken from a part of Tacitus's *Histories* which has long since been lost)[59] describes a council of war at which the fate of the Temple was debated. Some thought that the Romans would be charged with vandalism if they destroyed so magnificent a structure, 'but others, including Titus himself, expressed the opinion that the temple should most certainly be demolished, in order that the Jewish and Christian religions might be the more completely wiped out; for although these religions were mutually hostile, they nevertheless shared the same origin; the Christians were an offshoot of the Jews, and if the root were destroyed the stock would quickly perish'.

[56] *BJ* iv, 150, 157, 163ff, 318, 388; v, 16f; vi, 94, 109f, 126, 311. While Josephus mentions the sacrifices offered by the victorious Romans to their legionary standards in the Temple court (*BJ* vi, 316), he does not describe this action as an abomination, whatever he may have thought privately.

[57] See p. 100 with n. 26. [58] *BJ* vi, 236ff.

[59] *Chronicle* ii, 30. 6. See H. W. Montefiore, 'Sulpicius Severus and Titus' Council of War', *Historia* 11 (1962), pp. 156ff.

Perhaps there were some who cherished such a hope. But in fact both Judaism and Christianity survived the fall of the Temple and displayed a more vigorous life for its disappearance.

Josephus was not the only Jew who recognized Vespasian as the new master of the world. Yoḥanan ben Zakkai, a leading rabbi of the school of Hillel, is said to have been smuggled out of Jerusalem during the fighting and brought before Vespasian. He hailed him as emperor and predicted his conquest of Jerusalem on the strength of the Isaianic oracle: 'Lebanon shall fall by a mighty one' (Isa. 10:34). 'A mighty one' (Heb. *'addīr*), he said, 'is an epithet applied only to a king', while on the strength of Deut. 3:25, as interpreted in his school, he equated 'Lebanon' with the sanctuary.[60] Whether there is some historical substance in this tradition or not, this was believed of Yoḥanan ben Zakkai; yet his is a venerated name while the memory of Josephus has been execrated by patriotic Jews.

For Yoḥanan it was who, after the catastrophe, received permission from the Romans to set up a school of rabbinical study at Jamnia, in western Judaea. Here a new Sanhedrin of doctors of the law was established. The Second Jewish Commonwealth, the temple-state which had endured since the return from the Babylonian exile, was now at end; the old Sanhedrin, comprising chief priests and elders, with the reigning high priest as president, was no more. Judaea was now a full imperial province, governed by a legate with legionary forces at his command,[61] and there was no national administration entrusted with authority over internal Jewish affairs as there had been under the procurators. Yet the new Sanhedrin not only served as a focus for reassembling the shattered national life of Israel, but succeeded in establishing some degree of authority itself in the eyes of Rome. Its main function was to act as a supreme court for the organization of Jewish law. The accumulated tradition of generations which constituted the oral law was digested and codified. Since Yoḥanan and his principal colleagues belonged to the school of Hillel, there was now a greater measure of agreement on the main lines of legal interpretation than

[60] TB *Giṭṭin*, 56b. According to TB *Yoma*, 39b, Yohanan prophesied the destruction of the Temple on the basis of Zech. 11:1 ('Open your doors, O Lebanon, that the fire may devour your cedars!').
[61] The forces were those of Legio X Fretensis, whose commander was also governor of the province. Cf. Josephus, *BJ* vii, 5; Dio Cassius, *Hist.* lv, 23.

there had been in the days when the schools of Shammai and Hillel had stood over against each other, although the individual members of the new school were far from being unanimous on interpretative details, to the point where excommunication was resorted to.[62] The work of codification was prosecuted by successive leaders of the school—notably Rabbi Aqiba and Rabbi Me'ir—until towards the end of the second century, under Rabbi Judah the Prince, the completed work was reduced to writing in the corpus of religious jurisprudence which is called the Mishnah.[63]

The oral law had been largely designed to adapt the requirements of the early written Torah to the changing situation of later days;[64] and Yoḥanan and his colleagues carried this process of adaptation forward in the changed circumstances of the period following A.D. 70. Some conservative Pharisees felt that after the fall of the Temple they could no longer eat flesh or drink wine because there were no more animal sacrifices or libations of wine; but it was pointed out to them that on the same principle they could no longer eat bread or drink water, since the presentation of first-fruits and the ceremony of water-pouring had also been discontinued. The new Sanhedrin grasped the practical truth that 'new occasions teach new duties'.

If the new Sanhedrin provided the necessary cohesion for Jewish national existence, the cohesion at a local level was provided by the synagogue, and it was indeed through the synagogue that the Sanhedrin exercised its authority. An outstanding example of this is provided by the effective exclusion of Nazarenes and other 'heretics' from participation in Jewish worship when, about A.D. 90, a member of the Sanhedrin named Samuel the Less reworded one of the blessings recited daily in the synagogue so as to make it include

---

[62] The outstanding instance was the excommunication of Rabbi Eliezer ben Hyrkanos, Yoḥanan ben Zakkai's 'well-plastered cistern that does not lose a drop' (*Pirqē Abot* 2:8), because he was too intransigent a traditionalist to move with the times (TB *Baba Meṣia'* 59a–b).

[63] In the rabbinical schools of Palestine and Babylonia the Mishnah provided the basis for further study and commentary (*gemara*), which was ultimately codified in the Palestinian Talmud (c. A.D. 400) and Babylonian Talmud (c. A.D. 500) respectively.

[64] For the early beginnings of this process cf. J. Weingreen, 'Old Testament and Rabbinical Exposition', in *Promise and Fulfilment*, ed. F. F. Bruce (Edinburgh, 1963), pp. 107ff; 'Oral Torah and Written Records', in *Holy Book and Holy Tradition*, ed. F. F. Bruce and E. G. Rupp (Manchester, 1968), pp. 54ff.

a curse on such persons. In the present Jewish prayer book this blessing appears as the twelfth of the Eighteen Benedictions;[65] it runs thus:

> And for slanderers let there be no hope, and let all wickedness perish as in a moment; may all Thy enemies be speedily cut off, and the kingdom of arrogance do Thou speedily uproot and break in pieces, cast it down and humble it speedily, in our days. Blessed art Thou, O Lord, who breakest enemies in pieces and humblest the arrogant.

But towards the end of the first century it was given this form:

> For apostates let there be no hope, and the kingdom of arrogance do Thou speedily uproot in our days; and let Nazarenes and heretics (*minim*) perish as in a moment; let them be blotted out of the book of life and not be enrolled with the righteous. Blessed art Thou, O Lord, who humblest the arrogant.[66]

This revised edition of the prayer was authorized by the Sanhedrin and adopted in synagogues, so that Jewish Christians, by keeping silence at this point, might give themselves away and be excommunicated. The 'heretics' or *minim* were members of other sects of which the Sanhedrin disapproved. It is only after A.D. 70 that we can begin to talk about normative Judaism and of deviations from the norm; in the days of the Second Temple there was a much greater variety of Jewish religious life and practice, and no one form could claim to represent the standard by which others were to be judged.

When the rabbis of Jamnia discussed the recognition of canonical books and the rejection of others, one group to which they paid attention was 'the books of the *minim*'. These contained the name of God, and yet their contents were unacceptable. Some of these books might be documents such as have been discovered in the Qumran caves, but they certainly included Jewish Christian writings. These *gilyōnim*, as they are called in the rabbinical traditions, cannot be identified with any of our canonical gospels or with their sources; they appear to have been Hebrew or Aramaic documents bearing some kind of secondary relation to our Gospel of Matthew or to the work known to Christian writers in later generations as

---

[65] Cf. S. Singer, *The Authorised Daily Prayer Book* (London, 1939), pp. 94f.

[66] Cf. C. W. Dugmore, *The Influence of the Synagogue upon the Divine Office* (Oxford, 1944), p. 4; the Hebrew text was discovered in the Cairo genizah.

the 'Gospel according to the Hebrews'. Although in these debates
the canonicity of such works as Ezekiel, Ecclesiastes, Esther, the
Song of Songs, and the Wisdom of Jesus the son of Sira was discussed, it is unlikely that the idea of extending canonical recognition to the Christian books was seriously entertained: they were
mentioned only to be condemned. 'The *gilyōnīm* and the books of
the *minīm* are not sacred scripture'.[67] Some leading rabbis, like
Yohanan ben Zakkai and Aqiba's pupil Me'ir, made derogatory puns
on the word *euangelion*, altering the vowels to *'āwen-gillāyōn* or
'awōn-gillāyōn ('iniquity of the margin'). But 'the vehemence with
which the leading rabbis of the first generation of the second century express their hostility to the gospel and other books of the
heretics, and to their conventicles, is the best evidence that they
were growing in numbers and influence; some even among the
teachers of the Law were suspected of leanings towards the new
doctrine'.[68]

Not only was the canon of Hebrew scripture discussed and fixed
at Jamnia, but its text and interpretation also. The variety in Hebrew biblical text types which we find among the Qumran manuscripts is not reproduced after A.D. 70. The latest evidence on this
score confirms the belief which has long been held: that the con-
sonantal text on which the Massoretic edition is based was standard-
ized as the only acceptable text by Aqiba and his colleagues. In
the Qumran manuscripts this 'proto-Massoretic' text is represented
alongside the type of Hebrew text underlying the Septuagint version and (for the Pentateuch) a popular Palestinian type closely
akin to the Samaritan Bible.[69] But after the fall of the Second
Temple there is no evidence that Jews acknowledged or used any
text other than the 'proto-Massoretic'.[70] As for the Septuagint version, that was used so freely by Christians in their Gentile mission
that it came to be regarded by Jews as a Christian version. Many
of its renderings might have seemed to be providentially designed
to support Christian claims. If a Jew like Philo regarded the Septu-

[67] Tosefta, *Yadaim* 2:13.
[68] G. F. Moore, *Judaism in the First Centuries of the Christian Era*, 1 (Cambridge, Mass., 1927), p. 244.
[69] Cf. F. M. Cross, *The Ancient Library of Qumran and Modern Biblical
Studies* (New York, 1958), pp. 124ff.
[70] E.g. the biblical Hebrew texts found at Murabba'at and the En-gedi region (with a *terminus ad quem* of A.D. 135) are all of this type.

agint in his day as the product of divine inspiration, Greek-speaking Christians felt that they had even greater cause to regard it thus. To the Jews, on the other hand, the Christian appeal to the Septuagint brought a sense of disillusionment with that version, so that 'the day on which the seventy elders wrote the Law in Greek for the king' was compared to the day on which Aaron made the golden calf.[71] A good example of the Christian use of the Septuagint and Jewish refusal to admit the validity of the Christian premises and arguments is provided in Justin's *Dialogue with Trypho the Jew*, a work whose dramatic date is A.D. 135, soon after the suppression of the second Jewish revolt. New Greek translations of the Hebrew scriptures were made by Jews—notably those of Aquila and Theodotion—which avoided renderings that played into the hands of Christian apologists.

It may even be that similar considerations dictated the removal from the synagogue service of certain passages of scripture whose recital might in one way or another be exploited in a Christian sense. The Ten Commandments had once been recited daily in the synagogue liturgy, but this practice was discontinued—lest it should be said (so the explanation runs) that only the decalogue, and not the whole codification of Torah, together with the oral tradition, was committed to Moses by God.[72] We know that in some forms of Jewish Christianity the sacrificial regulations of the Pentateuch were rejected as a later and spurious accretion to the law given to Moses.[73] And the absence of the fourth Servant Song from the *haphṭārōṯ* (prophetic lessons) in the synagogue lectionary may have something to do with its popularity among Christians as a prophecy of the passion of Jesus.[74]

Lines of interpretation, too, were laid down by the rabbis of this period which carefully excluded the messianic exegesis favoured by Christians. Hence, for centuries to come, although the Hebrew scriptures in text or in translation were venerated as holy writ by Jews and Christians alike, they were read in accordance with two divergent and contradictory interpretative traditions, to a point

---

[71] Cf. Philo, *Vita Mosis* ii, 34–40 as against *Sopherim* i, 8f.

[72] TB *Berakot* 3c; cf. M. Simon, 'The Ancient Church and Rabbinical Tradition', in *Holy Book and Holy Tradition*, ed. F. F. Bruce and E. G. Rupp, p. 110.   [73] Cf. *Clem. Recogn.* i, 36–9; *Clem. Hom.* iii, 45.

[74] This is the explanation given by H. Loewe in C. G. Montefiore and H. Loewe, *A Rabbinical Anthology* (London, 1938), p. 544.

where what should have served as a bond of union might almost have been two different bodies of literature.

4

In the years between A.D. 73 and 132 some measure of resettlement on the site of the derelict city of Jerusalem took place. There was no Roman ban on Jewish settlement or worship there during these years as there was after A.D. 135. When, according to Epiphanius, Hadrian paid a visit to the site early in his reign, he found there seven poor synagogues and one small church;[75] if this statement is well founded, some Jewish-Christian as well as Jewish resettlement is implied, and this is corroborated by Eusebius.[76] But Jerusalem never again became the centre of Jewish Christianity. To what extent sacrificial worship was resumed in the Temple area is a debated subject.[77] It may well be that when the Jewish insurgents under Ben-Kosebah seized control of the region in A.D. 132 plans were made to rebuild the Temple;[78] but it is unlikely that Jewish Christians would have regarded either the maintenance of sacrifice on the site or the rebuilding of the Temple as anything but defiance of the revealed decree of God.

Galilaean Christianity continued to flourish for some generations after A.D. 73; the Nazarene communities there looked on the descendants of the holy family, the *desposynoi*, as their natural leaders.[79]

Vespasian's ruling that the half-shekel tax paid annually by Jews into the temple treasury at Jerusalem be paid after A.D. 70 into the temple treasury of Jupiter Capitolinus at Rome[80] may have affected Jewish Christians as well as other Jews. In fact the tax in its new form was exacted more widely than in its old form; women now

[75] Epiphanius, *Pan.* 29:7; *De mensuris et ponderibus* 14f; cf. H. J. Schoeps, *Theologie und Geschichte des Judenchristentums*, p. 284.
[76] *Demonstratio Evangelica* iii, 5.
[77] Cf. K. W. Clark, 'Worship in the Jerusalem Temple after A.D. 70', *NTS* 6 (1959–60), pp. 269ff.
[78] Such an attempt is envisaged in the Epistle of Barnabas 16:4. The association on coins of the second Revolt of 'Eleazar the high priest' with 'Simeon prince of Israel' (i.e. Ben-Kosebah) may or may not be relevant in this regard.
[79] See E. Lohmeyer, *Galiläa und Jerusalem* (Göttingen, 1936), pp. 54f, for the view that the church of Damascus was founded by Galilaean disciples soon after Jesus' death.   [80] Josephus, *BJ* vii, 218.

had to pay it as well as men; the upper age-limit of fifty was raised, or perhaps abolished, and Jewish children were liable to it from three years old and upwards.[81] The gospel story of the payment of the tetradrachm on behalf of Jesus and Peter together (Matt. 17:24–7) has no bearing on the payment of the Capitoline tax; it served rather as a model for Jewish Christians in the days when the tax went to Jerusalem, advising them to pay it so as not to give offence. According to Dio Cassius, it was Jews who followed their ancestral customs who were required by Vespasian to pay the Capitoline tax; this requirement possibly involved some Jewish Christians and exempted others.[82] But Jewish Christians—at least those who were circumcised—were probably rendered liable for payment when the scope of the tax was broadened under Domitian[83] so as to apply to all circumcised persons (including those who attempted to conceal their circumcision by *epispasmos*) and even Gentile adherents of Judaism who might not be circumcised at all, in addition to other Gentiles falsely accused of such adherence. This unconscionable extension of the tax, which gave great encouragement to informers, was repealed by Nerva, an act which is commemorated by the legend on his coinage FISCI IVDAICI CALVMNIA SVBLATA ('the removal of the perversion of justice in relation to the *fiscus Iudaicus*').[84]

When Hadrian issued his ban on circumcision in A.D. 132, which precipitated Ben-Kosebah's revolt,[85] Jewish Christians who maintained this covenant-sign must have been affected by it as much as other Jews; yet they were unable to take part wholeheartedly in the revolt because they could not acknowledge Ben-Kosebah's messianic claim. Perhaps they joined with others who rejected this claim in calling him Bar-koziba, 'the son of falsehood', as a counterblast to the designation Bar-kokhba, 'the son of the star', given him by Aqiba who hailed him as the messianic 'star out of Jacob' predicted by Balaam (Num. 24:17). At any rate their refusal to acknowledge Ben-Kosebah as the Messiah stamped them in the eyes of many of

[81] Cf. *CPI* II, 168, 169, 171, 223, 421.
[82] Dio Cassius, *Hist.* lxvi, 7. 2.
[83] Cf. Suetonius, *Domitian* 12:2. See E. M. Smallwood, 'Domitian's Attitude towards the Jews and Judaism', *Cl. Phil.* 51 (1956), pp. 1ff.
[84] See I. A. F. Bruce, 'Nerva and the *Fiscus Iudaicus*', *PEQ* 96 (1964), pp. 34ff.
[85] Spartianus, *Hadrian* 14; cf. Dio Cassius, *Hist.* lxix, 12.

their fellow-Jews as traitors to the national cause, and brought severe reprisals on them.[86]

When the revolt was put down and the pagan city of Aelia Capitolina was erected on the site of Jerusalem, Jewish Christians were no doubt excluded from it along with Jews in general. The new church of Jerusalem which arose in Aelia Capitolina was a completely Gentile-Christian community, even if it regarded itself in some degree as heir and successor to the apostolic church of Jerusalem.[87] As for the remnant of Jewish Christians, their subsequent history is but scantily documented. Some maintained relations with the Catholic Church, like the Nazarenes whom Jerome knew at Beroea (Aleppo) in Syria;[88] these may represent a dispersion from the early church of Damascus. Others, and these perhaps the majority, maintained their existence as the church of Jerusalem in dispersion, alienated alike from orthodox Jews and catholic Christians. They called themselves 'the poor'—*hā'ebyōnim*, the 'Ebionites' of the Greek and Latin Fathers. The church of Jerusalem in apostolic times used this designation of itself, and so did the Qumran community.[89] It has long been supposed that the distinctive features of Ebionite belief and practice may have owed something to the influence of Essene and related groups, and the discovery and study of the Qumran literature have added weight to this supposition. Justin in his day knew of two different kinds of Jewish Christians —those who practised circumcision and other requirements of the Jewish law but at the same time shared Justin's general view of the person of Christ, for whose salvation he could hope; and those who combined with their devotion to the Jewish law what came later

[86] Cf. Justin, *Apol.* i, 31:6. The name Ben-Kosebah is now attested from contemporary Hebrew documents; cf. the Murabba'at texts 24. B 3, C 3, 20, E 2, G 3; 43. 1, 8. It is not at all certain if the Galilaeans to whom reference is made in the last-mentioned passage (a letter from Simeon Ben-Kosebah to Yeshua Ben-Galgula) have anything to do with Jewish Christians.

[87] Cf. F. C. Burkitt, *Christian Beginnings* (London, 1924), pp. 65ff, for the suggestion that the church of Aelia, 'rather like a new purchaser that has bought the Old Manor House, who after a while begins to collect old family portraits and souvenirs', rescued from oblivion the text of an Aramaic discourse delivered by James the Just and produced the free Greek rendering which we know as the Epistle of James.

[88] Jerome, *De uiris illustribus*, 3; cf. Epiphanius, *Pan.* 29:7.

[89] Irenaeus, *Haer.* i, 22; iv, 52; v, 1, 3; Hippolytus, *Ref.* x, 22; Tertullian, *Praescriptio* 33. Cf. Gal. 2:10 (see p. 270); 1 QM xi, 9, 13; xiii, 13f; 1 QH v, 22; 1 QpHab. xii, 3, 6, 10.

to be called an 'adoptionist' Christology, for whom he could cherish no hope of salvation. The latter, of whom Trypho, Justin's Jewish interlocutor, knew something as well as Justin, believed Jesus to be a man of ordinary human descent, who was chosen by God to be Messiah.[90] If these latter are the Ebionites of other Christian writers, they also regarded Jesus' ministry mainly as that of a second Moses; he was, in their eyes, not only the prophet like Moses mentioned in Deuteronomy but also the reformer and purifier of the Law, who came to remove from it such unworthy accretions as the sacrificial ritual and to emphasize and apply its true and inward meaning. They refused to acknowledge Paul as a true apostle of Christ; to them the chief of the apostles was James the Just. Attempts have been made to wrest information about them from the sources which critical study has discerned as underlying the *Clementine Recognitions* and *Clementine Homilies*. One of these sources has been identified with *The Travels of Peter*, a work known to Origen in the first half of the third century and itself based on earlier documents and traditions: another, *The Ascents of James*, may have provided Hegesippus with the details of his account of James's martyrdom.[91]

The Ebionites appear to have lingered on in Transjordan, Syria and Egypt until the seventh century, when those who had not by that time been absorbed in Jewish or Christian orthodoxy lost their identity in the rising tide of Islam. The name of one Ebionite leader has been preserved—Symmachus, author or reviser of a Greek version of the Old Testament which was included in Origen's *Hexapla*. From him the Ebionites were sometimes called Symmachians.[92]

[90] Justin, *Dialogue* 48:2ff.

[91] Cf. H. J. Schoeps, *Theologie und Geschichte des Judenchristentums, passim*; J. Munck, 'Jewish Christianity in Post-Apostolic Times', *NTS* 6 (1959–60), pp. 103ff.

[92] Cf. Marius Victorinus, *Comm. on Gal.* 1:19; Ambrosiaster, *Prologue to Comm. on Gal.*; Augustine, *c. Faustum Manichaeum* 19:4, 17; *c. Cresconium Donatistam* i, 31.

29 Christianity in Rome

1

A new chapter in the history of Roman Christianity, as has been said above, opens in A.D. 54, with the death of Claudius and the succession of Nero, by which time Claudius's edict of five years earlier, expelling Jews (and Jewish Christians) from Rome, became a dead letter.[1] Less than three years after the accession of Nero, Paul could describe the Christian community of Rome as renowned for its faith throughout the world.[2] It was no longer confined to Jewish believers; it included a large number of Gentiles, most of whom had become Christians as a result of the Gentile mission in various parts of the Eastern Mediterranean and had subsequently settled in Rome. Some of these were perhaps inclined to view their fellow-believers of Jewish origin as poor relations and to think of themselves as fully committed and fully emancipated Christians by contrast. It is for their benefit that Paul emphasizes that the olive-tree which represents the people of God has the patriarchs of Israel as its root, and that even if some of the original (Jewish) branches have been broken off because of their unbelief, the new (Gentile) branches which have been grafted into the olive-tree from the oleaster to which they formerly belonged (a process 'contrary to nature', as he points out) owe their present position to the unmerited grace of God. 'Do not boast over the [original] branches', he warns the Gentile Christians. 'If you do boast, remember it is not you that support the root, but the root that supports you' (Rom. 11:18).

Although reference has just been made to the 'Christian community of Rome' at the time when Paul wrote the Epistle to the Romans, it may be worthy of note that this letter is not addressed 'to the church of God which is at Rome', 'but to all God's beloved

---

[1] See p. 299.   [2] Rom. 1:8.

at Rome, who are called to be saints' (Rom. 1:7). This may mean
that while there were many Christians in Rome at this time, meeting
in synagogues or 'house-churches' or other local groups, there was
no unified 'church of Rome' under a city-wide administration. Perhaps some local groups consisted of Jewish Christians and others
of Gentile Christians, and there were few, if any, in which Jewish
and Gentile Christians met together. Nor would it be surprising if
some groups were called synagogues[3] (or 'episynagogues')[4] while
others were designated *ekklēsiai.* One recent study adduces the
evidence of Romans 16:3–16 in this connexion: 'It was never Paul's
practice to list the individual members of a church to which he was
writing . . . , but if there was no church to address, he could do
nothing else but send his letter to all those individuals whose names
he knew in Rome. It is moreover suggestive of the way Christians
of Rome were associated with each other that no fewer than five
sets of names are included in a way that suggests household groups,
and specific use is made of the term *ekklēsia* in one such case'.[5]

It is Prisca and Aquila who have an *ekklēsia* in their house (v. 3);
the use of this term in connexion with associates of Paul is what
might be expected. Members of the household of Aristobulus and
of the household of Narcissus (vv. 10, 11) may have been slaves or
freedmen belonging formerly to Aristobulus (a brother of Herod
Agrippa I who lived as a private citizen in Rome) and to Tiberius
Claudius Narcissus (a freedman of Tiberius who was executed at
the instance of Nero's mother late in A.D. 54) who passed into the
possession of the emperor and would be distinguished from other
members of the imperial household as Aristobuliani and Narcissiani.
The two remaining groups are identified by reference to some
of their outstanding members: 'Asyncritus, Phlegon, Hermes, Pa-
trobas, Hermas, and the brethren who are with them' (v. 14) and
'Philologus, Julia, Nereus and his sister, and Olympas, and all the
saints who are with them' (v. 15).

[3] Cf. Hermas, *Shepherd*, Mandate 11:9, 13, 14. (See p. 206, n. 4.)
[4] A word used in Heb. 10:25 where, however, it may mean the act of gathering rather than the place of gathering (so RSV: 'not neglecting to meet together'). But see W. Manson, *The Epistle to the Hebrews* (London, 1951),
p. 69.
[5] E. A. Judge and G. S. R. Thomas, 'The Origin of the Church at Rome: A
New Solution?', *RThR* 25 (1966), p. 91; cf. E. A. Judge, *The Social Pattern of
Christian Groups in the First Century* (London, 1960), pp. 36f.

Yet the decentralized condition of the Roman Christians in A.D. 57 should not be exaggerated. The reports which reached Paul from Rome appear to have described their spiritual progress as a whole, and his directing his letter 'to all God's beloved at Rome'[6] implies that he expected them all to hear it read, though not necessarily at the same time.

If we are right in maintaining the minority view that the greetings in Romans 16 are intended for Rome and not for Ephesus,[7] it is plain that by the time Paul wrote some very interesting Christians from other parts of the empire had made their way to Rome. Who were Andronicus and Junias,[8] whom Paul calls 'my kinsmen and my fellow-prisoners'? 'They are men of note', he adds, 'among the apostles, and they were in Christ before me' (v. 7)— they must have been very early Christians, members probably of the Hellenist section in the primitive Jerusalem church. And what of 'Rufus, eminent in the Lord, also his mother and mine' (v. 13)? On the assumption of the Roman destination of Romans 16 and the Roman milieu of the Gospel of Mark, we should be inclined to identify him with the Rufus of Mark 15:21, the son of Simon of Cyrene. If from there we take a long, speculative step and suggest that this Simon was the same as 'Symeon who was called Niger', a leading prophet and teacher in the early church of Syrian Antioch (Acts 13:1), we should at once be provided with a setting in which the mother of Rufus could prove herself a true mother also to the disinherited Paul.[9]

It is nonetheless surprising that, not more than eight years after Claudius's edict, the Christian community in Rome should have been in such a flourishing condition as Paul's letter implies, however it was organized. Here a suggestion of T. W. Manson deserves to be considered. Discussing the origin of the gospel of Mark, he wrote: 'If Peter had paid a visit to Rome some time between

[6] Rom. 1:7.

[7] Cf. C. H. Dodd, *The Epistle to the Romans* (London, 1932), pp. xviiff; F. F. Bruce, *The Epistle of Paul to the Romans* (London, 1963), pp. 266ff; for arguments for the Ephesian destination see T. W. Manson, *Studies in the Gospels and Epistles* (Manchester, 1962), pp. 230ff.

[8] Or perhaps we should understand the feminine Junia, and render ἐπίσημοι by 'persons of note' rather than 'men of note'.

[9] Cf. J. A. Robertson, *The Hidden Romance of the New Testament* (London, 1920), pp. 203ff; A. B. Kinsey, 'Simon the Crucifer and Symeon the Prophet', *ExT* 35 (1923–4), pp. 84ff.

55 and 60; if Mark had been his interpreter then; if after Peter's
departure from the city Mark had taken in hand—at the request of
the Roman hearers—a written record of what Peter had said; then
the essential points in the evidence would all be satisfied'.[10]

This is a hypothetical reconstruction, but Peter does appear to
have embarked on a more extended ministry in the fifties of the
first century, and if, with the accession of a new emperor in 54, expelled Jews began to make their way back to Rome, a visit from
Peter, in his capacity as apostle to the Jews, would have been very
helpful in re-establishing the Christian fellowship within this wider
Jewish community. If indeed Paul had cherished some earlier
hope of being the first to preach the gospel in Rome, news of such
a development would have caused him to change his plans.[11] It
would be interesting to know more than we do about the background of his statement to the Roman Christians that he had
often intended to visit them but had been prevented thus far
(Rom. 1:13). But his principle of not building on another man's
foundation (Rom. 15:20) would make him dismiss any idea of
settling down in Rome and exercising an apostolic ministry there
as he had done in Corinth and Ephesus, although it would not
prevent his preaching to Gentiles in Rome during his brief halt
in the city (Rom. 1:13–15) or using Rome as a forward base for
his projected Spanish mission (Rom. 15:24, 28f).

In the year in which Paul wrote his letter to the Roman Christians, an incident is recorded which has been thought to cast
further light on the progress of Christianity in Rome. Pomponia
Graecina, wife of Aulus Plantius (who had added Britain to the
Roman Empire fourteen years previously), was examined by a
domestic court on a charge of having embraced a 'foreign superstition'. Colour was given to this charge, says Tacitus, by the fact
that for fourteen years she had worn mourning garb and

[10] T. W. Manson, *Studies in the Gospels and Epistles*, pp. 33ff. He points out
that Peter's 'departure' (*excessio*) mentioned in the Anti-Marcionite Prologue
to Mark need not be understood as his death, but as his leaving Rome after
his first visit there—although Irenaeus probably understood the term in the
sense of 'death' when he says that Mark's gospel was delivered in writing after
the departure (ἔξοδος) of Peter and Paul.
[11] In a lecture mentioned by E. A. Judge and G. S. R. Thomas in *RThR* 25
(1966), p. 90, n. 56, G. Bornkamm suggested that Paul was bound for Rome
along the Via Egnatia even earlier (*c.* A.D. 50; cf. Acts 17:1), when news that
he had been forestalled in Rome made him turn south to Achaia.

avoided the society which a lady of her class would naturally seek.[12] One commentator on Tacitus suggests that 'the retirement and sobriety of a Christian might well appear a kind of "perpetual mourning" to the dissolute society of the Neronian period'.[13] But the phrase 'foreign superstition' is quite general; it could, for example, refer to Judaism, which was favoured by a considerable number of Roman ladies. As it was, Pomponia was acquitted of the charge, and continued for the rest of her life to enjoy the esteem of her friends in spite of her retiring ways. It may be a mere coincidence, or it may have further significance, that one of the oldest Christian cemeteries in Rome, the 'Cemetery of Callistus' by the Appian Way, contains second-century inscriptions commemorating members of the *gens Pomponia*, one of whom, named Pomponius Graecinus, was presumably one of Pomponia's direct or collateral descendants.[14] Christianity had thus entered her family a century after her day, if not in her own lifetime.

2

Three years after Paul's despatch of his letter to Rome, he arrived there himself, under armed guard, to have his case heard by the supreme court. Luke relates how 'the brethren' from Rome, hearing of his approach, came as far as Appii Forum and Tres Tabernae (stations on the Appian Way, respectively some forty-three and thirty-three miles south of Rome) to greet him and his companions and escort them for the remainder of their journey. 'On seeing them', he adds, 'Paul thanked God and took courage' (Acts 28:15). But of further contact with the Roman Christians during Paul's two years of house-arrest Luke has nothing to say. He does report a non-committal remark made by the representatives of the Jews of Rome with whom Paul had an interview three days after his arrival in the city. They professed to have heard nothing about his arrest and trial in Judaea; 'but', they said, 'we desire to hear from you what your views are; for with regard to

[12] Tacitus, *Annals* xiii, 32. 3–5.
[13] H. Pitman (ed.), *Cornelii Taciti Annalium Libri XIII–XVI* (Oxford, 1904), Notes, pp. 29f.
[14] Cf. H. Leclercq, 'Aristocratiques (Classes)', in *DACL* 1, 2 (Paris, 1907), cols. 2847f.

this sect we know that everywhere it is spoken against' (Acts 28:
22). These words should not be pressed to mean that they knew
nothing of Christianity in Rome, whether Jewish or Gentile; they
were cautiously feeling their way with Paul, and 'everywhere'
might well include Rome itself.

Paul's freedom to proclaim the gospel to all who came his way
during his two years in Rome must have been a source of encouragement to many Christians in the city; whether the Epistle
to the Philippians was sent from Rome or not, the language of
Phil. 1:14 would certainly be true of Paul's Roman imprisonment:
'most of the brethren have been made confident in the Lord because of my imprisonment, and are much more emboldened to
speak the word of God without fear'. It could well be that the
following words, telling how some preached the gospel in a
spirit of loving fellowship with Paul, while others did so 'out of
partisanship, . . . thinking to afflict me in my imprisonment' (Phil.
1:16f), were also applicable to Paul's situation in Rome.

The relevance of the Epistle to the Hebrews to the history of
Roman Christianity must be doubtful because its provenance and
destination cannot be decided with certainty. One of the most
persuasive views of its purpose[15] regards it as written to a 'house-
church' or synagogue of Jewish Christians in Rome who found
themselves out of sympathy with the prevalent trend of Roman
Christianity, stimulated as it had been to fresh endeavour in the
Gentile mission by Paul's recent stay in the city, and began to
wonder if they might not have been too precipitate in committing
themselves to a new order which involved an increasing breach
with the cherished traditions of their old religion. The old religion enjoyed the protection of Roman law, but it was becoming
more and more difficult to try to keep a foot in either camp. They
would soon have to declare for the one or the other; and declaration
for the gospel would mean burning their boats and entrusting
themselves to the dangerous uncertainties of a new way of life in
company about which they did not feel completely happy. The
old familiar environment exerted a strong attraction. To them in
this predicament came this letter, urging them to cut loose from
their old attachments and face the unknown with Christ, gladly

[15] W. Manson, *The Epistle to the Hebrews* (London, 1951).

accepting the stigma that adhered to the Christian name for the
sake of the prize that lay before them. This way of faith was the
way chosen by their forefather Abraham, who 'went out, not knowing where he was to go' (Heb. 11:8). The old order with all its
dear and hallowed associations was in any case obsolescent and
on the point of disappearing; the future lay with Christ and with
those who followed him.

The writer reminds them of the persecution they had cheer-
fully faced in the first joyful days of their faith (Heb. 10:32-4)—a
reference perhaps to the circumstances of their banishment from
Rome in A.D. 49[16] (from which they had presumably returned)—
but mentions that they have not yet reached the point of shedding their blood in their struggle against sin, which suggests a date
for the letter not later than the middle of A.D. 64.

3

Some time after midnight on 19 July, A.D. 64, the night after full
moon, a fire broke out at the north-east end of the Circus Maximus
in Rome, adjoining the Palatine and Caelian hills. The shops
which stood in a colonnade round the outer face of the Circus
were full of combustible wares which provided fodder for the
flames, and the conflagration, securing a hold there and fanned by
the wind, raged throughout the city for five days. When at last it
was stamped out, a fresh outbreak started on the estate of Tigellinus. Of the fourteen districts into which the city was divided,
only four were spared; three were completely destroyed and the
remaining seven received severe damage. The imperial palace itself, on the Palatine hill, was burned out.

Nero was at Antium (Anzio), on the Tyrrhenian coast, when
the fire started. He hastened back to Rome and threw himself
vigorously into the organization of relief. The Campus Martius, on
the east bank of the Tiber, and the imperial gardens west of the
river were thrown open to the homeless multitudes; temporary
shelter was constructed for them, and they were provided with
grain at a greatly reduced rate.

But Nero received little thanks for these measures. People were

[16] See p. 297.

unwilling to believe that the fire was accidental, and many thought that Nero had arranged it in order that he might rebuild the city nearer to his heart's desire. A story spread around that during the fire he had indulged his histrionic propensities and sung of the burning of Troy. Rumour also told how men attempting to fight the fire were prevented by threatening gangs, while others could tell of men who were seen actively encouraging the flames to spread, claiming that they had their orders. 'Perhaps they had their orders', says Tacitus, 'or perhaps they just wanted to loot unhindered'.[17]

The rebuilding of the city was energetically undertaken; instead of the narrow, winding streets and irregular blocks of high tenements which had been a positive invitation to the flames, the broad streets and spacious buildings of the new city were regularly planned. The lower courses of every building had to be of approved stonework, semi-detached buildings were forbidden, and every householder was required to have fire-fighting appliances readily accessible.[18]

But the finger of popular suspicion continued to point at Nero. His new palace, 'the Golden House', which replaced the one lost in the fire, was so luxurious and extensive—it stretched from the Palatine hill to the Esquiline—that current pop songs described Rome as being rebuilt on what was left over from the palace.[19] Nero accordingly found it expedient to provide scapegoats. The Christians of Rome, by now a large community, were charged with instigating the fire. Why the Christians? First, no doubt, because they were unpopular 'haters of the human race', disliked by all for their anti-social attitude. So much of the Roman way of life was bound up with what Christians regarded as immorality and idolatry that they would not take part in it. Jews, of course, held equally aloof, but Jews had always been like that; besides,

[17] *Annals* xv, 38. 8. Tacitus is our principal authority for the fire and its sequel. Suetonius (*Nero* 38) is less careful than Tacitus about checking his statements; thus he reproduces without qualification the rumour that 'Nero fiddled while Rome burned' and the gossip which charged Nero with setting the city on fire. Pliny the Elder (*Nat. Hist.* xvii, 5) speaks of 'the Emperor Nero's conflagration' (*Neronis principis incendia*), which *might* imply that Nero started it.
[18] Tacitus, *Ann.* xv, 43. 4f; cf. Suetonius, *Nero* 16:1.
[19] Suetonius, *Nero* 39, 2; cf. 31:1f; Tacitus, *Ann.* xv, 42. 1; 52. 1.

they were members of a distinct nation, with their own ancestral religion. But the Gentile Christians of Rome had no such reason for holding aloof. In Juvenal's words, they belonged to the sewage of the Orontes which had discharged itself into the Tiber; in Suetonius's words, they were 'a race of men given to a novel and baneful superstition'; Tacitus describes them as notorious for their depravity.[20] Not only so, but popular Christian eschatology looked for the fiery dissolution of the current world-order—not on some remote, hypothetical 'last day', but soon, any time now. When Rome, the capital of the world, caught fire and blazed from end to end, what wonder if some of the simpler souls imagined that this was the expected day of the Lord, and welcomed it as such? Their own material possessions were consumed by the fire together with those of their neighbours; what matter, if the city of God, the kingdom of the saints, was to be erected on the ruins? If such sentiments were voiced during the fire, they would give some colour to the charge of incendiarism; but even so, it proved very difficult to make the charge stick.

'First of all', says Tacitus, 'those who confessed were arrested'. Confessed to what? To being Christians, or to being incendiaries? It is conceivable that one or two of them, in an excess of enthusiasm, were willing to give themselves up for having started the fire or helped it along; whatever form their confession took, they were compelled to divulge their associates' names, and in consequence 'a huge crowd was convicted not so much of arson as of hatred of the human race'.[21] Their execution was an occasion for popular entertainment; Nero's gardens were thrown open for the occasion. According to Tacitus, some were crucified, some were sewn up in the skins of animals and hunted down by dogs, some were covered with pitch and set alight to serve as living torches when darkness fell. Thirty years later, Clement of Rome recalls how 'a great multitude' of believers had to endure cruel sufferings, how Christian women were forced to act the parts of Dirce and the daughters of Danaus for the delectation of the spectators.[22] These atrocities went far to defeat their end; men began to feel that these wretched people, guilty as they were of

[20] Juvenal, *Satire* iii, 62; Suetonius, *Nero* 16:2; Tacitus, *Ann.* xv, 44. 3.
[21] Tacitus, *Ann.* xv, 44. 5.   [22] I Clem. 6:1f.

being Christians, and deserving the severest punishment, were nevertheless being sacrificed to glut the emperor's savage lust rather than in the public interest.

The horrible experiences of those days were not quickly forgotten by the Christians themselves. The last persecuting Antichrist in the Apocalypse of John is Nero come to life again;[23] he and his empire are doomed to destruction by the parousia of the true Christ. The imperial city is viewed as Babylon the great, the scarlet woman seated on the seven-headed beast, 'drunk with the blood of the saints and the blood of the martyrs of Jesus' (Rev. 17:6). And if Rome rose again after the fire of A.D. 64, 'the smoke of her burning' would once more ascend to heaven, and she would be found no more (Rev. 17:9, 18, 21).

Traditionally the apostles Peter and Paul are held to have been martyred in Rome during the Neronian persecution—if not in the pogrom that followed the fire, then a year or two later. Something has already been said about Paul's last days,[24] but our earliest references to his death couple it with Peter's.

The earliest reference of all is Clement of Rome's. Immediately before his account of the martyrs under Nero, he singles out Peter and Paul as pre-eminent examples of men who showed steadfastness in face of afflictions arising from envy. Clement has adduced seven examples from the Old Testament and goes on:

> But let us cease from examples of antiquity and come to those who contended thus in days nearest to our own. Through jealousy and envy the greatest and most righteous pillars of the church were persecuted and contended unto death. Let us place before our eyes the good apostles. Peter, because of wicked jealousy, suffered not one or two but many trials, and having borne witness there went to the place of glory which was his due.

This is followed by the account of Paul's apostolic labours and faithful witness quoted above; as with Peter, so with Paul, Clement says, it was on account of 'jealousy and strife' that he 'showed the way to the prize of endurance'.[25] Then he adds that 'to these men of holy manner of life was added a great multitude of the elect, who suffered because of jealousy and provided a most noble example among ourselves'—and goes on to describe what they en-

[23] See pp. 410f.   [24] See p. 367.   [25] I Clem. 5:1-4, 5.

dured under Nero. Nero indeed is not mentioned, but 'among ourselves' means 'in Rome', and his language matches Tacitus's account
of the Neronian persecution. When he says that this multitude of
martyrs 'was added' to Peter and Paul,[26] his words should not be
pressed to imply that the two apostles died before the others,
but rather that they were the most eminent of the Neronian martyrs.
It might even be questioned whether he necessarily means that
Peter and Paul, like the 'great multitude' of martyrs, bore their
testimony 'among ourselves'—i.e. in Rome—but in the light of other
evidence that Rome was indeed the place where the two apostles
died Clement probably intended to convey this; when he wrote,
the fact that the apostles had died in Rome was probably so well
known that it was sufficient to allude to it rather than to state it
explicitly.

It may be further asked what was the precise nature of the envy
and jealousy which, according to Clement, was responsible for
the death of the apostles and their fellow-martyrs. So far as Paul
is concerned, his prosecution by the Sanhedrin on the evidence of
Asian Jews may have been in Clement's mind. We have no comparable evidence relating to Peter. As for the Neronian martyrs in
general, we may recall what Tacitus says about those who 'confessed' on the morrow of the Great Fire and gave information
which led to the arrest of many others. This provides too slender
a foundation for any substantial reconstruction; one might wonder, however, whether some tension between Jewish and Gentile
members of the Roman church played some part here or, since
some of the Jewish members of the church probably still maintained a footing in the synagogue, whether the tension between
Jews and Christians in Rome was exploited by the imperial police
to procure the arrest of suspects. We cannot know for certain.

That Peter as well as Paul was put to death at Rome under
Nero is the unanimous testimony of Christian tradition so far as it
touches this subject.

In the course of his letter to the Roman church, written from
Smyrna about A.D. 110 to prepare the Christians of the capital for
his arrival in their city to be exposed to the wild beasts, Ignatius

[26] 'These men of holy manner of life' to whom the Roman martyrs were
'added' (I Clem. 6:1) may be not only Peter and Paul but also the Old Testament examples which precede them.

begs them not to do him an 'unseasonable kindness' by trying to use their influence to prevent his martyrdom. Yet he can only beg them to respect his wishes: he cannot give them orders. 'I do not command you, as Peter and Paul did; they were apostles, I am a convict; they were free men, I am a slave to this day'.[27]

This is the one place where Ignatius mentions Peter and Paul together—elsewhere in his correspondence there is one reference to each separately—and the natural sense is that Peter and Paul did as apostles give authoritative directions to the church of Rome. The Epistle to the Romans will satisfy the reference to Paul; we have no comparable evidence for Peter. Peter's one reasonably certain contact with Rome is his death there; but if Ignatius knew of no more than this, he would have sufficient ground for his general remark about Peter's exercise of apostolic authority in Rome. He, too, would have one contact with Rome, for he too was on his way to martyrdom there, but this (in his eyes) gave him no right to address the Roman church in such imperative terms as Peter would have been entitled to use. It might, indeed, be possible to construe Ignatius's language to mean more specifically that, while Peter and Paul had given the Roman church certain orders with reference to their martyrdom, he could only make a request of them regarding his.

Peter may indeed have paid an earlier visit to Rome at the beginning of Nero's principate, as has been suggested. But the evidence for such an earlier visit is nebulous indeed compared with that for his coming to Rome in Nero's later years.[28] On this latter point Hans Lietzmann summed up the situation thus:

> All the early sources about the year 100 become clear and easily intelligible, and agree with their historical context and with each other, if we accept what they clearly suggest to us, namely, that Peter sojourned in Rome and died a martyr there. Any other hypothesis regarding Peter's death piles difficulty upon difficulty, and cannot be supported by a single document.[29]

About A.D. 170 Dionysius, bishop of Corinth, writing a letter to

[27] *Ad Rom.* 4:3 (see pp. 418, 428).
[28] The identification of 'Babylon' in I Peter 5:13 with Rome, made by Clement of Alexandria in the sixth book of his *Hypotyposes* (according to Eusebius, *HE* ii, 15. 2), is by far the most probable.
[29] *Petrus und Paulus in Rom*[2] (Berlin, 1927), p. 238.

the Roman church, mentions as a bond of union between Corinth and Rome the fact that the churches in both these cities were planted by Peter and Paul, 'for both of them taught together in our Corinth, where they planted our church, and likewise they taught together in Italy also and were martyred about the same time'.[30] What Paul would have said could he have foreseen this naming of Peter alongside himself as co-founder of the church at Corinth is difficult to imagine! However, the balance was redressed somewhat, with equal distortion of historical fact, by his being traditionally claimed as co-founder of the Roman church with Peter.

Dionysius, of course, is a witness to current tradition, not to a historical situation preceding his time by a century and more. This is evident from his naming Dionysius the Areopagite, one of Paul's few converts among the Athenians (Acts 17:34), as first bishop of Athens.[31]

Another witness to current tradition around the same time is Irenaeus, who went to Gaul from the province of Asia about A.D. 177 to become bishop of Lyons. Irenaeus, in his treatise *Against Heresies*, appeals to the maintenance of the original apostolic teaching in those churches where a continuous succession of bishops could be traced back to apostolic founders. One of these churches was Rome where, he says, the church was founded and established 'by the two most glorious apostles Peter and Paul', who delivered the bishop's ministry to Linus, from whom it passed to Anencletus and then to Clement (author of the Epistle of Clement). This 'apostolic succession' is then traced down to Eleutherus, bishop of Rome in Irenaeus's own day, and is presented as an argument that the faith maintained by the Roman church when Irenaeus was writing is the faith inculcated by the apostles.[32] In fact, Irenaeus is probably committing an anachronism when he traces the monarchical episcopate at Rome back to apostolic times; the evidence of Ignatius and Hermas suggests that as late as the early years of the second century the Roman church was administered by a college of presbyter-bishops and not by a single bishop.[33] Irenaeus's list of Roman bishops, which served as a source for later lists, may itself go back to Hegesippus, the Palestinian Christian, who appears

[margin note: collegiate Roman rule in 2nd cent.]

---

[30] *Apud* Euseb. *HE* ii, 25. 8. [31] *Apud* Euseb. *HE* iii, 4. 10; iv, 23. 3.
[32] Irenaeus, *Haer.* iii, 3. 1–3. [33] See pp. 418f with nn. 8–10.

to have been a pioneer in the argument that the true and original
Christian faith could be identified if one ascertained the consensus
of belief in all the churches founded by apostles. He himself undertook this quest about A.D. 150 and travelled as far as Rome,
interrogating the churches which he visited about their beliefs and
recording his findings in five books of *Memoirs*, which (though
long since lost) provided Eusebius with valuable source-material.
He found that 'in each (episcopal) succession and in each city
the faith is just as the law and the prophets and the Lord proclaim it'.[34]

Here, then, we have a further witness to the tradition that Peter
and Paul were joint founders of the church of Rome, and the
practice of naming both apostles jointly as founders persisted into
the third century. But from the time of Hippolytus onwards (*c.*
220), when the founder of an apostolic church began to be reckoned as first in succession of bishops, the principle that there
could be one bishop only at one time began to lead to the sub-
stitution of Peter's name alone as apostolic founder for the names
of Peter and Paul together.[35]

Another writer towards the end of the second century, the Roman presbyter Gaius, gives a reference to something more tangible
than oral tradition. He engaged in a controversial correspondence
with a Phrygian Montanist named Proclus, who appealed to venerated names in support of his position: 'Philip's four daughters
who were prophetesses', he says, 'were at Hierapolis in Asia; their
tomb is there and so is their father's'.[36] But if venerated names
and tombs are to be invoked, Gaius can go one better: 'I can point
out the trophies of the apostles; for if you will go to the Vatican or
to the Ostian Way, you will find the trophies of those who
founded this church'.[37]

By 'trophies' Gaius means monuments marking the place of the
apostles' martyrdom or of their burial. The word (Gk. *tropaion*)
is military in origin; it denotes the pile of arms of various kinds
which the victors heaped on the battlefield to celebrate their put-

[34] *Apud* Euseb. *HE* iv, 22. 3.
[35] Cf. C. H. Turner, *Catholic and Apostolic* (London, 1931), p. 225; see also
his essay 'Apostolic Succession' in H. B. Swete (ed.), *Essays on the Early History of the Church and the Ministry* (London, 1921), pp. 93–214, especially
pp. 141f.
[36] *Apud* Euseb. *HE* iii, 31. 4 (see p. 376).   [37] *Apud* Euseb. *HE* iii, 25. 7.

ting the enemy to flight. The 'trophies' of Peter and Paul are accordingly their 'victory' monuments. It was in the belief that the apostles were actually buried at the places indicated by Gaius that Constantine in the fourth century built the basilica of St. Peter on the Vatican hill and that of St. Paul outside the walls on the road to Ostia—the former at immense trouble and expense, for it involved extensive excavation of the side of the hill to accommodate the foundations. Whether Gaius himself understood the 'trophies' to be 'funerary monuments' is not so certain. Perhaps he was not greatly concerned whether they marked the spot of martyrdom or of burial, if he supposed that the apostles were buried near the spots where they were executed. That Peter's 'trophy' should be located on the Vatican hill is the more interesting because Nero's gardens, where Tacitus says the Roman Christians were publicly executed after the Great Fire, were situated on that very hill—probably a short distance south of Constantine's basilica.

The 'trophy' of Peter to which Gaius refers was almost certainly discovered in the course of excavations beneath the *confessio*[38] in St. Peter's in 1940 and the following years; it was a simple columnar monument with reference to which Constantine manifestly oriented the whole basilica.[39] If (as seems likely) the monument was built at the same time as a small water channel in the immediate vicinity, it can be dated in the time of Marcus Aurelius, whose name is stamped on several bricks of the channel, and perhaps before his accession to the imperial throne in A.D. 161, since he is designated Caesar, not Augustus. If the monument was erected about A.D. 160, it was about a generation old when Gaius mentioned it in his letter to Proclus. It remains to learn whether a similar monument waits to be discovered some day beneath the high altar of San Paolo fuori le Mura.[40]

[38] The *confessio* is the chamber around the tomb together with the shaft connecting it with the altar.
[39] Cf. E. Kirschbaum, *The Tombs of St. Peter and St. Paul* (London, 1959), pp. 143ff; also J. M. C. Toynbee and J. B. Ward-Perkins, *The Shrine of St. Peter and the Vatican Excavations* (London, 1956); O. Cullmann, *Peter: Disciple, Apostle, Martyr* (London, 1953), pp. 132ff.
[40] The two slabs forming the floor under the high altar and bearing between them the inscription PAVLO APOSTOLO MART (in fourth-century lettering) perhaps stood upright in their original position, possibly as two of the four sides

The traditions responsible for the location of San Pietro in Vaticano and San Paolo fuori le Mura thus go back almost to the middle of the second century, and they may well be based on actual fact. But there is a rival site, associated with both the apostles, which, while it does not have such early attestation as those on the Vatican hill and the Ostian road, was for a time a very popular place of pilgrimage. This is the so-called Memoria Apostolorum ad Catacumbas, beneath the Church of St. Sebastian at the third milestone on the Appian Way.[41] Here, according to the *Depositio Martyrum* in the Calendar of Philocalus (A.D. 354) were placed the bones of Peter (? and Paul); the date (29 June, A.D. 258) mentioned in this connexion is probably that of the establishment of the shrine.[42] Evidence on the site makes it certain that in the third quarter of the third century and well into the fourth it was widely believed that the remains of both the apostles lay there. This evidence consists largely of *graffiti* invoking them by name ('Peter and Paul, remember us'; 'Peter and Paul, pray for Victor'; 'Paul [and] Peter, remember Sozomenos, and so do you who read this') and referring to the holding of *refrigeria* (memorial banquets) in their honour. The abundance of such references to the apostles forms a striking contrast to the absence of this sort of thing from the neighbourhood of the 'trophy' beneath St. Peter's, apart from the solitary and enigmatic Greek letters ΠΕΤΡ . . . ΕΝΙ (? 'Peter is in here') scratched on the wall beside it.[43] There are a number of Christian prayers for the departed written up in the neighbourhood of the 'trophy' (for there was a pre-Constantinian cemetery there), but these take such forms as 'Paulinus, may you live', 'Simplicius, may you live in Christ', and none of them refers to Peter.

The association of the two apostles with the site on the Appian Way is further attested by the hymn *Apostolorum Passio*, which

---

of a structure enclosing the *memoria* in the Constantinian basilica (E. Kirschbaum, *The Tombs of St. Peter and St. Paul*, pp. 179ff).

[41] On this *memoria* see especially H. Chadwick, 'St. Peter and St. Paul in Rome: The Problem of the Memoria Apostolorum ad Catacumbas', *JTS*, n.s. 8 (1957), pp. 31ff, an article to which this account is deeply indebted.

[42] The extant text of the entry runs: 'III Kal. Iul. Petri in Catacumbas et Pauli Ostense Tusco et Basso consulibus'.

[43] Cf. E. Kirschbaum, *The Tombs of St. Peter and St. Paul*, pp. 137f and pl. 24a.

goes back to the middle of the fourth century and indicates that
on 29 June their martyrdom was commemorated at all three sites
—the Vatican hill, the Ostian Way and the Appian Way:

> Tantae per urbis ambitum
> Stipata tendunt agmina;
> Trinis celebratur uiis
> Festum sacrorum martyrum.[44]

But this attempt to satisfy the competing claims of the rival sites
did not last long; when Pope Damasus, in the course of restoring
the Christian cemeteries of Rome, turned his attention to the
Memoria Apostolorum ad Catacumbas, he indicated an official line
in the opening words of an inscription which he set up in the
Basilica Apostolorum which was built on the site:

> Hic habitasse prius sanctos cognoscere debes
> Nomina quisque Petri pariter Paulique requiris . . .

'Here', he announced, 'you must know that the saints formerly
dwelt, whoever you are who ask for the names of Peter and
Paul'.[45] In other words, their bodies lay here once upon a time,
but they are here no longer. This, with its implication of a translation of the bodies from the Via Appia to the Vatican hill and
the road to Ostia, represents an attempt to harmonize the conflict-
ing traditions and to divert the attention of pious pilgrims to the
two Constantinian basilicas beneath which the apostles' bodies
were now believed to rest. Some students of later days, beginning
with John Pearson, seventeenth-century bishop of Chester,[46] have
proposed a more reasonable harmonization by envisaging a tem-

[44] 'The closely packed columns make their way on the circuit of the great
city; the festival of the holy martyrs is celebrated on three roads'. The hymn
is traditionally ascribed to Ambrose.
[45] The remainder of the inscription underlines the Roman church's claim to
primacy over the eastern churches on the ground that Peter and Paul came
from the east to Rome to be martyred and buried there.
[46] J. Pearson, *Annales Cyprianici*, p. 62 (included in *S.C.C. Opera*, ed. J.
Fell, Oxford, 1682), as H. Chadwick points out in *JTS*, n.s. 8 (1957), p. 41, n.
2. So, more recently, L. Duchesne (ed.), *Liber Pontificalis* i (Paris, 1886), pp.
civff; *Christian Worship* (London, 1919⁵), p. 277; H. Lietzmann, *Petrus und
Paulus in Rom*, pp. 122ff; 'The Tomb of the Apostles ad Catacumbas', *HTR* 16
(1923), pp. 147ff. E. Kirschbaum (*The Tombs of St. Peter and St. Paul*, pp.
198ff) suggests that only the heads of the two apostles were removed to the
Via Appia.

porary translation of the apostles' bodies from the other sites to the Via Appia—perhaps because of the circumstances of the persecution of Christians under Valerian (A.D. 253–9), when Christians were forbidden to hold their ordinary meetings and access to their cemeteries was prevented. But even this is a harmonizing reconstruction of two separate traditions—one enjoying official approval and the other popular favour—and there is no independent evidence in its support. The recent excavations on the Vatican have filled in details of what was known before, but most of what was unknown before remains unknown.

That Peter and Paul were the most eminent of many Christians who suffered martyrdom in Rome under Nero is certain; that they were claimed as co-founders of the Roman church and that this, together with their martyrdom there, conferred great religious (as distinct from political) prestige on that church, is likewise certain; but how far otherwise the elements of the growing tradition have a basis in the historical events of the sixties of the first Christian century is still uncertain.

4

Nero's attack on the Roman Christians came as a shock which they never forgot. But they survived it, and grew stronger because of it. The official execration of Nero's memory which followed his deposition and death (9 June, A.D. 68) provided them with a propaganda weapon; when later emperors took repressive action against them, they could be charged with following a Neronian precedent (*institutum Neronianum*).[47] This charge does not appear to have deterred emperors who saw fit to adopt a persecuting policy; still, it was a good point for a Christian apologist to emphasize that the first persecuting emperor was the worst of the emperors.

Not all Nero's subjects, however, thought so ill of him. Some refused to believe the reports of his death, and for twenty years after it there was a succession of pretenders who claimed to be Nero, and received a measure of support in the eastern provinces. The last of these was one Terentius Maximus, who for a time was

[47] The phrase is Tertullian's (*Ad Nationes* 1:7). Cf. E. T. Merrill, *Essays in Early Christian History* (London, 1924), pp. 131ff.

sponsored by the Parthians; at last they reluctantly agreed to his extradition to Rome (A.D. 88). Even after that, it was believed in some quarters that Nero would return from the dead and reoccupy Rome at the head of an army from the east.[48]

Echoes of this belief in *Nero rediuiuus* can be heard in the New Testament Apocalypse, where one of the imperial heads of the seven-headed beast (the Roman Empire), though it has suffered a mortal stroke, is destined to revive and rule as the last persecuting Antichrist. The seven heads, the seer is told, are 'seven emperors, five of whom have fallen, one is, the other has not yet come, and when he comes he must remain only a little while. As for the beast that was and is not, it is an eighth but it belongs to the seven, and it goes to perdition' (Rev. 17:10f).[49] The identification of these emperors is not certain, but probably the passage is written from the perspective of Vespasian's principate (A.D. 69-79) and it is expected that his next successor but one will be *Nero rediuiuus*. In the event, Vespasian's next successor but one was his younger son Domitian (81-96), and his identification by readers of the Apocalypse with the 'eighth' emperor who 'belongs to the seven' goes far to account for his reputation in Christian tradition as a persecutor and also, perhaps, for the dating of the Apocalypse in his principate. But it is plain that from the viewpoint of the Apocalypse this 'eighth' and last emperor is still to come.

The civil war in Italy which marked 'the year of the four emperors' between Nero's death and Vespasian's arrival in Rome in the summer of 70 to assume the imperial power which the Senate conferred upon him at the end of 69 may have suggested to the Roman Christians that swift judgement had overtaken the persecuting city. But with the arrival of Vespasian the traces of the civil war were quickly removed: the economy was placed on a stable footing; the Capitol in Rome, which had been burned down in the fighting at the end of Vitellius's reign, was rebuilt.

---

[48] Cf. Tacitus, *Hist.* i, 2; ii, 8; Suetonius, *Nero* 57; Dio Cassius, *Hist.* lxvi, 19. 3; *Sib. Or.* 4:119-24, 138f.

[49] For 'the beast that was and is not' cf. Rev. 13:3, 12, 14; there is some oscillation in the imagery and its interpretation between the empire ('the seven-headed beast') and the individual emperors (strictly the heads of the beast) who from time to time embodied the imperial power.

Vespasian, it is said, set an example by collecting the first basketful of rubble from the ruins and carrying it off on his shoulder.[50]

Little enough is known of the fortunes of Christians in Rome or elsewhere under the Flavian emperors. As members of an unauthorized religious association they were liable to summary penalties, but there was no express ban on Christianity as such. Even if Titus imagined that the destruction of the Jerusalem Temple would speed the disappearance of Judaism and Christianity alike,[51] neither he nor his father took any decisive action against the practice of either of these religions. (In fact, as late as the principate of Trajan, in A.D. 112, it is plain that there was no statutory precedent which even the emperor himself could quote with regard to Christians. As members of an illegal association they were law-breakers, but 'they must not be ferreted out'; on the other hand, 'if they are charged and convicted, they must be punished' —but anyone who recanted by sacrificing to the state gods was to be pardoned.)[52]

Domitian, as has been said, ranks as a persecutor in Christian tradition.[53] But evidence to justify this reputation is scanty. Clement of Rome, writing at the end of his reign (perhaps shortly after his death), indicates that he has been hindered in dealing with the dissension in the Corinthian church 'because of the sudden and repeated misfortunes and calamities which have befallen us';[54] but in the absence of more explicit information we cannot be sure that he refers to an outbreak of persecution.

Domitian's predilection for being styled *dominus et deus noster*,[55] 'our Lord and God', stimulated a satirical response in many of his subjects, but would have been regarded as plain blasphemy by Christians, for whom there was 'one God, the Father, . . . and one Lord, Jesus Christ' (I Cor. 8:6). But there is no record that this precipitated a clash between him and the Christians.

He suspected, not without reason, that many members of the Senate were plotting against him, and towards the end of his reign he took severe action against some of them, including certain

---

[50] Suetonius, *Vespasian* 8:5.   [51] See pp. 383f.
[52] Plin. *Ep.* x, 97 (see p. 424).
[53] Cf. Tertullian, *Apol.* 5:4. See E. T. Merrill, *Essays in Early Christian History*, pp. 148ff.
[54] I Clem. 1:1.   [55] Suetonius, *Domitian* 13:2.

members of the imperial family. Among the latter was his cousin Flavius Clemens, who was sentenced to death towards the end of his consulship in A.D. 95 on a charge of atheism, for which many others also were condemned who had drifted into Jewish ways'.[56] The wife of Clemens, Flavia Domitilla, Domitian's niece, was sentenced on the same charge to exile on the island of Pandateria, off the Campanian Coast.[57] Clemens and Domitilla had two young sons, who at this point disappear from history; they had actually been designated by Domitian as his heirs, and renamed by him Vespasian and Domitian.[58]

It was Domitilla's steward, Stephanus by name, who a few months later offered his services to a group of senatorial conspirators against Domitian's life and assassinated him (18 September, A.D. 96).[59] Domitian was replaced as emperor by Nerva, an elderly Senator (96–98), who reversed several of Domitian's tyrannical measures; Domitilla, for example, was released from banishment and resumed possession of her property in Rome.[60]

Roman tradition claims Clemens and Domitilla as Christians. Dio Cassius's description of their offence as 'atheism', combined with 'Jewish ways', is scarcely a strong enough foundation in itself for the establishment of this tradition. Domitian, we know, took various repressive measures against the Jews; not only did he exact the Jewish tax with untoward severity[61] but he penalized the proselytization of Roman citizens[62] and kept a sharp look-out against any sign of a renewal of Jewish insurgency. It is in this last connexion that we should appraise the story told by Hegesippus[63] about the two grandsons of Judas the brother of Jesus, who were examined by Domitian because they belonged to the royal line of David, but were dismissed when he found them to be humble working men quite uninterested in politics.

Christianity might indeed be regarded as a mixture of Judaism

[56] Dio Cassius, *Hist.* lxvii, 14; cf. Suetonius, *Domitian* 15:1, where Flavius Clemens is described as 'a man despised by all for his inactive life (*inertia*)'. Flavius Clemens was the son of Vespasian's brother T. Flavius Sabinus.

[57] Dio Cassius, *Hist.* lxviii, 14. 2.   [58] Suetonius, *Domitian* 15:1.

[59] Suetonius, *Domitian* 17:1; Dio Cassius, *Hist.* lxvii, 15–17.

[60] Eusebius, *HE* iii, 20. 8.   [61] See p. 391.

[62] Dio Cassius, *Hist.* lxvii, 14. 2. See E. M. Smallwood, 'Domitian's Attitude towards the Jews and Judaism', *Cl. Phil.* 51 (1956), pp. 1ff.

[63] *Apud* Euseb. *HE* iii, 20.

and atheism, but the strongest argument for the tradition claiming Clemens and Domitilla (especially Domitilla) as Christians is archaeological. There is inscriptional evidence that the 'Cemetery of Domitilla' on the Via Ardeatina, one of the oldest Christian burying-places in Rome (running south from the city), was hollowed out under land which belonged to Flavia Domitilla and her family: moreover, it contains epitaphs commemorating bearers of the Flavian name.[64] North of the city, on the Via Salaria, is another very early Christian burying-place, the 'Cemetery of Priscilla'. It contains a crypt belonging to the noble family of Acilii Glabriones.[65] One of Flavius Clemens's fellow-victims on the same charge of Judaism and atheism was one Acilius Glabrio, who had been consul in A.D. 91. In addition to his other offences, he had incurred Domitian's displeasure some time previously by showing a skill in lion-slaying which Domitian could not match.[66]

If indeed these pieces of evidence do point to the infiltration of Christianity into the noblest families of Rome, then Harnack's words are justified: 'Between fifty and sixty years after Christianity reached Rome, a daughter of the Emperor embraces the faith, and thirty years after the fearful persecutions of Nero, the presumptive heirs to the throne were brought up in a Christian house'.[67] We may hesitate to go so far, but Roman tradition in this regard is clearly based on something more substantial than thin air, and Christianity in Rome, having survived the first attack on its existence, was destined to advance, in spite of subsequent and more severely organized attacks by supreme authority, until at last it was the city and empire that capitulated to the church.

[64] See H. Leclercq, 'Aristocratiques (Classes)', *DACL* 1, 2, cols. 2850–2854.
[65] H. Leclercq, *DACL* 1, 2, cols. 2854–2860.
[66] Dio Cassius, *Hist.* lxvii, 14; cf. Suetonius, *Domitian* 10:2.
[67] A. Harnack, 'Christianity and Christians at the Court of the Emperors', *Princeton Review* 1 (1878), p. 269; cf. his *Mission and Expansion of Christianity* II (London, 1908), p. 46. This Flavia Domitilla was not a daughter of the Emperor (Vespasian) but his granddaughter (Domitian's niece).

30 Christianity at the End of the New Testament Period

1

By the end of the first century A.D. Christianity was well established in the Roman world. From its birthplace in Judaea it had spread west along the northern shore of the Mediterranean as far as Gaul, if not as far as Spain; it had spread along the North African coast to Cyrenaica, if it had not already reached the Roman province of Africa. Two hundred years were to elapse before the Roman state accepted the presence of the church; before that time intermittent attempts were made to repress and, if possible, extirpate Christianity, but the historian, looking back on the situation with all the advantages of hindsight, can see that by A.D. 100 Christianity had come to stay, that its abolition was no longer practicable.

By that year most of the New Testament documents had been written, although the New Testament as a recognized collection did not yet exist.[1] By that year the pattern of the catholic church as we find it in the later part of the second century was beginning to take shape. The apostolic age was no more, but conditions both within and without the churches were dictating ways of filling the vacuum left by the death of the apostles. Those churches which claimed an apostolic foundation attached great importance to the maintenance of the teaching which they had originally received. There were powerful forces at work in many of them which militated against the maintenance of that teaching; chief among these were those tendencies which in a few decades blossomed forth in the elaborate systems of the various schools of Gnosticism. One form of incipient Gnosticism is the syncretistic angel-cult of nonconformist Jewish foundation and pagan super-

[1] Cf. R. M. Grant, *The Formation of the New Testament* (London, 1965).

structure attacked in the Epistle to the Colossians. The Christians of Colossae and other cities of the Lycus valley are urged to remain true to the 'tradition' which was first delivered to them, not to be shifted from the foundation on which their Christian life had been originally based: 'As therefore you received[2] Christ Jesus as Lord, so live in him, rooted and built up in him and established in the faith, just as you were taught' (Col. 2:6f). Two or three decades later another form of incipient Gnosticism in some of the other churches in proconsular Asia led to a local schism which called forth the First and Second Epistles of John. This variety of Gnosticism is traditionally associated with a teacher named Cerinthus. Cerinthus, a man trained in Egypt but resident in the province of Asia, accepted the general dualistic world-view characteristic of Gnosticism (including the creation of matter by an inferior power or demiurge), but propounded a novel Christology. He distinguished the man Jesus (the son of Joseph and Mary, endowed with greater virtue and wisdom than other men), from 'the Christ', who descended on Jesus in the form of a dove after he was baptized, empowering him to perform miracles and proclaim 'the unknown Father', but who left him before he died, so that 'Jesus suffered and rose again, while the Christ remained immune from suffering, since he was a spiritual being'.[3] This view can be recognized as related to Docetism.[4] The Docetists, regarding matter as inherently evil, could not believe it possible for a divine being to come into such close association with the material order as was implied in incarnation in a human body. Jesus, as the manifestation of deity on earth, could not have a real human body; he only *seemed* to have one. (It is from *dokein*, the Greek verb meaning 'seem', that the term 'Docetism' is derived.) The biblical doctrines of creation and resurrection, as well as incarnation, were excluded by Docetism. Cerinthus, with his belief that the man Jesus rose again, was not a typical Docetist, but he did not identify the man Jesus outright with the divine being whom he called 'the Christ'.

[2] Gk. παρελάβετε. For the use of παραλαμβάνω as one of the two technical verbs used in reference to tradition see p. 244.

[3] Irenaeus, *Haer.* i, 21.

[4] Cf. Ignatius, *Ad Smyrn.* 3:2; Clement of Alexandria, *Strom.* 7. 17. 76. 26; Hippolytus, *Ref.* viii, 2, 11; x, 16; Serapion *apud* Euseb. *HE* vi, 12. 6, etc.

In the Epistles of John, as in the Epistle to the Colossians, the readers are encouraged to hold fast to their original foundation: 'Let what you heard from the beginning abide in you. If what you heard from the beginning abides in you, then you will abide in the Son and in the Father' (I John 2:24). Those former associates of theirs who had not adhered to the teaching which they had 'heard from the beginning' had severed themselves from the fellowship in which alone eternal life was to be had: 'they went out from us, but they were not of us; for if they had been of us, they would have continued with us' (I John 2:19).

How a Christian leader endeavoured to check the increasing influence of Gnostic teachers is seen in the Second Epistle of John, where the writer (who designates himself 'The Elder') addresses a local church corporately and its members individually ('the elect lady and her children') and warns them against the 'deceivers' who 'have gone out into the world, men who will not acknowledge the coming of Jesus Christ in the flesh; such a one is the deceiver and the antichrist' (II John 7). If any one visits the church and does not bring 'the doctrine of Christ'—the teaching which they had originally received and hitherto maintained— he is not to be admitted or given any countenance or encouragement, 'for he who greets him shares his wicked work' (II John 10f).

We cannot be sure whether the church paid heed to the Elder's admonition or not. But not all the churches to which he wrote submitted to his authority. It appears from the Third Epistle of John that the Elder had a number of travelling associates in whom he reposed great confidence and who went around the churches presumably to strengthen them in the apostolic faith. One church, at the instance of a self-appointed leader named Diotrephes, refused to accept the Elder's friends; Diotrephes indeed threatened with excommunication any members of the church who harboured them. So the treatment which the Elder recommended to the 'elect lady' as appropriate for Gnostic visitors was actually meted out in another church[5] to his own accredited

[5] There is nothing in III John to suggest that the church in question was that addressed in II John; they have been identified, however, by some students, e.g. by R. Eisler, *The Enigma of the Fourth Gospel* (London, 1938), pp. 170ff,

messengers. Diotrephes has sometimes been regarded as an early example of the monarchical bishop. (The monarchical bishop—one bishop in control of the administration of the church of a city—replaced the earlier government of each church by a body of elders or 'bishops'.) It is more probable that we should recognize in him a symptom of the disease which the monarchical bishop was intended to cure.[6]

The first clear references to the monarchical episcopate appear a few years after the beginning of the second century in the letters which Ignatius, bishop of Antioch, wrote on his journey to Rome to be exposed to the wild beasts in the arena. Ignatius was acquainted in his own and other churches with various forms of Gnostic and Docetic teaching—especially the latter. The safeguard against the spread of such teaching, Ignatius emphasized, was the authority of the bishop. If in each church no one was allowed to administer baptism or the eucharist, or even preside at an *agapē*, except the bishop or someone specifically approved by him, undesirable doctrines would be effectively excluded.[7] (The idea that a bishop might himself sponsor such doctrines does not seem to have occurred to Ignatius.)

The vehemence with which Ignatius in his letters emphasizes the authority of the bishop suggests that his view was not universally shared. He himself was monarchical bishop in the church of Antioch, as Polycarp was in Smyrna and Onesimus in Ephesus; but there were other churches in which the monarchical episcopate was not yet established. It is fairly clear when one reads between the lines of Ignatius's letter to the Roman church that the monarchical episcopate did not yet exist in that church. This conclusion seems to be confirmed by the *Shepherd* of Hermas, a popular allegory written by a Roman Christian early in the second century, where mention is made of 'the elders who preside over the church', or of 'the rulers and those who occupy the chief seats', but not of any one bishop.[8] Hermas refers to Clement as foreign secretary of the Roman church.[9] Clement, who figures in

---

according to whom it was the Fourth Gospel, recommended in I and II John, which the church referred to in III John 9 refused to receive.

[6] Cf. C. H. Dodd, *The Johannine Epistles* (London, 1945), pp. 161ff.

[7] Ignatius, *Ad Smyrn.* 8:1f.　　　[8] Vision 3. 9. 7.　　　[9] Vision 2. 4. 3.

the pontifical lists as one of the earliest Roman bishops,[10] is the traditional author of the anonymous letter sent about A.D. 96 by the Roman church to the church of Corinth, known as the First Epistle of Clement. In the light of Hermas's reference, he is to be regarded more probably as one of the collegiate presiding elders or bishops of the church than as *the* bishop.

It appears from the letter of Clement that the institution of the monarchical bishop was unknown also in the church of Corinth in A.D. 96; and it was equally unknown in the church of Philippi some years later when Polycarp wrote to it shortly after the death of Ignatius, for in his letter those in authority are addressed collectively as elders.

By the middle of the second century, however, the monarchical bishop was established in all these churches, and the 'catholic faith' was successfully maintained in them against the powerful attraction of the Gnostic systems, which owed much of their appeal to their being in harmony with current climates of intellectual opinion. One church where the collegiate principle survived longer than elsewhere was that of Alexandria in Egypt.[11]

The origins of the church of Alexandria are shrouded in even greater mystery than those of the church of Rome. The late account which ascribes the foundation of the Alexandrian church to Mark, the associate of the apostles,[12] may very well have been devised to replace one which implied a less reputable origin for Alexandrian Christianity—less reputable, that is to say, by the standards of catholic orthodoxy. Paul's friend Apollos was a Jew of Alexandria; if it was in his native city that he came to know the gospel story, then Alexandrian Christianity at that early date (*c.* A.D. 50) presumably shared the defects which Priscilla and Aquila detected in Apollos's understanding of 'the Way'. Indeed, it has

---

[10] Third after the apostles, according to Irenaeus, *Haer.* iii, 3. 2; next after Peter, who ordained him, according to Tertullian, *Praescr.* 32. See p. 405. Cf. M. Bévenot, 'Clement of Rome in Irenaeus's Succession-List', *JTS*, n.s. 17 (1966), pp. 98ff; D. F. Wright, 'Clement and the Roman Succession in Irenaeus', *JTS*, n.s. 18 (1967), pp. 144ff.

[11] At Alexandria until the beginning of the fourth century the presbyters regularly promoted one of their number to be bishop; cf. Jerome, *Ep.* 146. 1, translated and annotated in J. Stevenson, *A New Eusebius* (London, 1957), pp. 378f; see also W. Telfer, 'Episcopal Succession in Egypt', *JEH* 3 (1952), pp. 1ff.

[12] Eusebius, *HE* ii, 16.

been argued that the catholic faith as held in the apostolic churches did not take root in Alexandria until well into the second century.[13] The principal figures in Alexandrian Christianity during the first two-thirds of the second century were more gnostic than catholic in their doctrine—Basilides, Isidore and Valentinus, for example. Not until the last third of the century do we have clear evidence of catholic Christianity establishing its predominance in Alexandria with the foundation of the great catechetical school of that city under its successive leaders Pantaenus, Clement and Origen—and some of them were suspected (not without reason) of being unduly influenced by gnostic speculation.

The developed Gnosticism of the second century does not belong to New Testament history, and the pre-Christian gnostic myth which the *religionsgeschichtlich* school of Christian origins believes was used by several New Testament writers as a vehicle for the gospel is actually a reconstruction based to a large extent on much later material, especially on Mandaean texts.[14] The general pattern of the gnostic myth (if it is not too bold to speak of a general pattern amid such a rich proliferation of mythology as the gnostic systems present) portrays a heavenly essence which falls from the upper spiritual world of light into the lower material world of darkness and is imprisoned in a number of earthly bodies. To liberate this pure essence from its imprisonment a saviour descends from the world of light to impart the true knowledge (*gnosis*); he is at once redeemer and revealer. By acceptance of the revealed knowledge, the pure essence attains release from the thraldom of matter and re-ascends to its true abode. This myth may owe something to the Iranian conception of Gayomart,[15] the

13 Cf. W. Bauer, *Rechtgläubigkeit und Ketzerei im ältesten Christentum* (Tübingen, 1964²), pp. 49ff, and other works mentioned on p. 294, n. 6.

14 Cf. R. Bultmann, 'Die Bedeutung der neuerschlossenen mandäischen und manichäischen Quellen für das Verständnis des Johannesevangeliums', *ZNTW* 24 (1925), pp. 100ff; E. Peterson, 'Bemerkungen zur mandäischen Literatur', *ZNTW* 25 (1926), pp. 236ff; 'Urchristentum und Mandäismus', *ZNTW* 27 (1928), pp. 55ff; G. Bornkamm, *Mythus und Legende in den apokryphen Thomasakten* (Göttingen, 1933); R. McL. Wilson, *The Gnostic Problem* (London, 1958); R. M. Grant, *Gnosticism and Early Christianity* (New York, 1959); see also pp. 226–30.

15 Cf. R. Reitzenstein, *Das Iranische Erlösungsmysterium* (Bonn, 1921). In the Avesta Gayomart ('mortal life') appears occasionally as the ancestor of the Aryans and the first believer in the teaching of Ahura Mazda. Later he appears as a key figure in a cosmic drama: he is a heavenly being, primal man,

primal man, to whom a redemptive function is assigned; but it is much more likely that the distinctive outlines of the gnostic myth, including the identification of the redeemer-revealer with primal man, represent a mythologizing of the early Christian story than that the New Testament presentation of that story can be explained in terms of gnostic mythology. It may indeed be surmised that one of the earliest attempts to re-state the gospel in terms of gnostic mythology was made in the syncretism which is attacked in the Epistle to the Colossians.

2

Externally, the danger with which the church had to reckon was the hostility of the imperial power. This hostility was always latent, but manifested itself in active persecution only sporadically and in limited areas, now in the capital, now in this province, now in that.

In the New Testament itself two documents take the recent (Neronian) persecution of Christians in Rome as a warning that similar persecution may soon be experienced by Christians in Asia Minor. The First Epistle of Peter, sent from 'Babylon' to 'the exiles of the Dispersion in Pontus, Galatia, Cappadocia, Asia, and Bithynia', warns its readers of the 'fiery ordeal' which is about to test them, and instructs them about their attitude and behaviour when it breaks (I Peter 4:11–19). The Apocalypse of John, addressed in the first instance to seven churches in the province of Asia, portrays the city of Rome as the scarlet woman 'Babylon the great', in whom 'was found the blood of prophets and of saints' (Rev. 17:5; 18:24)—a reflection of the events of A.D. 64—and sees tribulation such as the Roman Christians had endured lying in store for their Asian brethren. Indeed, in some parts of Asia it has already begun: in Pergamum one Antipas has been killed some time previously as a faithful witness of Jesus (Rev.

---

the son of Ahura Mazda, who, after battling with the power of evil for a cycle of 3,000 years, is overcome and killed by it. But from him, after his death, the human race springs up; and when, at the end of time, the *saošyant* ('saviour') appears to raise the dead, Gayomart will be the first to rise and will be exalted to archangelic rank. But this myth makes its appearance in the 7th century A.D. and is likely neither chronologically nor materially to have influenced the Christian story.

2:13), and John himself writes from the Aegean island of Patmos, to which he has been sent 'on account of the word of God and the testimony of Jesus' (Rev. 1:9)—words which traditionally, and most probably, denote penal banishment by sentence of a Roman court. The relation of this John to the other bearers of the same name known in the church at this period is debatable; writing as a prophet in the name of the exalted Christ, he speaks to the churches with exceptional authority. Most, if not all, of the seven churches addressed were among those planted during Paul's Ephesian ministry of A.D. 52–55; the picture of them given in the Apocalypse confirms the impression given by all relevant evidence that in the province of Asia Gentile Christianity flourished in unsurpassed vigour, even if in some of them a measure of social and religious compromise with their pagan environment calls forth sharp criticism.

Not until the beginning of the third century was there anything like a general enactment, binding throughout the empire, proscribing the practice of Christianity. Legally, then, in our period the practice or profession of Christianity fell *extra ordinem*; it was dealt with by the procedure called *cognitio*, in which, where ordinary provincials were concerned, a magistrate had unlimited authority.[16] As for the beginning of the second century, we are fortunate in having an illuminating document from the imperial side in the exchange of letters on this subject between the Emperor Trajan (A.D. 98–117) and the younger Pliny (C. Plinius Secundus) during the latter's period of office as proconsul of Bithynia and Pontus (A.D. 111–12).[17] Pliny had at first taken summary action against Christians in his province, in the exercise of the very wide discretion which belonged to his proconsular *imperium*. But as further instances of Christianity were brought to his notice, he began to wonder if he was following the correct procedure. Nothing in his past experience helped him here, and there was no statute against Christians which his expert legal assessors could quote to him so as to set his doubts at rest. Accordingly, he consulted the emperor, as he did on many matters that called for his decision as provincial governor.

[16] Cf. A. N. Sherwin-White, 'The Early Persecutions and Roman Law Again', *JTS*, n.s. 3 (1952), pp. 199ff.
[17] Plin. *Epp.* x, 96, 97. Cf. E. T. Merrill, *Essays in Early Christian History* (London, 1924), pp. 174ff.

PLINY TO TRAJAN

My Lord: It is my custom to refer to you everything that I am in doubt about; for who is better able either to correct my hesitation or instruct my ignorance?

I have never taken part in trials (*cognitiones*) of Christians; consequently I do not know the precedents regarding the question of punishment or the nature of the inquisition. I have been in no little doubt whether some discrimination is made with regard to age, or whether the young are treated no differently from the older; whether renunciation wins indulgence, or it is of no avail to have abandoned Christianity if one has once been a Christian; whether the profession of the name is to be punished in itself, even if unaccompanied by disgraceful practices, or only the disgraceful practices commonly associated with the name.

So far this has been my procedure when people were charged before me with being Christians. I have asked the accused themselves if they were Christians; if they said 'Yes', I asked them a second and third time, warning them of the penalty; if they persisted I ordered them to be led off to execution. For I had no doubt that, whatever kind of thing it was that they pleaded guilty to, their stubbornness and unyielding obstinacy at any rate deserved to be punished. There were others afflicted with the like madness whom I marked down to be referred to Rome, because they were Roman citizens.

Later, as usually happens, the trouble spread by the very treatment of it, and further varieties came to my notice. An anonymous document was laid before me containing many people's names. Some of these denied that they were Christians or had ever been so; at my dictation they invoked the gods and did reverence with incense and wine to your image, which I had ordered to be brought for this purpose along with the statues of the gods; they also cursed Christ; and as I am informed that people who are really Christians cannot possibly be made to do any of those things, I considered that the people who did them should be discharged. Others against whom I received information said they were Christians and then denied it; they meant (they said) that they had once been Christians but had given it up: some three years previously, some a longer time, one or two as many as twenty years before.[18] All these likewise both did reverence to your image and the statues of the gods and cursed Christ. But they maintained that their fault or error amounted to nothing more than this: they were in the

---

[18] The 'twenty years before' would bring us back to Domitian's reign; but this provides at best the slenderest of evidence in support of the tradition stigmatizing him as one of the persecuting emperors (see pp. 411ff).

habit of meeting on a certain fixed day before sunrise and reciting an antiphonal hymn to Christ as God, and binding themselves with an oath—not to commit any crime, but to abstain from all acts of theft, robbery and adultery, from breaches of faith, from denying a trust when called upon to honour it. After this, they went on, it was their custom to separate, and then meet again to partake of food, but food of an ordinary and innocent kind. And even this, they said, they had given up doing since the publication of my edict in which, according to your instructions, I had placed a ban on private associations. So I thought it the more necessary to inquire into the real truth of the matter by subjecting to torture two female slaves, who were called 'deaconesses';[19] but I found nothing more than a perverse superstition which went beyond all bounds.

Therefore I deferred further inquiry in order to apply to you for a ruling. The case seemed to me to be a proper one for consultation, particularly because of the number of those who were accused. For many of every age, every class, and of both sexes are being accused and will continue to be accused. Nor has this contagious superstition spread through the cities only, but also through the villages and the countryside. But I think it can be checked and put right. At any rate the temples, which had been well-nigh abandoned, are beginning to be frequented again; and the customary services, which had been neglected for a long time, are beginning to be resumed; fodder for the sacrificial animals, too, is beginning to find a sale again, for hitherto it was difficult to find anyone to buy it. From all this it is easy to judge what a multitude of people can be reclaimed, if an opportunity is granted them to renounce Christianity.

The imperial rescript was brief and to the point.

TRAJAN TO PLINY

My dear Secundus: You have followed the correct procedure in investigating the cases of those who have been charged before you with being Christians. Indeed, no general decision can be made by which a set form of dealing with them could be established. They must not be ferreted out; if they are charged and convicted, they must be punished, provided that anyone who denies that he is a Christian and gives practical proof of that by invoking our gods is to be discharged on the strength of this repudiation, no matter what grounds for suspicion may have existed against him in the past. Anonymous documents which

[19] Lat. *ministrae.*

are laid before you should receive no attention in any case; they are a very bad precedent and quite unworthy of the age in which we live.

Pliny, it is clear, did not take the initiative as governor against the Christians in his province; he acted only when charges were brought against individuals by private prosecutors (by the process of *delatio*). But why was Christianity a matter for *delatio*? To begin with, Pliny appears to have taken it for granted that the charge of Christianity was a capital one, and executed the accused persons who admitted the charge and refused to recant. The question whether the *name* of Christian was sufficient for conviction or evidence of the 'disgraceful practices commonly associated with the name' (*flagitia cohaerentia nomini*) had to be forthcoming did not occur to him at first; he took it for granted that the 'name' was crime enough. This situation is the one implied in the second part of the First Epistle of Peter[20] (4:12–5:11), where the imminent probability is envisaged that a man may be penalized simply 'as a Christian',[21] 'for the name of Christ'; if so, far from counting this a public disgrace, 'under that name let him glorify God' (4:14, 16).

Pliny knew, as something which was generally recognized, that Christianity was disapproved of by the state; he was quite vague about the reason for this, but understood that Christianity could not be allowed to spread unchecked. Nero's action against them might be disallowed as a precedent because of his general *damnatio memoriae*; but antecedent to Nero's action was their social condemnation as 'haters of the human race'.[22] Public report associated certain disgraceful practices with the Christian profession, but these practices could be dealt with on their own demerits. One thing was clear to Pliny: if, after receiving every encouragement and opportunity for reconsideration which a humane and reasonable magistrate could give, those Christians who appeared before him would not renounce their profession but persisted in

[20] I Peter falls into two main parts: (*a*) a baptismal homily (1:3–4:11) and (*b*) a message of encouragement in persecution (4:12–5:11). While in the latter part persecution for the Christian name is an imminent certainty, in the earlier part suffering for righteousness' sake is a remote contingency (3:13f).

[21] See p. 268. Cf. *Letter of Churches of Vienne and Lyons, apud* Euseb. *HE* v, 1. 10, 19, 20, 44, 50; Tertullian, *Apol.* 2:13, for evidence that the statement 'I am a Christian' was sufficient ground for condemnation.

[22] Tacitus, *Annals* xv, 44. 5.

their superstition, they were guilty of *contumacia*, they had committed contempt of court, and for this, if for nothing else, they were liable to the death penalty if the governor saw fit to impose it.

If another charge were sought against the Christians, they could be prosecuted for belonging to an illegal association. Pliny says that, in accordance with the emperor's instructions, he had placed a ban on private associations. Trajan, like his predecessors, was very suspicious of such associations of his subjects. No matter how innocent and, indeed, positively beneficial the ostensible aim of one of these associations might be, long experience had shown how readily they lent themselves to the fomenting of political subversion. A good example of this is provided in another exchange of letters between Pliny and Trajan. There had been some serious outbreaks of fire in the chief cities of Pliny's province, so he wrote to ask Trajan if it would be a good thing to organize fire brigades. Trajan said No: it was better, he thought, to leave the extinguishing of fires to private initiative. However praiseworthy the organization of fire brigades might appear, the trouble was that, like so many other private associations, they could so easily be exploited for seditious ends.[23]

There is, indeed, some evidence that exemptions from the general ban on private associations were allowed—more particularly, that associations of poorer citizens for religious purposes (*collegia tenuiorum religionis causa*) were permitted from the time of the Julio-Claudian emperors.[24] But it is not clear that this permission extended beyond Italy, and in any case it would be necessary that the *religio* in question should not threaten public order or offend public morals. Christianity, as popularly and even officially envisaged, did both. The kind of disgraceful practices associated in current belief with the profession of Christianity may be hinted at in Pliny's remark to the emperor that the evidence he had been able to obtain from ex-Christians indicated that the food which Christians took at their common meal was 'food of an ordinary and innocent kind'—for Christians were widely suspected of ritual mur-

23 Pliny, *Epp.* x, 33, 34.
24 On this A. N. Sherwin-White (*Roman Society and Roman Law in the New Testament* [Oxford, 1963], p. 206) quotes F. de Robertis, *Il Diritto associativo Romano* (Bari, 1938), pp. 371–4.

der and cannibalism (as Jews had been suspected before them), and of ritual incest to boot.[25]

It was probably the discovery that the profession of Christianity did not inevitably connote the disgraceful practices popularly associated with it that moved Pliny to consult the emperor. If at first he shared the widespread opinion that Christians as such were guilty of these practices then he would without more ado exercise his powers of *coercitio* (magisterial compulsion) against them, except that those who were Roman citizens had their cases referred to the emperor—apparently whether they took the initiative in appealing to Caesar or not.[26] But when it became clear to him that this widespread opinion was not borne out by the evidence, he began to wonder if the profession of Christianity was in itself to be treated as a capital offence, and in default of any precedent or other form of guidance he turned to Trajan.

Trajan's reply to Pliny does not add much to our knowledge of the status of Christians before the law. He confirms the correctness of Pliny's moderate procedure. Christians were to be prosecuted on conviction, he confirmed, but they were not to be hunted down, nor should any attention be paid to anonymous letters accusing people of Christianity. (This was not so much intended to grant immunity to Christians as to protect pagans against attempts at calumniation.) Every encouragement, moreover, should be given to Christians to renounce their profession and put themselves in the right before the law.

Christian apologists naturally found this decision outrageous and inconsistent,[27] but Trajan, according to his lights, meant to deal firmly but reasonably with an anti-social cult. Plainly he was no fanatical persecutor, but a ruler who intended to maintain law and order throughout his dominions without interfering unduly with the liberty of his subjects. As he saw it, the spread of Christianity, especially on such a scale as Pliny's language implies for Bithynia and Pontus, was a menace to law and order and must be repressed, but without unnecessary severity. Pliny's language points incidentally to one possible reason for the accusations that were laid before him. The spread of Christianity threatened certain

[25] Cf. *Letter of Churches of Vienne and Lyons, apud* Euseb. *HE* v, 1. 14; Tertullian *Apol.* 7:1ff.   [26] See p. 358 with nn. 25, 26.
[27] Cf. Tertullian, *Apol.* 2:6–9.

forms of business in the province—the business, for example, of providing fodder for the animals destined for the altars of pagan temples. We are reminded of the indignation expressed by the silversmiths of Ephesus at the success of Paul's evangelization of their city with the consequent diminution of the demand for silverware associated with the cult of Artemis.[28]

Pliny's letter is interesting also because of the information it supplies about Christian worship in Asia Minor at the beginning of the second century. Even if the testimony is that of apostates, it agrees with the information gained from other sources. The 'certain fixed day' on which Christians met before sunrise was presumably Sunday—the *hēmera kyriakē* or *dies dominica*,[29] as they called it, because on it their Lord rose from the dead. The anthem which they sang 'to Christ as God'[30] recalls the New Testament injunction to Christians about 'addressing one another in psalms and hymns and spiritual songs' as they praise the Lord with all their hearts (Eph. 5:19; cf. Col. 3:16), and may be illustrated by some of the canticles of the Apocalypse, especially the 'new song' of Rev. 5:9f, 'Worthy art thou . . . for thou wast slain. . . .' The 'oath' (Lat. *sacramentum*) by which they bound themselves to abstain from wickedness of various kinds may have been the 'fencing of the table' in which purity of heart and conduct was insisted upon in those who would take the eucharist. The food which they came together later to eat was probably the *agapē*, the 'love-feast' or fellowship meal.

One notable Christian martyr in the reign of Trajan was Ignatius, who was sent under military guard from Syrian Antioch to Rome to be exposed to the wild beasts in the amphitheatre about A.D. 110.[31] To Trajan's reign belongs also the martyrdom of Symeon, successor to James the Just as leader of the church of Jerusalem;[32] Symeon, as a member of the holy family, may have been accused

28 Acts 19:24–7 (see pp. 328f).
29 So first called in Rev. 1:10; cf. *Didache* 14:1 ('the Lord's *kyriakē*').
30 Cf. R. P. Martin, *Worship in the Early Church* (London, 1964), pp. 28ff; *Carmen Christi* (Cambridge, 1967).
31 It was on his way to Rome that he wrote his seven letters which have survived (see p. 418), at Smyrna and Troas. He refers to his military guard as 'ten leopards' (*Ad Rom.* 5:1).
32 Eusebius, *HE* iii, 32. 2ff, reporting the testimony of Hegesippus.

of complicity in the Jewish revolts which broke out about the time of Trajan's Parthian campaign (A.D. 115).[33]

The precedent set by Trajan in his letter to Pliny was followed by his successor Hadrian (117–38), if we may judge from a rescript which the latter emperor sent in A.D. 124 to Minucius Fundanus, proconsul of Asia.

HADRIAN TO FUNDANUS

I have received a letter addressed to me by your illustrious predecessor, Serenus Granianus, and his report, I think, ought not to be passed over in silence, lest innocent people be molested and an opportunity for hostile action be given to malicious accusers. If the provincials plainly wish to support this petition of theirs against the Christians by bringing some definite charge against them before the court, let them confine themselves to this action and refrain from mere appeals and outcries. For it is much more just that, if anyone wishes to bring an accusation, you should examine the allegations. If then anyone accuses them and proves that they are doing anything unlawful, you must impose a penalty in accordance with the gravity of the crime; but if anyone brings such accusations simply by way of blackmail, you must sentence him to a more severe penalty in proportion to his wickedness.[34]

The genuineness of this document has been questioned, partly because it is preserved to us only as a quotation in Justin Martyr's *Apology* and partly because its purpose has been misunderstood. Even if the Greek form in which we have it is not a literal translation of the Latin original, its essential historicity and authenticity need not be doubted. Hadrian's purpose, like Trajan's, is not to protect Christians, but to protect against vexatious prosecution or blackmail people who were falsely accused of being Christians. Private prosecutors must be required to support their charges with positive evidence, and this may imply that explicit evidence of the 'disgraceful practices' as well as of the profession of Christianity must be adduced. If so, it is not surprising that an apologist like Justin should quote the rescript as constituting a charter of liberty for Christians, whom he knew to be innocent of the 'disgraceful

[33] Dio Cassius, *Hist.* lxviii, 17ff, 32.
[34] Justin, *Apol.* i, 68; cf. Eusebius *HE* iv, 8. 6ff. See E. T. Merrill, *Essays in Early Christian History*, pp. 202ff.

practices' alleged against them. But even if he was right in putting such a favourable construction on Hadrian's words, an imperial rescript strictly applied only to the province of the governor who sought a ruling, and need not bind an emperor's successors. Justin himself was to prove this when he was condemned to death in Rome by the urban prefect about the year 165 for persistent—it might have been described as 'contumacious'—refusal to renounce his Christian profession.[35] The advice given in I Peter 4:12ff on the proper behaviour in face of persecution 'for the name of Christ' was to be required from time to time by Christians here and there throughout the Roman Empire for several generations, until, after the severest persecution of all, the peace of the church was established by the toleration edicts of Galerius in the east (311) and of Constantine and Licinius in the west (313).

[35] The *Acts of Justin* are free from the conventional pieties of later martyrologies and give an impression of substantial historicity: morever, in Justin's replies to the magistrate a characteristic 'donnishness' has been detected (E. C. E. Owen, *Some Authentic Acts of the Early Martyrs* [Oxford, 1927], p. 48).

Bibliography

In addition to the New Testament documents, the principal primary sources for New Testament history are the works of Josephus and Philo (now conveniently accessible in full in the Loeb editions of both authors), Tacitus's *Annals* and *Histories* and Suetonius's *Lives of the Twelve Caesars*. Other primary material (including inscriptions and papyrus documents as well as literary excerpts) is available in a number of collections, of which the following deserve special mention:

Barrett, C. K., *The New Testament Background* (London, 1957)

Charlesworth, M. P., *Documents illustrating the Reigns of Claudius and Nero* (Cambridge, 1939)

Ehrenberg, V., and Jones, A. H. M., *Documents illustrating the Reigns of Augustus and Tiberius*² (Cambridge, 1955)

McCrum, M., and Woodhead, A. G., *Select Documents of the Principates of the Flavian Emperors, A.D. 68–96* (Cambridge, 1961)

Smallwood, E. M., *Documents illustrating the Principates of Nerva, Trajan, and Hadrian* (Cambridge, 1966)

Stevenson, J., *A New Eusebius* (London, 1957)

Theron, D. J., *Evidence of Tradition* (London, 1957)

OTHER WORKS

Abrahams, I., *Studies in Pharisaism and the Gospels* (Cambridge; Series 1, 1917; Series 2, 1924)

Anderson, H., *Jesus and Christian Origins* (New York, 1964)

Balsdon, J. P. V. D., *The Emperor Gaius* (Oxford, 1934)

Barrett, C. K., *Jesus and the Gospel Tradition* (London, 1967)

Bartlet, J. V., *The Apostolic Age* (Edinburgh, 1899)

Bauer, W., *Rechtgläubigkeit und Ketzerei im ältesten Christentum* (Tübingen, 1964²)

Bentzen, A., *King and Messiah*, E.T. (London, 1955)

Betz, O., *What do we know about Jesus?* E.T. (London, 1967)

Bishop, J., *Nero: The Man and the Legend* (London, 1964)

Black, M., *The Scrolls and Christian Origins* (London, 1961)

Blinzler, J., *The Trial of Jesus*, E.T. (Cork, 1959)

Bornkamm, G., *Jesus of Nazareth*, E.T. (London, 1960)

Borsch, F. H., *The Son of Man in Myth and History* (London, 1967)

Bousset, W., *Die Religion des Judentums im späthellenistischen Zeitalter*[3], ed. H. Gressmann (Tübingen, 1926)

Brandon, S. G. F., *The Fall of Jerusalem and the Christian Church* (London, 1951[1], 1957[2])

Brandon, S. G. F., *Jesus and the Zealots* (Manchester, 1967)

Brandon, S. G. F., *The Trial of Jesus of Nazareth* (London, 1968)

Bultmann, R., *Primitive Christianity in its Historical Setting*, E.T. (London, 1956)

Burkitt, F. C., *Christian Beginnings* (London, 1924)

Burkitt, F. C., *Church and Gnosis* (Cambridge, 1932)

Cadbury, H. J., *The Book of Acts in History* (New York, 1955)

Caird, G. B., *The Apostolic Age* (London, 1955)

Cole, A., *The New Temple* (London, 1950)

Conzelmann, H., *The Theology of Saint Luke*, E.T. (London, 1960)

Cook, S. A., Adcock, F. E., and Charlesworth, M. P. (edd.), *Cambridge Ancient History*, X: *The Augustan Empire, 44 B.C.–A.D. 70* (Cambridge, 1934); XI: *The Imperial Peace, A.D. 70–192* (Cambridge, 1936)

Cullmann, O., *The Early Church* (London, 1956)

Cullmann, O., *Peter: Disciple, Apostle, Martyr*, E.T. (London, 1953[1], 1962[2])

Cullmann, O., *Salvation in History*, E.T. (London, 1967)

Cullmann, O., *The State in the New Testament*, E.T. (London, 1955)

Danby, H., *Studies in Judaism* (Jerusalem, 1922)

Daube, D., *The New Testament and Rabbinic Judaism* (London, 1956)

Davies, W. D., *Paul and Rabbinic Judaism* (London, 1948)

Davies, W. D., *The Setting of the Sermon on the Mount* (Cambridge, 1964)

Davies, W. D., and Daube, D. (edd.), *The Background of the New Testament and its Eschatology* [C. H. Dodd *Festschrift*] (Cambridge, 1954)

Deissmann, A., *Light from the Ancient East*, E.T. (London, 1927)

Dibelius, M., *Paul*, E.T. (London, 1953)

Dibelius, M., *Studies in the Acts of the Apostles*, E.T. (London, 1956)

Dodd, C. H., *Parables of the Kingdom* (London, 1935)

Dodd, C. H., *The Apostolic Preaching and its Developments* (London, 1936)

Dodd, C. H., *New Testament Studies* (Manchester, 1953)

Dodd, C. H., *Historical Tradition in the Fourth Gospel* (Cambridge, 1963)

Dodd, C. H., *More New Testament Studies* (Manchester, 1968)

Dugmore, C. W., *The Influence of the Synagogue upon the Divine Office* (Oxford, 1944)

Duncan, G. S., *Jesus, Son of Man* (London, 1947)

Duncan, G. S., *St. Paul's Ephesian Ministry* (London, 1929)

Dupont-Sommer, A., *The Essene Writings from Qumran*, E.T. (Oxford, 1961)

Easton, B. S., *Christ in the Gospels* (New York, 1930)

Ehrhardt, A., *The Apostolic Succession* (London, 1953)

Ehrhardt, A., *The Apostolic Ministry* (Edinburgh, 1958)

Ehrhardt, A., *The Framework of the New Testament Stories* (Manchester, 1964)

Ehrhardt, A., *The Beginning* (Manchester, 1968)

Farmer, W. R., *Maccabees, Zealots and Josephus* (New York, 1956)

Filson, F. V., *A New Testament History* (London, 1965)

Filson, F. V., *Three Crucial Decades* (London, 1964)

Finkel, A., *The Pharisees and the Teacher of Nazareth* (Leiden, 1964)

Finkelstein, L., *The Pharisees* (Philadelphia, 1946)

Förster, W., *Palestinian Judaism in New Testament Times*, E.T. (Edinburgh, 1964)

Gärtner, B., *The Areopagus Speech and Natural Revelation* (Lund, 1955)

Gärtner, B., *The Temple and the Community in Qumran and the New Testament* (Cambridge, 1965)

Goguel, M., *Au Seuil de l'Evangile: Jean-Baptiste* (Paris, 1928)

Goguel, M., *Life of Jesus*, E.T. (London, 1933)

Goguel, M., *The Birth of Christianity*, E.T. (London, 1953)

Goguel, M., *The Primitive Church*, E.T. (London, 1964)

Goodenough, E. R., *By Light, Light* (New Haven, 1935)

Goodenough, E. R., *The Politics of Philo Judaeus* (New Haven, 1938)

Goodenough, E. R., *An Introduction to Philo Judaeus* (New Haven, 1940)

Grant, F. C., *The Economic Background of the Gospels* (Oxford, 1926)

Grant, F. C., *Ancient Judaism and the New Testament* (Edinburgh, 1960)

Grant, F. C., *Roman Hellenism and the New Testament* (Edinburgh, 1962)

Grant, R. M., *Gnosticism and Early Christianity* (New York, 1959)

Grant, R. M., and Freedman, D. N., *The Secret Sayings of Jesus* (London, 1960)

Guterman, S. L., *Religious Toleration and Persecution in Ancient Rome* (London, 1951)

Harnack, A., *The Mission and Expansion of Christianity*, E.T. (London, 1908)

Hengel, M., *Die Zeloten* (Leiden, 1961)

Higgins, A. J. B., *Jesus and the Son of Man* (London, 1964)

Higgins, A. J. B. (ed.), *New Testament Essays* [T. W. Manson memorial volume] (Manchester, 1959)

Hooker, M. D., *Jesus and the Servant* (London, 1959)

Hooker, M. D., *The Son of Man in Mark* (London, 1967)

Jackson, F. J. F., and Lake, K., *The Beginnings of Christianity*, Part I, vols. i–v (London, 1922–33)

Jaubert, A., *La Date de la Cène* (Paris, 1957)

Jeremias, J., *Jerusalem in the Time of Jesus*, E.T. (London, 1969)

Jeremias, J., *The Parables of Jesus*, E.T. (London, 1954[1], 1963[2])

Jeremias, J., *The Eucharistic Words of Jesus*, E.T. (Oxford, 1955[1]; London, 1966[2])

Jeremias, J., *Abba: Studien zur neutestamentlichen Theologie und Zeitgeschichte* (Göttingen, 1966)

Jeremias, J., *The Central Message of the New Testament* (London, 1965)

Jones, A. H. M., *The Cities of the Eastern Roman Provinces* (Oxford, 1937)

Jones, A. H. M., *The Herods of Judaea* (Oxford, 1938)

Jones, A. H. M., *Studies in Roman Government and Law* (Oxford, 1960)

Judge, E. A., *The Social Pattern of Christian Groups in the First Century* (London, 1960)

Kilpatrick, G. D., *The Trial of Jesus* (Oxford, 1953)

Kirschbaum, E., *The Tombs of St. Peter and St. Paul*, E.T. (London, 1959)

Klausner, J., *Jesus of Nazareth*, E.T. (London, 1929)

Klausner, J., *From Jesus to Paul*, E.T. (London, 1944)

Klausner, J., *The Messianic Idea in Israel*, E.T. (London, 1956)

Knox, J., *Chapters in a Life of Paul* (New York, 1950)

Knox, W. L., *St. Paul and the Church of Jerusalem* (Cambridge, 1925)

Knox, W. L., *St. Paul and the Church of the Gentiles* (Cambridge, 1939)

Knox, W. L., *The Acts of the Apostles* (Cambridge, 1948)

Kraeling, C. H., *John the Baptist* (New York, 1951)

Lake, K., *The Earlier Epistles of St. Paul*[2] (London, 1914)

Lampe, G. W. H., *The Seal of the Spirit* (London, 1951)

Leaney, A. R. C., *The Rule of Qumran and its Meaning* (London, 1966)

Leon, H. J., *The Jews of Ancient Rome* (Philadelphia, 1960)

Lietzmann, H., *The Beginnings of the Christian Church*, E.T. (London, 1949)

Lietzmann, H., *The Founding of the Church Universal*, E.T. (London, 1950)

Lietzmann, H., *Petrus und Paulus in Rom*[2] (Berlin, 1927)

Lightfoot, R. H., *Locality and Doctrine in the Gospels* (London, 1937)

Lindars, B., *New Testament Apologetic* (London, 1961)

Lohmeyer, E., *Galiläa und Jerusalem* (Göttingen, 1936)

Lohmeyer, E., *Lord of the Temple*, E.T. (Edinburgh, 1961)

Lundström, G., *The Kingdom of God in the Teaching of Jesus*, E.T. (Edinburgh, 1963)

Manson, T. W., *The Teaching of Jesus*[2] (Cambridge, 1935)

Manson, T. W., *The Sayings of Jesus* (London, 1949)

Manson, T. W., *The Servant-Messiah* (Cambridge, 1953)

Manson, T. W., *Ethics and the Gospel* (London, 1960)

Manson, T. W., *Studies in the Gospels and Epistles* (Manchester, 1962)

Manson, W., *Jesus the Messiah* (London, 1943)

Manson, W., *The Epistle to the Hebrews* (London, 1951)

Martin, R. P., *Carmen Christi* (Cambridge, 1967)

Merrill, E. T., *Essays in Early Church History* (London, 1924)

Meyer, E., *Ursprung und Anfänge des Christentums* (Stuttgart-Berlin, 1921–3)

Momigliano, A., *Claudius: The Emperor and his Achievement* (Cambridge, 1961)

Montefiore, C. G., *Rabbinic Literature and Gospel Teachings* (London, 1930)

Montefiore, C. G., and Loewe, H., *A Rabbinic Anthology* (London, 1938)

Moore, G. F., *Judaism in the First Centuries of the Christian Era* (Cambridge, Mass., 1927–30)

Moule, C. F. D., *The Birth of the New Testament* (London, 1962)

Moule, C. F. D., *The Phenomenon of the New Testament* (London, 1967)

Mowinckel, S., *He That Cometh*, E.T. (Oxford, 1956)

Munck, J., *Paul and the Salvation of Mankind*, E.T. (London, 1959)

Munck, J., *The Acts of the Apostles* (New York, 1967)

Nickle, K. F., *The Collection* (London, 1966)

Nineham, D. E. (ed.), *Studies in the Gospels* [R. H. Lightfoot memorial volume] (Oxford, 1955)

Nock, A. D., *Early Gentile Christianity and its Hellenistic Background* (New York, 1964)

Nock, A. D., *St. Paul* (London, 1938)

Ogg, G., *The Chronology of the Public Ministry of Jesus* (Cambridge, 1940)

Ogg, G., *The Chronology of the Life of Paul* (London, 1968)

Otto, R., *The Kingdom of God and the Son of Man*, E.T. (London, 1943)

Perrin, N., *The Kingdom of God in the Teaching of Jesus* (London, 1963)

Perrin, N., *Rediscovering the Teaching of Jesus* (London, 1967)

Pfeiffer, R. H., *History of New Testament Times and an Introduction to the Apocrypha* (New York, 1949)

Pohlenz, M., *Paulus und die Stoa* (Darmstadt, 1964)

Ramsay, W. M., *St. Paul the Traveller and the Roman Citizen*[14] (London, 1920)

Reicke, B., *The New Testament Era*, E.T. (Philadelphia, 1968)

Rengstorf, K. H., *Apostleship* (London, 1952)

Repo, E., *Der 'Weg' als Selbstbezeichnung des Urchristentums* (Helsinki, 1964)

Robinson, J. A. T., *Twelve New Testament Studies* (London, 1962)

Ropes, J. H., *The Apostolic Age* (London, 1906)

Rowley, H. H., *From Moses to Qumran* (London, 1963): vii. Jewish Proselyte Baptism and the Baptism of John (pp. 209–35); viii. The Qumran Sect and Christian Origins (pp. 237–79)

Sandmel, S., *Herod: Profile of a Tyrant* (Philadelphia, 1967)

Schlatter, A., *The Church in the New Testament Period*, E.T. (London, 1955)

Schlatter, A., *Die Kirche Jerusalems vom Jahre 70–130* (Gütersloh, 1898)

Schoeps, H. J., *Theologie und Geschichte des Judenchristentums* (Tübingen, 1949)

Schoeps, H. J., *Aus frühchristlicher Zeit* (Tübingen, 1950)

Schoeps, H. J., *Urgemeinde, Judenchristentum, Gnosis* (Tübingen, 1956)

Schoeps, H. J., *Paul*, E.T. (London, 1961)

Schürer, E., *A History of the Jewish People in the Time of Jesus Christ*, E.T. (Edinburgh, 1886–90)*

Schürer, E., *A History of the Jewish People in the Time of Jesus*, abridged and edited by N. N. Glatzer (New York, 1961)

Scobie, C. H. H., *John the Baptist* (London, 1964)

Sérouya, H., *Les Esséniens* (Paris, 1959)

Sevenster, J. N., and van Unnik, W. C. (edd.), *Studia Paulina* [J. de Zwaan *Festschrift*] (Haarlem, 1953)

Sherwin-White, A. N., *Roman Society and Roman Law in the New Testament* (Oxford, 1963)

* A revised edition is being prepared under the editorship of M. Black and G. Vermes.

Simon, M., *Jewish Sects at the Time of Jesus*, E.T. (Philadelphia, 1967)

Simon, M., *St. Stephen and the Hellenists in the Primitive Church* (London, 1958)

Simon, M., *Verus Israel* (Paris, 1948)

Simon, M., and others, *Aspects du Judéo-Christianisme* (Paris, 1965)

Simon, M., and Benoit, A., *Le Judaïsme et le Christianisme Antique* (Paris, 1968)

Smith, J., *The Voyage and Shipwreck of St. Paul*[4] (London, 1880)

Stauffer, E., *Christ and the Caesars*, E.T. (London, 1955)

Stauffer, E., *Jesus and His Story*, E.T. (London, 1960)

Steinmann, J., *St. John the Baptist and the Desert Tradition*, E.T. (London, 1958)

Stendahl, K. (ed.), *The Scrolls and the New Testament* (London, 1958)

Stewart, R. A., *Rabbinic Theology* (Edinburgh, 1961)

Sutcliffe, E. F., *The Monks of Qumran* (London, 1960)

Taylor, V., *The Life and Ministry of Jesus* (London, 1954)

Tcherikover, V. A., *Hellenistic Civilization and the Jews*, E.T. (Philadelphia, 1959)

Tödt, H. E., *The Son of Man in the Synoptic Tradition*, E.T. (London, 1965)

Turner, C. H., *Catholic and Apostolic* (London, 1931)

van Unnik, W. C., *Tarsus or Jerusalem: The City of Paul's Youth*, E.T. (London, 1962)

Williamson, G. A., *The World of Josephus* (London, 1964)

Wilson, R. McL., *The Gnostic Problem* (London, 1958)

Wink, W., *John the Baptist in the Gospel Tradition* (Cambridge, 1968)

Winter, P., *On the Trial of Jesus* (Berlin, 1961)

Wolfson, H. A., *Philo* (Cambridge, Mass., 1947)

Wood, H. G., *Jesus in the Twentieth Century* (London, 1960)

Yates, J. E., *The Spirit and the Kingdom* (London, 1963)

Zahrnt, H., *The Historical Jesus*, E.T. (London, 1963)

Zimmerli, W., and Jeremias, J., *The Servant of God*, E.T. (London, 1965[2])

1 Index of Authors

2 Index of Persons (other than authors)

3 Index of Places

4 Index of Principal Subjects